Islamic Thought and the Art of Translation

Islamic History and Civilization

STUDIES AND TEXTS

VOLUME 202

The titles published in this series are listed at *brill.com/ihc*

William C. Chittick and Sachiko Murata
PHOTO BY MOHAMMED RUSTOM

Islamic Thought and the Art of Translation

Texts and Studies in Honor of William C. Chittick and Sachiko Murata

Edited by

Mohammed Rustom

BRILL

LEIDEN | BOSTON

Cover illustration: Art work by Behnaz Karjoo.

The Library of Congress Cataloging-in-Publication Data is available online at https://catalog.loc.gov
LC record available at https://lccn.loc.gov/2022048693

Typeface for the Latin, Greek, and Cyrillic scripts: "Brill". See and download: brill.com/brill-typeface.

ISSN 0929-2403
ISBN 978-90-04-52902-1 (hardback)
ISBN 978-90-04-52903-8 (e-book)

This book is printed on acid-free paper and produced in a sustainable manner.

The author has no share save the post of translator, and no portion but the trade of speaker.

From the preface of Jāmī, *Lawā'iḥ*, trans. William C. Chittick in Sachiko Murata, *Chinese gleams of Sufi light: Wang Tai-yü's* Great learning of the pure and real *and Liu Chih's* Displaying the concealment of the real realm, Albany, NY: SUNY Press, 2000, 134

Contents

هو

Foreword

In the Name of God, the All-Good, the All-Merciful

∵

I have known William Chittick and Sachiko Murata for over half a century as their teacher, friend, colleague, and scholarly collaborator. It was in 1964, when I was the Aga Khan Professor of Islamic Studies at the American University of Beirut, that I first met a young American student named Chittick in one of my classes and during a public lecture I gave at the University. He drew my attention as a gifted student and potentially a serious scholar. During that year he also visited historical Islamic cities in Syria and became deeply attracted to the Islamic intellectual and spiritual tradition. After returning to America for his senior year and having received his bachelor's degree, he came to Iran where he spent the next dozen years finishing his doctorate at the University of Tehran, becoming later an instructor at Aryamehr University of Technology and the Imperial Iranian Academy of Philosophy when I headed both institutions.

It is remarkable how quickly he mastered Persian and later Arabic. I know of no Western scholar who speaks, reads, and writes Persian as well as Chittick does. Soon after he arrived, he came to see me about the subject for his PhD thesis and I suggested to him that he edit and comment upon ʿAbd al-Raḥmān Jāmī's commentary upon Ibn ʿArabī's *Nasqh al-fuṣūṣ*. He wondered at that time who Jāmī was but in a few years he produced a remarkable work that was soon published and remains to this day one of the major works on theoretical Sufism (*ʿirfān-i naẓarī*). This work also marks the beginning of Chittick's special interest in Ibn ʿArabī whose works he also studied with some leading Persian masters. I had the occasion to introduce him to such well-known authorities of Islamic thought as Sayyid Muḥammad Kāẓim ʿAṣṣār, ʿAllāma Ṭabāṭabāʾī, and Sayyid Jalāl al-Dīn Āshtiyānī, the latter becoming a very close friend of Chittick. The young Chittick also came to know the famous Japanese scholar Toshihiko Izutsu who was one of our main teachers at the Imperial Academy and with whom Chittick also studied the *Fuṣūṣ*. The Chitticks also helped the Izutsus in countless material ways when the Japanese scholar and his wife were in Tehran. Before long Chittick became immersed in the works of Ibn ʿArabī. I remember that after I wrote *Three Muslim Sages*, the last part of which is devoted to al-Shaykh al-Akbar, I told him that I was now leaving Ibn ʿArabī for him to pursue. He went on to produce several seminal works on him, works that have established him as the leading scholar of Ibn ʿArabī in the English-speaking world.

As for Sachiko Murata, she had come to Persia from Japan to study Shiʿite Law, especially as related to family matters; but she also devoted herself to Islamic and Iranian studies in general at the University of Tehran, where she met Chittick, an encounter that led to their marriage. While in Tehran, Murata wrote a short treatise on *mutʿa* or temporary marriage in both Japanese and Persian. The treatise is so well written and clear that it has been reprinted numerous times and is still widely read in Persia. She also became fluent in Persian and at home she and Chittick speak Persian together rather than English.

While in Tehran the Chitticks began to collect a wonderful set of traditional *kilim* rugs and traditional curtains. Their apartment was more Persian than most Persian homes besides housing a very rich library devoted to Islamic and Japanese studies. Fortunately, at the time of the Iranian Revolution in 1979, when they were forced to leave the country, they were able to save all their belongings and books.

As in my own case, the Iranian Revolution of 1979 changed the trajectory of the lives of the Chitticks. After a few months in Turkey, they returned to New York where Chittick worked for a while with the late Ehsan Yarshater on the *Encyclopaedia Iranica* which the latter was editing. Fortunately, a professorial position opened for both of them at the State University of New York at Stony Brook, where they have been teaching to this day—Chittick in Islamic studies and Murata in Buddhism and Far Eastern religions. Their home in Long Island became a haven for scholars and others seeking knowledge of religion. It is a piece of traditional Persia far away from the land that they were forced to leave. Over the past few decades when I have had the nostalgia for my homeland from which I am exiled, I have gone often to their Persian home for a few days. Besides the intellectual feast that I have found there in an ambience of great friendship, I have always been treated by Sachiko Murata's exceptionally fine Japanese cooking in which she is a master. She has always prepared the best Japanese dishes this side of Tokyo.

Once well settled, the Chitticks began their serious scholarly activities anew. Chittick himself produced his several masterly works on Ibn ʿArabī and Qūnawī, Rūmī, Bābā Afḍal Kāshānī, Maybudī, and many other prominent Sufis and Islamic philosophers. He even critically edited and commented upon some very salient works which were not known by the general scholarly community in Persia itself. He became famous not only in the West but also in Persia where he is recognized as a major Islamic scholar and where he has received several national awards. In a sense he is a living presence in Persian intellectual circles although residing far away. Many of his English works as well as those of Murata have been translated into Persian.

Among Murata's works, I must mention especially her *The Tao of Islam* which remains widely popular in scholarly circles. Applying such basic Chinese ideas as *yin-yang* to the study of Islamic metaphysical, cosmological, and mystical teachings, she provides in this book both a fresh look at Islamic doctrines and also a profound work on comparative philosophy matching in significance the work of Izutsu.

A new intellectual and spiritual continent was revealed with the discovery by members of the international scholarly community of the works of Chinese Muslim thinkers such as Wang Daiyu, and Murata was one of the main actors in this event. When the gaze of a few scholars turned to this rich tradition, it came to the attention of the famous Chinese scholar Tu Weiming who was Professor at Harvard but later returned to China where a special institute was established for him by the Chinese government. He suggested to me to organize a conference together at Harvard on this late Chinese Islamic school. We decided that we would each invite a number of scholars for our "team." Of course, I invited both Chittick and Murata and that event led to the publication of several major works on this late Islamic intellectual tradition in China. Tu Weiming participated at the beginning but the work was carried out primarily by Murata who is still continuing this ground-breaking scholarly effort.

Fortunately, both Chittick and Murata are still very active as both teachers and creative scholars and the influence of their work continues to spread in both East and West as the background of those who have contributed to this volume reveals. I pray that they be given many more years of physical health and intellectual fortitude to continue to enrich the fields of Islamic and Far Eastern studies and in fact traditional studies in general. And God knows best.

Seyyed Hossein Nasr
Washington, June 2022

Preface

William C. Chittick was born in Milford, Connecticut, USA in 1943. He did his undergraduate degree in history at the College of Wooster in Ohio and came into contact with the field of Sufi studies at the American University of Beirut (AUB) while spending the 1964–1965 academic year as a study abroad student. After attending Seyyed Hossein Nasr's public lectures at the AUB, the young Chittick resolved to enroll into the University of Tehran's Faculty of Letters to do graduate work under Nasr's supervision. Having written his honors thesis on Rūmī during his senior year in 1965–1966, Chittick then devoted the next eight years of his life (1966–1974) to his doctoral studies in Persian literature at the University of Tehran. He also worked as a research assistant in Tehran's Center for the Study of Islamic Science from 1971 to 1972. His PhD dissertation, published in 1977 and reprinted in 1992, was a study and critical edition of Jāmī's *Naqd al-nuṣūṣ*, a major commentary on Ibn ʿArabī's own abridgement of his *Fuṣūṣ al-ḥikam* entitled *Nasqh al-fuṣūṣ*.

Sachiko Murata was born in Asahikawa, Hokkaido, Japan in 1943. She did her undergraduate degree at Chiba University, where she obtained a BA in family law in 1965. After serving as a lawyer's assistant from 1965–1966 at the Iimura Law Firm based in Tokyo, Murata joined the University of Tehran's Faculty of Letters as a doctoral student in 1967. She obtained her PhD in 1971 with a thesis on the role of women in Niẓāmī's *Haft paykār*. During this time, she also served as a teacher of Japanese at the Japanese Embassy in Tehran. Murata then set out to do a second doctoral degree at the University of Tehran's Faculty of Theology. She thus first completed an MA in Islamic law in 1975. Her MA thesis, which was published in Persian in 1978 and revised into an English monograph in 1987, was on the institution of temporary marriage (*mutʿa*) in Islamic jurisprudence. By 1977, she had finished all of her PhD course work and was well on her way to completing a second PhD, this time with a thesis on the theme of family law in Islam and Confucianism. Unfortunately, the revolution of 1979 spelt an end to the realization of this goal.

Chittick and Murata met and married during their time in Iran. While after their studies Murata served as Assistant Director for the Japanese Institute for West Asian Studies in Tehran and Chittick as Assistant Professor of Comparative Religion at Aryamehr University of Technology (now called the Sharif University of Technology), they both eventually took up positions at the Imperial Iranian Academy of Philosophy (now called the Iranian Institute of Philosophy) in the late 1970s. As students and then teachers in Tehran, Chittick and Murata had the very fortunate opportunity to study with a number of Iran's most illustrious scholars. Amongst their teachers were such noteworthy names as Sayyid Jalāl al-Dīn Āshtiyānī, Badīʿ al-Zamān Furūzānfar, Abū l-Qāsim Gurjī, Jalāl al-Dīn Humāʾī, Toshihiko Izutsu, Seyyed Hossein Nasr, Sayyid Muḥammad Ḥusayn Ṭabāṭabāʾī, and Sayyid Ḥasan Iftikhārzāda Sabziwārī. The kind of academic training Chittick and Murata received was thus quite unparalleled, which partly explains why their writings display such a profound level of insight and technical know-how.

They made their permanent move to the United States before the 1979 revolution. Chittick served as Assistant Editor for the *Encyclopaedia Iranica* from 1981–1984, and he and Murata joined SUNY Stony Brook as Assistant Professors of Religious Studies (and eventually Comparative Studies) in 1983. At present, Chittick is Distinguished Professor in the Department of Asian and Asian American Studies and Affiliate Professor of Philosophy, and Murata is Full Professor in the Department of Asian and Asian American Studies.

Throughout the course of their long and distinguished careers, Professors Chittick and Murata have received many academic honors. These include Kenan Rifai Distinguished Professorships at Peking University's Institute of Advanced Humanistic Studies and Honorary Professorships at Minzu University's School of Philosophy and Religious Studies, as well as fellowships from the National Endowment for the Humanities, the John Simon Guggenheim Foundation, the Harvard Centre for the Study of World Religions, and the École des Hautes Études en Sciences Sociales (EHESS).

∴

Over the past five decades William Chittick and Sachiko Murata have contributed in major ways to changing the landscape of not only their fields of concentration—Sufism and Islamic philosophy—but also the broader disciplines of religious studies and global philosophy. Together, they have published more than forty books in the form of monographs, edited volumes, and translations, and over 300 original articles. Their writings have been translated into some fifteen languages and are taught at every major academic institution worldwide.

Perhaps the most distinctive feature of their books is the manner in which they approach premodern texts of Islamic thought. They place great emphasis on the robust analysis and concrete English translation of these texts over and against any kind of simplistic and convenient theorizations of them. Indeed, one of the reasons why their writings have been widely accessible to so many different types of people is because they cut to the chase, taking their readers to the heart of the texts themselves with impressive explanatory clarity and careful attention to rendering their technical language in terms that are cogent and consistent.

As partners in life and scholarship, Chittick and Murata have collaborated on many important projects. The best-known of their co-authored works is their introductory textbook on Islam, *The vision of Islam* (1994). This work has significantly informed the discursive categories through which scholars present and explain the Islamic tradition in the classroom, and it continues to do so.

Among Chittick's monographs that delve into the worldview of key figures in Islamic thought, three titles that typify his unmatchable skills in translation and rigorous textual analysis are *The Sufi path of love: The spiritual teachings of Rumi* (1983), *The Sufi path of knowledge: Ibn al-ʿArabī's metaphysics of imagination* (1989), and *The heart of Islamic philosophy: The quest for self-knowledge in the teachings of Afḍal al-Dīn Kāshānī* (2001). Some of his more recent books include *Divine love: Islamic literature and the path to God* (2013) and his complete translation of Aḥmad Samʿānī's Persian masterpiece *Rawḥ al-arwāḥ* under the title, *The repose of the spirits: A Sufi commentary on the divine names* (2019). These two works demonstrate how central love has been to the spiritual and intellectual quest in Islam, and this over 100 years before the appearance of such great lovers as Rūmī and ʿAṭṭār.

Sachiko Murata's ongoing research on the Han Kitab and its major representatives has opened up an entirely new universe to scholars of Islamic studies and non-Western philosophy. Her first book on Chinese-language Islam, *Chinese gleams of Sufi light: Wang Tai-yü's* Great learning of the pure and real *and Liu Chih's* Displaying the concealment of the real realm (2000), and her more recent study and translation entitled *The first Islamic classic in Chinese: Wang Daiyu's* Real commentary on the true teaching (2017), are major landmarks of scholarship. With great erudition and a linguistic range that is second to none, these works highlight how Sufi metaphysics was integrated into the language and worldview of Neo-Confucianism, thereby providing a window for Islamicists and cross-cultural philosophers into the unique nature of Islamic thought in Chinese. Murata's best-known work, *The Tao of Islam: A sourcebook on gender relationships in Islamic thought* (1992), remains an essential resource for the study of Islamic cosmology, Sufi psychology, and divine names theology.

As teachers, Chittick and Murata have trained a variety of graduate students and have always kept the doors of their home open to those seeking to read Arabic, Persian, and Chinese texts with them. Those who have had the fortunate opportunity to study with them would readily note their characteristic hospitality, humility, and humor. Then there are of course an even wider number of people who are their students by virtue of having been significantly influenced by their scholarship.

A *Festschrift* that brings together these various kinds of *ṭullāb* in addition to including Chittick and Murata's countless friends and colleagues across the globe would easily take up six or seven large volumes. The essays in *Islamic Thought and the Art of Translation* are therefore limited to people who have learned from them, in one way or another, over the past twenty-five years. Many of these authors are established scholars of Islamic studies today, others advanced graduate students, and still others professional educators and artists across various domains in the humanities. Suffice it to say, despite their diverse approaches to and understandings of the field of Islamic thought, one thing these contributors have in common is the profound debt of gratitude they owe to the present volume's recipients.

Mohammed Rustom
Toronto, September 2022

Acknowledgements

I am very grateful to Hinrich Biesterfeldt and Sebastian Günther for including this *Festschrift* in their prestigious Islamic History and Civilization Series; Teddi Dols for ensuring that the book pass through its various levels of review and publication swiftly and efficiently; Seyyed Hossein Nasr for writing the Foreword; the anonymous reviewers for their helpful suggestions; and the authors who contributed to this collection in a timely manner so that its publication would coincide with the eightieth birth year of both its recipients. My research assistant Jana Newiger and the volume's production editor Noralyne Alabdullah-Maranus worked tirelessly on the articles and saw to it that every dimension of this publication conformed to Brill's meticulous standards. A number of friends and colleagues also helped out in various ways. Thanks go to Kazuyo Murata for surreptitiously obtaining essential biographical information about her aunt, and Nosheen Mian, Nariman Aavani, Muhammad Faruque, Atif Khalil, Munjed Murad, Bilal Orfali, and Cyrus Zargar for their feedback on the volume's conception and content. A publication grant awarded by the Persian Heritage Foundation allowed me to commission the stunning piece on the front cover, which was handcrafted by Behnaz Karjoo.

Mohammed Rustom
Toronto, September 2022

List of Figures

Notes on the Contributors

Mukhtar H. Ali
is Lecturer in Islamic Studies at the University of Chicago Divinity School. He specializes in Islamic philosophy, ethics, Sufism, Quranic studies, and comparative religion.

Mohammed Mehdi Ali
is a PhD student at the University of Chicago. His areas of interest include Persian and Arabic poetry, Islamic philosophy, and the school of Ibn ʿArabī.

Khalil Andani
is Assistant Professor of Religion at Augustana College. He specializes in Quranic studies, Islamic theology and philosophy, Shiʿi Ismaʿili history and thought, and Sufism.

Rosabel Ansari
is Assistant Professor of Philosophy at Stony Brook University. She specializes in Graeco-Arabic and Islamic philosophy, with an emphasis on the philosophy of language and metaphysics.

Masoud Ariankhoo
is an Islamic studies doctoral candidate at Harvard University. His interests are in the fields of Islamic intellectual history and Sufism.

Alireza Asghari
is an Islamic studies doctoral candidate at the University of Leiden. His interests are in Avicennan and Safavid philosophy, Shiʿi mysticism, and Islamic metaphysics.

Justin Cancelliere
completed graduate work at the University of Georgia, where his research addressed the problem of universals in Islamic metaphysics. His areas of interest include Islamic philosophy, Sufism, and the Platonic-Aristotelian tradition.

Yousef Casewit
is Associate Professor of Quranic Studies at the University of Chicago Divinity School. His research interests include commentaries on the divine names, Sufi *tafsīr*, and the intellectual history of North Africa and al-Andalus.

Davlat Dadikhuda
is a Postdoctoral Researcher in Islamic philosophy at the University of Jyvaskyla. His research interests are in Islamic philosophy, rational theology, and Sufism.

Maria Massi Dakake
is Associate Professor of Religious Studies at George Mason University. Her research interests are in the fields of Quranic studies, Shiʿi thought, Sufism, and female approaches to religion.

Marlene DuBois
is Professor of English at the State University of New York at Suffolk County Community College. Her research interests are in comparative religion, Sufism, and mythic narratives.

Naser Dumairieh
obtained a PhD in Islamic studies from McGill University's Institute of Islamic Studies. His areas of interest include Islamic philosophy, theology, and Sufism, with particular emphasis on intellectual and spiritual life in the Hijaz.

Omar Edaibat
obtained a PhD in Islamic studies from McGill University's Institute of Islamic Studies. He specializes in the Bā ʿAlawī Sufi tradition of Yemen's Hadhramawt valley, Islamic law, and contemporary Islamic thought.

Muhammad U. Faruque
is Inayat Malik Assistant Professor of Arabic and Islamic Studies at the University of Cincinnati. He specializes in Islamic ethics and philosophy, Quranic studies, philosophical Sufism, and the history and theory of subjectivity.

Atif Khalil
is Associate Professor of Religious Studies at the University of Lethbridge. He specializes in Sufism, Islamic philosophy, and Islamic theology.

Amer Latif
is Associate Professor of Religion at the Marlboro Institute for Liberal Arts and Interdisciplinary Studies at Emerson College. His research areas include Sufism, comparative religion, and translation studies.

Sayeh Meisami
is Associate Professor of Islamic Philosophy at the University of Dayton. She specializes in Islamic philosophy in its socio-cultural and religious contexts.

Matthew Melvin-Koushki
is Associate Professor of History at the University of South Carolina. He specializes in early modern Islamicate intellectual and imperial history, with a focus on the theory and practice of the occult sciences in Timurid-Safavid Iran and the broader Persianate world to the 19th century.

Kazuyo Murata
is Senior Lecturer in Islamic Studies at King's College London. She specializes in pre-modern Sufism in the Persianate world as well as the thematic and conceptual study of Muslim thought.

Shankar Nair
is Associate Professor of Religious Studies at the University of Virginia. His research interests include Sufism and Islamic philosophy; Quranic exegesis; Hindu philosophy and theology; Hindu-Muslim interactions in South Asia; Arabic, Persian, and Sanskrit literatures; and the general intellectual history of the Indian subcontinent.

Seyyed Hossein Nasr
is University Professor of Islamic Studies at The George Washington University. He specializes in Islamic philosophy, Sufism, Islamic art, Islamic science, religion and the environment, and comparative religion.

Oludamini Ogunnaike
is Associate Professor of African Religious Thought and Democracy at the University of Virginia. He specializes in Sufism and Yoruba religious traditions in West Africa, particularly their intellectual and aesthetic dimensions, as well as cross-cultural and decolonial philosophy.

Alireza Pharaa
is a doctoral candidate in philosophy at Stony Brook University. His research focuses on Islamic philosophy, Sufism, and continental philosophy.

Tahera Qutbuddin
is Abdulaziz Saud AlBabtain Laudian Professor of Arabic at the University of Oxford. She specializes in Arabic oratory, the sermons of Imam ʿAlī, and Fatimid-Tayyibi Shiʿi doctrine, history, and poetry.

Ali Karjoo-Ravary
is the Richard W. Bulliet Assistant Professor of Islamic History at Columbia University. He specializes in the history of Sufism, multilingual poetry, Islamic discourses on kingship and governance, and Sufi art.

Mohammed Rustom
is Professor of Islamic Thought at Carleton University and Director of the Carleton Centre for the Study of Islam. He specializes in Islamic philosophy, Sufism, Quranic exegesis, and cross-cultural philosophy.

Laury Silvers
obtained a PhD in comparative studies at Stony Brook University. Before retiring to write mysteries set in the time and place of her research specialization in early Sufism, she taught Islamic studies at Skidmore College and the University of Toronto.

Gregory Vandamme
is a doctoral candidate in religious studies at the University of Louvain. He specializes in Akbarian Sufi thought, Islamic theology, and Quranic hermeneutics.

Cyrus Ali Zargar
is Al-Ghazali Distinguished Professor of Islamic Studies at the University of Central Florida. He specializes in classical Sufi literature, Iranian intellectual history, and ethics in Islamic philosophy and Sufism.

Books by William C. Chittick and Sachiko Murata

The chronological list below does not include translations of William C. Chittick and Sachiko Murata's books, as well as their many abridged and complete translations of Sufi texts that have been published in various journals and anthologies over the past several decades.

Books by William C. Chittick

Co-edited with Alireza Asghari, Saʿīd al-Dīn al-Farghānī, *Muntahā l-madārik*, 2 vols., Leiden: The Islamic Manuscripts Press of Leiden (forthcoming).

Rumi et Shams: La voie spirituelle de l'amour, trans. Jean Annestay, Paris: Editions i, 2021.

Muqārabāt fī l-taṣawwuf wa-l-ḥubb wa-l-insān, trans. Muhammad ʿAli Jaradi and Dima El-Mouallem (a special issue of *al-Maḥajja* 36 (2021), ed. Ahmad Majed).

Translator of Aḥmad Samʿānī, *The repose of the spirits: A Sufi commentary on the divine names*, Albany, NY: SUNY Press, 2019.

Translator of Rashīd al-Dīn Maybudī, *The unveiling of the mysteries and the provision of the pious*, Louisville: Fons Vitae, 2015.

Divine love: Islamic literature and the path to God, New Haven: Yale University Press, 2013.

In search of the lost heart: Explorations in Islamic thought, eds. Mohammed Rustom, Atif Khalil, and Kazuyo Murata, Albany, NY: SUNY Press, 2012.

Co-authored with Sachiko Murata and Tu Weiming, *The sage learning of Liu Zhi: Islamic thought in Confucian terms*, Cambridge, MA: Harvard University Asia Center, 2009.

Science of the cosmos, science of the soul: The pertinence of Islamic cosmology in the modern world, Oxford: Oneworld, 2007.

Editor of *The essential Seyyed Hossein Nasr*, Bloomington: World Wisdom, 2007.

Editor of *The inner journey: Views from the Islamic tradition*, Sandpoint: Morning Light Press, 2007.

Ibn ʿArabi: Heir to the prophets, Oxford: Oneworld, 2005.

The Sufi doctrine of Rumi, Bloomington: World Wisdom, ^{2}2005.

Me & Rumi: The autobiography of Shams-i Tabrizi, Louisville: Fons Vitae, 2004.

Translator of Mullā Ṣadrā, *The elixir of the gnostics*, Provo, UT: Brigham Young University Press, 2003.

The heart of Islamic philosophy: The quest for self-knowledge in the teachings of Afḍal al-Dīn Kāshānī, New York: Oxford University Press, 2001.

Translator of Jāmī, *Gleams*, in Sachiko Murata, *Chinese gleams of Sufi light: Wang Tai-*

yü's Great learning of the pure and real *and Liu Chih's* Displaying the concealment of the real realm, Albany, NY: SUNY Press, 2000, 128–210.

Sufism: A short introduction, Oxford: Oneworld, 2000.

The self-disclosure of God: Principles of Ibn al-ʿArabī's cosmology, Albany, NY: SUNY Press, 1998.

Varolmanın Boyutları [*The dimensions of existence*], ed. and trans. Turan Koç, Istanbul: Insan Yayınları, 1997.

Co-authored with Sachiko Murata, *The vision of Islam*, New York: Paragon House, 1994.

Imaginal worlds: Ibn al-ʿArabī and the problem of religious diversity, Albany, NY: SUNY Press, 1994.

Critical edition of ʿAbd al-Raḥmān Jāmī, *Naqd al-nuṣūṣ fī sharḥ Naqsh al-fuṣūṣ*, Tehran: Cultural Studies and Research Institute, ^{2}1992.

Faith and practice of Islam: Three thirteenth century Sufi texts, Albany, NY: SUNY Press, 1992.

The Sufi path of knowledge: Ibn al-ʿArabī's metaphysics of imagination, Albany, NY: SUNY Press, 1989.

Translator of ʿAlī b. al-Ḥusayn, *The psalms of Islam*, London: Muhammadi Trust, 1988.

Translator of Javad Nurbakhsh (comp.), *Sufism IV: Repentance, abstinence, renunciation, wariness, humility, humbleness, sincerity, steadfastness, courtesy*, London: Khanaqahi Nimatullahi Publications, 1988.

The Sufi path of love: The spiritual teachings of Rumi, Albany, NY: SUNY Press, 1983.

Translator of ʿAlī b. al-Ḥusayn, *Supplication: Makārim al-akhlāq*, London: Muhammadi Trust, 1983.

Translator of ʿAlī b. Abī Ṭālib, *Supplications* (*duʿā*), London: Muhammadi Trust, 1982.

Co-translated with Peter L. Wilson, Fakhr al-Dīn ʿIrāqī, *Divine flashes*, New York: Paulist Press, 1982.

Translator of Javad Nurbakhsh (comp.), *Sufism II: Fear and hope, contraction and expansion, gathering and dispersion, intoxication and sobriety, annihilation and subsistence*, New York: Khanaqahi Nimatullahi Publications, 1982.

Translator of Javad Nurbakhsh (comp.), *Sufism I: Meaning, knowledge, and unity*, New York: Khanaqahi Nimatullahi Publications, 1981.

A Shiʿite anthology, Albany, NY: SUNY Press, 1981.

Indices to Saʿīd al-Dīn Farghānī, *Mashāriq al-darārī*, ed. Sayyid J. Āshtiyānī, Mashhad: Dānishgāh-i Firdawsī, 1978, 651–811.

Editor of *The works of Seyyed Hossein Nasr through his fortieth birthday*, Uppsala: University of Utah Press, 1977.

Co-edited with Seyyed Hossein Nasr (vols. 1–3) and Peter Zirnis (vols. 2–3), *An annotated bibliography of Islamic science*, Tehran: Imperial Iranian Academy of Philosophy, 1975–1978 (vols. 1–2); Tehran: Cultural Studies and Research Institute, 1991 (vol. 3).

Translator of Sayyid Muḥammad Ḥusayn Ṭabāṭabā'ī, *Muhammad in the mirror of Islam*, Tehran: Dār al-Kutub al-Islāmiyya, 1970.

Books by Sachiko Murata

The first Islamic classic in Chinese: Wang Daiyu's Real commentary on the true teaching, Albany, NY: SUNY Press, 2017.

Co-authored with William C. Chittick and Tu Weiming, *The sage learning of Liu Zhi: Islamic thought in Confucian terms*, Cambridge, MA: Harvard University Asia Center, 2009.

Chinese gleams of Sufi light: Wang Tai-yü's Great learning of the pure and real *and Liu Chih's* Displaying the concealment of the real realm, Albany, NY: SUNY Press, 2000.

Co-authored with William C. Chittick, *The vision of Islam*, New York: Paragon House, 1994.

The Tao of Islam: A sourcebook on gender relationships in Islamic thought, Albany, NY: SUNY Press, 1992.

Translator of Ḥasan b. Zayn al-Dīn al-ʿĀmilī, *Isuramu Hōriron Josetsu* [*Principles of Islamic law*], Tokyo: Iwanami, 1985.

Izdiwāj-i muwaqqat, Tehran: Hamdami, 1978; rev. English version published as *Temporary marriage in Islamic law*, London: Muhammadi Trust, 1987.

PART 1

Sufism in Persianate Contexts

CHAPTER 1

ʿAyn al-Quḍāt's *Tamhīdāt*: An Ocean of Sufi Metaphysics in Persian

Masoud Ariankhoo and Mohammed Rustom

Readers of William Chittick and Sachiko Murata's writings often note their unique ability to discern and effectively communicate the visions of reality animating the various texts in Islamic thought that they study. This is surely because they do not see these works as mere repositories of ideas that make no demands on those who engage with them. Rather, they are akin to shoreless oceans inviting onlookers to plunge in, provided they have no hope of returning. In keeping with this characterization, and as a tribute to our beloved teachers and friends, in this article we would like to offer a drop from one of the deepest of these oceans belonging to the pre-modern period.

1 Life and Times

ʿAyn al-Quḍāt was born in Hamadan in 490/1097 into a scholarly family with roots going back to present-day East Azerbaijan.[1] He dedicated himself to learning at a young age, and particularly excelled in scholastic theology, philosophy, jurisprudence, and Arabic and Persian poetry. Having already authored several major Arabic treatises in fields as diverse as mathematics and poetry, at the age of twenty-four ʿAyn al-Quḍāt wrote his most important and influential Arabic work, the *Zubdat al-ḥaqāʾiq* (*The essence of reality*). This book is likely the first full-fledged defence of Sufi metaphysics in the Arabic language, and was remarkably written in a matter of two to three days.[2]

The *Essence* was the result of a long period in which our author carefully read the work of Abū Ḥāmid al-Ghazālī (d. 505/1111) and also took the Sufi Path from al-Ghazālī's younger brother Aḥmad al-Ghazālī (d. 520/1126). Upon the

1 For his life, education, and times, see the introduction in Rustom, Mohammed, *Inrushes of the heart: The Sufi philosophy of ʿAyn al-Quḍāt*, Albany, NY: SUNY Press, 2023.

2 A new Arabic edition and translation of this work is now available: ʿAyn al-Quḍāt, *The essence of reality: A defense of philosophical Sufism*, ed. and trans. Mohammed Rustom, New York: New York University Press, 2022.

 | DOI:10.1163/9789004529038_002

death of his master, ʿAyn al-Quḍāt succeeded him in his function as Sufi shaykh and continued his profession as legal judge in his native city of Hamadan. As a Sufi master himself, ʿAyn al-Quḍāt trained many students, both through oral instruction and written correspondences, the latter of which amount to over 150 letters that have been published under the title *Nāma-hā* (*The letters*).[3]

ʿAyn al-Quḍāt had gotten into trouble with a group of religious scholars in Hamadan in roughly 522/1128. A number of charges were laid against him, mostly having to do with his being a "heretic" on account of his alleged claim to some sort of divine status, his being deemed a sorcerer by his contemporaries, and his supposed belief that he had attained a degree of knowledge that was beyond that of God's Prophets. He was thus imprisoned for a short while in Baghdad in 523/1129. While in prison, ʿAyn al-Quḍāt was given the opportunity to defend himself against these and other related charges, which resulted in his penning a beautiful Arabic literary treatise, *Shakwā l-gharīb* (*The exile's complaint*).[4] Despite the convincing nature of ʿAyn al-Quḍāt's defence, he was sent to Hamadan in 523/1129, where he was executed by the Seljuq state at the age of thirty-four in 525/1131. Present-day Hamadan is host to a memorial complex in honor of ʿAyn al-Quḍāt; but his tomb, which had originally been a site of pilgrimage for several centuries after his death, has not survived.

Readers may notice an uncanny similarity between ʿAyn al-Quḍāt's fate and that of the great Sufi figure al-Ḥallāj (d. 309/922), to whom ʿAyn al-Quḍāt had a particular attachment. Like al-Ḥallāj, ʿAyn al-Quḍāt was accused of heresy; and, like al-Ḥallāj, his status as a "heretic" was invoked as the reason underlying his state-sponsored execution. But, as is now well-known, al-Ḥallāj's death was due to deeper, political causes. And the same was the case with ʿAyn al-Quḍāt. In ʿAyn al-Quḍāt's eyes, many scholars had become exceedingly jealous of his accomplishments. We cannot ascertain whether or not these envious scholars were directly involved in bringing him down. But we can rest assured that they were at least not sympathetic to ʿAyn al-Quḍāt's cause, and likely helped fan the flames of the charges made against him.

These charges were a foil for the real reasons behind our author's execution, which had to do with his strident public condemnation of the Seljuq government's corrupt administrative and financial practices.[5] At the same time, ʿAyn

3 ʿAyn al-Quḍāt, *Nāma-hā*, ed. ʿAlī Naqī Munzawī and ʿAfīf ʿUsayrān, 3 vols., Tehran: Intishārāt-i Asāṭīr, 1998. A discussion of their nature and content can be found in the introduction in Rustom, *Inrushes of the heart*.

4 For a translation of this text, see ʿAyn al-Quḍāt, *A Sufi martyr*, trans. A.J. Arberry, London: Keagan and Paul, 1969.

5 See Rustom, *Inrushes of the heart*, ch. 2 and Safi, Omid, *The politics of knowledge in premodern*

al-Quḍāt also discerned another kind of jealousy at work in bringing about his demise—not human jealousy, but divine jealousy.[6] Like al-Ḥallāj, ʿAyn al-Quḍāt had revealed the secret of God's unity and the truth concerning the utter nothingness of human beings before God. He did this in his *Nāma-hā* and public sermons, and especially in his magnum opus in Persian, the *Tamhīdāt* (*Paving the path*).

2 Paving the Path

Paving the path was completed in 521/1127 and easily ranks among the greatest classics of Sufi literature. It is a work of incredible profundity and sophistication, and can be said to supply some of the stock imagery and expressions that would come to be associated with the classical Persian poetic tradition as seen in the writings of such giants as Farīd al-Dīn ʿAṭṭār (d. ca. 617/1220), Jalāl al-Dīn Rūmī (d. 672/1273), and Maḥmūd Shabistarī (d. ca. 720/1320). At the same time, this book anticipates many of the doctrinal formulations, themes, and concerns that characterize the perspective of the highly influential Spanish metaphysician Ibn ʿArabī (d. 638/1240) and the many generations of his followers.

In its modern printed edition, *Paving the path* is just over 350 pages long, and is divided into ten unequal parts. Although ʿAyn al-Quḍāt wrote this work as a stand-alone text, it also incorporates sections from his aforementioned letters and his oral discourses given to his students.

To a certain extent, ʿAyn al-Quḍāt drew inspiration from Aḥmad al-Ghazālī's Persian masterpiece on the metaphysics of love, the *Sawāniḥ al-ʿushshāq* (*Apparitions of the lovers*). But the scope and style of *Paving the path* defies classification. It is entirely unique in its method of delivery and in the directness with which the author addresses his points. Although there is a good deal of (mostly) Persian poetry in *Paving the path*, it is by and large a Persian prose work. Yet even the prose in question is of a different order of writing all together. Many of the arguments and topics broached by ʿAyn al-Quḍāt in *Paving the path* not only depend on this book's inner logic, but the very language in which and through which his points are made.

Islam: Negotiating ideology and religious inquiry, Chapel Hill: University of North Carolina Press, 2006, ch. 6.

6 The details of this argument are given in Rustom, Mohammed, "ʿAyn al-Quḍāt between divine jealousy and political intrigue," in *Journal of Sufi Studies* 7.1–2 (2018), 47–73.

For lack of a better term, we may characterize ʿAyn al-Quḍāt's unique language in *Paving the path* as something like "Persian Quranic prose." Thus, on any given page of this text, one is sure to encounter multiple references to Quranic verses, both overt and covert, which is to say nothing of our author's extensive use of Prophetic traditions and the sayings of earlier Sufi masters. This Persian Quranic prose, which ʿAyn al-Quḍāt develops to great rhetorical effect, allows him to paradoxically maintain his own authorial voice (in Persian) while coalescing the Arabic of the Quran with his own words, thereby eliminating his personal voice from the equation. To demonstrate what this looks like, we can do no better than to cite one typical example from *Paving the path*. In this passage, ʿAyn al-Quḍāt tackles one of his favourite subjects, namely "habit-worship" (*ʿādat-parastī*), to which we shall return in due course. Notice how, in the span of only several lines, ʿAyn al-Quḍāt weaves a number of Quranic verses and a couple of Prophetic sayings into the fabric of his argument:

> O dear friend! If you want the beauty of these mysteries to be disclosed to you, then let go of habit-worship, for habit-worship is idol-worship. Do you not see how the arrow of this group goes? "We found our fathers upon a creed, and we are surely following in their footsteps" [Q 43:23].[7] Whatever you have heard from creatures, forget it! "A vile guide for man is his conjecture."[8] Whatever you have heard, ignore it, for "The tale-bearer shall not enter the Garden."[9] Whatever appears, do not look at it! "And do not spy upon one another" [Q 49:12]. Whatever is difficult for you, only ask with the tongue of the heart, and be patient until you arrive: "Had they been patient until thou camest out unto them, it would have been better for them" [Q 49:5]. Accept the advice of Khiḍr: "Question me not about anything until I make mention of it to thee" [Q 18:70].[10]

Apart from the unique use of language we find in *Paving the path*, ʿAyn al-Quḍāt's style is also distinct in that his statements are at once exhilarating,

7 All translations of Quranic verses in this article are taken, with modifications, from Nasr, Seyyed Hossein et al. (eds.), *The study Quran: A new translation and commentary*, New York: HarperOne, 2015.

8 Abū Dāwūd, *Sunan*, in *Jamʿ jawāmiʿ al-aḥādīth wa-l-asānīd wa-maknaz al-siḥāḥ wa-l-sunan wa-l-masānīd*, v, Vaduz: Jamʿiyyat al-Maknaz al-Islāmī, 2000, Adab, 80, no. 4974.

9 Muslim, *Ṣaḥīḥ*, in *Jamʿ jawāmiʿ al-aḥādīth*, iv, Īmān, 47, no. 303.

10 ʿAyn al-Quḍāt, *Tamhīdāt*, ed. ʿAfīf ʿUsayrān, Tehran: Intishārāt-i Manūchihrī, 1994, 12–13, §18. All translations from the *Tamhīdāt* in this article are adapted from Rustom, *Inrushes of the heart*.

enthralling, and even extemporaneous. Readers get the sense at every turn of the page that the work before them is due to a creative genius that transcends and yet subsumes the personhood of its author. Thus, we find passages peppered throughout *Paving the path* in which ʿAyn al-Quḍāt tells us that he is not in control of the words that appear on the pages before him and which come through him. In fact, he is often as bewildered over his statements as are his listeners:

> Where is this meddling judge of Hamadan from? Where are these words of mysteries from? The speaker does not know what he is saying, so how can the hearer know what he is hearing?![11]

As ʿAyn al-Quḍāt saw it, *Paving the path* was a gift given to him by God, which is why he says, "Alas! Whoever wants to hear of the divine mysteries without an intermediary, say, 'Listen to ʿAyn al-Quḍāt!'"[12] The divine mysteries which ʿAyn al-Quḍāt speaks of in this work are many. It contains most of his mature mystical, philosophical, cosmological, theological, epistemological, anthropological, and aesthetic doctrines, not to mention his many musings on the nature of love, language, the function of the spiritual master, the origins of the Quran, and the inner meanings of the rites and symbols of the *sharīʿa*. One example of the latter shall suffice:

> In the *sharīʿa*, fasting is an expression of refraining from food and drink, namely the fast of the body. But in the world of reality, fasting is a teaching of consuming food and drink .... This is called "the fast of meaning," and is the fast of the soul. It is God's fast: "The fast is Mine."[13] Why? Because in this fast there is nothing but God.[14]

In many ways, *Paving the path* does not really have a beginning, middle, and an end. The experience of reading this masterpiece of Sufi metaphysical literature is more like being thrown into the middle of an ocean than it is like starting out on a journey by foot. The person engulfed by the billows of this majestic ocean will inevitably be taken in by another of its waves even as he struggles for air. The surest strategy, then, is to allow the ocean to be one's guide.

---

11 ʿAyn al-Quḍāt, *Tamhīdāt* 15, § 22.
12 ʿAyn al-Quḍāt, *Tamhīdāt* 300, § 394.
13 Bukhārī, *Ṣaḥīḥ*, in *Jamʿ jawāmiʿ al-aḥādīth*, ii, Tawḥīd, 35, no. 7584.
14 ʿAyn al-Quḍāt, *Tamhīdāt* 91, § 129.

What one finds the more they learn to swim in this manner is that *Paving the path* ties themes and concepts together in such a seamless and natural way that it becomes almost pointless to try to capture this vast ocean into any kind of conceptual jar. This calls to mind the famous lines from the *Mathnawī* of Jalāl al-Dīn Rūmī:

> Were you to pour the ocean into a pitcher,
> how much could it hold? Enough for but one day.[15]

For our purposes, we will have to make do with a schematization of some of the major doctrinal themes and ideas in *Paving the path* as suffices "for but one day." For those who are as yet unable to swim in this ocean, such an undertaking will give them a sense of the interconnectedness of the ideas that inform ʿAyn al-Quḍāt's worldview.[16] In the following sections, therefore, we will offer one reading of *Paving the path*, attempting to outline how some of its key metaphysical ideas build off of and flow into one another.

3 Imagination and Imaginalization

That *Paving the path* accounts for a coherent metaphysical vision can be demonstrated with recourse to one major idea linked to every other dimension of the work, namely imaginalization (*tamaththul*). In classical Islamic thought, the imaginal world came to refer to an intermediary space that brings opposites together, and this allowed Muslim thinkers of various intellectual persuasions to offer new solutions to age-old theological problems. Imagination (*khayāl*) primarily provided them with an objective means to express the manner in which the realm of forms (*ṣūra*) flows into the world of meaning (*maʿnā*), and the world of meaning into the realm of forms. Although imagination can be traced to a number of earlier Islamic sources, it is commonly acknowledged that it came to the forefront of the discussion largely due to the influence of Ibn ʿArabī.

Yet many Persian Sufi authors had been drawing on notions of imagination and imaginalization a century before Ibn ʿArabī. Their source has perplexed scholars for the past several decades. But when we turn to ʿAyn al-Quḍāt, the

15 Rūmī, Jalāl al-Dīn, *Mathnawī-yi maʿnawī*, ed., trans., and comm. Reynold A. Nicholson, 8 vols., i, London: Luzac, 1925–1940, 20.

16 A detailed presentation of the full range of ʿAyn al-Quḍāt's spiritual and intellectual teachings can be found in Rustom, *Inrushes of the heart*.

missing piece of the puzzle emerges. Indeed, he was the first Persian author to discuss imaginalization at length, and this in a manner that would leave an indelible mark upon the later tradition. In explaining the function of imaginalization, ʿAyn al-Quḍāt makes reference to several well-known instances wherein the angel Gabriel appeared in the form of a man:

> See how the discussion drags me from one place to another! … The foundation of the existence of the next world is through imaginalization, and recognizing imaginalization is no trifling matter! Most divine mysteries are known through imaginalization and are seen through it. Alas! "He imaginalized himself to her as a mortal man, well-proportioned" [Q 19:17] is a complete answer. Gabriel showed himself to Mary from the spiritual world in the garb of a mortal man by way of imaginalization, and she saw him as a man in human form.
>
> One time, Muṣṭafā's Companions saw Gabriel in the form of a Bedouin. There was another time when Gabriel showed himself to Muṣṭafā in the form of Diḥya al-Kalbī. If it was Gabriel, who is spiritual, how did he assume form so that he could be seen as a Bedouin in the garment of a mortal man? And if it was not Gabriel, who then was seen? Know that it was imaginalization, pure and good.[17]

When ʿAyn al-Quḍāt says that the "foundation of the existence of the next world is through imaginalization," he takes this to refer to all eschatological realities, including the very states cultivated by human beings during their time on earth. In the afterlife, these states reappear to them in imaginalized forms: "When a person looks, he sees his own attributes imaginalized. His existence is his punishment, yet he thinks that somebody else is punishing him! But the punishment is his self and is from himself!"[18]

ʿAyn al-Quḍāt also sees in imaginalization the ability to envision God's manifest and embodied reality:

> Alas! "I saw my Lord on the night of the Ascension in the most beautiful form."[19] This "most beautiful form" is imaginalization. If it is not imaginalization, then what is it? "God created Adam and his offspring in the form of the All-Merciful" is also a kind of imaginalization. Alas! One of

17 ʿAyn al-Quḍāt, *Tamhīdāt* 293, § 385.
18 ʿAyn al-Quḍāt, *Tamhīdāt* 289, § 377.
19 Cf. Tirmidhī, *Sunan*, in *Jamʿ jawāmiʿ al-aḥādīth*, vi, 2000, Tafsīr, 39, no. 3541.

His names is "the Form-Giver" [Q 59:24], that is, He is the maker of forms. But I am saying that Form-Giver means the displayer of forms.[20]

4 Light and Darkness

The concept of imaginalization, or what ʿAyn al-Quḍāt also refers to as the result of the "alchemy" of God's desire and love,[21] is invoked in *Paving the path* to account for the diversity inherent in the cosmic order:

> "He it is who created you; among you are unbelievers and among you are believers" [Q 64:2]. The diversity in the colors of existents is no trifling matter! And one of God's signs is the diversity in the creation of people: "And amongst His signs is the diversity in your languages and colors" [Q 30:22].[22]

As the above passage suggests, the diversity we see all around us boils down to two positions, namely faith (*īmān*) and disbelief (*kufr*). Through the function of imaginalization our author shows us how these two seemingly antithetical terms are closely related to one another by virtue of their being linked to the two principles responsible for the emergence of the cosmic order: the light of the Prophet Muhammad and the darkness of Iblis, both of which are imaginalizations of the divine Sun:

> Do you know what this sun is? It is the light of Muhammad that comes forth from the East of Beginninglessness. Do you know what moon this is? It is the black light of ʿAzāzīl that emerges from the west of Endlessness.[23]
>
> The upshot of this discussion is that God is a substance and light an accident. Substance was never without accident and will not be. Thus, I have spoken about the heavens and the earth through symbols, namely that two of His lights are the roots of the heavens and the earth—their reality is these two lights. One is the light of Muhammad, and one the light of Iblis.[24]

20 ʿAyn al-Quḍāt, *Tamhīdāt* 296, § 388.
21 ʿAyn al-Quḍāt, *Tamhīdāt* 181, § 239.
22 ʿAyn al-Quḍāt, *Tamhīdāt* 181–182, § 239.
23 ʿAyn al-Quḍāt, *Tamhīdāt* 126, § 175.
24 ʿAyn al-Quḍāt, *Tamhīdāt* 258, § 340.

> O dear friend! This is wisdom: whatever is, was, and will be must not and cannot be otherwise. Whiteness could never be without blackness. Heaven cannot be without earth. Substance is inconceivable without accident. Muhammad could never be without Iblis. Obedience without disobedience and unbelief without faith cannot be conceived. Likewise is it with every opposite.[25]

We are thus presented in *Paving the path* with a metaphysics of light and darkness of the first order, and one in which Iblis is seen as a vital piece to the puzzle of a cosmic plan necessitating that his darkness offset and complement the light of the Prophet. Related to this observation is the fact that, as a master of the outward and inward Islamic sciences, ʿAyn al-Quḍāt is a firm critic of those whom he labels as "form-seers" (*ṣūrat-bīnān*). He links this group of people to habit-worship and idol-worship, and even identifies habit-worship with what he calls "legalism" (*sharīʿat-warzī*):

> The world of habit-worship is the *sharīʿa*, and legalism is habit-worship. So long as you do not perceive habit-worship and let go of it, you will not be in realism (*ḥaqīqat-warzī*). These words are known in the *sharīʿa* of reality, not in the *sharīʿa* of habit![26]

In short, habit-worship entails selfishness, not selflessness. A person who is given to his deeply ingrained habits, such as his neurotic and excessive knit-picking over matters of religion and law, is a self-lover and not a lover as such. But if he can relinquish all manner of habit, then he will enter the tavern of ruins (*kharābāt*):

> How much do you hear? Come out of habit-worship! Even though you have been in school for seventy years, you have not become selfless for one moment! Be in the tavern of ruins for one month to see what the tavern and the tavern-dwellers do with you! O metaphorical drunkard! Become a tavern-dweller. Come so that we can go along for one moment![27]

Establishing the groundwork for ʿAyn al-Quḍāt's metaphysics of light and darkness and his stance against habit-worship sets the stage for his deep critique of

---

25 ʿAyn al-Quḍāt, *Tamhīdāt* 186, § 245.
26 ʿAyn al-Quḍāt, *Tamhīdāt* 320, § 419.
27 ʿAyn al-Quḍāt, *Tamhīdāt* 340–341, § 452.

any individual who understands religion on a purely exoteric level. Approaching matters in this way allows us to discern unity to ʿAyn al-Quḍāt's thought amid what seem like disparate remarks and stray comments: ʿAyn al-Quḍāt's critique of religious formalism turns out to be a direct corollary to his conception of light and darkness, which itself is connected to his theodicy and theory of human agency on the one hand,[28] and his doctrine of imaginalization on the other. At minimum, this multi-layered reading enables us to see that the religious formalists for ʿAyn al-Quḍāt account for the outward and "dark" aspect of religion, which is personified by Iblis and his misguidance:

> Do you know what that black light is? "He was among the unbelievers" [Q 2:34] was his robe of honor, and the sword of "'By Thy exaltedness, I shall certainly cause them to err'" [Q 38:82] was unsheathed. Without choice, he was cast as a meddler into the darknesses of "the darknesses of land and ocean" [Q 6:97]. The guardian of exaltedness came, serving as the doorkeeper of the presence of "I seek refuge from Satan the accursed."[29]

> You call him "Iblis." He has taken misguidance as his profession, and curses have become his nourishment: "'By Thy exaltedness, I shall certainly cause them to err, all together'" [Q 38:82].[30]

At the same time, those who have penetrated the inner meaning of religion account for its inward and luminous aspect, which is personified by the Prophet and his guidance:

> Alas! Perhaps you have never read that God has an attribute called "the most special attribute," and which is hidden from all people? Perhaps this most special attribute that is hidden from all is the light of Muhammad? Do you know what I am saying?[31]

> Anyone who suffers and is half-slain in the world of Iblis is cured in the world of Muhammad; for unbelief is the stamp of annihilation, and faith the stamp of subsistence. As long as there is no annihilation, subsistence

---

28 See Rustom, Mohammed, "Devil's advocate: ʿAyn al-Quḍāt's defence of Iblis in context," in *SI* 115.1 (2020), 65–100. For an inquiry into ʿAyn al-Quḍāt's complex understanding of religion in general and Islam in particular, see Boylston, Nicholas, "Islam from the inside out: ʿAyn al-Quḍāt Hamadānī's reconception of Islam as vector," in *JIS* 32.2 (2021), 161–202.

29 ʿAyn al-Quḍāt, *Tamhīdāt* 119, § 168.

30 ʿAyn al-Quḍāt, *Tamhīdāt* 30, § 43.

31 ʿAyn al-Quḍāt, *Tamhīdāt* 268, § 351.

> will not be found. In this path, the more the annihilation, the more perfect the subsistence.[32]

These points also significantly relate to another dimension of ʿAyn al-Quḍāt's thought, namely his unique understanding of the Quran. Just as Iblis (whose tragic image ʿAyn al-Quḍāt develops like none other) accounts for misguidance and darkness, so too does he symbolize the black letters in which the Quran is written. And, just as Muhammad accounts for guidance and light, so too does he symbolize the white paper upon which the black letters of the Quran are written. Moving away from misguidance and towards guidance, away from Iblis and towards Muhammad, and away from the black letters of the Quran to their supra-formal, white aspect, one comes face to face with the primordial Quran itself:

> Perhaps you have not read or heard this verse in the Quran: "There has come unto you, from God, a light and a clear Book" [Q 5:15]. It calls Muhammad "light" and it calls the Quran, which is the Word of God, "light": "and those who follow the light that has been sent down with him" [Q 7:157]. In the Quran you see black letters on white parchment. But parchment, ink, and lines are not light![33]

> Alas! We see in the Quran nothing but black letters and white paper! When you are in existence, you can see nothing but blackness and whiteness. But when you come out of existence, the Word of God will obliterate your own existence. Then, from obliteration, you will be taken to affirmation. When you reach affirmation, you will not see another blackness—all you will see is whiteness, and will recite, "and with Him is the Mother of the Book" [Q 13:39].[34]

5 Self-Reflexive Love

ʿAyn al-Quḍāt's doctrine of beauty and love as found in *Paving the path* is inextricably linked to the foregoing discussion. For starters, our author argues that the hearts and spirits of God's servants can act as mirrors in which He sees His own beautiful image:

32 ʿAyn al-Quḍāt, *Tamhīdāt* 233, § 302.
33 ʿAyn al-Quḍāt, *Tamhīdāt* 2, § 2.
34 ʿAyn al-Quḍāt, *Tamhīdāt* 173, § 229.

> The heart knows what the heart is and who it is. The heart is the object of divine gaze, and itself is worthy: "God looks at neither your forms nor your actions, but He looks at your hearts."[35] O friend! The heart is God's looking-place.[36]

> "My Lord, what is the wisdom in my being created?"[37] The answer came: "The wisdom in your being created is that I should see Myself in the mirror of your spirit and My love in your heart." He said, "The wisdom is that I see My own beauty in the mirror of your spirit and cast love for Myself into your heart."[38]

ʿAyn al-Quḍāt's main point of emphasis in these kinds of discussions is upon what we can call the "Muhammadan mirror." Unlike everything in creation, each of which serves as an imperfect and partial site for God's Self-manifestation, the Muhammadan mirror is the perfect and total site for it:

> Anyone who searches for the path of recognition of His Essence, a mirror is prepared for the spirit of his own reality, and he looks in that mirror—he recognizes the spirit of Muhammad. Thus, the mirror is prepared for the spirit of Muhammad. The mark of this mirror has come: "I saw my Lord on the night of the Ascension in the most beautiful form." In this mirror, "Faces that Day shall be radiant, gazing upon their Lord" [Q 75:22–23] is found, and a cry is given in the world: "They did not measure God with His true measure" [Q 6:91]; that is, they did not recognize God with His true recognition.[39]

In other words, ʿAyn al-Quḍāt maintains that a dimension of God's infinity involves what we can call Self-negation, which allows for divine delimitation and particularization. Objectively beholding His beautiful form vis-à-vis the particularities of His Self-manifestation, God displays Himself in the mirrors of human souls (which are imperfect). At the same time, He objectively beholds His beautiful form vis-à-vis the totality of His Self-manifestation by displaying Himself in the Muhammadan mirror (which is perfect). What all of this entails is that, even outside of His subjective Self-knowledge, God's

35 Cf. Muslim, *Ṣaḥīḥ*, Birr, 10, no. 6707.
36 ʿAyn al-Quḍāt, *Tamhīdāt* 146, § 198.
37 This question is posed by Abū Bakr al-Nassāj (d. 487/1094), the master of Aḥmad al-Ghazālī.
38 ʿAyn al-Quḍāt, *Tamhīdāt* 272, § 356.
39 ʿAyn al-Quḍāt, *Tamhīdāt* 58–59, § 79.

gaze is still fixed upon His creatures only because it is really fixed upon Himself qua manifestation:

> Alas! O listener of these words! By the spirit of Muṣṭafā, people have imagined that God's beneficence and love of creation is for them. It is not for them! Rather, it is for Himself. When a lover gives a gift to his beloved and is gentle to her, that gentleness he shows is not for her as much as it is out of love for himself. Alas! From these words you imagine that God's love for Muṣṭafā is for Muṣṭafā. But this love for him is for Himself![40]

The logic which informs this perspective is straight-forward: just as God can only know Himself both subjectively and objectively, so too can He only love Himself both subjectively and objectively. With respect to God's Self-seeing, ʿAyn al-Quḍāt explains it in this way:

> Just as God can only recognize God, so too can God only see God. "Show me!" [Q 7:143] had the color of jealousy. "Thou shalt not see Me" [Q 7:143].[41] He said, "O Moses! With your exertion and striving, you will not see Me; with your selfhood alone, you cannot see Me. You can only see Me through Me."[42]

Yet insofar as God sees His own imaginalized beautiful image through the myriad forms in creation, human beings can likewise contemplate God's beauty amidst the constellation of refracted images which emerge from His Self-seeing love and beauty onto the mirror of the cosmos. The interplay between love, seeing, and beauty takes us back, once again, to the function of imaginalization:

> When one sees increase in beauty and an added form at every instance or every day, love becomes greater and the desire to see the object of one's yearning becomes greater. At every instant, "He loves them" [Q 5:54] is imaginalized for "they love Him" [Q 5:54], and "they love Him" is, likewise, imaginalized. Thus, in this station, the lover sees the Beloved at every instant in another form of beauty and sees himself in a more perfect and complete form of love.[43]

---

40 ʿAyn al-Quḍāt, *Tamhīdāt* 217, § 278.

41 These two verses respectively convey Moses' request to see God and God's response to Moses.

42 ʿAyn al-Quḍāt, *Tamhīdāt* 305–306, § 402.

43 ʿAyn al-Quḍāt, *Tamhīdāt* 124–125, § 173.

6 Conclusion

If this article amounts to nothing but a drop from the vast ocean of *Paving the path*, from one perspective it will have accounted for the ocean itself. As ʿAyn al-Quḍāt puts it, "A drop from the ocean can itself be called the 'ocean.'"[44] From another perspective, our attempt has surely been feeble, unlike many others who have successfully taken the plunge into *Paving the path* and have even emerged with some of its precious pearls. Among these successful divers we may count such important medieval Persian authors as ʿAzīz al-Dīn Nasafī (d. before 699/1300) and ʿAbd al-Raḥmān Jāmī (d. 898/1492). But it was the Sufis of India who were especially skilled at treading its waters. This was particularly true among authors in the Chishtī and Suhrawardī orders.

The popular reception of *Paving the path* in Indian Sufi circles is evidenced in the writings of such figures as Niẓām al-Dīn Awliyāʾ (d. 725/1325), Naṣīr al-Dīn Chirāgh Dihlawī (d. 757/1356), Rukn al-Dīn Kāshānī (d. after 738/1337), and Masʿūd Bakk (d. 789/1387). The great Sufi master Sharaf al-Dīn Manīrī (d. 782/1380) also draws on this tradition in his oral discourses wherein he speaks of ʿAyn al-Quḍāt with admiration. The culmination of the Indian reception of *Paving the path* comes over two hundred years after ʿAyn al-Quḍāt's death in the form of a detailed Persian commentary upon it by the Indian spiritual teacher Sayyid Muḥammad Gīsūdarāz (d. 825/1422). We also know that, in the 11th/17th century, *Paving the path* was translated into Dakhini by Mīrān Ḥusayn Shāh (d. 1070/1669), and into Ottoman Turkish at around the same time, where it was a staple text of the Mevlevi Sufi order. During this same time period, the great Safavid philosopher and mystic Mullā Ṣadrā (d. 1050/1640) also drew on *Paving the path* in his highly developed Quranic commentaries.[45]

Even in our own times, a great wave of interest has been generated around *Paving the path* in intellectual and spiritual circles in countries such as Canada, England, France, Iran, Pakistan, Turkey, and the United States. Past or present, what all readers of *Paving the path* would surely acknowledge is that it is a testimony to the originality of its author, whose soul, like the book itself, was an ocean without a shore:

44 ʿAyn al-Quḍāt, *Tamhīdāt* 336, § 443.

45 For ʿAyn al-Quḍāt's historical reception, see the introduction in Rustom, *Inrushes of the heart*.

Whatever is learned from people is land and land-like, and whatever is learned from God—"The All-Merciful taught the Quran" [Q 55:1–2]—is ocean and ocean-like. And the ocean has no end.[46]

Bibliography

Abū Dāwūd, *Sunan*, in *Jamʿ jawāmiʿ al-aḥādīth wa-l-asānīd wa-maknaz al-siḥāḥ wa-l-sunan wa-l-masānīd*, v, Vaduz: Jamʿiyyat al-Maknaz al-Islāmī, 2000.

ʿAyn al-Quḍāt, *A Sufi martyr*, trans. A.J. Arberry, London: Keagan and Paul, 1969.

ʿAyn al-Quḍāt, *Tamhīdāt*, ed. ʿAfīf ʿUsayrān, Tehran: Intishārāt-i Manūchihrī, 1994.

ʿAyn al-Quḍāt, *Nāma-hā*, ed. ʿAlī Naqī Munzawī and ʿAfīf ʿUsayrān, 3 vols., Tehran: Intishārāt-i Asāṭīr, 1998.

ʿAyn al-Quḍāt, *The essence of reality: A defense of philosophical Sufism*, ed. and trans. Mohammed Rustom, New York: New York University Press, 2022.

Bukhārī, *Ṣaḥīḥ*, in *Jamʿ jawāmiʿ al-aḥādīth wa-l-asānīd wa-maknaz al-siḥāḥ wa-l-sunan wa-l-masānīd*, ii, Vaduz: Jamʿiyyat al-Maknaz al-Islāmī, 2000.

Boylston, Nicholas, "Islam from the inside out: ʿAyn al-Quḍāt Hamadānī's reconception of Islam as vector," in *JIS* 32.2 (2021), 161–202.

Ibrāhīmī Dīnānī, Ghulām Ḥusayn, *ʿAql-i mast: Tamhīdāt-i ʿAyn al-Quḍāt Hamadānī*, ed. Iḥsān Ibrāhīmī Dīnānī, Isfahan: Mīrāth-i Kuhan, 2021.

Jamʿ jawāmiʿ al-aḥādīth wa-l-asānīd wa-maknaz al-siḥāḥ wa-l-sunan wa-l-masānīd, Vaduz: Jamʿiyyat al-Maknaz al-Islāmī, 2000.

Muslim, *Ṣaḥīḥ*, in *Jamʿ jawāmiʿ al-aḥādīth wa-l-asānīd wa-maknaz al-siḥāḥ wa-l-sunan wa-l-masānīd*, iv, Vaduz: Jamʿiyyat al-Maknaz al-Islāmī, 2000.

Nasr, Seyyed Hossein et al. (eds.), *The study Quran: A new translation and commentary*, New York: HarperOne, 2015.

Rūmī, Jalāl al-Dīn, *Mathnawī-yi maʿnawī*, ed., trans., and comm. Reynold A. Nicholson, 8 vols., London: Luzac, 1925–1940.

Rustom, Mohammed, "ʿAyn al-Quḍāt between divine jealousy and political intrigue," in *Journal of Sufi Studies* 7.1–2 (2018), 47–73.

Rustom, Mohammed, "Devil's advocate: ʿAyn al-Quḍāt's defence of Iblis in context," in *SI* 115.1 (2020), 65–100.

Rustom, Mohammed, *Inrushes of the heart: The Sufi philosophy of ʿAyn al-Quḍāt*, Albany, NY: SUNY Press, 2023.

Safi, Omid, *The politics of knowledge in premodern Islam: Negotiating ideology and religious inquiry*, Chapel Hill: University of North Carolina Press, 2006.

Tirmidhī, *Sunan*, in *Jamʿ jawāmiʿ al-aḥādīth wa-l-asānīd wa-maknaz al-siḥāḥ wa-l-sunan wa-l-masānīd*, vi, Vaduz: Jamʿiyyat al-Maknaz al-Islāmī, 2000.

46 ʿAyn al-Quḍāt, *Tamhīdāt* 8, § 11.

CHAPTER 2

The Life of the Breath of Life in Rūmī

Kazuyo Murata

"I was dead, I became alive; I was crying, I became laughing,"[1] says Rūmī (d. 672/1273) in one of his famous *ghazal*s, describing his transformation from a sober scholar to a passionate lover of God after spending some intense years with his spiritual companion, Shams-i Tabrīzī.[2] Becoming alive (*zinda*) through passionate love of God is a prominent theme in Rūmī's thought, and it entails intensification of the human experience of both the pain of separation from and the pleasure of union with God. Choosing to live in such inner turmoil[3] as a passionate lover of God is the opposite of living in indifference or weariness (*malūlī*), which Rūmī sees as a major hindrance on the path to God: "Beware, do not sigh coldly in your indifference! Seek pain! Seek pain, pain, pain!"[4]

One of the motifs Rūmī uses in speaking about becoming alive is "breath" (*nafas*, *nafkha*, *nafḥa*, *dam*, etc.), which has roots in the Quran and Hadith. The Quran describes how human life begins with God's breath: "I breathed into him of My spirit" (Q 15:29; 38:72). However, in relation to human beings, the work of the divine breath does not end with this initial impartation of life to lifeless clay. In Rūmī's tales, the divine breath appears again and again in various forms and occasions over the course of human life to guide, console, and revive human

1 Rūmī, Jalāl al-Dīn, *Kulliyyāt-i shams: Dīwān-i Jalāl al-Dīn Muḥammad Balkhī (Mawlawī)*, ed. Badīʿ al-Zamān Furūzānfar, Tehran: Hirmis, 2007, *ghazal* 1393, line 1 (the *ghazal* number indicated here is according to the standard Furūzānfar numbering presented in parentheses in the Hirmis edition); here I follow Arberry's translation in Rūmī, *Mystical poems of Rumi*, trans. Arthur J. Arberry, Chicago: University of Chicago Press, 2009, 184, poem 170. I indicate where I have adopted existing translations of Rūmī's works; otherwise translations are mine.

2 The most extensive work on Shams' life and thought to date is by Chittick, William C., *Me and Rumi: The autobiography of Shams-i Tabrizi*, Louisville, KY: Fons Vitae, 2004.

3 One might recall that "fluctuation" (*taqallub*) is the root meaning of "heart" (*qalb*) as it oscillates between "two of the fingers of the All-Merciful," as the Prophet said. See Chittick, *The Sufi path of knowledge: Ibn al-ʿArabī's metaphysics of imagination*, Albany, NY: SUNY Press, 1989, 106.

4 Rūmī, *Mathnawī-yi maʿnawī*, ed. and trans. Reynold A. Nicholson, 2 vols., Tehran: Būta, 2002, IV, 4304. This is Chittick's translation of the verse in Chittick, *The Sufi path of love: The spiritual teachings of Rumi*, Albany, NY: SUNY Press, 1983, 208.

 | DOI:10.1163/9789004529038_003

beings. This brief study looks at the "life" of the divine breath in the course of human existence from creation to resurrection as presented by Rūmī.

On the aforementioned verse, "I breathed into him of My spirit" (Q 15:29; 38:72), Rūmī writes,

> God said to the angels, *See, I am creating a mortal of clay. When I have shaped him and breathed My Spirit into him, fall you down, prostrating yourselves to him* (XXXVIII 71–2). He connected the body to dark clay and the spirit to the breath of His own Spirit, so that the light and divine Breath would make this dark clay its instrument for righteousness, justice, and guarding God's Trust; so that it might be a means of salvation, elevation, and high degrees. The purpose was not that the dark clay, through its greed for the light of *I breathed My spirit into him*, should make the lamp its instrument for treachery and theft.
>
> When a thief comes with a lamp,
> he takes the better goods.
>
> On the contrary, that lamp and candle of the Breath-Spirit should illuminate the clay of the body with the light of religion and hold it back from its greed for clay, ignorance, and heaviness.[5]

God's spirit breathed into clay thus represents not only life but also the intellect that allows human beings to discern the right from the wrong and follow divine guidance.

There are passages in the Quran and Hadith that indicate various ways in which the divine breath reappears in the course of the earthly life of human beings. For instance, the Prophet said, "Indeed, I find the breath of the All-Merciful (*nafas al-raḥmān*) from the direction of Yemen."[6] Rūmī alludes to this *ḥadīth* by employing various terms including "scent" (*bū*) and "wind" (*bād*) in reference to the breath of the All-Merciful. For example, "God's scent (*bū-yi yazdān*) reaches Muhammad from the direction of Yemen."[7]

Rūmī also points out that prophets not only perceive God's scent but also convey it to others by emitting sweet scent, which in turn has a special effect on its perceiver:

---

5 Chittick, *The Sufi path of love* 151–152; this is Chittick's translation of Rūmī, *Maktūbāt*, ed. Yūsuf Jamshīdīpūr and Ghulām Ḥusayn Amīn, Tehran: Bungāh-i Maṭbūʿātī-yi Pāyanda, 1956, 189–190.

6 While this is the formulation of the prophetic saying commonly found in Sufi literature, it is not found in this exact wording in major Hadith collections.

7 Rūmī, *Kulliyyāt, ghazal* 2003, line 11.

> Like the breath of the All-Merciful that, without mouth, comes to Muhammad from Yemen
> Or like the scent of Ahmad the Messenger that, in intercession, comes to the sinner
> Or like the scent of goodly, gentle Joseph [that] strikes upon the soul of lean Jacob.[8]

The last verse refers to the Quranic episode of Jacob sensing Joseph's smell from a distance before Joseph's shirt reaches Jacob to restore his eyesight:

> "Go, take this shirt of mine, and cast it over my father's face; he will recover his sight. Then bring me your family all together." So, when the caravan departed, their father said, "Indeed I find Joseph's wind/smell (*rīḥ*), if you do not think me doting" (Q 12:93–94).

Among the prophets in Islam, Jesus stands out in his strong association with "breath" because of the following two Quranic depictions. First, God impregnated Mary by breathing His spirit into her: "And Mary, Imran's daughter, who guarded her virginity—so We breathed into her of Our spirit" (Q 66:12). On this Rūmī writes,

> A spiritual Form, purified of the elements, reached the heart's Mary from God's Court—
> A passing messenger impregnated the heart with a breath concealing the spirit's mystery.[9]

Second, Jesus' breath gives life to the dead:

> "I have come to you with a sign from your Lord. I will create for you from clay like the shape of a bird and breathe into it, and then it will become a bird with God's permission. I will heal the blind and the leper and bring the dead back to life with God's permission" (Q 3:49).

Rūmī often speaks of the power of Jesus' breath in giving relief and imparting life: "At the door of that cell of Jesus in the morning, that he might deliver them from sin by his breath;"[10] and "So that the breath of Jesus may make you

8 Rūmī, *Mathnawī* ii, 1199–1201.
9 This is Chittick's translation of Rūmī's *ghazal* 3072, lines 7–8 in *The Sufi path of love* 344.
10 Rūmī, *Mathnawī* iii, 300.

alive, fair, and blessed like itself."[11] In many of Rūmī's poems, Jesus appears as a reviver of body and spirit.

Not only the prophets but also saints or friends (*awliyā'*) of God—some of whom are Sufis—have the power to detect and convey God's breath as sweet scent. Rūmī presents an extensive reflection on this topic in the *Mathnawī* in his tale of the Sufi Bāyazīd (or Abū Yazīd) Basṭāmī (d. 234/848 or 261/875), who predicted the birth of a great Sufi, Abū l-Ḥasan Khāraqānī (352–425/963–1033), nearly a century earlier by sensing a sweet scent (*bū-yi khwush*) coming from Khāraqān:

> One day that sultan of god-wariness was passing
> with his disciples toward the desert.
> Suddenly a sweet scent came to him
> in the district of Rayy from the direction of Khāraqān.
> Right there he made a lament of the one who yearns;
> he smelled a scent from the wind.
> He was inhaling the sweet scent lovingly;
> his soul was tasting wine from the wind ....
> When traces of intoxication became apparent in him,
> a disciple inquired him about that breath (*dam*) ...
> "You are inhaling a scent when no flower is manifest;
> without doubt it is from the Unseen and from the rose garden of the All.
> O you who are the aim of every soul that reaches its aim,
> at every moment/breath (*dam*) there is a message and a letter from the Unseen.
> Like Jacob, at every moment/breath, from a Joseph
> the cure is reaching your nose."[12]

After the disciple finishes posing his long question, Bāyazīd answers:

> He said, "A marvelous scent came to me,
> just like [it did] to the Prophet from Yemen,
> As Muhammad said, 'On an easterly breeze,
> the scent of God is coming to me from Yemen.'"[13]

11 Rūmī, *Mathnawī* i, 1909.

12 Rūmī, *Mathnawī* iv, 1803–1806; iv, 1810; iv, 1813–1815.

13 Rūmī, *Mathnawī* iv, 1826–1827.

As Bāyazīd's "soul was tasting wine from the wind," we can see an intoxicating effect of the sweet scent of God only on those who can sense it. Rūmī then adds: "From Uways and from Qaran a marvelous scent made the Prophet intoxicated and rapturous."[14] He also writes elsewhere: "Since our life is from 'I blew into him of My spirit' [Q 15:29; 38:72], it is permissible that His 'I blew' be wine and nourishment;"[15] and "From that breath by which Adam became astonished and the wits of the folk of Heaven became witless."[16]

Another key *ḥadīth* on God's breath is the following: "In the days of your time, your Lord has breathings (*nafaḥāt*); so expose yourselves to them."[17] A section of the *Mathnawī* is devoted to an exploration of this *ḥadīth*:

> The Prophet said that the breathings of the Real
> prevail in these days.
> Keep ear and intelligence attentive to these moments;
> seize such breathings.
> A breathing came, saw you, and went;
> it gave life to whomever it wanted and then went.
> Another breathing arrived; be vigilant
> so that you will not miss this one too, o mister![18]

Rūmī points out that whether people are aware or not, the fact is that God keeps sending His breath their way throughout their earthly existence. This leads Rūmī to emphasize the importance of cultivating the power of the "nose" to detect the faintest of God's sweet scent:

> The nose is what catches a scent
> and is taken by the scent toward a highway.
> Whoever has no scent is without a nose;
> a scent is that scent that is of religion.[19]

Once one develops a nose that is receptive to the scent of God, one will find many spiritual benefits, one of which is removal of sorrow: "The wind of the

14 Rūmī, *Mathnawī* iv, 1829.
15 Rūmī, *Kulliyyāt*, *ghazal* 1734, line 9.
16 Rūmī, *Mathnawī* i, 1987.
17 This *ḥadīth* is not found in standard collections but is in secondary collections such as al-Haythamī, *Majmaʿ al-zawāʾid wa-manbaʿ al-fawāʾid*, Beirut: Muʾassasat al-Maʿārif, 1986, 10.234.
18 Rūmī, *Mathnawī* i, 1950–1953.
19 Rūmī, *Mathnawī* i, 440–441.

breath burnishes the breast of sorrow; if the breath stopped for a moment, annihilation would come upon the soul;"[20] "He is the one who takes your hand and the burden-bearer; from moment to moment have hope for that breath from Him;"[21] and

> Wherever I shine from the niche of a breath,
> there the difficulties of a world are resolved.
> That darkness not removed by the sun
> becomes like morning through Our breath.[22]

In fact, the divine breath not only takes away sorrow but also gives joy to its perceiver:

> Is there any soul that is not joyful through His sweet scent,
> even if the soul has no sense of whence it has become joyful?
> Many a happy rose is laughing through the breath of the Real,
> but not every soul knows whence it has become laughing.[23]

While the majority of Rūmī's discussions on "breath" is about God's breath, he also speaks about "bad breaths" of some creatures, which need to be avoided and eliminated. The Quran gives one instance of bad breathing in Q 113:4: "From the evil of the women who blow on knots" (*al-naffāthāt fī l-ʿuqad*). The historical reference may be to black magic that was being practiced during the time of the Prophet, from which people are urged to take refuge in God.[24] When Rūmī refers to this verse, he indicates that it is not only the practitioners of black magic that one must guard against but also this entire world that casts hot spells of temptations:

> The Prophet called this world of yours a sorceress
> because through her spells she put humankind in the pit.
> Beware! The hag has hot spells;
> her hot breath has taken kings captive.

---

20 Rūmī, *Kulliyyāt*, *ghazal* 26, line 8.
21 Rūmī, *Mathnawī* ii, 2518.
22 Rūmī, *Mathnawī* i, 1940–1941.
23 Rūmī, *Kulliyyāt*, *ghazal* 423, lines 3–4.
24 See Nasr, Seyyed Hossein et al. (eds.), *The study Quran: A new translation and commentary*, New York: HarperOne, 2015, 1581–1582.

> She is "the women who blow" [Q 113:4] within one's breast;
> she is the one who fastens the knots of sorcery.[25]

The antidote to the bad breaths of this world that tighten knots to ensnare humanity, according to Rūmī, is the "sweet-breathed" (*khwush damī*) "knot-loosener" (*ʿuqda gushā*)—that is, God:

> Behold! Seek the sweet-breathed knot-loosener,
> one who knows the secret of "God does what He wills" [Q 14:27] ....
> Her breathing (*nafkh*) has tightened these knots;
> so seek the breath (*nafkha*) of the sole Creator
> So that "I breathed into him of My spirit" [Q 15:29; 38:72]
> may liberate you from this and say, "Come higher!"
> The breathing of sorcery is not consumed except by the breathing of the Real;
> the former is the breathing of wrath, while the latter is the breathing of mercy.[26]

Foul breath thus pulls human beings toward this world and therefore toward God's wrath, while the sweet breath of God takes them to His mercy.[27]

Rūmī warns that it is wrong to assume that all bad breaths are external to human beings, for they themselves can emit bad breaths: "A smell of a bad inmost heart (*sirr*) comes from your breath, and your sorrow glares from your head and face, o braggart!"[28] Rūmī points out how God and His friends can see through the hearts of people, and no pretense can deceive them because it is like claiming to have eaten rose-scented sugar when in fact one has eaten garlic.[29] Moreover, the bad-breathed will not have their prayers answered because their bad breath is an indicator of their vices, which only deserve God's wrath:

---

25 Rūmī, *Mathnawī* iv, 3193–3195.

26 Rūmī, *Mathnawī* iv, 3198; iv, 3202–3204.

27 Rūmī speaks about the need to loosen these "knots" in various places, and a similar discussion is found in Ibn ʿArabī, who compares individual beliefs (*iʿtiqād*, *ʿaqīda*) to knotting (*ʿaqd*) and knots (*ʿuqda*) because of their shared root, *ʿ-q-d*. Chittick explains, "To the extent that a person ties his belief into a tighter knot, he will be further from the Divine Reality, which is Nondelimited by definition. To the extent he loosens all knots, he will be nearer to God," *The Sufi path of knowledge* 336. Also see Chittick, *The Sufi path of knowledge* 340, 347, 352.

28 Rūmī, *Mathnawī* iv, 1773.

29 Rūmī, *Mathnawī* iv, 1776.

The smell of arrogance, the smell of greed, and the smell of concupiscence
will come through speech like [the smell of] onions ….
Supplications, then, will be rejected because of that smell;
that crooked heart shows in tongue.[30]

The process of refreshing our breaths to eliminate the bad odor coincides with realizing that we do have a good breath inside us, i.e., the divine breath blown into us at the moment of creation:

This frame of Adam is a face cover;
we are the *qibla* of all prostrations.
Regard that breath; do not see Adam
so that we may snatch your soul with gentleness.[31]

You make the form of a person from filth and blood [cf. Q 16:66]
such that he would flee two farsangs from the smell of the filth.
You make him food out of dust that turns into pure verdure;
he escapes from impurity when You breathed spirit into him.[32]

To help human beings remember that the divine breath lies at their core, Rūmī makes the analogy of the human being as a reed through which the breath of God blows: "The heart said, 'I am His reed, lamenting by His breaths,'"[33] and "Because by God's gentleness I was [the object of] 'I breathed' [Q 15:29; 38:72], I am the breathing of the Real (*nafkh-i ḥaqq*), separate from the body's reed."[34] Thus the imagery of the reed that famously opens the *Mathnawī* with its lament of having been cut off from the divine reedbed now reveals another aspect of the human being: it is hollow inside so that the divine breath may blow through it.

Once human beings realize their identity as God's breath, every other breath—including the breath of the human body—becomes something worth obliterating. Rūmī compares human beings' relation to God to the flea's relation to the wind in a tale of Solomon hearing the complaint of the flea against the wind:

30 Rūmī, *Mathnawī* iii, 166; iii, 169.
31 Rūmī, *Kulliyyāt*, *ghazal* 1576, lines 5–6.
32 Rūmī, *Kulliyyāt*, *ghazal* 2820, lines 9–10.
33 Rūmī, *Kulliyyāt*, *ghazal* 2135, line 10.
34 Rūmī, *Mathnawī* iii, 3933.

> When [the wind] comes, where shall I find rest,
> for it wrings breath (*damār*) out of me?
> Such is the seeker of God's court:
> when God comes, the seeker becomes naught.
> Although that union is subsistence in subsistence,
> at the beginning that subsistence is in annihilation.[35]

Giving up one's own breath becomes necessary in order for the human being to be filled with the divine breath entirely. When one is empty of one's own breath, God fills the void with His own breath, just like the butcher slaughtering sheep, according to another of Rūmī's parables:

> When no more breath remains in the sheep, [the butcher] fills it with his own breath;
> you will see where the breath of God takes you.
> I have spoken this in parables; otherwise, His generosity
> kills no one and lets go of killing.[36]

Rūmī repeatedly speaks of annihilation (*fanā'*) of the individual self[37] in terms of giving up of one's individual breath. Rūmī's instructions for this voluntary death to the self are the following: "Become His dust and get buried out of grief over Him so that your breath gains replenishments from His breath."[38]

Giving up one's own breath can mean two things: (1) annihilating one's individual identity apart from God, which is a way of becoming alive in spirit; and (2) giving up the bodily breath, meaning death of the body. Here it seems worth laying out four types of life and death: bodily life, bodily death, spiritual life, and spiritual death. Throughout Rūmī's writings, what he cares most about among these four is spiritual life, i.e., being alive in spirit. Conversely, what he abhors most is spiritual death. Being alive or dead in body is of secondary importance to Rūmī. But does that mean that the body is unnecessary and meaningless in his view? The answer is no. In reading Rūmī, Sachiko Murata points out the complementary relationship between body and spirit:

35 Rūmī, *Mathnawī* iii, 4655–4657.

36 Rūmī, *Kulliyyāt, ghazal* 765, lines 5–6.

37 This is the state of voluntary death to the self as described by the *ḥadīth*, "Die before you die!" See Chittick, *The Sufi path of love* 183.

38 Rūmī, *Mathnawī* iii, 132.

> [T]he analogue of heaven within the human microcosm, the "spirit," can do nothing without a body, which acts as its vehicle and instrument. Just as God created the universe to manifest His own perfections—the Hidden Treasure—so also the spirit needs the body to bring its own potentialities into actuality. As Rūmī puts it,
>
> The spirit cannot function without the body,
> and without the spirit, the body is withered and cold.
> Your body is manifest and your spirit hidden:
> These two put all the world's business in order.[39]

In the circle of human life from birth to death to resurrection, what matters in Rūmī's view is the aliveness of the spirit throughout the process of embodiment. The aliveness of each human spirit is judged by how it utilizes each bodily breath, that is, the time that is given for its embodied existence.

After the body gives up its breath and meets its death, there occurs a key event that involves yet another breathing: the resurrection of all human beings through the blowing of the horn (Q 18:99; 39:68) so that they can face God for the final judgement. Despite the terrifying connotations of the blowing of the horn at the end of times as depicted in the Quran, Rūmī notices and highlights the life-giving power of the breathing into the horn. In fact, the blowing of the horn often functions as a symbol of spiritual revival in his writings:

> You are for me the breathing into the horn and the resurrection, so what shall I do?
> Dead or alive, wherever you are, there I am.
> Without Your lips, I would be like an inanimate and silent reed;
> what melodies shall I play the moment You breathe into my reed?[40]

Rūmī often calls whoever has the power to revive the human spirit—e.g., God, prophets, and saints—"Isrāfīl," the angel who blows the horn to resurrect the dead: "Because You are the Isrāfīl of my heart who makes water and clay alive, breathe the breath (*nafkha*) of God into our ear from the fortunate path!;"[41]

39 Murata, Sachiko, *The Tao of Islam: A sourcebook on gender relationships*, Albany, NY: SUNY Press, 1992, 14. This is her translation of Rūmī, *Mathnawī* v, 3423–3424.

40 Rūmī, *Kulliyyāt, ghazal* 1641, lines 2–3.

41 Rūmī, *Kulliyyāt, ghazal* 11, line 6.

"Behold, for the saints are the Isrāfīl of the time; from them the dead attain life and flourish."[42]

Rūmī's depictions of the life-giving breath of God show how it accompanies the human being at each moment, from creation to resurrection. Rūmī refers to the ever-present nature of God by employing a unique Persian term, *ham-dam* or *ham-nafas*, literally meaning "co-breather," with a sense of intimacy and being in unison:[43] "In the two worlds there is no co-breather other than God."[44] As human beings are empty containers for the divine breath like the reed, their sole co-breather and intimate friend who accompanies them at each breath can only be God, the provider of their bodily and spiritual breath. Rūmī says, "Be like the fish in the ocean of meaning, who becomes a co-breather of none but sweet water."[45]

∴

If students and scholars are also like fish in the ocean of knowledge, Professors Chittick and Murata have thrown many students and readers into that ocean, only to make them realize that they had been fish out of water all along, now growing ever thirstier for the sweet water of the shoreless ocean of knowledge. The search for knowledge that Chittick and Murata commenced more than half a century ago has taken them literally unto China and many other places. Their example and work are invitations to become *ham-dam* in their search for knowledge, which can be seen as a chain of breaths that sustain and are sustained by scholars from generation to generation. Out of gratitude and heartfelt wishes for "their warm breaths" to continue to guide us all for many years to come, may I say, *damishān garm*!

42 Rūmī, *Mathnawī* i, 1929.

43 Nurbakhsh translates *ham-dam* as "friend-in-breath:" "This expression indicates an intimate friend of like temper and a companion on the Way," Nurbakhsh, Javad, *Spiritual poverty in Sufism* (faqr & faqir)*: Including some definitions of spiritual stations, mystical states, time, and breath*, trans. Leonard Lewisohn, London: Khaniqahi-Nimatullahi Publications, 1984, 137.

44 Rūmī, *Kulliyyāt, ghazal* 2284, line 6.

45 Rūmī, *Kulliyyāt, ghazal* 658, line 7.

Bibliography

Chittick, William C., *The Sufi path of love: The spiritual teachings of Rumi*, Albany, NY: SUNY Press, 1983.

Chittick, William C., *The Sufi path of knowledge: Ibn al-ʿArabī's metaphysics of imagination*, Albany, NY: SUNY Press, 1989.

Chittick, William C., *Me and Rumi: The autobiography of Shams-i Tabrizi*, Louisville, KY: Fons Vitae, 2004.

al-Haythamī, *Majmaʿ al-zawāʾid wa-manbaʿ al-fawāʾid*, Beirut: Muʾassasat al-Maʿārif, 1986.

Murata, Sachiko, *The Tao of Islam: A sourcebook on gender relationships*, Albany, NY: SUNY Press, 1992.

Nasr, Seyyed Hossein et al. (eds.), *The study Quran: A new translation and commentary*, New York: HarperOne, 2015.

Nurbakhsh, Javad, *Spiritual poverty in Sufism* (faqr & faqir)*: Including some definitions of spiritual stations, mystical states, time, and breath*, trans. Leonard Lewisohn, London: Khaniqahi-Nimatullahi Publications, 1984.

Rūmī, Jalāl al-Dīn, *Maktūbāt*, ed. Yūsuf Jamshīdīpūr and Ghulām Ḥusayn Amīn, Tehran: Bungāh-i Maṭbūʿātī-yi Pāyanda, 1956.

Rūmī, Jalāl al-Dīn, *Divani Shamsi Tabriz*, trans. Reynold A. Nicholson, San Francisco: Rainbow Bridge, 1973.

Rūmī, Jalāl al-Dīn, *Mathnawī-yi maʿnawī*, ed. and trans. Reynold A. Nicholson, 2 vols., Tehran: Būta, 2002.

Rūmī, Jalāl al-Dīn, *The Masnavi*, trans. Jawid Mojaddedi, books 1–4, Oxford: Oxford University Press, 2004–2017.

Rūmī, Jalāl al-Dīn, *Kulliyyāt-i shams: Dīwān-i Jalāl al-Dīn Muḥammad Balkhī (Mawlawī)*, ed. Badīʿ al-Zamān Furūzānfar, Tehran: Hirmis, 2007.

Rūmī, Jalāl al-Dīn, *Mystical poems of Rumi*, trans. Arthur J. Arberry, Chicago: University of Chicago Press, 2009.

CHAPTER 3

Mirrors in the Dream of the Alone: A Glimpse at the Poetry of Bīdil

Ali Karjoo-Ravary

1 Introduction

Mīrzā ʿAbd al-Qādir b. ʿAbd al-Khāliq, known as Bīdil-i Dihlawī, was born in ʿAẓīmābād (modern day Patna, India) in 1054/1644. His family was of Turkic descent from the Arlās tribe of the Chaghatay and was, in keeping with the time, multilingual.[1] He moved to Delhi at the age of twenty and took it up as place of residence, though he travelled widely throughout his life and, in his own recounting, met many scholars and sages from different religious communities. His works are extant and well-preserved. In addition to the collection of his *ghazal*s and shorter *mathnawī*s, he has an autobiography titled *Chahār ʿunṣur* (*The four elements*) written between 1094/1683 and 1116/1704, and four large *mathnawī*s.[2] The longest of these, entitled *ʿIrfān*, is 11,000 verses long and was completed in 1122/1711. Mīrzā Bīdil died nine years after *ʿIrfān*'s completion in Delhi in 1133/1720, and the reputed (but recently recovered) site of his burial is now a shrine devoted to poetic performance and competition (*mushāʿara*).[3]

Mīrzā Bīdil's influence is a subject in and of its own.[4] Of the many poets indebted to him, Mīrzā Ghālib (d. 1285/1869) and ʿAllāma Iqbāl (d. 1357/1938) are two notable examples, and through them he left his mark on Urdu liter-

1 For his basic biographical sketch in English, see Siddiqi, Moazzam, "Bīdel, ʿAbd-al-Qāder," in *EIr Online*, iv.3, 244–246, https://iranicaonline.org/articles/bidel-bedil-mirza-abd-al-qader-b (last accessed: 31 October 2021).

2 On his autobiography, see Qasemi, Sharif H., "Čahār onṣor," in *EIr Online*, iv.6, 623–624, http://www.iranicaonline.org/articles/cahar-onsor (last accessed: 31 October 2021) and Keshavmurthy, Prashant, *Persian authorship and canonicity in late-Mughal Delhi: Building an ark*, New York: Routledge, 2016, 15–60. On *Chahār ʿunṣur*'s designation as an autobiography, see 16–17. Keshavmurthy also analyzes Bīdil's refrains and devotes a chapter to the tale of Madan and Kāmdī in *ʿIrfān*.

3 Safvi, Rana, "Bagh-e Bedil," https://ranasafvi.com/bagh-e-bedil/ (last accessed: 31 October 2021).

4 On Bīdil's afterlives, see Schwartz, Kevin L., "The local lives of a transregional poet: ʿAbd al-Qāder Bidel and the writing of Persianate literary history," in *Journal of Persianate Studies* 9.1 (2016), 83–106.

 | DOI:10.1163/9789004529038_004

ature.[5] He has been the poet par excellence in Afghanistan and Central Asia for over the past two centuries and remains so even in the diaspora. In Iran, where modernists criticized his work in the 20th century, there has been a major revival of interest in his poetry over the last few decades. This has led to a robust body of secondary literature on Bīdil in Persian and Urdu, as well as multiple European languages.[6]

The present paper is primarily an exploration through translation of some aspects of Ibn ʿArabī's (d. 638/1240) influence as enshrined in Bīdil's *ʿIrfān*.[7] The influence of Ibn ʿArabī on Bīdil was clearly stated in 1992 by William C. Chittick, who identified *ʿIrfān* as the prime locus of this influence.[8] Since then, it has been explored in depth by Prashant Keshavmurthy and ʿAlī Akbar Shūbkulāyī.[9] The principle behind the translations presented below is simply to give a

5 On Ghālib and Bīdil, see Aḥsan al-Ẓafar, Sayyid [also: Ahsan-uz-Zafar, Syed], *Bīdil wa-Ghālib*, New Delhi: Ghalib Institute, 2012.

6 On his life and work, see ʿAbdulghanī, *Rūḥ-i Bīdil*, Lahore: Majlis-i Taraqqi-i Adab, 1968; Shafīʿī Kadkanī, Muḥammad R., *Shāʿir-i āyina-hā: Barrisī-yi sabk-i hindī wa-shiʿr-i Bīdil*, Tehran: Āqā, 1989; Aḥsan al-Ẓafar, Sayyid [also: Ahsan-uz-Zafar, Syed], *Mīrzā ʿAbd al-Qādir Bīdil: Ḥayat aur kārnāmah*, 2 vols., Rampur: Rampur Raza Library, 2009. On another one of his *mathnawīs*, see Kovacs, Hajnalka, *"The tavern of the manifestation of realities": The Maṣnavī muḥīṭ-i aʿẓam by Mīrzā ʿAbd al-Qādir Bedil (1644–1720)*, Chicago (PhD Diss.): University of Chicago, 2013; Fiṭrat, Muḥammad Ḥusaynī, *Jahān-i Bīdil*, Tehran: Intishārāt-i ʿIrfān, 2014. In terms of poetics, see Gould, Rebecca, "Form without a home: On translating the Indo-Persian Radīf," in *Translation Review* 90 (2014), 15–28; Ṭabāṭabāʾi, Mahdī, "Bunmaya-yi ḥubāb wa-shabaka-yi taṣwīrhā-yi ān dar ghazaliyyāt-i ʿAbd al-Qādir Bīdil-i Dihlawī," in *Matnpizhuhī-yi Adabī* 18.62 (2014), 82–123; Mikkelson, Jane, "Of parrots and crows: Bīdil and Ḥazīn in their own words," in *Comparative Studies of South Asia, Africa and the Middle East* 37.3 (2017), 510–530; Mikkelson, Jane, "Flights of imagination: Avicenna's Phoenix (ʿAnqā) and Bedil's figuration for the lyric self," in *Journal of South Asian Intellectual History* 2 (2019), 28–72; and Pellò, Stefano, "Two passing clouds: The rainy season of Mīrzā Bīdil and Amānat Rāy's Persian version of Bhāgavata Purāṇa 10.20," in *Iran and the Caucasus* 24.4 (2020), 408–418 as well as Pellò, Stefano, "The portrait and its doubles: Nāṣir ʿAlī Sirhindī, Mīrzā Bīdil and the comparative semiotics of portraiture in late seventeenth-century Indo-Persian literature," in *Eurasian Studies* 15.1 (2017), 1–35. On this phase of Persian poetry see Losensky, Paul, *Welcoming Fighānī: Imitation and poetic individuality in the Safavid-Mughal Ghazal*, Costa Mesa, CA: Mazda Publishers, 1998; Faruqi, Shamsur Rahman, "A stranger in the city: The poetics of Sabk-e Hindi," in *Annual of Urdu Studies* 19 (2004), 1–93 and the introduction to Keshavmurthy, *Persian authorship*.

7 This is rooted in a project that first began under the tutelage of Professor William C. Chittick and Professor Sachiko Murata as an undergraduate and which later expanded under the guidance of Professor Jamal J. Elias during my graduate education.

8 Chittick, William C., "Notes on Ibn al-ʿArabī's influence in the subcontinent," in *MW* 82.3–4 (1992), 218–241, 237.

9 Keshavmurthy, *Persian authorship*; Shūbkulāyī, ʿAlī A., *Ṣulḥ-i kull: Jāygāh-i ʿirfān-i Ibn ʿArabī dar shiʿr-i Bīdil-i Dihlawī*, Tehran: Intishārāt-i Mawlā, 2019. Ibn ʿArabī is, of course, not the only influence on Bīdil, and Keshavmurthy shows how Bīdil's lyric masterfully interweaves Indic

taste of the ways in which Bīdil stretches and articulates, through verse, unarticulated or implied aspects of Ibn ʿArabī's thought. I will begin with Bīdil's cosmology (with a touch of my own commentary) and end with some of his prescriptive verses that address the human situation.

2 The Loneliness of God

The world arrived as proof of oneness
because loneliness brings imagination.
The Essence has neither defect nor perfection,
but whoever is alone never lacks imagination. (lns. 522–523)
Love keeps so many images with itself;
a lonely person imagines so much.
Here, multiplicity is the affirmation of unity.
Here, awareness is effaced in bewilderment. (lns. 525–526)[10]

God being "alone" before creation is a standard feature of Islamic theology connected to His oneness (*tawḥīd*). Bīdil's perspective considers the implication of this solitude by drawing a parallel with the human experience of loneliness. The consolation of loneliness is the imagination. Thus, even the solitude associated with God's utter unity caused Him to imagine. What did He imagine? Everything that exists. Bīdil takes a standard aspect of Ibn ʿArabī's thought, the cosmos as God's imagination, and connects it to God's being alone and His love for another.[11] In so doing, he links imagination not only to creation, but to a love that brings about imaginal worlds without cease.

Aware of the full implications of human loneliness, Bīdil is quick to assert that "the Essence has neither defect nor perfection." The Essence (*dhāt*) is a technical term referring to God's selfness or He-ness, and is the referent to

---

philosophy and cosmology. See also, in this regard, Pellò, Stefano, "Black curls in a mirror: The eighteenth-century Persian Kṛṣṇa of Lāla Amānat Rāy's *Jilwa-yi ẕāt* and the tongue of Bīdil," in *Hindu Studies* 22 (2018), 71–103. On other possible influences and thinking through Bīdil with Avicenna (as well as complicating the notion of influence itself), see Mikkelson, "Flights."

10 All translations of Bīdil are mine and from the following edition: Bīdil, ʿAbd al-Qādir, *Shuʿla-yi āwāz: Mathnawīhā-yi Bīdil-i Dihlawī*, ed. Akbar Bihdārwand, Tehran: Nigāh, 2009, 48.

11 On the cosmos as God's imagination, see Chittick, William C., *The sufi path of knowledge: Ibn al-ʿArabī's metaphysics of imagination*, Albany, NY: SUNY Press, 1989, 112–129.

which all of God's names point. It is ontologically prior to any designation, manifestation, or relationship. While Bīdil affirms that the Essence is without any lack, he also marks that it is without any perfection. Rather, it is beyond any sense of either, and there is no room in that utter unity for any duality, distinction, or hierarchy.

The turn towards imagination is not out of any fundamental lack, but rather, is simply part of being alone. This is a clear reference to a well-known *ḥadīth qudsī* wherein God says, "I was a Hidden Treasure and I loved to be known, so I created creation so that they may know Me."[12] For Bīdil, in keeping with Ibn ʿArabī, this creation is identical to God's imagining. He was a hidden treasure, that is, a storehouse for limitless beauties, and His love drew these things out. Ultimately, these are nothing but Him; He simply loved for His own self to be known by Himself. But He is also limitless, and the Essence in its utter unity can never fully be known. Thus, the drawing out of all things, God's imagination, is the way through which every possible thing comes to be known. The never-ending world of multiplicity is God's journey of self-knowledge, and every self-disclosure is an image from His imagination. This is why multiplicity is the proof of His unity, and the relationship between the two effaces understanding in "bewilderment." Bewilderment, in keeping with Ibn ʿArabī and his followers, is the ultimate form of knowledge.[13]

> In every disclosure, in this expanse of self-disclosure,
> the Real has no need for appearing as two.
> Behind every work, there is an illusionless face;
> and where He is the face, the back is He too.
> The drunkenness of your unity is without sobriety—
> this means duality is effaced from your face. (lns. 289–291)
> The seed of unity does not bring two flowers:
> from reality, duality does not laugh. (ln. 293)[14]

Behind every existent thing there is God's face, an allusion to the Quranic verse "Wherever you turn, there is the face of God" (Q 2:115). The inward reality of existence is one, and thus, all its manifestations are one even as they differ in

12 On the use of this *ḥadīth* in Ibn ʿArabī's school, see Murata, Sachiko, *The Tao of Islam: A sourcebook on gender relationships in Islamic thought*, Albany, NY: SUNY Press, 1992, 61–63.

13 On bewilderment as the ultimate response to the way things are, see Chittick, William C., *The self-disclosure of God: Principles of Ibn al-ʿArabī's cosmology*, Albany, NY: SUNY Press, 1998, 78–83.

14 Bīdil, *Shuʿla* 40.

accord with standing and perspective. Every face and what lies behind it is He. His drunkenness, that is, the intoxication of His bewildering and continuous presence, is without sobriety.[15] By sobriety, Bīdil means the capacity to distinguish twoness. Everything that appears as different is not different yet also not the same—there is no possibility for anything but bewilderment. The limitless is fully present in the limited.

> When He falls into attachment, He is named "corporeal."
> When He leaves entification, He is named "untouchable."[16]
> When He converses, He adorns temporality.
> When He holds His breath, He constructs eternity.
> Servanthood is with Godhood here.
> The trap is opening your wings here.
> The Real is apparent through him and he through the Real:
> Unbounded from bounded and bounded from Unbounded. (lns. 62–65)[17]

Bīdil says that all phenomenal differences are merely aspects of the Real. The "corporeal" marks attachment to form, the process through which something becomes an entity. When He leaves "entification," He is named the opposite, that which is without body or form. Entification is a technical term taken from Ibn ʿArabī. The entities are the possible things, that is, the objects of God's knowledge. "The fixed entities" are the individual things as known by God, while the "possible" or "actual" entities refer to their status in creation. Entification is the process whereby an undifferentiated part of God's knowledge (the Hidden Treasure) is differentiated and distinguished.[18] Attachment means that God drapes the possible things with His own being and attributes so that they may exist.

God's speech is the adornment of temporality, that is, the entire phenomenal cosmos, which is the canvas of His imagination. When He holds His breath

15 To read more about what this specific intoxication may mean, cf. Chittick, *The Sufi path* 199.

16 This is the Arabic word *ṣamad*, a name of God presented here as the opposite of *jasad*, corporeal body. *Ṣamad* has a sense of everlasting refuge, a safe haven which is inaccessible. On the difficulties of this word, see Rosenthal, Franz, "Some minor problems in the Qurʾān," in *The Joshua Starr memorial volume: Studies in history and philology*, New York: Conference on Jewish Relations, 1953, 67–84.

17 Bīdil, *Shuʿla* 31.

18 On the entities, see Chittick, *The self-disclosure* 29–46.

and remains silent, He "constructs eternity." The image here is taken from Ibn ʿArabī's identification of the cosmos with the breath of God, calling it "the Breath of the All-Merciful." He writes, "the Breath of the All-Merciful bestows existence upon the forms of the possible things, just as the human breath bestows existence upon letters. Hence the cosmos is the words of God in respect to this breath …"[19] On His breath, He articulates every possible thing. But every exhalation, as Bīdil points out, has an inhalation. He holds His breath and marks eternity, where everything remains undifferentiated, hidden, and non-manifest. But He breathes, so His inhalation and exhalation are perpetual, and thus, creation is perpetual. Ibn ʿArabī calls this "the Renewal of Creation."[20] Since everything is forever changing and in flux, one needs to witness reality from the widest perspective possible through the eyes of bewilderment, not understanding. Only this perspective allows one to grasp that ultimately, servanthood is godhood. In other words, when He, through His breath, made manifest the cosmos, He manifested both "god" and "servant," two aspects of the same reality.[21] Bīdil uses an ambiguous line to warn that "opening your wings," that is, affirming your own identity and choice at this level, is a trap, for it affirms duality. This is because from the perspective of sheer unity, the differences of identity and personhood are effaced. At the same time, that line also means that "opening your wings," that is, freedom, can only be found in the "trap," that is, the world of delimitation. Being demands a locus for manifestation.

The ambiguous "he" refers, in one aspect, to every created thing, pointing out thereby that the relationship between God and the cosmos is reciprocal.[22] But it also specifically refers to the "Muhammadan Reality" or the "Perfect Human Being." God loved to be known, so the manifestation of His knowledge demands a perfect knower. This reality is the "image" upon which humanity was created, and thus, ultimately, nothing other than God-as-Divinity (as opposed to God-as-Essence). For the sake of this reality, God created the cosmos so that He could truly be known, and it is ultimately nothing other than God knowing Himself through love. Ibn ʿArabī writes: "The Breath of the All-Merciful made the cosmos manifest in order to release the property of love and relieve what the Lover found in Himself. So He knew Himself through witnessing in

19 Chittick, *The Sufi path* 131.
20 Chittick, *The Sufi path* 97–98.
21 On the mutual need between servant and God, see Murata, *The Tao* 190–191.
22 This ambiguity is increased by the Persian language wherein the word is ungendered and can also mean "it."

the Manifest …"[23] The Perfect Human Being is the one who loves, knows, and witnesses God, or, in other words, he is God in the form of lover, knower, and witnesser.

> Action, the flowering of His signs;
> Names, the form of His stations.
> He let out a breath and morning dawned.
> He let His tears fall and clouds rained.
> The meadow: a page from the lesson of His color.
> The ocean: a drop of sweat from the heat of His yearning.
> Eternity-without-beginning: the fable of His start.
> Eternity-without-end: the thought of His finish.
> The meaning of the words: knower and known,
> body and spirit, apparent and secret,
> from the world of necessity to possibility itself,
> whatever you think, hidden or visible,
> He is spring and these are all His color.
> He is the instrument and all this His song. (lns. 104–110)[24]

Actions and Names refer to aspects of God. The Names, also called the Attributes, designate the different aspects through which God becomes manifest. Actions are how those aspects relate to creation. God's action is the flowering of the Muhammadan Reality in the cosmos, and the Names of God are the forms of that reality's stations. Station is a technical term from Sufism designating the waypoints of the path to (or with) God. Bīdil is pointing out that God's creation and self-disclosure are all for the sake of this reality, a reality that is simultaneously what it means to be God and what it means to be human. The cosmic world is but a manifestation of the states of this reality.

Eternity-without-beginning is a translation of the Arabic word *azal* and signifies the eternity preceding the now. It is a direction that is ontological, not temporal, and signifies a relationship with the eternally present. Bīdil identifies it with the fable or myth of creation and beginning, in other words, where we came from, marking that the origin of the human being is rooted in the imagination of God. Eternity-without-end, *abad*, is eternity in the other direction. It is the thought of the end, the imagination of consummation and fulfilment which will forever continue. As the other side of the story, Bīdil is saying that the

23 Chittick, *The Sufi path* 131.
24 Bīdil, *Shuʿla* 33.

tale of return is also within the imagination and thus, a place that will never be reached, only eternally sought. Coming and going are all rooted in God, whose own Essence is where every opposite is rooted and every path is completed. That is why Bīdil calls Him "spring" and the phenomenal world His "color." Like "spring," that reality appears only through other things. God's instrument plays, but all we hear is the music.

> He is a sun but kneads dust,
> He has a heaven but never boasts.
> Lord, what is this play of bewilderment?
> Who is this Resurrection-seller of possibility?
> The dust of a sigh carries heaven;
> a tear drop holds the ocean in embrace. (lns. 71–73)
> A glance spreads its wings before the eyelashes,
> with all, without all, not this, not that.
> His work is outside the exertion of choice.
> His color is outside the garment of spring.
> With every negation of an other, still thinking of another;
> the circling of His flirtation draws him closer to Himself.
> This means that in that place where nothing can be found,
> besides this wave and curl,
> nothing can be found. (lns. 75–78)[25]

Bewilderment, as mentioned before, is the only proper response to the way things are for Ibn ʿArabī and his followers. The reason for this is that reality is the union of all opposites. Everything in the cosmos is God and not God simultaneously. Ibn ʿArabī is clear that "this is a place of bewilderment: He/not He." Then, commenting on Q 8:17, "you did not throw when you threw, but God threw," he writes:

> He is saying, "You are not you when you are you, but God is you." This is the meaning of our words concerning the Manifest and the loci of manifestation and the fact that He is identical with them, even though the forms of the loci of manifestation are diverse … The "other" is in reality affirmed/not affirmed, He/not He.[26]

25 Bīdil, *Shuʿla* 31–32.
26 Chittick, *The Sufi path* 115.

Thus, for Bīdil, the cosmos is a "play of bewilderment" wherein God's appearance is also a veil. He is the sun of existence but He molds with His own hands the form of an earthly body, the lowest of the low. The heavens belong to him but His most perfect manifestation is the form of a slave. Ibn ʿArabī makes it doubly clear: "knowledge of God is bewilderment, and knowledge of creation is bewilderment."[27] God is a "Resurrection-seller," that is, He sells to the world of possibility, aka the objects of His knowledge, a "Resurrection," an entering into forms. But Bīdil keeps asking who He is because the answer is both clear and unclear. The name of that reality conceals as much as it reveals. And in all of this, Bīdil reminds, He is "with all, without all, not this, not that." He has a work that is outside all exertion, let alone choice, though "each day He is upon a task" (Q 55:29). And He has a color, though outside of all the colors of the phenomenal world (spring) which is, "the coloring of God, and who colors better than God?" (Q 2:138). Despite all His negation of what is other than Him ("there is no god but God"), He is forever thinking of "the other," an other He always wanted. Bīdil thus depicts creation as flirtation, as the play of love, where God as both Lover and Beloved, veils and unveils, chases and hides. He constantly seeks what is other than Him and leaves the objects of His affection, if receptive, in wonder, bewilderment, and awe. God, alone, imagines an entire cosmic order wherein human beings, in their every love, find and lose parts of Him. All this is a dream, God's dream, which is identical with reality itself. And in this dream, what are human beings?

> We are the imaginings of the veil of the Unseen,
> the conversation of the book "wherein is no doubt" [Q 2:2].
> The goal of this image is an illusion.
> The meaning of this speech is non-existent.
> Silence: the lesson of our signlessness.
> Lament: the composition of our inability. (lns. 471–473)
> Finding is nonexistent while seeking subsists;
> the cup is in dust and conversation pours drinks. (ln. 475)

The Unseen is God's knowledge and the veil is God's imagination, and human being are pictures drawn upon the veil. God breathes, and human beings are His articulations, the conversation of God, each individual an act of revelation. The goal of the image of their being is "illusion," that is, imagination itself is the goal. And their meaning, as words of God, is fundamentally non-existent,

27 Chittick, *The Sufi path* 380.

for it resides in God's knowledge where nothing has yet reached "existence." Their silence shows that they, in themselves, have no signs. They only operate based on the signs given to them, that is, based on how they are articulated by Being itself. Their lament is the admission of their inability, that is, their fundamental poverty towards God. Bīdil is saying that human beings are nothing but an image, or rather, streams of images that come in and out of the Unseen. The image itself has no access to the Unseen, only receiving what comes out of it. Thus, they never find because that would mean reaching the end of God's knowledge, which does not exist. Rather, they are always seeking, for seeking itself was the goal of creation. The cup, that is, the receptivity which defines the human being, is in dust, earth, the lowest of the low. And conversation, that is, God's articulations upon the breath, pours wine and is the Saqi who determines the portion of each. All existence is the play of images which "loved to be" seen, and humanity exists only for this game of love.

> Us and I are entirely the measuring out of yearning;
> there are no sides, it is just the exploration of oneness.
> This means that the grasping and holding of love and desire
> are ultimately nothing but the imagination of unity. (lns. 517–518)[28]

Human identity was measured in and out of passion, that is, the only goal of individual identity is love. Human and divine identity are not sides but rather, perspectives of and upon unity, just like how what a dreamer sees in their dream is nothing but their own self, even if they see someone else. All the game of love and desire, the story of creation and its end, is all the imagination of unity, or, as mentioned before, the imagination of God, God's dream. As Ibn ʿArabī writes, "… the forms of the cosmos … are the forms of a dream to the Dreamer. The interpretation of the dream is that those forms are His states, nothing else."[29] The play of the cosmos, with all its characters and relations, is nothing but the infinite states and stations of the One who dreamt and forever dreams it all.

> Because that signless instrument subsists,
> the melodies too subsist.
> The imaginings have no end:
> shorelessness cannot be tied by any limit. (lns. 508–509)[30]

28 Bīdil, *Shuʿla* 49.
29 Chittick, *The Sufi path* 120.
30 Bīdil, *Shuʿla* 49.

The instrument, God's form-bestowing imagination, is outside of time and forever subsists, even as it perpetually changes due to its limitless nature.

> Our melody is the clamor of the entities
> appearing from the instrument of eternity.
> The entities are not outside the eternal instrument;
> the fermentation of wine is in wine itself. (lns. 499–500)[31]

Creation is not outside of God but, as already mentioned, resides within Him as His dream.

> The ocean of engendered things and all it contains
> is the churning restlessness of His reality.
> His outward and inward are temporality and eternity.
> His form and meaning are existence and nonexistence. (lns. 6–7)
> His substance is the meaning of intellects and souls.
> His accident: the color of the sensible world. (ln. 10)[32]
> The East and West of which they speak
> are the front and back of His turning face. (ln. 22)
> The tumult of the nine oceans, with all its pomp and pride,
> drowns beneath the image-wave of but one of His pearls. (ln. 25)
> From His form, meaning is the springtime of witnessing.
> From His meaning, form is the paradise of appearing.
> The garden of the Names is full of roses through His Essence.
> The feast of the things is radiant through His light. (lns. 27–28)
> His nearness and farness: the presence and absence of self.
> Understanding His self leads to bewilderment of self. (ln. 32)[33]

The cosmos is an ocean in which the engendered things are never at rest, just like God's imagination, according to Bīdil. Restlessness is a characteristic of love, and, in this context, connected to God's original love to be known.

God's substance, a term taken from philosophy, is the meaning of souls and intellects, their intelligible reality as known by God. Accident, the opposite of substance in philosophy, refers to a property that is secondary to a thing's existence. Bīdil uses the pair to say that the color of the world (everything that can be

31 Bīdil, *Shuʿla* 48.
32 Bīdil, *Shuʿla* 29.
33 Bīdil, *Shuʿla* 30.

sensed in it) is an accidental property of the reality of Being. While the meaning of a thing does not change, its color and how it is perceived always changes.

Like Ibn ʿArabī, reality is a matter of perspective for Bīdil. East and west derive meaning from the turning of God's face and need each other to make sense. Similarly, the classic pair of opposites in Sufi literature, form and meaning, are two interdependent aspects of the same reality. The form of God is what allows meaning to be witnessed while the meaning of God is what allows His form to appear. All language about God is either a perspective on the Real or a relational aspect of it. The Real is the ground of all identity. Nearness to and farness from God is also nearness and farness from the self, and Persian allows it to refer to either the human self or the self of God. Ultimately, the ambiguity is intentional as the two are one and the same. And since human beings are the imaginings of one who is Alone, they too find themselves alone in the world.

> Because creation's place of solitude is so narrow,
> The heart of solitude is where creation finds ease. (ln. 537)[34]

The word translated as "solitude," *waḥsha*, also means wilderness and dread. This place, that is the world wherein human beings have been imprisoned, is narrow and constricted. In one sense, this is a reference to the Quranic verse: "We created man in the most beautiful of statures, then we reduced him to the lowest of the low" (Q 95:4–5). Man was sent to the lowest of the low, that is, the most constricted of the constricted, a reference to their embodiment in a form that is more or less fixed.[35] As Ibn ʿArabī writes,

> here is nothing wider than the reality of man, and nothing narrower. As for its wideness, that is because it is not too narrow for anything at all, except one thing. As for its narrowness, that is because it cannot embrace two incoming thoughts at once, since it is one in essence, so it does not accept manyness.[36]

Being made in the image of God means that every human being is its own solitude. But being an image of something means that humans are its reflection, and like any mirror, humanity can only accept one image at a time. This is why the only ease for a human heart is in the heart of solitude, where one's state most resembles the reality of their being.

34 Bīdil, *Shuʿla* 50.
35 Whatever is dominated by a single form is more constricted.
36 Chittick, *The Sufi path* 376.

What is man? The self-disclosure of perception:
understanding the meaning of "were it not for you …" (ln. 3)[37]

Self-disclosure is a translation of the Arabic word *tajallī*. Disclosure is an unveiling, revelation, or manifestation of something hidden. All disclosure is God's self-disclosure because all creation happens "within" God. Perception is the means by which a thing is known, so man is the self-disclosure of God's knowing of Himself. That is, they are the meaning of another popular *ḥadīth* in which Muhammad quotes God as saying to him, "were it not for you I would not have created the spheres."[38] Bīdil uses this to say that God created the cosmos for the sake of that reality so that it may perceive the Real. Human beings are thus defined based on their capacity to know God and to witness His unbounded imagination and its never-repeating flow and change, an ocean which has always been and will always be.

From their ancient flowing, the departing waves
have bound a form of stability (ln. 538)[39]

This short analysis aimed only to show glimmers of how Ibn ʿArabī's cosmology features in Bīdil's poetry. Bīdil is, in fact, the premier lyricist of Ibn ʿArabī's school, and his poems stretch and play with language itself so as to furnish a new perspective for his audience. In what follows, I will offer thematic selections from *ʿIrfān* without commentary. Whereas the previous selections focused on Bīdil's cosmology ("the Origin"), what follows are Bīdil's prescriptions for how to go back to God ("the Return").

3 Impediments

What path lies there in that direction? Look here, this way;
in this direction see the indication of He.
What appears there, belongs here:
farseeing is the perfection of seeing.
His otherness is nothing but slander,
who can grasp man's flirtatious glances? (lns. 79–81)

---

37 Bīdil, *Shuʿla* 29.

38 Furūzānfar, Badīʿ al-Zamān (ed.), *Aḥadīth-i Mathnawī*, Tehran: Intishārāt-i Dānishgāh-i Tihrān, 1955, no. 546.

39 Bīdil, *Shuʿla* 50.

The eye is awake and the dream, an interpretation.
The lips are silent and the lament, a discourse.
This gardener is intensely colorless.
This world of disclosure—sheer deception.
Happy the heart that placed before Him a mirror!
The Rose Garden is an eye that saw His gait. (lns. 83–85)[40]

You've perceived a garden but there is no color.
There is a mountain before your eyes,
but not of stone. (ln. 168)[41]
You bind similarity to incomparability.
You join metaphor to reality.
You were beauty, but you held a mirror to yourself
and imagined that you were what you saw. (lns. 173–174)
Your being a mirror is duality:
to be before an "I" involves being a "You."
Become a clear mirror; this is perfection!
Efface your own picture; this is beauty! (lns. 176–177)[42]

Far from self but near to all,
a light in every place but dark before yourself. (ln. 223)
The cosmos is rid of the picture of love and hate:
your war and peace are but against yourself.
You are what you call out to, yet you still seek?
Home is in your arms, yet you still run away?
If you are hunted, you are hunted by yourself;
the moment you run, you fall into your own trap.
There is no trace of any other before or behind you.
You run, but from your own shadow.
You've dragged yourself into darkness;
how far you think yourself to be. (lns. 225–229)
No cup had this much residue.
No morning suffered such an assault of night.
Some dust rose and appeared from your body
and it covered you from your own sight.
Heedless of faith, on the verge of sleep,

40 Bīdil, *Shuʿla* 32.
41 Bīdil, *Shuʿla* 35.
42 Bīdil, *Shuʿla* 36.

who but you was ever trampled by their own shadow? (lns. 236–238)
From this sleep, your life-work was thrown upside down.
Now, even shadows attack you by night. (ln. 240)[43]
Strive until this talisman that controls you melts;
until this shadow disappears and becomes a sun. (ln. 251)[44]

4 Seeing Correctly

The substance of modesty is nothing but water:
become water and grasp the meaning of shame.
In the lesson of self-understanding,
no eyeglasses are better than covering the eyes.
Modesty does not see the air above one's head,
water sees nothing but what is before its feet.
Being this and that is nonsensical;
it is shamelessness to see others. (lns. 219–222)[45]

The cause of your running this way and that
is because you do not look before your own feet. (ln. 446)[46]

Your sleep is the mirror-holder of deprivation,
even if it is life, it is non-existence.
You have given death the name "life,"
you have turned your own day, like a shadow, into night (lns. 241–242).
What a storm ignorance threw upon your knowledge;
that, from your dawning, even the night cloister falls.
O illusion-caster of white and black,
night is your lashes and day, your glance.
Though you appear by a hundred veils at night,
when you open your eyes, you yourself are dawn.
For how long will you drink the cup of sleep?
You have shut your lashes to never open them again.
The time of sleep has passed, lift your head.
Lift your lashes from the path of vision.

43 Bīdil, *Shuʿla* 38.
44 Bīdil, *Shuʿla* 39.
45 Bīdil, *Shuʿla* 37.
46 Bīdil, *Shuʿla* 46.

Closed lashes are the darkness of deprivation;
until you open your eyes, it is still night. (lns. 244–249).[47]
Ignorance keeps your mirror black;
God keep you from this affliction.
Do not set the table of doubts through illusion,
you are the mirror of the beauty of certainty.
I fear that your heart will be lost in passing breaths,
and in place of your mirror, only rust will grow.
Before the mirror goes to dust,
there is still a chance to polish it. (lns. 257–260)
There is no ill but your sleep.
If the eye opens,
there is no darkness left. (ln. 262)[48]

Before the candle of realization can be lit,
the eye must be fixed on traversing the self.
That which distracts it is a futile flight;
illusion is to run away from the self.
You seek another, but no other is visible;
these mannerisms are foolish and mistaken.
What is other? That which, at present, you are not;
or, in other words,
the very thought of the future. (lns. 410–413)[49]

5 Being Yourself

Creation, with all this manifestation of perfection,
is nothing but the mirror of an impossible thought. (ln. 266)
You become Him? What an impossible imagining.
He becomes you? This too is illusion and imagination.
Servanthood is not the world of Godhood,
the cage is not the mirror of freedom. (ln. 270–272)[50]

You are outward, let go of sorrow over the inward;
the possible cannot find the necessary.

47 Bīdil, *Shuʿla* 38.
48 Bīdil, *Shuʿla* 39.
49 Bīdil, *Shuʿla* 45.
50 Bīdil, *Shuʿla* 39.

You want to unite heaven and earth?
There is no thought more impossible than this. (lns. 287–288)[51]

If you are heaven or if you are earth,
whatever you are, right now, you are that.
Until another time comes and you take another color,
becoming a rose or wine, a rock or clay. (lns. 415–416)[52]

The ease of the wounded is in impatience;
here, the ship is always in a whirlpool. (ln. 464)[53]

For as long as you are captive, desire not freedom.
For as long as you suffer, sorrow not happiness.
In lamentation, carry not the grief of silence;
for as long as crying is your coin, buy not laughter.
The goal is that you not rush forward
from the enclosure of self through the incantation of desire.
If, in pursuit of meaning, your self is not lost
even a wound is not empty of a smile.
And if your heart looks at your own state,
the wound becomes but a stroll through another rose-garden.
What an affliction, an abandonment, a racing madness,
that you are not content with yourself for even a moment.
You are an ocean but, from this fever and its heedlessness,
all your waves crash upon the shore.
Nested at home and you yearn for travel;
travel far and your glance is towards home.
A jewel and a restless heart together?
A house full of sun yet need for a candle?
All your profits are taken from yourself.
Everything you find, in reality, you lose. (lns. 272–281)[54]
Whatever you are, you are far from yourself;
far from self and utterly forsaken. (ln. 284)[55]

51 Bīdil, *Shuʿla* 40.
52 Bīdil, *Shuʿla* 45.
53 Bīdil, *Shuʿla* 47.
54 Bīdil, *Shuʿla* 39–40.
55 Bīdil, *Shuʿla* 40.

Journey one meadow, whether leaves or flowers.
Swim one direction, whether glass or wine.
You are all light, why think of darkness?
You are all awareness, why bring forth ignorance?
Until you know that end is beginning,
life remains an instrument with an uncouth song. (lns. 294–296)[56]

You are the workshop of high and low,
if you become naught, all that exists is you. (ln. 178)
Seek clarity from this obscurity;
leave your self and find union.
It is better to find meaning without writing.
It is better to receive disclosure without qualification or quantification.
Water has neither outward nor inward:
water writes a simple page. (lns. 180–182)
The wave of your flowering became separation.
Lifting your head became the form of duality. (ln. 185)
Every bubble and foam that rises up,
is nothing but froth, the rest is all wave. (ln. 189)
Both wave and whirlpool are nothing but the ocean;
other than this name, no other can be found.
Grasp the essence, names are many.
Become cooked, raw thoughts are many. (lns. 191–192).

Beholder of the world of imagination,
the disclosure is without veil, rub your eyes!
For how long will you look through your lashes?
For how long will the feet of your yearning trip on your skirt?
Rip off your skirt! Escape the trap!
Part your lashes and rid yourself of raw thoughts.
What is the skirt? The dust of the illusion of duality.
What are the lashes? The veil of what you are.
For how long will you carve duality out of your self?
For how long will you throw dust in the face of disclosure? (lns. 158–162)[57]

56 Bīdil, *Shuʿla* 40.
57 Bīdil, *Shuʿla* 35.

6 Finding Home

Prepare for subsistence, where is perishing?
Dive into the ocean whether waves or foam. (ln. 305)[58]

In your infancy, adolescence is not seen.
In your youth, old age is not there.
If you are night, day cannot be found in you.
If you are dawn, evening cannot fall upon you.
For as long as you are, awareness has no currency;
the zenith has no ascent for as long as you are base.
Ancient instrument of renewal's melody,
the repetition of disclosure cannot be seen from you.
In every breath of yours
one reality spreads its wings into the garment of soul.
That reality is your unbounded subsistence
which, through your talisman, appears bounded.
Through the bounded, be for the unbounded.
This and that are both unreal, be with the Real.
Home is from you, go no further;
gather yourself so you do not lose yourself. (lns. 418–425)[59]

Everyone is left behind yet they pass ahead;
on a journey, yet effaced in their own bosom.
Like a candle, lives have left as you journey on.
Every step, another home.
Every step, another world, a place of refuge.
Once you pass, that is no longer your place.
The candle's goal is traversing its self.
Wherever the eyes open,
that is your homeland. (lns. 406–409)[60]

A homeland other than the present moment is an illusion.
Whatever lies in that direction is non-existent.
Whoever remembered the desert at home,

58 Bīdil, *Shuʿla* 41.
59 Bīdil, *Shuʿla* 45.
60 Bīdil, *Shuʿla* 45.

built hellfire in the middle of paradise. (lns. 385–386)
Whoever remembered home in the desert,
built a nest in hopelessness. (ln. 389)
Not only did the desert journey not bring presence,
but they remained deprived of the joy of home too. (ln. 388)[61]

Even those with feet stuck in mud move forward like bolts of lightning.
Even home has taken the road.
A world has downed the cup of madness;
it plays a song out of scale.
Wine pours glass into the vine.
Water sifts flame into stone.
Here, an entire creation chases vain desire.
Here, no one is in the house. (lns. 330–333)[62]

The fruit of the garden of your disposition is raw,
otherwise, how could existence be a place for rest? (ln. 448)[63]
When the road is not your home,
you will not find ease anywhere. (ln. 298)[64]

7 Love

Intellect and sense, hearing and seeing, spirit and body:
all are love, "He is God, the One" [Q 112:1].
From a fistful of Adam's earth, love spilled
so much blood
that the world lost its color. (lns. 1–2)[65]

From eternity-without-beginning to eternity-without-end
this seed of bewilderment has led thought to roots.
Wherever disclosure appears, it faces Him
until that breath where He is with Him.

61 Bīdil, *Shuʿla* 44.
62 Bīdil, *Shuʿla* 42.
63 Bīdil, *Shuʿla* 46.
64 Bīdil, *Shuʿla* 40.
65 Bīdil, *Shuʿla* 29.

When He leaves self, only love knows—
only flames can read the lines of firewood. (lns. 35–37)[66]

Love says, "Move beyond duality,
hold unto me and move beyond you-ness."
Love has neither head nor foot,
it holds no difference between hearing and sight.
For as long as you are unaware of the submission of love,
the problem is with you, even if you are completely a jewel.
What is submission? Abiding by contentment;
staying away from the meddling of I and us.
If the heart wears the skirt of contentment
even bleeding still has colors. (lns. 300–304)[67]

What is love? The root of the substance of His essence.
Disclosure: the rising splendor of His signs.
Beauty visible but love, hidden;
the flame veiled but the candle waxing proud.
The eye open, its glance cast that way;
the ear and lip unaware of speaking or hearing. (lns. 38–40)
The flash of the Essence was the killer's blade;
Attribute and Name were the blood of sacrifice. (ln. 44)[68]

Beauty: a color that joined His rose.
Love: a fervor that escaped His mind.
Awareness: the opening of His eyes
Ignorance: the batting of His lashes. (lns. 54–55)[69]

8 The Footsteps of God

From the beginning hear the clamor of the end;
see the footprint and hear the footstep.
Everywhere, the dust of the departed rises.
The six directions are filled with the sound of a single footstep.

66 Bīdil, *Shuʿla* 30.
67 Bīdil, *Shuʿla* 41.
68 Bīdil, *Shuʿla* 30.
69 Bīdil, *Shuʿla* 31.

The high points are nothing but the dust of low points:
it is a footprint, not the picture of being.
To realize the meaning of the world,
there is no model better than a footprint.[70]
If you're caught up in the footprint,
your journey through the possible is worthless to awareness. (lns. 555–559)
Without doubt, form is the ambush of annihilation;
it is the frowning brow of the snare of desire. (ln. 561)[71]
The power of the workshop of our being
at times gave forth a dewdrop, at times a breeze.
When, from swooning, the breezes struck one another,
a footprint came to be from the dewdrop.
The dewdrop was effaced, it became air,
and the footprint became the sound of a footstep.
Before this, the imaginal dewdrop
opened its wings in the veil of air.
In this time, the dewdrop subsists through the air;
we have left and the footprint remains.
So through a footstep's sound and a footprint,
for how long will you ponder existence and nonexistence? (lns. 564–569)[72]

If there are no eyes, find ears:
watch the disclosure of those who have left.
Consider these songs that reach your ears—
treasure them! Strive in their intellection.
What trace is there of the ancestors? What appearance?
Those images were without sign.
A few sparks and they opened their eyes,
only to shut them soon again.
Now, all those pictures of imagination
are effaced through devotion in the world of majesty.
Whoever seeks a sign from those disclosures,
seeks an illusory dust from no-place.

70 This is playing on the word for foot (*qadam*) in Arabic which, without voweling, looks the same as eternity (*qidam*).

71 Bīdil, *Shuʿla* 50.

72 Bīdil, *Shuʿla* 51.

If you have a sign of your companions,
you still gaze at those who have gone.
All of these are the same in kind;
they are fairies in human form.
Though they are drawn on the page of sobriety,
as soon as you blink, they are effaced.
Your eyes are short-sighted:
you perceive absence as presence.
In a single moment, consider the being and subsistence
of this rootless world
gone from memory.
All of our seeing and hearing
is but a footprint and a footstep. (lns. 542–553)[73]

No matter how much exertion counts its steps,
the end sleeps within the beginning.
We are birds with no sign of wing or feather,
we are a caravan that leaves no trace.
We go, but leave no footsteps.
We leap in fear,
but there is no trap, no ambush. (lns. 480–482)[74]

Know: the flame is sought and the spark seeks;
the description of the Essence dominates the Attribute.
Where the sun discloses itself,
what can a shadow gain from its own shape?
When a shadow is dominated, it becomes light:
bounty is a flood on the structure of the Unseen.
What does a shadow dominated by light mean?
Open your eyes, what does awareness mean?
When lightning dominates over tinder,
tinder's picture is wiped away from the tablet of being. (lns. 145–149)[75]

Whatever was dominated, its existence left.
The perspectives of its being and subsistence left.
More so the one dominated by the presence of God

73 Bīdil, *Shuʿla* 50.
74 Bīdil, *Shuʿla* 47–48.
75 Bīdil, *Shuʿla* 34.

to whose understanding duality can never reach.
If the Real dominates, where is the unreal?
Layla has unveiled herself;
where is the veil? (lns. 151–153)[76]

Bibliography

ʿAbdulghanī, *Rūḥ-i Bīdil*, Lahore: Majlis-i Taraqqi-yi Adab, 1968.

Aḥsan al-Ẓafar, Sayyid [also: Ahsan-uz-Zafar, Syed], *Bīdil wa-Ghālib*, New Delhi: Ghalib Institute, 2012.

Aḥsan al-Ẓafar, Sayyid [also: Ahsan-uz-Zafar, Syed], *Mīrzā ʿAbd al-Qādir Bīdil: Ḥayat aur kārnāmah*, 2 vols., Rampur: Rampur Raza Library, 2009.

Bīdil, ʿAbd al-Qādir, *Shuʿla-yi āwāz: Mathnawīhā-yi Bīdil-i Dihlawī*, ed. Akbar Bihdārwand, Tehran: Nigāh, 2009.

Chittick, William C., *The Sufi path of knowledge: Ibn al-ʿArabī's metaphysics of imagination*, Albany, NY: SUNY Press, 1989.

Chittick, William C., "Notes on Ibn al-ʿArabī's influence in the subcontinent," in *MW* 82.3–4 (1992), 218–241.

Chittick, William C., *The self-disclosure of God: Principles of Ibn al-ʿArabī's cosmology*, Albany, NY: SUNY Press, 1998.

Faruqi, Shamsur Rahman, "A stranger in the city: The poetics of Sabk-e Hindi," in *Annual of Urdu Studies* 19 (2004), 1–93.

Fiṭrat, Muḥammad Ḥusaynī, *Jahān-i Bīdil*, Tehran: Intishārāt-i ʿIrfān, 2014.

Furūzānfar, Badīʿ al-Zamān (ed.), *Aḥadīth-i Mathnawī*, Tehran: Intishārāt-i Dānishgāh-i Tihrān, 1955.

Gould, Rebecca, "Form without a home: On translating the Indo-Persian Radīf," in *Translation Review* 90 (2014), 15–28.

Keshavmurthy, Prashant, *Persian authorship and canonicity in late-Mughal Delhi: Building an ark*, New York: Routledge, 2016.

Kovacs, Hajnalka, *"The tavern of the manifestation of realities": The Maṣnavī muḥīṭ-i aʿẓam by Mīrzā ʿAbd al-Qādir Bedil (1644–1720)*, Chicago (PhD Diss.): University of Chicago, 2013.

Losensky, Paul, *Welcoming Fighānī: Imitation and poetic individuality in the Safavid-Mughal Ghazal*, Costa Mesa, CA: Mazda Publishers, 1998.

Mikkelson, Jane, "Of parrots and crows: Bīdil and Ḥazīn in their own words," in *Comparative Studies of South Asia, Africa and the Middle East* 37.3 (2017), 510–530.

76 Bīdil, *Shuʿla* 35.

Mikkelson, Jane, "Flights of imagination: Avicenna's Phoenix (ʿAnqā) and Bedil's figuration for the lyric self," in *Journal of South Asian Intellectual History* 2 (2019), 28–72.

Murata, Sachiko, *The Tao of Islam: A sourcebook on gender relationships in Islamic thought*, Albany, NY: SUNY Press, 1992.

Pellò, Stefano, "The portrait and its doubles: Nāṣir ʿAlī Sirhindī, Mīrzā Bīdil and the comparative semiotics of portraiture in late seventeenth-century Indo-Persian literature," in *Eurasian Studies* 15.1 (2017), 1–35.

Pellò, Stefano, "Black curls in a mirror: The eighteenth-century Persian Kṛṣṇa of Lāla Amānat Rāy's *Jilwa-yi ẕāt* and the tongue of Bīdil," in *Hindu Studies* 22 (2018), 71–103.

Pellò, Stefano, "Two passing clouds: The rainy season of Mīrzā Bīdil and Amānat Rāy's Persian version of Bhāgavata Purāṇa 10.20," in *Iran and the Caucasus* 24.4 (2020), 408–418.

Qasemi, Sharif H., "Čahār onṣor," in *EIr Online*, iv.6, 623–624, http://www.iranicaonline.org/articles/cahar-onsor (last accessed: 31 October 2021).

Rosenthal, Franz, "Some minor problems in the Qurʾān," in *The Joshua Starr memorial volume: Studies in history and philology*, New York: Conference on Jewish Relations, 1953, 67–84.

Safvi, Rana, "Bagh-e Bedil," https://ranasafvi.com/bagh-e-bedil/ (last accessed: 31 October 2021).

Schwartz, Kevin L., "The local lives of a transregional poet: ʿAbd al-Qāder Bidel and the writing of Persianate literary history," in *Journal of Persianate Studies* 9.1 (2016), 83–106.

Shafīʿī Kadkanī, Muḥammad R., *Shāʿir-i āyina-hā: Barrisī-yi sabk-i hindī wa-shiʿr-i Bīdil*, Tehran: Āqā, 1989.

Shūbkulāyī, ʿAlī A., *Ṣulḥ-i kull: Jāygāh-i ʿirfān-i Ibn ʿArabī dar shiʿr-i Bīdil-i Dihlawī*, Tehran: Intishārāt-i Mawlā, 2019.

Siddiqi, Moazzam, "Bīdel, ʿAbd-al-Qāder," in *Eir Online*, iv.3, 244–246, https://iranicaonline.org/articles/bidel-bedil-mirza-abd-al-qader-b (last accessed: 31 October 2021).

Ṭabāṭabāʾi, Mahdī, "Bunmaya-yi ḥubāb wa-shabaka-yi taṣwīrhā-yi ān dar ghazaliyyāt-i ʿAbd al-Qādir Bīdil-i Dihlawī," in *Matnpizhuhī-yi Adabī* 18.62 (2014), 82–123.

CHAPTER 4

Sufi Gleams of Sanskrit Light

Shankar Nair

The field of South Asian Studies has exhibited a growing interest in the phenomenon of translation, with scholars in recent decades turning increasing attention to the multitudes of creative retellings and vernacular iterations of classical Indian texts and tales that pepper the archive.[1] One particular current of translation activity that has captured especial attention is the so-called Mughal "translation movement," referring to the Mughal Empire's efforts to patronize and facilitate the translation of a large corpus of Sanskrit texts into the Persian language, an initiative spanning primarily the 10th/16th and 11th/17th centuries. To accomplish these translations, Mughal nobles often brought together different translation "teams," for which Persophone Muslim scholars would work alongside one or more Sanskrit *paṇḍit*s, typically the bearers of a traditional Hindu or Jain scholarly formation.[2]

When, as a young, aspiring scholar many years ago, I first set out to pursue my own study of the Mughal translation movement, there was accordingly a considerable body of books and articles to consult and after which to attempt to model myself. Yet none of these models quite suited me, as I struggled to formulate my research questions and how best to pursue them. To my surprise, it was a chance encounter with a book not located within South Asian Studies at all, but rather, within Chinese Studies, that finally provided the key to unlock my eventual scholarly trajectory: Professor Sachiko Murata's *Chinese gleams of Sufi light*, with Professor William C. Chittick's new translation of ʿAbd al-Raḥmān Jāmī's *Lawāʾiḥ* included therein (some nine years later, their *The sage learning of Liu Zhi* would provide even further guidance and inspiration). There was simply no work in South Asian Studies the likes of what I had encountered in these remarkable monographs; at last, I had before me a framework and model

1 See, e.g., Paula Richman's (ed.) landmark volume, *Many Rāmāyaṇas: The diversity of a narrative tradition in South Asia*, Berkeley, CA: University of California Press, 1991, as well as the more recent volume in many ways inspired by it, Hawley, Nell Shapiro and Sohini Sarah Pillai (eds.), *Many Mahābhāratas*, Albany, NY: SUNY Press, 2021.

2 For more, see, e.g., Truschke, Audrey, *Culture of encounters: Sanskrit at the Mughal court*, New York: Columbia University Press, 2016 and Nair, Shankar, *Translating wisdom: Hindu-Muslim intellectual interactions in early modern South Asia*, Oakland, CA: University of California Press, 2020.

 | DOI:10.1163/9789004529038_005

of scholarship to adapt for my own intellectual purposes. Although I have never had the privilege of studying under Professors Murata and Chittick directly, my own work would simply not have been possible without the foundations their scholarship provided for me (however inadvertently—and with all shortcomings being fully my own!). I am delighted to be able to express my gratitude, in some small measure, through this contribution to a richly deserved *Festschrift* in their honor.

∵

In the spirit of Professors Murata and Chittick's publications that guided me so, I translate below one passage hailing from the era of the Mughal translation movement. On the left, I translate the original Sanskrit source text, known as the *Laghu-Yoga-Vāsiṣṭha* (*The abridged "Vasiṣṭha's Yoga"*[3]), composed by one Gauḍa Abhinanda in likely the 4th/10th or 5th/11th century. On the right is my rendition of one of the several Persian translations of this treatise that were produced under Mughal patronage, known as the *Jūg bāsisht* (a Persian transliteration of the Sanskrit title "*Yoga-Vāsiṣṭha*"), composed in 1006/1597 by the Muslim scholar Niẓām al-Dīn Pānīpatī (d. 1018/1609–1610) and the Hindu Sanskrit *paṇḍit*s Jagannātha Miśra Banārasī (d. unknown) and Paṭhān Miśra Jājīpūrī (d. unknown) at the behest of Prince Salīm (the soon-to-be Emperor Jahāngīr, d. 1037/1627). Since comparison and contrast between the two texts is a desideratum of the exercise, I have erred on the side of literality in my translation style for the purposes of this piece. Professors Murata and Chittick possess a remarkable ability in their translation work of keeping their footnotes and explanatory interjections to a minimum (a talent I have not at all begun to master): I attempt to emulate this practice to a certain extent below, in the hopes that both the Sanskrit and Persian iterations of the treatise might speak for themselves while still remaining lucid to the reader. I do provide some explanatory annotations, however, at points where it might help to deepen the reader's appreciation of the nuances of the two texts. These annotations are also, in part, a compensation for the rigors so often posed by a literal-leaning mode of translation.

3 The *Laghu-Yoga-Vāsiṣṭha* itself being a substantially abridged and modified redaction of a prior, much lengthier Sanskrit treatise known as the *Mokṣopāya* (*The means to liberation*), hailing from the tenth-century Kashmir Valley. The *Mokṣopāya*-cum-*Laghu-Yoga-Vāsiṣṭha* would subsequently be further revised and redacted in the form of the well-known *Yoga-Vāsiṣṭha* (*Vasiṣṭha's Yoga*); see Hanneder, Jürgen, *Studies on the Mokṣopāya*, Wiesbaden: Harrassowitz, 2006.

In this passage, the complete twelfth chapter of the *Laghu-Yoga-Vāsiṣṭha*'s sixth and final book,[4] the sage (*ṛṣi*) Vasiṣṭha counsels prince Rāma—the same Rāma who is also the hero of the epic tale of the *Rāmāyaṇa*—as Vasiṣṭha does throughout the majority of the treatise's duration. In answering Rāma's numerous queries, Vasiṣṭha has occasion to touch upon a number of topics that have threaded throughout the treatise, including the nature of the self (*ātman*), ultimate Reality (*Brahman*), and the world (*jagat*); the nature of knowledge (*jñāna*) and ignorance (*ajñāna*); and the phenomena of suffering, bondage, liberation (*mokṣa*), desire, misperception, and imagination. Vasiṣṭha characteristically illustrates his teachings via a narrative anecdote, in this case, an encounter between a figure by the name of Bhṛṅgīśa and the Hindu deity Śiva. Bhṛṅgīśa, bewildered and stricken by the countless vicissitudes to be encountered within mundane existence, approaches Śiva for advice. Śiva's discourse in response centers on three ideal modes of conduct to be cultivated by the spiritual aspirant: that of the great agent (*mahākartṛ*), the great enjoyer (*mahābhoktṛ*), and the great renouncer (*mahātyāgin*).

Providing the backdrop for Śiva's discourse is the *Laghu-Yoga-Vāsiṣṭha*'s own characteristic metaphysics, which I have treated at greater length elsewhere.[5] Suffice it to say for our purposes here, the foundation of all reality, according to the *Laghu-Yoga-Vāsiṣṭha*, is pure consciousness (*saṃvid*), identified in the text with *Brahman* or absolute Reality. At the same time, this pure consciousness is furthermore identified with the highest Self (*ātman* or *paramātman*), alternately depicted in microcosmic terms (i.e., the innermost self hidden within the depths of each individual soul) or in macrocosmic terms (i.e., "the self of the world"). This pure consciousness/*Brahman*/*ātman*, although eternally unchanging and unalterable, is nevertheless a dynamic reality that, through its self-directed "pulsation" and "vibration" (*spanda*), appears to undergo change and modification, voluntarily manifesting itself in the manifold forms and appearances that constitute the phenomenal world (*jagat*). The phenomenal world hence bears an ambiguous status in relation to *Brahman*, like a wave upon the ocean: from a certain perspective, only the ocean is real while the wave is merely transient, fleeting, and effectively unreal; from another perspective, however, the wave is no different from the ocean and, indeed, identical with it. The *Laghu-Yoga-Vāsiṣṭha* anchors the entire drama of pure consciousness's (seeming) self-manifestation in the form of the world via the multivalent notion of *saṃkalpa*, a Sanskrit term denoting meanings as varied as "wish,"

4 This sixth book is entitled the *Nirvāṇa prakaraṇa* or "section on extinction" (*Nirbān parakaran* in Persian transliteration).

5 See Nair, *Translating wisdom* 30–42.

"desire," "intention," "thought," "mental construction," "conceptualization," and "imagination," among other senses. The author, Abhinanda, appears to have all of these significations in mind when he attributes to the highest Self a capacity of "desire/imagination" (*saṃkalpa*), which accordingly moves and stirs the Self to give rise to the world; at the same time, on a more microcosmic scale, we individual selves too possess our own capacities of "desire/imagination/conceptualization/mental construction" (again, *saṃkalpa*), as when a combination of misperception, memory, our own prior mental concepts and categories, and personal aversion or fear leads us, upon encountering a rope in a dark room, to imagine a snake—an act of "creation" in its own right, albeit within an individual scope.

The three translators faced a considerable task in their mandate to render such complex Sanskrit doctrines and teachings into Persian, though their abundant and vibrant resort to the conceptual vocabulary of Ibn ʿArabī (d. 638/1240) and his interpreters facilitated the endeavor wonderfully. The translators' decision to correlate the Hindu/Sanskrit *saṃkalpa* with the Islamic/Persian *khwāhish* ("desire")—rendered in such a way as to invoke the famous *ḥadīth* of the Hidden Treasure, so expertly expounded by Professors Murata and Chittick so many times across their prolific careers—is but one of numerous inspired translational choices to be savored within the passage below.

Laghu-Yoga-Vāsiṣṭha[6] 6:12:1–45	***Jūg bāsisht***[7] *Bihringīs Upākhiyān* (*Bhṛṅgīśa Upākhyāna*)[8]
Vasiṣṭha said:	[Vasiṣṭha said]
	Know [O Rāma] that, by reason of the ego (*ahankār*; Skt. *ahaṃkāra*), the living creature (*jān-dār*) becomes captive to the afflictions of the world (*dunyā*) and bound to endless rebirths (*janam*; Skt. *janma*). Now, I will tell you

6 Abhinanda, Gauḍa, *Laghuyogavāsiṣṭhaḥ: Vāsiṣṭhacandrikāvyākhyāsahitaḥ*, ed. Vāsudeva Śarma Panaśīkara, Delhi: Motilal Banarsidass, 1985, 775–782.

7 Nāʾīnī, Sayyid Muḥammad Riżā Jalālī and Narayan Shanker Shukla (eds.), *Jūg bāsisht* (*Yoga Vasistha*)*: Dar falsafa wa-ʿirfān-i Hind, tarjuma-yi Niẓām al-Dīn Pānīpatī*, Tehran: Shirkat-i Offset, 1981, 441–446.

8 "The story of Bhṛṅgīśa." At times when the three translators have preserved a given Sanskrit term within the body of the Persian text, I will accordingly provide the translators' Persian transliteration of the Sanskrit term in question, followed by the more standard Sanskrit transliteration labeled with the abbreviation "Skt."

(*cont.*)

Laghu-Yoga-Vāsiṣṭha	*Jūg bāsisht*
	the *Bihringīs upākhiyān* ("story of Bhṛṅgīśa"). The upshot and aim of the story is [to affirm] that, so long as the intellect (*ʿaql*) does not arrive at knowledge of the Nourisher (*parwardagār*) and one does not become effaced (*maḥw*) and drowned (*mustaghriq*) in witnessing the beauty of the Real (*mushāhada-yi jamāl-i ḥaqq*), then one will not be liberated (*khalāṣ*) from arrival and departure and birth and death in this world (*ʿālam*).[9]
	O Rāmchand![10] You know not why the tumult of this world (*dunyā*) was [originally] constituted and for what reason this world—an abode of forgetfulness (*ghaflat*)—became inhabited and flourishing? The boundaries of this [world] constitute the confines of where living beings dwell: the cause for the gathering of living creatures here is due to their remoteness from knowledge of the Real and their forgetfulness concerning the remembrance of absolute Being (*ghaflat az yād-i hastī-yi muṭlaq*) such that they have not and do not attain knowledge (*gyān*; Skt. *jñāna*) of the Real and comprehension (*dar-yāft*) of the nature of *Brahman* (*Barahman-rūp*; Skt. *Brahman-rūpa*). For that reason, those souls each time journey along the path of [re]birth (*janma-zāda*), falling helplessly into the fetters and bondage of transmigration (*tanāsukh*), and [then] pass away. By reason of the [limited]

9 The first of several references to the Hindu notion of reincarnation or transmigration, wherein a soul is ceaselessly caught within a repeating cycle of rebirth and re-death unless and until the advent of liberation from that cycle, known as *mokṣa*.

10 I.e., the name "Rāmacandra," the fuller name of prince Rāma.

(*cont.*)

Laghu-Yoga-Vāsiṣṭha	*Jūg bāsisht*
	conceptualizations of the intellect (*taṣawwur-i ʿaql*) and deficiency in knowledge of the Real, they cannot escape from bondage to the circumstances of the world (*asbāb-i dunyā*). Even more surprising, they understand this same bondage to be the very means of life, and so their perception and understanding never pass beyond the station of water and clay. And then there is time—time becomes an even firmer chain and fetter upon them.
By reason of forgetting the true nature of the imperceptible self, this world (*jagat*) appears to be enduring. O Rāma! This world has not [actually] come into being from any other [cause], just like a snake from a rope.[11]	Know that deficiency in knowledge of the origins [of the world] is the cause of living creatures' confusion and distress, just as the existence of a rope and its appearance becomes the occasion to falsely imagine the form of a snake (*wahm-i ṣūrat-i mārī*). For, if the rope did not exist and did not appear, no one would fall into false imagining, since, at first, the form of the rope enters into one's vision; from that form, one [mistakenly] supposes that "this is a snake." In the same way, if there were no deficiency in knowledge of the Nourisher and the veil of forgetfulness had not seized one's path, this confusion of arrival and departure, birth and death would be laid aside and the chain of existents' successive births (*janma*) would be broken.

11 A standard analogy deployed in Hindu philosophy, particularly the Advaita Vedānta tradition, to illustrate ignorance's (*avidyā*) capacity to illusorily effect the appearance of the phenomenal world. In a dark room, one may see a rope and mistakenly believe it to be a snake; the beholder's own ignorance of the real state of affairs, in other words, falsely projects the appearance of an entity "snake" onto the rope.

(*cont.*)

Laghu-Yoga-Vāsiṣṭha	*Jūg bāsisht*
He who, O Rāma, regards[12] this multitude of rays as distinct from the sun, for him, that multitude is indeed as if other than the sun. He by whom the bracelet is regarded as distinct from the gold [of which it is made], for him, indeed, that gold is not the same as that bracelet. [But] he by whom the rays would be regarded as indistinct from the sun, for him, those rays are the same as the sun. He is said to be unwavering (*nirvikalpa*[13]). He by whom the bracelet is regarded as indistinct from the gold, he is said to be unwavering, possessing the great understanding of the oneness of gold.	Know that all these variegated and determined (*taʿayyun*) existents that come into sight, innumerable and without limit, are all occasions for the appearance of the essence of the Real (*maẓāhir-i dhāt-i ḥaqq*) and loci of manifestation for absolute Being (*majālī-yi jilwa-yi hastī-yi muṭlaq*). The root of all of these appearances is the one essence of *Brahman*, just as with ornaments and gold pieces, such as bracelets, earrings, anklets, rings, and so forth, each of which has its own distinct determination and form: the root of all of those ornaments is the one essence of gold, which remains the very same gold even after those forms are shattered. Or just as, upon the rising of the exalted sun, thousands upon thousands of scattering beams, radiance, and rays can be seen, [still] the root of all those limitless and endless beams and rays is the one essence of the exalted sun. When one attains knowledge of *Brahman* (*gyān-i barahm*; Skt. *brahma-jñāna*) and arrives at complete knowledge of the Essence, he becomes effaced

12 The particularly fecund Sanskrit term *bhāvanā*, a causative form derived from the verbal root *bhū*, "to be" or "become." *Bhāvanā* thus literally means "bringing into being" or "causing to be," but comes to acquire multifarious nuances across diverse Sanskrit contexts. The term's significations include varieties of "mental attention," "meditation," and "imagination," among other senses. (See e.g., Shulman, David, *More than real: A history of the imagination in South Asia*, Cambridge, MA: Harvard University Press, 2012, 17–23, 64–71 and Ollett, Andrew, "What is *Bhāvanā*?," in *Journal of Indian Philosophy* 41.3 (2013), 221–262). Hence, what I have translated as "regards" over the next several verses could just as well be translated as "imagines," the idea being that, in our intellectual conceptualization of a given phenomenon or object, we "create" or construct that object or "bring it into being" in a certain way—certainly subjectively (for instance, in a dream), but arguably even objectively, at some level, as the *Laghu-Yoga-Vāsiṣṭha* tantalizingly indicates repeatedly across its length (for instance, in the projection of a snake onto a rope). The potential resonances with the Islamic notion of *khayāl*, as interpreted by Ibn ʿArabī and his later exegetes, are evident.

13 A term meaning "unwavering," "unchanging," or "free from doubt," *nirvikalpa* is also

(*cont.*)

Laghu-Yoga-Vāsiṣṭha	*Jūg bāsisht*
Having left aside all multiplicity, stand firm in the condition of real consciousness (*saṃvid*)—which is completely free from any object of consciousness—fixed within the womb of pure consciousness.	in the vision of *Brahman* and becomes annihilated (*fānī*) in Its essence, like a drop which falls into the ocean and becomes the ocean. O Rāmchand! Having relinquished one's distress over counting good and bad acts and reckoning base and exalted deeds—having passed beyond all those fetters, one becomes effaced in the quintessence of the knowledge of *Brahman* (*brahma-jñāna*) and the grasping of the Real. Do not give way to any doubt within yourself; evade the [cycle of] arrival and departure from this world! When you become entirely removed from the world and the essence of *Brahman* becomes the *qibla*[14] of your resolve, then you will never again return to this world (*dunyā*) and the afflictions of the cycle of rebirth (*janma*) will no longer encircle you.
When, just like the wind which enacts a pulsating power of vibration (*spanda-śakti*), the self (*ātman*), entirely on its own, suddenly enacts a power (*śakti*) called "desire/imagination" (*saṃkalpa*),	O Rāmchand! Know this pure Being and essence of *Brahman*—which is singular, one, and transcendent (*munazzah*), no name, mark, color, or form having any path to It—after the desire to create (*khwāhish-i āfarīnish*)

associated in several Sanskritic schools of thought with a variety of meditation known as *nirvikalpa samādhi*, wherein meditative absorption reaches such a degree that individual self-consciousness disappears and the distinctions between knower, knowing, and object of knowledge dissolve. In certain contexts, particularly the Buddhist Yogācāra school, the term *nirvikalpa* also describes a form of knowledge, cognition, or perception that is devoid of mental and conceptual constructs or interpretive overlay—a kind of "direct knowing," itself typically cast as the fruit of a particular regimen of meditation or spiritual practice. For more, see, e.g., Thompson, Evan, "What's in a concept? Conceptualizing the nonconceptual in Buddhist philosophy and cognitive science," in Christian Coseru (ed.), *Reasons and empty persons: Mind, metaphysics, and morality. Essays in honor of Mark Siderits*, London: Springer (forthcoming), and Bronkhorst, Johannes, "A note on Nirvikalpaka and Savikalpaka perception," in *Philosophy East and West*, 61.2 (2011), 373–379.

14 I.e., the direction of the Islamic daily prayers towards the Kaʿba in Mecca.

(*cont.*)

Laghu-Yoga-Vāsiṣṭha	*Jūg bāsisht*
At that time, [this] self of the world, making itself as if in the form of a discrete semblance (*ābhāsa*) that abounds in the drive toward desire/imagination (*saṃkalpa*), becomes mind (*manas*[15]).	appears to It, It Itself by Itself desires to display Its own perfections and to manifest all these forms and colors. There occurs to that singular Essence, without name or mark, a determination (*taʿayyun*) which they call "mind" (*man*; Skt. *manas*).
This world, which is just pure desire/imagination (*saṃkalpa-mātra*), enjoying the condition of being perceived (*dṛśyatā*), is neither real (*satyam*) nor false (*mithyā*[16]), arising like the snare of a dream. While one sees, hears, touches, smells, speaks, wakes, and dreams—none of it is a novel (*apūrva*[17]) [creation]. One thus regards it to be real (*satya*).	This *manas* becomes the occasion for the appearance of creation (*khalq*) and the cause for the existence of the world (*jahān*). That absolute Essence, having alighted and descended from Its own level of undelimited absoluteness and having become all these essences [here], It shines forth [Its] effulgence and manifests [Itself] to the world of appearance and witnessing (*ʿālam-i ẓāhir wa-shuhūd*). A distinct *manas* is manifested to each essence and to each individual entity.
Whatsoever one does, know that to be pure consciousness, stainless and diffused. *Brahman* has assumed swelling forms; there exists naught else than that.	Know that the *manas* and *cit* ("mind"; Skt. *citta*) of each individual has its root and origin in the *manas* of *Brahman*. When this *manas* and *citta* has passed beyond all [worldly] attachments and fetters, it returns to its own root, comes to know the essence of *Brahman*, and becomes

15 *Manas* refers roughly to the individual faculty of the "mind," but, in certain Sanskritic cosmologies, can also refer to a particular macrocosmic function or entity. The *Laghu-Yoga-Vāsiṣṭha* frequently probes the evanescent boundary between this individual *manas* and its "cosmic" counterpart.

16 Although the terminology differs in relevant ways not to be elided, compare with the notion of *anirvacanīya* ("inexpressible" or "indescribable"), one of Advaita Vedānta's preferred labels for worldly phenomena, said to enjoy some degree of relative or conventional reality since they are neither truly real (*sat*)—because they are transient—nor entirely unreal (*asat*)—because they are encountered in conventional experience, unlike more genuine fictions such as the "son of a barren woman" or a "square circle."

17 I.e., genuinely new and unprecedented; something which had no existence whatsoever

(*cont.*)

Laghu-Yoga-Vāsiṣṭha	*Jūg bāsisht*
Since the whole array of existent objects (*padārtha*) abides [only] through having consciousness as their essence, this world entire is simply consciousness. There is nothing else that is [actually] produced/imagined.	effaced in knowledge of It. Having passed beyond the characteristics of water and clay,[18] it becomes annihilated (*fānī*) in the essence of *Brahman*, subsists (*bāqī*) in It, and attains liberation (*mūja*; Skt. *mokṣa*). And [so] the original objective is obtained, just as rings, earrings, and all [types of] golden jewelry, after their forms are shattered and they are removed from [their] determination (*taʿayyun*), they become [simply] gold and there remains no other thing except the essence of gold.
There is no object of consciousness at all, since its source is the one consciousness by way of all its forms. What, then, is bondage and liberation (*mokṣa*)?	O Rāmchand! All these existents of the world and determined entities of every form and color which come into sight: know these to be nothing other than the form of the Real's desire and thought (*ṣūrat-i khwāhish wa-andīsha-yi ḥaqq*)—that very desire and thought of *Brahman* which shines forth [Its] effulgence in so many forms, images, and colors and comes into appearance.
	One cannot call these appearances a "thing" in origin and in actuality, since they are perishing (*fānī*) and not enduring (*nā-pāyanda*)—they are [merely] waves upon the ocean of forgetfulness (*ghaflat*) and ignorance (*agyānī*; Skt. *ajñāna*). But one also cannot call them "nothing" and entirely disregardable (*bī-iʿtibār*), since

prior to its coming into being. The *Laghu-Yoga-Vāsiṣṭha* rejects that any object or event could fit this label, since all worldly phenomena have their root in *Brahman*/pure consciousness.

18 A reference to the material constitution of humankind, whom God created out of water and clay (see, e.g., Q 32:7–8).

(*cont.*)

Laghu-Yoga-Vāsiṣṭha	***Jūg bāsisht***
Having endured the [misleading] thoughts "this is liberation; that, then, is bondage!," and having cast aside all anxious apprehensions, may you then arise, O great soul, in enacting your own duty—with withering conceit, observing silence, mastering the passions with vanquished pride, free from individualistic self-regard (*ahaṃkṛti*).	they do [indeed] enter into sight and possess full appearance and manifestation. The upshot is that the occupations and affairs of the world and the tumult of all this here is like a long and extended dream (*khwāb*), fit to be seen. For, the seer of a dream causes the affairs within his own dream to come to pass and becomes occupied with the occurrences and happenings [therein]. In that moment, he does not imagine (*khayāl*) those affairs to be [anything] else than genuine, actual reality. But after waking, he realizes that all that he saw and all that appeared within the world of dream was not real (*aṣlī*) or to be given [genuine] consideration (*iʿtibārī*). Likewise, when one arrives at understanding of the Nourisher and complete knowledge (*jñāna-yi kāmil*) appears, and he becomes effaced in witnessing the light of the Real, then he knows with certainty (*yaqīn*) that all this is [merely] a certain level of being (*wujūd*) which has come before him—that he had caused all that to come to pass; it was not a [real] thing and did not possess concrete, genuine actuality.
Having abandoned all doubts, O sinless one, and having gathered your courage forevermore, may you become the great agent (*mahākartā*), the great enjoyer (*mahābhoktā*), and the great renouncer (*mahātyāgī*).	Know that the crux of the matter is to become effaced in the essence of *Brahman*. For, when one arrives at one's own origin (*aṣl*)—like a drop which has fallen into the ocean and become effaced in it—then he has attained the goal. For him there will not be anything more to do with this world nor with rebirth (*janma*) therein. Delivered from all confusions, he will abide in unceasing tasting (*dhawq*) and joy (*surūr*).

(*cont.*)

Laghu-Yoga-Vāsiṣṭha	*Jūg bāsisht*
	O Rāmchand! In waking and dreaming, sitting and standing, eating and sleeping, stopping and going—in all circumstances and times, whatever you see and whatever comes before you, having entrusted all that to the essence of *Brahman*, may you become a witness of [*Brahman*'s] beauty in all its completeness. May you behold the one perfect Light (*nūr-i kāmil*) in everything and every place, and may you not sit for a single moment, a single instant, negligent in remembering It. You should know your own sight to be Its sight and your own hearing and speaking to be Its hearing and speaking. Likewise, every act and deed that comes from you, know it to [truly] be from It. In all conditions, moments of activity, and moments of rest, you must see yourself to be without agency (*bī-ikhtiyār*), like a pen in the writer's hand. You mustn't attribute any quality, act, or deed to yourself. Make your own being and essence effaced in Its being and essence. Do not conceive of this world, along with all its multiplicity, clamor, and tumult—including the heavens, the stars, and the earth; the mountains and the oceans; towns and forests full of wild and aquatic animals, beasts, and birds, including grazers, reptiles, flighted fowl, and all [other] species of creatures and existents which you might see—to be anything other than the epiphany (*jilwa*) of the one perfect essence of *Brahman*. Know with certainty (*yaqīn*) that that pure Essence—which is sheer intellect (*ʿaql-i khāliṣ*)—displays [Itself] within the totality of the determinations (*taʿayyun*) and in the entirety of the existents' loci of manifestation

(*cont.*)

Laghu-Yoga-Vāsiṣṭha	*Jūg bāsisht*
	(*maẓāhir*). This world received existence (*wujūd*) and became existent (*mawjūd*) by reason of Its thought (*andīsha*) and desire (*khwāhish*).
Rāma said:	Afterwards, Rāmachandra asked Vasiṣṭha:
What are these that you mention: the great agent, the great renouncer, the great enjoyer? O master, explain these to me properly.	O Vasiṣṭha! In the revered books[19] of the Indians and in the Purān (Skt. Purāṇas[20]), they have spoken of the "great agent" (*mahākartā*)—i.e., an extraordinary doer such that there is no doer or actor like him—the "great enjoyer" (*mahābhoktā*)—i.e., an exceptional partaker in life's pleasures and delights and an extraordinary obtainer of happiness and tasting (*dhawq*) such that there is no companion of pleasure and taste like him—and the "great renouncer" (*mahātyāgī*)—i.e., an exceptional renouncer and relinquisher such that there is no renouncer (*tārik*) or folk of relinquishment (*ahl-i gudhasht*) like him. What is the meaning of these three expressions? What qualities are described for each of these three? What sort of a person would [each of these] be? Please explain this to me; render the significance of these expressions firm in my mind.
	Bhṛṅgīśa's Questions to Mahādeva[21]:
Vasiṣṭha replied:	Vasiṣṭha replied to Rāmchand:

19 I.e., the four Vedas.

20 A large body of Sanskrit works containing the great tales and myths of Hindu deities, heroes, and kings. The Purāṇas are typically given the status of *smṛti,* that is, authoritative scripture that is nonetheless secondary in authority to the *śruti,* i.e., the Vedas.

21 An appellation of the Hindu deity Śiva.

(*cont.*)

Laghu-Yoga-Vāsiṣṭha	*Jūg bāsisht*
Long ago, O Rāma, the Lord of the half-moon crown (Śiva) explained to Bhṛṅgīśa these three modes of conduct (*vrata*[22]), through which one can abide free from affliction. The Moon-Bearer, [Śiva,] accompanied by His entire retinue, had stood upon the peak at the summit of Mount Sumeru, resembling fire.	O Rāmchand! What you have asked of me, there was [a man] among the servants and chiefs of Mahādeva (Śiva) by the name of Bhṛṅgīśa who before you had [already] asked Mahādeva about these very same expressions and appellations. Mahādeva had rendered the meaning of these expressions in a manner that became firm in Bhṛṅgīśa's mind and cast aside the doubts in his heart. I will tell you, so listen!
Desirous of knowledge, that Bhṛṅgīśa, possessing great splendor, respectfully asked Śiva about the nature [of these three modes of conduct]. Bhṛṅgīśa, his hands joined in greeting, bowed reverentially to Umā's husband (Śiva).	At one time, Mahādeva—from whose head shines forth the moon's radiance—had seated Himself near Mount Sumeru, at its northern face, along with the attendants and auxiliaries among the servants and lords of His court.
Bhṛṅgīśa said:	Bhṛṅgīśa approached in utter supplication. With both palms joined together, he petitioned:
O Lord, having observed this arrayed world of *saṃsāra*,[23] wavering like a billowing wave, I am left bewildered, bereft of any solace concerning the true nature of things.	O grandest Lord of lords! I am bewildered (*ḥayrānī*) at the vicissitudes of this world, which, like the appearances of waves upon the ocean or the gleams and flashes of the sun's rays, possess no end or limit. Each of its appearances and epiphanies is in a certain hue, yet no single gleam or flash is enduring, but [rather] comes into view in each moment in a different mode (*nawʿ*); at each instant, a different occurrence or phenomenon shows forth. The intellect (*ʿaql*) becomes incapable and despairing of

22 A *vrata* is a religious vow or some form of pious observance, meritorious act of devotion, or regimen of spiritual practice or voluntary austerities.

23 I.e., the indefinitely recurring cycle of reincarnation, and the world of mundane existence more generally.

(*cont.*)

Laghu-Yoga-Vāsiṣṭha	*Jūg bāsisht*
What inner resolution (*niścaya*), desirable and firmly fixed, can I adopt that will allow me to stand within this dilapidated house of the world without grief and affliction?	grasping the reality of this condition (*ḥaqīqat-i īn ḥāl*). This world is seen in itself to be like an old house upon which [showers] drop with every rain from every direction, and so it becomes the cause of all sorts of grief and anguish due to the house's old age and dilapidated state. Could there be a certain mode; might there be some regimen (*tadbīr*) at one's disposal—a regimen and subtle means (*ḥīla*) through which liberation (*khalāṣ*) from the griefs of the world could become easy, wherein one could live one's life inhabiting a corner of that house in restful ease (*farāghat*), able to pass the time in security?
Lord [Śiva] replied:	Mahādeva (Śiva), in response to Bhṛṅgīśa, extended an explanation in the tongue of realities (*zabān-i ḥaqā'iq*), asserting:
Having abandoned all doubts, O sinless one, and having gathered your courage forevermore, may you become the great agent, the great enjoyer, and the great renouncer.	O Bhṛṅgīśa! Establishing yourself in a single orientation (*jihat*) and mode of conduct (*dall*), cleansing your breast of the weeds of doubt (*shubha*) and delusion (*wahm*), and making your resolve firm and your intention total, you should become in this world (*dunyā*) a "great agent" (*mahākartā*), a "great enjoyer" (*mahābhoktā*), and a "great renouncer" (*mahātyāgī*) who has escaped from the griefs of the world (*'ālam*). No anguish or vexation in any form will find a way to you.
Bhṛṅgīśa said:	Bhṛṅgīśa, after reverencing Mahādeva and showing assurance in His prescription, asked Him:

(*cont.*)

Laghu-Yoga-Vāsiṣṭha	*Jūg bāsisht*
What are these that you mention: the great agent, the great enjoyer, the great renouncer? O master, explain these to me properly.	O most perfect of the perfect! Please explain to me the significance of these three expressions and the meaning of these three appellations so that it becomes firm in my mind.
Lord [Śiva] replied:	Mahādeva replied:
He who acts with utter indifference to passion and enmity, pleasure and pain, righteousness and unrighteousness,[24] the fruits [of action] or lack thereof, he is called the "great agent." He who, practicing silence, free from selfishness, agitation, and passion, acts without pride or self-regard, he is called the great agent. He who, standing apart like a witness (*sākṣin*) over all having severed all clinging attachment (*sneha*), engages in what needs to be done without desire (*icchā*), he is called the great agent. Entirely free from both agitation and happiness, through pellucid, equanimous understanding, he neither grieves over nor hastens excitedly toward [any object]—he is called the great agent.	O Bhṛṅgīśa! "Great agent" means that, for every act and deed of the seeker on the path to God (*ṭālib-i rāh-i khudā*) that may come about, one should not perceive, related to that act and deed, any connection with individual self-agency (*ikhtiyār*) or any [selfish] intention, occupation, desire, inclination, or aversion within one's mind. At that time, one will become the great agent. Furthermore, having become silent (*mūnī*; Skt. *muni*)—i.e., constraining your speech and all your senses—relinquishing the ego (*ahaṃkāra*) and passing beyond anger and malice, in every act that you do, at that time, you will become the great agent. Moreover, you must also become without desire (*khwāhish*) and will (*irāda*), not having the fruits and results [of action] as your intended goal, and not holding in mind any reward or compensation.[25] In every act that you do [at that time], you will become the great agent.
Whose mind bears equanimity towards birth, life, and death, equal to arising and vanishing, he is called the great agent.	Additionally, you should not become sorrowful at the disappearance of some sought-after goal or intended object, nor should you become

24 I.e., *dharma* and *adharma*.
25 Cf. *Bhagavad Gītā* 2:38–53.

(*cont.*)

Laghu-Yoga-Vāsiṣṭha	***Jūg bāsisht***
	delighted at the obtaining of some desired thing. By way of pure intellect (*ʿaql-i khāliṣ*), distant from any doubt (*shubha*), there having entered into sight the reality of the [world's] condition, in every act you do and deed you accomplish, you will become the great agent. It must also be that birth and death; arrival in this world, being and living in the world, and departure from it; achieving esteem and reaching a station of veneration, or becoming unesteemed and falling out of rank, honor, and glory; [all these] must be equal (*barābar*) before you. [If you do so,] in every act you do and deed you exhibit, you will become the great agent.
Likewise, he [who] in no way loathes nor longs for anything, but enjoys all that has come to pass, he is called the "great enjoyer." He who is not excited nor agitated by pleasures or pains, ritual activities or bodily labors, the existence or nonexistence [of objects], that which causes confusion or that which is enjoyed, he is called the great enjoyer. Old age, death, and calamity, both sovereignty and poverty alike, are [all] to be delighted in—he who enjoys thus is called the great enjoyer.	"Great enjoyer" (*mahābhoktā*) means that, in your living and livelihood, you do not yearn for long perdurance in this world (*dunyā*) possessed of power and glory. You do not give space within yourself for desire and avarice. You never hold in mind [such thoughts as] "I should be like this" or "I should behave like that," nor "through worldly possessions, I can attain distinction among the folk of the world (*ahl-i dunyā*)." Having understood each thing and affair that might come about as being on account of your own allotted destiny (*sarnuwisht-i naṣīb*), and having reckoned your own entrustment (*ḥawāla*[26]) in that affair from the realm of the unseen (*ʿālam-i ghayb*), at that

26 A financial term in reference to a "trust," i.e., a sum of money entrusted to an individual to be then transported and transferred to a designated recipient, often residing in a different, foreign region or city.

(*cont.*)

Laghu-Yoga-Vāsiṣṭha	*Jūg bāsisht*
He [who] encounters pungent, sour, salty, and bitter foods—whether unpleasant, pleasant, or delectable—with equanimity, he is called the great enjoyer. That tranquil one who sees both the pleasureful and the pleasureless, both the one engaging in amorous sport and likewise the one abstaining from it, to be equal, he is called the great enjoyer.	time, you will become the great enjoyer. Youth and old age, death and life, moreover, will be the same for you; there will be no distinction for you between the glory of dominion and sovereignty, on the one hand, and wretchedness, poverty, and destitution, on the other. You should be consonant with every circumstance that might come about—at that time, you will become the great enjoyer.
He who maintains steady equanimity with respect to milk or even a sweet candy, with respect to the righteous and likewise the unrighteous, he is called the great enjoyer. "This object is to be enjoyed and not to be enjoyed"[27]—having relinquished that which wavers thus, he who enjoys, with his covetous desire vanished, is called the great enjoyer. He who, with equanimous intellect (*buddhi*), uninterruptedly enjoys both misfortune and success, bewilderment and joy, he is called the great enjoyer.	Likewise, when you know sweet, sour, bitter, astringent, and so forth to be equivalent flavors and you draw no distinction [between them]; when something towards which the dispositions (*ṭabīʿat*) of men compulsively incline, something which they abhor and from which their dispositions flee, something from which they can acquire profit, and something from which they could not profit—when [all those] are equal (*barābar*) to you, at that time, you may be called the great enjoyer.
Likewise, he who, through understanding (*dhī*), has completely renounced both righteousness and unrighteousness, pleasure and pain, birth and death, he is called the "great renouncer."	The meaning of "great renouncer" (*mahātyāgī*) is someone who passes beyond being a performer of good deeds or bad deeds and relinquishes [both] living and dying. He does not understand any thing to be from himself. He

27 I take this phrase to refer to the vacillating character of our relationship with worldly objects—even the most delectable of desserts can give way to disgust if eaten to excess, only to appear delicious again the very next day.

(*cont.*)

Laghu-Yoga-Vāsiṣṭha	***Jūg bāsisht***
	[who] passes beyond all fetters, he can be called the great renouncer.
He who, with understanding, has abandoned all desires, all exertions, every doubt, and all certainties, he is called the great renouncer. He who has inwardly abandoned all—righteousness and unrighteousness, the reflective mind (*manas*), and that which is sought after—he is called the great renouncer. All this incitement toward perceivable objects (*dṛśya*) that is observed [here], he who rightly relinquishes [all] that is called the great renouncer.	One who passes beyond all desires (*khwāhish*) and wishes (*ārzū*); who makes himself free of concern for whatever fear (*tars*) and fanciful delusion (*wahm*) may call to mind, as well as whatever might reckon his own [personal] benefit; who makes himself unwavering (*bī-taghyīr*) and indifferent (*bī-tafāwut*) to that which ornaments and adorns his body, as well as that which brings scorn and disgrace; who keeps his intellect (*ʿaql*) far from reckoning's dispersive discriminations (*tafriqa*); and who does not shackle his attention (*tawajjuh*) to any thing or any fetter—he would be the great renouncer.
Vasiṣṭha said:	Vasiṣṭha said to Rāmchand:
Thus spoke the Lord of lords (Śiva) to Bhṛṅgīśa long ago, O sinless one. Having recourse to this vision, O Rāma, arise, with your anguish departed! *Brahman*—the eternally [self-]arisen, unblemished in nature—is the end and the beginning [of all things]. For, no thing is stirred even the slightest bit by any other. Imagine/regard/consider[28] thus! Having [yourself] attained to purity, of entirely spotless and tranquil disposition, come to extinction (*nirvāṇa*)!	O Rāmchand! In this way, Bhṛṅgīśa acquired this guidance and instruction from Mahādeva, and grasped this kind of *upadīsh-gyān* ("knowledge through instruction"; Skt. *upadeśa-jñāna*) [from Him]. He performed act and deed in accordance with Mahādeva's injunctions, firmly maintained himself in consonance (*nisbat*) with [them], and, having resolved [himself] to the path (*ṭarīq*) displayed before his eyes, did not transgress it by even a single step. You too must act in accordance with those [three] teachings! Having oriented yourself to a single course and direction, you must live according to that path and way, for your welfare will be there.

28 Once again, a verbal form of the Sanskrit term *bhāvanā*. See note 12 above.

(*cont.*)

Laghu-Yoga-Vāsiṣṭha	*Jūg bāsisht*
Brahman, free of any blemish, the singular seed that gives rise to the totality of phenomena in every *kalpa*,[29] is of the nature of the highest Self (*paramātman*). That vast *Brahman*, from whom all existence sprouts and grows, is like the sun, which indeed shines forth.	O Rāmchand! The pure essence of *Brahman*, absolute Being, is without name, mark, form, or color, without end or limit, without change or alteration. It is transcendent (*munazzah*), free and clear of all relations and constraints; It is subtle (*laṭīf*) to the extent that perfection (*kamāl*) and magnificence arise [within It]. It does not perish or disappear. No other thing possesses being and existence alongside Its being and existence. You must make [It] the *qibla* of your resolve. Having removed all doubts concerning the attributes of Its perfection and omnipotence, in the same way that the perfected ones and master sages (*rikhīshur*; Skt. *ṛṣīśvara*[30])—having attained to the utmost of ease and tranquility in their belief (*iʿtiqād*) and understanding—become effaced in witnessing Its beauty and perfection, just so must you be upon that very same path and conviction (*ʿaqīda*), drowned in Its remembrance, so that you may attain the stage of liberation (*mūja*; Skt. *mokṣa*), which is the most exalted stage of the God-seekers (*khudā-ṭalab*).
No other thing present here, whether real or unreal, in any place or at any time, can possibly exist. O virtuous one (*sādhu*)! Having established [yourself] thus in the inward, fixed firmly in certainty (*niścaya*), persist in	O Rāmchand! Having understood everything among the variegated determinations and existents [of the world], beyond limit or reckoning—the high and the low, the black and the white, the red and the yellow, of every

29 I.e., a cosmic age—one grand "segment" of cyclical cosmic time, according to Hindu thought, of which infinite multitudes have and will come to pass. A *kalpa* is sometimes referred to as a "day of Brahmā," said to contain one thousand *mahāyugas* (each *mahāyuga* being one complete cycle of the four *yugas* or "world ages").

30 Lit., lord (*īśvara*) of sages (*ṛṣis*).

(*cont.*)

Laghu-Yoga-Vāsiṣṭha	*Jūg bāsisht*
joyful pleasure (*vilāsa*) with [your] apprehensions departed.	genus and species that may fall into your sight or be seen in this world—to be through and through loci of manifestation for the Real Essence's self-disclosures and epiphanies of the absolute Light's perfections, you should fix this belief within your heart: in [all] these appearances of various sorts and in [each of] these displays without end or limit, there is no existence or being other than Its [existence and being]. It is that very same Essence, perfect and singular, that displays Its own beauty in every color and self-discloses Its own perfection in every scent.
Constantly turned inward, while also accomplishing all that needs to be accomplished outwardly, you will never fall into distress; [rather,] you will become one for whom individualistic self-regard (*ahaṃkṛti*) has been dispelled.	Fixed in this conviction and firm repose, you will keep the ego (*ahaṃkāra*) distant from yourself and will no longer perceive yourself in the midst [of the world]. Once you become without ego, you will inevitably reach the stage of liberation (*mokṣa*). You will no longer have anything more to do with this world, and the rope of rebirth's fetters (*qayd-i janma*) around the neck of your soul will be severed.

Bibliography

Abhinanda, Gauḍa, *Laghuyogavāsiṣṭhaḥ: Vāsiṣṭhacandrikāvyākhyāsahitaḥ*, ed. Vāsudeva Śarma Panaśīkara, Delhi: Motilal Banarsidass, 1985.

Bronkhorst, Johannes, "A note on Nirvikalpaka and Savikalpaka perception," in *Philosophy East and West*, 61.2 (2011), 373–379.

Hanneder, Jürgen, *Studies on the Mokṣopāya*, Wiesbaden: Harrassowitz, 2006

Hawley, Nell Shapiro and Sohini Sarah Pillai (eds.), *Many Mahābhāratas*, Albany, NY: SUNY Press, 2021.

Murata, Sachiko, *Chinese gleams of Sufi light: Wang Tai-yü's* Great learning of the pure and real *and Liu Chih's* Displaying the concealment of the real realm, Albany, NY: SUNY Press, 2000.

Murata, Sachiko, William C. Chittick and Tu Weiming, *The sage learning of Liu Zhi: Islamic thought in Confucian terms*, Cambridge, MA: Harvard University Asia Center, 2009.

Nā'īnī, Sayyid Muḥammad Riżā Jalālī and Narayan Shanker Shukla (eds.), *Jūg bāsisht* (*Yoga Vasistha*)*: Dar falsafa wa-ʿirfān-i Hind, tarjuma-yi Niẓām al-Dīn Pānīpatī*, Tehran: Shirkat-i Offset, 1981.

Nair, Shankar, *Translating wisdom: Hindu-Muslim intellectual interactions in early modern South Asia*, Oakland, CA: University of California Press, 2020.

Ollett, Andrew, "What is *Bhāvanā*?," in *Journal of Indian Philosophy* 41.3 (2013), 221–262.

Richman, Paula (ed.), *Many Rāmāyaṇas: The diversity of a narrative tradition in South Asia*, Berkeley, CA: University of California Press, 1991.

Shulman, David, *More than real: A history of the imagination in South Asia*, Cambridge, MA: Harvard University Press, 2012.

Thompson, Evan, "What's in a concept? Conceptualizing the nonconceptual in Buddhist philosophy and cognitive science," in Christian Coseru (ed.), *Reasons and empty persons: Mind, metaphysics, and morality. Essays in honor of Mark Siderits*, London: Springer (forthcoming).

Truschke, Audrey, *Culture of encounters: Sanskrit at the Mughal court*, New York: Columbia University Press, 2016.

CHAPTER 5

Re-reading the Quranic Maryam as a Mystic in Nuṣrat Amīn's *Makhzan-i ʿirfān*

Maria Massi Dakake

1 Introduction*

One of the most consistent and insistent claims of many contemporary scholars wrestling with patriarchal or even misogynist aspects of traditional Islamic scholarship is that these aspects do not derive essentially from the Islamic scripture, the Quran, itself. Rather, they are attributable in whole or in large part to the exclusively male voices and perspectives historically responsible for explaining and commenting upon the Quran, and for transferring the content of its often-multivalent verses into established systems of law and theology. Many contemporary scholars have identified a disconnect between the Quranic assertion of the essential moral and spiritual equality of the genders on the one hand, and the assumption of a moral hierarchy between men and women that seems to inform many of the traditional commentaries upon it, on the other. Part of the solution to this problem, these scholars rightly suggest, is the increased participation and inclusion of Muslim women in contemporary processes of interpretation of the Quran. The Quran explicitly addresses itself to both men and women, and according to several accounts of the circumstances in which various verses were revealed to the Prophet (*asbāb al-nuzūl*), some of these verses came specifically in response to questions posed by women companions of the Prophet. The Quran spoke to and responded to women in its earliest audience, and insofar as it continues to speak and respond to people through time—that is, to the extent that it continues to provide meaningful answers to contemporary concerns—women's understandings of the Quran continue to be essential for the fullest possible *human* understanding of the Quran.

Of course, women's views on the Quran are not entirely absent. Some of the Prophet's companions, including his wives, and especially ʿĀʾisha, are fre-

* I would like to acknowledge the generous support of the National Endowment for the Humanities whose summer grant facilitated this research.

DOI:10.1163/9789004529038_006

quently cited as authorities in Quranic commentaries. Their views are preserved, but also mediated, by male transmitters and writers who wrote these classical commentaries. Beginning in the mid-20th century with the Egyptian scholar Bint al-Shāṭi'’s (d. 1998) partial, literary commentary on the Quran,[1] an increasing number of women have become engaged in Quranic study and commentary. Most, however, approach the Quran selectively, commenting on a subset of verses oriented around a particular theme. Some of these works by contemporary Muslim female scholars focus on the Quran's views on women, specifically;[2] or offer a distinctively women's reading of the Quranic position on other issues.[3] More generally, female scholars are increasingly engaged in modern forms of scholarship and analysis of the Quran at the academic level, while there are also increasing numbers of informal women's Quranic study or reading groups at the broader communal level. But rarely do we see a truly comprehensive, written commentary on the Quran produced entirely by a female scholar. Nuṣrat Amīn's *Makhzan-i ʿirfān* (*The treasury of true knowledge*) is one of those rare examples: a complete 15-volume Persian translation and commentary on the Quran, initially published serially between 1957–1975.[4]

2 Nuṣrat Amīn: Her Life and Her Work

Nuṣrat Amīn (1886–1983), who often wrote under the pen name Bānū-yi Īrānī, was a conservative religious scholar who lived and worked nearly all her life in pre-revolutionary Iran. She was deeply versed in the sciences of the Quran and Hadith, as well as the more mystical discipline of *ʿirfān*, while also being one of only two women in her time who held the position of *mujtahida*, the highest rank of religious legal authority in Shiʿism. She was one of a small number of advanced Shiʿi female religious scholars, almost all of whom, unlike herself, were the scions of prominent families of religious scholars within the

1 See Bint al-Shāṭi', ʿĀ'isha ʿAbd al-Raḥmān, *al-Tafsīr al-bayānī li-l-Qur'ān al-karīm*, 2 vols., Cairo: Dār al-Maʿārif, 1966.

2 Two of the earliest works in this regard are Wadud, Amina, *Qur'an and woman: Rereading the sacred text from a woman's perspective*, Oxford: Oxford University Press, 1999 and Barlas, Asma, *Believing women in the Quran: Unreading patriarchal interpretations*, Austin: University of Texas Press, 2002. More recently, see the work of the Moroccan scholar, Lamrabet, Asma, *Women in the Quran: An emancipatory reading*, Leicestershire: Kube Publishing, 2016, as well as Ibrahim, Celene, *Women and gender in the Quran*, Oxford: Oxford University Press, 2020.

3 See, for example, the recent work of Lamptey, Jerusha, *Never wholly other: A Muslima theology of religious pluralism*, Oxford: Oxford University Press, 2014.

4 Amīn, Nuṣrat B., *Makhzan-i ʿirfān dar tafsīr-i Qur'ān*, 15 vols., Isfahan: Gulbahār, n.d.

Shiʿi religious establishment. Yet none of Amīn's male relatives, including her spouse, were members of the Shiʿi religious clergy or intellectual community, and her work as a religious scholar seems to have been motivated entirely by her own personal religious and scholarly interests. As a Shiʿi religious scholar writing during the reign of the secularizing Pahlavi Shahs of Iran (1941–1979), she advocated for conservative religious positions regarding social and family norms, and strenuously objected to Reza Shah's ban on women's veiling. Yet she was also committed to the advancement of women's religious education, opening a network of schools for girls and teaching many young women during regular sessions in her own home. Her Quran commentary likely has its origin in teaching sessions with her students.

3 The Commentary

Nuṣrat Amīn's Quran commentary is entitled *Makhzan-i ʿirfān*, a title that seems to derive from a *ḥadīth* attributed to the fourth Shiʿi Imam, ʿAlī Zayn al-ʿĀbidīn (d. 95/713), in which he refers to the Quran as a "treasury of true knowledge." Amīn quotes this *ḥadīth* in the commentary's substantial introduction,[5] which seeks to establish the legitimacy of her engagement in Quranic exegesis and lays out her exegetical philosophy. She claims initially to have equivocated over the idea of writing a Quranic commentary, but finally resolved that she would do so by relying on established works of exegesis, and most importantly, on the teachings of the Shiʿi Imams.[6] All of this sounds very cautious and conservative indeed, but as the introduction goes on, it becomes clear that she does not intend to compose a Quranic commentary that merely reproduces existing exegetical views. Like other exegetes, she spends some time in her introduction discussing the traditional warnings against interpreting the Quran according to one's own opinion (*tafsīr bi-l-raʾy*),[7] as well as the importance of relying on transmitted exegetical traditions, and the difference between *tafsīr* and *taʾwīl*.[8] But in the end, she invokes the Quranic verse that enjoins its readers to contemplate the Quran (*tadabbur al-Qurʾān*)[9] as a justification for her efforts. She

5 Amīn, *Makhzan-i ʿirfān* i, 12. She attributes this quote to the early Safavid era Quran commentary *Manhaj al-ṣādiqīn* by Fatḥ Allāh Kāshānī (d. 988/1550).

6 Amīn, *Makhzan-i ʿirfān* i, 12.

7 Amīn, *Makhzan-i ʿirfān* i, 9–11.

8 Amīn, *Makhzan-i ʿirfān* i, 8.

9 Q 47:24: "Do they not contemplate the Quran? Or do hearts have their locks upon them?" All Quranic quotations are taken, with occasional modifications, from Nasr, Seyyed Hossein et al. (eds.), *The study Quran: A new translation and commentary*, New York: HarperOne, 2015. See Amīn, *Makhzan-i ʿirfān* i, 9.

argues that it makes no sense to claim that it is impermissible to consider and contemplate the Quran, when the Quran is meant to be a source of teaching and instruction for people.[10] Such sincere contemplation is what she intends to manifest in her commentary, and this kind of contemplation, she argues, does not constitute the forbidden *tafsīr bi-l-raʾy*.[11]

In the 15 volumes of writing that follow, Amīn reproduces the Quranic text in the original Arabic, in segments that average about 5–10 verses in length. Each segment is followed by her Persian translation of the Quranic passage, and then her own commentary. Like other exegetes, she will sometimes take the opportunity to digress from straightforward commentary on the text to offer a brief discussion on an adjacent topic under a separate heading. As she promises in her introduction, her Quranic commentary eruditely cites the works of a range of traditional Shiʿi and non-Shiʿi scholars. The work of these earlier exegetes informs and at times inspires her own exegesis, but does not delimit it, or act as a set of authoritative parameters for her own, often free-flowing commentary on the Quranic verses. Moreover, her work evinces a deep, personal attachment to the Quran, as well as a devotional and mystical view of the human relationship with God.

Amīn's Quranic commentary offers us a uniquely comprehensive presentation of a Muslim woman's understanding of, and relationship with, her scripture. Despite this, it has received very little scholarly attention. Several scholars have researched Nuṣrat Amīn's life and reception in both pre- and post-revolutionary Iran, but their work has largely focused on her life and career as a religious legal authority, and as an advocate for women's education.[12] These scholars note that while her legacy has been celebrated in some official conferences promoted by the government of Iran, her scholarly publications have received little critical attention, and are often not found in the seminary libraries in Iran. The only serious study in English of her commentary is an article by Travis Zadeh, which provides an initial, illuminating introduction to some key features of her commentary, including the way in which it is informed by her training in *ʿirfān*.[13]

10 Amīn, *Makhzan-i ʿirfān* i, 11.

11 Amīn, *Makhzan-i ʿirfān* i, 9.

12 See, for example, Künkler, Mirjam and Roja Fazaeli, "The life of two *mujtahidahs*: Female religious authority in twentieth-century Iran," in Masooda Bano and Hilary E. Kalmbach (eds.), *Women, leadership and mosques: Changes in contemporary Islamic authority*, Leiden: Brill, 2011, 127–160 and Rutner, Maryam, "Religious authority, gendered recognition, and instrumentalization of Nusrat Amin in life and after death," in *Journal of Middle East Women's Studies* 11.1 (2015), 24–41.

13 See Zadeh, Travis, "Persian Qurʾanic networks, modernity, and the writings of ʿan Iranian

I am only at the beginning of my own study of Amīn's *tafsīr*, but in this article I would like to present a focused examination of her commentary on those passages of the Quran that recount the story of Maryam (Mary, the mother of Jesus). Even this limited, thematic study of Amīn's commentary offers a meaningful look at her exegetical method: the way her work is informed by existing works of *tafsīr*, while also demonstrating exegetical independence; the way in which her commentary is shaped (but not determined) by her Shiʿi confessional commitments; the influence of her mystical views, particularly on the nature of divine love and the human attachment to God; and the more intimate and personal perspective she brings, as a woman, to the Quran's account of its most prominent and heroic female figure, Maryam bt. ʿImrān, Mary the mother of Jesus.

4 The Story of Maryam

The story of Maryam is primarily recounted in two substantial passages of the Quran. The first is located in Sūra Āl ʿImrān (Q 3:35–48), which begins with an account of Maryam's mother consecrating her unborn child to God and continues with Maryam's dedication as a child to the Temple, and her later encounter with the angel who announces the miraculous birth of her son, Jesus, the Messiah. The second is found in Sūra Maryam (Q 19:16–33), where the story of the angelic annunciation is retold, and followed by an account of the difficulties Maryam suffered in giving birth to Jesus alone in the wilderness and bringing him to her people. In both passages, Maryam's story is entwined with that of her uncle, the prophet Zakariyyāʾ (who cares for her in the Temple); and in both accounts, Maryam's encounter with the angel serves as the climactic point of the narrative. Maryam is also mentioned in several places as a paragon of purity and chastity, and as a "sign for humankind" (along with her son). In various passages throughout the Quran, Maryam is the recipient of a variety of divine favors (*karāmāt*), in addition to her miraculous conception of Jesus (described as a "word" from God) without a male intermediary. This has led to some debate about the status of Maryam: Is she a prophet, given her direct encounter with the angel of revelation and the various miracles she is granted by God?; or is she a saint, granted a special standing and relationship with God because of her extraordinary purity and devotion?; or is she simply a righteous woman?

---

lady', Nusrat Amin Khanum (d. 1983)," in Suha Taji-Farouki (ed.), *The Qur'an and its readers worldwide: Contemporary commentaries and translations*, Oxford: Oxford University Press in association with The Institute of Ismaili Studies, 2015, 275–323.

Amīn's commentary does not directly engage this question. She does not acknowledge the minority position regarding the possible prophethood of Maryam, clearly stating, at one point, that Maryam was not a prophet.[14] However, Amīn's discussion of Maryam suggests that she occupied a spiritual rank that was unusually close to the station of prophethood. She compares Maryam's pious struggles with those of well-known Quranic prophets, and repeatedly emphasizes the high mystical station she attained through a combination of her own spiritual devotion, and her extraordinary "chosenness" by God. In what follows, I will first discuss more traditional elements in Amīn's commentary, including her perspective as a Shiʿi traditionist, specifically. Then I will consider some of the more mystical elements in Amīn's commentary on Maryam's story, some of which go beyond what is found in other mystical commentaries, in part because of the psychological "intimacy" she evinces as a spiritual woman herself, contemplating Maryam's extraordinary situation.

5 *Makhzan-i ʿirfān* as a Traditional Shiʿi Commentary

As we noted above, Nuṣrat Amīn claims in the introduction to her commentary that she will rely heavily upon the established works of traditional Quranic commentators. It is clear, when reading her commentary, that she does indeed hew close to the discussions of several classical exegetes, most notably the 6th/12th-century Twelver Shiʿi commentator, al-Ṭabarsī (d. 548/1154). She sometimes cites him by name, or by the name of his commentary, *Majmaʿ al-bayān*, although in other places she seems to broadly reproduce the structure and content of parts of al-Ṭabarsī's commentary translated or paraphrased in Persian. Amīn also relies very heavily on the work of her Shiʿi contemporary, Muḥammad Ḥusayn Ṭabāṭabāʾī (1904–1981) and his massive 20th-century commentary, *al-Mīzān*. In addition to Shiʿi sources, she also cites some classical Sunni works, including al-Ṭabarī's *Jāmiʿ al-bayān ʿan taʾwīl āy al-Qurʾān*, and regularly references early exegetical opinions, including those of Ibn ʿAbbās (d. 68/687), al-Suddī (d. 128/745), Ḥasan al-Baṣrī (d. 110/728) and others. In her inclusion of both Shiʿi and Sunni sources, she is following a tradition well-

14 This comes in connection with a discussion about the possibility of non-prophets receiving not just divine favors (*karāmāt*), but also evidentiary miracles (*muʿjizāt*). In this case, she is reproducing al-Ṭabarsī's argument that non-prophets can receive such miracles—a position that stands in opposition to those who claimed that it was precisely because Maryam received such miracles that she must be considered a prophet. See Amīn, *Makhzan-i ʿirfān* viii, 107.

established among Twelver Shiʿi exegetes from the time of Shaykh al-Ṭāʾifa al-Ṭūsī (d. 460/1066) onward. In her introduction, Amīn also indicates that she will seek understanding of the Quran from those whose wisdom derives directly from the "niche of lights,"[15] by whom she means the Shiʿi Imams. To this end, she often cites *aḥādīth* attributed to the Imams directly, or through the medium of other works, commonly al-Kulaynī's (d. 329/941) *al-Kāfī*, or the Hadith-based Shiʿi *tafsīr* of the early Shiʿi scholar, al-ʿAyyāshī (d. 3rd/9th century). She also engages more mystical or Sufi-oriented commentaries, including the *Rūḥ al-bayān* of Ismāʿīl Ḥaqqī Burūsawī (d. 1137/1725), Rashīd al-Dīn al-Maybudī's (fl. 6th/12th century) *Kashf al-asrār*, and the *Tafsīr-i ṣāfī* of Fayḍ Kāshānī (d. 1091/1680), although she does not cite any of these directly in the passages on Maryam that we will examine here.

One of the issues that naturally arises in discussions about Maryam in a Shiʿi context is her relationship and comparison with Fāṭima, the daughter of the Prophet and wife of ʿAlī b. Abī Ṭālib. As the crucial link between the Prophet, ʿAlī, and the Imams, Fāṭima has mythical status in the Shiʿi tradition. She is celebrated (as she is in the Sunni tradition) for her closeness to her father, the Prophet, as well as for her piety, humility, and poverty, and devotion as a wife and mother. But as the wife and mother to the Imams, Fāṭima is also considered by Shiʿis to be among the 14 infallibles (the Prophet, the twelve Imams, and herself), who were the recipients of special knowledge from the Prophet, and to have had her name (along with that of her husband, ʿAlī, and her sons Ḥasan and Ḥusayn), inscribed on the very throne of God.[16] Her purity is emphasized in the epithet often attributed to her, *al-batūl* (the virgin), and she is sometimes said to have never menstruated or experienced postpartum bleeding.[17] The reference to Fāṭima as "virgin" and the emphasis on her purity makes for a natural comparison with Maryam. Moreover, she is included, along with Maryam, Khadīja, the wife of the Prophet, and Āsiya, the wife of Pharaoh, among the four greatest women of the world in spiritual rank according to both Shiʿi and

---

15 Amīn, *Makhzan-i ʿirfān* i, 3 and 12.

16 See Amir-Moezzi, Mohammad Ali, *The divine guide in early Shiʿism: The sources of esotericism in Islam*, trans. David Streight, Albany, NY: SUNY Press, 1994, 30–31.

17 See Thurkill, Mary, *Chosen among women: Mary and Fāṭima in medieval Christianity and Shiʿite Islam*, Notre Dame, IN: University of Notre Dame Press, 2007, 60; McAuliffe, Jane Dammen, "Chosen among women: Mary and Fāṭima in Qurʾanic exegesis," in *Islamochristiana* 7 (1981), 1–28; and Pierce, Matthew, *Twelve infallible men: The imams and the making of Shiism*, Cambridge, MA: Harvard University Press, 2016, 120. In one Shiʿi *ḥadīth*, the exemption from menstruation is said to be a characteristic of all daughters of the prophets; see al-Kulaynī, Muḥammad, *al-Kāfī*, ed. Muḥammad J. Shams al-Dīn, 7 vols., Beirut: Dār al-Taʿāruf li-l-Maṭbūʿāt, 1990, i, 530.

Sunni tradition. The comparison also raises the thornier issue, for Shiʿis, of how to understand the Quranic assertion that Maryam was chosen and preferred above "all women." If this Quranic statement is understood literally and absolutely, this would give Maryam precedence over all women (past and future), including Fāṭima—a position that traditional Shiʿi thinkers and commentators generally rejected. How does Nuṣrat Amīn treat this comparison?

Nuṣrat Amīn is effusive in her discussion of Maryam's high spiritual station, her closeness to God as His "beloved," and her unique position among women, but as a Shiʿi, she also has a deep attachment to Fāṭima. In Amīn's discussion of the miraculous food that comes to Maryam in her prayer niche, she mentions, like other commentators, the way in which this miracle surprised her guardian Zakariyyāʾ and inspired him to ask for his own miracle from God (a son for him and his aging, barren wife). She also notes the widespread extra-Quranic tradition that the food that came to her was usually "fruits out of season," emphasizing the truly miraculous nature of this provision, and the impossibility of it having been provided by another human being. However, she also includes in her commentary on Maryam's miraculous food a similar story about miraculous provisions granted to Fāṭima—a story clearly meant to establish a connection and even parity between the two women. According to this story, the Prophet had no food to eat, and could not find any food with his wives. When he went to the house of his daughter, Fāṭima, to ask if she had anything to give him, she indicated that she could indeed help him. Earlier, a neighbor had sent her some food intended for her husband and sons, but she put it away, knowing presciently that this food was divinely intended for the Prophet. When the Prophet arrived, therefore, she was prepared, and immediately sent one of her sons to fetch a little bit of the food and put it in a container for the Prophet. When the Prophet opened the container, it miraculously overflowed with food (an account that also bears parallels with the Gospel story of the loaves and the fishes). Even Fāṭima seems to have been surprised; but when the Prophet asked her where the food came from, she responds by citing Maryam's own words from Q 3:37: "It is from God. Truly He provides for whomever He wills without reckoning." The Prophet responds by thanking God for allowing him to witness the miracle that Zakariyyāʾ saw from Maryam.[18]

We see a similar invocation of Shiʿi tradition when directly discussing the question of whether Maryam's precedence and chosenness, as articulated in Q 3:42, places her above the station of Fāṭima. The verse reads: "And remem-

18 Amīn, *Makhzan-i ʿirfān* iii, 103.

ber when the angels said, 'O Mary, truly God has chosen you and purified you, and chosen you above the women of the worlds.'" In discussing the question of precedence associated with this verse, Amīn follows Ṭabāṭabā'ī's discussion in *al-Mīzān* closely. She notes that Maryam's chosenness is mentioned twice. The first time the chosenness is expressed without qualification, "God has chosen you," whereas the second mention of chosenness is relational, saying that God has "chosen you above the women of the worlds." Amīn states that while the first mention of Maryam's chosenness established her precedence over all of the people *of her time*, the second one, where her precedence is explicitly over *all the women of the worlds*, is related to the unique miracle whereby she conceived Jesus through the divine spirit that was breathed into her. In this, Amīn asserts, Maryam is truly unique, and she acknowledges that the most natural reading of the verse would indicate that Maryam takes precedence over *all women*, meaning "from the beginning of the world to the end."[19] And yet, Amīn feels compelled to mention the existence of sound *aḥādīth* from the Prophet and the Imams that suggest that Fāṭima had to be considered an exception to Maryam's otherwise universal precedence over all women of the world. She says that "some of the *mufassirīn*" cite the *ḥadīth* found in both Sunni and Shiʿi sources wherein the Prophet says that Fāṭima is a "part of me" (*biḍʿa minnī*),[20] the "light of his eye," and the fruit of his inmost heart (*fu'ād*). Since Fāṭima was part of the Prophet, whereas Maryam was only "part" of her father, ʿImrān, Maryam's station could not exceed Fāṭima's, at least in this regard.[21] She also cites the well-known *ḥadīth* in which the Prophet declares Fāṭima to be the "*sayyida* (mistress) of the women of the world."[22] She says that on the basis of such statements, the *mufassirīn* have declared that Maryam's precedence was indeed universal over all women, but for the single exception of Fāṭima.

Amīn ultimately takes a similar position—upholding the (near) universality of Maryam's spiritual precedence over all the women of the world, but retaining the exception made for Fāṭima in Shiʿi tradition. Continuing to follow

---

19 Amīn, *Makhzan-i ʿirfān* iii, 108.

20 This is also found in al-Bukhārī, Muḥammad, *Ṣaḥīḥ al-Bukhārī*, Liechtenstein: Thesaurus Islamicus Foundation, 2000, *Kitāb Faḍā'il aṣḥāb al-nabī*, n. 3714 and Ibn al-Ḥajjāj, Muslim, *Ṣaḥīḥ Muslim ibn al-Ḥajjāj*, Liechtenstein: Thesaurus Islamicus Foundation, 2000, *Kitāb Faḍā'il al-ṣaḥāba*, n. 2449.

21 Amīn, *Makhzan-i ʿirfān* iii, 109. We might note that this line of reasoning assumes that the Prophet's reference to Fāṭima as "part of me" is a reference to the fact that she was his daughter, since it is compared to Maryam being "part of ʿImrān" (her father). However, such a line of reasoning seems to neglect the fact that the Prophet had other biological daughters, even if they were not as close to him as Fāṭima was.

22 Amīn, *Makhzan-i ʿirfān* iii, 109. For this tradition, see also al-Kulaynī, *al-Kāfī* i, 381–382.

Ṭabāṭabāʾī's discussion closely, she says that it was only the miraculous conception of Jesus that put Maryam in a completely unique and separate category from all other women. She notes that the other qualities that collectively constitute her particular excellence (*faḍīlat*)—including the rigorous maintenance of her purity, her confirmation of the words of God and the heavenly books, and even her status as *muḥaddatha* (one spoken to by God)—great as they are, have also been attributed to others. Indeed, the very next verse, Q 3:43, enjoins Maryam to be devoutly obedient to God and "bow with those who bow," indicating that others shared a similar station of worship with her, and that she was enjoined to worship humbly along with them.[23] On this issue, then, Amīn's commentary takes a very traditional approach, both in method and content, relying directly upon other Shiʿi commentators and upholding the unique status of Fāṭima in the broader Shiʿi tradition.

6 Reading the Story of Maryam as a Mystic and as a Woman

Nuṣrat Amīn, in addition to holding more "exoteric" scholarly credentials, including *ijāza*s in Hadith and law, was also trained in the esoteric mystical and intellectual science of *ʿirfān*. This may not have been a merely academic interest, however, as she claimed to have experienced spiritual visions herself.[24] Throughout her commentary on Maryam's story in the Quran—a story filled with accounts of extraordinary divine miracles and powerful spiritual encounters, but also moments of great suffering and loneliness—Nuṣrat Amīn discusses Maryam's interior spiritual and psychological states in a way few other commentators do, and Amīn seems intent on establishing her spiritual rank. When she speaks of Maryam's spiritual "station" (*maqām*) she usually refers to her as possessing the *maqām* of servanthood (*ʿubūdiyya*). She does not entertain notions of Maryam's possible prophethood, as we noted, nor does she refer to her explicitly as a "saint." While she has much to say about the meaning of Maryam's Quranic epithet, *ṣiddīqa*, she does not connect it with the notion of sainthood (with which it is sometimes associated), but rather reads it more literally to mean that she was a "confirmer" of God's words (more on this shortly). At the same time, she is careful to make sure that the various ways

23 Amīn, *Makhzan-i ʿirfān* iii, 110; see also Ṭabāṭabāʾī, Muḥammad Ḥusayn, *al-Mīzān fī tafsīr al-Qurʾān*, 21 vols., Beirut: Muʾassasat al-Aʿlamī, 1970–1985, commentary on Q 3:42–43.

24 See Amīn, Nuṣrat B., *Nafaḥāt al-raḥmāniyya fī l-wāridāt al-qalbiyya*, Beirut: Dār al-Maʿārif al-Ḥikmiyya, 2018, 60-64.

that Maryam's story parallels that of the prophets, and the many distinctions she shares with them, are not lost on her readers.

One of the places where Amīn clearly connects Maryam's story with that of other prophets is in her discussion of the opening lines of the passage in Sūra 19 (Maryam): "And [remember] Mary in the Book, when she withdrew from her family to an eastern place. And she veiled herself from them. Then We sent unto her Our Spirit …." (Q 19:16–17). Amīn begins her commentary on these verses by presenting some of the existing commentary on them by other "*mufassirīn*." These unnamed commentators expanded on the elliptical statements in these verses, explaining that they refer to the time when Maryam first began to menstruate, and so had to leave the Temple and stay in the house of her aunt until it had passed. After she had cleaned herself and washed her clothes, the angel appeared to her. Amīn does not directly discredit or reject this account, despite the fact that it would seem to be at odds with the thoroughgoing purity attributed to Maryam in other parts of the commentary tradition—a contradiction she does not mention. Amīn herself, however, thinks that it is more in keeping with what the Quran actually says to interpret Maryam's "withdrawal" and separation as having a purely spiritual purpose. She suggests that Maryam was voluntarily undertaking a radical form of spiritual seclusion in the wilderness in order to devote herself entirely to God and be completely free of interactions with other people. Even the "veil" that the verse says she drew between herself and her people may not be merely a cloth covering, according to Amīn, but might instead refer to a more dramatic physical barrier she placed between herself and others—possibly a wall, or even a mountain cave. She mentions that similar periods of spiritual seclusion in the wilderness preceded the onset of the prophetic missions of Moses, Jesus, and Muhammad. She reminds her readers that another verse of the Quran (Q 23:50) says that God gave *both* Jesus and Maryam "refuge in a high place of stillness" (*āwaynāhumā ilā rabwatin dhāti qarārin wa-maʿīn*). Amīn uses this to suggest that Maryam sought spiritual solitude in a mountain cave, specifically, and she connects this directly with the story of Muhammad himself, who received his initial revelation, and his initial encounter with Jibrīl, in a cave on Mount Ḥirāʾ.[25]

Amīn does not refute the views of the earlier "*mufassirīn*" directly, but she does not have to. The stark contrast between the earlier (male) commentators' more pedestrian and mundane speculation about Maryam leaving the Temple to stay with her aunt while she was experiencing the very normal female state

25 Amīn, *Makhzan-i ʿirfān* viii, 105.

of menstruation and subsequent purification, and Amīn's own interpretation that Maryam left the Temple in search of the radical spiritual seclusion necessary for intensive prayer and spiritual exercises in the wilderness, makes her point very clearly. This is not the story of a timid young girl menstruating for the first time and in need of motherly guidance, but the story of a spiritual warrior who needs no one, seeking out God alone in the most forbidding of environments. And the reward for her rigorous spiritual endeavor is an encounter with the Spirit that is as powerful and overwhelming as that of the prophets Moses and Muhammad. Moreover, she presents Maryam's example as a spiritual lesson for her readers, telling them in a concluding exhortation:

> Until the house of the heart is completely emptied of everything else, it will not become the locus of the dawning of divine light. We are the same. If we want to find the path to truth, we must empty our own hearts of "it was said" and "he said" and our preoccupation with the world, so that we might become recipients of the illumination of the light of knowledge.[26]

Her reference to emptying one's heart of "it was said" and "he said" suggests the need to transcend the ordinary means of acquiring knowledge in the Islamic tradition—the transmission of statements attributed to this or that scholar—so that one might be illuminated by the light of knowledge (*maʿrifa*) itself. Indeed, she has just offered something of an example of this in her own commentary, as she goes beyond the transmitted speculations of the *mufassirīn*, overly concerned as they are with mundane female bodily processes, to offer a spiritual interpretation of Maryam's story that is not only more compelling and inspiring, but one that she claims is more consistent with the literal meaning of the Quranic text itself.[27]

In other ways, and equally as subtlely, Amīn's commentary on the story of Maryam aims to convey Maryam's elevated spiritual station in a way that goes beyond existing exegetical treatments. For example, several accounts of Maryam's encounter with the angel(s) and her miraculous and sudden conception of Jesus mention "the Spirit" (*rūḥ*) as both the angel that takes the form of a man and speaks with her (Q 19:17–18) and that which is "breathed into her" to generate the miraculous child in her womb, "We breathed into her of Our Spirit" (Q 21:91).[28] Commentators have debated the meaning of "Our Spirit" in

26 Amīn, *Makhzan-i ʿirfān* viii, 105.

27 Amīn, *Makhzan-i ʿirfān* viii, 105.

28 Or "We breathed into *it* of Our Spirit" (Q 66:12), with the "it" possibly being a reference to the opening in her shirt into which the Spirit was blown. The closest male-gendered

these contexts, since the idea that it might refer to God's very Spirit was widely dismissed as an unacceptable delimitation of God. Some therefore considered it to be the spirit of Jesus himself, as he is referred to elsewhere in the Quran as a "spirit from [God]" (Q 4:171), while others argue that the attribution of this Spirit to God was simply meant as an honorific statement, as when one describes the Kaʿba as the "House of God." Amīn cites these different explanations in her commentary, but then offers her own suggestion—namely that this Spirit that was breathed into Maryam was nothing less than the original, primordial *rūḥ*—that greatest Spirit, under whose light all of the other spirits fall, and the very first creature that God created, also described as the First Intellect or the primordial Pen. In Islamic thought, this "greatest Spirit" is often understood to take the form of Jibrīl, the Angel of revelation; and in a more ultimate sense, it is the very conduit of divine light and intellect to the human realm. The recipients of this divine Spirit, or Intellect, or Light are naturally the prophets, who receive it in the form of revelation. Thus, for Amīn to assert that "Our Spirit" in these verses refers to this most transcendent *rūḥ*, that Maryam received this *rūḥ* into herself in the form of a "breath," and that from this *rūḥ*, Jesus, also described as a "word from God," was engendered within her, would seem to bring her very close to the station of prophethood indeed.

In general, Amīn is not content to have Maryam presented merely as the instrumental vessel through which the Prophet Jesus was conveyed into the world (as unique as that makes her), but is also eager to establish her spiritual station in ways that are independent of her son. As an example, we might look at her commentary on Q 21:91, in which Maryam is mentioned (although not by name) at the end of a long list of prophets. After briefly mentioning Moses, Aaron, Abraham, Lot, Isaac, Jacob, Noah, David, Solomon, Job, Ismāʿīl, Idrīs, Dhū l-Kifl, Dhū l-Nūn, Zakariyyāʾ, and John, the Sūra, which is entitled "The Prophets" (al-Anbiyāʾ), concludes this list by mentioning "she who preserved her chastity" (i.e., Maryam), saying that she and her son were made "a sign for the worlds." Some commentators explain the mention of Maryam at the end of a long line of prophets as simply a way to ensure that the list ends with Jesus, the last prophet before Muhammad. Amīn, however, chooses to emphasize the significance of having Maryam herself being given a place in this

referent for the "it" in Q 66:12 is *farj*, a word that means an opening. It may be a reference to one's private parts (as when the Quran talks about the believers being those who "guard their private parts") and in these cases, as in Q 66:12, it is often metaphorically and euphemistically translated as "guarding or preserving chastity." Commentators (including Amīn) generally understand the *farj* in reference to Maryam's encounter with the angel as the opening in her shirt through which the "breathed spirit" was cast upon her.

long line of sent prophets. She notes that the purpose of the statement in this verse that she and her son together constitute a "sign for the worlds" is not only to demonstrate God's power to bring a human being like Jesus into existence without intermediary, but also to establish the honor and spiritual precedence of Maryam who enjoys the *maqām* of "infallibility" and is described with a purity that is like no other—a purity that has afforded her a place in the "divine holiness," where she resides even now, after her death.[29]

To offer a third example of the way in which Amīn's commentary on the story of Maryam goes beyond other exegetical treatments, we might consider her discussion of one of the Quranic titles given to Maryam, *ṣiddīqa*[30]—a term that means either "truthful one" or "confirmer," and may simply refer to her righteous character. Amīn connects the epithet *ṣiddīqa* in Q 5:75 with the later statement in Q 66:12 that Maryam "confirmed (*ṣaddaqat*) the words of her Lord and His Books." Most other commentators assume that what is meant by this latter statement is that Maryam was a true believer in the divine words of revelation as found in "His Books," that is, the scriptures. Amīn does not reject this understanding, but rather expands upon it. She suggests that Maryam's confirming the "words of her Lord" may also refer to her confirmation of "words" that came specifically and directly to her from God, through personal inspiration (*ilhām*) or through a theophanic communication made possible by her extraordinary purity and moral perfection. As Amīn says, "A pure heart that is empty of psychic impurities [such as Maryam's] becomes a receiver of divine self-manifestation (*tajalliyyāt*) through which are transmitted the lights of knowledge and gnosis (*ʿulūm wa-maʿārif*)."[31]

Despite the transcendent spiritual qualities of Maryam that Amīn emphasizes in her commentary, and her claim that she was free of "psychic impurities," she also engages with the more emotional, affective, and intimate aspects of Maryam's spiritual journey and her relationship with God. For example, when discussing Maryam's distress as she labors to give birth to Jesus in the wilderness, Amīn tells us that there were three reasons for Maryam's anguish at that moment: first, she was alone; second, she was in pain from labor; and third (and most disturbingly) she was afraid of the accusations of fornication that were likely to be leveled against her pure person unjustly. Here, Amīn allows herself to imaginatively inhabit the mind of Maryam at this time—something she can

29 Amīn, *Makhzan-i ʿirfān* viii, 301–302.

30 Q 5:75. Note that Amīn does not deal with the term extensively in her commentary on this verse, but only in her commentary on Q 66:12, in connection with the statement that Maryam "confirmed the words of her Lord."

31 Amīn, *Makhzan-i ʿirfān* xii, 404.

perhaps do as a woman and a mother herself. Knowing herself the pain of labor, she can now imagine how this would be compounded by being utterly alone during the experience; and as a spiritual person herself, she can imagine the overwhelming pain of facing such an unjust accusation. In the Quran, Maryam cries out at this moment, longing for death, and to be utterly forgotten. This expression of longing for death and oblivion by Maryam might seem to some to reflect a sudden loss of trust in God on the part of Maryam. But this is not how Amīn reads the account. For her, this is the moment when Maryam's spiritual character is tested under maximum pressure, and (Amīn suggests) from which she emerges purified and worthy of an even higher spiritual station. She tells us:

> Until a human being drinks from the cup of adversity, the joy of union cannot arise. Witness the saints (*awliyāʾ*) and the near ones (*muqarrabīn*) and the calamities and adversity with which they were tried, each according to his ability … They were tested under pressure, and they remained as pure as the purest gold, completely radiant and purified of all uncleanness, so that they became worthy of the station of divine holiness.[32]

Amīn here discusses the transformative and purifying effect of adversity in the context of the "saints" more generally; but her mention of this in connection with Maryam's own moment of adversity and great anguish clearly implies that she, too, emerged pure and radiant from the experience. This was not a moment of weakness for Maryam, but a moment of spiritual triumph and purification forged in the crucible of great physical and spiritual struggle.

Amīn balances assertions of Maryam's personal heroism in this moment by also emphasizing the extraordinary care and intimacy that God demonstrates toward Maryam in her suffering. As Maryam struggles in labor in the wilderness, the Quran says that a voice called to her, telling her to shake the trunk of a date palm so that ripe fruits would fall down upon her and to drink from a river that had miraculously appeared beneath her feet. Commentators have traditionally debated whose voice it is that calls to her, with some considering it to be Jesus himself, and others the angel who first brought her the news of the miraculous birth. Amīn comes down in favor of the position that the voice comes from the angel or "Spirit" himself, whom she says was commanded by God to function as a "midwife (*qābila*)" for Maryam, "attending to her condition until the pregnancy could be delivered and making her heart content

32 Amīn, *Makhzan-i ʿirfān* viii, 107–108.

through divine favors (*alṭāf-i ilāhī*)."[33] God's concern for Maryam's personal suffering and fear is such that He sends the "greatest Spirit," His first creation, to serve as a personal "midwife" to Maryam. Such divine intimacy and solicitousness for Maryam is also demonstrated, according to Amīn, by the fact that God (sometimes through the angels) calls Maryam by name on several different occasions. Maryam is, in fact, the only woman mentioned *by name* (rather than referred to by title or relation) in all of the Quran. Some have speculated the mention of Maryam's name in the Quran (a distinction usually reserved for prophets) is simply a matter of necessity: since Jesus did not have a father, and people were usually identified through the names of their fathers, he had to be identified through the name of his mother, and so this name had to be specified. But Maryam is called by, and indeed given, her name in the Quran, independent of any relation to Jesus. For Amīn, this is a sign of great honor, but more importantly, it is a sign that Maryam is the "beloved of God (*maḥbūba-yi Allāh*)."[34]

7 Conclusion

In this brief study, we have tried to elucidate some of the salient features of Nuṣrat Amīn's commentary on the Quran through a close study of her commentary on the Quranic story of Maryam. Amīn's completion of a comprehensive, 15-volume Persian translation and commentary on the Quran is a unique achievement in itself. But her impressive combination of scholarly competencies—from law to Hadith, to philosophy, mysticism, and *ʿirfān*—affords her the ability and the authority to comment richly on the text. In addition to these traditional resources, Amīn also draws deeply from her own spiritual life and experience to offer intimate, and moving discourses on the nature of divine love and the path to seeking it. She is respectful of the broader Islamic (and especially Shiʿi) tradition, eruditely citing a good number of Shiʿi, as well as Sunni sources, including both exoteric and esoteric works. But she is also, in places, unsatisfied by this transmitted tradition. In these places, she feels free to go beyond the limitations of these sources and their occasionally mundane or theologically pedantic concerns, and to draw upon her own rich inner experience to elucidate what she considers to be most meaningful and powerful in the scripture, and in what speaks to her and what she clearly hopes will speak to her audience as well.

33 Amīn, *Makhzan-i ʿirfān* viii, 108.

34 Amīn, *Makhzan-i ʿirfān* viii, 108. See also Amīn, *Makhzan-i ʿirfān* viii, 110, where she is described as the "beloved of the Real" (*maḥbūba-yi ḥaqq*).

Bibliography

Amīn, Nuṣrat B., *Makhzan-i ʿirfān dar tafsīr-i Qurʾān*, 15 vols., Isfahan: Gulbahār, n.d.

Amīn, Nuṣrat B., *Nafaḥāt al-raḥmāniyya fī l-wāridāt al-qalbiyya*, Beirut: Dār al-Maʿārif al-Ḥikmiyya, 2018.

Amir-Moezzi, Mohammad Ali, *The divine guide in early Shiʿism: The sources of esotericism in Islam*, trans. David Streight, Albany, NY: SUNY Press, 1994.

Barlas, Asma, *Believing women in the Quran: Unreading patriarchal interpretations*, Austin: University of Texas Press, 2002.

Bint al-Shāṭiʾ, ʿĀʾisha ʿAbd al-Raḥmān, *al-Tafsīr al-bayānī li-l-Qurʾān al-karīm*, 2 vols., Cairo: Dār al-Maʿārif, 1966.

al-Bukhārī, Muḥammad, *Ṣaḥīḥ al-Bukhārī*, Liechtenstein: Thesaurus Islamicus Foundation, 2000.

Ibn al-Ḥajjāj, Muslim, *Ṣaḥīḥ Muslim Ibn al-Ḥajjāj*, Liechtenstein: Thesaurus Islamicus Foundation, 2000.

Ibrahim, Celene, *Women and gender in the Quran*, Oxford: Oxford University Press, 2020.

al-Kulaynī, Muḥammad, *al-Kāfī*, ed. Muḥammad J. Shams al-Dīn, 7 vols., Beirut: Dār al-Taʿāruf bi-l-Maṭbūʿāt, 1990.

Künkler, Mirjam and Roja Fazaeli, “The life of two *mujtahidah*s: Female religious authority in twentieth-century Iran,” in Masooda Bano and Hilary E. Kalmbach (eds.), *Women, leadership and mosques: Changes in contemporary Islamic authority*, Leiden: Brill, 2011, 127–160.

Lamptey, Jerusha, *Never wholly other: A Muslima theology of religious pluralism*, Oxford: Oxford University Press, 2014.

Lamptey, Jerusha, *Divine words, female voices: Muslima explorations in comparative feminist theology*, Oxford: Oxford University Press, 2018.

Lamrabet, Asma, *Women in the Quran: An emancipatory reading*, Leicestershire: Kube Publishing, 2016.

Lamrabet, Asma, *Women and men in the Quran*, London: Palgrave-Macmillan, 2018.

McAuliffe, Jane Dammen, “Chosen among women: Mary and Fāṭima in Qurʾanic exegesis,” in *Islamochristiana* 7 (1981), 1–28.

Nasr, Seyyed Hossein et al. (eds.), *The study Quran: A new translation and commentary*, New York: HarperOne, 2015.

Pierce, Matthew, *Twelve infallible men: The imams and the making of Shiism*, Cambridge, MA: Harvard University Press, 2016.

Rutner, Maryam, “Religious authority, gendered recognition, and instrumentalization of Nusrat Amin in life and after death,” in *Journal of Middle East Women's Studies* 11.1 (2015), 24–41.

al-Ṭabarsī, al-Faḍl b. al-Ḥasan, *Majmaʿ al-bayān fī tafsīr al-Qurʾān*, 6 vols., Beirut: Muʾassasat al-Aʿlamī, 2005.

Ṭabāṭabāʾī, Muḥammad Ḥusayn, *al-Mīzān fī tafsīr al-Qurʾān*, 21 vols., Beirut: Muʾassasat al-Aʿlamī, 1970–1985.
Thurkill, Mary, *Chosen among women: Mary and Fāṭima in medieval Christianity and Shiʿite Islam*, Notre Dame, IN: University of Notre Dame Press, 2007.
Wadud, Amina, *Qurʾan and woman: Rereading the sacred text from a woman's perspective*, Oxford: Oxford University Press, 1999.
Zadeh, Travis, "Persian Qurʾanic networks, modernity, and the writings of 'an Iranian lady', Nusrat Amin Khanum (d. 1983)," in Suha Taji-Farouki (ed.), *The Qurʾan and its readers worldwide: Contemporary commentaries and translations*, Oxford: Oxford University Press in association with The Institute of Ismaili Studies, 2015, 275–323.

PART 2

The Akbarian Tradition

CHAPTER 6

Some Notes on Ibn ʿArabī's Correlative Prophetology

Gregory Vandamme

1 Introduction*

In his *Kitāb al-Isfār ʿan natāʾij al-asfār* (*The secrets of voyaging*), Muhammad and Adam are presented by Ibn ʿArabī (d. 638/1240) as "respectively father and son to one another."[1] In this early treatise in which Ibn ʿArabī describes a series of journeys taking place at certain ontological and cosmological levels of a perpetually moving universal existence, the journey of Adam is described as being the exact opposite of the preceding journey of Muhammad, "yet following the same course."[2] These unusual ascriptions contrast with the classical qualifications of Adam as the father of mankind and Muhammad as the Seal of the Prophets, and clearly indicate an intricate correlation between the two figures that exceeds their chronological succession.

As I have already shown elsewhere,[3] the notions of "relation" (*nisba*) and "correlation" (*munāsaba*) are absolutely central to the ontology of Ibn ʿArabī. Only the infinite being of God truly "is," whereas everything else is but a web of intertwined relations in that unique being. Ibn ʿArabī often asserts in a famous provocative formulation that everything that is found in existence is at the same time "Him not Him" (*huwa lā huwa*). In consequence, every existing reality is thus implicated in ambiguous ontological correlations which Ibn ʿArabī sometimes describes in the classical philosophical and theological terms of his time, but above all by resorting to the symbolic discourse of the Quran, Hadith, and the Sufi tradition. It is therefore necessary to consider carefully the mul-

* I want to express my gratitude to Professor Cécile Bonmariage for her careful reading of the article and her useful comments that greatly improved this work.

1 Ibn ʿArabī, Muḥyī al-Dīn, *Kitāb al-Isfār ʿan natāʾij al-asfār* (*The secrets of voyaging*), ed. Denis Gril, Abrar A. Shahi, and Angela Jaffray, Oxford: Anqa Publishing, 2016, 71. All translations are mine in order to retain consistency in technical vocabulary.

2 Ibn ʿArabī, *Kitāb al-Isfār* 71.

3 Vandamme, Gregory, "L'ontologie corrélative d'Ibn ʿArabī: Métaphysique de l'être et de ses relations," in Jean-Michel Counet (ed.), *La non-dualité: Perspectives philosophiques, scientifiques, spirituelles*, Leuven: Peeters, 2021, 89–102.

 | DOI:10.1163/9789004529038_007

tiple aspects and the peculiar formulations of Ibn ʿArabī regarding any given reality described in his works. Ibn ʿArabī himself gives this clear advice in the chapter dedicated to Adam in his *Kitāb al-Isfār*: "Connect what we have left unsaid with what we already said, according to the correspondence, and you will be well guided, God willing!"[4]

In this study, we will see through the example of the relation between Adam and Muhammad that this correlative approach seems also crucial to understand the intricacies of Ibn ʿArabī's prophetology. By applying his own advice, gathering, and collecting the scattered common elements shared by Adam and Muhammad in several of his writings, we will see how these two figures appear correlated, and ultimately depend on each other. Rather than provide a comprehensive survey and a thorough analysis of the question, this paper will propose some introductory notes to a problem that merits much closer scholarly consideration.[5]

2 Adam and Muhammad: A Meta-History

The first thing we need to consider in order to understand the correlation between the figures of Adam and Muhammad in Ibn ʿArabī's prophetology is their respective ahistorical—or more precisely meta-historical—dimension. Since the very beginning of Quranic exegesis, Adam has been considered as a cosmological figure and a historical prophet, and the father of mankind. His story usually begins long before his creation and is filled with legends involving angels and *jinns*. As demonstrated by Cornelia Schöck in her *Adam im Islam*, the formative period of Islamic theology has given great importance to the figure of Adam in questions regarding universal salvation, eschatology, and freewill, as well as the prophetical and cosmological functions of Muhammad.[6] Early Sufi literature already used those motifs to evoke the divine aspect of

---

4 Ibn ʿArabī, *Kitāb al-Isfār* 79.

5 I should mention here the article by Singh, David E., "An onto-epistemological model: Adam–Muhammad as the traditional symbols of humanity's all-comprehending epistemic potential," in *MW* 94.2 (2004), 275–301. Although this study presents some interesting aspects of the question, it is above all based on commentaries on the *Kitāb Shajarat al-kawn* (*The tree of existence*) usually attributed to Ibn ʿArabī, but which has proven to be by ʿAbd al-Salām Ibn Ghānim al-Maqdisī (d. 678/1280). See Alaoui Mdaghri, Younes, "Critical study of the erroneous attribution of the book Shajarat al-kawn to Ibn ʿArabī instead of to Ibn Ghānim al-Maqdisī," in *The Journal of Rotterdam Islamic and Social Sciences* 1 (2010), 1–16.

6 Schöck, Cornelia, *Adam im Islam: Ein Beitrag zur Ideengeschichte der Sunna*, Berlin: Schwarz, 1993.

human nature, as exemplified in a verse of al-Ḥallāj (d. 309/922): "What is Adam if not yourself? And the one who stands in between is Iblīs."[7]

It is thus not surprising to see Ibn ʿArabī describing Adam in his *Fuṣūṣ al-ḥikam* (*The bezels of the wisdoms*) as a reality out of time that largely exceeds the usual mythical-historical figure: "He is the new (*ḥādith*) and eternal (*azalī*) human, the continuous and perpetual emergence (*nash'*), and the dividing and synthetic word."[8] It is probably more unexpected to see Ibn ʿArabī declaring elsewhere that "God created one hundred thousand Adams."[9] This appears in chapter 367 of his *al-Futūḥāt al-Makkiyya* (*The Meccan illuminations*), where he gives an account of his spiritual journey through the heavens, which clearly reminds of the spiritual ascension (*miʿrāj*) of the Prophet Muhammad. In the first heaven, Ibn ʿArabī faces Adam and all the blessed and the damned among his progeny, before seeing himself at the right of the father of mankind, troubled by this sudden ubiquity. Later, in the fourth heaven, Ibn ʿArabī discusses with Idrīs the eternity of the world and the age of Adam. Among other things, Ibn ʿArabī tells him of a visionary experience he had during which one of his ancestors—older than forty-thousand years—explained to him that God created many Adams. The number "one hundred thousand" is drawn by Ibn ʿArabī from a *ḥadīth* that is absent from the canonical collections, but which he considers authentic according to his own spiritual unveiling.[10]

These two contrasting dimensions of the figure of Adam, who is presented by Ibn ʿArabī both as a unique meta-historical reality and as multiple historical instances, should probably be approached from the perspective of the microcosmic and macrocosmic aspects of the "Perfect Man" (*al-insān al-kāmil*).[11] Ibn

7 Al-Ḥallāj, al-Ḥusayn b. Manṣūr, *Kitāb al-Ṭāwasīn* (*Le livre "Tâwasîn" de Hallâj*), ed. Stéphane Ruspoli, Paris: Albouraq, 2007, 346.

8 Ibn ʿArabī, Muḥyī al-Dīn, *Fuṣūṣ al-ḥikam* (*Facsimile of oldest copy* (*dated 630H, TIEM 1933*) *and édition critique*), ed. Mahmud Erol Kılıç and Abdurrahim Alkış, Istanbul: Litera Yayıncılık, 2016, 28 (50). (From now on, abbreviated as *"Fuṣ."* The pages correspond to the recent edition by Kılıç and Alkış, while the pages in the classical ʿAfīfī edition are indicated between hyphens).

9 Ibn ʿArabī, Muḥyī al-Dīn, *al-Futūḥāt al-Makkiyya*, 4 vols., iii, Cairo: Dār al-Fikr, n.d., 549. (From now on, abbreviated as *"Fut."*)

10 It should be noted that we find a close *ḥadīth* in Shiʿi collections, where the Imam Abū Jaʿfar al-Bāqir is quoted thus: "God created a million (*alf alf*) worlds, and a million Adams." See Ibn Bābawayh al-Qummī, *al-Tawḥīd*, ed. Hāshim al-Ḥusaynī al-Tihrānī, Qom: Mu'assasat al-Nashr al-Islāmī, 2008, 271.

11 See Chittick, William C., *Imaginal worlds: Ibn al-ʿArabī and the problem of religious diversity*, Albany, NY: SUNY Press, 1994, 31–38, and Takeshita, Masataka, *Ibn ʿArabī's theory of the Perfect Man and its place in the history of Islamic thought*, Tokyo: Institute for the Study of Languages and Cultures of Asia and Africa, 1987.

ʿArabī repeatedly claims in the *Fuṣūṣ* and the *Futūḥāt* that Adam is a name for the Perfect Man, which is the focal point of the whole process of Creation: "God condensed the cosmos in a synthetic existence that contains all its meanings in the most perfect aspects, and He named him Adam."[12] The synthetic function of the Adamic Perfect Man is often described by Ibn ʿArabī as the "mirror" created by God to contemplate Himself.[13] More precisely, it is the world in its entirety that acts as "an unpolished mirror" for the Divine Manifestation, while Adam is "the shine of this mirror and the spirit of this form."[14] The mirror of the Adamic Perfect Man is described as a double-sided mirror, one face reflecting the image of God and the other reflecting the image of the Perfect Man: "Whenever we contemplate Him, we contemplate ourselves. Whenever He contemplates us, He contemplates Himself."[15] Only the Adamic Perfect Man is able to see those two aspects together, whereas "the world is a veil on itself," for contrary to Adam, "it cannot perceive the Real through its perception of itself."[16] We will see further that this duality plays a central role in the articulation between the Adamic and Muhammadan aspects of the Perfect Man.

The synthetic cosmological function of the Adamic Perfect Man is also symbolized by the motif of the "seal" (*khatm*) throughout the opening chapter of the *Fuṣūṣ*: "He is the Seal of the treasures of the other world from all eternity … He is called 'Caliph' for that reason, because [God] Most High guards His Creation by him, like the seal guards the treasures."[17] We will have to come back to the notion of the seal that is well known for being associated with the figure of Muhammad, and to its relation to the "Caliphate" of the Perfect Man.[18]

For Ibn ʿArabī, every human being inherits the synthetic Adamic nature from the "supreme parent" (*al-wālid al-akbar*), and the perfect human mode of existence is nothing but the actualization of this potentiality inherited from him. The human being who does not completely realize that perfect Adamic nature is only "an animal whose form resembles the outward appearance of

12 *Fut.* iii, 10.

13 *Fuṣ.* 27 (48).

14 *Fuṣ.* 27 (49).

15 *Fuṣ.* 31 (53). Ibn ʿArabī comments elsewhere on the famous *ḥadīth*: "The faithful (*al-mu'min*) is the mirror of the faithful," by saying that because the name "the Faithful" is one of the Divine names, we can actually read the *ḥadīth* either as: "God is the mirror of the faithful," or "The faithful is the mirror of God," *Fut.* i, 112. See also Chodkiewicz, Michel, *Un océan sans rivage: Ibn ʿArabî, le livre et la loi*, Paris: Éditions du Seuil, 1992, 175.

16 *Fuṣ.* 32 (54).

17 *Fuṣ.* 28 (49–50).

18 See Chodkiewicz, Michel, *Le sceau des saints: Prophétie et sainteté dans la doctrine d'Ibn Arabî*, [Paris]: Gallimard, 2012, 70–82.

humans,"[19] because he does not acknowledge the eminence of his reality, and his cosmological function in the Divine Manifestation. In other words, only those who recognize and realize the reality of the Perfect Man actually inherit from Adam the cosmological function of Caliph: "Every human being is not Caliph. For us, the animal human being is not Caliph."[20]

The figure of Adam in Ibn ʿArabī should therefore always be read as alluding to both the universal and cosmological reality of the Adamic Perfect Man, as well as to the fundamental aspect of the Adamic human condition that is potentially shared by every individual. As a matter of fact, Ibn ʿArabī seems to be principally concerned with the later aspect of the Adamic reality, as he declares in his *Kitāb ʿAnqāʾ mughrib* (*The stupefying phoenix*):

> My goal, in everything I write in accordance with that spiritual art (*fann*), is not knowledge (*maʿrifa*) of Creation (*kawn*). Rather, it is the instruction of the heedless about what constitutes the essence (*ʿayn*) of the human being and the Adamic individual (*al-shakhṣ al-Ādamī*).[21]

In short, the figure of Adam seems to designate three distinct yet correlative dimensions for Ibn ʿArabī: the meta-historical Perfect Man, the mythical-historical father of humanity, and the commonly shared Adamic nature, potentially inherited from him by every human being. Remarkably, those three dimensions seem to have some precise correspondences with his use of the figure of Muhammad.

As it is the case with Adam, we can also find expressions of a meta-historical dimension of Muhammad in early sources of the Islamic tradition, as for example in the famous canonical *ḥadīth*, often commented upon by Ibn ʿArabī, in which the Prophet states, "I was a prophet while Adam was between spirit and body;" or according to a variant to which Ibn ʿArabī gives preference, "between water and clay."[22] The fact that such a "Muhammadan light" (*nūr Muḥammadī*) pre-existed the historical life of the Prophet has been treated in several Quran commentaries, and then gradually became a widespread

---

19 See *Fut.* ii, 293–296; iii, 154 and 296. See also Chittick, William C., *The Sufi path of knowledge: Ibn al-ʿArabī's metaphysics of imagination*, Albany, NY: SUNY Press, 1989, 275–276.

20 Ibn ʿArabī, Muḥyī al-Dīn, "Kitāb ʿUqlat al-mustawfiz," in Henrik S. Nyberg (ed.), *Kleinere Schriften des Ibn ʿArabī (Nach Handschriften in Upsala und Berlin zum ersten Mal herausgegeben und mit Einleitung und Kommentar versehen*), Leiden: Brill, 1919, 39–99, 45–46.

21 Ibn ʿArabī, Muḥyī al-Dīn, *ʿAnqāʾ mughrib fī maʿrifa khatm al-awliyāʾ wa-shams al-maghrib*, ed. ʿAbd al-ʿAzīz Ṣultān al-Manṣūb, Cairo: Shirkat al-Quds, 2016, 56.

22 See, e.g., *Fuṣ.* 39 (64), 202 (214), and *Fut.* iii, 23; iv, 58.

motif in Sufism, as well as in classical theology and popular Islamic culture.[23] Then, on the basis of that tradition, Ibn ʿArabī elaborated the complex notion of "Muhammadan reality" (*ḥaqīqa Muḥammadiyya*), which presents a metahistorical vision of the Prophetic mission and assigns to Muhammad a primordial status in the economy of Creation that appears in several points intertwined with what we have seen about the Adamic Perfect Man. The Muhammadan reality is presented at length in the *Kitāb ʿAnqāʾ mughrib* as "the origin of the beginning (*aṣl al-budʾ*) and the first emergence (*nashʾ*),"[24] from which the whole cosmos subsequently emerged.[25] In the *Futūḥāt*, this primordial function is openly associated with the notion of "First Intellect" (*ʿaql*) which, as we will see, is also associated with Adam:

> The beginning of Creation was the dust (*al-habāʾ*), in which the first existent (*mawjūd*) was the Muhammadan reality [proceeding] from the All-Merciful (*al-raḥmān*). There was no "where?" enclosing it, because there was no spatial location (*ḥayyiz*) ... Then, He disclosed Himself—Glory to Him—by His light to this dust—which people of rational inquiry call "materia prima" (*al-hayūlā al-kull*)—in which the entire universe was in its full potentiality (*bi-l-quwwa wa-l-ṣalāḥiyya*). Everything that was in this dust received [from the Divine Manifestation] according to its capacity and its predisposition. And nothing, in this dust, was closer to Him in order to receive [this Manifestation] than the reality of Muhammad—Peace and Blessings be upon him—which is also called "the Intellect" (*al-ʿaql*). He is thus the master of all the universe, and the first to appear in existence.[26]

A clear correlation between the Adamic and the Muhammadan realities seems to take shape in Ibn ʿArabī's depiction of the primordial function of the Perfect Man. In the chapter of Muhammad that closes his *Fuṣūṣ al-ḥikam*, Ibn ʿArabī relates the two figures by evoking the *ḥadīth* mentioned earlier:

---

23 See Gril, Denis, *Le serviteur de Dieu: La figure de Muhammad en spiritualité musulmane*, Paris: Éditions du Cerf, 2022; Addas, Claude, *La maison muhammadienne: Aperçus de la dévotion au Prophète en mystique musulmane*, Paris: Gallimard, 2015; and Schimmel, Annemarie, *And Muhammad is His messenger: The veneration of the Prophet in Islamic piety*, Chapel Hill, NC: The University of North Carolina Press, 1985.

24 Ibn ʿArabī, *ʿAnqāʾ mughrib* 103.

25 Ibn ʿArabī, *ʿAnqāʾ mughrib* 109.

26 *Fut.* i, 118–119.

> [Muhammad] is the most perfect creature of the human species. That is why things began by him and are sealed by him. He was indeed a prophet while Adam was between water and clay and then [when he appeared] in his elementary form, he was the Seal of the Prophets.[27]

This passage illustrates all the ambiguity of the question, as Ibn ʿArabī alludes both to the meta-historical Muhammadan reality and to the historical Prophet by the single name "Muhammad."

We see that the motif of the seal, already encountered in the opening chapter of Adam to describe the cosmological function of the Perfect Man, reappears in the closing chapter of Muhammad to describe his perfection. Another shared motif is their respective mediating function as vectors of the Divine Mercy (*raḥma*), ascribed to Adam in the opening chapter[28] even though it is usually the privilege of the figure of Muhammad, because of the verse: "We only sent you as a Mercy for the worlds" (Q 21:107). At this point, we can already realize how these two figures seem intimately intertwined in Ibn ʿArabī's view. Above all, there seems to be no clear precedence between their respective pre-existence. In a certain way, Adam and Muhammad appear to merge obscurely in the notion of the Perfect Man, so that we can barely distinguish them in their meta-historical aspect. Some precious indications that allow us to sensibly distinguish between them can however be found, as we will now see.

3 The Two Fathers

A first key distinction that proves helpful to clarify the correlation between the two meta-historical figures of Adam and Muhammad can be found in the *Kitāb al-Isfār*. Muhammad is described there by Ibn ʿArabī as "the first father among the spiritual entities, father of Adam and the world," while Adam is described as "the corporeal father, father of Muhammad and of all the sons of Adam."[29] Ibn ʿArabī seems thus to draw a clear line between the meta-historical and spiritual Muhammadan reality—which is designated here as "the father of Adam"—and his human embodiment in the Prophet Muhammad—which is one of "the sons of Adam." Nonetheless, in this passage again he seems to willingly preserve the ambiguity between the meta-historical and the historical realities by naming them both "Muhammad," even though he finally adds that the first designates

27 *Fuṣ.* 202 (214).
28 *Fuṣ.* 28 (50).
29 Ibn ʿArabī, *Kitāb al-Isfār* 71.

"the essential reality and spirit of Muhammad—Peace and Blessings be upon him."[30] But more importantly, this passage seems to bring into light the specific aspects of each reality: Muhammad is the spiritual father of mankind whereas Adam is its corporeal father.

Another passage illustrating the correlation between the spiritual Muhammadan reality and the corporeal Adamic nature can be found in the *Kitāb ʿAnqāʾ mughrib*. Here, Ibn ʿArabī alludes to the corporeal embodiment of Muhammad by referring to the clay in which Adam was created, according to the Quranic narrative and the aforementioned *ḥadīth* that speaks of the precedence of Muhammad over the Adamic clay: "[The Prophet] is the supreme genus (*al-jins al-ʿālī*) for all the genera, and the greatest father (*al-ab al-akbar*) for all existents and human beings (*nās*), even though his clay (*ṭīna*) appeared later."[31] In another revealing passage of the same book, Ibn ʿArabī comments on the Quranic verse describing the creation of Adam—"He fashioned him in due proportion and breathed into him something of His spirit" (Q 32:9)—by declaring: "The spirit attributed to the Real, which was breathed out from Him into the world of Creation, is the Muhammadan reality."[32]

What is remarkable here is that Ibn ʿArabī adds a comment which presents these two qualities as constitutive of the reality of the Perfect Man: "According to this definition, he is the [Perfect] Man (*insān*) in the two abodes (*dār*), and His manifestation in the two worlds."[33] This dual quality should be related to the motif of the double-sided mirror that we have already encountered with respect to the Perfect Adamic Man. It is a constitutive element of the Adamic reality for Ibn ʿArabī, just as a mirror is only such because of the image it reflects: "[God] knew that His own existence was a 'thing,' thus He created Adam in His form. Hence Adam was a duality."[34] That dual quality is that of the "interface" (*barzakh*),[35] a famous notion used by Ibn ʿArabī to characterize that which allows one to connect two separate realities through a third emerging entity—the interface—which participates of the nature of the two, without being reduced to either of them. Because of its dual—Adamic and Muhammadan—nature, the Perfect Man is thus the mirroring interface which

30 Ibn ʿArabī, *Kitāb al-Isfār* 71.
31 Ibn ʿArabī, *ʿAnqāʾ mughrib* 111.
32 Ibn ʿArabī, *ʿAnqāʾ mughrib* 108.
33 Ibn ʿArabī, *ʿAnqāʾ mughrib* 108.
34 *Fut.* iv, 307. See also Chittick, William C., *The self-disclosure of God: Principles of Ibn al-ʿArabī's cosmology*, Albany, NY: SUNY Press, 1998, 180.
35 See Chittick, *The self-disclosure*, xxv–xxvii, 331–339, and Bashier, Salman H., *Ibn al-ʿArabī's 'barzakh': The concept of the limit and the relationship between God and the world*, Albany, NY: SUNY Press, 2004.

connects the spiritual and corporeal levels of being, as it appears clearly in this passage from the *Kitāb Inshāʾ al-dawāʾir* (*The emergence of the circles*):

> It is as if he is an interface (*barzakh*) between the cosmos and the Real, and a synthesis between the creature and the Real. He is the line that separates the Presence of God from that of the becoming [existence], like the line that separates the shadow from the sun. That is his reality, and that is why absolute perfection is due to him in temporal existence (*ḥudūth*) and in eternity (*qidam*), whereas absolute perfection is due to the Real only in eternity, for He has no entry in temporal existence: He is too Sublime for this![36]

According to Ibn ʿArabī, the dual constitution of the Perfect Man notably appears in the Quranic narrative of Adam's creation, through the motif of the "two Hands" of God (Q 38:75):[37] "It is nothing but the synthesis of the two forms: the form of the cosmos and the form of the Real, which are the two Hands of the Real."[38] Ibn ʿArabī also uses the symbol the "two Feet" to describe how everything appears in existence as dual couples (*zawjān ithnayn*) emerging from the Divine Pedestal (*kursī*), as another verse affirms: "And of all things We created couples" (Q 51:49).[39] But it is yet another Quranic symbol that is most often used by Ibn ʿArabī to denote the synthetic dual quality of the Perfect Man: "the Pen" (*al-qalam*) mentioned in Q 68:1,[40] which designates for him the First Intellect (*ʿaql*). A major overlap between the two figures of Adam and Muhammad appears in their respective link to that motif of the Pen, for if we have already seen that Ibn ʿArabī clearly identifies the Intellect with the Muhammadan reality in the *Futūḥāt*, we also find it associated in the same work with Adam, while its necessary counterpart, "the Preserved Tablet" (*al-lawḥ al-maḥfūẓ*),[41] is identified with Eve:

---

36 Ibn ʿArabī, Muḥyī al-Dīn, *Kitāb Inshāʾ al-dawāʾir al-iḥāṭa* (*La production des cercles*), trans. Maurice Gloton and Paul Fenton, Paris: Éditions de l'Éclat, 1996, 25.

37 There are also numerous *ḥadīths* mentioning one or two Hands of God involved in the creation of Adam. See Gimaret, Daniel, *Dieu à l'image de l'homme: Les anthropomorphismes de la sunna et leur interprétation par les théologiens*, Paris: Éditions du Cerf, 1997, 190–205.

38 *Fuṣ.* 32 (55). See also *Fut.* ii, 67 and iii, 150.

39 *Fut.* iv, 100. On the implications of this principial polarity on the human genders, see Murata, Sachiko, *The Tao of Islam: A sourcebook on gender relationships in Islamic thought*, Albany, NY: SUNY Press, 1992.

40 On the motif of the Pen and its association with the notion of the Universal Intellect (*al-ʿaql al-kullī*) as first emanation of God, see Wisnovsky, Robert, "Heavenly book," in *EQ*.

41 See Madigan, Daniel A., "Preserved tablet," in *EQ*.

> For rational thinkers, the name of the Preserved Tablet is "the Universal Soul." It is the first existence demanded by the Intellect, like Eve regarding Adam: She was created from him and was coupled with him. It became therefore two, just as being (*wujūd*) became two by the thing that came into being, and knowledge became two through the Pen that came into being.[42]

Ibn ʿArabī alludes here to the Quranic verses presenting the creation of mankind coming from a "unique soul," from which a double (*zawj*) is created, before "spreading from the two a multitude of men and women" (Q 4:1, 6:98 and 39:6). But more importantly, he emphasizes the fact that it is the dual nature of the Adamic Perfect Man that manifested itself, so that it "became two."

Just as Adam was created by God to contemplate Himself, the creation of Eve proceeds from the reality of Adam, for him to contemplate his own dual nature.[43] Eve is a mirror for Adam, just as Adam is a mirror for God:

> Adam was a duality ... So when God created Eve from him, He did not increase the dual nature that Adam possessed ... Rather, his dual form made Eve manifest, and so she was the first thing born from that dual nature, just as He created Adam with His two Hands.[44]

In other words, because the Adamic mirror of Creation is a double-faced mirror receiving the Divine image and reflecting it both towards God Himself and towards His Creation, it in turn demands another mirror to reflect his own image, both towards himself and towards what is beyond this new mirror, and so on in the processing chain of Creation.

4 The Muhammadan Tree and the Adamic Birds

The articulation between the Muhammadan reality and the multiple manifestations of the dual nature of the Adamic Perfect Man is the object of an early

---

42 *Fut.* iii, 399.

43 "He married none other than himself. From him came the companion and the child, and the affair (*amr*) is one in the multiple." *Fuṣ.* 57 (70). This explains in a sense why Ibn ʿArabī affirms that the form of the Perfect Man is a sphere. See Ibn ʿArabī, Muḥyī al-Dīn, "al-Tadbīrāt al-ilāhiyya fī iṣlāḥ al-mamlaka al-insāniyya," in Henrik S. Nyberg (ed.), *Kleinere Schriften* 101–240, 225.

44 *Fut.* iv, 307. See also Chittick, *The self-disclosure* 179–181.

poetic and allusive treatise by Ibn ʿArabī the *Risālat al-Ittiḥād al-kawnī*.[45] In this short epistle, Ibn ʿArabī depicts the relations between a tree and four birds (in the order of their appearance in the text: a dove, a royal eagle, a phoenix, and a crow), each one of them describing its own nature that is a particular aspect of the Perfect Man. A quick overview of some elements characterizing the tree, the eagle, and the dove will illustrate what we already encountered about Muhammad, Adam, and Eve.

The declaration of the tree seems to designate the Muhammadan reality, for it reminds us of the way we already saw Ibn ʿArabī describe it as emerging from the Primordial dust: "I became like the *materia prima*, the receptacle of every form in this world and the other. There is nothing I do not bear in myself."[46] The tree has been "planted by the Hand of the One (*aḥad*) in the garden of eternity (*abad*),"[47] so that his radical unity contrasts with the duality of Adam: It is "at the same time shadow and light," its time is "the now," its function is "that of the equator," and of "the equilibrium of the humors."[48] The account of the royal eagle seems on the other hand to insist on the dual nature of Adam, and to emphasize both his receptive and emanative functions:

> The eagle asked: "How could something be manifested from me, when my station is that of deficiency (*ʿajz*) and I am not endowed with authority nor power?"—He was answered: "Continue to tell your moan, and this will appear to you face to face. That is the second harmony and the conjunction of the doubles (*mathānī*)."[49]

45 Its full title is *The epistle of the unification of creation in the presence of the essential testimony through the presence of the human tree and the four spiritual birds* (*Risālat al-Ittiḥād al-kawnī fī ḥaḍrat al-ishhād al-ʿaynī bi-maḥdar al-shajara al-insāniyya wa-l-ṭuyūr al-arbaʿa al-rūḥāniyya*). The epistle is quoted in *Fut*. ii, 351 and was thus composed before Ibn ʿArabī's departure for the East in 598/1201. See Ibn ʿArabī, Muḥyī al-Dīn, "Risālat al-Ittiḥād al-kawnī: Le livre de l'Arbre et des quatre Oiseaux d'Ibn ʿArabī," ed. Denis Gril, in *AI* 17 (1981), 53–111, 67–68.

46 Ibn ʿArabī, *Risālat al-Ittiḥād* 79.

47 Ibn ʿArabī, *Risālat al-Ittiḥād* 78.

48 Ibn ʿArabī, *Risālat al-Ittiḥād* 79. It should be noted that the tree also declares: "My emerging constitution (*nashʾa*) is spherical, like the [celestial] sphere (*falak*);" Ibn ʿArabī, *Risālat al-Ittiḥād* 79, which reminds us of what we just mentioned about the sphericity of the Perfect Man.

49 Ibn ʿArabī, *Risālat al-Ittiḥād* 80. The Adamic eagle of the *Risālat al-Ittiḥād* also describes himself in a way that alludes to the Quranic polemical arguments regarding Christology (Q 5:116): "By confusing eternity with anteriority, they declared me eternal and affirmed that my existence was not outside non-being ... I deny their worshiping of me;" Ibn ʿArabī, *Risālat al-Ittiḥād* 83. This is to be linked with the parallel between Adam and Jesus men-

As for the dove, she expresses the fact that her creation is manifesting the inner duality of the Adamic eagle rather than the apparition of a distinctive nature, just as Eve proceeds directly from the nature of Adam:

> Essential being in the visible world, my existence is only through dualities. I am called "second" yet I am not additional … My existence is the limit of all creatures. I come after the one whose essence transcends the eyesight. That nature which is peculiar to me is found in every being, close or distant.[50]

We find however some clear overlaps between the Muhammadan and the Adamic realities in the epistle. For example, the eagle declares that his existence was "the very beginning," as he is the "Manifestation of Himself to Himself," "the sublime emanation and the light of His existence,"[51] all of which reminds us clearly of the motifs of the Muhammadan reality mentioned earlier. Eventually, Ibn ʿArabī warns us about the limits of the rational categorization of the Adamic reality of the eagle:

> Some philosophers invented lies about me. Some others, men of merit, joined their forces to capture me … by using means that I was myself providing them … Satan sowed confusion in their minds. They imagined themselves at the top while they were still in the bottom of the valley … They only captured an eagle in my image, coming from the country of conjecture. "Here is the evident truth!," they claimed. Do they not understand that truth did not appear to them, and actually cannot appear?[52]

5 From the Adamic Duality to the Muhammadan Triplicity

The self-mirroring of the Adamic Perfect Man and his relation to his double is described in detail in the *Fuṣūṣ al-ḥikam*, although interestingly not in the chapter dedicated to Adam, but rather in the closing chapter dedicated to Muhammad. The tense articulation between the unity and the multiplicity of the Adamic Perfect Man actually seems to underlie the structure of the book.

---

tioned in the Quran: "Truly the likeness of Jesus in the sight of God is that of Adam" (Q 3:59).

50 Ibn ʿArabī, *Risālat al-Ittiḥād*.

51 Ibn ʿArabī, *Risālat al-Ittiḥād*.

52 Ibn ʿArabī, *Risālat al-Ittiḥād* 83.

The opening chapter, dedicated to the "divine wisdom in an Adamic word," ends with a table of contents of the whole work, as if his "synthetic existence" (*kawn jāmiʿ*) was containing every other prophet mentioned after him. It is probably no accident that this chapter addresses precisely the interdependent correlation between universals and existent things. As for the closing chapter, dedicated to the "singular wisdom in a Muhammadan word," it is marked by triplicity rather than duality. Muhammad is qualified there as the "primordial singularity" from which all the following numbers proceed, for "the first of the singulars (*afrād*, i.e., "the odds") is three" and "his emerging constitution is triple."[53] Because there are 27 chapters in the *Fuṣūṣ*, each dedicated to a prophetic figure—or "word" (*kalima*)—the triplicity underlying this closing chapter also seems to contain the whole book, just as Muhammad is said to be endowed with "the all-comprehensive words" (*jawāmiʿ al-kalim*).[54] Mathematically speaking, as 27 is 3 to the power of 3, we can consider that all the chapters of the book only result from the self-multiplication of the Muhammadan Perfect Man.

The articulation between the Muhammadan reality and the historical instances of the Prophets must be considered in the perspective of the precedence of the prophetic reality over its human embodiment, as claimed by the aforementioned *ḥadīth* in which Muhammad affirmed that he "was a prophet when Adam was still between water and clay." A strong example for that is given by Ibn ʿArabī regarding the Quranic narrative of the primordial "Covenant" (*mīthāq*) of all the human souls, extracted from the loins of Adam to testify of their faithfulness before their Lord.[55] The second Covenant mentioned in the Quran, in which—following the same pattern—the Prophets affirm their mission,[56] is considered as coming before that of the children of Adam, which Ibn ʿArabī calls "the second Covenant."[57]

Therefore, in Ibn ʿArabī's view, the qualities and functions of the Adamic Perfect Man are nothing but a manifestation of the Muhammadan reality:

---

53 *Fuṣ*. 202 (214).

54 *Fuṣ*. Ibn ʿArabī adds that those words are actually "the names of Adam," alluding to the motif of the Divine names taught by God to Adam and then by Adam to the angels, which is at the center of the opening chapter. See *Fuṣ*. 28–29 (50–51).

55 Q 7:172.

56 Q 3:81.

57 *Fut*. iv, 58. See Addas, *La maison muhammadienne* 52. A third Covenant, between God and the "Children of Israel," is mentioned in Q 5:12. The pledge between Muhammad and the believers can also be related to those covenants: "Those who pledge allegiance to you pledge allegiance only to God. The Hand of God is over their hands" (Q 48:10).

> When God taught the names to Adam, he was in a secondary station compared to Muhammad, for Muhammad already knew the all-comprehensive words (*jawāmiʿ al-kalim*), and all the names are but words. When Muhammad was not apparent in the concrete, he already appeared in the names, for he is endowed with them. Then, this appeared in the first human existent, which is Adam.[58]

Before being the children of Adam and Eve, the human beings are thus the children of two fathers, and the history of mankind is the history of that double heritage:

> Adam, and all those who came after him, were but inheritors of Muhammad, for he was a prophet when Adam—who was still "between water and clay"—was not yet existent. The Prophethood belonged to Muhammad when there was no Adam, just as the human natural Adamic form belonged to Adam when the Prophet did not yet have a form. Thus, for Adam and for all the Prophets, Adam is the father of the human bodies, while Muhammad is the father of the heritage. This is from Adam until the inheritor who will seal the affair. Any revealed law that appeared, any knowledge, was thus an inheritance from Muhammad.[59]

According to Ibn ʿArabī, when the corporeal manifestation of Muhammad finally occurred, it brought a temporal revolution that allowed for all humanity to access the primordial state of Creation. This is the meaning of a canonical *ḥadīth* quoted in the first chapter of the *Futūḥāt*: "Time returned to its original state (*al-zamān qad istadāra*), that of the creation by God of the heavens and the earth."[60] In other words, for Ibn ʿArabī, the historical Muhammad is nothing but the manifestation of the Muhammadan reality in the cosmic dimension of the Adamic Perfect Man. Therefore, his historical manifestation is the most perfect Adamic mirror available to humanity to contemplate its original perfection:

---

58 *Fut.* ii, 88.

59 *Fut.* iii, 456–457.

60 *Fut.* i, 80. See also Ibn ʿArabī, *ʿAnqāʾ mughrib* 124. The *ḥadīth* is quoted by al-Bukhārī, *Ṣaḥīḥ al-imām al-Bukhārī al-musammā bi-l-Jāmiʿ al-musnad al-ṣaḥīḥ al-mukhtaṣar min umūr rasūl Allāh wa-sunnatihi wa-ayyāmihi*, ed. Muḥammad Z. Ibn Nāṣir al-Nāṣir, 9 vols., Jedda: Dār al-Minhāj, 2015, *Badʾ al-khalq* 59, 8.

> When God discloses Himself in the mirror of your heart, your mirror only reflects Him according to its capacity and its configuration ... Persevere therefore in faith and in observance of the prophetic model, and place the Prophet in front of you, like a mirror ... because the manifestation of God in the mirror of the Prophet is the most perfect, the most right, and the most beautiful. Whenever you see Him in the mirror of the Prophet, you perceive a perfection that you cannot perceive when you contemplate Him in your own mirror ... Do not seek to contemplate Him anywhere but in the mirror of the Prophet. Do not try to contemplate Him in your own mirror, nor to contemplate the Prophet and what is manifested in his mirror in your own mirror.[61]

It is thus through the perfect combination of the Muhammadan and the Adamic aspects of the Perfect Man, which are both manifested in the historical Prophet, that human beings can finally contemplate the image of God: "When you arrive at Muhammad, it is not Muhammad that you find, but God in a Muhammadan form."[62]

6 The Two *mīm*s of the *basmala*

To end this introductory overview of the correlation between the figures of Adam and Muhammad, we should mention the illuminating passages of the *Kitāb al-Mīm*, an epistle dedicated to the science of letters in which Ibn ʿArabī exposes the symbolism of the letters *mīm*, *wāw* and *nūn*. Those three letters share the common characteristic of having a palindromic name, constituted by the doubling of their own consonant and the mediation of one of the three vowels of the Arabic language.[63] Ibn ʿArabī uses this symbolic context to formulate the articulation between the two complementary realities of Adam and Muhammad by using the motif of the letter *mīm* that is present in their names.

The correlation between the corporeal Adamic aspect and the spiritual Muhammadan aspect of the Perfect Man is symbolized here by the letter *ī* that connects the two presences of the letter *mīm* in the names of Adam and Muhammad:

---

61 *Fut.* iii, 251–252. See Addas, *La maison muhammadienne* 54.

62 *Fut.* ii, 127.

63 Interestingly, we find Ibn ʿArabī explaining in the long chapter 2 of the *Futūḥāt*, dedicated also to the science of letters, that the nature of the *mīm* is radically triple, for its name is composed of three letters (*mīm-yāʾ-mīm*), whose names are themselves in turn composed of three letters (*mīm-yāʾ-mīm* and *yāʾ-alif-hamza*); *Fut.* i, 74.

> The *mīm* belongs to both Adam and Muhammad while the *ī* is the cause of the connection between the two … Muhammad operates spiritually in Adam by the *ī*, and it is through this operation that his spiritual [influence] (*ruḥāniyya*) and that of all those who manage Creation happens, from the Universal Soul to the last existent, which is the human spirit: "I was a prophet while Adam was still between water and clay." As for Adam, he operates corporeally in Muhammad by the mediation of the *ī*, and it is through this operation that the corporeality of every human in the world—including Muhammad—happens. Adam is thus the father of Muhammad, our father, and the father of Jesus, corporeally. As for Muhammad, he is the father of Adam, our father, and the father of Jesus, spiritually.[64]

That is why the spiritual history of mankind, that is usually called by Ibn ʿArabī "the cycle of Dominion" (*dawrat al-mulk*), is also qualified by him as "the cycle of the sphere of our master Muhammad" (*dawrat falak sayyidinā Muḥammad*).[65]

Ibn ʿArabī adds that we can find an indication of this cycle in "the prolongation existing in the *mīm*" of the *basmala* ("In the name of God, the All-Merciful the Merciful": *Bi-smi Llāh al-raḥmān al-raḥīm*).[66] The term "prolongation" (*madd*) alludes to a rule of Quranic recitation, according to which one should emphasize certain letters (usually vowels rather than consonants) and sustain it longer in the recitation.[67] But here, Ibn ʿArabī seems rather to suggest a subtle prolongation from the *mīm* of the first word—*ism* ("name")—to that of the last word—*raḥīm* ("Merciful"):

---

64 Ibn ʿArabī, Muḥyī al-Dīn, *Kitāb al-Mīm* (*Le Livre du Mîm, du Wâw et du Nûn*), ed. Charles-André Gilis, Beirut: Albouraq, 2002, 80.

65 Chapter 10 of the *Futūḥāt* is dedicated to "the knowledge of the cycle of Dominion," and chapter 12 to "the cycle of the sphere of our master Muhammad," *Fut.* i, 134–138 and i, 143–147. See also *Fut.* ii, 9 and iii, 514.

66 Ibn ʿArabī, *Kitāb al-Mīm* 84. Chapter 5 of the *Futūḥāt* is dedicated to the symbolism of the *basmala* and the *fātiḥa*. Ibn ʿArabī presents there some other symbolic interpretations of the *mīm* of the *basmala*, among which we find an interesting affirmation concerning the Covenant, the cycle of Dominion, and the *mīm*: "[Man] entered the Dominion by the *mīm* of 'Am I not your Lord?' (*a-lastu bi-rabbikum*)," that is, the testimonial question asked by God to the children of Adam (Q 7:172); *Fut.* i, 74.

67 It should be noted that there is an actual prolongation (*madd*) in the recitation of the *mīm* (though precisely speaking, a prolongation of the *ī* that is in the *mīm*) in the three isolated letters opening the second Quranic Sūra: "*alif, lām, mīm*" (Q 2:1). Ibn ʿArabī considers those three opening letters as "the synthesis of the interface (*barzakh*), the two abodes, the link, and the two realities;" *Fut.* i, 65.

> The *mīm* of *bi-smi* ("in the name") belongs to Adam, for he is endowed with the names. It is by the prolongation existing in him that the world of bodies exists: "He created you from a unique soul" [Q 4:1]. Eve was created from Adam, and if she were created from other than him [the affirmation] "He created you from a unique soul" would not be true regarding corporeality. As for the *mīm* of *al-raḥīm* ("the Merciful"), it belongs to Muhammad, for he is endowed with Mercy: "[The Messenger is] kind and merciful (*raḥīm*) to the believers" [Q 9:128], that is the mercy of faith (*īmān*); and "We only sent you as a Mercy for the worlds" [Q 21:107], that is the mercy of origination (*ījād*). It is by the prolongation (*madd*) existing in him that the continuing support (*istimdād*) of the world of spirits exists.[68]

As we just saw, the existence of the human world is sustained both by the continuous corporeal presence of the Adamic reality and the continuous spiritual presence of the Muhammadan reality:

> The corporeal appearance of Muhammad in history is therefore the completion of the spiritual cycle of manifestation of the Muhammadan reality: His station appeared later in the world of bodies, whereas the station of Adam appeared first, and that is why we say *Bi-smi Llāh al-raḥmān al-raḥīm*. [Muhammad] is last in corporeity (*jismiyya*) and first in spirituality, whereas Adam is first in corporeality (*jismāniyya*) and last in spirituality.[69]

Just as the "name" in the beginning of the *basmala* is already alluding to the name "the Merciful" at the end of the sentence, the reality of Adam is the prefiguration of the manifestation of the reality of Muhammad. In other words, the Muhammadan reality of Adam only appears with the Adamic existence of Muhammad, just as the meaning of the *basmala* precedes its enunciation and is already virtually contained in its first word, but only appears effectively at the end of its formulation, with the name "the Merciful."

68 Ibn ʿArabī, *Kitāb al-Mīm* 84.

69 Ibn ʿArabī, *Kitāb al-Mīm* 84.

7 Conclusion

The foregoing has brought to light the extent of the correlation between the figures of Adam and Muhammad in Ibn ʿArabī's prophetology. We have seen that, in his view, the two figures should be considered both as aspects of the Perfect Man and as historical human beings. Their respective natures are revealed to be combined and intertwined, both in their meta-historical and historical instances. For Ibn ʿArabī, the historical Muhammad is the Adamic form of the spiritual Muhammadan reality, and the meta-historical Adam is the Muhammadan form of the corporeal Adamic reality. The Muhammadan spiritual fatherhood precedes the Adamic corporeal fatherhood, and the history of the children of Adam is therefore in a way the corporealization of the spiritual meta-history of the children of Muhammad.

What we have shown here regarding the figures of Adam and Muhammad should be extended to other Prophets. Such a correlative approach has proven to be particularly relevant to bring to light some of the intricacies of Ibn ʿArabī's doctrine of the Perfect Man. Indeed, it is hoped that further research on other Prophets (following the same line of inquiry taken up in this study) will help bring about a more comprehensive understanding of Ibn ʿArabī's prophetology and spiritual anthropology.

Bibliography

Addas, Claude, *La maison muhammadienne: Aperçus de la dévotion au Prophète en mystique musulmane*, Paris: Gallimard, 2015.

Alaoui Mdaghri, Younes, "Critical study of the erroneous attribution of the book Shajarat al-kawn to Ibn ʿArabī instead of to Ibn Ghānim al-Maqdisī," in *The Journal of Rotterdam Islamic and Social Sciences* 1 (2010), 1–16.

Bashier, Salman H., *Ibn al-ʿArabī's 'barzakh': The concept of the limit and the relationship between God and the world*, Albany, NY: SUNY Press, 2004.

al-Bukhārī, *Ṣaḥīḥ al-imām al-Bukhārī al-musammā bi-l-Jāmiʿ al-musnad al-ṣaḥīḥ al-mukhtaṣar min umūr rasūl Allāh wa-sunnatihi wa-ayyāmihi*, ed. Muḥammad Z. Ibn Nāṣir al-Nāṣir, 9 vols., Jedda: Dār al-Minhāj, 2015.

Chittick, William C., *The Sufi path of knowledge: Ibn al-ʿArabī's metaphysics of imagination*, Albany, NY: SUNY Press, 1989.

Chittick, William C., *Imaginal worlds: Ibn al-ʿArabī and the problem of religious diversity*, Albany, NY: SUNY Press, 1994.

Chittick, William C., *The self-disclosure of God: Principles of Ibn al-ʿArabī's cosmology*, Albany, NY: SUNY Press, 1998.

Chodkiewicz, Michel, *Un océan sans rivage: Ibn ʿArabî, le livre et la loi*, Paris: Editions du Seuil, 1992.

Chodkiewicz, Michel, *Le sceau des saints: Prophétie et sainteté dans la doctrine d'Ibn Arabî*, [Paris]: Gallimard, 2012.

Gimaret, Daniel, *Dieu à l'image de l'homme: Les anthropomorphismes de la sunna et leur interprétation par les théologiens*, Paris: Éditions du Cerf, 1997.

Gril, Denis, *Le serviteur de Dieu: La figure de Muhammad en spiritualité musulmane*, Paris: Éditions du Cerf, 2022.

al-Ḥallāj, al-Ḥusayn b. Manṣūr, *Kitāb al-Ṭāwasīn* (*Le livre "Tâwasîn" de Hallâj*), ed. Stéphane Ruspoli, Paris: Albouraq, 2007.

Ibn ʿArabī, Muḥyī al-Dīn, *al-Futūḥāt al-Makkiyya*, 4 vols., Cairo: Dār al-Fikr, n.d.

Ibn ʿArabī, Muḥyī al-Dīn, "Kitāb ʿUqlat al-mustawfiz," in Henrik S. Nyberg (ed.), *Kleinere Schriften des Ibn ʿArabī* (*Nach Handschriften in Upsala und Berlin zum ersten Mal herausgegeben und mit Einleitung und Kommentar versehen*), Leiden: Brill, 1919, 39–99.

Ibn ʿArabī, Muḥyī al-Dīn, "al-Tadbīrāt al-ilāhiyya fī iṣlāḥ al-mamlaka al-insāniyya," in Henrik S. Nyberg (ed.), *Kleinere Schriften des Ibn ʿArabī* (*Nach Handschriften in Upsala und Berlin zum ersten Mal herausgegeben und mit Einleitung und Kommentar versehen*), Leiden: Brill, 1919, 101–240.

Ibn ʿArabī, Muḥyī al-Dīn, "Risālat al-Ittiḥād al-kawnī: Le livre de l'Arbre et des quatre Oiseaux d'Ibn ʿArabī," ed. Denis Gril, in *AI* 17 (1981), 53–111.

Ibn ʿArabī, Muḥyī al-Dīn, *Kitāb Inshāʾ al-dawāʾir al-iḥāṭa* (*La production des cercles*), trans. Maurice Gloton and Paul Fenton, Paris: Éditions de l'Éclat, 1996.

Ibn ʿArabī, Muḥyī al-Dīn, *Kitāb al-Mīm* (*Le Livre du Mîm, du Wâw et du Nûn*), ed. Charles-André Gilis, Beirut: Albouraq, 2002.

Ibn Bābawayh al-Qummī, *al-Tawḥīd*, ed. Hāshim al-Ḥusaynī al-Tihrānī, Qom: Mu'assasat al-Nashr al-Islāmī, 2008.

Ibn ʿArabī, Muḥyī al-Dīn, *ʿAnqāʾ mughrib fī maʿrifa khatm al-awliyāʾ wa-shams al-maghrib*, ed. ʿAbd al-ʿAzīz Ṣulṭān al-Manṣūb, Cairo: Shirkat al-Quds, 2016.

Ibn ʿArabī, Muḥyī al-Dīn, *Fuṣūṣ al-ḥikam* (*Facsimile of oldest copy* (*dated 630H, TIEM 1933*) *and édition critique*), ed. Mahmud Erol Kılıç and Abdurrahim Alkış, Istanbul: Litera Yayıncılık, 2016.

Ibn ʿArabī, Muḥyī al-Dīn, *Kitāb al-Isfār ʿan natāʾij al-asfār* (*The secrets of voyaging*), ed. Denis Gril, Abrar A. Shahi, and Angela Jaffray, Oxford: Anqa Publishing, 2016.

Madigan, Daniel A., "Preserved tablet," in *EQ*.

Murata, Sachiko, *The Tao of Islam: A sourcebook on gender relationships in Islamic thought*, Albany, NY: SUNY Press, 1992.

Nyberg, Henrik S. (ed.), *Kleinere Schriften des Ibn ʿArabī* (*Nach Handschriften in Upsala und Berlin zum ersten Mal herausgegeben und mit Einleitung und Kommentar versehen*), Leiden: Brill, 1919.

Schimmel, Annemarie, *And Muhammad is His messenger: The veneration of the Prophet in Islamic piety*, Chapel Hill, NC: The University of North Carolina Press, 1985.

Schöck, Cornelia, *Adam im Islam: Ein Beitrag zur Ideengeschichte der Sunna*, Berlin: Schwarz, 1993.

Singh, David E., "An onto-epistemological model: Adam–Muhammad as the traditional symbols of humanity's all-comprehending epistemic potential," in *MW* 94.2 (2004), 275–301.

Takeshita, Masataka, *Ibn ʿArabī's theory of the Perfect Man and its place in the history of Islamic thought*, Tokyo: Institute for the Study of Languages and Cultures of Asia and Africa, 1987.

Vandamme, Gregory, "L'ontologie corrélative d'Ibn ʿArabī: Métaphysique de l'être et de ses relations," in Jean-Michel Counet (ed.), *La non-dualité: Perspectives philosophiques, scientifiques, spirituelles*, Leuven: Peeters, 2021, 89–102.

Wisnovsky, Robert, "Heavenly book," in *EQ*.

CHAPTER 7

Beautiful-Doing (*iḥsān*) as the Station of No Station (*maqām lā maqām*) and the Genesis of the Perfect Human (*al-insān al-kāmil*)

Alireza Pharaa

The Human Ultimate is the great
completion
equipped with every beauty.
When the form is beautified,
the subtlety's beauty goes back.[1]

As for a Perfect Human Being who
arrives,
every beauty is arranged within him.
For, when he beautifies his apparatus,
the beauty of the light of the Real
returns.[2]

Akbarian studies owe a tremendous debt to the translated works and interpretations of Professors Chittick and Murata, who are referred to by close colleagues and students as the *mashāyikh al-mutarjimīn* (the Masters of the Translators).[3] It is a testament to the unmatched range, consistency, and depth of their contributions to the study of Ibn ʿArabī (d. 638/1240), al-Shaykh al-Akbar (the Greatest Master), and his Akbarian school of thought, which after the first generation of Muslims is the most popular and influential propagator of Islamic thought, practice, and spirituality. On numerous occasions, I have heard speakers of Islamic languages (Arabic, Persian, Turkish, Urdu, etc.) as well as speakers of modern European, African, and Asian languages tell me how they were able to successfully approach the Greatest Shaykh and his school of thought after reading the works of William C. Chittick and Sachiko Murata.

∴

1 Liu Zhi, *The root classic*; trans. Murata, Sachiko, William C. Chittick, and Tu Weiming, *The sage learning of Liu Zhi: Islamic thought in Confucian terms*, Cambridge, MA: Harvard University Asia Center, 2009, 134.

2 Nūr al-Ḥaqq, *al-Laṭāʾif* (*The subtleties*); trans. Murata, Chittick, and Weiming, *The sage learning* 135.

3 In fact, Mohammed Rustom was the first person I heard articulate this title, which he says originates with Yousef Casewit. This designation has since been adapted by me and other colleagues and students to express what we admire most about Chittick and Murata's momentous scholarly achievements.

 | DOI:10.1163/9789004529038_008

One of the most significant ways Chittick and Murata have opened Akbarian studies to a broader audience is by shifting focus away from highly popular yet terribly misunderstood concepts, such as *waḥdat al-wūjūd* (Oneness of Being),[4] toward what Ibn ʿArabī and his disciples have discussed and written about. *Al-insān al-kāmil* (the Perfect Human) is one such key term, which to this day is commonly explained in terms of the many fanciful applications of *waḥdat al-wūjūd*—a term not even developed by Ibn ʿArabī. Chittick and Murata articulate the Akbarian understanding of "the perfect human" within every one of their main publications as well as many of their articles. Among the numerous ways of approaching the perfect human, two terms stand out as uniquely fruitful in understanding it: *iḥsān* (beautiful-doing or the work of beauty) and *maqām lā maqām* (the station of no station). The perfect human is less of a term than a title for the ultimate goal, which everything and everyone aims for in Akbarian thought. It is a name given to the dynamic telos of man and the cosmos, thus, everything can be viewed in relation to it and it has a trace in everything. Human perfection never finishes as it remains ever imperfect in its perfection. Thus, perfection is an endless path and not a settled definition or formula.

Thanks to Chittick and Murata, the station of no station has been placed at the forefront of Akbarian thought, since Ibn ʿArabī frequently makes use of this key term to explain many of his other key ideas, in particular "the perfect human." So, it should come as no surprise to anyone acquainted with Chittick and Murata's writings to see the perfect human brought together in this article alongside the station of no station. The odd term in this triad is beautiful-doing. For the most part, I treat *jamāl* and *ḥusn* as equivalent terms expressing beauty, which I group together under *iḥsān* (beautiful-doing or the work of beauty), since any role played by beauty in the literature is also an instance of beautiful-doing. However, when the context calls for it, I draw out distinctions between these terms.

Chittick and Murata devote a good deal of attention to beautiful-doing alongside the perfect human. Both beautiful-doing and beauty are undeniable cornerstones of Islamic thought, ethics, art, poetry, theology, and philosophy. Yet, for all of its prominence, the work of beauty is easily overlooked and often dismissed as one among many ways to express approval. In contrast, this article

4 For a historical analysis of *waḥdat al-wūjūd* (Oneness of Being) and an explanation of its different meanings, see Chittick, William C., *In search of the lost heart: Explorations in Islamic thought*, ed. Mohammed Rustom, Atif Khalil, and Kazuyo Murata, Albany, NY: SUNY Press, 2012, 71–88.

brings out the work of beauty in the genesis, understanding, and applications of the two aforementioned terms: the station of no station and the perfect human.

The opening verses to this article are translations by Chittick and Murata from the original Chinese writings of Liu Zhi's (d. 1730) *The root classic* (left-side) and this book's corresponding Arabic translation offered by Nūr al-Ḥaqq (Ma Lianyuan, b. al-Sayyid Luqmān al-Ṣīnī) (d. 1904), *The subtleties* (right-side). The verses offer a glimpse into the easternmost part of the Akbarian school's understanding of the intertwined relation between the perfect man and the work of beauty. While I roughly follow the trajectory of the sun, moving from the easternmost to the western roots of the Akbarian school, historically, the diffusion of the tradition starts in the West with Ibn Arabi in Andalusian Spain and moves through Persia onward to China and the Indian Subcontinent.

The opening verses draw upon an axiomatic Sufi saying about beauty, the *ḥadīth*: "God is beautiful, and He loves beauty."[5] The perfect man "is equipped with every beauty" because he achieves the ultimate goal of the traveler on the Sufi path, which is "deiformity" (*ta'alluh*) or "assuming the character traits of God" (*al-takhalluq bi-akhlāq Allāh*).[6] By assuming the character traits of God, the perfect human becomes beautiful and loved for beauty, since he recognizes that all beauty belongs to the Real and "returns"/"goes back" to the Real. Moreover, everything is beautiful when witnessing creation as the unveiling of the Real and Being, which is a witnessing and tasting achieved only by the perfect human.

Why single out beauty in relation to the Real, the perfect man, and deiformity? Is God not also Good, Perfect, Just, Merciful, and so on? Firstly, all these names belong to God, yet beauty is uniquely described by God's love, as expressed in the axiomatic *ḥadīth*. Ibn ʿArabī reformulates this very idea as: "Love, its cause is beauty (*jamāl*) … and its other cause is beautiful-doing (*iḥsān*)."[7]

Secondly, beauty is used to describe the perfect man in both general terms and particular individuals. At the most general level, the perfect man is discussed in relation to God's names, the famous 99 names of God. All of God's names are brought together under the designation, "To Him belong the Most Beautiful Names" (Q 17:110), as opposed to the most perfect, good, honorific, or majestic names. Once Adam's creation was complete, the first thing God did

5 Muslim, *Ṣaḥīḥ*, in *Jamʿ jawāmiʿ al-aḥādīth wa-l-asānīd wa-maknaz al-siḥāḥ wa-l-sunan wa-l-masānīd*, iv, Vaduz: Jamʿiyyat al-Maknaz al-Islāmī, 2000, Īmān, 41, no. 275.
6 Chittick, William C., *The Sufi path of knowledge: Ibn al-ʿArabī's metaphysics of imagination*, Albany, NY: SUNY Press, 1989, 22.
7 Ibn ʿArabī, Muḥyī al-Dīn, *al-Fūtūḥāt al-Makkiyya*, 4 vols., ii, Beirut: Dār Ṣādir, 1968, 326.24.

was to teach Adam all the names: "He taught Adam the names, all of them …" (Q 2:31). Why? To increase Adam in knowledge!? Surely, but more crucially because "… He presented them [the names] unto the angels …" (Q 2:31). Adam was one of those names presented to the angels. Adam was presented as the presenter of all the names. God completes creation with Adam, who is uniquely designated by knowledge of all the names. Put another way, only after God wraps Adam in the most beautiful of things, which are the names or the Most Beautiful Names, does He present him for the prostration of all the angels. The Most Beautiful Names are the sign of Adam's perfection, who is the archetype of the perfect human. Therefore, Adam transforms into God's image and assumes God's form by way of learning the Most Beautiful Names and possessing them as his character-traits. So, to him belong the Most Beautiful Names. If not for this deiformity, the angels would be prostrating to other than God and fall into idolatry and association. Ibn ʿArabī explains:

> He said, "He taught Adam the names, all of them" (Q 2:31), that is, the divine names [the Most Beautiful Names] from which all things in engendered existence come into being.[8]
>
> It is not that the meanings of the Most Beautiful Names stand-forth through He-ness, rather He-ness stands-forth through the meanings of the names … and He was not named except through the properties of his acts, by way of meaning. So all of them are most beautiful names, other than among them are those that are vocalized, and among them are those that are known but not vocalized, due to the application of blame upon it from its property in common-usage.[9]

All acts belong to God and he is the Agent (*fāʿil*) of every act, as the frequently quoted verse states: "You did not throw when you threw, but God threw" (Q 8:17). As Ibn ʿArabī explains in the quote above, all names are derived from acts that belong to Him; thus, all names are most beautiful, just not known or acknowledged as *the Most Beautiful Names*. God is not known in common-usage (*ʿurf*) as "the Thrower," which can justifiably be derived from the aforementioned verse. He is not called by names of severity (*qahr*) as it is blameworthy for humans to possess them. Nonetheless, God calls Himself by those names in the Quran, such as "the Slayer" or "the Terrible in Punishment." So they too are most beautiful names.

8 Ibn ʿArabī, *al-Fūtūḥāt* i, 216.9; trans. Chittick, *The Sufi path* 276.

9 Ibn ʿArabī, *al-Fūtūḥāt* ii, 412.17.

Acknowledged divine names or not, the perfect man assumes all the character-traits of God, whether their application in common-usage to humans carries praise or blame. As the Quran states, Adam was taught all the names, which as Ibn ʿArabī explains "are the divine names" and "all of them are most beautiful."

Nonetheless, the *sharīʿa* prevents the perfect human from acting unlawfully. Furthermore, courtesy demands that the perfect man act out of servanthood and pure love for the Real—never for one's ego. The perfect human acts with blameworthy and praiseworthy names; thus, he remains invisible within visible acts and is not singled out as a saint or sage by common people.

Finally, deiformity does not mean becoming one with God in his Essence (*dhāt*) or gaining knowledge of God's He-ness (*huwiyya* or ipseity). Both Essence (*dhāt*) and He-ness (*huwiyya* or ipseity) are pronouns in Arabic, thus they are without content, but act as pointers to something other than themselves, to God; but God is a thing such that "Nothing is as His likeness" (Q 42:11). Chittick explains: "the Shaykh [Ibn ʿArabī] often cites the Koranic verse, 'God warns you about His Self' (3:28,30), which he frequently explains in terms of the prophetic saying, 'Reflect (*tafakkur*) upon all things, but reflect not upon God's Essence.'"[10] Silence is most befitting to God's Essence, which is what pronouns do (Essence and ipseity)—silently indicate and point to other than themselves without adding any content.

Adam was created in God's image and form, that is God's Divinity (Divine Names), not His Essence. As Ibn ʿArabī frequently puts it—Everything is Him/not-Him. In the eye of similitude (*tashbīh*), the perfect man assumes God's form and the divinity of his Most Beautiful Names. Through the eye of incomparability (*tanzīh*), only God knows Himself in His Essence and He-ness.

As mentioned before, beauty not only describes the most general (the Divine Names), but also it describes the perfect human in particular. This requires understanding the perfect human through the individual perfect men and women, who each are in their unique ways "*a* Perfect Human Being,"[11] as Nūr al-Ḥaqq puts it in the opening verses. Chittick explains: "There are many different types of perfect men … [The] prophets and great friends of God, as human beings, manifest the name Allah in its relative fullness. Then, in their specific functions, they display one or more of the Most Beautiful Names."[12] On the one

10 Chittick, *The Sufi path* 62.

11 Nūr al-Ḥaqq, *al-Laṭāʾif* (*The subtleties*); trans. Murata, Chittick, and Weiming, *The sage learning* 135.

12 Chittick, *The Sufi path* 27.

hand, each perfect human traces their perfection to Adam, as the template for all humans, who learned all the names and assumed the Most Beautiful Names as character-traits. Yet, each perfect human is different and unique; as the Sufi axiom states, "There is no repetition in self-disclosure." Therefore, each perfect human assumes all of the Most Beautiful Names, yet manifests them or a single one each time in different, unique, and diverse ways. Abraham is described by beauty in the Quran as is Jesus in many Islamic sources, sayings, and poems. Muhammad, as the Seal of the Prophets and the telos of all perfect humans in the Islamic and Sufi tradition, is characterized by beauty and beautiful-doing:

> You have a beautiful example in God's Messenger for whosoever hopes for God and the Last Day, and remembers God abundantly. (Q 33:21)
>
> You have a beautiful example in Abraham, and those with him … (Q 60:4)
>
> You have a beautiful example in them for whoever hopes for God and the Last Day … (Q 60:6)

Beauty describes both the perfect human in general Divinity (the Most Beautiful Names) and as seen in these verses, in their particular example. Muhammad is the paragon to the archetype of humanity, Adam, as well as the seal to the chain of prophets, exemplified by Abraham and his progeny of prophets. At the ontological level, the story of Adam's creation and learning all the names is realized in its utmost beauty and perfection with Muhammad. At the individual level, Muhammad is the inheritor of the prophets and the culmination of the perfect human being. Abraham here stands as a second Adam as the father to the most well-known chain of prophets, giving birth to all the Jewish prophets and Jesus. Although, "those with him" are not limited to his progeny, and instead include every example of a perfect human being, prophet or not. So Muhammad as inheritor and seal of all the prophets is the most perfect and beautiful human. Beauty not only describes Muhammad's praiseworthy acts, but importantly those acts that common usage consider blameworthy. Chittick and Murata translate and discuss the following well-known *ḥadīth*, which makes this point clear:

> God has prescribed doing what is beautiful for everything. When you kill, do the killing beautifully, and when you slaughter, do the slaughtering beautifully. You should sharpen your blade so that the victim is relieved.[13]

---

13 Murata, Sachiko and William C. Chittick, *The vision of Islam*, New York: Paragon House, 1994, 226.

Chittick and Murata point out that this *ḥadīth* begins with beauty as a universal rule for all acts, then continues by listing acts that are commonly deemed as ugly or blameworthy and not normally considered beautiful, and ends with specific moral advice and ethical considerations in doing things beautifully. So this *ḥadīth* places beauty and beautiful-doing as the task of the perfect human. It is beauty that brings together the universal and engendered command (*amr takwīnī*) with the particular acts and the prescriptive command (*amr taklīfī*).[14]

Now that we have established the key importance of beauty and beautiful-doing for the perfect human in its particular and universal roles, we can begin to move westward on our path to understanding the work of beauty in the genesis of the perfect human in Ibn ʿArabī and the perfect human's station of every station and station of no station. Here, I revisit the article's opening verses of Liu Zhi and Nūr al-Ḥaqq, by way of the two Persian works cited by Lui Zhi as the direct inspiration for his verses: *Mirṣād al-ʿibād* of Najm al-Dīn Rāzī (d. 654/1256) and *Maqṣad-i aqṣā* of ʿAzīz al-Dīn Nasafī (d. ca. 699/1300). While I did not find any particular passage that explicitly corresponded to Lui Zhi's verses, the discussion of beauty (*jamāl*) in *Mirṣād al-ʿibād* and *Maqṣad-i aqṣā* leave clear traces in Lui Zhi's verse.

All things originate from God and return to Him, known as the origin and the return or the descent and the ascent. When discussing this universal rule in terms of beauty, Rāzī and Nasafī repeatedly draw upon the metaphor of the heart as a mirror, which aims at the ideal of receiving and returning light without distortion or loss, yet each individual is distinguished by those unique reflections and even perfect humans have their unique reflections of the Most Beautiful Names. The heart is the seat of the intellect and the soul is a mirror that once cleaned from all dust and imperfection can reflect God's beauty in each individual's uniqueness. Ironically, one achieves this uniqueness by striving for absolute dissolution of the ego and self. As Rāzī puts it:

> Know that once the mirror of the heart is polished from all things other than the Presence [of the Beloved] and limpidness reaches perfection, it becomes the shining-place for the sun of the Presence's Beauty and the world-displaying goblet of the Essence of high attributes.[15]

The polishing of the heart's mirror helps explain the last two verses of Lui Zhi's opening poem: "When the form is beautified / the subtlety's beauty goes

14 See Chittick's *The Sufi path* 292–293, for further discussion of the engendered and prescriptive commands.

15 Rāzī, Najm al-Dīn, *Mirṣād al-ʿibād*, Tehran: Ṭūs, 1982, 150.

back."[16] Interestingly, Nūr al-Ḥaqq's rendition of the play between beauty and light makes the mirror metaphor all the more pertinent: "For, when he beautifies his apparatus / the beauty of the light of the Real returns."[17] Everything originates from God and returns to Him under the commands of creation and resurrection, yet beauty unveils this originating and returning to be taking place now, at this and every moment. Rāzī eloquently references the axiom, "everything beautiful is from God's beauty,"[18] in the midst of his analysis of Adam's first encounter of God's beauty as Eve's beauty.

Becoming a mirror to God's beauty is to assume God's image and form, which as discussed is to be characterized by all the names, since all are most beautiful names. Such a perfect soul is what Rāzī calls "the beauty-displaying mirror of Divine Presence,"[19] that is, the soul of the perfect human realizing itself as the Most Beautiful Names.

Nasafī in turn draws upon the mirror metaphor to analyze beauty in relation to perfection by focusing on beauty's quality of bringing diverse things together. Early on in *Maqṣad-i aqṣā*, Nasafī lays down the definitions of his terms, where for human perfection he lists four aspects that must be perfected: "beautiful words (*aqwāl-i nīk*), beautiful acts (*afʿāl-i nīk*), beautiful character-traits (*akhlāq-i nīk*), and the known-things (*maʿarif*)."[20] The first three "beauties" listed here reminds any Persian speaker of the threefold Zoroastrian axiom of beautiful deeds, beautiful thoughts, and beautiful words. Nasafī's gathering of these three beauties under his definition of perfection resonates with this article's opening poem, particularly Lui Zhi's first and second verses, "The Human Ultimate [Perfect Human] is the great completion / equipped with every beauty."[21]

Nasafī describes the first three aspects of his definition of perfection as beautiful, while not extending the ascription of beauty to the fourth aspect of perfection, "the known-things." This subtlety runs remarkably consistent across the classical works of Sufism and Islamic Philosophy. Beauty (Arabic *jamāl* and Persian *nīk*) can be witnessed in manifest and visible things, whereas God's knowledge is non-manifest and unseen. Thus, beauty (*jamāl*) on its own

16 Liu Zhi, *The root classic*; trans. Murata, Chittick, and Weiming, *The sage learning* 134.
17 Nūr al-Ḥaqq, *al-Laṭāʾif* (*The subtleties*); trans. Murata, Chittick, and Weiming, *The sage learning* 135.
18 Rāzī, Najm al-Dīn, *Mirṣād al-ʿibād*, Tehran: Ṭūs, 1982, 64.
19 Rāzī, *Mirṣād al-ʿibād* 35.
20 Nasafī, ʿAzīz al-Dīn, *Maqṣad-i aqṣā*, Tehran: Kitābkhāna-yi ʿIlmiyya-yi Ḥāmidī, 1972, 80.
21 Liu Zhi, *The root classic*; trans. Murata, Chittick, and Weiming, *The sage learning* 134.

falls short of perfect or complete inclusiveness. Yet, the story is different for beautiful-doing or the work of beauty (*iḥsān*), as I shall elaborate on shortly.

From the very definition of his terms, Nasafī draws together perfection with beauty and aspects beyond beauty. Nasafī comes full circle when ending his book by restating his four aspects of perfection, yet not to describe the perfect human, but God:

> As God's Essence said, "I was a hidden treasure, so I loved to be recognized." He desired to see His beauty and to witness His attributes, names, acts, and wisdoms. And beauty can be seen in a mirror, so He made a mirror for Himself. A mirror is of two types: one for them to see their beauty's reflection, and one for them to see their entity itself [or exact selves], [just as] "the faithful is a mirror to the faithful." O Dervish, God made one such mirror in which to see His own entity [exact self] in it, and that mirror is Adam [humans].[22]

Here, Nasafī lists his four aspects of human perfection in relation to God: "beautiful character-traits" of the perfect human go back to God's "names" (His Most Beautiful Names), the perfect human's "beautiful words" to His "attributes," the perfect man's "beautiful acts" to His "acts," and "the known-things" to His "wisdoms." At first, beauty seems unrelated to this list, where "wisdoms" are indistinguishably listed alongside attributes, names, and acts. Yet, Nasafī goes on to separate the mirror of beauty from the mirror of entity, which reestablishes the three beauties and known-things' distinction of perfection. The mirror of entity reflects non-manifestation, God's knowledge, and Essence whereas the mirror of beauty reflects manifestation, creation, and Divinity. Non-manifest entities are God's knowledge of things, which have not been commanded into existence or uttered the engendered command (*amr takwīnī*). Yet, what becomes manifest is exactly what was non-manifest in God's knowledge.

The above quote from Nasafī begins with God's Essence, which is God in Himself, at Himself, and God's knowledge of Himself; inaccessible to anyone other than God. God creates because He loves to be known and to be witnessed in the beauty of His Divinity (names, attributes, acts). It has been already discussed how Adam, an archetype for the perfect human, is the mirror for God's attributes, names, and acts, which is to say the mirror of beauty. Here, Nasafī singles out Adam as also a mirror for the non-manifest, the mirror of entity.

---

22 Nasafī, *Maqṣad-i aqṣā* 80.

I refer back to the story of Adam's creation, where the angels object to the bloodshed and corruption that will ensue from Adam and his progeny. God replies, "I know what you know not" (Q 2:30). This story reaffirms the inaccessibility of God's knowledge, God's Essence, and knowledge of the entities even to the angels. Then, the story of creation continues with God teaching Adam "the names, all of them" (Q 2:30), which as previously discussed, are the Most Beautiful Names. So, none other than God had known the Most Beautiful Names beforehand and Adam is distinguished by firsthand knowledge of them. The story of Adam's creation sheds light on knowledge in both its non-manifest character and later manifestation as Divine Beauty of the names, attributes, and acts are all rooted in the Most Beautiful Names.

Let us now delve deeper into how the non-manifest (God in His Essence and His knowledge of Himself and the entities) relates to the manifest (the beauty of Divinity and creation), by turning all the way westward to the work of beauty in Ibn ʿArabī's perfect human. It is important to notice that beauty (*jamāl*) is different from *the work of beauty* or *beautiful-doing* (*iḥsān*), where the former operates within the latter; but beautiful-doing involves both the manifest and non-manifest, the visible and invisible, and the existent things and non-existent things. I show how Ibn ʿArabī brings these opposites together when discussing beautiful-doing's role related to submission, faith, and love, beginning with an analysis of Ibn ʿArabī's development of the perfect human from beauty and beautiful-doing.

Ibn ʿArabī's concept of the perfect human is rooted in his understanding of stations (*maqām*), where the station of the perfect human is both the station of no station and the station of every station. Ibn ʿArabī develops the station of no station directly from beauty, whereas he derives the station of every station from beauty through an intermediary understanding of courtesy. As to the station of no station, Ibn ʿArabī states:

> The highest of all human beings are those who have no station … This belongs to no human being except only the Muhammadans, as a divine solicitude already given to them. God has said concerning their likes, "But as for those unto whom the most beautiful … has already gone forth from Us, they shall be kept far from it" (Q 21:101), that is, from the Fire, since the Fire is one of these stations. So in reality, they are kept far from the stations.[23]

23 Ibn ʿArabī, *al-Fūtūḥāt* iii, 506.30; trans. Chittick, *The Sufi path* 376.

Ibn ʿArabī derives the station of no station, identified here as the Muhammadan station, directly from "the most beautiful" (*al-ḥusnā*). Muhammad here and in the Sufi tradition designates the ultimate goal of human perfection and in this passage Ibn ʿArabī shows beauty's negative role in keeping one far from existence, creation, fire, and all the stations. Beauty is the gift of non-delimitation and freedom from existence—a gift that is given without request, but "has already gone forth from Us" (Q 21:101). This negative role of beauty is often ignored and rarely mentioned, since the analysis of *iḥsān* (beautiful-doing) or *ḥusn* and *jamāl* (beauty) invokes similitude (*tashbīh*) with God in the literature. Yet, beauty's negative role gives rise to arguably Ibn ʿArabī's most prominent analysis of human perfection—the station of no station: the perfect humans are "those who have no stations," which is to say their station is the station of no station. The above quote shows that beauty's negative gift is the place of emergence for this station of no station.

One can generally call this negative beauty, a *tanzīh* (incomparable) aspect, which makes the perfect human incomparable to all of existence, the stations, the Divinity, and the Most Beautiful Names. This is in contrast to the previous discussion of the perfect human's similitude to God's Divinity and all of creation in the story of Adam. However, *tashbīh* (similitude/immanence) and *tanzīh* (incomparability/transcendence) are more soundly used when discussed in relation to God. While being kept far from the stations removes all delimitations from the perfect human with respect to the stations and existence, it does not claim anything about the perfect human in relation to God's Essence. In fact, the perfect human's non-delimitation and unqualified existence resemble and are in similitude to God, since "Nothing is as His likeness" (Q 42:11). So even the dissimilitude and non-delimitation of the perfect human is within similitude to God. Humanity at its most perfect is incomparable within similitude—an Akbarian rendition of transcendence in immanence.

Similitude operates more clearly and straightforwardly when describing the perfect human at the station of every station, which is the ever complementary and logically penultimate station to the perfect human's station of no station. Here, beauty works through the intermediary discussion of courtesy within Ibn ʿArabī's analysis:

> One is called a "Muhammadan" … who brings together all the stations, then emerges from them, entering "no station."[24]

24 Ibn ʿArabī, *al-Fūtūḥāt* i, 223.2; trans. Chittick, *The Sufi path* 377.

> The first thing which God commanded for His servant is "bringing together" (*jamʿ*), which is courtesy. "Courtesy" (*adab*) is derived from "banquet" (*maʾdaba*), which is to come together for food. Likewise courtesy is to bring together all good. The Prophet said, "God taught me courtesy." In other words: He brought together in me all good things (*khayrāt*); for he then says, "How beautiful is my courtesy!" In other words: He made me a locus for every beautiful thing (*ḥusn*).[25]

The perfect human enters the station of no station by first being characterized by all the stations and becoming a locus for all beautiful things through courtesy. Since all things are created by God, and as mentioned, all acts and names belong to God, everything is, ontologically speaking, beautiful. Thus by way of courtesy, the perfect human brings together all beauty within himself, thereby making all things beautiful. This gathering is not totalizing or finished; it gives place to diversity and the non-repetitive disclosures of the Real, each moment different and unique, all by becoming a place for courteous beauty.

The station of every station offers a *tashbīh* (similitude) aspect of beauty to understand and derive the perfect human. Ibn ʿArabī compares the perfect human to God's Divinity: "The relationship of the stations to the Muhammadan is the same as the relationship of the names to God … in every breath, in every moment, and in every state he takes the form which is required by that breath, moment, and state."[26] This is similitude: just as God is "each day upon some task" (Q 55:29), so too the perfect man is upon some task, state, breath, moment, and movement. Yet, at the same time, possessing the station of every station is epi-phenomenal with leaving all the stations and not being delimited by any one station. Thus, the station of no station. The perfect human is both similar to God's non-delimitation from every name, station, attribute, and act—similar in a *tanzīh* (incomparability) aspect—as well as similar in possessing all stations, acts, names, and the Most Beautiful Names.[27] Therefore, *tanzīh* never absolutely or unboundedly applies to humans even in perfection, but only to God's Essence.

Ibn ʿArabī's discussion of the perfect human as the possessor of the station of every station helps explain how Jāmī's *Fifth gleam* brings together perfection and beauty under the title of "the owners of levels." The beautiful (*al-ḥusn*) makes the perfect human a locus for the gathering of all the stations by way

25 Ibn ʿArabī, *al-Fūtūḥāt* ii, 640.23; trans. Chittick, *The Sufi path* 175.
26 Ibn ʿArabī, *al-Fūtūḥāt* iv, 76.27; trans. Chittick, *The Sufi path* 377.
27 Ibn ʿArabī, *al-Fūtūḥāt* iv, 76.27; trans. Chittick, *The Sufi path* 377.

of courteous beauty, as the *ḥadīth* says: "God taught me courtesy, and made my courtesy most beautiful (*aḥsana*)!"[28] This beautiful-doing (*iḥsān*) gathers all things in the perfect human through the banquet of courtesy—a banquet that is open to all, never-ending, non-repetitive, and giving place to the praiseworthy and blameworthy, conflict and peace.

Understanding the perfect human as the beautiful gatherer of "all the stations," levels of creation, and the Most Beautiful Names explains why Murata translates the Confucian virtue, *ren*, as *iḥsān*, when she explains: "The most important of the five virtues, the one that embraces all, is *ren*, humaneness ... If I had to translate it into Arabic, I would choose the word *iḥsān*, 'beautiful-doing.' "[29] Not only does Murata identify *iḥsān* (the work of beauty or beautiful-doing) for its power of gathering together all the other virtues, but she equates beautiful-doing with humaneness. From what has been discussed about the perfect human and beautiful-doing, it is clear to see that the perfect human embodies humaneness as one who possesses the Most Beautiful Names and is the place that opens to beautifully gather all of existence. Furthermore, by actualizing and attaining the station of every station, one steps beyond it and into the station of no station; but also the work of beauty is to ever strive to gather diverse and conflicting things in non-repetitive ways, which means stepping back into all the stations and the station of every station.

Beauty's negative role of keeping all of existence away from the perfect human in the station of no station, as well as the positive role of finding similitude to all of existence, stations, names, levels, and acts, takes place without eliminating differences or subsuming any concept under another for the sake of manufacturing agreeability or forced harmony. Rather, the work of beauty gathers by encouraging difference, non-repetition, and conflict, in what Ibn ʿArabī calls Divine Conflict:

> He who looks at the divine names will maintain that there is a Divine Conflict. That is why God said to His Prophet, "Dispute with them in the most beautiful way" (Koran 16:125). God commanded him to dispute in the manner demanded by the divine names, that is, in the way that is "most beautiful."[30]

---

28 al-Sakhāwī, Muḥammad b. ʿAbd al-Raḥmān, *al-Maqāṣid al-ḥasana*, ed. ʿAbd Allāh Muḥammad al-Ṣiddīq, Beirut: Dār al-Kitāb al-ʿArabī, 1985, 73–74.

29 Murata, Sachiko, *The first Islamic classic in Chinese: Wang Daiyu's* Real commentary on the true teaching, Albany, NY: SUNY Press, 2017, 21.

30 Ibn ʿArabī, *al-Fūtūḥāt* ii, 93.19; trans. Chittick, *The Sufi path* 55.

The discussion of Divine Conflict as being most beautiful belongs to similitude (*tashbīh*) within the work of beauty or beautiful-doing, because it brings forth the perfect human as a place for beautifully gathering all the divine names, the Most Beautiful Names, and all of existence without eliminating diversity or difference. That is, not just accepting conflict, but celebrating it by continuously finding new ways of bringing opposing and contrasting things together without neutralizing either or finding another term to settle conflicts. That is the work of beauty in its positive aspect.

To further understand both the positive and negative roles of beauty I turn to explore the role of beauty in relation to submission, faith, knowledge, and love. First, let us consider the implications of our discussion on the most famous and classical description of *iḥsān* (beautiful-doing) provided by the famous *ḥadīth* of Gabriel: "[Beautiful-doing is to] Worship God as if you see Him, for if you do not see Him, He sees you."[31]

The first part (first beautiful-doing) of this description has traditionally attracted the most attention and analysis in scholarship, whereas the second part (second beautiful-doing) is often ignored or immediately brushed aside as a principle for moral prescriptions. Commonly, second beautiful-doing is not even mentioned in the literature. This common reading sets both segments of beautiful-doing as a one-sided moral prescription: first beautiful-doing is taken as what one should strive toward, while second beautiful-doing works as a safeguard in case of failure. So, if you fail to see God, at least act out of shame and fear to achieve what first beautiful-doing prescribes. This is a well-established reading for both ethics and the general masses, especially for educating children. Yet, the perfect human brings together both the engendered command (*amr takwīnī*) and the religious/prescriptive command (*amr taklīfī*) by way of the beautiful.

As a first step, let us complicate the religious/prescriptive view by drawing on points of intentional contradiction within Ibn ʿArabī's work. As mentioned, the perfect human does not shy away from blameworthy acts/names. Instead, perfect humans beautifully gather together all acts and names, both the blameworthy and praiseworthy. For Ibn ʿArabī, attaining a praiseworthy station is often accompanied by attaining its opposite or forgoing the acquired praiseworthy station, as one way of understanding the intertwined relation between the station of no station and the station of every station. For example, in Ibn ʿArabī's magnum opus, the *al-Fūtūḥāt al-Makkiyya* (*Meccan openings*),

---

31 Reference to the famous *ḥadīth* of Gabriel according to which the angel came in human form and asked the Prophet several questions. Chittick and Murata's *Vision of Islam* presents the entire Islamic worldview through the prism of this tradition.

his chapter on "The station of shame" is immediately followed by "The station of abandoning shame,"[32] the latter sounding bizarre to the uninitiated as a station or character-trait on the path to human perfection. Yet, the perfect human employs shame in its appropriate place and abandons shame in another. Each time differently and each place uniquely. According to Ibn ʿArabī, the perfect human is not delimited by shame nor lack of shame, so reading the famous *ḥadīth* of Gabriel's description of beautiful-doing as chiefly about achieving shame or any other prescriptive command is missing the target. Although, the prescriptive remains valid in its own particular use.

A more nuanced understanding takes into account both beauty's positive and negative role, what I broadly identified as a *tashbīh* (similitude) and *tanzīh* (incomparability) aspect of beauty. So the *ḥadīth* of Gabriel's description of beautiful-doing can be read as first beautiful-doing speaking about seeing God through the eye of similitude and second beautiful-doing about seeing Him through the eye of incomparability, as Ibn ʿArabī explains:

> When the servants of the Real witness Him, they see Him as possessing two relationships, the relationship of incomparability, and that of descent to the imagination through a kind of similarity. The relationship of incomparability is His self-disclosure in ["Nothing is as His likeness"] (42:11). The other relationship is His self-disclosure in the Prophet's words, "Worship God as if you see Him" … you are urged to turn the attentiveness of your heart and your worship toward these two, then you should not turn away from them, if you are perfect.[33]

These are "the two eyes of the heart," where the heart is the traditional locus of the intellect within Islamic thought. The perfect human gives each eye and beat of the heart its due, never eliminating one for the other. Human perfection is to live according to both segments of beautiful-doing—seeing God's incomparability and similitude, then assuming both incomparability and similitude as character-traits, even if the perfect human is incomparable in similitude (transcendence in immanence). The two-fold description of beautiful-doing lays out the never-ending path of human perfection.

As to first beautiful-doing (*iḥsān*), Ibn ʿArabī identifies the phrase, "as if," with imagination, since everything other than God is imaginal. Imagination is the way to similitude and beautiful-doing is to see God in every realm of imagin-

32 Ibn ʿArabī, *al-Fūtūḥāt*, ch. 139.

33 Ibn ʿArabī, *al-Fūtūḥāt* ii, 3.28, 4.3, 26; trans. Chittick, *The Sufi path* 227.

ation, from one's faculties to the cosmos. However, "if you are perfect," as the above quote states, means to counter-balance similitude with incomparability. Therefore, Ibn ʿArabī draws on knowledge as the path to second beautiful-doing, in contrast to the similitude in imagination:

> Whoever has his knowledge identical to his seeing is a beautiful-doer (*muḥsin*) continually; surely He sees you continually, since He knows you continuously, and there is no beautiful-doing (*iḥsān*) in the Law (*sharʿ*) [established way] except this, as he had said concerning it: "For if you do not see Him, surely He sees you."[34]

God's knowledge is inward and non-manifest (*bāṭin*), which is countered by His outward manifestation (*ẓāhir*) of His Names and all of existence. Imagination gathers God's outward manifestation, while knowledge opens us to the inward and non-manifest.[35] God knows you by your "fixed entity" (*ʿayn thābita*) or "specific face" (*wajh khāṣṣ*), which is your uncreated and most hidden face. Your face is God's face turned to see you uniquely in His knowledge and your unique reflection of God's face. Ibn ʿArabī and his followers call this *al-maʿlūmāt al-maʿdūmāt* (the known non-existent things),[36] which is the specific face of each thing in God's knowledge.

All of this helps explain the quote mentioned early on in this article: "Love, its cause is beauty (*jamāl*) … and its other cause is beautiful-doing (*iḥsān*)."[37] The first cause relates to similitude, imagination, and manifestation: love is caused by the manifest and outward beauty of *jamāl*, which is also expressed in first beautiful-doing's description given to Gabriel. Yet, now we can see that first beautiful-doing is possible because of second beautiful-doing: if not for the non-manifest, inaccessible, and incomparable there would not be the separation and endless striving needed to sustain love. Second beautiful-doing falls under divine majesty or sublimity (*jalāl*), as a counterpart to first beautiful-doings' beauty (*jamāl*). Ibn ʿArabī explains:

---

34 Ibn ʿArabī, *al-Fūtūḥāt* ii, 344.10.

35 I only realized the significance of the second part of *iḥsān* after reading Farghānī, Saʿīd b. Muḥammad, *Muntahā l-madārik fī sharḥ Ṭāʾiyya Ibn al-Fāriḍ*, ii, Tehran: Āyāt-i Ishrāq, 2011, 117–118.

36 Ibn ʿArabī, *al-Fūtūḥāt* ii, 489.21: "And as to the rays of the names, they assign entities to the known things, which is a light embracing over the non-existent things and the existent things …"

37 Ibn ʿArabī, *al-Fūtūḥāt* ii, 326.24.

> Love attaches itself only to a nonexistent thing, and that is its permanence. How beautifully the Koran has expressed this with His words, *He will love them and they will love Him* [5:54]. For it employs pronouns of absence and the future tense verbs. Hence it ascribes love's connection only to that which is absent and nonexistent ... Every entity was nonexistent in itself and known to Him, and He loved to bring it into existence.[38]

Love never ends, nor does the journey of the lover, since the end is nonexistent and the Beloved never reached. Stepping into a path that promises full accessibility and attaining of the subject is not a path of love. So, the perfect human is always imperfect and incomplete, because he strives toward "what is absent and nonexistent." The lover endlessly looks for "the nonexistent Beloved"[39] on the twofold path of beautiful-doing (*iḥsān*): the eye of similitude seeing the beauty (*jamāl*) of manifestation in imagination and the eye of incomparability witnessing non-manifestation through knowledge. One cannot love without a glimpse at manifestation, yet one also cannot begin or continue to love without the majesty/sublimity (*jalāl*), separation, and the inaccessibility of non-manifestation. This is the twofold path of beautiful-doing traveled by the perfect human. Second beautiful-doing states that "if you do not see Him, He sees you," but does this second beautiful-doing only describe the Beloved!? How does the perfect human embody second beautiful-doing as a character-trait? How does the heart open to witness the non-manifest and invisible? Only by annihilating the subject, ego, and self do you subsist. You see Him as He sees you, as the Beloved says in the *ḥadith*: "When I love him, I am his hearing by which he hears, his sight by which he sees, his hand by which he holds, and his foot upon which he walks."[40]

38 Ibn ʿArabī, *al-Fūtūḥāt* ii, 327; trans. Chittick, William C., *The self-disclosure of God: Principles of Ibn al-ʿArabī's cosmology*, Albany, NY: SUNY Press, 1998, 21–22.

39 Ibn ʿArabī, *al-Fūtūḥāt* ii, 332.15.

40 This is part of the famous *ḥadīth al-nawāfil*, for which, see Rustom, Mohammed, "Ibn ʿArabī on Proximity and Distance: Chapters 260 and 261 of the *Futūḥāt*," in *Journal of the Muhyiddin Ibn ʿArabi Society* 41 (2007), 93–107.

Bibliography

Chittick, William C., *The Sufi path of knowledge: Ibn al-ʿArabī's metaphysics of imagination*, Albany, NY: SUNY Press, 1989.

Chittick, William C., *The self-disclosure of God: Principles of Ibn al-ʿArabī's cosmology*, Albany, NY: SUNY Press, 1998.

Chittick, William C., *In search of the lost heart: Explorations in Islamic thought*, ed. Mohammed Rustom, Atif Khalil, and Kazuyo Murata, Albany, NY: SUNY Press, 2012.

Farghānī, Saʿīd b. Muḥammad, *Muntahā l-madārik fī sharḥ Ṭāʾiyya Ibn al-Fāriḍ*, Tehran: Āyāt-i Ishrāq, 2011.

Ibn ʿArabī, Muḥyī al-Dīn, *al-Fūtūḥāt al-Makkiyya*, 4 vols., Beirut: Dār Ṣādir, 1968.

Murata, Sachiko and William C. Chittick, *The vision of Islam*, New York: Paragon House, 1994.

Murata, Sachiko, William C. Chittick and Tu Weiming, *The sage learning of Liu Zhi: Islamic thought in Confucian terms*, Cambridge, MA: Harvard University Asia Center, 2009.

Murata, Sachiko, *The first Islamic classic in Chinese: Wang Daiyu's* Real commentary on the true teaching, Albany, NY: SUNY Press, 2017.

Muslim, *Ṣaḥīḥ*, in *Jamʿ jawāmiʿ al-aḥādīth wa-l-asānīd wa-maknaz al-siḥāḥ wa-l-sunan wa-l-masānīd*, iv, Vaduz: Jamʿiyyat al-Maknaz al-Islāmī, 2000.

Nasafī, ʿAzīz al-Dīn, *Maqṣad-i aqṣā*, Tehran: Kitābkhāna-yi ʿIlmiyya-yi Ḥāmidī, 1972.

Rāzī, Najm al-Dīn, *Mirṣād al-ʿibād*, Tehran: Ṭūs, 1982.

Rustom, Mohammed, "Ibn ʿArabī on Proximity and Distance: Chapters 260 and 261 of the *Futūḥāt*," in *Journal of the Muhyiddin Ibn ʿArabi Society* 41 (2007), 93–107.

al-Sakhāwī, Muḥammad b. ʿAbd al-Raḥmān, *al-Maqāṣid al-ḥasana*, ed. ʿAbd Allāh Muḥammad al-Ṣiddīq, Beirut: Dār al-Kitāb al-ʿArabī, 1985.

CHAPTER 8

Fear, Deeds, and the Roots of Human Difference: A Divine Breath from al-Qūnawī's *Nafaḥāt*

Justin Cancelliere

1 Introduction

Throughout the history of Islam, the Sufis have laid great emphasis on the nexus between knowledge and experience. For them, the acquisition of knowledge in the truest sense of the word transpires at a level of existence situated above that of the mind, ontologically speaking. It is therefore interesting—if not surprising given the mores governing mainstream Sufism[1]—that the number of texts detailing the spiritual experiences of Sufis are comparatively so few in number relative to treatises motivated in the first instance by doctrinal or practical concerns.

In the case of Ṣadr al-Dīn al-Qūnawī (d. 673/1274), not only does his treatise *al-Nafaḥāt al-ilāhiyya* (*The divine breaths*), a translated excerpt from which is given below, offer accounts of a large number of separate visionary experiences, but its chapters also go into a level of detail for each experience that distinguishes this book from other works with which it might be compared. As Richard Todd has noted, al-Qūnawī's "precise chronicle of epiphanies and intuitions would appear to be unique in the annals of Sufi literature."[2] Comprising over 250 pages in the printed edition and containing material spanning three decades of al-Qūnawī's life,[3] this second-longest of his books was also among his most important.[4]

The title of the work is an allusion to the *ḥadīth*, "Verily your Lord has breaths of His Mercy in the days of your time—so expose yourselves to them!"[5]

1 "The hearts of the free are the graves of secrets," as it is said (*qulūb al-aḥrār qubūr al-asrār*).

2 Todd, Richard, *The Sufi doctrine of man: Ṣadr al-Dīn al-Qūnawī's metaphysical anthropology*, Leiden: Brill, 2014, 9. Todd does not explicitly mention the *Nafaḥāt* here, but the allusion to it is obvious.

3 Clark, Jane, "Toward a biography of Ṣadr al-dīn al-Qūnawī," in *Journal of the Muhyiddin Ibn 'Arabi Society* 49 (2011), 1–34, 29; Todd, *Sufi doctrine* 42.

4 Clark, "Biography" 18; Todd, *Sufi doctrine* 42.

5 Trans. Chittick, William C., *In search of the lost heart: Explorations in Islamic thought*, ed. Mohammed Rustom, Atif Khalil, and Kazuyo Murata, Albany, NY: SUNY Press, 2012, 349n12.

 | DOI:10.1163/9789004529038_009

Immediately after citing this saying in the introduction, al-Qūnawī explains the impetus for the book's composition[6] as follows:

> I turned toward my Lord in the gnosis of [this] exposure and its types, and He—glory be to Him—revealed to me its reality and its universal subdivisions. So I saw them restricted (*maḥṣūr*) in what I was shown of the exposure, and I will mention all of them [for you], God-willing.[7]

Then, after spending several paragraphs delineating the different modalities of such "exposure" (*al-taʿarruḍ*), he concludes the introduction thus:

> Know that I will mention in this book some of the breaths of the All-Merciful and fruits of the preeminent and lordly self-disclosures—[that is,] some of what the Real so bounteously bestowed upon me in this nearness and whose remembrance He made easy. So reflect upon that which reaches your hearing and which your mind (*lubb*) brings to light. Recognize its worth that you might be blessed with the great felicity and the dignity of drawing nigh. To God belong the facilitation and excellence [in this affair].[8]

As Chittick also points out in this note, al-Qūnawī comments upon this same *ḥadīth* in his *Sharḥ al-arbaʿīn*, with the expository text (about a page and a half's worth) being the same in both works (see al-Qūnawī, Ṣadr al-Dīn, *al-Nafaḥāt al-ilāhiyya*, ed. Muḥammad Khwājawī, Tehran: Intishārāt-i Mawlā, 1996, 3–5; al-Qūnawī, Ṣadr al-Dīn, *Sharḥ al-arbaʿīn ḥadīth*[an], ed. Hasan Kamil Yılmaz, Qom: Intishārāt-i Bīdār, n.d., 171–173). It may also be of interest that al-Qayṣarī mentions this *ḥadīth* in a discussion of the different types of unveiling (*kashf*), of which one is "olfaction" (*istinshāq*), or "the inhalation of the divine breeze and the aroma of Lordship" (al-Qayṣarī, Dāwūd, *The horizons of being: The metaphysics of Ibn al-ʿArabī in the* Muqaddimat al-Qayṣarī, trans. Mukhtar H. Ali, Leiden: Brill, 2020, 163).

6 According to Clark, it was Ibn ʿArabī himself who instructed al-Qūnawī to start recording his spiritual experiences, but in the passage she cites from the *Nafaḥāt*, the Shaykh al-Akbar's command pertains only to one epiphany in particular. In this last part of the *nafḥa*, al-Qūnawī is recounting an extensive visionary conversation he had with his master, in the midst of which he sees an inscription. Intending to write it down in the form in which he witnessed it, he is stopped by Ibn ʿArabī, who tells him not to rush and not to write it in that form, whereupon al-Qūnawī asks, "So how should I write?" The Shaykh then expresses the same truth in a pithier and more refined way, after which he says, "Write it and preserve it, and do your utmost to exhort [the people to the truth]" (*bāligh fī l-waṣiyya*). Perhaps this last phrase could be taken as a general injunction to write, but I believe the translation just provided is correct. See Clark, "Biography" 18; al-Qūnawī, *al-Nafaḥāt* 126–127.

7 Al-Qūnawī, *al-Nafaḥāt* 3–4.

8 Al-Qūnawī, *al-Nafaḥāt* 5.

The chapter I have translated[9] is representative in that it is comprised of a number of loosely related sections—a characteristic that stands to reinforce in the sympathetic reader the sense that al-Qūnawī was indeed writing at the behest of his inspired states.[10] The first, main section opens with a discussion of the differences between awe (*khashya*), fear (*khawf*), and the fear of God (*taqwā*) before proceeding to an elaborate exposition of human action and its relation to the one divine Act. The next section, which bears the heading "a great secret," is a brief excursus that provides metaphysical descriptions of Islam, faith, and *walāya* as well as comments regarding the nature and significance of Jesus. The following section—also "a great secret"—refers the differences perceived in the world back to the intelligible constitutions of things, which vary in their degrees of proximity to "the inclusive equilibrium" (*al-iʿtidāl al-shāmil*). The final section, which is cosmological and eschatological in nature, gives the reader some sense of what al-Qūnawī takes to be the larger context and ultimate stakes of all of the preceding.

As for the particular way in which al-Qūnawī is endeavoring to edify the reader in this chapter, it could be described on a basic level as an encouragement to turn from an experience of the world dominated by awareness of mere appearances to a vision of existence in its aspect of verticality. He is beckoning the spiritual aspirant to repentance (*tawba*), as it were. For the person who does this in earnest and so is aided by God, it becomes apparent that a much greater degree of vigilance, or a more profound sense of what vigilance entails, is required of the seeker than might have been supposed previously. Since the happenings comprising the integral cosmos are determined in large part by causes whose existence and modes of operation tend to be invisible to human consciousness in its ordinary, "fallen" modalities, one should be exceedingly wary of judging anyone or anything in the absence of the requisite criteria. Moreover, given the innate human tendency toward lassitude—hence the prevalence of the vice of settling for comfortable conventions—such circumspection entails a certain independence on the part of the gnostic vis-à-vis not only the common people but also those scholars who are habitually susceptible to forgetting that God "does whatever He will" (Q 3:40).[11] It might therefore be said

9 Al-Qūnawī, *al-Nafaḥāt* 179–186.

10 What may at first appear as disjointedness reveals itself upon repeat readings to be superficial in nature. The chapters' sections are subtly and intimately interconnected, with this fact potentially being obscured only by al-Qūnawī's method of circling around a point—"architectonically," as it were—rather than proceeding linearly.

11 All subsequent translations of Quranic terms and verses, with the exception of Q 55:37

that al-Qūnawī is participating in the activity known as *tajdīd*, or what is said to be the perennially necessary "making new" or revival of tradition on the basis of the direct verification of eternal truths.

∴

Notwithstanding this description of *tajdīd*, it would not be far from the truth to say that William Chittick and Sachiko Murata each deserve the title of *mujaddid* within their own respective spheres of influence, namely the academic study of Islam and cross-cultural philosophy. Surely their many accomplishments have contributed greatly to making the discipline "new," and in my own case an author like al-Qūnawī would not be comprehensible without the aid of their writings. Indeed, it was Chittick who in 1978 drew attention to the fact that al-Qūnawī was "still virtually unknown and unstudied in the West"[12]—a lacuna that he has since done much to fill through his lucid analyses and expert translations. I hope that the following contribution toward furthering this line of study will be pleasing to these esteemed scholars.

2 Translation

2.1 *A Universal Breath*

Awe is a specific [type of] fear that occurs only to the one who knows the consequences of actions and that it is undoubtedly the Real who bestows existence upon them, since nothing obstructs [such bestowal] save from the standpoint of the recipient. [Such a person] has found the root, namely the action, which necessitates the manifestation of the fruit [thereof], and that is the consequence in any case. It is from this point of view that the scholar's being in awe of the Real [should be understood]. And the fruit of awe in the one to whom it occurs is [his] being uninterested in any act[13] whose consequence—were it to manifest itself to him and become joined to him—he knows would neither agree with nor please him.

As for fear, it does not presuppose knowledge of every act and its consequence, but rather the love of well-being and belief in the possibility of the

below, are taken from Nasr, Seyyed Hossein et al. (eds.), *The study Quran: A new translation and commentary*, New York: HarperOne, 2015.

12 Chittick, William C., "The last will and testament of Ibn ʿArabi's foremost disciple and some notes on its author," in *Sophia Perennis* 4.1 (1978), 43–58, 43.

13 I will consistently translate *fiʿl* as "act" and *ʿamal* as "action."

occurrence of that which is unfavorable due to the commission of this act which is forbidden to him.

As for the fear of God, it is a vigilance and a cautiousness necessitated by the ruling of contingency and allowance [of choice]. It strives for a total severance [of attachment] to matter, and it is on its guard against whatever it is that might happen.

Regarding knowledge, know that just as it necessitates awe and abstention from involvement in a matter whose consequence is known to be harmful and disagreeable, so too does it sometimes require boldness in engaging with matters whose entailment of harmful consequences is supposed by the fearful person to be general in ruling (*ʿāmm al-ḥukm*) relative to whoever pursues them, while [in point of fact] the matter is the opposite of that. So it is in this respect only that the harmful effect expected [to follow from such matters] becomes manifest when the locus of the actor is predisposed to receive it, and it is on account of the expectation of the reception [of this effect] that it is necessary to suppose the absence of the one averse [to it] and victorious [over it] as well.[14]

Do you not see that many bad foods, or rather poisonous things [in general], are eaten by people possessing strong constitutions and noble souls adorned by consummate faith, veracity, and reliance [upon God], and they are not harmed by that in the least? And that fire does not burn whatever comes into contact with it without qualification, but rather on condition that the body in contact with it be capable of being burned?

It is for this reason that [fire] has an effect on neither the salamander nor ruby, nor on many benevolent individuals possessed of veracity and forcible strength, such that this property—through the ruling of adjacency—pervades even their garments, and they are not touched by the fire.[15] The evidence of this from the *sharīʿa* is his saying, peace and blessings be upon him: "The Fire does

---

14 Absence (*ʿadam*), that is, from what would be the effect's locus of manifestation (*maẓhar*) were the actor to be characterized in any given moment by the particular preparedness that "eternally necessitates," as it were, the occurrence of this or that effect.

15 By "the ruling of adjacency" (*ḥukm al-mujāwara*), al-Qūnawī is referring to the property of a reality (*ḥaqīqa*) that, in virtue of its subordinating "power" (*tabaʿiyya*), subsumes the rulings of the realities subordinate to it (*tābiʿ*) and thereby "dyes" them with its characteristic "color" (*inṣibāgh*). So, in the present example, since according to the worldview of al-Qūnawī the clothes of a person in a very real sense manifest and thus are causally connected to his or her reality, the rulings of that reality determine the states through which the clothes pass. This is only one of an innumerable number of examples of what one might call the metaphysics of *tabarruk* (i.e., the obtaining of blessings through the intermediary of a blessed person or thing).

not consume man's places of prostration," despite the fact that these places belong to the parts of his body admitting of being burned. And [there is also] his saying regarding Hell, according to which [Hell] says, "Enter O believer, for your light has extinguished my blaze."

Just as "good deeds remove those that are evil" [Q 11:114], thus is it with the secret in the servant who is the source (*maṣdar*) of that good deed which erases the harm of that evil deed.

For us, the erasure in this station[16] is twofold: the erasure of the form of the evil deed and the erasure of its consequence and harm after death wherever God wills among the homesteads and standing-places through which the creation passes, and in Hell—God protect us from it.

Perhaps the cause of both erasures is an essential matter within man, and perhaps it is a good act following upon a blameworthy act that abrogates its ruling and changes its form,[17] just as he has said, peace and blessings be upon him: "Follow an evil deed with a good deed. It will erase it."[18]

And I saw in this station—when I was made to enter it and acquainted with it—the difference between the outward and inward consequences of actions, where it is that they ultimately lead to, and the extent of the perplexity of [people's various] endings.[19] I was made acquainted with the reality of taking-to-task and of pardoning and forgiveness. I saw the effect of each one differing from the effect of the other, and I saw the secret of substitution and the destruction of the forms of the actions so that they become "scattered dust" [Q 25:23].

I saw the actions pure in evil and in good, and those mixed from both with a greater portion of evil or of good. I saw the good deed erase the good deed, and I saw some of the actions called evil erase other evils. I saw the substitution and the erasure occurring sometimes all at once and sometimes [only] gradually, after a while, little by little, like the transformations in this cosmos of ours. And I saw the actions' spirits and their configuration (*intishāʾ*) between the father-

16 This of course in the technical, Sufi sense of the word (*maqām*).

17 In sketching these two alternatives, which are not mutually exclusive, al-Qūnawī is alluding to the extrinsic nature of all human actions vis-à-vis a person's underlying, or transcendent, reality, which in Akbarian thought is said to be uncreated (*ghayr majʿūl*). As will become clear in what follows, this reality can exercise its effects in the cosmos through modes of causation that approach or even coincide with "pure verticality," hence certain seeming anomalies.

18 Tirmidhī, *Sunan*, in *Jamʿ jawāmiʿ al-aḥādīth wa-l-asānīd wa-maknaz al-siḥāḥ wa-l-sunan wa-l-masānīd*, vi, Vaduz: Jamʿiyyat al-Maknaz al-Islāmī, 2000, Birr, 55, no. 2115.

19 I.e., posthumous destinations.

hood of the scholar's knowledge and the motherhood of his presence[20] despite what he knows and despite his believing it to be correct when it was [a case of] a correct belief agreeing with the matter at hand.

Regarding action [considered] from the perspective of its form and its cadence in a noble locus, or in the locus of presence (*maḥḍar*) of a truthful actor drawn nigh [unto God], I saw that sometimes its ruling prevails over the ruling of its spirit, which is worthy of blame on account of a corrupt intention and deficient [state of] presence. [And I saw] the opposite of that as well, so that the form of the deficient action is rectified on account of the righteousness of the action's spirit through soundness of knowledge, sincerity of intention, and beautiful gatheredness (*ḥusn al-jamʿiyya*) at the time of presence.[21] So the righteousness of the corrupt action is brought about both from the point of view of its form and from that of its spiritual reality (*rūḥāniyya*).

I saw the righteous action of Zayd rectify the corrupt action of ʿAmr as well as the opposite of that when the ruling authority (*salṭana*) of the corrupt becomes manifest, as He, the Exalted, says: "And be mindful of a trial that will not befall only those among you who do wrong" [Q 8:25]. This does not contradict the principle derived from His saying, exalted is He: "And none shall bear the burden of another" [Q 35:18]. For this effect does not occur or come about through the ruling of that through which there is distinction between the righteous and the wicked, but rather in accordance with the ruling of that through which there is unification and participation between Zayd and ʿAmr. His saying "And none shall bear the burden of another" is [spoken with] the tongue of the prevailing of that through which there is distinction over the ruling of that through which there is participation. So understand!

I saw in this station, from among the secrets of actions and actors and their requital—in respect of evil and of good, of this life, the isthmus (*barzakh*), and the Hereafter, of intention and presence, and in respect of knowledge, witnessing, and intellection—that which is unable to be expounded owing to its magnitude, the impossibility of expressing it, and the explanation's being insufficient to elucidate it.

I saw some of the actions occupied with fading away and another action appearing and stabilizing it. Perhaps that stabilizing action comes from that actor [himself], or perhaps it comes from other than him. As for that which comes from other than him, perhaps it is intentional and perhaps not—rather

20 The contrast is between understanding something theoretically and bringing that understanding to bear on one's state of being.

21 I.e., that of the actor.

it is through the characteristic property of a [given] participation and correspondence between two individuals in state, act, or station, or because of participation in some essential attributes, or in a single attribute whose ruling prevails over [the two individuals][22] at the time of the donning of that action.[23]

I saw the types of actions linked, some of them with others, such that perhaps an individual intends a certain action[24] in accordance with a certain belief about some matter or other, and he is prevailed over by the ruling of a [given] moment and state—or that of a station also—that is, by the ruling of another action in a form other [than what he intended]. So there appears an unknown consequence regarding which [only] a few people recognize whence it was configured (*intasha'at*) and how it is that it came about. And that is due to the coming-into-effect and prevailing of the ruling of another type of action possessing a hidden ascendancy (*salṭana*) having gained its force[25] through the ruling of the actor's moment and state even though it be contrary to his aim and intention.

I saw the universal [realities] of the secrets of the disobediences and obediences, and I looked down from the presence of the dawning-place upon the secrets of their consequences and preludes. I found that relative to some people they were proofs of the secret of predestination such that on the morrow experience corroborates the report. Relative to others they were causes and instruments whereby the rulings of negligence and circumspection and the secret of justice in rewards and requitals become manifest. And relative to others they were snares and imaginalizations (*khayālāt*) by which some of them pursued the Hereafter from this life,[26] and some of them [pursued] from the Hereafter the comprehensive affair, which is the secret of the perfections of both this life

22 Lit. "a single attribute prevailing over both of them with respect to ruling" (*ṣifa wāḥida hiya al-ghāliba ḥukm^{an} 'alā kull minhumā*).

23 The example of a battle may be helpful here. If a warrior is losing his courage, perhaps he is able to muster it back up himself, or perhaps his brother notices his state and intentionally encourages him, or perhaps the failing warrior simply sees the courage of his brother and is inspired by it, in which case the effect is attributable to one of the causes given in the rest of the sentence.

24 The Arabic reads *'ilm* here, but it is clear that it was supposed to be *'amal*. See al-Qūnawī, *Tarjuma-yi Nafaḥāt-i ilāhiyya*, trans. Muḥammad Khwājawī, Tehran: Intishārāt-i Mawlā, 1996, 186.

25 This participle phrase is a past-tense verb in the Arabic. Its subject is "a hidden ascendancy."

26 This passage was difficult to get into English. The image is one of a "hunting ground" that spans multiple levels of reality such that, from one's starting point in a lower level, one is able to "trap" realities belonging to a higher level using the "snares" of one's obedient actions.

and the Hereafter, and some of them [pursued] from these three affairs realization through them and through recognition of what is in them, and [they pursued] the blessing of beholding them as well as the ruling and the secrets to which they are consigned.

I saw that some abandon their specified allotment of all of what has been mentioned for their absolute and most complete allotment, discovering [thereby] the perfection of lucidity laid away (*mūdaʿ*) in all of that[27] and passing on to the elucidation of the oneness of the principial Act and free disposal. So he sees the oneness of the One who disposes freely and the free disposal, and [he sees] the cause of the pluralizations of that one Act in the different recipients as well as Its acquisition, in relation to the pluralizations, of manifold descriptions on whose account that unitary Act, upon becoming plural, is called obedience and disobedience and has beauty and ugliness, and effects both eternally befitting and unbefitting, attributed to it—for a fixed time finite in ruling, or indefinitely.

Then, in my return from this lofty place of witnessing, I saw while descending some of the acts that are called actions relative to the one unfit for gnosis of the Real,[28] and [I saw] his witnessing [that] out of faith and fair dealing. And I saw [some of the acts] relative to someone else as causes of his profiting[29] due to his renunciation or adornment, or the removal of a harm [issuing] from an innate heedlessness, or authority, or the attraction of a benefit, the alleviation of some distress, and the seeking of deliverance from a tribulation.

And as this was the closing of the circuit of the sphere of actions, and it was joined to its beginning and apogee, I found the actions of the greatest of men proceeding in the stations revelatory of the justice of the Real and His good pleasure, and [I found them] entering into the levels of knowledge and ignorance and junction and separation through His protection. He manifests Himself and dons the rulings of His tasks in accordance with His knowledge of the pluralizations.

So understand and ponder these secrets. I do not think they have reached your hearing, and perhaps they have not been mentioned until now. And God is the Guide.

---

27 The image is one of unearthing a treasure.

28 Here al-Qūnawī is reserving the word act (*fiʿl*) for God, whereas action (*ʿamal*) pertains to the level of the creature. He is saying that the gnostic knows all of what are conventionally called actions to be the acts of God Himself.

29 This word (*nuhba*) literally means spoils or loot (from *nahaba,* to plunder or take by force). Khwājawī, who gives manuscript variants in a note, glosses it as *ghalaba* or "victory" (al-Qūnawī, *al-Nafaḥāt* 183). If *nuhba* is correct, al-Qūnawī would be likening this life to an enemy that the God-fearing person should seek to "despoil."

2.2 *A Great Secret*

Islam is the form of the level of being acted upon;[30] faith pertains to the meaning of absolute Being;[31] and contingency[32] and friendship (*walāya*) are for the witnessing of general existence in respect of its general form,[33] which is the locus of manifestation of the inclusive equilibrium following from the universal, general composition effected by the primal marriage.[34] The disposer of the general form of existence[35] is the Universal Spirit, and Its preservation [of it] is through knowledge.[36] It is necessary that [the Spirit] possess at all times a human locus of manifestation, and that is the spirit of the reality that is in certain respects akin to the human subtlety,[37] the last of whose loci of manifestation is a perfect end, and that is Jesus, peace be upon him. The ruling of

---

30 That is, the practice of the Islamic religion constitutes the outward sign of one's having opened oneself to being acted upon by the Divine, namely by doing what is commanded by God's Law. Esoterically, this statement could also be taken to mean that all things are always already in submission to God whether they realize it or not, since nothing can contravene the divine Will.

31 At the highest level, the object of faith is God conceived not as the supreme being, but as Being Itself, which for al-Qūnawī transcends the distinction between transcendence and immanence. Regarding the term *wujūd*, I will translate it as "Being" when it denotes divinity without qualification and as "existence" in all other cases.

32 This word (*imkān*) can also be translated as "possibility." The meanings and connotations of the two terms in English are different in certain respects, but both would work in this particular passage.

33 According to the famous *ḥadīth* of the Hidden Treasure, God created the world because He loved to be recognized. For al-Qūnawī, the ultimate purpose of the entire creation is only fulfilled in the direct witnessing of the Divine. But since only God can know God, such witnessing is not possible without God's self-revelation, which goes by a very great number of names in Akbarian texts. Here, "general existence" (*al-wujūd al-ʿāmm*) would be synonymous with the Muhammadan Reality (*al-ḥaqīqa al-Muḥammadiyya*), the Breath of the All-Merciful (*nafas al-raḥmān*), etc. In Akbarian metaphysics, this level of reality constitutes the mysterious "point of contact" between the Absolute and the relative, or the Necessary and the contingent.

34 The marriage, that is, between the active and passive principles of manifestation, which are operative at all levels of the cosmos. Here al-Qūnawī is referring specifically to the first such marriage (*al-nikāḥ al-awwal*), which transpires at the divine level. For discussion of this concept in al-Qūnawī, see Todd, *Sufi doctrine* 66–68, 121–122; for Ibn ʿArabī, see Chittick, William C., *The self-disclosure of God: Principles of Ibn al-ʿArabī's cosmology*, Albany, NY: SUNY Press, 1998, 304.

35 I will sometimes translate *nisba* adjectives as genitives to avoid awkwardness or problematic translations.

36 The synonymy of the terms Universal Spirit and First Intellect for al-Qūnawī is worth mentioning in this connection.

37 In Sufism, the psychological term "human subtlety" or "subtle human reality" (*al-laṭīfa al-insāniyya*) "can denote the soul as it has become more aligned with the heart and the spirit" (Rustom, Mohammed, *Inrushes of the heart: The Sufi philosophy of ʿAyn al-Quḍāt*,

the common man after his departure—that is, the departure of Jesus—is the ruling of the animal forms, which do not possess rational souls.[38]

2.3 *A Great Secret Containing a Weighty Symbol*

[Say that] we have found two plants participating in [the same] constitution. Both of them are hot and dry in the third or fourth degree, for example. They are growing from the same soil in the same region, [but] one of them is flourishing and the other is withering. Whether the effect be due to a specificity attributable to one of them from the point of view of its quiddity, or from that of the [particular] spiritual power in virtue of which it exists, or from the perspective of the constitution it acquired from the elements subsequent to its quiddity's having become clothed with existence, or [whether] a particular influence from the powers of the heavens becomes attached to that, the manifestation of its ruling depends upon the moment comprising the starting point for that plant's growth and existentiation. [So] that effect is obtained from the coalescence of the spiritual powers exerting their influence through the mediation of the planetary fashionings, and the reception of this specific constitution is that [very] effect [occurring] in that manner at that moment. This is an intelligible constitution to which the form of the constitution of the plant is subordinate in ruling due to an invisible correspondence established between the two constitutions. The matter is doubtless thus.

It is possible that there be effects occurring on the basis of the constitutions of human beings, such as sciences, morals, and the likes of these from what is blameworthy or praiseworthy, influencing or influenced. The things observed among some people that are unusual and do not occur otherwise are attributable to the aforementioned principle. The ruling mentioned above is general to all of what [exists] in the elemental world: wherefore it is not correct to rely upon something merely on the basis of its being regarded as commendable or shameful by the intellect.[39] In reality, the [correct] judgment regarding something is not that it is such and such while some other thing is not such and such.[40]

Albany, NY: SUNY Press, 2023, ch. 5). It is also, according to Chittick, "equivalent to the 'rationally speaking soul' (*al-nafs al-nāṭiqa*)" (Chittick, *Self-disclosure* 269).

38 For Jesus as the "Seal of Universal Sainthood" in Akbarian thought, see Chodkiewicz, Michel, *Seal of the saints: Prophethood and sainthood in the doctrine of Ibn ʿArabī*, trans. Liadain Sherrard, Cambridge: Islamic Texts Society, 1993, 116–127.

39 Lit. "reliance upon a thing from among [the things] regarded as good by the intellect or [the things] regarded as shameful by it is not correct."

40 Since, from the highest point of view, there is only one Actor, one should not make distinctions that are not made by the Actor Himself.

Since it is possible that there appear one possessing a particular constitution the relation of which to equilibrium is closer [than that of others], and whose reception of spiritual influences and heavenly powers is more complete, it is necessary for him that he judge things by rulings that differ from the rulings of the one who proceeds according to [the conventions of] the majority. His motive is the principle that he bases himself on, and so they oppose him. He does not give preference to them; rather, it may be that the one judging a thing at this or that time [does so] in accordance with his perception of it, with [this perception] being subordinate to the ruling of his constitution at the time [of the occurrence] of the judgment, which is subordinate to the ruling of his reception of spiritual influences and constitutional conditionings, [so that] his constitution shifts into a mode different from the first mode.[41]

That shifting necessitates his constitution's assumption of a mode [of being] more complete than the first, such that the manifestation of the influences of the Names, of spirituality, and of heavenly powers is more perfect in him. He judges the thing [in question] by that which differs from his preceding ruling, and he sees [it] through this perfective description obtained at the later time in spite of the prior deficiency. Or rather, perhaps there comes to him the establishment of a demonstration for that, so that the very thing he denied at first is confirmed, as well as the opposite of that.

It may also happen that his constitution assumes a mode [of being] whose relation to equilibrium is more distant than that of the mode his constitution was in before, so that his reception of spiritual influences is weaker, less complete, and severer in deficiency. He then judges in a manner contrary to his prior ruling, even though he is mistaken. For these two forms there exist similitudes: [for example,] the youth advancing in age who advances in understanding and awareness, and the decline of the old man experiencing decrepitude and senility. The thing becomes a locus for the two opposite rulings arriving from the single ruler,[42] or rather for myriad rulings that are well-nigh infinite in accordance with the two rulers, or in accordance with the one ruler differing in state at two [different] moments. The variation in the soul's governing of the body and its influencing it at every moment are likewise in accordance with the state

41 Despite some ambiguity in this sentence (mainly regarding the precise meaning of the second instance of the word *ḥukm*, which I have translated as "judgment" instead of "ruling"), the basic idea is clear. Given that the gnostics, instead of basing themselves upon convention, make themselves available to God, their spiritual poverty renders them receptive to especially direct modes of guidance.

42 Lit. "the thing becomes an arriving place (*mawrid*) for the two opposite rulings from the single ruler."

of the body. That then is a well-known matter, and if the matter be thus, judging things to be beautiful or ugly and their being negated and affirmed[43] become relative, attributional matters that differ through the disparity of the states of the two rulers for the reasons indicated. So understand!

2.4 *A Gleam*

The seven heavens are elemental, and every elemental [thing] has spiritual powers that are the ruling properties of the realities of nature insofar as these realities are garbed with the elements, or rather insofar as these realities are themselves.

The eighth celestial sphere is the Heights,[44] and its surface is the ground of the Garden, which is the Pedestal,[45] and its ceiling is the Throne of the All-Merciful, and its dais discloses the All-Merciful Name and the Presence of being made to witness [God] at the Dune, which is the last of the gardens and the first of the gates of the Presence and the residence (*maskan*) indicated in the *ḥadīth*;[46] and [it is] the loftiest of the habitations attained by the people of the Garden—not the perfect from among the people of the Real and His elite.

The seven heavens are like the shadows of the gardens, while the eighth, which is the Garden of Eden, is the shadow of the Presence of the All-Merciful. The transference of the felicity and spirituality found in the heavens is completed at the Resurrection and upon their[47] becoming joined to the gardens. And that which is found in them of sorrow and of the preponderance of the elemental qualities demanding generation and corruption liquefies and separates, as He, the Exalted, has made known: "reddish, like the dregs of oil" [Q 55:37]. And it flows back, belonging to Hell in virtue of its attachment to the elements, which turn into fire and bitter cold, as mentioned in the reports and established through witnessing. Every heaven comprises one of the gates of Hell to which a particular people belongs,[48] and the gardens are eight [in number]

43 Lit. "judging things by beauty and ugliness and negation and affirmation."

44 See Q 7:46–48.

45 See Q 2:255.

46 For the "Dune of Vision" and discussion of the *ḥadīth* in question, see Chittick, *Self-disclosure* 440. See also Chittick, *In search* 119, 256.

47 I.e., the felicity and spirituality found in the heavens.

48 This juxtaposition of the celestial and the infernal brings the chapter full circle, since it not only conveys a "cut-and-dried" cosmological truth (viz., the separative function of each *barzakh* or isthmus by which the different levels of reality are distinguished from each other) but also serves to remind the intended audience of their vulnerability vis-à-vis God regardless of how high one has managed to climb spiritually. According to a *ḥadīth qudsī*, which echoes Q 7:99, "God, ever exalted is He, says: 'No-one, except those who are lost,

on account of their being on the surface of the eighth celestial sphere, and on account of what we pointed out [above]. This is an august exposition, and this is a reminder.

Bibliography

Ali, Mukhtar H., *Philosophical Sufism: An introduction to the school of Ibn al-ʿArabī*, London: Routledge, 2022.

Chittick, William C., "The last will and testament of Ibn ʿArabi's foremost disciple and some notes on its author," in *Sophia Perennis* 4.1 (1978), 43–58.

Chittick, William C., *The self-disclosure of God: Principles of Ibn al-ʿArabī's cosmology*, Albany, NY: SUNY Press, 1998.

Chittick, William C., *In search of the lost heart: Explorations in Islamic thought*, ed. Mohammed Rustom, Atif Khalil, and Kazuyo Murata, Albany, NY: SUNY Press, 2012.

Chodkiewicz, Michel, *Seal of the saints: Prophethood and sainthood in the doctrine of Ibn ʿArabī*, trans. Liadain Sherrard, Cambridge: Islamic Texts Society, 1993.

Clark, Jane, "Toward a biography of Ṣadr al-dīn al-Qūnawī," in *Journal of the Muhyiddin Ibn ʿArabi Society* 49 (2011), 1–34.

Dagli, Caner, *Ibn al-ʿArabī and Islamic intellectual culture: From mysticism to philosophy*, New York: Routledge, 2016.

Ibn ʿArabī, Muḥyī al-Dīn, *Divine sayings: 101 hadith qudsi* (Mishkāt al-anwār), trans. Stephen Hirtenstein and Martin Notcutt, Oxford: Anqa Publishing, 2004.

Nasr, Seyyed Hossein et al. (eds.), *The study Quran: A new translation and commentary*, New York: HarperOne, 2015.

al-Qayṣarī, Dāwūd, *The horizons of being: The metaphysics of Ibn al-ʿArabī in the* Muqaddimat al-Qayṣarī, trans. Mukhtar H. Ali, Leiden: Brill, 2020.

al-Qūnawī, Ṣadr al-Dīn, *Sharḥ al-arbaʿīn ḥadīth^{an}*, ed. Hasan Kamil Yılmaz, Qom: Intishārāt-i Bīdār, n.d.

al-Qūnawī, Ṣadr al-Dīn, *al-Nafaḥāt al-ilāhiyya*, ed. Muḥammad Khwājawī, Tehran: Intishārāt-i Mawlā, 1996.

al-Qūnawī, Ṣadr al-Dīn, *Tarjuma-yi Nafaḥāt-i ilāhiyya*, trans. Muḥammad Khwājawī, Tehran: Intishārāt-i Mawlā, 1996.

Rustom, Mohammed, *Inrushes of the heart: The Sufi philosophy of ʿAyn al-Quḍāt*, Albany, NY: SUNY Press, 2023.

---

feels safe from the ruse of God'" (Ibn ʿArabī, Muḥyī al-Dīn, *Divine sayings: 101 hadith qudsi* (Mishkāt al-anwār), trans. Stephen Hirtenstein and Martin Notcutt, Oxford: Anqa Publishing, 2004, 53).

Tirmidhī, *Sunan*, in *Jamʿ jawāmiʿ al-aḥādīth wa-l-asānīd wa-maknaz al-siḥāḥ wa-l-sunan wa-l-masānīd*, vi, Vaduz: Jamʿiyyat al-Maknaz al-Islāmī, 2000.
Todd, Richard, *The Sufi doctrine of man: Ṣadr al-Dīn al-Qūnawī's metaphysical anthropology*, Leiden: Brill, 2014.

CHAPTER 9

Being with a Capital *B*: Ibn Turka on Ibn ʿArabī's Lettrist Cosmogony

Matthew Melvin-Koushki

Back in graduate school, I regularly made the pilgrimage from New Jerusalem (aka New Haven) to Mount Sinai—in its Long Island manifestation—to read Ibn ʿArabī (d. 638/1240) and Ibn Turka (d. 835/1432) with Professor Chittick, often followed by dinner and shisha. Even more than his oceanic erudition and that of Professor Murata, it was these encounters that helped form me as a scholar and philologist-to-the-death. Their bookhoard home is a magical portal onto an alternate, paradisaical, Qajar dimension; I remain awed and inspired by their total commitment to the beauty of the text. In honor of Professor Chittick and Professor Murata's watershed scholarship and equally generous mentorship, I can think of no offering more meet than an investigation into Ibn Turka's take on Ibn ʿArabī's take on *magical text*—or *text as magic*.

∴

1 Introduction

Lettrism (*ʿilm al-ḥurūf*) was a science central to both sages' life projects.[1] Indeed, more than any of Ibn ʿArabī's innumerable commentators and intellectual heirs, Ibn Turka was responsible for the philosophical systematization and sociopolitical mainstreaming of this occult science, with sweeping ramifications for the history of science, the history of empire, and the history of the book alike. His *Sharḥ Fuṣūṣ al-ḥikam* is the first and only commentary on the Supreme Master's most seminal work to be thoroughgoingly lettrist in focus.[2] His *Book of investigations* (*Kitāb al-Mafāḥiṣ*), the first summa

1 See, e.g., Gril, Denis, "The science of letters," in Muḥyī al-Dīn Ibn al-ʿArabī, *The Meccan revelations*, ed. Michel Chodkiewicz, trans. Cyrille Chodkiewicz and Denis Gril, 2 vols., ii, New York: Pir Press, 2004, 105–219; Rašić, Dunja, *The written world of God: The cosmic script and the art of Ibn ʿArabī*, Oxford: Anqa Publishing, 2021.

2 Melvin-Koushki, Matthew, *The quest for a universal science: The occult philosophy of Ṣāʾin*

 | DOI:10.1163/9789004529038_010

of Islamic Pythagoreanism, definitively synthesizes, fully works out, and productively extends the lettrist implications littering Ibn ʿArabī's oeuvre, defined by the classic esotericizing principle of *tabdīd al-ʿilm*, 'scattering knowledge,' which principle he rejects.[3] To make them scientifically and technologically usable to his royal patrons specifically and the scholarly community generally, Ibn Turka penned over a dozen Persian and Arabic books and treatises on lettrism, stylistically gorgeous, philosophically cutting-edge, and wonderfully accessible in a way no previous treatments had been.

This corpus exemplifies a new, specifically early modern sensibility, whereby the esoteric and elitist discourse of medieval and ancient thinkers was systematically de-esotericized and democratized in the service of empirical science and world empire.[4] For Ibn Turka, lettrism is simultaneously the most valid form of metaphysics *and* physics, the epitome of *taḥqīq*, the ultimate proof of the superiority of the Moderns to the Ancients. The perennialist yet progressivist "lettrist consciousness" or "cosmic philology" this Isfahani occult philosopher fostered came to inform everything from Persianate riddle (*muʿammā*) culture to imperial architecture, to arts of the book. Most notably, it was an important engine of the *mathesis* turn that would define the "Scientific Revolution," whereby Muslims, Jews, and Christians, respectfully departing from Aristotle and returning to Pythagoras, began to read and write the world as a mathematical, magical text.[5]

To give a taste (*dhawq*) of this transformative textual process, this Pythagorean paradigm shift, I offer a translation and brief contextualization of Ibn Turka's Arabic treatise *On the* B (*al-Risāla al-Bāʾiyya*). It was written in answer to a colleague's question as to why *B* opens the Quran; that the same letter also opens the Torah made this question an equally pressing concern for Jewish and Christian kabbalists, and hence a productive site for comparative early mod-

---

al-Dīn Turka Iṣfahānī (1369–1432) and intellectual millenarianism in early Timurid Iran, New Haven (PhD Diss.): Yale University, 2012, 112–113. Professor Chittick, needless to say, served as a reader of my dissertation.

3 Melvin-Koushki, *The quest*, ch. 7; Gardiner, Noah D., *Esotericism in a manuscript culture: Aḥmad al-Būnī and his readers through the Mamlūk period*, Ann Arbor (PhD Diss.): University of Michigan, 2014, ch. 2.

4 On this definition of early modernity see Melvin-Koushki, Matthew, "*Taḥqīq* vs. *taqlīd* in the renaissances of Western early modernity," in *Philological Encounters* 3.1 (2018), 193–249.

5 Melvin-Koushki, Matthew, "Powers of One: The mathematicalization of the occult sciences in the High Persianate tradition," in *IHIW* 5.1 (2017), 127–199. On this simultaneously mathematical and linguistic cosmology as a patrimony of Hellenistic late antiquity see Acevedo, Juan, *Alphanumeric cosmology from Greek into Arabic: The idea of* stoicheia *through the medieval Mediterranean*, Tübingen: Mohr Siebeck, 2020.

ern Western intellectual historiography. In his own remarkable treatment of the subject, our Timurid lettrist does what he does best: he stitches together Ibn ʿArabī's freewheeling insights on the subject into a conceptually precise and usable product. Ibn Turka's only other identified source is the Kubrawi shaykh Saʿd al-Dīn Ḥamūya (d. 649/1252), Ibn ʿArabī's Iranian contemporary, whose oeuvre is even more centrally lettrist, and even more slippery. Indeed, Ḥamūya—who talismanically blessed the Ilkhanid ruler Ghāzān Khan's (r. 694–703/1295–1304) conversion to Islam, prefiguring Ibn Turka's own service to the Timurid dynasty—went so far as to personally criticize Ibn ʿArabī in a letter as being too rigid in his lettrism![6] What this critique makes clear, however, is that both Ibn ʿArabī and Ḥamūya can be usefully read as *jazz philosophers*—and Ibn Turka, their systematizing and Pythagoreanizing lettrist heir, as a *philosopher of jazz*.[7]

2 Betic Cosmogony in Premodern Lettrist and Kabbalist Thought

> If you are indeed a teacher, and if you know the letters well,
> tell me the power of *alpha* and I will tell you that of *beta*.
>
> *The infancy gospel of Thomas*[8]

B is not among the light (*nūrānī*) letters—the 14 isolated letters (*muqaṭṭaʿāt*) opening 29 Sūras, naturally a primary matrix of lettrism, representing exactly half the Arabic alphabet—but rather first of the dark (*ẓulmānī*) ones and fountainhead of all duality. Why, then, does it open both the Quran and the Torah, those mathematical-linguistic models of the cosmos? Surely the primordial singularity of *A*, as avatar of both divine Oneness and the beginning of creation, is far better suited to this monotheistic, monotheurgic purpose?

This is the central cosmogonic conundrum Ibn Turka addresses in the *R. al-Bāʾiyya*. To riddle it, he deftly combines rational and traditional arguments in

6 See now Uy II, Cyril V., *Lost in a sea of letters: Saʿd al-Dīn Ḥamūya (d. 1252) and the plurality of Sufi knowledge*, Providence (PhD Diss.): Brown University, 2021, 14, 89–91 and *passim*.

7 My thanks to Prof. Uy for this analogy. His masterful dissertation is the first on Ḥamūya, of equal importance to Ibn ʿArabī in the history of lettrism. We eagerly await the critical edition of Ḥamūya's seminal *Kitāb al-Maḥbūb*—one of Ibn Turka's favorite sources—by Elizabeth Alexandrin and Paul Ballanfat. Jacques Derrida (d. 2004) has also been called a jazz philosopher, for equally obvious reasons; see, e.g., Ramshaw, Sara, *Justice as improvisation: The law of the extempore*, New York: Routledge, 2013, 111.

8 Translated in Acevedo, *Alphanumeric cosmology* 128.

the standard scholarly manner, drawing on Ibn ʿArabī and Ḥamūya in particular, who drew in turn on centuries of Sufi speculation on the subject. Their eastern authorities include such luminaries as Sahl al-Tustarī (d. 282/896), al-Ḥakīm al-Tirmidhī (d. ca. 295–300/907–912), Manṣūr al-Ḥallāj (d. 309/922), Abū Naṣr al-Sarrāj (d. 377/988) and Abū ʿAbd al-Raḥmān al-Sulamī (d. 412/1021); their western authorities include Ibn Masarra (d. 319/931) and Ibn Barrajān (d. 536/1141).[9] Taken together, a recurring theme in these early lettrist speculations is the status of the dot (*nuqṭa*) under the *B* as ultimate symbol of divine creation.[10] But their tenor is strictly allusive and alliterative, rather than philosophical or Pythagorean, with emphasis on the simple occurrence of the letter in various Arabic terms or divine names, and talismanic applications are not discussed. This approach is epitomized in Sulamī's treatise *Explication of the meaning of the letters* (*Sharḥ maʿānī l-ḥurūf*), which synthesizes many earlier sources, usually without attribution:

> The *Bāʾ* … symbolizes that through God (*bihi*) all things are brought forth and made to perish. It can also indicate that God is the Eternal (*al-abadī*) for whom eternity a parte ante (*azal*) and a parte post (*abad*) has no reality. This thought is illustrated by a verse of Abū ʿAlī al-Rūdhabārī, "You are troubled because He conceals from Himself His affection for you, hides from you His affection for you, and hides from you your affection for Him. Like a beam that flashes up from a beacon, He wanders aimlessly about in passionate love for you, unless you yourself are the flash." The *Bāʾ* can also signify the divine names that begin with the letter *Bāʾ*. With regard

9 On Ibn Barrajān and his doctrine of world as scripture see Casewit, Yousef, *The mystics of al-Andalus: Ibn Barrajān and Islamic thought in the twelfth century*, Cambridge: Cambridge University Press, 2017. On Ibn Masarra, whose more philosophical, Neoplatonizing approach to the letters was an especially important model for Ibn ʿArabī, see Garrido Clemente, Pilar, "The science of letters in Ibn Masarra: Unified word, unified world," in *Journal of the Muhyiddin Ibn ʿArabi Society* 47 (2010), 47–61; Ebstein, Michael, *Mysticism and philosophy in al-Andalus: Ibn Masarra, Ibn al-ʿArabī and the Ismāʿīlī tradition*, Leiden: Brill, 2014, ch. 2. The authorship of the two lettrist treatises attributed to Ibn Masarra in modern scholarship is not secure; however, as José Bellver has shown, Ibn ʿArabī's citation of his *Kitāb al-Ḥurūf*, aka *al-Lisān al-ʿaẓīm fī l-ḥurūf*—presumably a different work—confirms him as an important lettrist authority in any case (see Bellver, José, "The beginnings of rational theology in al-Andalus: Ibn Masarra and his refutation of al-Kindī's *On first philosophy*," in *Qanṭara* 41.2 (2020), 323–371).

10 This summary is given in Böwering, Gerhard, "Sulamī's treatise on the science of the letters (*ʿilm al-ḥurūf*)," in Bilal Orfali (ed.), *In the shadow of Arabic: The centrality of language to Arabic culture. Studies presented to Ramzi Baalbaki on the occasion of his sixtieth birthday*, Leiden: Brill, 2011, 339–397, 352.

> to human beings, the *Bāʾ* refers to them as God's servants who follow His commands with loyalty and zeal or, in the words of Ibn ʿAṭāʾ, it manifests God's kindness (*birr*) toward the prophets.[11]

A similarly allusive approach to the *B* features in the earliest texts of kabbalah, which also synthesize eastern and western authorities. The *Sefer ha-Bahir* (*Book of illumination*) is a case in point: it too dwells on the *B* in relation to the *A* as cosmogonic agent. As Elliot Wolfson summarizes in his analysis of this key medieval Hebrew work: "Before *alef* comes *beit*—here in a nutshell lies the wisdom of kabbalah."[12] This paradoxical principle became a central focus of subsequent kabbalist meditations on the mechanics of creation, reaching a crescendo in the Italian Renaissance with such systematizing humanist scholars as Rabbi Yohanan Alemanno (d. after 1504) and his student Giovanni Pico della Mirandola (d. 1494), father of Christian kabbalah.[13] These meditations pivot on the concept of the *coincidentia oppositorum* as famously formalized by the German Pythagorean cardinal Nicholas of Cusa (d. 1464): the *B* as 2 is both the engine of duality and the tool for return to singularity through the marriage of all opposites.[14]

The same concept runs like a red thread through Ibn ʿArabī's vast, kaleidoscopic oeuvre and gives it a measure of thematic coherence, as Professor Chittick and Professor Murata have definitively shown. To this end, he frequently invokes the classic Sufi—and Empedoclean and Plotinian—phrase *al-nikāḥ al-sārī fī jamīʿ al-dharārī*, 'the marriage act pervading all atoms,' to explain the mechanics of creation.[15] And what is more atomic than the dot under the *B*? For it is the origin of all letters, even the *A*, composed of three dots.

---

11 Böwering, "Sulamī's treatise" 357.

12 Wolfson, Elliot R., *Alef, mem, tau: Kabbalistic musings on time, truth, and death*, Berkeley: University of California Press, 2006, 118.

13 On both figures see especially Ogren, Brian, *The beginning of the world in renaissance Jewish thought:* Ma'aseh Bereshit *in Italian Jewish philosophy and kabbalah, 1492–1535*, Leiden: Brill, 2016.

14 Albertson, David, *Mathematical theologies: Nicholas of Cusa and the legacy of Thierry of Chartres*, Oxford: Oxford University Press, 2014, *passim*.

15 Indeed, one of Ibn ʿArabī's lost works bears precisely this title. On this and related themes see, of course, Murata, Sachiko, *The Tao of Islam: A sourcebook on gender relationships in Islamic thought*, Albany, NY: SUNY Press, 1992, 147–151 and *passim*; Chittick, William C., *The Sufi path of knowledge: Ibn al-ʿArabī's metaphysics of imagination*, Albany, NY: SUNY Press, 1989, ch. 20; Chittick, William C., *The self-disclosure of God: Principles of Ibn al-ʿArabī's cosmology*, Albany, NY: SUNY Press, 1998, 5–6, 173–181. Its most salient precedent would seem to be Plotinus's (d. 270) doctrine of *erotic*-cum-*numeric* emanation of the many from the transcendent One, well known to arabophone philosophers through the pseudepigraphal

What the perceptive reader might glean from Ibn ʿArabī's scattered treatments of the letters generally and *A* and *B* specifically, especially in his monumental *Meccan revelations* (*al-Futūḥāt al-Makkiyya*), is that the latter letter is intimately connected to his (in)famous theory of the superiority of *walāya* to *nubuwwa*, of sainthood to prophethood.[16] While a stumblingblock for more puritan scholars, this theory became hegemonic by the early modern period, and indeed the basis for radical new theories of saint-philosopher-kingship that defined post-Mongol Persianate imperial discourse, whether Mughal, Safavid, or Ottoman.[17] As preeminent theoretician of human sainthood generally and Islamic sainthood specifically, Ibn ʿArabī identified Jesus as Seal or ultimate model of the first, and himself as Seal of the second.[18] But many of his otherwise faithful intellectual heirs, both Sunni and Shiʿi, begged to differ with the Doctor Maximus on this point, arguing instead for the historical superiority of ʿAlid sainthood to Muḥammadan prophecy—in precisely betic terms.

The first to do so was Sayyid Ḥaydar Āmulī (d. ca. 787/1385), who combined lettrist, astrological, and alchemical proofs to demonstrate the identity of Sufism and Shiʿism.[19] Central to his cosmogonic argument is the *B*: graphically a straight line indistinguishable from the *A*, its distinguishing lower dot rep-

---

Theology of Aristotle (*Uthūlūjiyā*), a partial translation of the *Enneads*. The Empedoclean doctrine of Love and Strife similarly informed Suhravardī's (d. 587/1191) Illuminationist philosophy. See Banner, Nicholas, *Philosophic silence and the 'One' in Plotinus*, Cambridge: Cambridge University Press, 2018, *passim*; Walbridge, John, *The leaven of the ancients: Suhrawardī and the heritage of the Greeks*, Albany, NY: SUNY Press, 2000, 48–51.

16 Contrary to Ibn ʿArabī's usual scattering procedure, the long second chapter of the *Futūḥāt* is mostly lettrist in tenor; for translated sections, see Gril, "The science of letters;" Ibn al-ʿArabī, Muḥyī al-Dīn, *The openings revealed in Makkah* (al-Futūḥāt al-Makkīyah)*: Books 1 and 2*, trans. Eric Winkel, New York: Pir Press, 2018, 161–324. For a summary of his cosmology more generally see Chittick, William C., *Ibn ʿArabi: Heir to the prophets*, Oxford: Oneworld, 2005. On Ḥamūya's equivocal, cyclic approach to the same question see Alexandrin, Elizabeth R., "Seals and sealing of *walāyah* in Ṣūfī and Shīʿī texts: The cases of al-Ḥakīm al-Tirmidhī and Saʿd al-Dīn Ḥamūyah," in Saiyad Nizamuddin Ahmad and Sajjad H. Rizvi (eds.), *Philosophy and the intellectual life in Shīʿah Islam*, London: The Shīʿah Institute Press, 2017, 69–93; Uy, "Lost in a sea of letters," ch. 4.

17 Melvin-Koushki, Matthew, "Early modern Islamicate empire: New forms of religiopolitical legitimacy," in Armando Salvatore et al. (eds.), *The Wiley-Blackwell history of Islam*, Hoboken: Wiley-Blackwell, 2018, 353–375.

18 See, e.g., Elmore, Gerald T., *Islamic sainthood in the fullness of time: Ibn al-ʿArabī's* Book of the fabulous gryphon, Leiden: Brill, 1999, *passim*.

19 Mansouri, Mohammad Amin, "*Walāya* between lettrism and astrology: The occult mysticism of Sayyid Ḥaydar Āmulī (d. c. 787/1385)," in *Journal of Sufi Studies* 9.2 (2020), 161–201.

resents the transformation of Creator into created. As such, the second letter is the first being, "which is called Intellect, Spirit, Pen, Substance, Light, Element, Cause, Isthmus, Presence of Oneness, Presence of Names, First Entification, First Manifestation, Caliph, and First Imam."[20]

For the Twelver Shiʿi sage Āmulī, the *B* thus represents prophethood, and its dot sainthood, without which the eternal divine effluxion must remain cosmically unmanifest. Hence the saying of the First Imam himself, ʿAlī b. Abī Ṭālib (d. 40/661): "I am the dot beneath the *B* (*anā l-nuqṭa allatī taḥt al-bāʾ*)." Here Āmulī takes Ibn ʿArabī to task for failing to correctly ascribe to ʿAlī this seminal tradition, which served as prooftext for all later lettrists, regardless of confessional affiliation.[21]

So much for theory; what of practice? While a cosmogonist in his own right, the Sufi sage-mage Aḥmad al-Būnī (d. btw. 622–630/1225–1232) came to epitomize applied lettrism from the 9th/15th century onward, in contrast with the theoretical lettrism of Ibn ʿArabī, due not least to the categorizing efforts of Ibn Turka. The Andalusian lettrist famously swore not to practice his art; his Ifriqiyan counterpart swore no such thing.[22] Al-Būnī's treatments of the *B* therefore combine both theory and practice, though later Būnian pseudepigrapha—especially the *Great sun of knowledge* (*Shams al-maʿārif al-kubrā*), a grimoire even more ubiquitous in Islamdom than Maslama al-Qurṭubī's (d. 353/964) bestselling *Goal of the sage* (*Ghāyat al-ḥakīm*), aka the Latin *Picatrix*—reflect his reception as Ibn ʿArabī's complement and twin, and so are more resolutely technological. As that may be, both theory and practice are on display in his *Subtle allusions* (*Laṭāʾif al-ishārāt*), an authentic work.[23] Therein he first provides and explicates this cosmogonic diagram of the *B*, graphically representing the lettrist theory al-Būnī shares with Ibn ʿArabī—

---

20 For the technical terms in this passage and their significance see the translation in Mansouri, "*Walāya*" 183.

21 Mansouri, "*Walāya*" 189–190. On Āmulī's complex diagrams of his lettrist cosmogony and cosmology see Viengkhou, Aaron, "*Tawḥīd* divided: The esoteric orthodoxy of Sayyid Ḥaydar Āmulī (d. after 782/1380)," in *La Rosa di Paracelso* 2 (2020 [2022]), 27–51; Viengkhou, Aaron, "Sayyid Ḥaydar Āmulī's scripturalization of reality," in *IOSOTR*, http://islamicoccult.org/aaron_viengkhou (last accessed: 25 October 2021). Cf. Winters, Zach, "Reading the Book of Creation in the *Miftāḥ al-Asrār* of Āẕarī Isfarāyinī," in *La Rosa di Paracelso* 2 (2020 [2022]), 13–25.

22 As Dunja Rašić shows, however, several talismanic diagrams nevertheless occur in his oeuvre (*The written world*).

23 Gardiner, *Esotericism, passim*. For an (unreliable) edition of the *Laṭāʾif al-ishārāt* see Coulon, Jean-Charles, *La magie islamique et le corpus bunianum au Moyen Âge*, 4 vols., iv, Paris (PhD Diss.): University of Paris IV—Sorbonne, 2013, 64–180/394.

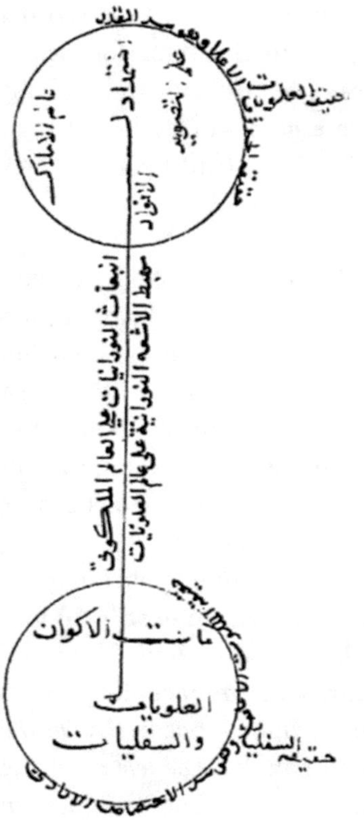

FIGURE 9.1
B diagram in al-Būnī, *Laṭāʾif al-ishārāt*, Paris, BnF, MS Arabe 2657, f. 28[a]
REPRODUCED IN COULON, “LA MAGIE ISLAMIQUE” IV, 103/394, FIG. 23

note the letter’s representation as a second *A* joining the celestial realm to the terrestrial (see Fig. 9.1 above). He then details its practical applications—including medical—as follows:

> Know that whoever writes this form [of the *B*] on a Friday, fasting on Thursday as well as Friday and giving alms, then binds it to his right upper arm, God shall open his breast and, having removed all lassitude, show him the secret inherent in the *B* and its angelic radiances. Therefore understand what the leading authorities have discoursed on with respect to the *B*—i.e., the letter itself—as to the fact that its formal manifestations, both supernal and infernal, together manifest an individual upright figure perfect of form and gorgeous of scent. As such, there is no authority that has not discoursed on the *B*, whose radiance is perpetual and unwavering. Upon any mention of its secret that radiance shines upon its essence, which essence inheres in certain divine names whose meaning is safely preserved, so that no motion is possible to it except through [the names of] God Most High. When this letter occurs in a divine

> name it therefore serves as a conduit of divine grace to its user. Writing such a divine name [in order to wear it] is particularly useful [for easing] pains caused by [an excess of] dryness or easing any difficult undertaking, for God Most High will thereby ease it. These names of God Most High include the Kind (*al-birr*), the Creator (*al-bāriʾ*), the Perduring (*al-bāqī*), and the Resurrector (*al-bāʿith*).[24]

This is the context and sourcebase for Ibn Turka's synthetic, systematic treatise on the *B*. Focused on lettrist theory only, it is profoundly Akbarian (and Ḥamūyan) in tenor, as are most of his other lettrist works. Indeed, as noted, Ibn Turka is responsible for the overneat identification of Ibn ʿArabī with lettrist theory and al-Būnī with lettrist practice that would become standard thereafter.[25] Yet his partially successful quest to transform his Timurid warlord patrons into philosopher-kings made him a powerful advocate of its practice too, such as in his *Query of kings* (*Suʾl al-mulūk*), which sets forth a full system of imperial talismanic lettrism, with medical, military, and other applications.[26]

But to synthesize and systematize is also to create and contest.[27] All four operations are on display here as elsewhere in Ibn Turka's oeuvre. A committed Sunni imamophile and perennialist-progressivist, he embraces Ibn ʿArabī's doctrine of the superiority of sainthood to prophethood—but in his *On the dot* (*Risāla-yi Nuqṭa*) follows Āmulī in declaring Imam ʿAlī the avatar of the dot under the *B* and epitome of Muḥammadan *walāya*.[28] The introduction

---

24 Coulon, *La magie islamique* iv, 102–104/394 (translation mine).

25 This most explicitly in his *Risāla-yi Ḥurūf*, which proposes an *ahl-i ḥaqāyiq* vs. *ahl-i khawāṣṣ* binary, the latter group of practical lettrists being the majority; see Melvin-Koushki, *The quest* 278–279, 478–479.

26 This work is edited and translated in my forthcoming *The lettrist treatises of Ibn Turka: Persian Pythagoreanism and imperial occultism in the Timurid renaissance*, Leiden: Brill (forthcoming).

27 Cf. the equally lettrist but encyclopedic project of Ibn Turka's Anatolian counterpart, ʿAbd al-Raḥmān al-Basṭāmī (d. 858/1454), on which see Gardiner, Noah D., "The occultist encyclopedism of ʿAbd al-Raḥmān al-Bisṭāmī," in *MSR* 20 (2017), 3–38. On early modern Islamic commentary culture as often creative and subversive rather than merely scholastic and imitative see, e.g., Ingalls, Matthew B., *The anonymity of a commentator: Zakariyyā al-Anṣārī and the rhetoric of Muslim commentaries*, Albany, NY: SUNY Press, 2021; Melvin-Koushki, "*Taḥqīq* vs. *taqlīd*."

28 Melvin-Koushki, *The quest* 344; for an edition and translation see my forthcoming *The lettrist treatises*. He expands on this point in the same treatise, citing Ḥamūya's *Kitāb al-Maḥbūb* (Tehran, MS Majlis 10196/10, f. 125^{a-b}):

> [*W*]*alāya* refers to the dot under the *B*. This is demonstrated through the fact that the dot here under discussion has two aspects in its written form. First, it is the point of

to his *Book of investigations* is even more explicit on this point: it celebrates ʿAlī as the inventor of lettrism, a Muslim Pythagoras standing to Muḥammad as the Samoan sage did to Solomon. His mathematizing marriage of lettrism with Pythagoreanism by this device and others—centered on the doctrine of the *coincidentia oppositorum*—is likewise unprecedented, yet also calculated to fully Islamicize the Pythagorean project of the original Brethren of Purity (Ikhwān al-Ṣafāʾ), with whom he and his wide network of students strongly identified.[29]

Two passages suffice to show his Pythagoreanizing approach to lettrism as enshrined in his *R. al-Bāʾiyya*. From the *Book of investigations*:

> Although multiplicity is fully expressed by 9, which comprises the totality of its degrees, its power and virtue first erupt in 2: for only in 2 is multiplicity pure, untainted by any other "unitness" whether actually or through comprehensive ascription that, commixed, would make it 3, which does not concern us here. No other number has this property, since all other numbers have a merely relative, comprehensive unitness and unitive, uniting form, which is as distant as possible from the originary 1, which is yet intimately joined thereto.
>
> Twain is twain, and nothing but them remain:
> a true saying—or rather, the finest wine!
>
> *B* signifies this 2. It is the terminus of [numerical] relations and yet their very origin, as was discussed above. It is likewise that which combines firstness with coupling as the *coincidentia oppositorum* (*muʿtanaq al-*

origin of all insofar as it is a dot, which is the origin of all letterforms, as the author of [the *Book of the*] *Beloved* sings:

One dot became an *A* and *A* became all the letters
and so *A* occurs in each of their names.

Second, it is the point of return of all insofar as it is the cause of knowledge of its own characteristics and the source for distinguishing between all ambiguities. The consequence in this context is that *sacral power* refers to the origin of perception and witnessing of a one that is singular in its [expression of] true Oneness, just as the circumference of a circle is both point of origin and of return.

29 See, e.g., Melvin-Koushki, Matthew, "The New Brethren of Purity: Ibn Turka and the renaissance of Pythagoreanism in the early modern Persian cosmopolis," in *IHIW* 11 (2023), forthcoming. It must be noted, however, that Ḥaydar Āmulī does gesture in the same direction, twice citing Pythagoras by way of the Ikhwān al-Ṣafāʾ, albeit in passing; see Viengkhou, "Scripturalization of reality."

> *aḍdād*), one of the properties peculiar to the Prophet wherewith his heirs, "men of main and vision" [Q 38:45], provision themselves.[30]

And from *On the dot* (his imamophilic citation of ʿAlī is here significant):

> It will be clear to those who understand lettrist allusions that it is established on the pages of numerological analysis that *B* refers to the first entification, also known as the Muḥammadan Reality, this being clear by way of the connecting ties of correspondence. For the *coincidence of opposites* (*taʿānuq-i aṭrāf*)—one of the features that most distinguishes this exalted Presence, as has been sung:
>
> > For me opposites embrace, the rug of otherness
> > rolled away: all things are equal.[31]
> >
> > Devotedly, my lover closes a door she never opened,
> > cuts the cord of a friendship already severed.
> > Alas that her arrival that never happened never will!
> > Alack that she broke her false pledge!
>
> —becomes most explicit on this level and here is most realized, insofar as it is the level of *secondness*, and as such the closest possible to and hence ultimate level after the One, as discussed in [my *Book of*] *investigations*. This is a thing so evident as to not admit of the slightest doubt. Thus the dot beneath it refers to the true Oneness that is the occult aspect of that entification and its reality, which can be neither the referent of any statement nor the import of any allusion. For as the Commander [of the Faithful] himself said in his answer to the questions of Kumayl: "[Ultimate reality] is the revealing of the glories of [divine] Majesty [directly], without allusion."[32]

---

30 *Mafāḥiṣ*, 1.12, Tehran, MS Majlis 10196/2, ff. 62a–b. Ibn Turka clarifies in his *Risāla-yi Shaqq al-qamar wa-bayān-i sāʿat* that this category refers in the first place to the House of the Prophet (*ahl-i bayt*), including the Twelve Imams and their Sufi heirs. It is likewise significant that his fellow Timurid Sunni imamophile lettrist, Ḥusayn Vāʿiẓ Kāshifī, quotes from the *Mafāḥiṣ* verbatim precisely on the *B* in his own thoroughgoingly lettrist *Jawāhir al-tafsīr*. See Melvin-Koushki, *The quest* 264–266, 315–320.

31 Ibn Turka often cites this line (227) from Ibn al-Fāriḍ's (d. 632/1235) *al-Tāʾiyya al-kubrā*, famed as "The poem of the way" (*Naẓm al-sulūk*), on which he wrote a full, prosimetric commentary, *Sharḥ-i Naẓm al-durar*; see Melvin-Koushki, *The quest*, excursus.

32 Tehran, MS Majlis 10196/10, f. 125a.

Ibn Turka's most radical departure from Sufi lettrist precedent, however, is in his valorization of the written and mathematical letter over the spoken.[33] Mapping Ibn ʿArabī's cosmology onto contemporary social, political, and scientific reality, in which book culture defined scholarly accreditation and affiliation, and mathematical occult science was booming, he pursued imperial and scholarly objectives foreign to those of his esotericizing sources.

Most subversively, he recast lettrism in Illuminationist terms in order to formally displace both Peripatetic and Illuminationist philosophy as the supreme form of metaphysics. Ironically, however, his challenge to Illuminationism in particular only served to integrate lettrism into the same. Preeminent *ishrāqī* philosophers like Jalāl al-Dīn Davānī (d. 908/1502) and Mīr Dāmād (d. 1040/1631) influentially embraced Ibn Turka's lettrist metaphysics, which synthesizes the Avicennan-Ṭūsian doctrine of the transcendental modulation of being (*tashkīk al-wujūd*) with its Suhravardian upgrade, the transcendental modulation of light (*tashkīk al-nūr*), to produce his signature doctrine of the transcendental modulation of letter (*tashkīk al-ḥarf*): letters of light as uncreated, all-creative matrix of the cosmos, gradually descending from the One in extramental, mental, spoken, and finally written form. This doctrine is the most philosophically robust defense of the book and the book arts in Islamic intellectual history—and imperial architecture by extension. As I have argued, its Pythagorean project was most fully embodied in the design schemes of the Shaykh Luṭf Allāh Mosque in Isfahan, the new Safavid capital city itself and the Tāj Maḥal in Mughal Agra, those epitomes of the Timurid imperial mode.[34]

Ibn Turka's lettrist metaphysics-physics likewise served as a fitting preface to the 9th/15th-century boom in book culture and encyclopedism throughout the Islamic heartlands. Arabic and Persian manuals on a panoply of sciences—occult or otherwise—proliferated expressly as a means to relieve the reader of the need for a teacher. The era of *deep reading* had begun.[35] Exemplifying this new, early modern culture, his own Arabic and Persian manuals of

33 Here again, however, his departure does have Shiʿi precedent: Ḥaydar Āmulī and even Nāṣir-i Khusraw (d. 481/1088) both make a similar intervention, although less explicitly and systematically. See Mansouri, "*Walāya*"; Mansouri, *Spiritual hierarchy*. On the later Persianate reception of this revised lettrist hierarchy see, e.g., Cole, Juan, "The world as text: Cosmologies of Shaykh Ahmad al-Ahsa'i," in *SI* 80 (1994), 145–163, 145–146.

34 Melvin-Koushki, Matthew, "Of Islamic grammatology: Ibn Turka's lettrist metaphysics of light," in *al-ʿUṣūr al-Wusṭā* 24 (2016), 46–117.

35 El-Rouayheb, Khaled, "The rise of 'deep reading' in early modern Ottoman scholarly culture," in Sheldon Pollock, Benjamin A. Elman, and Kuming Kevin Chang (eds.), *World philology*, Cambridge, MA: Harvard University Press, 2015, 201–224.

lettrism, several of which enjoyed wide popularity across the Persianate world, are unprecedentedly user-friendly, designed to train their readers—especially royal readers—in the science.

With such works as the *R. al-Bāʾiyya* as precedent, the lettrist manuals produced during the 9th/15th and 10th/16th centuries are likewise accessible and systematic. They include those of the Aqquyunlu philosopher Davānī, the Timurid polymath Ḥusayn Vāʿiẓ Kāshifī (d. 910/1505) and his son ʿAlī Ṣafī (d. 939/1533). The latter's *Amulet of protection from the trials of time* (*Ḥirz al-amān min fitan al-zamān*), written for the Qizilbash governor of Khurasan, represents a summa of political lettrism; it became a bestseller during the high Safavid period, despite its dependence on Sunni authorities only—including Ibn Turka.[36] That his Sunni imamophilic brand of philosophical-scientific lettrism became a prime means of Shiʿizing Iran under the Safavids is best seen in the oeuvre of Maḥmūd Dihdār Shīrāzī (fl. 985/1576), the most prolific Persian author on applied lettrism of the 10th/16th century, and teacher in the occult sciences to Shaykh Bahāʾī (d. 1030/1621) himself, the sage-mage architect of the Safavid state. Similarly drawing on al-Būnī and Ibn ʿArabī by way of Āmulī and Ibn Turka, Dihdār's works are studded with theoretical mediations on the *B*, as in this passage from his Twelverizing prosimetric treatise *Unveiling secrets* (*Kashf al-asrār*), in encomium to the First Imam:

> For ʿAlī (*ʿLY* = 110 > 11 > 2 > *B*) is two 1s as shown by this *B*
> whose dot manifests therefrom.
> When the two 1s are properly joined
> they become wholly one in form:
> any who beholds its form
> must immediately count it the letter *B*,
> for the dot beneath it
> removes the veil of that letter.
> How wondrous to witness this—
> these two manifesting in existence as one!
> Two become one to manifest two 1s,
> thereby moving multiplicity to unveil herself.
> Oneness sits veiled in the *A*
> while manyness shows her face in the *B*—

36 Subtelny, Maria, "Kāshifī's *Asrār-i qāsimī*: A late Timurid manual of the occult sciences and its Safavid afterlife," in Liana Saif et al. (eds.), *Islamicate occult sciences in theory and practice*, Leiden: Brill, 2020, 267–313; Melvin-Koushki, *The quest* 248–280.

yet it is the dot that is [primordial] Oneness
that manifests so mightily to distinguish the *B*![37]

Dihdār's thoroughgoingly lettrist project does much to explain the status of Safavid philosophers like Ghiyās̱ al-Dīn Manṣūr Dashtakī (d. 949/1542) and Shaykh Bahāʾī as master talismanists in service to the Safavid Empire, as well as the transformation of Ibn Sīnā (d. 428/1037) himself—no booster of the occult sciences—into a Pythagoreanizing occultist in the early 11th/17th century. It is likewise largely responsible for the sudden explosion in popularity of Rajab al-Bursī's (d. after 813/1411) *Dawnings of the lights of certain knowledge* (*Mashāriq anwār al-yaqīn*), a controversial work that, for all its Twelver theological extremism, draws on the same Akbarian lettrist lineage.[38]

That Ibn Turka's lettrism successfully entered the Persianate philosophical mainstream is best seen in the oeuvre of Mīr Dāmād, which features no less than three lettrist works. Chief among them is *Firebrands and epiphanies* (*Jaẕavāt va-mavāqīt*), an ornate Persian summary of his Illuminationist philosophy as a whole, commissioned by Shāh ʿAbbās the Great (r. 995–1038/1587–1629). By contrast, his Arabic *Lamp of illumination and keeping the balance* (*Nibrās al-ḍiyāʾ wa-taswāʾ al-sawāʾ*) is focused on a thorny Twelver theological problem, the question of apparent change in the divine will (*badāʾ*): it deploys lettrist theory as the best means of riddling his signature doctrine of perpetual creation or meta-time (*ḥudūth dahrī*), which he proposed as a new philosophy of history. (This proposal was directly inspired by Ibn Turka's own promotion of a new Pythagorean imperial historiography, enshrined in the *Book of conquest* (*Ẓafar-nāma*) of Sharaf al-Dīn ʿAlī Yazdī (d. 858/1454), his closest friend and student. Combining lettrism and conjunction astrology, it became a model for persophone historians down to the colonial period. Its basic premise: history can be a *science*[39]). Here Mīr Dāmād's succinct treatment of the *B*—that engine of creation—characteristically reframes the ontological function of this letter in Avicennan-Illuminationist terms:

---

37 Tehran, MS Millī 12653/4, ff. 152^{a-b}.

38 Subtelny, "Kāshifī's *Asrār-i qāsimī*"; Lawson, Todd, "A 14th century Shiʿi gnostic: Rajab Bursī and his *Mashāriq al-anwār*," in *Ishraq: Islamic Philosophy Yearbook* 1 (2010), 422–438; Melvin-Koushki, Matthew, "World as (Arabic) text: Mīr Dāmād and the Neopythagoreanization of philosophy in Safavid Iran," in *SI* 114.3 (2019), 130–183; Melvin-Koushki, "Maḥmud Dehdār Širāzi," *EIr*.

39 On this new classificatory ethos more generally, peculiar to 9th/15th-century Persian and Arabic historiography, see Markiewicz, Christopher, "History as science: The fifteenth-century debate in Arabic and Persian," in *Journal of Early Modern History* 21 (2017), 216–240.

> The degree of *B* is the spirit of twoness: it is the mate of the first and first of the repetitions of oneness. Its written form as ب is the first permutation and self-manifestation of ا, leading back thereto in its degree of precision, the supreme form of explication. As such, this letter was designated that of the realm of the intellect, indeed the First Intellect itself, chief of all things created. It is likewise the first of seconds, the Supreme Pen, the Right Hand—and the two extended hands of the All-merciful (whose power is exalted) are both right.
>
> That its essence is at base the coupling of separating multiplicity and the doubling of the bond that is "the marriage act between all atoms"—as is signified in the holy revelation by the Most High's saying "And of everything We created pairs, that haply you may remember" [Q 51:49]—can only be understood according to two senses, potential or actual, whereby the essential freedom of the substance of the essence (*dhāt*) itself becomes constrained by the other with respect to the actual effluxion of the doer; according to two degrees, quiddity (*māhiyya*) or quoddity (*inniyya*); and according to two respects, genus or species, which twain constitute a quiddity, whose Creator is the Constituter (His mention be glorious) through His own essence, which is exclusive Oneness (*aḥadiyya*)—sole Actor and end of all action, Origin and Return, First and Last.[40]

Space does not allow us to follow the many further iterations and evolutions of Ibn ʿArabian, Ḥamūyan, Būnian, and Ibn Turkian lettrist theory on the *B* after the 11th/17th century; suffice it to say that, in Iran alone, the Shaykhiyya and Bābī and Bahāʾī movements of the 19th century were all profoundly lettrist and indeed often talismanic in tenor.[41] What the above examples show, however, is the remarkable degree to which Ibn Turka succeeded in making lettrist metaphysics and physics philosophically coherent and scientifically and politically usable over the long term.

This he did in the teeth of inquisition and intrigue, as the present treatise's preface attests. It was written to combat the "baseless constructs and devious

40 Mīr Dāmād, *Nibrās al-ḍiyāʾ wa-taswāʾ al-sawāʾ fī sharḥ bāb al-badāʾ wa-ithbāt jadwā l-duʿāʾ*, with glosses by Mullā ʿAlī Nūrī, ed. Ḥāmid Nājī Iṣfahānī, Tehran: Hijrat, 1995, 81–82; see Terrier, Mathieu, "The wisdom of God and the tragedy of history: The concept of appearance (*badāʾ*) in Mīr Dāmād's *Lantern of brightness*," in Saiyad Nizamuddin Ahmad and Sajjad H. Rizvi (eds.), *Philosophy and the intellectual life in Shīʿah Islam*, London: The Shīʿah Institute Press, 2017, 94–133; Melvin-Koushki, "World as (Arabic) text."

41 For references see Melvin-Koushki, *The quest* 280–281.

propagandizing" of the contemporary Sufi Ḥurūfiyya movement in particular, whose anti-Timurid anarchism threatened his life's project. Its longer-lived Nuqṭavī offshoot represented a similar threat.[42] At the same time, such movements reflected the new salience of lettrism among scholarly and political elites and the general populace alike throughout the early modern Persianate world, for whom Ibn Turka's theory of the letter as light and light as being simply made cultural and cosmogonical sense.[43]

3 Ibn Turka, Imperialist-Empiricist Philosopher of Akbarian Jazz

The first modern scholars to recognize the centrality of lettrism to Ibn Turka's life's project, Professor Muḥammad-Taqī Dānishpazhūh (d. 1996) and Ayatollah Sayyid ʿAlī Mūsawī Bihbahānī (d. 1975), made a strong case for his importance within the history of Western philosophy, and hence the need to finally edit and publish his oeuvre.[44] Dānishpazhūh even styled him the "Spinoza of Iran" to jumpstart research on this front. This presentation of one of Ibn Turka's minor lettrist treatises is in modest answer to their call. But he was hardly a Spinoza (d. 1677), putative father of biblical criticism.

While certainly a monist in the Akbarian mode, Ibn Turka was no Quranic critic. To the contrary, he vehemently championed the Quran as blueprint for reality, departing, sometimes radically, from philosophical and mystical precedent in his systematic reformulation of lettrism as a simultaneously Pythagorean and ʿAlid universal science—and technology of universal empire. As such, he is comparable instead to the infamous Anglo-Welsh occultist John

42 See, e.g., Bashir, Shahzad, *Fazlallah Astarabadi and the Hurufis*, Oxford: Oneworld, 2005; Mir-Kasimov, Orkhan, *Words of power: Ḥurūfī teachings between Shiʿism and Sufism in medieval Islam. The original doctrine of Faḍl Allāh Astarābādī*, London: I.B. Tauris/Institute of Ismaili Studies, 2015; Babayan, Kathryn, *Mystics, monarchs and messiahs: Cultural landscapes of early modern Iran*, Cambridge, MA: Harvard University Press, 2002; Kiyā, Ṣādiq, *Nuqṭaviyān yā Pasīkhāniyān*, Tehran: Anjuman-i Īrānvīj, 1941. As Uy observes, however, the even more radical Ḥurūfī embrace of sheer linguistic *play* can be seen as an organic continuation of Ḥamūya's project as well (*Lost in a sea of letters* 223).

43 That this "lettrist consciousness" permeated the Persianate world even through the colonial and reformist period is suggested by Pickett, James, *Polymaths of Islam: Power and networks of knowledge in Central Asia*, Ithaca: Cornell University Press, 2020; Morgan, Daniel J., *Spokesman of the unseen world: Shāh Walī Allāh (1703–1762), Islamic reform and applied cosmology in late-Mughal Delhi*, Chicago (PhD Diss.): University of Chicago, 2021; Zadeh, Travis, *Wonders and rarities: The marvelous book that traveled the world and mapped the cosmos*, Cambridge, MA: Harvard University Press (forthcoming).

44 For references see Melvin-Koushki, *The quest* 21.

Dee (d. 1608), model of Faust, who sought to weaponize Cusanus's *coincidentia oppositorum* for similarly imperial-scientific, kabbalist-alchemical purposes.[45]

In broader Western intellectual-historical terms, his project is likewise reminiscent of those of other, far better studied Latin Christian scholars, like Pico and Giordano Bruno (d. 1600), and Jewish ones, like Alemanno, kabbalists to a man: they too called for the investigation of the world as another mathematical-linguistic scripture.[46] But none of them served sovereigns of the caliber of Ulugh Beg (r. 811–853/1409–1449), the most famous sultan-scientist in Islamic history, whose Samarkand Observatory—founded the same year, 823/1420, that Ibn Turka completed his *Book of investigations*—produced the most accurate star tables of the 9th/15th century, so accurate that they were still being used in London in the 19th. This epochal push for mathematical precision in astronomy has not a little to do with Ibn Turka's dedication to Ulugh Beg of his book-length lettrist analysis of the *basmala*, whose preface explicitly fashions him as saint-philosopher-king in Akbarian, Alexandrian, Platonic, and Solomonic terms, and which dwells at greater length on the *B* as cosmogonic agent.[47]

Perhaps, then, we should begin to read celebrated kabbalists like Pico, Alemanno, Dee, and Bruno—philosophers of jazz—as Jewish or Christian Ibn Turkas. Their synthesizing, creative, subversive, and indelibly Pythagorean meditations on the Arabic, Hebrew, and Greek letter *B* are at the heart of Western metaphysics and physics alike, and deserve comparative investigation by historians of science, empire, and the book as such.

4 Note on the Text

The *R. al-Bāʾiyya* is preserved in Iran in two known manuscripts: Tehran, MS Majlis 10196/13, ff. 122b–124a, copied in 828/1425 from a comprehensive *majmūʿa* of Ibn Turka's works most likely copied by Sharaf al-Dīn ʿAlī Yazdī himself, and wholly reliable and authoritative; and Tehran, MS Sipahsālār 2930/1, ff. 1b–6a, copied in 845/1441 from another, less comprehensive collection of

45 Melvin-Koushki, "The New Brethren."

46 See, e.g., Killeen, Kevin and Peter J. Forshaw (eds.), *The word and the world: Biblical exegesis and early Modern science*, Basingstoke: Palgrave Macmillan, 2007; Håkansson, Håkan, *Seeing the word: John Dee and renaissance occultism*, Lund: Lund University Press, 2001; de León-Jones, Karen Silvia, *Giordano Bruno and the Kabbalah: Prophets, magicians, and rabbis*, New Haven: Yale University Press, 1997; Ogren, *The beginning of the world.*

47 Melvin-Koushki, "The New Brethren."

Ibn Turka's works. Since the latter manuscript has unfortunately been stolen in the meantime, as I found to my alarm when on site, the translation below is based on my edition of the Majlis 10196 copy, for which see my forthcoming *The lettrist treatises of Ibn Turka*. Stylistically, that this treatise is in Arabic makes it more technical and less prosimetrical than its Persian counterparts in the author's oeuvre, following his general procedure. As such, its ten sections are titled according to the epistemic and generic scheme organizing the *Mafāḥiṣ*, according to the pattern "*wajh*^{un} x *fī naẓm*^{in} x." Thus, for example, section 5: *wajh ḥisābī fī naẓm dhawqī*, "a calculative aspect as to direct experience."

∴

***On the* B (ب)**
In the name of God, All-merciful, Ever-merciful.

After rendering praise to God, Lord of all creatures and Creator of His intimates among those who ponder the evidence of His manifest signs, and after invoking His blessings upon him in whose niche of prophetical Sealhood and through whose perfect words appeared that which was hidden of the supernal realities from out their letter coverts, and upon his House and Companions, guides on the paths of certitude by means of their rational arguments and experiential allusions:

I chanced to meet an individual free of the vice of status-seeking whose noble aspiration impelled him to seek beyond merely posited significations and their circumscribed, improvised nutriment, which cannot satiate one's hunger on the quest for the meaning of celestial revelations and revelatory written forms; he asked me as to why the letter *B* opens the holy Quran and the nature of the characteristics it exclusively enjoys among the other letters which give it this precedence. I was initially hesitant to offer them my views on the subject given the intensity of his desire and the little I had to offer in the marketplace of composition—but then I came across the teachings of certain Sufis on the *B* that are detestable to any seeking guidance, given their use of baseless constructs and devious propagandizing, utterly devoid of edificatory value. The exigency of the moment therefore prompted me to give him but a taste of the various ripe fruits of the age pendulous on its highest branches and as yet unpicked.

Let me therefore present the matter in such a way as to be recognizable to those accustomed to the exoteric approach of the acquired, incremental sciences, thereby allowing those students with pure souls and quick minds to understand it:

The principles that inform the science of letters, despite the clarity of its method and the reliability of its arguments, appear recondite to most people. This is because the All-wise and All-knowing (whose wisdom is exalted) has distracted them from an evaluation of these principles in order to preserve the dignity of His inviolable might and out of solicitude for the majesty of His work, until time issues forth with the battle-standards of His rule.

[Now these principles are as follows:]

1. *A sapiential aspect as to the nature of Arabic*

Know that the letters have [certain natural] divisions that reveal those aspects which they share and in which they are distinct from one another. It is therefore necessary when plumbing their real meanings—which are free from the mediation of any artificial designation or positing by a designator or transmitter—to inquire into these aspects. For these meanings and the understanding of the same can only obtain from the letters themselves, whence the necessity of investigating the various aspects of their correspondences and characteristics essential to each letter individually according to the three forms they possess, from their points of articulation in manifestation to the disclosures of knowledge and perception, as has been shown at length elsewhere. What is clear [for our purposes here], however, is that this cannot be achieved without invoking the letters' abovementioned shared and distinguishing aspects, the former clarifying their [unitive] source in reality and the latter revealing their specific property according to how they may be used within the context of these divisions, both in the most explicit way possible. The purpose of my discourse having impelled me to instruct and inform [the reader] in a comprehensible way, I shall begin with [a list of] most of these aspects according to these divisions, rendering them the basis of our investigation here.

Thus: The letters include some that have an independent signification in common usage, this by way of convention, like *S* and *M*. Others have no such signification, except in compound with another [letter] of their namewords, like ʿ and *Ṣ*. First among the latter are those that only have this at the beginning of their namewords, like *B* and *S*. Others have it only at their end, like *H*. Still others have it only in their middle, like *Y* and *T*. Finally, there are the letters [whose namewords] have this signification completely, whether beginning, end, or middle, like *A*.

This principle being established, know that whatever has such a perfected terminus will have it arranged accordingly in those positions where it can occur. Such a position wherein [the letter] is enabled to achieve its terminal perfection requires its primordial reality and stronghold of essential receptivity, as with, for example, *B* and *S*, whose terminal perfection signifies [spiritual] meanings, which become most manifest when they initiate words and phrases.[48] As such, their primordial receptivity requires preeminence and firstness. The *B*, however, has a further signification as to how all things began—hence its being singled out to open the known [Quranic] text.

2. *A sapiential aspect as to inductive reasoning*

There is no offspring in the realms of contingency that is born and manifests on the pages of stripe and engendered being but that it is preceded by two parents or two premises, or the like among the various expressions of opposition according to the opposition of expressions. This is what is technically referred to as *the marriage act pervading all atoms*. From this it is manifest that duality has precedence over everything in natural terms, since it is not possible for a thing to manifest, whether epistemologically or essentially, without its being preceded by duality. It is precisely this that is the meaning form of the *B*, which has precedence as such.

3. *A discursive aspect as to direct experience*

Among the categorizations revealing aspects of the particular characteristics of the letters is that dividing them into *high [letters] of light*, which are those revealed by their own names in separate fashion at the beginning of the Quranic Sūras relating to the Sealing of prophethood, and *low [letters] of darkness*, which are those revealed only according to their referents in the constructions and words [of normal language]; both divisions are equal in number and balance each other as opposites.[49] [By this principle], it is clear that the *A* has preeminence within the first group, while *B* has preeminence in the second, and so is perfectly fitted to open the written and arranged [Quran] that people are familiar with.

But you may ask: How can it be fitting for a dark [letter] to open [the Quran] rather than a light one, given the latter's special association with transcendent holiness and nobility?

I answer: In the written Quran circulating among the public in book form are two orders of arrangement. The first is the primordial, holy, revelatory one, according to which He originally revealed it to His servant the Seal (God bless and keep him), who himself said that the first [verse] to be revealed to him was

---

48 Note that *B* opens the Quran and *S* closes it. By contrast, the Torah, which also opens with *B*, closes with *L*; these letters reversed give the word *lev* (= Ar. *lubb*), 'heart,' the focus of much kabbalistic speculation.

49 That is, the light letters are the *muqaṭṭaʿāt*, representing half the Arabic alphabet, and the dark letters the remaining half.

the saying of the Most High “Read (*iqra’* = *AQR’*) in the name of your Lord Who created!” [Q 96:1]. The second is arbitrary, conventional, and intermixed, and is that agreed upon by the Companions during the tenure of ʿUthmān (God be pleased with him); its order was determined according to the lower letters. It is therefore clear that the order of the written [text of the Quran] that people are familiar with is the second one, and so the only letter fit to open it is the *B*—the same principle being likewise operative in the first order as to the preeminence of [the *A*, the letter] that was commanded to be recited at the very first.

4. *A verbal aspect as to exhortation*

The letters have another categorization, that according to their respective points of articulation. They include the labial [letters], which manifest from that point exclusively; the faucal-glottal, which manifest from that point; and the middling, which are uvular to dental. Among these divisions, the most manifest is of course the labial, especially when combined with a long vowel, as may be seen with the *B* (*bā’*). Now it is clear that the fundamental point of the [Quranic text as so] written and arranged is to communicate and to manifest, nothing else—and foremost among all the letters competing for preeminence on the racecourse of making-manifest is the *B*, as you have been apprised; it wins that race.

5. *A calculative aspect as to direct experience*

The *second* [of anything] that is specifically described as such always refers to the *first* [of the same], which is what makes it second. This principle being established, it is evident that the *B* (= 2), for all that it refers to the Origin in the same way as all the other letters, at least in its external aural form—for speech as such necessarily presupposes a speaker—possesses a further indication of the Origin in its mental, [that is, mathematical,] form, complementing its external aural and visual forms. As such, the *B* contains within it [not just one but] two gates onto the first principle, unlike all the other letters, which makes it worthy of preeminence in the Speech of the Guide: for “God speaks the truth and He guides on the way” [Q 33:4].

6. *A written aspect as to direct experience*

Among the categorizations that explicate the realities of all the letters is that based on their dottedness: is their associated dot manifest or occult, above or below, and single or multiple? Now the dot is the form of distinguishing entification and the aspect of engendered existence; every letter therefore concentrates it, manifesting with it, making it singular, encompassing it, incorporating it into its own existential reality. Thus [the letter] becomes perfect in its ability to refer to that desired as a necessary consequence of the manifestation of the aspects of correspondence between signifier and signified.

It is evident that the *B* comprises these aspects, unique [among the letters] in its placement of the dot below it, a single one. For as it has been said [by ʿAlī himself]: "*I am the dot beneath the* B."[50] It is precisely the lower placement of the dot and hence the occultation of its properties that allows the letter to refer to absolute all-comprehensiveness [preceding delimited manifestation], of which there is no external form more perfect than the Quranic revelation. It is likewise evident that whatever letters are most explicit in their significations must be given precedence for the purposes of instruction and clarification—hence the precedence of the *B*.

7. *Another written aspect in sapiential terms*

Among the categorizations pertaining to the letter is that based on the [direction of] movement when writing it, which is the source of its manifestation. Some letters are produced by a descending, [vertical] motion of the pen from high to low, like *A* (ا), while others are produced by an extending, [horizontal] motion from right to left or the reverse. (This is the subset of this categorization that will concern us here; a full account of the various categorizations in all their significations may be found in [my *Book of*] *investigations*.) Supreme among the extending letters is the *B*.

Now the Quranic revelation, from the dawning horizon of its glad tidings to the noon terminus of its commands and the exposition of the figures of its lines, has various levels, whether general ones concerned with knowledge or differentiating ones concerned with revelation. [As that may be], all its levels were perfected through its manifestation to His servant Muḥammad (God bless and keep him). And it has further levels, to wit, those concerned with *extension*, given [his charge to] manifest and communicate it to all peoples. The most perfect and most manifest of all its levels among the general populace is the [Quranic] text as spoken and written, the one familiar to people. It is therefore necessary that [that letter] possessing precedence and preeminence in the [Quranic] text have supremacy in terms of extension, this in order to facilitate its communication and act as an instructive guide on the path. Hence it is necessary that the *B* open this text in its role as the most extended of the extensive letters.

50 That Ibn Turka, departing from Ibn ʿArabī, attributes this saying to Imam ʿAlī, may be inferred from his analysis of the same in *R. Nuqṭa*.

8. *A written aspect in mental terms*
When the descending motion whereby the *A* manifests is combined with the extending motion whereby the *B* manifests, their combination produces the *L*, which is the perfection of the revelation: for *ALM* has preeminence at the level of revelation. Given that the *L* is the most general expression of this form, and that the station of its textual recording and instructional arrangement requires differentiation whereby it may be distinguished, the *B* was made to open [the Quranic text], since it is the differentiating form of the *L*. Therefore do you see its form as fully spelled out to be the heart of the form of the *L*:

FIGURE 9.2
B as *L*

9. *A mental aspect as to exhortation*
It is evident from the above aspect that the father [or progenitor] takes precedence with respect to differentiating manifestation. But the precedence of the *L* has to do with the general and still occult [aspect] of the same. For as it has been sung:

> My mother birthed my father—
> a marvel among marvels![51]

The first characteristic is possessed rather by the *B*, and the latter by the *M*. Therefore just as the *M* takes precedence over its two brothers at the level of general revelation, so too does the *B* take precedence at the level of differentiating textualization, in accordance with the principle of the balancing of opposites, as will be evident to the intelligent.

10. *Another mental aspect as to calculation*
The realities either pertain to the multiplicity of the [divine] Names or to the essential [divine] Oneness; there are no other poles than these two that may be signified or indicated. Now it is evident that the terminus of multiplicity is the *A*, in the same way that the form of Oneness is 1. As for the *B*, some of its simpler occult folds signify both of these poles, and it so merits precedence whenever the discourse relates to communication and instruction: for giving precedence to the general significance of what is intended is here required, as is evident.

51 This line is variously attributed to al-Ḥallāj or Imam ʿAlī.

As to how it signifies this, it is immediately evident upon the calculation of the name of its numerical value in clear Arabic, as may be seen from the following figures:

FIGURE 9.3
The value of the word "two"

11. *A further mental aspect as to calculation*
The *A*, which has precedence in every [other] comprehensive or specific arrangement, has a general form, which is that of its referent, as well as other distinguishing and differentiating forms according to the differentiation of its aspects, whether manifest or occult. The first of these forms is therefore *A* (= 1), whose very form expresses its signified; among its forms that reveal its reality is [the Quranic construction] *In the name of* (بسم), [wherein the *A* is elided]. Thus you see its division by 2 and its multiplication by 2 resulting in the same [equation], which is the [mathematical] relationship that best shows the nature of its object and is operative in all its parts; this is because the same relationship is one of likeness and similitude, which does not give onto any aspect of ambiguity with respect the subject of its likeness, as is evident. Whoever wishes for a proof testifying to this principle, let him consider these figures:

FIGURE 9.4
The values of *A* and of *A* plus 1, which equals *In the name of*

Let this be the final point I raise in this treatise as to the aspects of the letters. May God Most High increase us in awareness of the intricate occult folds of the [Quranic] verses and grant us success in explicating such occult matters—this through the sanctity of him whose noble name has sealed the treasurehouses of perfection, Muḥammad, God bless and keep him and all his House.

Completed on 14 Ramadan 828 [8 August 1425].

Bibliography

Acevedo, Juan, *Alphanumeric cosmology from Greek into Arabic: The idea of* Stoicheia *through the medieval Mediterranean*, Tübingen: Mohr Siebeck, 2020.

Albertson, David, *Mathematical theologies: Nicholas of Cusa and the legacy of Thierry of Chartres*, Oxford: Oxford University Press, 2014.

Alexandrin, Elizabeth R., "Seals and sealing of *walāyah* in Ṣūfī and Shīʿī texts: The cases of al-Ḥakīm al-Tirmidhī and Saʿd al-Dīn Ḥamūyah," in Saiyad Nizamuddin Ahmad and Sajjad H. Rizvi (eds.), *Philosophy and the intellectual life in Shīʿah Islam*, London: The Shīʿah Institute Press, 2017, 69–93.

Babayan, Kathryn, *Mystics, monarchs and messiahs: Cultural landscapes of early modern Iran*, Cambridge, MA: Harvard University Press, 2002.

Banner, Nicholas, *Philosophic silence and the 'One' in Plotinus*, Cambridge: Cambridge University Press, 2018.

Bashir, Shahzad, *Fazlallah Astarabadi and the Hurufis*, Oxford: Oneworld, 2005.

Bellver, José, "The beginnings of rational theology in al-Andalus: Ibn Masarra and his refutation of al-Kindī's *On first philosophy*," in *Qanṭara* 41.2 (2020), 323–371.

Böwering, Gerhard, "Sulamī's treatise on the science of the letters (*ʿilm al-ḥurūf*)," in Bilal Orfali (ed.), *In the shadow of Arabic: The centrality of language to Arabic culture. Studies presented to Ramzi Baalbaki on the occasion of his sixtieth birthday*, Leiden: Brill, 2011, 339–397.

Casewit, Yousef, *The mystics of al-Andalus: Ibn Barrajān and Islamic thought in the twelfth century*, Cambridge: Cambridge University Press, 2017.

Chittick, William C., *The Sufi path of knowledge: Ibn al-ʿArabī's metaphysics of imagination*, Albany, NY: SUNY Press, 1989.

Chittick, William C., *The self-disclosure of God: Principles of Ibn al-ʿArabī's cosmology*, Albany, NY: SUNY Press, 1998.

Chittick, William C., *Ibn ʿArabi: Heir to the prophets*, Oxford: Oneworld, 2005.

Cole, Juan, "The world as text: Cosmologies of Shaykh Ahmad al-Ahsaʾi," in *SI* 80 (1994), 145–163.

Coulon, Jean-Charles, *La magie islamique et le corpus bunianum au Moyen Âge*, 4 vols., Paris (PhD Diss.): University of Paris IV—Sorbonne, 2013.

de León-Jones, Karen Silvia, *Giordano Bruno and the Kabbalah: Prophets, magicians, and rabbis*, New Haven: Yale University Press, 1997.

Dihdār Shīrāzī, Maḥmūd, *Kashf al-asrār*, Tehran, MS Millī 12653/4, ff. 140b–160b.

Ebstein, Michael, *Mysticism and philosophy in al-Andalus: Ibn Masarra, Ibn al-ʿArabī and the Ismāʿīlī tradition*, Leiden: Brill, 2014.

Elmore, Gerald T., *Islamic sainthood in the fullness of time: Ibn al-ʿArabī's* Book of the fabulous gryphon, Leiden: Brill, 1999.

El-Rouayheb, Khaled, "The rise of 'deep reading' in early modern Ottoman scholarly culture," in Sheldon Pollock, Benjamin A. Elman, and Kuming Kevin Chang (eds.), *World philology*, Cambridge, MA: Harvard University Press, 2015, 201–224.

Gardiner, Noah D., *Esotericism in a manuscript culture: Aḥmad al-Būnī and his readers through the Mamlūk period*, Ann Arbor (PhD Diss.): University of Michigan, 2014.

Gardiner, Noah D., "The occultist encyclopedism of ʿAbd al-Raḥmān al-Bisṭāmī," in *MSR* 20 (2017), 3–38.

Garrido Clemente, Pilar, "The science of letters in Ibn Masarra: Unified word, unified world," in *Journal of the Muhyiddin Ibn ʿArabi Society* 47 (2010), 47–61.

Gril, Denis, "The science of letters," in Muḥyī al-Dīn Ibn al-ʿArabī, *The Meccan revelations*, ed. Michel Chodkiewicz, trans. Cyrille Chodkiewicz and Denis Gril, 2 vols., ii, New York: Pir Press, 2004, 105–219.

Håkansson, Håkan, *Seeing the word: John Dee and renaissance occultism*, Lund: Lund University Press, 2001.

Ibn al-ʿArabī, Muḥyī al-Dīn, *The openings revealed in Makkah* (al-Futūḥāt al-Makkīyah)*: Books 1 and 2*, trans. Eric Winkel, New York: Pir Press, 2018.

Ibn Turka, Ṣāʾin al-Dīn ʿAlī, *Kitāb al-Mafāḥiṣ*, Tehran, MS Majlis 10196/2, ff. 52–118.

Ibn Turka, Ṣāʾin al-Dīn ʿAlī, *Risāla-yi Nuqṭa*, Tehran, MS Majlis 10196/10, ff. 124^b–126^a.

Ingalls, Matthew B., *The anonymity of a commentator: Zakariyyā al-Anṣārī and the rhetoric of Muslim commentaries*, Albany, NY: SUNY Press, 2021.

Killeen, Kevin and Peter J. Forshaw (eds.), *The word and the world: Biblical exegesis and early modern science*, Basingstoke: Palgrave Macmillan, 2007.

Kiyā, Ṣādiq, *Nuqṭawiyān yā Pasīkhāniyān*, Tehran: Anjuman-i Īrānwīj, 1941.

Lawson, Todd, "A 14th century Shiʿi gnostic: Rajab Bursī and his *Mashāriq al-anwār*," in *Ishraq: Islamic Philosophy Yearbook* 1 (2010), 422–438.

Mansouri, Mohammad Amin, "*Walāya* between lettrism and astrology: The occult mysticism of Sayyid Ḥaydar Āmulī (d. c. 787/1385)," in *Journal of Sufi Studies* 9.2 (2020), 161–201.

Mansouri, Mohammad Amin, *Spiritual hierarchy: Reading ʿAzīz Nasafī in his Sufi, Ismaili and occult milieus*, Toronto (PhD Diss.): University of Toronto, 2022.

Markiewicz, Christopher, "History as science: The fifteenth-century debate in Arabic and Persian," in *Journal of Early Modern History* 21 (2017), 216–240.

Melvin-Koushki, Matthew, "Maḥmud Dehdār Širāzi," in *EIr.*

Melvin-Koushki, Matthew, *The quest for a universal science: The occult philosophy of Ṣāʾin al-Dīn Turka Iṣfahānī (1369–1432) and intellectual millenarianism in early Timurid Iran*, New Haven (PhD Diss.): Yale University, 2012.

Melvin-Koushki, Matthew, "Of Islamic grammatology: Ibn Turka's lettrist metaphysics of light," in *al-ʿUṣūr al-Wusṭā* 24 (2016), 46–117.

Melvin-Koushki, Matthew, "Powers of One: The mathematicalization of the occult sciences in the High Persianate tradition," in *IHIW* 5.1 (2017), 127–199.

Melvin-Koushki, Matthew, "Early modern Islamicate empire: New forms of religiopolitical legitimacy," in Armando Salvatore et al. (eds.), *The Wiley-Blackwell history of Islam*, Hoboken: Wiley-Blackwell, 2018, 353–375.

Melvin-Koushki, Matthew, "*Taḥqīq* vs. *taqlīd* in the renaissances of Western early modernity," in *Philological Encounters* 3.1 (2018), 193–249.

Melvin-Koushki, Matthew, "World as (Arabic) text: Mīr Dāmād and the Neopythagoreanization of philosophy in Safavid Iran," in *SI* 114.3 (2019), 130–183.

Melvin-Koushki, Matthew, "The New Brethren of Purity: Ibn Turka and the renaissance of Pythagoreanism in the early modern Persian cosmopolis," in *IHIW* 11 (2023), forthcoming.

Melvin-Koushki, Matthew, *The lettrist treatises of Ibn Turka: Reading and writing the cosmos in the Timurid renaissance*, Leiden: Brill (forthcoming).

Mīr Dāmād, *Nibrās al-ḍiyāʾ wa-taswāʾ al-sawāʾ fī sharḥ bāb al-badāʾ wa-ithbāt jadwā l-duʿāʾ*, with glosses by Mullā ʿAlī Nūrī, ed. Ḥāmid Nājī Iṣfahānī, Tehran: Hijrat, 1995.

Mir-Kasimov, Orkhan, *Words of power: Ḥurūfī teachings between Shiʿism and Sufism in medieval Islam. The original doctrine of Faḍl Allāh Astarābādī*, London: I.B. Tauris/Institute of Ismaili Studies, 2015.

Morgan, Daniel J., *Spokesman of the unseen world: Shāh Walī Allāh (1703–1762), Islamic reform and applied cosmology in late-Mughal Delhi*, Chicago (PhD Diss.): University of Chicago, 2021.

Murata, Sachiko, *The Tao of Islam: A sourcebook on gender relationships in Islamic thought*, Albany, NY: SUNY Press, 1992.

Ogren, Brian, *The beginning of the world in renaissance Jewish thought:* Ma'aseh Bereshit *in Italian Jewish philosophy and Kabbalah, 1492–1535*, Leiden: Brill, 2016.

Pickett, James, *Polymaths of Islam: Power and networks of knowledge in Central Asia*, Ithaca: Cornell University Press, 2020.

Ramshaw, Sara, *Justice as improvisation: The law of the extempore*, New York: Routledge, 2013.

Rašić, Dunja, *The written world of God: The cosmic script and the art of Ibn ʿArabī*, Oxford: Anqa Publishing, 2021.

Subtelny, Maria, "Kāshifī's *Asrār-i qāsimī*: A late Timurid manual of the occult sciences and its Safavid afterlife," in Liana Saif et al. (eds.), *Islamicate occult sciences in theory and practice*, Leiden: Brill, 2020, 267–313.

Terrier, Mathieu, "The wisdom of God and the tragedy of history: The concept of appearance (*badāʾ*) in Mīr Dāmād's Lantern of brightness," in Saiyad Nizamuddin Ahmad and Sajjad H. Rizvi (eds.), *Philosophy and the intellectual life in Shīʿah Islam*, London: The Shīʿah Institute Press, 2017, 94–133.

Uy II, Cyril V., *Lost in a sea of letters: Saʿd al-Dīn Ḥamūya (d. 1252) and the plurality of Sufi knowledge*, Providence (PhD Diss.): Brown University, 2021.

Viengkhou, Aaron, "Sayyid Ḥaydar Āmulī's scripturalization of reality," in *IOSOTR*, http://islamicoccult.org/aaron_viengkhou (last accessed: 25 October 2021).

Viengkhou, Aaron, "*Tawḥīd* divided: The esoteric orthodoxy of Sayyid Ḥaydar Āmulī (d. after 782/1380)," in *La Rosa di Paracelso* 2 (2020 [2022]), 27–51.

Walbridge, John, *The leaven of the ancients: Suhrawardī and the heritage of the Greeks*, Albany, NY: SUNY Press, 2000.

Winters, Zach, "Reading the Book of Creation in the *Miftāḥ al-Asrār* of Āẕarī Isfarāyinī," in *La Rosa di Paracelso* 2 (2020 [2022]), 13–25.

Wolfson, Elliot R., *Alef, mem, tau: Kabbalistic musings on time, truth, and death*, Berkeley: University of California Press, 2006.

Zadeh, Travis, *Wonders and rarities: The marvelous book that traveled the world and mapped the cosmos*, Cambridge, MA: Harvard University Press, 2023.

CHAPTER 10

Jāmī and the Wine of Love: Akbarian Sparks of Divine Light

Marlene DuBois

The Arabic poem *Khamriyya* (*Wine ode*) of Ibn al-Fāriḍ (d. 632/1235) also known as the *Mīmiyya* (poem rhyming with the letter *m*), has been much discussed in the Islamic world and has 25 surviving commentaries. I would like to discuss one of them, the Persian commentary written by ʿAbd al-Raḥmān Jāmī (d. 898/1492) called the *Lawāmiʿ* (*Sparks*). Almost 20 years ago, I read Professor William Chittick's article on the *Lawāmiʿ* entitled "Jāmī on divine love and the image of wine" (1981). It was the first time I had seen an excerpt of Jāmī's *Lawāmiʿ* in English, but over the course of the next few years as I wrote my PhD dissertation, I translated the whole of the text and was able to see the rest of what Jāmī had to say. This article will serve as another installment of translated text and commentary, following 40 years behind Professor Chittick's article discussing the *Lawāmiʿ*. I plan to present the full translation soon.

1 Introduction

Jāmī was an inheritor of the legacy of the school of Ibn ʿArabī and played a role in bringing Ibn ʿArabī's thought to the Persian-speaking world. Jāmī's commentary on the *Khamriyya* is 85 pages long, including a 26-page introduction on the topics of wine and love, and then 59 pages of line-by-line explication. Jāmī makes use of the theoretical frameworks established by Ibn ʿArabī (d. 638/1240), specifically the philosophical terminology, and also brings his own poetry into the commentary, giving it quite a different flavor from those of his contemporaries. For example, Dāwūd al-Qayṣarī (fl. 8th/14th century), whose commentary on the *Khamriyya* is called the *Sharḥ Khamriyyat Ibn al-Fāriḍ* (*Commentary on the Wine ode of Ibn al-Fāriḍ*), tends to infer practical advice from the *Khamriyya* that would assist the Sufi adept in his practices, rather than further discuss themes with technical philosophical language.[1]

1 For more on al-Qayṣarī's commentary, see Homerin, Th. Emil (ed. and trans.), *The wine of love*

 | DOI:10.1163/9789004529038_011

Jāmī's influence reached as far as East China, where two of his texts are known to have been translated into Chinese. In recounting the history of Islam in China, Professor Sachiko Murata names four texts as having been translated from Islamic languages (all Persian) into Chinese before the 20th century. Jāmī wrote two of the four texts, *Lawā'iḥ* (*Gleams*) and *Ashi''at al-lama'āt* (*The rays of the Flashes*). In *Chinese gleams of Sufi light*, Professor Murata presents a Chinese version of Jami's *Lawā'iḥ* by Liu Chih/Liu Zhi (d. 1730), *Displaying the concealment of the real realm*.[2] The text uses expressions more familiar to Neo-Confucian thought, for the benefit of Chinese Muslims who could not read Arabic or Persian, but who wanted to read the Islamic classics. Thanks to the work of Professor Murata, it has become clear that when one refers to Islamic civilization as "reaching all the way to China," it is possible to observe the school of Ibn 'Arabī's presence there, and to see Jāmī as one of its great representatives.[3]

In the *Lāwami'* Jāmī explains, among other things, how the wine metaphor in the *Wine ode* does not merely function to demonstrate Ibn al-Fāriḍ's excellence as a poet, poetic excellence notwithstanding. Rather, it demonstrates that Ibn al-Fāriḍ was privy to the reality of wine beyond any physical form through tasting (*dhawq*). Some of the passages I am including here on what Jāmī calls "the clothing of form" were presented in my dissertation (2010). However, my commentary there was limited, and I did not elucidate Jāmī's view on wine as gnostic states that arise from God's love, which he says are not known until tasted. In keeping with both Professor Chittick and Professor Murata's tradition of maintaining the primacy of the text, I will preserve the translated passages from the *Lawāmi'* contiguously where possible, indicating them with italics.[4]

In the tradition of the school of Ibn 'Arabī, the discussion of wine begins within the Quranic universe, where the signs of wine are many: the forbidden nature of its physical form, the prominence of its imagery as a reward in the paradise of the next world, and a Quranic command to seek it in this world.

---

and life: Ibn al-Fāriḍ's al-Khamrīyah *and al-Qayṣarī's quest for meaning*, Chicago: Middle East Documentation Center, 2005.

2 Murata, Sachiko, *Chinese gleams of Sufi light: Wang Tai-yü's* Great learning of the pure and real *and Liu Chih's* Displaying the concealment of the real realm, Albany, NY: SUNY Press, 2000.

3 For other relevant source texts, see Murata, Sachiko, William C. Chittick and Tu Weiming, *The sage learning of Liu Zhi: Islamic thought in Confucian terms*, Cambridge, MA: Harvard University Asia Center, 2009, 3–19.

4 The translation follows the edition by Ḥikmat Ā. Āqā, Tehran: Bunyād-i Mihr, 1962.

Wine-drinking is prohibited by the *sharīʿa*. But while other prohibited things have a usefulness in the Quranic worldview, for example dogs guard properties and herd animals in the field, and pigs consume garbage, wine is not like them. It has no function in everyday life, besides some limited medicinal use. However, those who are familiar with poetic tropes in the Islamic world know that wine appears prominently in poetry, whether such poetry is referred to later as Sufi poetry or secular poetry. Here our concern is the poetry as it was passed down in Sufi circles.

Though there are many definitions of Sufism, for practicality's sake, I will use one that seems most practical in the discussion of this text. It is found in Professor Murata's Introduction to *The first Islamic classic in Chinese*: "[Sufism is] an approach to Islamic learning that looks for inner meaning when dealing with outward forms and that emphasizes the need to undergo transformation of the soul to achieve a constant personal engagement with God."[5] Poets like Ibn al-Fāriḍ, Jāmī, and others who were understood by their readerships to be Sufi poets, seem readily to see wine as a metaphor for Divine Love. In other words, they see an inner meaning in its outward form. In the instance of wine, though, the inner meaning happens to be a surprising one because of its prohibition.

One could note this conjunction of forbidden-meets-the-sought-after as merely an anomaly within Islamic civilization; however, I would like to examine why wine stands out in the Quranic universe as ontologically special. And for Jāmī especially, I would like to examine why it seems to appear in the world quite explicitly as a pointer, pointing to the Real (*al-ḥaqq*).

2 Translation

The Wine Ode
Ibn al-Fāriḍ

We drank wine in the remembrance of the Beloved;
We were drunk with it before the vine was created.
It had the full moon as a cup, and it was a sun;
It was passed around by a crescent moon, and so many stars appeared when it was mixed!

5 Murata, Sachiko, *The first Islamic classic in Chinese: Wang Daiyu's* Real commentary on the true teaching, Albany, NY: SUNY Press, 2017, 3.

But for its fragrance, I would never have been guided to its tavern;
 But for its resplendence, imagination could not have conceived of it.
Time has left nothing of it but a ghost,
 As if its vanishing were concealed in the breasts of the aware.
Yet if it is mentioned in the tribe, its folk
 Become drunk, and no shame on them or sin.
It has ascended from the insides of the jugs,
 And nothing is left of it but the name.
But if one day it should enter into a man's mind,
 Joys will settle down therein and grief will depart.
Had the boon companions but gazed on the container's seal,
 That seal would have made them drunk without the wine.
Were they to sprinkle a dead man's grave with its drops,
 His spirit would return to him and his body would revive.
If they threw into the shadow of its vine's wall
 Someone ill, on the verge of death, his illness would go.
If a cripple were brought near its tavern, he would walk;
 If a dumb man recalled its taste, he would speak.
If the whiffs of its fragrance were to spread in the East,
 Smell would return to someone with a stuffed nose in the West.
A touching palm tinged by its cup
 Will never be lost at night while the star is in hand.
If it were secretly disclosed to the blind man, he would come
 To see, and by its strainer, the deaf man would hear.
If riders set out for the earth of its land,
 And among them is one snake-bitten, the venom would not harm him.
If the sorcerer traced the letters of its name on
 The brow of someone struck by the *jinn*, the script would free him.
And if its name were inscribed on the banner of the army,
 That inscription would intoxicate all those beneath the banner.
It refines the character traits of the boon companions, so by it is guided
 To the path of resolve he who had no resolve.
He whose hand knew no generosity will be munificent,
 And he who had no clemency will be clement despite anger.
If the stupid man of the tribe should kiss its strainer,
 That kiss would convey to him the meaning of its virtues.
They say to me, "Describe it, for you are acquainted with its description."
 Yes, I have knowledge of its attributes:

Limpid, but not water; subtle, but not air;
Light, but not fire; spirit, but not body.
Beautiful traits that guide the describers to describe it,
So their prose and poetry about it is beautiful.
And he who does not know it becomes joyful at its mention,
Like the one longing for Nuʿm at the mention of Nuʿm.
They say, "You have drunk sin!" Not at all—I have only
Drunk that whose abandonment would be a sin for me.
Good health to the folk of the monastery! How they were drunk with it,
Though they did not drink of it, only aspiring to do so.
I was drunk with it before I came to be.
It will stay with me forever, though my bones rot away.
So take it unmixed. If you want to, mix it—
It is wrong for you to turn away from the Beloved's mouth.
Watch for it in the tavern and seek its disclosure there
Amidst the melodies of the songs, with which it is booty.
Wine and worry never dwell in one place,
Just as sorrow never dwells with song.
If it makes you drunk once, even for the length of an hour,
You will see time as an obedient servant, yours to command.
There is no life in this world for the one who lives sober;
And when someone does not die drunk on it, resolve has passed him by.
Let him weep for himself, he whose life has been wasted
And who has never had a share or portion of it.[6]

3 Commentary

To start, the first two lines of the *Khamriyya* of ʿUmar Ibn al-Fāriḍ disallow the reading of *wine* as an ordinary wine:

We drank wine in the remembrance of the Beloved;
We were drunk with it before the vine was created.[7]

6 Ibn al-Fāriḍ's *Khamriyya*, trans. Marlene DuBois, from DuBois, Marlene R. (trans.), *ʿAbd al-Rahman Jami's Lawāmiʿ: A translation study*, Ann Arbor: UMI, 2010, 1–2.

7 DuBois (trans.), *ʿAbd al-Rahman Jami's* Lawāmiʿ. There are many translations to be found English, for example, Nicholson, Reynold A., *Studies in Islamic Mysticism*, Cambridge: Cambridge University Press, 1921, 184–188; Arberry, Arthur J., in Ibn al-Fāriḍ, ʿUmar b. ʿAlī, *The mystical*

If readers happened to make their way past the first two lines without noticing the logical impossibility of the speaker's assertion about being drunk with a substance that has not found existence yet, surely after reading the full 66-line poem they would see the impossibility of this wine's being an earthly vintage.

There are several associations established for wine by Quranic passages which bear mention. First, there is the mention of the river of wine in the next world's paradise, and also the prohibition of it in this world. Together, the passages make wine something to strive for in the next world and avoid in this world. Later in the cumulative tradition, but also based on Quranic passages, there comes the meaning of wine established by the school of Ibn ʿArabī, for which Jāmī is a key representative, that all created things are representations of themselves and also manifestations of God. In other words, wine is like everything else in the world, functioning as *His signs* in the earth.

> We shall show them our signs, in the horizons and in themselves,
> until they recognize that He is the Real. (Q 41:53)[8]

The *Lawāmiʿ* is an example of how the school of Ibn ʿArabī sees physical wine as a sign among many signs, but also as a metaphor (*majāz*), manifesting the Real (*al-ḥaqq*).

The Quran prohibits wine-drinking specifically for the community of Muhammad. It mentions wine-drinking along with gambling as known human activities, in that it *has* a use, for example medicinal use, but that "its sinfulness is greater" than its use.

> They will ask thee concerning wine and gambling. Answer, in both there is great sin and also some things of use unto men: but their sinfulness is greater than their use. (Q 2:216)

---

poems of Ibn al-Farid, trans. Arthur J. Arberry, London: Walker, 1952, 84–90; Lings, Martin, "The wine-song (*al-Khamriyyah*) of ʿUmar Ibn al-Fārid," in *Studies in Comparative Religion* 14.3–4 (1980), 131–134; and Homerin, Th. Emil, *From Arab poet to Muslim saint: Ibn al-Fāriḍ, his verse, and his shrine*, Cairo: American University in Cairo Press, 2001, 47–51. Each translation carries the meaning that I refer to here, that sets the wine referred to in the poem apart from earthly wine.

8 I have primarily used translations of the Quran from Arberry, Arthur J., *The Koran interpreted*, New York: MacMillan Publishers, 1955, in some cases modifying the translation for consistency with Ibn al-Fāriḍ or Jāmī's meaning, or when quoting from another text.

There is also an assumption that there will inevitably be those in the community who will drink for various reasons—in celebration or in forgetting pain—so it gives instructions on waiting for a clear head before prayers.

> O true believers! come not to prayers when ye are drunk, until ye understand what ye say. (Q 4:46)

However, overall, earthly wine is described by the Quran as among the works of the devil, who is the source of misguidance for human beings in the world.

> O true believers! Surely wine, gambling, stone pillars, and divining arrows are an abomination, of the work of Satan; therefore avoid them that ye may prosper. (Q 5:92)

In Hadith literature, wine appears in the narrative of the Prophet's miraculous night journey (*miʿrāj*), when Muhammad is shown three containers: wine, milk, and honey. Upon his taking the container of milk, the angel Gabriel says that it represents the religion (*dīn*).[9]

What milk might represent here is an interesting topic on its own, and a qualitative discussion of the symbolism of milk within the tradition would be valuable. But as wine is the focus here, it will be enough to note for our purposes that Muhammad took the milk in the *miʿrāj* narrative, and not the wine or the honey.

As Gabriel says in the narrative, what was "owed" to God through the practice of the religion (*dayn/dīn*) by Muhammad and his followers, has a character likened to milk, as opposed to wine or honey. "Religion" (*dīn*) encompasses all realms of life, including ways of doing (*sharīʿa*), ways of thinking (*īmān*), and ways of being (*iḥsān*). The Quran here implicitly acknowledges the *dīn* of other traditions, in other words, those other traditions may have ways (of doing, thinking, and being) that are characterized through wine or honey, but Islam's is instead characterized through milk.

Wine also makes an appearance in the Quranic story of Joseph, when first his prison-mate has a dream that foretells his own demise, and later when the king has a dream that foretells years of plenty and years of want. Both dreams include an image of wine-drinking that indicates good fortune. The *sharīʿa* of Joseph's time, not having a prohibition on wine, allows the earthly vintage to be a symbol of celebration and times of plenty.

---

9 Cf. Rustom, Mohammed, "Ibn ʿArabī's letter to Fakhr al-Dīn al-Rāzī," in *JIS* 25.2 (2014), 113–137, 129, n. 72.

> And there entered the prison with him two youths. Said one of them, "I dreamed that I was pressing grapes." Said the other, "I dreamed that I was carrying on my head bread, that birds were eating of. Tell us its interpretation; we see that thou art of the good-doers." (Q 12:36)

> "Fellow-prisoners, as for one of you, he shall pour wine for his lord; as for the other, he shall be crucified, and birds will eat of his head. The matter is decided whereon you enquire." (Q 12:41)

> "Then thereafter there shall come a year wherein the people will be succoured and press in season." (Q 12:49)

Where the Quran does offer imagery of wine in relation to those in the community of Muhammed, it is strictly in terms of the next world, in a similitude of Paradise, which is three types of rivers in Paradise: milk, wine, and honey—the same substances as in the three containers showed to the Prophet in the *miʿrāj* narrative.

> This is the similitude of Paradise which the godfearing have been promised: therein are rivers of water unstaling, rivers of milk unchanging in flavour, and rivers of wine—a delight to the drinkers, rivers, too, of honey purified; and therein for them is every fruit, and forgiveness from their Lord (Q 47:16)

Another similitude of Paradise is that of a prepared wine, sealed with musk. This wine is described specifically as something for those in this world to strive for.

> Surely the pious shall be in bliss, upon couches gazing; thou knowest in their faces the radiancy of bliss as they are given to drink of a wine sealed whose seal is musk—so after that let the strivers strive. (Q 83:23)

Echoing these verses, Ibn al-Fāriḍ makes mention of a wine jug and its seal in the *Khamriyya*, in particular, the effect of its seal on the person who gazes upon it.

> Had the boon companions but gazed on the container's seal,
> that seal would have made them drunk without the wine.[10]

---

10 Jāmī, *Lawāmiʿ* 151.

When Jāmī explicates the lines, he says the seal represents those who are the "carriers of essential love" in the world, specifically the corporeal bodies of the perfect human beings:

> [152] It may be that the poet means by container the hearts of the perfect and the spirits of the arrivers,[11] for it is these that in reality are the carriers of essential love.
>
> And what he means by the seal of the container is the elemental corporeal body that is enwrapped in the human configuration. The knower and the ignorant, the deficient and the perfect, are equal in this. Therefore, the veiled ones, based on formal equivalence, judge the state of them by their own state, and gain no cognizance of their inner states.[12] On the contrary, they insist on negating that.[13]

Jāmī calls the ones who seek the wine successfully through their associations with the perfect human beings "receptive seekers." When the seekers drink the wine, they are able to see the traces of wine in the perfect ones. This is their gaze upon the container's seal, as it were, and when they do this, they increase the effect of the wine on themselves:

> Through bestowed preparedness and acquired receptivity, the receptive seekers and disciples possessing the heart are the boon companions of this group's assembly, and the comrades of their session. Through the eminence[14] of drinking this wine, they witness its traces on the pages of their faces and the slips of their tongues.[15]

Jāmī says the eyesight of this group becomes piercing after drinking the wine, and they are able to perceive evidence of the wine in others, in their faces, and the things that they say.

His description is reminiscent of the verse describing the pious in Paradise: "Thou knowest in their faces the radiancy of bliss" (Q 83:23). Seeking the radiance of bliss is a fair summary of the spiritual path as Sufis have often expressed it: a pursuit of the vision of God in this world, without waiting until

11 Those in union (*wiṣāl*).

12 I.e., the state of the perfect; *qiyās bi-nafs*, or "judging by your own situation," is criticized in Sufism.

13 Their inner states.

14 That is, excellence.

15 Jāmī, *Lawāmiʿ* 151–152.

the next world. The Quranic passage, “they are given to drink of a wine sealed whose seal is musk—so after that let the strivers strive” (Q 83:24–26), carries immediate practical advice to those on the spiritual path: seek the wine now. The act of taking these verses of the Quran at face value and applying its words in a direct manner is characteristic of the school of Ibn ʿArabī.

Ibn ʿArabī's school stands out in the intellectual history of Islam partly because he and those who followed him offered these sorts of explanations for Sufi imagery. For example, Ibn ʿArabī explains in Quranically-sound language the imagery of wine and lovers that might not have seemed straightforward to the ears of the general population. He uses prose and direct Quranic references to explain things Sufis had previously expressed through poetry in symbolic language and metaphors—how God loved human beings, and was therefore the first Lover, and that God manifested himself in and through the world.

> He loves them and they love Him. (Q 5:54)

> I was a Hidden Treasure and I loved to be known, so I created the creatures.[16]

His Quran-based explanations give the experiential, symbolic thinking of the Sufis more visible roots in philosophical or theological principles. As a result, Sufi thought and practice after Ibn ʿArabī could more easily be expressed in a theoretical manner.[17]

Ibn al-Fāriḍ, for example, although contemporary with Ibn ʿArabī, wrote in an image-rich manner, with no explanation for outsiders. But as we have seen, there is actually concrete language in the Quran about wine, and Ibn ʿArabī and his followers convey the concrete understanding of Quranic language through their explanations. Ibn ʿArabī's foremost student, Ṣadr al-Dīn al-Qūnawī (d. 673/1274), commented on and adopted the image-rich poetry of Ibn al-Fāriḍ into the education of his students, and the intellectual heritage

16 Graham, William A., *Divine word and prophetic word in early Islam*, The Hague: Mouton, 1977, 72. This *ḥadīth qudsī* does not appear in the standard collections, however it is well-known, and often cited as being the key to understanding God's intention behind creating the world.

17 Chittick, William C., "Jami on divine love and the image of wine," in *Studies in Mystical Literature* 1.3 (1981), 193–209. "With Ibn al-ʿArabi and his school the images employed to describe the experiences of Love and Union came to be explained in the language of philosophical and metaphysical discourse."

that followed, beginning with al-Qūnawī, which has often been called by Western scholars the "school of Ibn ʿArabī," thus incorporated Ibn al-Fāriḍ's poetry as part of its foundation.[18]

William Chittick's article "Jāmī on divine love and the image of wine" included the first translation of an excerpt of Jāmī's commentary in English.[19] There, Professor Chittick recounts that when references to wine appeared in poetry of the Islamic world in the past, especially in what were thought to be Sufi works, readers tended to argue whether they should be interpreted as pointing to *wine in its mystical reality*, as in the wine of God, or pointing to *wine as profane*, as in the earthly vintage. The sacred vs. profane argument is still common enough today, though Annemarie Schimmel suggested in her *Mystical dimensions of Islam* that one's interpretation of the meaning of the wine should be rather an oscillation between the two, that "sometimes they mean the mystical wine and sometimes they mean the sensual or profane"[20] Since the meaning can change at any moment, Professor Schimmel's suggestion is that it is not useful to pinpoint it: "It seems futile … to look for either a purely mystical of a purely profane interpretation … their ambiguity is intended, the oscillation between the two levels of being is consciously maintained …"[21]

Professor Chittick's suggestion was that later study of Ibn ʿArabī and his school of thought offers additional understanding, in that it compels one to go beyond either of those two approaches and keep in mind that each thing, ontologically speaking, is both at once. In other words, wine in and of itself, whether it is represented as the word "wine" on the page, or whether it is the physical reality, always refers to both the mystical and the profane at the same time. As he describes,

> the things of this world are not just things, rather they are created by God, derived from God, and ultimately Self-Manifestations of God, loci of His Theophany, places in which He reveals the 'Hidden Treasure,' mirrors in which the Beauty of the Beloved can be contemplated.[22]

18 For more on the school and its legacy, see Chittick, William C., "The school of Ibn ʿArabi," in Oliver Leaman and Seyyed Hossein Nasr (eds.), *History of Islamic philosophy*, New York: Routledge, 1996, 510–523.

19 Chittick, "Jami on divine love."

20 Schimmel, Annemarie, *Mystical dimensions of Islam*, Chapel Hill, NC: University of North Carolina Press, 1975, 288.

21 Schimmel, *Mystical dimensions* 288.

22 Chittick, "Jami on divine love."

In other words, the meaning of any single thing in the world, and likewise the meaning of wine, is *both/and*—both the thing itself in the physical sense, and the thing as God's self-manifestation.

For the one on the spiritual path, who is striving to see the second meaning, God reveals Himself. It is this understanding of reality that Jāmī demonstrates in the *Lawāmiʿ*—how the second meaning is accessible through God's self-manifestation alone:

> Until one tastes it, one does not know, and once one knows, one cannot explain. So, expressing it is concealed from other than its finder, and making it manifest is hidden from other than its taster.
>
> Everyone who catches the scent of love's wine
> moves his bedroll from the lane of wisdom to the tavern.
> And when someone has not savored that wine in the mouth of tasting,
> his understanding will never reach that wine's secret.
> Last night in bewilderment to the old man of the Magi
> I said, "Give me a symbol of the wine in secret."
> He said, "It is a reality of finding.
> O precious son! How will you know it if you don't taste it?"[23]

Here the speaker of Jāmī's poem asks for a symbol of the wine, something by which one can understand it. To explain, Jāmī calls to mind the Arabic saying, "Metaphor is the bridge to reality." God may disclose Himself at will, but the earthly wine remains in the world as the metaphor, the bridge.

The *Khamriyya* recognizes the confusion between the earthly and the unseen wines, with a couplet staging some imaginary complainants who protest the poet's praising of wine-drinking:

> They say, "You have drunk sin!" Not at all—I have only
> drunk that whose abandonment would be a sin for me.

Jāmī explains the comprehension problem: some people do not understand meanings clothed with forms:

> Those unable to understand meanings in the midst of form, and those incapable of perceiving realities in the clothing of metaphor, have said:

23 Jāmī, *Lawāmiʿ* 108–109.

> "What you mean by the wine which you acknowledged drinking at the beginning of the ode and whose characteristics and traces you have spoken about in the rest of the verses is the wine which in language is called sin, and the drinker of which, in the *sharīʿa*, is called a sinner. You mean the wine of form, the grape wine whose drinking is the result of misguidance and whose drinker deserves punishment and chastisement."
>
> Hence, he combines repelling that with forbidding it: Not at all—God forbid! I never imbibe that wine nor repose in drinking it. I have drunk wine from the cup of love and have striven to drink it constantly. In my view, abandoning that wine is a sin, and he who abandons drinking it is far from the path of the aware and the wise.[24]

Ibn al-Fāriḍ's couplet is an example of the mystical vs. profane argument, wherein the poet's meaning is interpreted by others as being profane, but he defends himself, saying that his meaning is that of the sacred. Jāmī explains that the listeners are incapable of perceiving realities in the clothing of metaphor. Their eyesight cannot reach God's self-disclosures wrapped inside mundane forms.

In one section, Jāmī enumerates the specific and varied uses of metaphorical language. The first use is the one already mentioned, that metaphors aid in understanding ("metaphor is the bridge to reality"). But he goes on to say that the human being has an innate preference for the senses, that human beings are accustomed to understanding things through the five senses, and then to develop further understanding based on what they experienced:

> The point of expressing the meanings in the clothing of forms can be several things. (1) One is that at the beginning, human beings arrive at intelligible objects from sensory ones and at universals from particulars by means of applying the tools of sense perception and imagination. Hence, the perception of meanings other than in the midst of forms is not customary for their souls or familiar to their natures. If they should do otherwise, it is possible that their understanding will not be strong enough to reach it and they will not have the capacity to perceive it.
>
> However much you're not aiming for cruelty
> and have no wish to torment the heart,

24 Jāmī, *Lawāmiʿ* 176.

Don't come toward your lover without a veil,
  for he doesn't have the capacity for you to lift it.[25]

Even abstract thinkers have noted the relationship between the senses and thought. Ananda Coomaraswamy, in his essay on literary symbolism, quotes Aristotle from *De anima*: "even when one thinks speculatively, one must have some mental picture with which to think."[26] It seems Jāmī would agree, as he says few people are able to perceive ideas presented in abstract language, or meanings without forms. Metaphorical language offers what is concrete to represent ideas in a visual, auditory, or tactile manner, and in this manner, it is an aid for all to be able to understand:

> (2) Also, only the Folk of Meaning can profit from the expression of the meanings without the clothing of forms. [128] But, when they are expressed in the clothing of forms, the benefit will be public and the usefulness complete.
>
> It is meaning that steals the heart, and religion, too.
>   It is meaning that increases love, and hate, too.
> But it is disclosed in the clothing of form,
>   so the eyes of the form-seer will profit, too.[27]

The primary benefit of the use of metaphorical language, however, according to Jāmī, is that it transports a person from the world of form to the world of meaning. Since metaphors point to what is beyond them, they can draw people into the world of meanings. He says metaphors can make their comprehension sharper and give them a desire to spend more time in the world of meanings rather than the world of form. Once that happens, and the person spends more time in the world of meanings, there is a further use: metaphor creates ease in conversation among those who also dwell together in the world of meanings:

> It often happens that a form-worshiper, having heard certain meanings expressed in the clothing of form, begins to have an inclination. The beauty of meaning casts a ray from behind the curtain of form, making

---

25 Jāmī, *Lawāmiʿ* 127.

26 Coomaraswamy, Ananda K., *The door in the sky: Coomaraswamy on myth and meaning*, ed. Rama P. Coomaraswamy, Princeton: Princeton University Press, 1997, 184.

27 Jāmī, *Lawāmiʿ* 127–128.

> the person's understanding keen and his secret heart subtle: he flees from the form and clings to the meaning.
>
> Many have traveled in vain, suffering—
> suddenly their foot hits treasure in the path.
> Many have split mountains, looking for stone—
> suddenly the mine makes them into jewelers.[28]

Since the states of the Folk of Tasting are incomprehensible to others, the Folk of Tasting use conventional language and employ metaphors that are acceptable to most people as a poetic style of speaking, but not discernable as unusual to any outsiders:

> It is also the case that not everyone is an intimate of the secrets of reality, or aware of the states of the Folk of the Path. Therefore, to conceal those secrets and hide those states, they borrow the terms and expressions that are in common use and well-known for metaphorical purposes in the conversations of the Folk of Form so that the beauty of those meanings remains far from the sight of strangers, and concealed from the gaze of the non-intimates.
>
> Last night that moon combed the curls of her locks,
> and placed over her face her amber-fragrant tresses.
> With this trick she hid her comely face,
> so that whoever was not an intimate would not recognize her.[29]

The last usage of metaphorical language Jāmī mentions is one that he cites as belonging only to the Folk of Tasting, that is, he says that poetic language is somehow a special property of those on the path. The view is perhaps consistent with Ibn ʿArabī's own description of the function of poetry in the preface to his *Dīwān al-maʿārif* (*Gnostic collection of poems*). Claude Addas has suggested on the basis of the passage that Ibn ʿArabī believes poetry is the exclusive language of the gnostics.

> The *Shaykh al-Akbar* observes [that] the world is a work endowed with rhyme and rhythm. Moreover, he adds, God placed the jewels of spiritual knowledge, and the secrets of the Lord, in language. He then entrusted

28 Jāmī, *Lawāmiʿ* 128.
29 Jāmī, *Lawāmiʿ* 128.

> this treasure to the *ʿārifūn*, the gnostics, who, for fear of it being plundered, hid the secrets under the veil of poetry, disguising them with allusive and symbolic terms. And on top of all that, Ibn ʿArabī observes at the end of this unusual *khutba*, is the Prophet not referred to as the Master of language and the holder of the "sum of words" (*jawāmiʿ al-kalim*)?[30]

Addas' suggestion is that the passage establishes both the legitimacy and the necessity of poetic language from the point of view of Ibn ʿArabī. Jāmī may be expressing this very perspective through his explanation on expressing meanings in the clothing of forms and also in his habit of using his own poetry to explain most of his line-by-line explications in the *Lawāmiʿ*.

Lastly, in describing the uses of metaphorical language, Jāmī describes how the language of allusion can exercise an even more powerful effect than the verses of the Quran:

> It is also the case that the tastings and ecstatic findings of the Lords of Love, and the secret sciences [129] of the possessors of gnosis, when mentioned in the language of allusion, have a greater effect on the souls of the listeners than if they were clearly expressed. Consequently, the state of many of this group will not change when they listen to the verses of the Quran and the words of the Furqan,[31] but after listening to one or more couplets in Arabic or Persian containing a description of the tresses and the moles of beautiful women, or the coquetry and winking of loved ones, or the mention of wine, taverns, goblets, and cups, their state changes and they fall into turmoil.

> When she divulges her beauty with a fairy-like face,
> the lover's mind is at ease from her blandishments.
> When she glances secretly with coquetry and winks,
> she changes the state of the hapless lover.[32]

Jāmī's point about the powerful effect of poetry may be related to the first principle he raised, in which he says human beings naturally respond to sensory experience. But here he seems to be saying that those who dwell in the world of

30 Addas, Claude, "The ship of stone," in *Journal of the Muhyiddin Ibn ʿArabi Society*, https://ibnarabisociety.org (last accessed: 10 October 2022).

31 The discernment, usually meaning the Quran.

32 Jāmī, *Lawāmiʿ* 128–129.

meaning have a heightened response to the language of metaphor, and therefore may be seen as supporting the idea that Addas discerned from Ibn ʿArabī's *Dīwān al-maʿārif*, that he saw poetry as the exclusive legacy of the gnostics, holding "the jewels of spiritual knowledge."

In the passage that follows, the language of wine and love are inseparable. While Jāmī comments on Ibn al-Fāriḍ's lines, he illustrates all the functions of metaphorical language that he explains, while employing the linguistic richness of Persian and Arabic, and a combined language of poetry and metaphysics.

Spark

Building on the directives and preferences concerning the explication of meanings in the clothing of forms mentioned in these two Sparks, the poet displays the meaning of love and affection in the robe of the wine of form. Among the terms and expressions that are employed in this subject, he chose *mudāma* (wine) in order to suggest constancy (*mudāwama*) and perseverance in drinking it. Which constancy can be greater than for the drinking to begin in eternity without beginning and extend to eternity without end?

Saki, pour me wine from that enormous cup!
  Don't stop—give it to me constantly.
Since wine came into Arabic as *mudām*,
  O Persian Moon, you also, give me *mudām*.[33]

Given that the perfect ones of the Tribe have realized the essential love that is connected to [130] the Essence, and the word essence (*dhāt*) is feminine; and given that whatever the truthful lover says he says in correlation with his beloved and whatever he seeks he seeks in conformity with his sought one, the poet uses as a metaphor the feminine form of the word, *mudāma*, rather than *mudām*,[34] to refer to essential love.

Everyday my custom is to walk in the garden—
  perhaps the tulip and the rose will be my comfort.
Wherever I see a flower, its color, its fragrance
  I smell and pick that flower in the garden.

33 Both "wine" and "constantly."

34 The masculine form.

Flowers and gardens recall a paradisial state, another example of how what is found in this world is but a reminder of another reality.

Returning again to the "remembrance" in the first two lines of the *Khamriyya*,

> We drank wine in the remembrance of the Beloved
> We were drunk with it before the vine was created.

The speaker and his friends were drunk with this wine before creation even occurred. It is an other-worldly vintage whose qualities can only be *pointed to* by the earthly vintage and by the words of the poet. In mythic language, the wine might be called a *primordial* wine, a wine that existed (and exists) beyond time.[35] In this case, it is not only the wine that seems supernatural, but the speaker himself, as he was present in the time of beginnings as well and taking part in a supernatural activity. As for the Beloved in the poem, it is a Beloved who pre-existed the lovers, and therefore pre-existed primordial time. It is the Real (*al-ḥaqq*/God).

Al-Qayṣarī, another of Ibn al-Fāriḍ's commentators from the school of Ibn ʿArabī, says these lines refer to the primordial event of remembrance, of the *Covenant of Alast*, wherein all human beings attested to God as their Lord, and the corresponding practice of remembrance (*dhikr*), which is one of the core rituals of Sufi practice.

> And when thy Lord took from the Children of Adam, from their loins, their seed, and made them testify concerning themselves, "Am I not your Lord?" They said, "Yes, we testify." (Q 7:172)

So common is this reference that the exchange is referred to as the *Wine of Alast*, the drink that filled the pre-existent spirits, and gave them a piercing awareness of their true state. Coming into the world, they were bereft of this awareness, and left only with the metaphors, signs, and allusions that might guide them, if they could only remember.

After Jāmī's words on wine and love, flowers and gardens, he begins his line-by-line exegesis of the *Khamriyya*:

---

35 Eliade, Mircea, *Myth and reality*, trans. Willard R. Trask, New York: Harper & Row, 1963, 5–6. Eliade describes the nature of myth: "Myth narrates a sacred history; it relates an event that took place in primordial Time, the fabled time of the 'beginnings' … myths describe the various and sometimes dramatic breakthroughs of the sacred (or the "supernatural") into the World …"

The shaykh, Sharāf al-Dīn Abū Ḥafṣ ʿUmar b. ʿAlī al-Saʿdī, known as Ibn al-Fāriḍ the Egyptian, said:

We drank wine in the remembrance of the Beloved;
We were drunk with it before the vine was created.

He says that we drank, and in the remembrance of the Friend, toward whom is directed the face of everyone's love with each other, we drank a wine to our mutual love, [a wine] by which we became drunk. Rather, because of a whiff of it we lost ourselves; and this was before the creation of the vine, [131] that is, the grapevine and the stuff[36] of the well-known wine, full of evil and passion.

On the day when the heavens and spheres were not yet turning,
when water, fire, and dust were not yet mixed,
I was drunk in remembering you, a worshipper of wine—
even without sign of wine or vine.

It is us, the draft-drainers from the cup of your love—
for your draft-drainers—pour a draft!
In remembrance of you that morning, we drank the morning cup—
without any sign of vine or vine-planter.[37]

According to Jāmī, Ibn al-Fāriḍ's poem is about awakening to reality, the remembering of the Friend, and the eventual immersion in what is truly Real. He says once a person sees the Divine Beauty, and falls in love, there is no other way to be, think, or do:

Many saw the faces of the fine beauties
and fell into burning and melting from the brand of love.
They became the intimate of the mysteries and sat with the Folk of Tasting,
drinking the wine of reality from the cup of metaphor.[38]

Corporeal reality—handsome men and women, wine, and gardens—are all things that point to what is *beyond them*; they are only likenesses of what is

36 Matter, material.
37 Jāmī, *Lawāmiʿ* 127–131.
38 Jāmī, *Lawāmiʿ* 117.

truly Real. According to the Quran, it is God's habit to strike similitudes in the world. And in the Quran, there is offered the famous extended metaphor of God as a Light:

> God is the Light of the heavens and the earth; the likeness of His Light is as a niche wherein is a lamp; the lamp in a glass, the glass as it were a glittering star kindled from a Blessed Tree, an olive that is neither of the East nor of the West whose oil wellnigh would shine even if no fire touched it; Light upon Light. God guides to His Light whom He will. And God strikes similitudes for men, and God has knowledge of everything. (Q 24:35)

If every corporeal thing is God's self-manifestation, as the school of Ibn ʿArabī maintains, every existent thing is a kind of metaphor. In fact, God verifies His potential use even of minor similitudes: "God is not ashamed to strike a similitude even of a gnat, or aught above it." (Q 2:26) And the metaphorical beloveds, for as long as they exist in the world, point back to the true Beloved (God).[39] As the Prophet said, "God is Beautiful, and He loves beauty."[40] And so anything beautiful in the world can be called "trace beauty" according to Jāmī.

In the passage that follows, Jāmī explains how a person can be led from the trace beauties, or the metaphorical beloveds, toward real Beauty and the True Beloved, as "God guides to His Light whom He will":

> **Spark**
> Just as trace-beauty, which is taken as the object of metaphorical love, is a shadow and branch of the beauty of the Essence, which is the object of real love, so also metaphorical love is the shadow and branch of real love; and, in keeping with "metaphor is the bridge to reality,"[41] it [140] is the path of its actualization[42] and the means of reaching it. This is because, if a fortunate person, in keeping with his root creation, should have the receptivity for the essential love of the absolutely Beautiful, but has remained in the courtyard of concealment by the accumulated, dark veils of nature; then, if all at once a ray of that beauty's light should

39 The physical reality as a symbol that corresponds to an invisible reality is similar to the Platonic idea of forms and archetypes.

40 Muslim, *Ṣaḥīḥ*, in *Jamʿ jawāmiʿ al-aḥādīth wa-l-asānīd wa-maknaz al-siḥāḥ wa-l-sunan wa-l-masānīd*, iv, Vaduz: Jamʿiyyat al-Maknaz al-Islāmī, 2000, Īmān, 41, no. 275.

41 A famous saying in Arabic.

42 I.e., the actualization of real love.

begin to show itself from the curtain of water and clay in the form of a heart-taker with balanced qualities, proportionate members, harmonious parts, elegant stature, comely cheek, noble character traits, and good bloodlines—

You're sweet acting, fine speaking, and agile,
  you put salve on the brand of every sorrowful heart.
Like a freshly opened bud, you're pure
  of the stain of anyone's impudent touch.

—surely the bird of the heart of that fortunate man will turn toward it[43] and will spread its wings and feathers in the wind of His love. It will become the captive of His bait and the prey of His snare. It will turn its face away from every goal, or rather it will have no other goal.

From mosque and *darwīsh*-house, he comes to the vintner—
  he drinks the wine and comes drunk to the door of the beloved.
He becomes disgusted with everything but love for the beloved—
  he buys it at the price of a thousand souls.

The fire of love and the flame of yearning begin to be kindled in his make-up, and the dense veils, which consist of the heart's being imprinted by the engendered forms, start to burn away. The covering of heedlessness is lifted from the eye of his insight and the dust of multiplicity is swept away from the mirror of his reality. His eyes become sharp-seeing and his heart comes to recognize the reality. [141] He grasps the defects and deficiencies of swift-fading loveliness and he perceives the subsistence and perfection of the Possessor of Majesty. He flees from the former and clings to the latter, and the precedent solicitude of God comes forth to meet him.

First the beauty of the unity of the acts becomes manifest to him. Once he becomes firmly established in beholding the acts, the beauty of the attributes is unveiled. When he becomes deeply rooted in the unveiling of the attributes, the beauty of the Essence discloses itself, and he realizes essential love. The doors of witnessing are opened for him, and he sees existence from its first to its last as one reality.

Since its manifest has disclosed itself through all of its tasks and standpoints to his inward reality, the realities of the divine knowledge have

43 The ray of beauty's light; or her, the girl with those qualities.

become distinct. Since it has become colored by the ruling properties of the nonmanifest realities of knowledge, the external entities have become entified. Whatever he passes by, he finds Him, and whatever he gazes upon, he sees Him. At every moment he turns his face toward the Witnessed One and says:

In the breast You were hidden; I was heedless—
to the eyes You were plain; I was heedless.
For a lifetime I sought the world for a sign of You—
the whole world was in fact You; I was heedless.

When he arrives here, he knows that metaphorical love is like a whiff of the tavern of real love, and that love for the traces is like a ray of the sun of Essential Love. If you had not smelled that whiff, you would not have reached the tavern, and if this ray had not shone forth, you would not have found a portion of this sun.

Happy is the one who smelled the scent of the tavern;
he went off on the trail of that scent and arrived at the tavern.
A flash appeared from the tavern's lane,
and in its rays, he saw the tavern's sanctuary.[44]

The secrecy of lovers is another reason for metaphor and allusion. Because wine is tied to Divine Love it is necessarily bound up in the privacy of lovers. Andi Herawati in her "A semantic analysis of Ibn ʿArabī's account of metaphysical love" cites numerous scholars to the effect that Sufi authors have preferred, from the early days of Islam, to speak of their experiences on the spiritual path using indirect language and imagery because the esoteric knowledge, or the World of Meaning, is beyond the ken of those who dwell in the world of exoteric dogma, or the World of Form, but also because it was personal.[45] This is where wine finds its niche, as it is unique among metaphors.

44 Jāmī, *Lawāmiʿ* 139–141.

45 Herawati, Andi, "A semantic analysis of Ibn ʿArabī's account of metaphysical love," in *Journal of Islamic and Muslim Studies* 5.2 (2020), 48–64, 48. Herawati cites numerous scholars as having observed reticence from Sufi authors in speaking about love. Poetry and the language of allusion, however, was "able to express and convey esoteric knowledge without coming into direct conflict with the uncompromising formulations of exoteric dogma."

In the Quranic universe, wine stands apart from other created things: forbidden by the *sharīʿa*, yet held aloft by the Quran as an image of paradise. It is a familiar trope for poetry, yet a secret allusion for the Folk of Meaning. And in the school of Ibn ʿArabī, though it is a created thing like all other created things that manifest God, wine is unique. It is a *prohibited thing* that has a special ontological significance in its *ability to point to what is beyond it* and to guide human beings from the World of Form to the World of Meaning. But God must reveal the pointing. So even though Jāmī says "metaphor is the bridge to reality," he suggests that it is God alone who allows the crossing. The description of wine, Jāmī says, is understood only by the Folk of Tasting who have been given leave to enter the tavern. They are the seals of the jugs and the inheritors of the treasure; they dwell in privacy in the world of meaning and speak a language that glitters with the "jewels of spiritual knowledge."

Bibliography

Addas, Claude, "The ship of stone," in *Journal of the Muhyiddin Ibn ʿArabi Society*, https://ibnarabisociety.org (last accessed: 10 October 2022).

Arberry, Arthur J., *The Koran interpreted*, New York: MacMillan Publishers, 1955.

Chittick, William C., "Jami on divine love and the image of wine," in *Studies in Mystical Literature* 1.3 (1981), 193–209.

Chittick, William C., "The school of Ibn ʿArabi," in Oliver Leaman and Seyyed Hossein Nasr (eds.), *History of Islamic philosophy*, New York: Routledge, 1996, 510–523.

Coomaraswamy, Ananda K., *The door in the sky: Coomaraswamy on myth and meaning*, ed. Rama P. Coomaraswamy, Princeton: Princeton University Press, 1997.

DuBois, Marlene R. (trans.), *ʿAbd al-Rahman Jami's* Lawāmiʿ*: A translation study*, Ann Arbor: UMI, 2010.

Eliade, Mircea, *Myth and reality*, trans. Willard R. Trask, New York: Harper & Row, 1963.

Graham, William A., *Divine word and prophetic word in early Islam*, The Hague: Mouton, 1977.

Herawati, Andi, "A semantic analysis of Ibn ʿArabī's account of metaphysical love," in *Journal of Islamic and Muslim Studies* 5.2 (2020), 48–64.

Homerin, Th. Emil, *From Arab poet to Muslim saint: Ibn al-Fāriḍ, his verse, and his shrine*, Cairo: American University in Cairo Press, 2001.

Homerin, Th. Emil (ed. and trans.), *The wine of love and life: Ibn al-Fāriḍ's* al-Khamrīyah *and al-Qayṣarī's quest for meaning*, Chicago: Middle East Documentation Center, 2005.

Ibn al-Fāriḍ, ʿUmar b. ʿAlī, *The mystical poems of Ibn al-Farid*, trans. Arthur J. Arberry, London: Walker, 1952.

Jāmī, ʿAbd al-Raḥmān, *Lawāmiʿ*, ed. Ḥikmat Ā. Āqā, Tehran: Bunyād-i Mihr, 1962.
Lings, Martin, "The wine-song (*al-Khamriyyah*) of ʿUmar Ibn al-Fāriḍ," in *Studies in Comparative Religion* 14.3–4 (1980), 131–134.
Murata, Sachiko, *Chinese gleams of Sufi light: Wang Tai-yü's* Great learning of the pure and real *and Liu Chih's* Displaying the concealment of the real realm, Albany, NY: SUNY Press, 2000.
Murata, Sachiko, *The first Islamic classic in Chinese: Wang Daiyu's* Real commentary on the true teaching, Albany, NY: SUNY Press, 2017.
Murata, Sachiko, William C. Chittick and Tu Weiming, *The sage learning of Liu Zhi: Islamic thought in Confucian terms*, Cambridge, MA: Harvard University Asia Center, 2009.
Muslim, *Ṣaḥīḥ*, in *Jamʿ jawāmiʿ al-aḥādīth wa-l-asānīd wa-maknaz al-ṣiḥāḥ wa-l-sunan wa-l-masānīd*, iv, Vaduz: Jamʿiyyat al-Maknaz al-Islāmī, 2000.
Nicholson, Reynold A., *Studies in Islamic Mysticism*, Cambridge: Cambridge University Press, 1921.
Rustom, Mohammed, "Ibn ʿArabī's letter to Fakhr al-Dīn al-Rāzī," in *JIS* 25.2 (2014), 113–137.
Schimmel, Annemarie, *Mystical dimensions of Islam*, Chapel Hill, NC: University of North Carolina Press, 1975.

CHAPTER 11

Al-Qushāshī and al-Kūrānī on the Unity of God's Attributes (*waḥdat al-ṣifāt*)

Naser Dumairieh

1 Introduction

The concept of *waḥdat al-ṣifāt,* the "unity or oneness of attributes," was coined to resemble the famously controversial concept of *waḥdat al-wujūd* or the "unity or oneness of Being." Indeed, when in the 11th/17th century Mullā Ibrāhīm al-Kūrānī (d. 1101/1690), influenced by his teacher Ṣafī al-Dīn al-Qushāshī (d. 1071/1661), introduced and elaborated the concept of *waḥdat al-ṣifāt,* he considered it the twin sister of the concept of *waḥdat al-wujūd.* This article takes a closer look at the concept of the "unity of attributes" and investigates the different meanings of "unity" that were part of Akbarian discussions of God's unity occurring in 11th/17th-century Hijaz. In these discussions, some Hijazi scholars sought to demonstrate that Akbarian thought was, in fact, the correct interpretation of all Islamic teachings revolving around the main doctrine expressed in the article of faith or the word of unity (*kalimat al-tawḥīd*), *lā ilāha illā Allāh.* By revolving their doctrinal discussions around *tawḥīd,* these scholars made it clear that the Akbarian ideas encapsulated in the idea of *waḥdat al-wujūd* formed the correct interpretation of Islamic doctrines, rooted as they are in the concept of God's unity.

In his studies on Ibn ʿArabī (d. 638/1240), William Chittick has discussed *waḥdat al-wujūd* extensively, and has also presented the most comprehensive study of the term's history.[1] As Professor Chittick has shown, *waḥdat al-wujūd* has historically been identified with the perspective of Ibn ʿArabī and his followers, despite the fact that Ibn ʿArabī did not use this term in his writings. Nevertheless, both his advocates and his adversaries accepted the term as referring to the school that evolved around Ibn ʿArabī and his students and followers, even though, as Chittick points out, they have also understood it in different ways.[2]

---

1 Chittick, William C., *In search of the lost heart: Explorations in Islamic thought,* ed. Mohammed Rustom, Atif Khalil, and Kazuyo Murata, Albany, NY: SUNY Press, 2012, 71–88.

2 See Chittick, "A history" 86.

 | DOI:10.1163/9789004529038_012

Chittick's discussion and analysis of the concept of *waḥdat al-wujūd* proceeds via explaining the two terms that form it, an example I will follow in explaining the concept of *waḥdat al-ṣifāt*. Starting with a brief exploration of the two terms will situate al-Qushāshī and al-Kūrānī's ideas within their broader intellectual context and reveal the transitional shift toward Akbarian ideas that happened in 11th/17th-century Hijaz when scholars were not attempting to avoid controversial Akbarian ideas, but rather were discussing central Islamic doctrines using Akbarian terminology and with reasoning based on Ibn ʿArabī's ideas. This essay will thus start with a general introduction to the concepts of *waḥda* and *ṣifāt*; then, after a short biography of both al-Qushāshī and al-Kūrānī, I will discuss the term *waḥdat al-ṣifāt* and its function in these two scholars' intellectual systems. I will then conclude with some remarks that seek to clarify the interconnectedness of Islamic doctrines and how most of them are indeed based on the concept of unity.

2 *Tawḥīd*

Waḥda is the term common to *waḥdat al-wujūd* and *waḥdat al-ṣifāt*. As already stated, Ibn ʿArabī did not used the expression *waḥdat al-wujūd*; but he did use terms such as *waḥda*, and *waḥdāniyya*, *aḥadiyya*,[3] which are derived from the same root as *waḥda*.

Tawḥīd literally means "unification," or "making something one," but when *tawḥīd* is used to refer to God, it means believing and affirming God's unity, that God is one and unique (*wāḥid*). This affirmation is the first article of the *shahāda*, which is known as *kalimat al-tawḥīd*: "[There is] no god but God" (*lā ilāh illā Allāh*).[4] God is one and unique, and as He describes Himself, "nothing is like Him" (*laysa ka-mithlihi shayʾ*) (Q 42:11). Since there is no similarity between God and His creatures, He is unknowable to human beings, except to the extent that He reveals Himself. God has made some aspects of Himself known through His revelation, and the Quran describes God by His "most beautiful names" (*al-asmāʾ al-ḥusnā*), which became the basis for understanding the divine essence (*dhāt*) and attributes (*ṣifāt*).[5] But since God is one and nothing

3 Chittick, "A history" 73.

4 For the general meaning of *tawḥīd*, with a short reference to Sufism and to the contemporary usage of the term, see Gimaret, Daniel, "Tawḥīd," in *EI*² and Belhaj, Abdessamad, "Tawhid (oneness)," in Cenap Çakmak (ed.), *Islam: A worldwide encyclopedia*, Santa Barbara, CA: ABC-CLIO, 2017, 1553–1555, 1553.

5 Böwering, Gerhard, "God and His attributes," in *EQ*.

is like Him, nothing is like His essence, either, and there can be no similarity to Him in His attributes or His actions. In other words, God is utterly one in His essence, or *tawḥīd al-dhāt*, utterly one in His attributes, or *tawḥīd al-ṣifāt*, and utterly one in His actions, or *tawḥīd al-afʿāl*. This classification of different categories of *tawḥīd* means affirming that God's essence, attributes, and actions are unique and incomparable to any creatures' essence, attributes, and actions.

This classification of *tawḥīd* resulted from those early Muslim theologians who debated about God's attributes and attempted to classify them into different categories. This classification of the attributes and *tawḥīd* was known in Sufi literature as early as the 5th/11th century.[6] Some Sufis were concerned with how affirming God's unity was reflected in human consciousness, or, as Chittick explains, with "the assumption of the traits of the divine names as the very definition of the spiritual life."[7] One early Sufi who focused much of his attention on *tawḥīd* was Junayd al-Baghdādī (d. 298/910).[8] His definition of God's unity as "the isolation of the eternal from the temporal" became a standard definition in later Sufi texts.[9] Although this definition seems to have been influenced by the theological idea of God's transcendence (*tanzīh*), Junayd also classified *tawḥīd* into four categories:

> The first is the *tawḥīd* of the ordinary people; the second is the *tawḥīd* of those who are well versed in formal religious knowledge. The third and fourth stages are experienced by the elect who have esoteric knowledge (*maʿrifa*).[10]

Later, many Sufi manual texts, such as *al-Risāla al-Qushayriyya*,[11] *al-Lumaʿ* (*Flashes*) by al-Sarrāj (d. 378/988),[12] and *Kashf al-maḥjūb* (*Revelation of the*

6 Al-Qushayrī, ʿAbd al-Karīm b. Hawāzin, *al-Qushayrī's epistle on Sufism* (*al-Risāla al-Qushayriyya fī ʿilm al-taṣawwuf*), trans. Alexander D. Knysh, Reading: Garnet Publishing, 2007, 11. Since al-Qushayrī was Ashʿarī in doctrine, it can be expected that he would argue for the Ashʿarī understanding of God's attributes, which was that it cannot be said whether they are Him or they are not Him. Al-Qushayrī, *al-Qushayrī's epistle* 14.

7 Chittick, William C., *Ibn ʿArabi: Heir to the prophets*, Oxford: Oneworld, 2005, 30.

8 For a problematic but still useful study of Junayd's life, work, and thought, see Abdel-Kader, Ali H., *The life, personality and writings of al-Junayd: A study of a third/ninth century mystic*, London: Luzac, 1962.

9 Abdel-Kader, *The life* 70.

10 Abdel-Kader, *The life* 72.

11 Al-Qushayrī, *al-Qushayri's epistle* 14.

12 Al-Ṭūsī, Abū Naṣr al-Sarrāj, *al-Lumaʿ*, ed. ʿAbd al-Ḥalīm Maḥmūd and Ṭāhā A.B. Surūr, Cairo: Dār al-Kutub al-Ḥadītha, 1960, 49.

veiled) by al-Hujwīrī (d. 465/1072),[13] had sections on the meaning and categories of *tawḥīd*.[14] For Ibn ʿArabī and his students, as Chittick explains, *tawḥīd* was the governing theme,[15] and most of his students and followers discussed the term as the first principle of Islam and as part of the concept of *waḥdat al-wujūd*.[16]

Different ways of considering God's unity had thus been established long before the 11th/17th century. Among the most widely spread ideas concerning God's unity was that of confirming God's essence, attributes, and acts. Al-Ghazālī (d. 505/1111) in *al-Risāla al-qudsiyya* (*The Jerusalem epistle*) stated that the pronouncement of the full *shahāda*, "There is no god but God, and Muḥammad is the messenger of God," affirms God's essence, God's attributes, and God's acts, in addition to affirming the truthfulness of His messenger.[17] Ibn al-Humām (d. 861/1457) in *al-Musāyara* (*The pursuit*) stated that "the unity of God is the belief in unity in [God's] essence, attributes, and acts."[18] Sufis, as Chittick explains, also identified faith in God as entailing faith in His essence, attributes, and acts.[19]

Among the classifications of unity cited by al-Kūrānī is al-Dawānī's (d. 918/1502) classification in *Risālat Khalq al-aʿmāl* (*Treatise on the creation of human acts*). In this work, al-Dawānī classifies *tawḥīd* into three hierarchical categories. The lowest (*al-adnā*) is *tawḥīd al-afʿāl*, which means to believe with certainty that there is no effective agent (*muʾaththir*) in existence except God. Al-Kūrānī quotes only this category to argue for human efficacy in action. Al-Dawānī's second category is *tawḥīd al-ṣifāt*, which he describes as seeing that

13 Al-Hujwīrī, ʿAlī b. ʿUthmān, *The Kashf maḥjūb: The oldest Persian treatise on Ṣūfiism*, trans. Reynold A. Nicholson, Leyden and London: Brill, 1911, 278.

14 For al-Ghazālī's classification of people into four levels with regard to God's unity (*tawḥīd*), see Abrahamov, Binyamin, *Ibn al-ʿArabi and the Sufis*, Oxford: Anqa Publishing, 2014, 121. Chittick also mentions al-Anṣārī's five levels of *tawḥīd*; see Chittick, "A history" 72. Among other famous classification of *tawḥīd* is Ibn Taymiyya's classification into three categories: *tawḥīd al-rubūbiyya*, "oneness of God's lordship;" *tawḥīd al-ulūhiyya*, "oneness of worship;" and *tawḥīd al-asmāʾ wa-l-ṣifāt*, "oneness of God's names and attributes."

15 Chittick, *Ibn ʿArabi* 40.

16 For discussion of some aspects of the concept of *waḥda* among some of Ibn ʿArabī's commentators see Ali, Mukhtar H., *Philosophical Sufism: An introduction to the school of Ibn al-ʿArabī*, New York: Routledge, 2022, 44.

17 Tibawi, Abdel Latif, "Al-Ghazālī's sojourn in Damascus and Jerusalem," in *IQ* 9.3–4 (1965), 65–122, 79.

18 Ibn al-Humām, Muḥammad b. ʿAbd al-Wāḥid, *al-Musāmara fī sharḥ al-Musāyara fī ʿilm al-kalām*, Cairo: al-Maktaba al-Azhariyya li-l-Turāth, 2006, 47.

19 Chittick, William C., *Faith and practice of Islam: Three thirteenth century Sufi texts*, Albany, NY: SUNY Press, 1992, 39–47.

every power (*qudra*) is absorbed in God's omnipotence and every knowledge is taken in by God's perfect knowledge, and every perfection is a glimpse of the reflection of the lights of God's perfection. This level, according to al-Dawānī, is higher than the first and entails it. The third level is *tawḥīd al-dhāt*, in which all signs erase and expressions blur.[20]

3 God's Attributes (*ṣifāt Allāh*)

The classification of *tawḥīd* into different categories resulted from the classification of God's attributes. God describes Himself in the Quran with qualities such as "the Powerful" (*al-qādir*), "the Self-Sufficient" (*al-ghanī*), "the All-Knowing" (*al-ʿālim*), and other "most beautiful names,"[21] which, as Chittick states, are "referred to as attributes, since they designate qualities and characteristics."[22] God is also described in the Quran as possessing sensory attributes, such as a hand (Q 48:10) or an eye (Q 20:39), and with phrases that speak of Him, for example, as sitting on the Throne. These verses are classified by exegetes and theologians as "ambiguous" (*mutashābihāt*). As mentioned above, God is one and unique and "there is nothing like Him." So what is the proper way to conceive of divine attributes without entailing some kind of similarity (*tashbīh*) between God and His creatures, while also affirming what God affirms with respect to Himself, thereby not undermining divine transcendence and unity?

Among the earliest arguments regarding divine attributes in Islamic history was the refutation of anthropomorphism, which means that the literal meaning of the ambiguous verses had received some acceptance requiring a reply from other scholars. Several theological groups were accused by later Muʿtazilites and Ashʿarites of anthropomorphism and corporealism, in addition to certain individuals among the early theologians who were also accused of defending such views.[23] The groups and individuals who developed a corporealist description seemed to advocate a finite God who literally possessed

20 Dawānī, Jalāl al-Dīn, *Risālat Khalq al-aʿmāl*, in *al-Rasāʾil al-mukhtāra*, ed. Aḥmad Tūysirkānī, Isfahan: Emam Alī Public Library, 1985, 75–76.

21 Böwering, "God and His attributes," in *EQ*.

22 Murata, Sachiko and William C. Chittick, *The vision of Islam*, New York: Paragon House, 1994, 64.

23 Among the early groups that were accused of anthropomorphism were adherents of the Hadith (*ahl al-ḥadīth*), followers of Ibn Ḥanbal, some of the early Imami (Twelver) Shiʿis, and the Karrāmiyya. See Martin, Richard C., "Anthropomorphism," in *EQ*.

dimensions, altitude, a hand, and a face.[24] The earliest refutations of anthropomorphism are ascribed to al-Jaʿd b. Dirham (d. 124/742) and his student Jahm b. Ṣafwān (d. 128/746). While Jaʿd denied some of God's attributes, such as seeing and hearing,[25] Jahm argued that sharing means similarity (*tashbīh*). Thus, all attributes that are ascribed to God and shared by creation are themselves created. Jahm took transcendence to a level of an abstract idea in an effort to distance God from any kind of likeness to created beings.[26] Distancing God from human attributes, along with the ideas of absolute divine transcendence and the negation of God's attributes led to a reduction of God to a pure existence devoid of any positive substance.

Between these two extremes, a spectrum of different theological positions attempted to describe God in a proper way without compromising His transcendence or His attributes.[27] More traditional Hanbalite scholars argued that God's attributes should be confirmed with conviction and sincerity in belief and without asking why or how, because human understanding is restricted whenever it attempts to elucidate the essence-attributes issue.[28] Muʿtazilites argued that God is free of any impurities, such as the ascription of human attributes to Him, so they advanced the concept of *tanzīh* and took the position that the true meaning of the anthropomorphic and ambiguous passages must be understood through allegorical interpretation (*taʾwīl*). They classified attributes as *ṣifāt al-dhāt*, "attributes of the essence," which refer to God on account of His eternal existence without considering His acts, and *ṣifāt al-fiʿl*, "attributes of God's actions," which refer to God on account of His acts.[29] For the Muʿtazilites, who called themselves *ahl al-ʿadl wa-l-tawḥīd*, "the people of justice and unity," the unity of God was their most important doctrine. Thus, *tanzīh* should be applied to all Quranic verses and Hadiths that have corporeal descriptions, which means that any anthropomorphic references to God

---

24 Winter, Tim, "Introduction," in Tim Winter (ed.), *The Cambridge companion to classical Islamic theology*, Cambridge: Cambridge University Press, 2008, 1–16, 9.

25 Ibn Ḥanbal, Aḥmad, *al-Radd ʿalā l-Jahamiyya wa-l-Zanādiqa*, Riyadh: Dār al-Liwāʾ, 1977, 41–43.

26 Ibn Ḥanbal phrases the idea of Jahm about God as: "He is not described or known by any attribute or act, nor has He any term or limit; He is not grasped by the mind … and whatever may occur to your thought as a being, He is contrary to it." Ibn Ḥanbal, *al-Radd* 98.

27 Blankinship, Khalid, "The early creed," in Tim Winter (ed.), *The Cambridge companion to classical Islamic theology*, Cambridge: Cambridge University Press, 2008, 33–54, 46.

28 El-Bizri, Nader, "God: Essence and attributes," in Tim Winter (ed.), *The Cambridge companion to classical Islamic theology*, Cambridge: Cambridge University Press, 2008, 121–140, 125.

29 Gimaret, Daniel, "Ṣifa," in *EI*².

are to be interpreted allegorically.[30] In principle, the Muʿtazilites reduced God's attributes to His essence in order to negate a "plurality of eternals."[31]

In response to the Muʿtazilite reductive overemphasis on transcendence, the Ashʿarites argued that the affirmation of God's attributes should be coupled with the negation of implied anthropomorphic determinations. But for them, all descriptions of God in the Quran and Hadith were actual and to be accepted "without specifying how" (*bi-lā kayf*). The Ashʿarites also established a refined nuance between attributes of action (*ṣifāt al-fiʿl*), which come to be when God intends something and acts, and those of essence (*ṣifāt al-dhāt* or *ṣifāt al-nafs*).[32] However, later Ashʿarites from at least the 5th/11th century maintained that such passages in the Quran and Hadith should *not* be interpreted literally; one should either reinterpret them figuratively (*taʾwīl*) or entrust their meaning to God (*tafwīḍ*).[33]

Ibn ʿArabī's idea regarding God's attributes, as Chittick explains, is that people need to maintain the balance between God's transcendence and similarity by seeing with "both eyes," namely reason and imagination.[34] God is both transcendent and immanent, and "when reason grasps God's inaccessibility, it 'asserts his incomparability' (*tanzih*). When imagination finds him present, it 'asserts his similarity' (*tashbih*)."[35] In different contexts, Chittick emphasises that for Ibn ʿArabī knowing God is through both incomparability and similarity, because "on the one hand, God is unknowable; on the other, we can understand Him through the Names. True knowledge of Him must combine the two points of view."[36]

This attempt to keep the balance between divine transcendence and immanence in the Akbarian tradition was interpreted in a negative way by

30 El-Bizri, "God" 122.

31 Wāṣil b. ʿAṭāʾ (d. 131/748) is believed to have rejected the affirmation of the attributes of knowledge (*ʿilm*), power (*qudra*), will (*irāda*), and life (*ḥayāt*). Al-Naẓẓām denied that God has power over evil and Muʿammar refuted will and knowledge in order to free God's essence from multiplicity, while al-Jubbāʾī and Abū Hāshim asserted that God possesses a knowledge that is identical with His essence and not subsisting beside it. See El-Bizri, "God" 123–124.

32 El-Bizri, "God" 128.

33 El-Rouayheb, Khaled, *Islamic intellectual history in the seventeenth century: Scholarly currents in the Ottoman empire and the Maghreb*, New York: Cambridge University Press, 2015, 275–276.

34 Chittick, *Ibn ʿArabi* 19.

35 Chittick, *Ibn ʿArabi* 19.

36 Chittick, William C., "Ibn ʿArabī and his school: Life, works, and influence," in Seyyed Hossein Nasr (ed.), *Islamic spirituality: Manifestations*, New York: Crossroad, 1997, 49–79, 58.

scholars who emphasised one aspect over the other, and Ibn ʿArabī was thereby variously accused of reducing God to a mere abstract idea and of identifying God with the world. Before turning to these accusations, I will first introduce al-Qushāshī and al-Kūrānī, the two main scholars who weighed in on the question of the balance between divine transcendence and immanence in the 11th/17th-century Hijaz.

4 Ṣafī al-Dīn al-Qushāshī and Mullā Ibrāhīm al-Kūrānī

Ṣafī al-Dīn Aḥmad b. Muḥammad b. Yūnus al-Dajānī al-Qushāshī studied with his father and several Yemeni and Hijazi scholars, including Aḥmad b. al-Faḍl b. ʿAbd al-Nāfiʿ; ʿAbd al-Karīm al-Kujarātī, the student of al-Ghawth, the author of *al-Jawāhir al-khams* (*The five jewels*); and al-Sayyid Ghaḍanfar al-Nahrawālī al-Sīrāwī, who studied with Muḥammad Amīn, the nephew of the great Sufi Mullā ʿAbd al-Raḥmān Jāmī. Al-Qushāshī's main teacher and spiritual guide was Abū l-Mawāhib al-Shinnāwī (d. 1028/1619). Al-Qushāshī married al-Shinnāwī's daughter and became his *khalīfa* in several Sufi orders; he was also a *muftī* of both the Maliki and Shafiʿi *madhhab*s in Medina.

Al-Qushāshī was a prolific author, writing more than 50 works in Hadith, *uṣūl*, and Sufism. Among his works are the *Sharḥ al-ḥikam al-ʿAṭāʾiyya* of Ibn ʿAṭāʾ Allāh al-Iskandarī (d. 709/1309), *Sharḥ ʿaqīdat Ibn Khafīf al-Shīrāzī*, *Sharḥ ʿaqāʾid al-Nasafī*, a gloss on *al-Mawāhib al-ladunniyya* by al-Qasṭallānī, a gloss on *al-Insān al-kāmil* by ʿAbd al-Karīm al-Jīlī (d. ca. 832/1428), *Kalimat al-jūd fī l-qawl bi-waḥdat al-wujūd*, *al-Durra al-thamīna fī-mā li-zāʾir al-Madīna*, a *dīwān* of poetry, and his famous *thabat al-Simṭ al-majīd*. His students included most of the prominent scholars of the Hijaz in the 11th/17th century, among the most distinguished were, Mullā Ibrāhīm al-Kūrānī, Muḥammad b. Rasūl al-Barzanjī (d. 1101/1691), Abū Sālim al-ʿAyyāshī (d. 1090/1679), and Ḥasan al-ʿUjaymī (d. 1113/1702).

Mullā Ibrāhīm b. Ḥasan al-Kūrānī was born in the Kurdish mountains and studied most of the intellectual disciplines including *kalām*, logic, philosophy, geometry, and astronomy, mainly with two local teachers: ʿAbd al-Karīm b. Abī Bakr b. Hidāyat Allāh al-Kūrānī (d. 1050/1640) and Mullā Muḥammad Sharīf al-Kūrānī (d. 1078/1667). When he was around thirty years old, he spent about a year and a half in Baghdad. He then moved to Damascus, where he would stay for some four years. He taught in both of these cities and also continued his own education, this time with a newfound interest in Hadith and Sufism. Al-Kūrānī's immersion in Sufism led him to the works of al-Qushāshī and, after a period of correspondences with him, al-Kūrānī moved to the Hijaz where he settled in Medina, living there until his death. Al-Kūrānī was a prolific author as well: he wrote around one hundred works covering a wide range of Islamic disciplines including Sufism, theology, philosophy, *fiqh*, grammar, and Hadith.

Al-Kūrānī's encounter with al-Qushāshī was a turning point in his life. He continued his studies with al-Qushāshī, who was by that time famous as a theologian and Hadith scholar on the one hand, and as a Sufi deeply influenced by Ibn ʿArabī on the other. Al-Qushāshī's influence on al-Kūrānī was very strong, to the extent that it is difficult to talk about al-Kūrānī's thought independent of the influence of his teacher. All of al-Kūrānī's works were written after his meeting with al-Qushāshī and the latter's Akbarian tendency is very clear in all of al-Kūrānī's works. The only text that al-Kūrānī began to compose before his meeting with al-Qushāshī was later edited with the addition of new chapters that clearly reflect the influence of al-Qushāshī.

5 Classifying *Tawḥīd*

Al-Qushāshī was familiar with the traditional classifications of God's unity and attributes.[37] Indeed, in one of his treatises, he starts with a citation from Ibn Ḥajar al-Haytamī (d. 909/1566), *al-Tuḥfa ʿalā l-minhāj* (*The gift on the method*), in which Ibn Ḥajar says that God is one in His essence, with no multiplicity in any aspect, and that His attributes have no similarity in any aspect, nor do His acts have a companion in any respect.[38] However, al-Qushāshī's main concern was to emphasise the concept of unity in the Akbarian sense that there is no existence by itself and for itself except for God's existence;[39] that everything else exists through God, not by itself, so that everything other than God is nonexistent in one way or another. Thus, al-Qushāshī confirms the unity of existence by arguing that there is only one existence—God's—through which everything else exists.[40] Existence is essentially one (*al-wujūd wāḥid bi-l-dhāt*); everything other than God is nonexistent by its essence, but through God it possesses the attributes that God gave to it, and "we are by Him, and without

37 See for example Ṣafī al-Dīn Aḥmad al-Qushāshī, *al-Ifāda bi-mā bayna l-ikhtiyār wa-l-irāda*, MS. Istanbul, Residefendi428, fols. 35^a–45^a, 40^a, 43^a.

38 Al-Qushāshī, Aḥmad, *Risāla tataʿallaq bi-qawl laysa fī l-imkān abdaʿ mimmā kān*, MS. Residefendi428, fols. 135^a–138^a, 135^a.

39 Ibn ʿArabī, Muḥyī al-Dīn, *al-Futūḥāt al-Makkiyya*, 4 vols., iii, Beirut: Dār Ṣādir, 1968, 162.

40 Al-Qushāshī, Aḥmad, *Kalimat al-jūd bi-l-bayyina wa-l-shuhūd ʿalā l-qawl bi-waḥdat al-wujūd*, MS. Residefendi428, fols. 1^a–33^b, 2^b.

Him we would not be. He was, and nothing was with Him, and He is now as He was: there is nothing other than Him and nothing is with Him."[41]

Al-Kūrānī's definition of unity is similar to the traditional definitions wherein the term *tawḥīd* means ascribing unity to God and not making Him one, because His unity is essential, uncreated (*ghayr majʿūla*), and for Him.[42] Al-Kūrānī explains the different categories of unity in several texts, starting from his very first treatise entitled *Inbāh al-anbāh ʿalā iʿrāb lā ilāh illā Allāh* (*Alerting the vigilant to the grammatical nuances of the phrase "There is no God but God"*).[43] In this treatise, and in every context in which al-Kūrānī discusses this topic, he mentions that the first part of the word of unity (*kalimat al-tawḥīd*), *lā ilāh illā Allāh*, encompasses and entails all the different categories of unity. Although *Inbāh al-anbāh* is a grammar text, al-Kūrānī later added three chapters as a modification of the text, which demonstrate the clear Akbarian-theological influence of his teacher al-Qushāshī.[44] Chapter ten discusses the unity of God in the necessity of His existence (*tawḥīd Allāh fī wujūb wujūdihi*), chapter eleven the unity of acts (*tawḥīd al-afʿāl*), and chapter twelve the unity of existence (*tawḥīd al-wujūd*). Al-Kūrānī did not use the terms *tawḥīd al-ṣifāt* or *waḥdat al-ṣifāt* in this treatise, but his explanation of the unity of God as being the necessity of His existence includes an explanation of the idea of *waḥdat al-ṣifāt*, which I will discuss more fully below.

In his treatise *al-Mutimma li-l-masʾala al-muhimma* (*Complement to the important issue*), al-Kūrānī discusses the categories of unity in a very systematic way, classifying unity into four types (*marātib*):

i. *Tawḥīd al-ulūhiyya*, "unity of worship," is the first category, and it was established by Quranic verses and was agreed upon by all the prophets who called the people to worship God: "We never sent a messenger before you [O Prophet] without revealing to him: 'There is no deity except Me, so worship Me.'" (Q 21:25). This unity negates polytheism and confirms that God is the only deity worthy of worship.[45] God alone deserve to be

41 Al-Qushāshī, Aḥmad, *al-Intiṣār li-Imām al-Ḥarmayn*, MS. Istanbul, Residefendi428, fols. 112ᵃ–138ᵃ, 125ᵃ.

42 Al-Kūrānī, Ibrāhīm, *Qaṣd al-sabīl ilā tawḥīd al-ḥaqq al-wakīl*, MS. KSA: Maktabat al-Malik ʿAbd al-ʿAzīz, ʿĀrif Ḥikmat Collection, *ʿaqāʾid*/231, 126 fols., 19ᵃ.

43 This work was edited by Ahmet Gemi as part of his Ph.D. Dissertation, Ibrâhîm Kûrânî, *Inbâhu'l-enbâh ʿalâ taḥḳîḳi Iʿrâbi lâ ilâhe Illallah*, ed. Ahmet Gemi (PhD Diss.): Atatürk Üniversitesi, 2013; henceforth al-Kūrānī, *Inbāh al-anbāh*.

44 Al-Kūrānī started to compose *Inbāh al-anbāh* in Damascus in 1061/1651 and finished its first draft in Medina in 1062/1652, then edited the work again in 1071/1661.

45 Al-Kūrānī, Ibrāhīm, *al-Mutimma li-l-masʾala al-muhimma*, MS. Sehidalipasa2722, 129ᵃ–161ᵇ, 129ᵇ–130ᵃ.

worshiped because He is the Creator of everything, and He is the Benefactor (*al-nāfiʿ*), the one who causes distress (*al-ḍārr*), and since no one other than God can bring good or prevent harm, no one other than God deserves to be worshiped.[46]

ii. *Tawḥīd al-afʿāl*, "unity of actions," means that God has no companion in His acts, and this category is mentioned using several Quranic verses as well, including "God is the Creator of all things" (Q 39:62) and "God created you and whatever you do" (Q 37:96).

iii. *Tawḥīd al-ṣifāt*, "unity of attributes," which al-Kūrānī suggests can also be phrased as *tawḥīd al-wujūb al-dhātī*, the "unity of essential necessity" that entails all attributes of perfection. God's oneness entails that He be described by all the attributes of perfection, including the necessity of existence. Being described by all the attributes of perfection is called "the unity of the attributes of perfection" (*tawḥīd ṣifāt al-kamāl*). The third category is also mentioned in the Quran, for instance, "O mankind, you are in need of God, while God is the Self-Sufficient, the Praiseworthy" (Q 35:15).

iv. *Tawḥīd al-dhāt*, "unity of the essence," or unity of the true existence (*tawḥīd al-wujūd al-ḥaqīqī*).[47] This category of unity is also mentioned in the Quran; in explaining this type of unity, al-Kūrānī lists several verses: "He is the First and the Last, the Most High and Most Near, and He has knowledge of all things" (Q 57:3); "He is the One who encompasses everything" (Q 41:54); and "He is with you wherever you are" (Q 57:4). This type of unity for al-Kūrānī is related to the ideas 1) that God is absolute existence in the real sense of absoluteness that is neither restricted nor conditioned by anything apart from Himself, and 2) that He is able to manifest Himself in any restricted form without His absoluteness being affected in any way whatsoever. These ideas form the basis of al-Kūrānī's argument for God's manifestation in forms and his acceptance of the ambiguous verses (*mutashābihāt*) without allegorical interpretation.

All four of these categories, al-Kūrānī argues, are indicated by the word of *tawḥīd*, *lā ilāha illā Allāh*, which affirms divinity as exclusively belonging to God and negates it from anything other than Him; doing so entails the unity of God's acts, attributes, and essence.[48] Since the word of *tawḥīd* contains all the categories of God's unity, al-Kūrānī and indeed all Muslim theologians consider it to be the most fundamental aspect of the Islamic creed.

---

46 This explanation is the same al-Kūrānī used in *Inbāh al-anbāh* 222.

47 Al-Kūrānī, *al-Mutimma* 129^{b}.

48 Al-Kūrānī, *al-Mutimma* 130^{b}.

In *al-Mutimma*, after explaining the categories of unity through Quranic verses, al-Kūrānī returns to the argument that these four categories are also confirmed by reason (*ʿaql*) and unveiling (*kashf*). The first two categories are confirmed by reason through the thinking faculty, while the last two categories are confirmed by reason through its ability to perceive what is given to it. So, this kind of knowledge is based on faith and *kashf*, not independent reasoning.[49] By arguing that the unity of attributes is based on both the Quranic text and *kashf*, while also factoring into the equation the unity of divine attributes as the basis for man's effective agency and the theory of *kasb* (acquisition), it is clear that our author is under Ibn ʿArabī's influence. Ibn ʿArabī states that he found it difficult to distinguish between the Ashʿarite notion of the acquisition of actions and the Muʿtazilite position on their creation; the solution to this dilemma came to Ibn ʿArabī through a visual unveiling (*kashf baṣarī*).[50]

While al-Kūrānī discusses different categories of unity, al-Qushāshī emphasises the idea that attributes and actions are only mentally (*iʿtibārī*) multiple and that this mental multiplicity does not entail any multiplicity in the essence. He repeatedly explains that the world with all its greatness, multiplicity, attributes, and its beginning and end, is nothing if compared to the glory of God, because "the world's existence is not for itself, being a mirage in a desert ... The real is that whose existence is by virtue of itself; and since the existence of the world is not by virtue of itself, it is nonexistent."[51] Al-Qushāshī's citation from al-Farghānī's (d. 699/1299) commentary on *Fuṣūṣ al-ḥikam* (*The bezels of wisdom*) provides a good summary of his ideas about unity:

> Because His existence is from Himself, He is eternal, while the existence of all other things are not from themselves; they are thus created. All the attributes of the First are from His essence without needing anything else, unlike the attributes of the second. The attributes that the First has are in the form of perfection, while in the second they are in the form of reflections and borrowed shadows; rather, they are nothing more than a mirage, an illusory existence. But in reality, they are nothing.[52]

---

49 Al-Kūrānī distinguishes between rational knowledge that can be obtained by reason, and a higher kind of knowledge, namely the intellect's divinely gifted ability to receive this divine knowledge. See al-Kūrānī, *Itḥāf al-Dhaki: Tafsir wahdatul wujud bagi Muslim nusantara*, ed. Oman Fathurahman, Jakarta: Miza, 2012, 197.

50 Chittick, William C., *The Sufi path of knowledge: Ibn al-ʿArabī's metaphysics of imagination*, Albany, NY: SUNY Press, 1989, 206.

51 Al-Qushāshī, Aḥmad, *Risāla fī waḥdat al-wujūd*, Ataturk Library, Istanbul Municipality, Osman Ergin, 1083, 12 fols., 2ª.

52 Al-Qushāshī, *Kalimat al-jūd* 19ª.

6 Unity of Attributes (*tawḥīd al-ṣifāt*)

Al-Kūrānī states that the idea of *waḥdat al-ṣifāt* is one of al-Qushāshī's doctrines and that no one has explained this idea better than him; indeed, al-Qushāshī's effort in establishing this concept, he declares, is similar to Ibn ʿArabī's effort in establishing the unity of Being.[53] Al-Qushāshī's relationship to *waḥdat al-ṣifāt* is indeed similar to Ibn ʿArabī's relationship to *waḥdat al-wujūd* at least in one respect: neither of them used the term that has been attributed to him, although the idea itself is diffuse through their respective works. After examining fifteen of al-Qushāshī's main theological texts, I found that the idea of the unity of divine attributes appears often in his writings, but that the term itself, i.e., *waḥdat al-ṣifāt*, is not used.

Nevertheless, the concept permeates his work: al-Qushāshī, as mentioned above, argues that true existence only belongs to God, whose existence is essentially one (*al-wujūd wāḥid bi-l-dhāt*), while everything other than Him does not exist by itself. Since God is necessarily existent, He should be described using all the attributes of perfection, because being necessarily existent entails perfection.[54] Or, we can say, God cannot be necessarily existent unless He is described using all the attributes of perfection. Al-Qushāshī explains that the fact that man was created in the image of God means that man can be characterized by divine attributes such as knowledge, power, and life. But ascribing these attributes to contingents does not make them similar to God's attributes or actions, because these attributes belong to God essentially while man obtains these attributes through God.[55] There can be no doubt that the existence of contingents is through God, which means that all attributes, actions, or perfections are also given to them by God, because perfection (*kamāl*) for the contingent is a branch of its existence, and before its existence a contingent has nothing but its readiness (*istiʿdād*) for existence. Thus, a contingent thing's life, knowledge, power, will, hearing, seeing, speaking, and all other attributes that can be obtained after becoming existent are given to it from those perfections that are God's.[56] This means that all the attributes of perfection are exclusively ascribed to God. Contingents do not have any attributes by themselves, because they

53 Al-ʿAyyāshī, Abū Sālim, *al-Riḥla al-ʿAyyāshiyya 1661–1663*, ed. Saʿīd al-Fāḍilī and Sulaymān al-Qurashī, 2 vols., i, Abu Dhabi: Dār al-Suwaydī, 2006, 590. See also Ramli, Harith, "Ashʿarism through an Akbarī lens: The two "*taḥqīqs*" in the curriculum vitae of Ibrāhīm al-Kūrānī (d. 1019/1690)," in Ayman Shihadeh and Jan Thiele (eds.), *Philosophical Theology in Islam: Later Ashʿarism East and West*, Leiden: Brill, 2020, 371–396, 389–390.

54 Al-Kūrānī, *al-Mutimma* 130[a].

55 Al-Qushāshī, *al-Ifāda* 38[b].

56 Al-Kūrānī, *Qaṣd* 45[b].

exist through God, so they are in need of Him for their existence, and since existence is the basis for any attribute or any perfection, all the perfections of contingents are from God. And any thing's perfection that is not from itself has no perfection. Thus, its perfections should be ascribed to its source, namely God.

Some attributes can thus be ascribed to God or to man, but for God they are essential, uncreated attributes, while in contingent beings these attributes are not essential. When an attribute is ascribed to man, that means it has been given to him by God, because whoever does not have true existence does not have true attributes. For example, knowledge can be ascribed to God or to man, but ultimately all knowledge is one, God's. Power can also be ascribed to God or to man, but ultimately all power is God's. Al-Qushāshī says that the attributes that are ascribed to created being are themselves created, and when they are ascribed to God they are eternal because they are uncreated and do not renew; thus, there are not two powers, nor are there two wills, or two knowledges, or two hearings.[57] Al-Kūrānī explains further by saying that essences differ in their characteristics or properties (*aḥkām*) according to the attributes they possess; for example, if an essence possess the attribute of knowledge it will be described as knowing. The properties of attributes also differ depending on the essence to which they are attributed. Knowledge can be characterised as eternal if it is ascribed to an eternal essence and can be characterized as generated (*ḥādith*) if it is ascribed to a generated being; but the reality of knowledge is one and what remains different are its properties. All attributes are similar in this respect. Thus, power is one reality, which is eternal if it is ascribed to an eternal essence and generated if it is ascribed to a generated essence.[58] Simply, if anything has an attribute through another, this attribute essentially belongs to the other. So, there is no real power except for God, a conclusion al-Kūrānī supports with Quranic verses that confirm that "all power belongs to God" (Q 2:165), "God is the Self-Sufficient, Praiseworthy" (Q 35:15), "He is the Knowing, the All-Aware" (Q 30:54), and "the All-Powerful, Almighty" (Q 57:25). Every attribute of perfection thus belongs essentially and exclusively to God as the essential, necessary existent. Through this argument, it becomes clear that the unity of essence entails the unity of attributes; in al-Qushāshī and al-Kūrānī's articulation, the unity of attributes in turn entails the unity of actions.

57 Al-Qushāshī, *al-Intiṣār* 119[b].
58 Al-Kūrānī, *al-Mutimma* 134[a].

7 From the Unity of Attributes to the Unity of Actions

Since contingents do not have existence by themselves, they essentially need God to exist. In other words, the essential attribute of contingents is being in need, just as the essential attribute of God is being Self-Sufficient and Omnipotent. Thus, the attributes that contingents have belong truly to God, who bestows attributes upon them in accordance with their readiness. The Prophet is told in the Quran to say, "*lā amliku li-nafsī naf*ʿ*an* *wa-lā ḍarr*an" (Q 7:188); and while the verse is usually translated as, "I have no power to benefit or harm myself," al-Qushāshī understands the word "*li-nafsī*" to mean "*by* myself," not "*for* myself." The verse goes on to say: "by myself I have no power ... except what God wills." Al-Qushāshī understands, in this case, "I will have power to benefit or harm myself." What the Prophet possesses thus does not belong to him, because the only entity who essentially possesses power is God.[59]

Here we find al-Qushāshī connecting the idea of God's attributes to one of his main controversial ideas, that while man produces effects through his actions, his effective power is not due to his essence; rather, it is given to him by God, and man uses his effective power by God's permission in a way that accords with God's will. This connection explains why most of the discussion of the idea of the unity of attributes in both al-Qushāshī and al-Kūrānī's works occurs in the context of their discussion of man's freedom of action and predestination. However, the move from the unity of attributes to the discussion of freedom of action and predestination passes through the idea of the unity of actions. Al-Kūrānī clearly says that "since the level (*martaba*) of unity of attributes is higher than the level of unity of acts, and the former includes the latter, the entry into the unity of acts through the gate of the unity of attributes is clearer and easier."[60] Al-Kūrānī explains the connection between the unity of attributes and the unity of acts in the following way: if we say that power is one in essence and multiple with respect to relations and standpoints (*nisab wa-iʿtibārāt*), then we generalize and say that every attribute of perfection that God has and that He may manifest is also one in essence and multiple with respect to relations and standpoints.

God is Omnipotent, the necessarily existent through Himself and perfect through His essence (*kāmil bi-l-dhāt*).[61] Humans can have power, will, and knowledge, but only as reflections of their divine counterparts. Human powers

59 Al-Qushāshī, *al-Intiṣār* 125ᵃ.

60 Al-Kūrānī, *al-Mutimma* 133ᵃ.

61 Al-Kūrānī, Ibrāhīm, *Maslak al-sadād ilā masʾalat khalq afʿāl al-ʿibād*, MS. Istanbul: Veliyuddin1815, fols. 32ᵇ–64ᵃ, 34ᵇ.

are instances of divine power; they are loci of manifestation (*maẓāhir*), entifications (*taʿayyunāt*), and revelations (*tanazzulāt*).[62]

On the level of the unity of actions, we can say that al-Qushāshī and al-Kūrānī agree with the traditional Ashʿarite theory of *kasb* that maintains that the only effective agent is God. But for both of them, power is also effective when it manifests in human acts, with God's permission. Ascribing effective power to man does not negate God's power as being solely effective, because power, as is the case with all attributes, is by essence one with respect to relations and standpoints. In *Maslak al-sadād* (*The path of rectitude*), al-Kūrānī says that accepting that human power (*qudra*) has an effect on human actions—by God's permission, not independently—does not contradict the claim that God is the Creator of everything, which is the unity of actions.[63] All the actions of all creatures are ultimately reducible to God's power. The human power that causes an action is therefore not independent of God's power, as the early Muʿtazilites wrongly supposed, but is instead a manifestation of God's absolute power. The human act simply results from a particular manifestation or instance of divine power and is thus not independent of God's power. Al-Kūrānī states that it is clear that power is one in essence but manifold in its entifications. If that is the case, he argues, it is correct to say that acts are one while also affirming the human's acquisition of his acts by virtue of the effect this power occurring by God's permission, and not independently.[64]

Attributes such as power are not essential to human beings but are instead bestowed on them by God. Humans have power only through God. What is given to humans by God belongs essentially only to God; thus, power is only one by essence, but it can be multiplied by its entifications. Man cannot act without power, and "there is no power except through God" (Q 18:39); thus, there is no human action except through God's power. This is how "God is the creator of all things" (Q 13:16) while at the same time man produces effects through his actions.[65]

In sum, the unity of attributes confirms that there is no power by essence except God's power. Thus, confirming the unity of attributes negates any true power except God's. How does this idea help al-Qushāshī and al-Kūrānī argue that man also has effective power in his actions, if there is no effective power in the world except God's? The unity of attributes entails the unity of actions, which, according to al-Kūrānī, allows us to confirm human capacity to act *by*

62 El-Rouayheb, *Islamic intellectual history* 301.
63 Al-Kūrānī, *Maslak* 32^{b}.
64 Al-Kūrānī, *Maslak* 34^{b}.
65 Al-Kūrānī, *Maslak* 34^{b}.

God's permission. Man has power that is given to him by God, but the true attribute of power belongs only to God; man does not have power and cannot act except by the power granted to him by God.[66]

8 From the Unity of Actions to Human Freedom

The question of human actions arose from attempts to keep the balance between human freedom of action and God's omnipotence, and the concept of the unity of acts helped al-Kūrānī to argue that man produces effects through his actions while "all power belongs to God." After establishing in his discussion of the unity of actions that God is the only creator of everything and that "all power belongs to God," al-Kūrānī argues that man produces effects through his actions, an idea that seems to contradict the idea of the unity of actions. But al-Kūrānī considers the idea of the unity of actions to be a demonstration of man's effect in his actions by God's permission.

Similar to all other attributes, power by essence belongs only to God. He is described by all the attributes of perfection essentially, so any perfection attributed to something other than God has been given to it by God. So, power by essence belongs only to God, and it effects are there only according to God's will. When God wants to act through a man, He makes their will attached to the act through His will, because "you do not will except that God wills" (Q 81:29). Thus man's will attaches to an action through God's will, and then God's power manifests in him to create the act. One can say that the effect of power is exclusively God's; or one can say that man has power by God's power and permission, not independently. The meaning of *kasb* is that a man acquires his effective agency by God's permission. Power in reality and essence is one, and differs in its standpoints. God's permission here means giving man the power to act, if his will agrees with God's will.[67]

Arguing for man's effective power over his actions was one of the most controversial topics in al-Qushāshī and al-Kūrānī's teachings. The Ashʿarites taught that since God is the sole creator, He creates human acts. Their doctrine of *kasb* allowed them to maintain God's sole creative agency while also allowing human beings to be legally responsible for their actions.[68] The Ashʿarite belief

66 Al-Kūrānī, Ibrāhīm, *Takmilat al-qawl al-jalī fī taḥqīq qawl al-Imām Zayd b. ʿAlī*, MS. Istanbul: Sehidalipasa 2722, fols. 296ᵃ–346ᵇ, 303ᵇ.

67 Al-Kūrānī, *al-Mutimma* 134ᵃ⁻ᵇ.

68 Abrahamov, Binyamin, "A re-examination of al-Ashʿarī's theory of 'kasb' according to 'Kitāb al-Lumaʿ'," in *JRAS* 2 (1989), 210–221, 210.

that only God has causal power came to be known as "occasionalism," which means there is no causal necessity between a cause and its effect; it is God who in fact brings about the effect in conjunction with the cause, thereby negating any kind of necessary causation in nature.

Al-Qushāshī and al-Kūrānī wanted to refute the two extreme positions, that human beings act independently and that their acts are completely determined by God. They rejected both the Muʿtazilite view that humans create their actions independently of God (*bi-l-istiqlāl*), and the mainstream Ashʿarite view that human actions are the direct creations of God and that human intentions and abilities have no effect (*ta'thīr*) on the created action.[69] Their middle position was to accept the idea that man produces effects through his actions, but with God's permission.[70]

In *Maslak al-sadād*, in which al-Kūrānī discusses the controversial topic of human effects over their own actions by God's permission, he states that affirming human agency by God's permission does not contradict the idea that God is the Creator of everything, which is referred to as the unity of actions.[71] In fact, establishing the unity of attributes and unity of actions was necessary for al-Kūrānī to argue that man produces effects through his actions; thus, the first chapter of *Maslak al-sadād* is entitled *Fī ithbāt tawḥīd al-ṣifāt al-muṣaḥḥiḥ li-tawḥīd al-afʿāl* ("On proving the unity of attributes that confirms the unity of actions"). The independent by itself and the perfect by itself is only God. And since independence and perfection are limited exclusively to God, that means everything other than Him is in need of Him, in their existence and their perfection; al-Kūrānī again grounds this argument in a Quranic verse, "O mankind, you are in need of God, while God is the Self-Sufficient, the Praiseworthy" (Q 35:15). Among the perfections of God is that He is omnipotent; God has power in Himself, and if any other creature has power, it is through God. "There is no power except through God" (Q 18:39), because "all power belongs to God" (Q 2:165). Thus, all the powers manifested in the created world are given by God, and what is given belongs truly only to the Giver. Otherwise, it would be essential for creatures, which is untenable. Thus, power essentially is one and belongs only to God, but its manifestations or entifications (*taʿayyunāt*) are multiple, which confirms the unity of actions, since all actions return to God's power. Confirming the unity of actions also confirms, on the other hand,

---

69 El-Rouayheb, *Islamic intellectual history* 298.

70 Al-Kūrānī's argument for his interpretation of *kasb* is examined closely in El-Rouayheb's *Islamic intellectual history* 294.

71 Al-Kūrānī, *Maslak* 32^{b}.

that humans have power that affects their acts, power given to them by God. This assertion that humans affect their actions by God's permission should not be confused with the Muʿtazilite idea that humans act by their own independent power, since there is no independent power except the one that is possessed by He who has power by the virtue of His essence, which is only God. By asserting that humans affect their actions by God's permission, al-Qushāshī and al-Kūrānī were able to refute predestination, since man produces effects through his actions and has independent free will but does so by virtue of God's permission.[72]

Thus, the unity of attributes is an essential idea for al-Kūrānī's argument for the unity of actions, and for the defense of his idea that man produces effects through his actions by God's permission. There is no contradiction between attributing the effect to a man and saying that there is no effect except via God's power, because the unity of attributes allows us to combine these two ideas. Thus, man was given effective power by God's permission; so there is no predestination. And his power to act is by God's permission; so he does not act independently. This middle path, for al-Kūrānī, lies in correctly conceiving of the doctrine of *kasb*.[73]

In reply to criticisms directed against him, al-Kūrānī says that those who have claimed that his ideas are similar to the Muʿtazilites' have not considered his position that man produces effects through his actions. He wonders how a person who believes in the unity of attributes and that power essentially belongs only to God could be understood as saying that there can be an essentially effective agency other than God's.[74]

9 Conclusion

Different categories or levels of unity are interconnected: the highest level of unity entails the one beneath it, and the lowest one refers to and indicates the higher. Confirming that there is "no god but God" is a first stage of unity, the unity of worship, which confirms that God alone deserves to be worshiped and negates the divinity of anything other than Him. He is the only truly divine being because His existence is essentially necessary for Him, while everything other than Him is in need of Him. Since He is the

---

72 Al-Kūrānī, *Maslak* 34[a]–36[a].

73 Al-Kūrānī, *Inbāh al-anbāh* 223.

74 Al-Kūrānī, *al-Mutimma* 133[b].

only true existence, He is the only effective power in the world. Realizing that no action can happen in the world without God's power confirms the unity of actions. Power is one attribute among other attributes of perfection that belong exclusively and essentially to God since He is the only true existence. God, as we saw in the fourth category of al-Kūrānī's classification of unity, *tawḥīd al-dhāt*, "unity of the essence," is described by all the attributes of perfection; the Quranic verses that al-Kūrānī quotes say that God is the First and the Last, the Most High and Most Near, the One who encompasses everything, and He is with us wherever we are. God's essence cannot be defined or conditioned because God is absolute existence in the sense that nothing can restrict Him. Since God's essence is identical to His existence, we can say that the unity of the essence is the unity of existence, or *waḥdat al-wujūd*, which compasses all levels of unity.

The unity of attributes seems to be the cornerstone of many of al-Qushāshī and al-Kūrānī's controversial positions. From one side it leads to the unity of existence and from the other side it confirms the unity of acts; it was between these categories of unity that al-Qushāshī and al-Kūrānī discussed most of their theological ideas.

On the level of the unity of existence, God is absolute existence and is able to manifest Himself in sensory and conceivable forms without His absoluteness being affected. Thus, any description of God in restricted forms in the Quran should be understood as God's manifestation, and therefore there is no need for figurative interpretation of the ambiguous verses, because they refer to divine manifestation. These two ideas, God as absolute existence and that there is no need to figuratively interpret the verses that describe God as taking on sensory forms, were interpreted by detractors of Akbarian thought in an extreme way. By describing God as absolute existence, Ibn ʿArabī and his followers were accused of reducing God to an abstract idea without actual existence. And the idea of God's manifestations in forms, or *tajalliyyāt* in Sufi terms, and the acceptance of the ambiguous verses (*mutashābihāt*) without allegorical interpretation were together read as a kind of anthropomorphism and even pantheism. Chittick describes the Akbarian awareness of the need to keep the balance between transcendence and immanence by seeing with "both eyes," which can serve to offset historical misreadings of the Akbarian perspective.

The unity of attributes in turn confirms the unity of actions because all attributes of perfection belong essentially to God and therefore power belongs essentially to God. But God's power can manifest in man's effective power, an idea that allowed al-Qushāshī and al-Kūrānī to argue that man produces effects through his actions. Thus, the unity of attributes is clearly related to the ideas of human freedom of action and, simultaneously, of God's omnipotence and foreknowledge. Mention of free will and predestination will raise the possibility that man may act against God's will; thus, questions of good and bad according to the intellect and legal responsibility should be discussed. Indeed, human freedom and predestination were clearly connected to the treatment of God's attributes even outside of the Akbarian tradition, since the Muʿtazilite argument for human freedom of action was motivated by the idea of preserving God's justice, which for them was inseparable from any discussion of God's unity.

Al-Kūrānī was aware of the complexity of the topic of unity and the interconnectedness of all Islamic doctrines. In one of his later works entitled *Imdād dhawī l-istiʿdād* (*Spiritual succour to the prepared*), he stated that he continued to receive questions about *kasb* because the main principle (*aṣl*) of the unity of attributes that he had explained in previous works was unclear. To clarify the unity of attributes, al-Kūrānī repeated his ideas about accepting the ambiguous verses without allegorical interpretation and said that this principle resulted from conceiving of God as absolute existence.[75]

In one of Professor Chittick's explanations of the Akbarian idea of *waḥdat al-wujūd*, he states it does not lie in any simple formulation. If people want a simple statement, he suggests, they should be satisfied with "There is no god but God."[76] This study has hopefully shown that this short formula of *tawḥīd* does, in fact, lie at the center of Islamic theology, and has articulated some of the reasons why Akbarian scholars considered the logical result of this idea to be *waḥdat al-wujūd*. Al-Qushāshī and al-Kūrānī's discussions of central Islamic doctrines within the framework of Akbarian thought were part of their effort to demonstrate that Ibn ʿArabī's ideas, encapsulated in the idea of *waḥdat al-wujūd*, provide the correct understanding of Islamic doctrines. Akbarian scholars of the 11th/17th century were discussing almost all the subjects that were widely treated in the Islamic theological tradition of their day. In the final analysis, the discussion of the unity of divine attributes was a means whereby the two main topics in Islamic theology, God's oneness and His attributes, could be shown as clearly resulting from and leading back to *waḥdat al-wujūd*.

75 Al-Kūrānī, Ibrāhīm, *Imdād dhawī l-istiʿdād li-sulūk maslak al-sadād*, MS. USA, Princeton University Library, GarretY3867, fols. 31^{a}–87^{b}, 32^{a}.

76 Chittick, "A history" 73.

Bibliography

Abdel-Kader, Ali H., *The life, personality and writings of al-Junayd: A study of a third/ninth century mystic*, London: Luzac, 1962.

Abrahamov, Binyamin, "A re-examination of al-Ashʿarī's theory of 'kasb' according to 'Kitāb al-Lumaʿ'," in *JRAS* 2 (1989), 210–221.

Abrahamov, Binyamin, *Ibn al-ʿArabi and the Sufis*, Oxford: Anqa Publishing, 2014.

Ali, Mukhtar H., *Philosophical Sufism: An introduction to the school of Ibn al-ʿArabī*, New York: Routledge, 2022.

al-ʿAyyāshī, Abū Sālim, *al-Riḥla al-ʿAyyāshiyya 1661–1663*, ed. Saʿīd al-Fāḍilī and Sulaymān al-Qurashī, 2 vols., Abu Dhabi: Dār al-Suwaydī, 2006.

Belhaj, Abdessamad, "Tawhid (oneness)," in Cenap Çakmak (ed.), *Islam: A worldwide encyclopedia*, Santa Barbara, CA: ABC-CLIO, 2017, 1553–1555.

Blankinship, Khalid, "The early creed," in Tim Winter (ed.), *The Cambridge companion to classical Islamic theology*, Cambridge: Cambridge University Press, 2008, 33–54.

Böwering, Gerhard, "God and His attributes," in *EQ*.

Chittick, William C., *The Sufi path of knowledge: Ibn al-ʿArabī's metaphysics of imagination*, Albany, NY: SUNY Press, 1989.

Chittick, William C., *Faith and practice of Islam: Three thirteenth century Sufi texts*, Albany, NY: SUNY Press, 1992.

Chittick, William C., "Ibn ʿArabī and his school: Life, works, and influence," in Seyyed Hossein Nasr (ed.), *Islamic spirituality: Manifestations*, New York: Crossroad, 1997, 49–79.

Chittick, William C., *Ibn ʿArabi: Heir to the prophets*, Oxford: Oneworld, 2005.

Chittick, William C., *In search of the lost heart: Explorations in Islamic thought*, ed. Mohammed Rustom, Atif Khalil, and Kazuyo Murata, Albany, NY: SUNY Press, 2012.

Dawānī, Jalāl al-Dīn, *Risālat Khalq al-aʿmāl*, in *al-Rasāʾil al-mukhtāra*, ed. Sayyid Aḥmad Tūysirkānī, Isfahan: Emam Ali Public Library, 1985.

El-Bizri, Nader, "God: Essence and attributes," in Tim Winter (ed.), *The Cambridge companion to classical Islamic theology*, Cambridge: Cambridge University Press, 2008, 121–140.

El-Rouayheb, Khaled, *Islamic intellectual history in the seventeenth century: Scholarly currents in the Ottoman empire and the Maghreb*, New York: Cambridge University Press, 2015.

Fathurahman, Oman, *Itḥāf Al-Dhaki: Tafsir wahdatul wujud bagi Muslim nusantara*, Jakarta: Miza, 2012.

Gimaret, Daniel, "Ṣifa," in EI^2.

Gimaret, Daniel, "Tawḥīd," in EI^2.

al-Hujwīrī, ʿAlī b. ʿUthmān, *The Kashf maḥjūb: The oldest Persian treatise on Ṣūfiism*, trans. Reynold A. Nicholson, Leyden and London: Brill, 1911.

Ibn ʿArabī, Muḥyī al-Dīn, *al-Futūḥāt al-Makkiyya*, 4 vols., Beirut: Dār Ṣādir, 1968.

Ibn Ḥanbal, Aḥmad, *al-Radd ʿalā l-Jahamiyya wa-l-Zanādiqa*, Riyadh: Dār al-Liwāʾ, 1977.

Ibn al-Humām, Muḥammad b. ʿAbd al-Wāḥid, *al-Musāmara fī sharḥ al-Musāyara fī ʿilm al-kalām*, Cairo: al-Maktaba al-Azhariyya li-l-Turāth, 2006.

al-Kūrānī, Ibrāhīm, *Imdād dhawī l-istiʿdād li-sulūk maslak al-sadād*, MS. USA, Princeton University Library, GarretY3867, fols. 31ª–87ᵇ.

al-Kūrānī, Ibrāhīm, *Maslak al-sadād ilā masʾalat khalq afʿāl al-ʿibād*, MS. Istanbul: Veliyuddin1815, fols. 32ᵇ–64ª.

al-Kūrānī, Ibrāhīm, *al-Mutimma li-l-masʾala al-muhimma*, MS. Sehidalipasa2722, 129ª–161ᵇ.

al-Kūrānī, Ibrāhīm, *Qaṣd al-sabīl ilā tawḥīd al-ḥaqq al-wakīl*, MS. KSA: Maktabat al-Malik ʿAbd al-ʿAzīz, ʿĀrif Ḥikmat Collection, *ʿaqāʾid*/231, 126 fols.

al-Kūrānī, Ibrāhīm, *Takmilat al-qawl al-jalī fī taḥqīq qawl al-Imām Zayd b. ʿAlī*, MS. Istanbul: Sehidalipasa2722, fols. 296ª–346ᵇ.

al-Kūrānī, Ibrāhīm, *Inbâhu'l-enbâh ʿalâ taḥḳîḳi Iʿrâbi lâ ilâhe Illallah*, ed. Ahmet Gemi, Erzurum (PhD Diss.): Atatürk Üniversitesi, 2013.

Martin, Richard C., "Anthropomorphism," in *EQ*.

Murata, Sachiko and William C. Chittick, *The vision of Islam*, New York: Paragon House, 1994.

al-Qushāshī, Aḥmad, *al-Ifāda bimā bayna l-ikhtiyār wa-l-irāda*, MS. Istanbul, Residefendi428, fols. 35ª–44ª.

al-Qushāshī, Aḥmad, *al-Intiṣār li-Imām al-Ḥarmayn*, MS. Istanbul, Residefendi428, fols. 112ª–138ª.

al-Qushāshī, Aḥmad, *Kalimat al-jūd bi-l-bayyina wa-l-shuhūd ʿalā l-qawl bi-waḥdat al-wujūd*, MS. Residefendi428, fols. 1ª–33ᵇ.

al-Qushāshī, Aḥmad, *Risāla fī waḥdat al-wujūd*, Ataturk Library, Istanbul Municipality, Osman Ergin, 1083, 12 fols.

al-Qushāshī, Aḥmad, *Risāla tataʿallaq bi-qawl laysa fī l-imkān abdaʿ mimmā kān*, MS. Residefendi428, fols. 135ª–138ª.

al-Qushayrī, ʿAbd al-Karīm b. Hawāzin, *al-Qushayrī's epistle on Sufism* (*al-Risāla al-Qushayriyya fī ʿilm al-taṣawwuf*), trans. Alexander D. Knysh, Reading: Garnet Publishing, 2007.

Ramli, Harith, "Ashʿarism through an Akbarī lens: The two "*taḥqīqs*" in the curriculum vitae of Ibrāhīm al-Kūrānī (d. 1019/1690)," in Ayman Shihadeh and Jan Thiele (eds.), *Philosophical Theology in Islam: Later Ashʿarism East and West*, Leiden: Brill, 2020, 371–396.

Tibawi, Abdel Latif, "Al-Ghazālī's sojourn in Damascus and Jerusalem," in *IQ* 9.3–4 (1965), 65–122.

al-Ṭūsī, Abū Naṣr al-Sarrāj, *al-Lumaʿ*, ed. ʿAbd al-Ḥalīm Maḥmūd and Ṭāhā A.B. Surūr, Cairo: Dār al-Kutub al-Ḥadītha, 1960.

Winter, Tim, "Introduction," in Tim Winter (ed.), *The Cambridge companion to classical Islamic theology*, Cambridge: Cambridge University Press, 2008, 1–16.

CHAPTER 12

The Akbarian Tradition in Hadhramawt: The Intellectual Legacy of Shaykh Abū Bakr b. Sālim

Omar Edaibat

1 Introduction

The intellectual and social history of Yemen's Hadhramawt valley and the pre-modern origins of Bā ʿAlawī Sufism, its largest and most influential spiritual tradition, remain poorly understood and understudied in the academy.[1] While the last few decades have witnessed a steady academic interest in the Banū ʿAlawī *sāda*'s (pl. of *sayyid*) large diasporic communities across the vast Indian Ocean region, with a number of historical and anthropological studies focusing on the social and political history of Hadhramawt since the 19th century,[2] the Hadhrami system of social stratification,[3] and on various communities or

1 See Edaibat, Omar, *The Bā ʿAlawī sāda of the Hadhramaut valley: An intellectual and social history from tenth-century origins till the late-sixteenth century*, Montreal (PhD Diss.): McGill Institute of Islamic Studies, 2021. The Banū ʿAlawī *sāda*, or Bā ʿAlawīs in the Hadhrami colloquial, are a large and famous Sunni tribe of the *ahl al-bayt* who trace their lineage back to their famed ancestor Imam Aḥmad b. ʿĪsā 'al-Muhājir' (d. 345/956), a descendant of the Prophet Muhammad's grandson al-Ḥusayn who migrated with several members of his family from his native Basra in Iraq to the Hadhramawt valley *circa* 317/929. As an organized Sufi brotherhood, the Bā ʿAlawī *ṭarīqa* was founded in the late-6th/12th-early-7th/13th century by Imam al-Muhājir's famed descendant 'al-Faqīh al-Muqaddam' Muḥammad b. ʿAlī (d. 653/1255), who was initiated with the Sufi *khirqa* into the spiritual lineage of the great North African Sufi Abū Madyan Shuʿayb (d. 594/1198). See Edaibat, *The Bā ʿAlawī sāda*, ch. 2.

2 For more on Hadhramawt's social and political transformations over the last two centuries, see Freitag, Ulrike, *Indian Ocean migrants and state formation in Hadhramaut: Reforming the homeland*, Leiden: Brill, 2003; Hartwig, Friedhelm, "Expansion, state foundation and reform: The contest for power in Hadhramaut in the nineteenth century," in Ulrike Freitag and William G. Clarence-Smith (eds.), *Hadhrami traders, scholars, and statesmen in the Indian Ocean, 1750s–1960s*, Leiden: Brill, 1997, 35–50; Boxberger, Linda, *On the edge of empire: Hadhramawt, emigration, and the Indian Ocean, 1880s–1930s*, Albany, NY: SUNY Press, 2002; Brehony, Noel (ed.), *Hadhramaut and its diaspora: Yemeni politics, identity and migration*, London: I.B. Tauris, 2017; Lekon, Christian, *Time, space and globalization: Hadhramaut and the Indian Ocean rim 1863–1967*, Gleichen: Muster-Schmidt, 2014; Collins, Brinston B., *Ḥaḍramawt: Crisis and intervention, 1866–1881*, Princeton (PhD Diss.): Princeton University, 1969.

3 An influential and pioneering work on the Hadhrami system of social stratification can be

 | DOI:10.1163/9789004529038_013

figures within the well-established ʿAlawī diaspora,[4] the premodern origins of their Sufi tradition and its contributions to the intellectual history of Sufism remain in need of a significant scholarly reappraisal.

2 Some Historiographical Considerations

The premodern intellectual and social history of Hadhramawt continues to pose a number of historiographical challenges for contemporary scholars. Serjeant's scholarship in the mid-20th century helped pave the way for much of the contemporary scholarship on Hadhramawt.[5] On the other hand, Knysh's "The Sāda in history"[6] offers a critical and bleak reflection on the current state of

---

found in Bujra, Abdalla S., *The politics of stratification: A study of political change in a South Arabian town*, Oxford: Clarendon Press, 1971. Bujra's findings on the rigidity of the social system in the valley are more recently critiqued in Sylvaine, Camelin, "Reflections on the system of social stratification in Hadhramaut," in Ulrike Freitag and William G. Clarence-Smith (eds.), *Hadhrami traders, scholars, and statesmen in the Indian Ocean, 1750s–1960s*, Leiden: Brill, 1997, 147–156.

4 Bang, Anne K., *Sufis and scholars of the sea: Family networks in East Africa, 1860–1925*, London: RoutledgeCurzon, 2003 and Ho, Engseng, *The graves of Tarim: Genealogy and mobility across the Indian Ocean*, Berkeley, CA: University of California Press, 2006 are two noteworthy and penetrating studies on members of the widely diffused ʿAlawī diaspora and their migratory patterns and scholarly networks across the Indian Ocean, with significant forays into the *sāda*'s early premodern history in Hadhramawt. However, given their scope and diasporic focus, their overviews of the *sāda*'s early intellectual history in the valley, while more helpful for our purposes, are far from comprehensive. Bang, *Sufis*; Ho, *Graves*. See also the essays in Freitag, Ulrike and William G. Clarence-Smith (eds.), *Hadhrami traders, scholars, and statesmen in the Indian Ocean, 1750s–1960s*, Leiden: Brill, 1997; Abushouk, Ahmed I. and Hassan A. Ibrahim (eds.), *The Hadhrami diaspora in Southeast Asia: Identity, maintenance or assimilation?*, Leiden: Brill, 2009.

5 Serjeant's historiographic and ethnographic fieldwork, in which he attempted to appraise the condition and scope of Hadhramawt's primary materials by providing an annotated catalogue of the major surviving MSS of its historic libraries, are no doubt valuable scholarly resources. See Serjeant, Robert B., "Materials for South Arabian history: Notes on new MSS from Ḥadramawt," in *BSOAS* 13.2 (1950), 281–307 and Serjeant, Robert B., "Materials for South Arabian history: Notes on new MSS from Ḥadramawt (Part II)," in *BSOAS* 13.3 (1950), 581–601. For his more detailed assessment of the general state of Hadhrami historiography, see Serjeant, Robert B., "Historians and historiography of Ḥaḍramawt," in *BSOAS* 25.1/3 (1962), 239–261.

6 Knysh, Alexander, "The Sāda in history: A critical essay on Ḥaḍramī historiography," in *JRAS* 9.2 (1999), 215–222. Based on his fieldwork in Hadhramawt, Knysh also authored a more recent study on the valley's modern Bā ʿAlawī tradition since the 1990 unification of Yemen, which offers a similarly bleak and pessimistic take on the current state of the *sāda*'s intellectual Sufi

Hadhrami historiography in which he questions the nature of the *sāda*'s intellectual Sufi tradition and our ability to reconstruct an accurate account of their early history, while Peskes's German study *al-ʿAidarūs und seine Erben*[7] remains perhaps the most informative and detailed academic study on the early ʿAlawīs to date, focusing on the intellectual and social history of their famous ʿAydarūs clan more specifically.

Upon examining the available Hadhrami primary sources, a recurring concern is their relatively late authorship, as nearly all the surviving biographical sources on the *sāda* were composed between the 9th/15th and 11th/17th centuries. As Knysh and Serjeant have noted, the 9th/15th century appears to be generally a terminus a quo with respect to pertinent biographical accounts (mostly hagiographic *manāqib*) and chronicles, among other relevant historical materials.[8] Another major concern with the surviving biographical works is their predominantly ʿAlawī authorship and their allegedly pro-*sāda* bias, in addition to their overwhelmingly hagiographic character, which renders them highly susceptible to exaggeration and embellishment. For Knysh, these works' pro-ʿAlawī accounts are so "riddled with underlying agendas and biases, which often hinge on considerations of genealogy and clannish honour," as to be patently unreliable.[9] His foray into the early historiography of Hadhramawt and his interpretation of the *sāda*'s historical materials is thus largely informed by

---

tradition. See Knysh, Alexander, "The 'tariqa' on a landcruiser: The resurgence of Sufism in Yemen," in *Middle East Journal* 55.3 (2001), 399–414.

7 Peskes, Esther, *al-ʿAidarūs und seine Erben: Eine Untersuchung zu Geschichte und Sufismus einer ḥaḍramitischen Sāda-Gruppe vom fünfzehnten bis zum achtzehnten Jahrhundert*, Stuttgart: Steiner, 2005. Another insightful essay on the major 9th/15th-century ʿAlawī Sufi and patron saint of Aden, Imam Abū Bakr al-ʿAydarūs al-ʿAdanī (d. 914/1508) can be found in Peskes, Esther, "Der Heilige und die Dimension seiner Macht: Abū Bakr al-ʿAydarūs (gest. 1509) und die Saiyid-Sūfīs von Ḥaḍramaut," in *QSA* 13 (1995), 41–72. The conclusions of these two German studies are more succinctly summarized in English in Peskes, Esther, "Sainthood as patrimony: ʿAbd Allāh al-ʿAydarūs (d. 1461) and his descendants," in Alexandre Papas and Catherine Mayeur-Jaouen (eds.), *Family portraits with saints*, Berlin: DeGruyter, 2020, 125–157.

8 The general neglect of manuscripts, exacerbated by low rates of literacy among the valley's mostly rural and Bedouin population, as well as the infestation of manuscripts by the voracious white ant, and the Wahhābī invasion of 1224/1809 appear to have collectively contributed to the destruction of several important libraries and the loss of thousands of volumes in Tarīm, ʿĪnāt, and elsewhere. Serjeant, "Materials" 281–283; Knysh, "Sāda in history" 216. The eminent ʿAlawī historian ʿAlawī b. Ṭāhir al-Ḥaddād also observes that, to the exception of its principal towns such as Tarīm, Say'ūn and Shibām, Hadhramawt's largely uneducated and mostly rural population may explain why Hadhrami histories and chronicles prior to the 9th/15th century have not survived. Al-Ḥaddād, ʿAlawī b. Ṭāhir, *Janī l-shamārīkh: Jawāb as'ila fī l-tārīkh*, ed. Muḥammad Yaslam ʿAbd al-Nūr, Tarīm: Tarīm li-l-Dirāsāt wa-l-Nashr, 2012, 53–56.

9 Knysh, "Sāda in history" 215.

a hermeneutics of suspicion, which at times appears to tilt towards the more critical and anti-ʿAlawī sentiments of the *sāda*'s modern Hadhrami detractors in the wake of the heated historiographical debates that were fueled by the ʿAlawī-Irshādī rivalries of the early 20th century.[10]

Knysh's generally pessimistic outlook on the historiography of Hadhramawt, which appears to be colored by his own negative encounters during his fieldwork in the valley,[11] may be contrasted with Serjeant's more nuanced and positive assessment of the *sāda* and the quality of their modern scholarship.[12] Though not entirely uncritical, in his opinion, the ʿAlawīs have generally fared better than their modern detractors, largely "owing to their superior scholarship."[13] Perhaps nowhere is this contrast more readily felt than in the lingering doubts concerning the authenticity of the ʿAlawīs' claimed descent from the Prophet Muhammad. Not only does Knysh question the authenticity of the *sāda*'s Prophetic ancestry, which Peskes also considers to be a dubious claim, but he goes further to question the very historicity of their famed ancestor Imam Aḥmad al-Muhājir (d. 945/956).[14] As for Serjeant, on the other hand, he displays no such concerns, "for it is difficult in Arabia to support a spurious pedigree, the more so, of course, when financial considerations enter."[15]

---

10 Knysh, "Sāda in history" 218. For more on the ʿAlawī-Irshādī controversies of the early-20th century, see Motoki, Yamaguchi, "Debate on the status of *sayyid/sharīfs* in the modern era: The ʿAlawī Irshādī dispute and Islamic reformists in the Middle East," in Morimoto Kazuo (ed.), *Sayyids and sharifs in Muslim societies: The living links to the Prophet*, London: Routledge, 2012, 49–71.

11 Thus, he describes his "shock" at the existence of illiterate *sāda* amongst the Bedouin rural tribes and at being "accosted by a persistent beggar in traditional *sayyid* garb." Motoki, "Debate" 217–218. The Banū ʿAlawīs are one of the largest and most diverse tribes in Hadhramawt today, consisting of at least 125 clans. Bā ʿAlawī, ʿAbd al-Raḥmān b. Muḥammad and ʿAlī Bā Ṣabrīn, *Bughyat al-mustarshidīn fī talkhīṣ fatāwā baʿḍ al-aʾimma min al-ʿulamāʾ al-mutaʾakhkhirīn*, 4 vols., iv, Tarīm: Dār al-Faqīh, 2009, 480. Certainly, not all these families took to the rigors of Sufi piety and scholarship, and indeed, a few of the *sāda's* clans in the rural areas took to the ways of their immediate Bedouin context.

12 Having visited Hadhramawt in the mid-20th century, Serjeant had the advantage of several personal encounters and fruitful exchanges with some of the *sāda's* most influential scholars and historians of the 20th century. For a brief description of these encounters and his positive take on the ʿAlawīs' scholarship, see Serjeant, "Historians" 252–257.

13 Serjeant, Robert B., *The saiyids of Ḥaḍramawt*, London: School of Oriental and African Studies, 1957, 28.

14 Knysh, "Sāda in history" 218. Peskes also notes the absence of non-ʿAlawī sources confirming the historicity of al-Muhājir, a claim which upon scrutiny is inaccurate. Peskes, *al-ʿAidarūs* 23, 201. For more on the historicity of Imam al-Muhājir, see Edaibat, *Bā ʿAlawī sāda*, ch. 1.

15 Serjeant, *Saiyids* 11.

As for Peskes, in her view, Serjeant reflects a clearly pro-*sāda* leaning, while Knysh's reading of their history and motives is unduly critical and unwarranted. Though she acknowledges the limitations of the biographical sources and at times shares in Knysh's general concerns, she nevertheless recognizes their value in allowing for at least a partial reconstruction of the *sāda*'s social and intellectual history.[16]

Such lingering scholarly concerns highlight the need to revisit the questions they raise and to re-examine the reliability of the available hagiographic biographies, among other primary materials, in allowing us to reconstruct a more accurate and complete picture of the *sāda*'s social and intellectual history.[17] Be that as it may, it suffices us here to note that other scholars have already successfully demonstrated that hagiographical materials can in fact be carefully mined in the service of historiography.[18] Indeed, most such materials are not exclusively concerned with the domains of the marvelous and the preternatural, offering us a wealth of valuable historical detail and biographical information.[19] Aside from addressing the historiographical concerns that are posed by the sources, which is beyond the immediate scope of this study, a more contextualized and comprehensive account of the ʿAlawī *sāda*'s contributions to the development of Hadhrami and Yemeni Sufism must also pay closer attention to the *sāda*'s scholarly networks and the various works that they studied, much of which can be readily gleaned from their primary biographical works. More importantly, such an account must also offer a broad survey and examination of their scholarly output so as to provide a more critical appraisal of their intellectual and spiritual canon.[20]

16 Peskes, *al-ʿAidarūs* 11–16.

17 These major historiographical concerns are exhaustively treated in Edaibat, *Bā ʿAlawī sāda*.

18 Despite some of its drawbacks, in addition to its more restrictive focus, Peskes's study on the *sāda*'s famous ʿAydarūs clan remains a helpful illustration of the overall value of the hagiographic genre for the field of Islamic historiography. For another powerful vindication of the use of hagiographic materials as an informative source of Sufi cultural history, see De Nicola, Bruno, "The ladies of Rūm: A hagiographic view of women in thirteenth- and fourteenth-century Anatolia," in *Journal of Sufi Studies* 3.2 (2014), 132–156.

19 Thus, John Renard draws our attention to the helpful distinction between 'hagiography' and 'biohagiography'—while 'hagiographies' are focused on the spiritual and moral qualities of the subject, with a special focus on elements of the preternatural and the marvelous, 'biohagiographies' add significant information concerning the subject's personal, public, and political life. Renard, John, *Friends of God: Islamic images of piety, commitment, and servanthood*, Berkeley, CA: University of California Press, 2008, 241–242.

20 See Edaibat, *Bā ʿAlawī sāda*, ch. 4–6.

It is these failures to adequately chart the *sāda*'s scholarly networks and curriculum of study and to carefully examine their significant intellectual writings, many of which continue to remain as unpublished MSS, that has led to our highly skewed academic understanding of the Bā ʿAlawī *sāda*'s premodern Sufi scholarship in a remote region that has been historically perceived as an intellectual and cultural backwater. Thus, for instance, much of the existing academic scholarship on Hadhramawt is of the inaccurate view that the works of Muḥyī al-Dīn Ibn ʿArabī (d. 638/1240), widely regarded as premodern Islam's preeminent authority on Sufi metaphysics and philosophical Sufism (*ḥaqāʾiq*), only managed to gain a "subterranean" following among the ʿAlawīs and Hadhramawt's Sufi elite.[21]

This study hopes to challenge this dominant scholarly narrative by focusing more specifically on the widely neglected intellectual and spiritual legacy of the ʿAlawī *sāda*'s leading Sufi authority of the 10th/16th century, Shaykh Abū Bakr b. Sālim (d. 992/1583), a major author on Sufi metaphysics who remains widely recognized as one of the Alawīs' most sophisticated exponents of philosophical Sufism. In doing so, it hopes to offer a much needed corrective to the received academic wisdom on the breadth and sophistication of the *sāda*'s premodern intellectual tradition, so as to re-interrogate the image of a scholarly family that was largely dominated by the interests of temporal and economic power and the strictly practical and legalistic concerns of religious orthopraxy and public preaching, where engagements with the more sophisticated intellectual scholarship of philosophical Sufism are deemed to have been mostly marginal.[22]

The 10th/16th century in many ways reflects a high point in the evolution of the ʿAlawīs' intellectual tradition and Hadhrami Sufism more generally, with the emergence of such important Sufi figures and their sophisticated works in philosophical Sufism as Shaykh b. ʿAbdallāh b. Shaykh b. ʿAbdallāh al-ʿAydarūs[23] (d. 990/1582), author of *Ḥaqāʾiq al-tawḥīd* (*The realities of divine unity*), and the

21 For examples of this popular academic perception, see Bang, *Sufis* 15; Ho, *Graves* 127n8; Peskes, *al-ʿAidarūs* 49, 190, 274–275; Peskes, "Der Heilige" 57. See also Knysh's generally critical assessment of the *sāda*'s Sufi tradition and his views on its relative lack of intellectual depth and sophistication in Knysh, "Sāda in history;" Knysh, "The 'tariqa'" 410.

22 This critical take on the *sāda*'s scholarly and Sufi credentials is forcefully voiced by Knysh, who concludes from a hasty examination of their hagiographic biographies that the premodern *sāda* were no more than "typical public figures who simply could not afford to dedicate themselves fully to the stringent demands of ascetic self-discipline and Sufi meditation … Once the camouflage is removed, the saint's religious clientele presents itself as an economic and political clientele of those in power." Knysh, "Sāda in history" 222.

23 For a biography of this major Hadhrami scholar, who settled in Ahmedabad in the Indian

famous scholar and disciple of the *sāda* Ḥusayn b. ʿAbdallāh b. ʿAbd al-Raḥmān Balḥajj Bā Faḍl[24] (d. 979/1571), author of *al-Fuṣūl al-fatḥiyya wa-l-nafathāṭ al-rūḥiyya* (*The sessions of* [*divine*] *openings and effusions of the spirit*). Not only did both of these major Hadhrami scholars display a clear fondness for Ibn ʿArabī's thought, reflecting a clear mastery of Akbarian themes within their writings, but as this study attempts to argue, their scholarship hardly represents a marginal stream within the Hadhrami Sufism of this period. Indeed, upon a closer reading of the *sāda*'s own biographical literature as is illustrated in the highly significant case of Shaykh Abū Bakr b. Sālim (d. 992/1583) below, it is safe to say that the study of Sufi works of *ḥaqāʾiq* and the positive reception of Ibn ʿArabī's thought, particularly the *Futūḥāt* and the *Fuṣūs*, was more broadly representative of the scholarly interests of Hadhramawt's Sufi elite across the 9th/15th and 10th/16th centuries.[25]

---

state of Gujarat, see al-Shillī, Muḥammad b. Abī Bakr, *al-Mashraʿ al-rawī fī manāqib al-sāda al-kirām Āl Abī ʿAlawī*, 2 vols., ii, Egypt: al-Maṭbaʿa al-ʿĀmira al-Sharafiyya, 1901, 119–122. *Ḥaqāʾiq al-tawḥīd* is an extensive commentary on the author's poem *Tuḥfat al-murīd*, which al-Shillī describes as a work of theology (*ʿaqāʾid*). Al-Shillī, *al-Mashraʿ* ii, 120. Given the commentary's title, *Ḥaqāʾiq al-tawḥīd*, it may easily be mistaken for a theological work, though a closer reading indicates that it is perhaps better described as an advanced work of philosophical Sufism (*ḥaqāʾiq*), as the topics of Sufi metaphysics frequently overlap with those of Islamic creed and *kalām* theology. The MS of this work is closely examined in Peskes, *al-ʿAidarūs* 222–233. While she makes no mention of Ibn ʿArabī's influences on the work, a close reading of her extensive quotations of the MS betrays clear Akbarian themes and a thoroughgoing Akbarian ontology. See Edaibat, *Bā ʿAlawī sāda*, ch. 4.

24 For more on this celebrated 10th/16th-century Hadhrami scholar of the *mashāyikh*, who was especially known for his strong preoccupation with the works of Ibn ʿArabī, see al-Shillī, Muḥammad b. Abī Bakr, *al-Sanāʾ al-bāhir bi-takmīl al-nūr al-sāfir*, ed. Ibrāhīm Aḥmad al-Maqḥafī, Sanaa: Maktabat Dār al-Irshād, 2004, 531–532; al-ʿAydarūs, ʿAbd al-Qādir b. Shaykh b. ʿAbdallāh, *al-Nūr al-sāfir ʿan akhbār al-qarn al-ʿāshir*, ed. Aḥmad Ḥālū, Maḥmūd al-Arnāʾūṭ and Akram al-Būshī, Beirut: Dār Ṣādir, 2001, 454–458. *Al-Fuṣūl al-fatḥiyya* is yet another Akbarian work of Sufi metaphysics, an MS of which survives in Tarīm, Yemen. See Edaibat, *Bā ʿAlawī sāda*, ch. 4.

25 To provide a couple of earlier overlooked examples, the famous ʿAlawī biographer Muḥammad b. ʿAlī Khirid (d. 960/1552) notes that the renowned 9th/15th-century ʿAlawī scholar al-Shaykh ʿAlī b. Abū Bakr al-Saqqāf (d. 895/1490) studied the *Futūḥāt* with Imam 'Jamal al-Layl' Muḥāmmad b. Ḥasan al-Muʿallim (d. 845/1442), the major scholar and famous progenitor of the Jamal al-Layl clan of *sāda*, while al-Shillī (d. 1132/1720) further notes that al-Shaykh ʿAlī's son ʿAbd al-Raḥmān b. ʿAlī (d. 923/1517) had a similarly strong preoccupation with the works of *ḥaqāʾiq*, especially those of al-Shaykh al-Akbar. Khirid, Muḥammad b. ʿAlī, *Ghurar al-bahāʾ al-ḍawī wa-durar al-jamāl al-badīʿ al-bahī*, ed. ʿAbd al-Qādir al-Jīlānī b. Sālim Khirid, Cairo: al-Maktaba al-Azhariyya li-l-Turāth 2002, 301; al-Shillī, *al-Mashraʿ* ii, 136. For a more complete historical survey of the reception of Ibn ʿArabī in Bā ʿAlawī Sufism, see Edaibat, *Bā ʿAlawī sāda*, ch. 4–6.

3 Biographical Background

Born in Tarīm in 919/1503, where he was raised, Shaykh Abū Bakr b. Sālim received a typical Islamic education from the leading *sāda* and *mashāyikh* clans of his time.[26] He began his intensive education from a young age with the Quran, after which he received an extensive exposure to the Islamic sciences with a number of different scholars. Among his notable teachers were ʿUmar b. Muḥammad Bā Shaybān (d. 944/1537), the *qāḍī* Aḥmad Sharīf (d. 10th/16th century), the jurist ʿAbdallāh b. Muḥammad b. Sahl Bā Qushayr[27] (d. 958/1551), with whom he studied the usual Shafiʿi *fiqh* works such as al-Nawawī's *al-Minhāj*, and the famous Sufi, jurist, and poet ʿUmar b. ʿAbdallāh Bā Makhrama[28] (d. 952/1545), with whom he studied al-Qushayrī's *Risāla*. More importantly, among the major Sufi masters who played a more influential role in his spiritual training were the famous Tarīmī *sayyid* Imam Aḥmad b. ʿAlawī Bā Jaḥdab[29] (d. 973/1566) and the renowned Sufi master of Shibām Maʿrūf Bā Jammāl (d. 969/1562).[30]

In addition to his daily routine of scholarly learning, Shaykh Abū Bakr would complement his education with a strict regimen of spiritual training, developing an affinity for long spiritual retreats at the popular gravesite of the Prophet Hūd. The hagiographic biographies also note that he regularly fasted the three hottest months of the year and that he would subsist for days on a mere diet of milk and coffee.[31] He eventually built himself a private residence near the vil-

26 The traditional biographies appear to be silent on the Imam's father and immediate family, and not much is known about them other than that he was a sixth-generation descendant of the highly celebrated Imam ʿAbd al-Rāhmān al-Saqqāf (d. 819/1416) through the Imam's son Imam ʿAbdallāh (d. 857/1453), for whom al-Shillī occasions a brief biography, noting that his main teacher in Sufism was his older brother Imam ʿUmar al-Miḥḍār (d. 833/1429), who taught him the works of *ḥāqāʾīq* and invested him with the Sufi *khirqa*. Al-Shillī, *al-Mashraʿ* ii, 179.

27 A major jurist and author of the popular *fiqh* work *Qalāʾid al-Khlāʾid*. For more on him, see Bā Dhīb, Muḥammad, *Juhūd fuqahāʾ Ḥaḍramawt fī khidmat al-madhhab al-Shāfiʿī*, 2 vols., i, Amman: Dār al-Fatḥ, 2009, 491–499.

28 For more on this famous Hadhrami Sufi scholar and for his views on Ibn ʿArabī, see al-Shillī, *al-Sanāʾ* 378–383; Edaibat, *Bā ʿAlawī sāda*, ch. 4.

29 For more on this major ʿAlawī, see al-Shillī, *al-Mashraʿ* ii, 69–73; Edaibat, *Bā ʿAlawī sāda*, ch. 3.

30 Al-Shillī, *al-Mashraʿ* ii, 26–27; al-Shillī, *al-Sanāʾ* 589. For the biography of the famous Hadhrami Sufi master Maʿrūf Bā Jammāl, see al-Mashhūr, Abū Bakr, "al-Shaykh Maʿrūf Bā Jammāl," in *Silsilat aʿlām Ḥaḍramawt al-kāmila*, Aden: Arbiṭat al-Tarbiya al-Islāmiyya (Farʿ al-Dirāsāt wa-Khidmat al-Turāth), 2002, 272–302; al-Shillī, *al-Sanāʾ* 456–462.

31 Buxton, Amin, *Imams of the valley*, Western Cape, South Africa: Dār al-Turāth al-Islāmī, 2012, 38.

lage of ʿĪnāt for his private retreats, where he permanently decided to settle.[32] The old city of ʿĪnāt had been initially built by the Kathīrīs in 929/1522, and soon after his settling in the area, news of his knowledge and generous hospitality attracted large numbers of seekers and visitors, with many deciding to settle around his new residence which would eventually become the Imam's *ḥawṭa* in the new ʿĪnāt.[33]

As the *manṣab* of the *ḥawṭa* of ʿĪnāt, Shaykh Abū Bakr b. Sālim was to also play an important role in the resolution of local political conflicts and tribal disputes.[34] Among the *sāda*, it was the Shaykh and his descendants who were destined to have the most extensive relations with the Kathīrī sultans, where their *ḥawṭa* served as a regular destination and meeting ground for the resolution of local political disputes and for seeking the *sāda*'s blessing and private counsel. In particular, the Imam and the *manṣabs* of his family after him would establish long-lasting ties with sultan al-ʿĀdil ʿUmar b. Badr (d. 1021/1612) and his descendants.[35]

Sometime after settling in ʿĪnāt, the Imam decided to visit the famous Sufi master Maʿrūf Bā Jammāl of Shibām and seek his permission to become his disciple. The Shaykh is said to have tested his zeal and determination by refusing to grant him permission to enter upon him for a period of forty days. Having passed this test, the Shaykh invested him with the *khirqa* and granted him an *ijāza*, and the Imam would go on to become the Shaykh's foremost disciple and his spiritual inheritor after him.[36] On other occasions, the Sufi master is known to have hinted at the Imam's status and promising future as the leading Sufi of his time, describing him variously with the exalted titles of *quṭb al-wujūd*, *ṣāḥib al-waqt*, and as the *khalīfa* of his time.[37]

32 Al-Shillī, *al-Mashraʿ* ii, 27; al-Shillī, *al-Sanāʾ* 590; Buxton, *Imams* 38.

33 Al-Shillī, *al-Mashraʿ* ii, 29.

34 The *ḥawṭa* as a politically neutral and sacred enclave, is a significant feature of the Hadhrami landscape and in later centuries becomes especially associated with the ʿAlawī *sāda*, who by the 9th/15th century begin to gradually displace the local *mashāyikh* clans in their growing temporal role as the neutral mediators and arbitrators of the valley's political and tribal conflicts. For more on the *ḥawṭa* and its associated social function of the *manṣab*, see Serjeant, *Saiyids* 14–19; Serjeant, Robert B., "*Haram* and *hawtah*, the sacred enclave in Arabia," in Francis E. Peters (ed.), *The Arabs and Arabia on the eve of Islam*, Aldershot: Ashgate, 1999, 167–184; Dostal, Walter, "The saints of Hadramawt," in Walter Dostal and Wolfgang Kraus (eds.), *Shattering tradition: Custom, law, and the individual in the Muslim Mediterranean*, London: I.B. Tauris, 2005, 233–253.

35 Ibn Hishām, Muḥammad, *Tārīkh al-dawla al-Kathīriyya*, ed. Muḥammad ʿAlī al-Jifrī, i, Tarīm: Tarīm li-l-Dirāsāt wa-l-Nashr, 2002, 89–90; al-Shillī, *al-Mashraʿ* ii, 28.

36 Al-Badawī, Mostafa, *A blessed valley: Wadi Hadramawt & the Alawi tradition*, UK: Guidance Media, 2013, 141–142.

37 Al-Shillī, *al-Sanāʾ* 590.

Shaykh Abū Bakr b. Sālim's fame in ʿĪnāt would soon spread to all the corners of the valley and beyond, where he became the subject of several hagiographic biographies. His teaching circles in the village soon began attracting scholars and seekers from as far as Iraq, Egypt, and Syria. His generosity towards his disciples and the poor was near legendary; his biographies note that he operated a public kitchen, wherein he would personally distribute some five hundred loaves of bread during lunch time and another five hundred during the evenings. As the most celebrated ʿAlawī Sufi authority of his day, the Imam taught a generation of major scholars and students from among the *sāda* and *mashāyikh*, which soon earned him the celebrated sobriquet of *fakhr al-wujūd*. Among his famous students were Imam Aḥmad b. Muḥammad al-Ḥabshī (d. 10th/16th century) and the famous Moroccan pilgrim and Ḥasanī *sayyid* and theologian Yusuf Ibn ʿĀbid al-Fāsī (d. 1048/1638), who met him near the end of his life and whose visit to Hadhramawt is said to have been foretold by the Imam.[38] The Imam's litanies continue to be widely read till this day, and his famous prayer of blessings upon the Prophet *ṣalāt al-tāj* continues to be widely recited in the Indian subcontinent and elsewhere.[39]

The story of Shaykh Abū Bakr b. Sālim's rise to fame (*ẓuhūr*) as the preeminent ʿAlawī spiritual authority of his day is unsurprisingly the subject of several preternatural tales. Al-Shillī relates a story where after wonderous tales of the Imam's renown and *karāmāt* in ʿĪnāt had reached Tarīm, a *sayyid* began complaining to his Sufi master Imam Aḥmad b. ʿAlawī Bā Jaḥdab that people were setting the young Abū Bakr above his ʿAlawī elders in Tarīm. Imam Bā Jaḥdab also disapproved of this and informed the *sayyid* to go out and remind people to refrain from such tales, for a young Shaykh possesses no more than a grain and is still a beginner on the path. Upon hearing of this news, Shaykh Abū Bakr b. Sālim is said to have been humbly pleased to receive confirmation that he possessed as much as a grain of attainment on the path. He then set out to meet with his master Imam Bā Jaḥdab in Tarīm, who gently reminded him that seeking fame and renown was something he did not need. Shaykh Abū Bakr responded that he could not contain the people from speaking about him and that Shaykh ʿAbd al-Qādir al-Jīlānī had come to him in a dream vision, along with a number of ʿAlawī masters, commanding him to expose himself and to

38 For al-Fāsī's rich travel memoir, which covers his journey to Hadhramawt, where he chose to settle for many years, and for his meetings with Shaykh Abū Bakr, see al-Fāsī, Yūsuf b. ʿĀbid b. Muḥammad, *Riḥlat Ibn ʿĀbid al-Fāsī min al-Maghrib ilā Ḥaḍramawt*, ed. Ibrāhīm al-Sāmrāʾī and ʿAbdallāh b. Muḥammad al-Ḥabshī, Beirut: Dār al-Gharb al-Islāmī, 1993, 99–140.

39 Buxton, *Imams* 38–40; al-Badawī, *A blessed valley* 145.

make his spiritual station known to the people. Imam Bā Jaḥdab is then said to have spoken to him in an equivocal and unintelligible language, which none understood, before reverting to his normal speech and ordering him to return to ʿĪnāt.[40]

In addition to his litanies, spiritual poetry, and gnostic writings on Sufi *ḥaqāʾiq*, the Imam is widely remembered for inaugurating the annual pilgrimage (*ziyāra*) and festival to the tomb site of the Prophet Hūd in the month of Shaʿbān, which had been previously arranged in smaller numbers according to the date harvest. As the largest spiritual festival in Hadhramawt, the *ziyāra* lasts for three days and is typically attended by the major scholars of the valley, with numerous processions, eloquent speeches, Mawlids, and sessions of spiritual poetry taking place, a tradition that continues to be led by the Imam's family till this day.[41]

Shaykh Abū Bakr b. Sālim had thirteen sons and four daughters, and his son Ḥusayn would become his spiritual heir after him. The Imam's family line would branch into several well-known and large *sāda* clans.[42] He died in 992/1583 and was buried in his family's cemetery in ʿĪnāt, where his tomb had a prominent dome erected over it and remains a popular destination today.

4 An Author of Sufi *ḥaqāʾiq*

Shaykh Abū Bakr b. Sālim continues to be celebrated today as one of the *sāda*'s most realized gnostics (*ʿārifūn*) and one of their most accomplished authors of philosophical Sufism. While his hagiographic biographies make no direct mention of his study of Ibn ʿArabī, it is nonetheless known that he was a contemporary of the scholar Ḥusayn b. ʿAbdallāh b. ʿAbd al-Raḥmān Balḥajj Bā Faḍl the famous author of Sufi *ḥaqāʾiq* and great admirer of Ibn ʿArabī who

40 Al-Shillī, *al-Mashraʿ* ii, 27.

41 It is believed that the visit to the Prophet Hūd as a devotional practice was first formalized by al-Faqīh al-Muqaddam (d. 653/1255), after whom the major ʿAlawī saints followed suit, making a habit of prolonged and isolated spiritual retreats at his tomb site. It was not until the 10th/16th century, however, that the tomb became formally the site of a major annual ʿAlawī pilgrimage (*ziyāra*) in the month of Shaʿbān, which was led for the first time by Shaykh Abū Bakr b. Sālim. Al-Badawī, *A blessed valley* 148–149. For more on this major annual pilgrimage (*ziyāra*), see Boxberger, *On the edge* 156–159; Buxton, *Imams* 37–38.

42 See al-Mashhūr, ʿAbd al-Raḥmān b. Muḥammad, *al-Shams al-ẓahīra fī nasab ahl al-bayt min Banī ʿAlawī*, ed. Muḥammad Ḍiyāʾ Shihāb, 2 vols., i, Jeddah: ʿĀlam al-Maʿrifa, 1984, 273–277.

was also known for his intimate relations with the *sāda* as one of their disciples.[43] While there is no clear indication from the biographical sources that these two major Hadhrami Sufis ever met and studied together, this was nonetheless very likely the case, as they were both disciples of the famous ʿAlawī Sufi master of Tarīm Imam Aḥmad b. ʿAlawī Bā Jaḥdab.[44] This connection suggests the possibility that they either studied the works of Ibn ʿArabī together or directly with their Sufi master, hinting at the likelihood, once again, that Ibn ʿArabī's works were more widely received within Hadhrami Sufi circles than we are led to believe. In any case, as we shall see below from a thematic survey of his two major works, the Imam's intimate familiarity with Ibn ʿArabī is unmistakable, where al-Shaykh al-Akbar's terminology, thought, and doctrines take center stage throughout his writings.

Shaykh Abū Bakr b. Sālim's *Miʿrāj al-arwāḥ wa-l-manhaj al-waḍḍāḥ* (*The ascension of spirits and the clarifying methodology*) and *Fatḥ bāb al-mawāhib wa-bughyat maṭlab al-maṭālib* (*Opening the door of* [*divine*] *gifts and the object of* [*spiritual*] *pursuits*) are among the most sophisticated works of philosophical Sufism within the *sāda*'s intellectual and spiritual canon, exhibiting a thoroughgoing mastery of Ibn ʿArabī's teachings and the highly technical and philosophical lexicon of the Sufi gnostics. Both works are also quite wide-ranging in their scope, though mostly similar in content, interweaving familiar Akbarian discussions on Sufi ontology, cosmology, theology, epistemology, hermeneutics, eschatology, and soteriology. *Miʿrāj al-arwāḥ* represents a more expanded discussion on many of the same themes found in *Fatḥ bāb al-mawāhib*, which is written in a more brief and condensed style. Both works, however, appear to be authored independently of one another, and the topics they address are not always an exact match.

Given their sophistication, the breadth of their topics, and their overall complexity, it is remarkable that both works continue to remain terra incognita within the academic study of Yemeni Sufism. A couple of factors can partially explain why they have received little to no scholarly attention thus far. Both works were only published in printed editions within the last decade, prior to which copies of their manuscripts were less accessible to foreign researchers. Furthermore, as advanced works of *ḥaqāʾiq*, the *sāda* have typically approached them in the same vein that they approach all works of Sufi metaphysics, by generally de-emphasizing their public reading and exposing them only to their worthy disciples within closed and private circles, a tendency that

43 See n. 24 above.

44 See n. 28 above.

has been witnessed and confirmed from first-hand conversations with some of their leading students in Hadhramawt.[45]

While these two works continue to remain relatively unknown, an exhaustive analysis of their contents is beyond the immediate scope and objectives of this study. Indeed, both works are divided into many small subsections on a plethora of topics that were dictated over a period of time in the inspired manner of the realized Sufis,[46] such that offering an independent and systematic analysis of each work would be too cumbersome and less helpful for our purposes. Rather, an attempt will be made here to treat both works holistically and provide a brief synopsis of the major recurring themes constituting the central features of Shaykh Abū Bakr b. Sālim's focus and attention. This approach seems justified in light of the more basic aim of this study, which is to cast a spotlight on the ʿAlawī *sāda*'s relatively ignored scholarly contributions, which in several cases, as with these two works in particular, demonstrate an intimate familiarity with Ibn ʿArabī's central teachings and doctrines.

From a brief analysis of both works, it becomes readily apparent that Shaykh Abū Bakr b. Sālim is deeply immersed in the Akbarian *weltanschauung*, displaying an intimate knowledge of the *Futūḥāt* and *Fuṣūṣ* in particular. Both works also reflect Ibn ʿArabī's inspired style, prioritizing the Divinely bequeathed supra-rational knowledge of the gnostics (*al-ʿilm al-wahbī* or *al-ʿilm al-ladunī*) over all other forms of acquired knowledge (*al-ʿilm al-kasbī*). Furthermore, like Ibn ʿArabī, nearly all his writing is consistently and organically interwoven with

45 In light of this general tendency, it is unsurprising to note Alexander Knysh's observation during his 1999 sojourn in the valley, where he remarks with a lack of enthusiasm concerning Dār al-Muṣṭafā, one of the *sāda*'s leading public seminaries in Tarīm, "It is in vain that one looks for works on Sufi metaphysics, epistemology or allegorical exegesis along the lines of Ibn ʿArabī and his followers. This initial impression was confirmed by Ḥabīb ʿUmar himself, who told me that, in accord with the tenets of the *ṭarīqa al-ʿAlawiyya*, they teach Sufism to their disciples primarily as morals and spiritual self-discipline." Knysh, "The 'tariqa'" 410.

46 As the editor notes on the book cover of *Miʿrāj al-arwāḥ*, "He dictated it in an inspired manner" (*amlāhu ʿalā sabīl al-wārid*). Indeed, a close reading of the two works does not readily reveal a clear structure guiding the arrangement of their contents. While their inspired style may at first glance appear to share much in common with Ibn ʿArabī's style in the *Futūḥāt*, as Chodkiewicz has masterfully revealed, the *Futūḥāt*, by contrast, does in fact have a clear logic behind its apparently unsystematic arrangement, which aims to closely mirror the structure and order of the Quran. For more on this topic, see Chodkiewicz, Michel, *An ocean without shore: Ibn ʿArabī, the book, and the law*, trans. David Streight, Albany, NY: SUNY Press, 1993, 64–76; Edaibat, Omar, "Muḥyī l-Dīn Ibn ʿArabī's personalist theory of the *sharīʿa*: An examination of his legal doctrine," in *Journal of Sufi Studies* 6.1 (2017), 1–46, 9–13.

verses from the Quran and Hadith traditions, which are frequently interpreted in a gnostic or esoteric light. Here, Shaykh Abū Bakr b. Sālim displays a remarkable similarity with al-Shaykh al-Akbar's scripturalistic hermeneutics where the Quran and *sunna* are taken as the absolute, central, and final authority on every aspect of his Sufi teachings.[47]

More concretely, the Imam employs a great deal of technical Sufi vocabulary, regularly providing definitions for his impressive array of terms relating to the Sufi states (*aḥwāl*), stations (*maqāmāt*), and other cosmological, theological, and gnostic concepts, most of which appear to be borrowed from al-Shaykh al-Akbar.[48] To provide but one example, throughout his ontological and cosmological discussions, he regularly employs Ibn ʿArabī's concept of immutable entities (*al-aʿyān al-thābita*), which may be defined as the objects of God's knowledge which include the nonexistent possible things (*mumkināt*) and the possible existent things (*mawjūdāt*) of the phenomenal world.[49] These entities (*aʿyān*) are immutable (*thābita*) because they never change, just as God's Knowledge never changes, and they are only brought into concrete existence when God gives preponderance to their existence over their nonexistence.[50]

While he relies heavily on Ibn ʿArabī's gnostic terminology, perhaps unsurprisingly, there are no direct references made to al-Shaykh al-Akbar throughout his works.[51] Instead, all his central reflections and explications are presented

47 The Imam is sure to stress this point emphatically on several occasions. See, for example, al-Saqqāf, Abū Bakr b. Sālim, *Miʿrāj al-arwāḥ wa-l-manhaj al-waḍḍāḥ*, ed. Aḥmad Farīd al-Mazīdī, Beirut: Kitāb Nāshirūn, 2013, 358, 454. For Ibn ʿArabī's 'scripturalism' in terms of his legal thought, see Edaibat, "Muḥyī l-Dīn Ibn ʿArabī's personalist theory" 22–39.

48 For a list of examples of his technical definitions, which is by no means exhaustive, see al-Saqqāf, *Miʿrāj al-arwāḥ* 291–292, 373–375, 377, 389, 391, 403–406, 429; al-Saqqāf, Abū Bakr b. Sālim, *Fatḥ bāb al-mawāhib wa-bughyat maṭlab al-maṭālib*, ed. Aḥmad Farīd al-Mazīdī, Beirut: Kitāb Nāshirūn, 2019, 41–44, 48, 65.

49 "*Ḥaqāʾiq al-mumkināt fī ʿilm al-ḥaqq taʿālā* …" al-Saqqāf, *Miʿrāj al-arwāḥ* 406.

50 For more on this Akbarian concept, see Chittick, William C., *The Sufi path of knowledge: Ibn al-ʿArabī's metaphysics of imagination*, Albany, NY: SUNY Press, 1989, 11–12, 83–86. For examples where this concept is employed by Abū Bakr b. Sālim, see al-Saqqāf, *Miʿrāj al-arwāḥ* 114, 116, 156, 204–206, 223, 256, 406. Additionally, a small section is devoted to '*al-ʿayān al-thābita*' in al-Saqqāf, *Fatḥ bāb al-mawāhib* 146–147.

51 Given his highly controversial status, where his ontological theological doctrine was the topic of fierce polemical debates, the deliberate omission of direct references to Ibn ʿArabī appears to be a historically common practice among his Hadhrami Sufi admirers and within the wider Arab Sufi scholarship. For more on this topic, see Chodkiewicz, *Ocean without shore* 1–18; Edaibat, *Bā ʿAlawī sāda*, ch. 4; Knysh, Alexander, *Ibn ʿArabi in the later Islamic tradition: The making of a polemical image in medieval Islam*, Albany, NY: SUNY Press, 1999.

as the fruits of spiritual realization, where references to other notable Sufi authorities are raised only sparingly to illustrate a particular point or provide an example. Be that as it may, upon closer analysis, his writing betrays an unmistakable and direct familiarity with the contents of Ibn ʿArabī's works, to the extent that he occasionally offers passing remarks or reflections which, upon closer scrutiny, appear to closely mimic the *ipsissima verba* of relevant passages from the *Fuṣūṣ*.

Two brief examples shall suffice us here to illustrate the point. In a discussion on the Prophet ʿĪsā's revival of the dead, the Imam offers the following explanation,

> And if Jibrīl had not appeared in the form of a human, ʿĪsā would not have been able to revive the dead without first appearing in that natural luminous elemental form in addition to the human form of his mother's side; for it was said of him upon reviving the dead, "He not He" (*huwa lā huwa*), and a state of bewilderment would befall those who gazed upon him.[52]

Elsewhere, in a brief passage discussing the mysterious Prophetic figure of Khālid, he offers the following remark,

> And Khālid had wanted the entire world to believe in what the Messengers had revealed, in order that he be a Mercy to everyone since he was honoured with the proximity of his Prophethood to that of Muhmmad, God's Peace and Blessings be upon him, and God sent him to all the worlds; even though Khālid was not the Messenger of God, God's Peace and Blessings be upon him, he nonetheless wanted to partake in this Mercy of the Muhammadan Message and obtain from it the greatest possible share.[53]

Both these passages are nearly identical in wording to passages from the chapters on the Prophet ʿIsā and Khālid in the *Fuṣūṣ*, proving conclusively that the Imam closely studied Ibn ʿArabī's works and must have consulted them diligently.

---

52 Al-Saqqāf, *Miʿrāj al-arwāḥ* 305. Cf. Ibn ʿArabī, Muḥyī l-Dīn, *Fuṣūṣ al-ḥikam*, Cairo: Dār Afāq, 2016, 140–141.

53 Al-Saqqāf, *Miʿrāj al-arwāḥ* 240. Cf. Ibn ʿArabī, *Fuṣūṣ* 213.

Though he is deeply indebted to Ibn ʿArabī, incorporating much of his terminology and teachings, Shaykh Abū Bakr b. Sālim's style and tone remains nonetheless that of an independent and realized master of spiritual realities, whose knowledge is drawn from experiential tasting (*dhawq*) and spiritual unveiling (*kashf*), which include regular visions of direct communion with the spirits of the Prophets and realized gnostics.[54] In the characteristic fashion of the Sufi mystics, the Imam thus repeatedly asserts throughout his writings that his words are not mere reflections emanating from one's passion or whim (*hawāʾ*) but are Divinely inspired, and such knowledge should remain generally concealed from the masses, who frequently lack the requisite courtesy (*adab*), sincere commitment (*ikhlāṣ*), and intellect (*ʿaql*) to benefit from it; as such, whatever he is permitted to reveal of his knowledge is out of mercy for his disciples and is meant to assist those sincere and worthy seekers on the path.[55]

Given what we know of similar writings on theoretical gnosis and Sufi metaphysics, it is rather unsurprising that the concept of *al-ʿilm al-ladunī* takes pride of place in both works. This form of supra-rational inner knowledge is only granted to the elect (*al-khawāṣṣ*) by Divine permission (*idhn*), and as a Divinely gifted knowledge (*ʿilm wahbī*), it is superior to all the rational Islamic sciences of the exoteric scholars (*ʿulamāʾ al-rusūm*) that are attained through personal training and toil (*ʿilm kasbī*).[56] Like Ibn ʿArabī, the Imam also warns his disciples that the exoteric scholars who have not tasted to the knowledge of inner realities are to be generally avoided, for they receive dead knowledge from a dead source, while this knowledge is received directly from the Real (*al-ḥayy*) who never dies.[57] The only way that the aspiring seeker can hope to attain to the reality of inner gnosis (*ḥaqīqa*) is by a strict adherence to the *sharīʿa* and an

54 The Imam's unveilings include numerous communions with the Prophet Muhammad, some of which were in a wakeful state. On one such occasion, after initially leaning towards concealing the knowledge that he had gained, the Prophet commanded him, "Speak of what has emanated from me to you to the rest of creation!" Elsewhere, he mentions his inner witnessing of the Night of Power (*laylat al-qadr*), which was unveiled to him in the year 991/1582. See al-Saqqāf, *Miʿrāj al-arwāḥ* 133; al-Saqqāf, *Fatḥ bāb al-mawāhib* 196, 244.

55 See discussions in al-Saqqāf, *Miʿrāj al-arwāḥ* 19, 29, 133, 144, 188–189, 259, 262, 361–362, 419, 427. These discussions are a further indication of the *sāda*'s general pedagogical inclination towards concealment when it comes to the teaching of advanced Sufi realities to the commoners and uninitiated.

56 Al-Saqqāf, *Miʿrāj al-arwāḥ* 23, 218, 274; al-Saqqāf, *Fatḥ bāb al-mawāhib* 115.

57 Al-Saqqāf, *Miʿrāj al-arwāḥ* 261. See also al-Saqqāf, *Fatḥ bāb al-mawāhib* 122.

emulation of the *sunna* of the Prophet (the *ṭarīqa*), with a deep sense of reverence and courtesy (*adab*) towards God and the knowers of God (*ʿārifīn*), a process that also necessitates submitting oneself fully to a realized spiritual master and guide with full love, devotion, and inner direction (*tawajjuh*); in this sense, the *sharīʿa* represents the tree from which the fruit of gnosis is reaped.[58] Such a spiritual journey can only be safely traversed on the boat of love (*markib al-maḥabba*) and with the provision and sustenance of God-consciousness (*zād al-taqwā*).[59]

4.1 *Theology and Ontology*

A major cornerstone of this realized knowledge (*maʿrifa*) and among the preeminent themes throughout both works, is an exhaustive explication of the ontological dimension of Ibn ʿArabī's theological doctrine, namely the realization that only God, as the Absolute Existent (*al-wujūd al-maḥḍ*) and Necessary Being (*wājib al-wujūd*), truly Exists; all other existing things may be said to 'exist' only in the relative and contingent sense as Self-disclosures (*tajalliyyāt*) of the Divine Presence. This understanding is affirmed by the Imam experientially through the process of spiritual unveiling and inner-witnessing of the Sufis (*mukāshafa*), but it is also affirmed textually on numerous occasions through his mystical exegesis of several Quranic verses and Hadith. Some of these textual sources are rather explicit and are simply affirmed literally; thus, as the Prophet Muhammad declares in a known *ḥadīth*, "The truest verse that the Arabs ever recited is that of Labīd, 'Indeed everything other than God is void (*bāṭil*)!'"[60] Others are more ambiguous or multivalent in meaning. In this respect, Q 28:88 "Everything comes to perish, save for His Face" is not simply a reference to the pending inevitability of death and the finality of creation but is also a reference to the "the Muhammadan spring (*mashrab*) of witnessing each thing in its disappearance (*iḍmiḥlāl*) in the Presence of the Real."[61] Similarly, as he explains, God's accompaniment to His creation in Q 57:4 "And He is with you wherever you may be" must be taken in this gnostic sense of witnessing, as it "cannot be understood with the meaning of association or comparison (*muqārana*), for how can this be when there is nothing other than His Existence

58 Al-Saqqāf, *Miʿrāj al-arwāḥ* 23, 87, 170, 375, 385, 397, 410; al-Saqqāf, *Fatḥ bāb al-mawāhib* 50, 71, 218, 255.
59 Al-Saqqāf, *Miʿrāj al-arwāḥ* 267–268.
60 Al-Saqqāf, *Miʿrāj al-arwāḥ* 296.
61 Al-Saqqāf, *Miʿrāj al-arwāḥ* 223.

in reality?"[62] Other examples of verses used to affirm this ontological doctrine include Q 24:35, "God is the Light of the Heavens and the Earth;" Q 41:54, "He Encompasses all things;" and Q 57:3, "He is the First and the Last, the Manifest and the Hidden, and He has Knowledge over all things."[63]

Certainly, like other authors of Sufi *ḥaqāʾiq*, Shaykh Abū Bakr b. Sālim is sure to stress the transcendence and incomparability (*tanzīh*) of God with respect to His creation, anticipating any potential detractors by emphatically dissociating himself from the usual polemical charges of *ḥulūl* (incarnation) or *ittiḥād* (union). Thus, as he states concerning God's transcendent nature,

> His individual Attributes are that God is One (*wāḥid*), Existing (*mawjūd*), Eternal (*qadīm*), Solitary (*aḥad*), Unique (*fard*), Self-Subsisting (*qāʾim bi-nafsihi*); He is unlike anything, and nothing is like Him. He is God, the One (*al-wāḥid*), the Subduer (*al-qahhār*). He is Powerful (*qādir*) by His Power, He Wills (*murīd*) by His Will, and He is dissociated (*munazzah*) from any charge of indwelling (*ḥulūl*) or physical touch (*mulāmasa*). He does not dwell in anything, and nothing dwells within Him. There is no God but He; He Encompasses all things in His Mercy (*raḥma*) and Knowledge (*ʿilm*), He Communicates with speech (*mutakallim*), He Hears (*samīʿ*), and He Sees (*baṣīr*).[64]

As for the recurring charge of God's union (*ittiḥād*) with His creation, the Imam is sure to appropriate and redefine the meaning of this polemical term on several occasions as follows,

> Union (*al-ittiḥād*): it is the witnessing of the One, Real, and Nondelimited Existence (*al-wujūd al-muṭlaq*), through Whom all things are made to exist in Truth, and each thing is united with Him (*ittaḥada bihi*) in the sense that it exists by Him, while being nonexistent in itself, and not in the sense that it has an independent existence that is united with Him, for this would be impossible (*muḥāl*).[65]

---

62 Al-Saqqāf, *Miʿrāj al-arwāḥ* 266. One can say that the verse can be understood in this comparative sense in a purely metaphorical or relative sense.

63 Al-Saqqāf, *Miʿrāj al-arwāḥ* 96.

64 Al-Saqqāf, *Miʿrāj al-arwāḥ* 117–118.

65 Al-Saqqāf, *Miʿrāj al-arwāḥ* 406.

Indeed, Shaykh Abū Bakr b. Sālim devotes significant attention to articulating a clear and detailed theological creed (*ʿaqīda*) that emphatically affirms God's transcendence and incomparability[66] and that is in many ways reminiscent of the Ashʿari occasionalism of the *mutakallimūn*, where actions are said to be 'acquired' (*kasbiyya*) from the human perspective and to be created (*khalqiyya*) from God's perspective.[67] Be that as it may, like Ibn ʿArabī and other controversial figures among the realized Sufis before him, the Imam repeatedly affirms that such a negative theology of Divine transcendence and incomparability (*tanzīh*) is only half the picture and must simultaneously be balanced by God's comparability (*tashbīh*) with His creation, where the Divine Being is able to relate to His creation without this necessitating any charge of anthropomorphism.[68]

It is here where the Imam's ontology is fully in line with the Akbarian doctrine of the 'oneness of being' (*waḥdat al-wujūd*). As he unequivocally explains,

> And the creation are in reality but imaginal forms (*ṣuwar khayāliyya*) that are moved by the Real, who is the true Speaker on their behalf, for they are directed and controlled by the rulings of (God's) power (*qudra*), and they [the forms] are in fact erased (*mahw*) in the state of their presence (*thubūt*), and they are nonexistent (*ʿadam*) in the state of their existence (*wujūd*)![69]

Elsewhere, he states,

> And know and understand what I say to you that every created entity is nonexistent, for all existence belongs to God, the Glorified and Exalted, and every delineated external image is delineated by Him with the affirmation of its nonexistence, and given its state of annihilation in its nonexistence, the Real decided to cloak it with the robe of external existence, and it thus came to exist.[70]

---

66 His theological creed is perhaps most comprehensively detailed in the subsection entitled *Faṣl fī ʿaqīda jāmiʿa* in al-Saqqāf, *Miʿrāj al-arwāḥ* 448–458. See also al-Saqqāf, *Miʿrāj al-arwāḥ* 428 where he argues that God's incomparability is necessitated by the *sharīʿa* by virtue of the degree of His Divinity (*ulūhiyya*).

67 Al-Saqqāf, *Miʿrāj al-arwāḥ* 290. See also, al-Saqqāf, *Fatḥ bāb al-mawāhib* 77–78.

68 For more on Ibn ʿArabī's views on the theological problem of *tashbīh* and *tanzīh*, see Chittick, *The Sufi path* 9, 58, 69, 110, 181.

69 Al-Saqqāf, *Miʿrāj al-arwāḥ* 259.

70 Al-Saqqāf, *Miʿrāj al-arwāḥ* 265.

On this occasion, the Imam is sure to also stress that this realized knowledge is a deep and treacherous ocean, and that none may enter upon it without the express permission of his teacher and spiritual guide, without whom the seeker is exposed to grave dangers.

Given this ontological reality, the multiplicity of creation (*al-kathra*) is in fact but the self-disclosure or manifestation of God's Names and Attributes (*ẓuhūr al-asmāʾ wa-l-ṣifāt*).[71] As such, to speak of the creation as being separate from God is to do so in a purely relative or metaphorical sense (*majāz*), a necessary and logical distinction that helps us account for the degree or station of His Divinity (*al-ulūhiyya*) as the Creator vis-à-vis His creation.[72] Here, it must also be noted that the Imam is sure to stress, following Ibn ʿArabī, that the Divine Names and Attributes are not in fact ontological in nature, meaning they have no external existence, but we may rather think of them in terms of relationships and correlations (*nisab*) with distinct traces and effects upon the creation.[73]

Interestingly, the Imam also briefly recounts a mythical disputation between the Names that appears to hint at a similar more expansive symbolic tale in the *Futūḥāt* between the immutable entities and the Divine Names in which the Names are personified and wish to manifest their effects within the cosmos. As their discussion unfolds, they gradually come to realize that they must ultimately return to the All-Comprehensive Name Allāh as an arbiter to resolve their dispute and bring a sense of balance and order to the creation by establishing the scale of the *sharīʿa*. Here Shaykh Abū Bakr b. Sālim further clarifies that the Divine decree necessitated a just arbiter to govern the Divine Names and their traces and that this task was granted exclusively to the Prophet Muhammad as represented in his cosmic and all-encompassing station of *al-ḥaqīqa al-Muḥammadiyya*.[74]

Given the foregoing considerations, Shaykh Abū Bakr b. Sālim argues the case that it is the Sufi gnostics alone who have the most complete realization of the cardinal monotheistic doctrine of God's unity (*tawḥīd*). As he explains, a negative theology that is strictly based on God's incomparability with his

---

71 Al-Saqqāf, *Miʿrāj al-arwāḥ* 114.

72 Al-Saqqāf, *Miʿrāj al-arwāḥ* 435.

73 Al-Saqqāf, *Miʿrāj al-arwāḥ* 172, 251. For more on the Divine Names as relationships, see Chittick, *The Sufi path* 35–36, 50, 52, 59, 60, 156.

74 Al-Saqqāf, *Miʿrāj al-arwāḥ* 271–272. Compare this summarized rendition with the more expanded mythical encounter between the Divine Names and the immutable entities in Chapter 66 of the first section (*faṣl*) of Ibn ʿArabī, Muḥyī l-Dīn, *al-Futūḥāṭ al-Makkiyya*, ed. Nawwāf al-Jarrāḥ, 9 vols., i, Beirut: Dār Ṣādir, 2004, 385–389. For more on *al-ḥaqīqa al-Muḥammadiyya*, see below.

creation, as is advocated by many among the masses and theologians, is an incomplete and deficient conceptualization of God that logically leads to His being divested of attributes (*taʿṭīl*):

> For the weak minds, once they stress the incomparability of the Real, their dissociation leads to a state of divestment (*taʿṭīl*), as when one would say: "God, the Exalted, has no direction and no place, nor is He a body or two, nor is He a substance (*jawhar*) or an accident (*ʿaraḍ*), and nor is He connected to or disconnected from anything." So understand from this that it leads to divestment due to the weak perception of the perceiver and his misguidedness; for the Most Exalted cannot be constrained by these constraints due to His Encompassing everything. Thus, directions, substances, accidents, and all things exist by the Real and subsist by His Self-Subsisting nature, for He is the source of everything in reality.[75]

As such, in the common manner of the Sufis, the Imam identifies two forms of *tawḥīd*: the *tawḥīd* of the common people (*al-ʿawāmm*) and the rationalists, who must rely on rational proofs and demonstrations for their knowledge of God, and the *tawḥīd* of the elite (*al-khawāṣṣ*) or the Sufi gnostics, whose knowledge of God is beyond rational proofs and is based on spiritual unveiling, where they come to directly witness the Divine Unity by erasing the forms of the phenomenal world (*maḥw al-rusūm*).[76] As he thus defines it in a pithy expression, pure *tawḥīd* consists of "casting the gaze away from the realms (of creation) by witnessing the One who is utterly dissociated from any imperfection."[77]

4.2 *Annihilation and Subsistence in God*

The experiential witnessing of this theological and ontological doctrine within the self is at the heart of the seeker's quest for spiritual realization, which is essentially to come to know and witness God as the Real. Central to this process of spiritual realization are the crucial Sufi concepts of annihilation (*al-fanāʾ*) and subsistence (*al-baqāʾ*) in God, which take center stage for Shaykh Abū Bakr b. Sālim as among the most foundational concepts of the Sufi path. *Fanāʾ* in

---

75 Al-Saqqāf, *Miʿrāj al-arwāḥ* 423.
76 Al-Saqqāf, *Miʿrāj al-arwāḥ* 423; al-Saqqāf, *Fatḥ bāb al-mawāhib* 34–35.
77 Al-Saqqāf, *Miʿrāj al-arwāḥ* 379.

this technical context is a reference to the servant's ability to gradually transcend the world of external forms, of which the greatest veil is none other than the human self, thereby witnessing God as the only abiding Reality behind the multiplicity of forms constituting the veils (*ḥijāb*) of the phenomenal world.[78] As the Imam explains, the greatest and highest form of Divine witnessing can only be attained through the servant's ability to transcend her attachment to the created forms:

> Proximity (to God) is in proportion to the ability to erase the forms, and distance (from God) is in proportion to what remains of the forms, for the veil (in reality) is none other than yourself.[79]

As he eloquently expresses it elsewhere in another pithy statement,

> Whoever witnesses that the creation has no action of its own has won, whoever witnesses that they have no life of their own has succeeded, and whoever views them as essentially nonexistent has reached (his destination).[80]

This Sufi concept of erasing the forms becomes later formalized as a general feature of the Bā ʿAlawī tradition by the major 12th/18th-century ʿAlawī authority Ḥabīb ʿAbd al-Raḥmān Balfaqīh (d. 1162/1749), who notes in a pithy expression in his popular description of the *sāda*'s spiritual method, "Their formalities consist of erasing the forms" (*rusūmuhum maḥw al-rusūm*).[81]

The process by which annihilation (*fanā*ʾ) is attained is through the gradual intensification of one's complete surrender to God and His constant invocation (*dhikr*) until He becomes all that is witnessed in one's vision.[82] As God declares in a popular *ḥadīth qudsī*,

> My servant continues to draw near to me with supererogatory (*nawāfil*) works until I come to love him. When I love him, I become his hearing

78 Al-Saqqāf, *Miʿrāj al-arwāḥ* 29.

79 Al-Saqqāf, *Miʿrāj al-arwāḥ* 402. See also, al-Saqqāf, *Fatḥ bāb al-mawāhib* 38, 72.

80 Al-Saqqāf, *Miʿrāj al-arwāḥ* 290.

81 Al-ʿAṭṭās, ʿAbdallāh b. ʿAlawī b. Ḥasan, *al-ʿAlam al-nibrās fī l-tanbīh ʿalā manhaj al-akyās*, Tarīm: Zāwiyat al-ʿAydarūs al-ʿIlmiyya, n.d., 22.

82 Here, the concept of worship (*ʿibāda*) in Q 51:56, "I did not create the Jinn and humankind except to worship Me (*li-yaʿbudūn*)," is interpreted to mean, following Ibn ʿArabī and earlier exegetical authorities, to come to know God. Al-Saqqāf, *Miʿrāj al-arwāḥ* 234.

> with which he hears, his sight with which he sees, his hand with which he strikes, and his foot with which he walks.[83]

The Imam repeatedly mentions this *ḥadīth* in conjunction with other traditions, such as the following tradition, which is taken as a popular spiritual maxim for the Sufis: "Whoever knows himself, knows his Lord" (*man ʿarafa nafsahu ʿarafa rabbahu*). As he explains, in his faithful confirmation of Ibn ʿArabī's ontology, the self does not truly exist but is rather the locus of the self-disclosure of the Real (*al-ḥaqq*); to overcome this major veil and realize the self's nonexistence is to become realized in God. This understanding is also supported through recourse to several other *ḥadīths*, such as the Prophet's statement, "I came to know my Lord through my Lord" (*ʿaraftu rabbī bi-rabbī*), in addition to other supporting verses from the Quran.[84]

Given the centrality of this concept and its specialized meaning, the Imam is sure to clarify that the term *fanāʾ* is only to be taken in the figurative sense from the perspective of one's experiential witnessing,

> The Prophet, God's peace and blessings be upon him, indicated by this that you are not truly yourself. Rather, it is He without you, for to connect the knowledge of God, the Exalted, to the annihilation of existence (*fanāʾ al-wujūd*) is but a mistake and a clear oversight ... since the knowledge of God does not necessitate the annihilation of existence ... for all things have no intrinsic existence ...; he did not say, God's peace and blessings be upon him, "Whoever annihilates himself, knows his Lord."[85]

Thus *fanāʾ* does not refer to an annihilation of the entity of the servant (*inʿidām ʿayn al-ʿabd*), as the servant does not exist in any independent sense to start; rather, given that the human self has two dimensions or faces (*wujūh*), one directed towards its human nature (*bashariyya*) and the other directed towards its Lord (*rabb*), *fanāʾ* is the process of annihilating the human dimension (*al-jiha*

83 See al-Saqqāf, *Miʿrāj al-arwāḥ* 39, 178, 180, 234, 298. In al-Saqqāf, *Miʿrāj al-arwāḥ* 39, the Imam seems to be quoting a similar variant of this *ḥadīth qudsī*, the more popular rendition of which can be found in the famous collection of al-Nawawī, Yaḥyā b. Sharaf and Ibn Rajab, *al-Arbaʿīn al-Nawawiyya wa-tatimmatuhā*, ed. ʿUmar ʿAbd al-Jabbār, Mecca: Maktabat al-Iqtiṣād, n.d., 26.

84 Al-Saqqāf, *Miʿrāj al-arwāḥ* 180, 234, 276; al-Saqqāf, *Fatḥ bāb al-mawāhib* 140.

85 Al-Saqqāf, *Miʿrāj al-arwāḥ* 234. This *ḥadīth* is very frequently referenced in both works.

al-bashariyya) in the Lordly dimension (*al-jiha al-rabbāniyya*) in terms of one's witnessing. In this initial station of *fanā'*, the servant becomes fully dissolved in the witnessing of God, such that he becomes a caller through God (*yad'ū bi-Llāh*). This is followed by exiting the ocean of 'annihilation' and entering into the ocean of 'subsistence' (*baqā'*), whereby the servant returns to his senses with the full knowledge and consciousness that all of creation subsists fully by God. In this latter station, the servant becomes a caller to God (*yad'ū ilā Allāh*) as a fully realized vicegerent (*khalīfa*) on the earth, and this is the first station that is acquired by the servant before coming to acquire some of the other Divine Attributes of his Lord.[86]

4.3 *The Muhammadan Reality*

Aside from his Akbarian ontological doctrine, another major recurring focus of both works is the cosmological and metaphysical doctrine of the Muhammadan Reality (*al-ḥaqīqa al-Muḥammadiyya*).[87] As Chittick helpfully clarifies, the Muhammadan Reality refers to a complex cosmological doctrine that is widely expounded upon by al-Shaykh al-Akbar using a variety of near-synonymous terms, such as the Supreme Isthmus (*al-barzakh al-a'lā*), the Breath of the All-Merciful (*nafas al-raḥmān*), the Cloud (*al-'amā'*), the Reality of Realities (*ḥaqīqat al-ḥaqā'iq*), the Universal Reality (*al-ḥaqīqa al-kulliyya*), and the Reality of the Complete Human (*ḥaqīqat al-insān al-kāmil*), among other names.[88]

Once again, Shaykh Abū Bakr b. Sālim's expansive exposition on the metaphysical concept of the Muhammadan Reality and its centrality in the Islamic cosmological hierarchy is solidly rooted in Ibn 'Arabī's ontological and cosmo-

---

86 Al-Saqqāf, *Mi'rāj al-arwāḥ* 58, 267–268, 434. Elsewhere, he provides analogies for the *fanā'* of the servant's dimension (*wajh al-'ubūdiyya*) in his Lordly dimension (*wajh al-rubūbiyya*) with the drop of water that ceases to exist upon returning to the sea or the ice that melts away once the sun of Reality has risen. Al-Saqqāf, *Mi'rāj al-arwāḥ* 433; al-Saqqāf, *Fatḥ bāb al-mawāhib* 37–38.

87 For more on the cosmological doctrine of the Muhammadan Reality, see Chittick, *The Sufi path* 125–143; Chodkiewicz, Michel, *Seal of the saints: Prophethood and sainthood in the doctrine of Ibn 'Arabī*, trans. Liadain Sherrard, Cambridge: Islamic Texts Society, 1993, 60–73; Rustom, Mohammed, "The cosmology of the Muhammadan Reality," in *Ishrāq: Islamic Philosophy Yearbook* 4 (2013), 540–545; Rustom, Mohammed, "Dāwūd al-Qayṣarī: Notes on his life, influence, and reflections on the Muḥammadan Reality," in *Journal of Muhyiddin Ibn 'Arabi Society* 38 (2005), 51–64.

88 As Chittick observes, "These are not exact synonyms, since each [term] is employed within a specific context and does not necessarily overlap with the others in all cases." *The Sufi path* 125, 139. See also, Chodkiewicz, *Seal* 68–69.

logical scheme. In outlining this scheme, the Imam draws upon variant Hadith traditions affirming the Prophet Muhammad's Light (*nūr*), Spirit (*rūḥ*), or the First Intellect (*ʿaql*)[89] as the first entity to be created by God, which are generally recognized by the Imam and the Sufi Gnostics as near-synonymous terms used to express the same reality.[90] This is also supported in yet another famous tradition in which the Prophet declares, "I was already a Prophet while Adam was still between water and mud."[91] As the first conscious creation and the most complete receptacle of the Divine Names, even the leader of the archangels Jibrīl is created from the Light of the Prophet Muhammad's Intellect, and it is also his Spirit (*al-rūḥ al-Muḥammadī*) that God blew into Adam and before which the angels fell prostrate (Q 38:72).[92]

As the first creation and primary locus for the self-disclosure of God's All-Comprehensive Name Allāh, the Muhammadan Reality stands as the 'Supreme Isthmus' (*barzakh*) that is the principal intermediary between God and the phenomenal world. As Mohammed Rustom summarizes this intermediary function and its cosmological significance,

> the Divine Essence cannot be diffuse throughout the cosmos, and, in Its manifest aspect, It requires an intermediary of some sort, who is none other than the Prophet. In other words, the function played by the Prophet is of the utmost significance. He manifests the Name Allah and acts as the intermediary through whom the Divine Names become diffuse throughout the cosmos.[93]

This intermediary function is reiterated by Shaykh Abū Bakr b. Sālim as follows,

---

89 Shaykh Abū Bakr on numerous occasions associates the First Intellect (*al-ʿaql al-awwal*) with the Muhammadan Reality. See al-Saqqāf, *Miʿrāj al-arwāḥ* 306–307, 336, 443, 457–458; al-Saqqāf, *Fatḥ bāb al-mawāhib* 19–20. While the term is more commonly associated with the Neoplatonic cosmology of Avicenna and al-Farābī, it must be borne in mind that the Sufi cosmological scheme differs in significant ways from the traditional Neoplatonic model articulated by the Islamic philosophers. The term's appropriation by the Sufi gnostics is thus primarily intended to highlight the role of the Light of Muhammad as the first created entity and conscious intelligence. Sitting at the apex of the cosmic hierarchy, it is the most complete receptacle of the totality of the Divine Names, frequently identified with the Breath of the All-Merciful (*nafas al-raḥmān*), out of which all the bodily forms were brought into existence. Rustom, "Cosmology" 542–543; Chittick, *The Sufi path* 159.

90 Al-Saqqāf, *Miʿrāj al-arwāḥ* 84, 90, 94, 110, 306–307, 457–458; al-Saqqāf, *Fatḥ bāb al-mawāhib* 19–20, 155, 168–169.

91 Al-Saqqāf, *Miʿrāj al-arwāḥ* 116, 207.

92 Al-Saqqāf, *Miʿrāj al-arwāḥ* 15, 94, 110, 167. See also, Chodkiewicz, *Seal* 68–69.

93 Rustom, "Cosmology" 542–543.

> Know that the Realities of all the realms are but loci of manifestation for the Human Reality (*al-ḥaqīqa al-insāniyya*), which is the locus manifesting the name Allāh, the Exalted; thus, their spirits are also but partial embodiments of the Great Human Spirit (*al-rūḥ al-aʿẓam al-insānī*), be it the spirit of an angel or otherwise. It is for this reason that the Intellect (*al-ʿaql*) is also called the Great World (*al-ʿālam al-kabīr*) according to people of the way (*ahl al-ṭarīqa*) ....[94]

As he further elaborates elsewhere,

> and the Divine Attributes must return to an essence (*dhāt*) to which they must be ascribed, for the essence is prior in existence, and the Messenger of God, God's Peace and Blessings be upon him, was the first in existence, as he is a pure essence (*dhāt maḥḍ*), and all the realms are but Attributes of this essence; this is what is meant by God creating the world from him, and his Spirit is thus referred to as the Great Pen (*al-qalam al-aʿlā*), and the First Intellect (*al-ʿaql al-awwal*) is but another aspect of this meaning.[95]

As is the case with Ibn ʿArabī, the Imam also employs several near-synonymous terms to describe the Muhammadan Reality and its cosmic role within the creation. Thus, the Prophet's Reality is variously described as the Locus of the Greatest Secret (*maẓhar al-sirr al-aʿẓam*), the Spirit of the World (*rūḥ al-ʿālam*), the Greatest Spirit (*al-rūḥ al-aʿẓam*), the Epicenter of the Circle of Existence (*markaz dāʾirat al-wujūd*), the Great World (*al-ʿālam al-kabīr*), the Human Reality (*al-ḥaqīqa al-insāniyya*), and the Form of the Greatest Name (*ṣūrat al-ism al-aʿẓam*), among other descriptive names.[96] In terms of its central purpose, the Prophet's Reality in the cosmic hierarchy also functions as the Heart of Existence (*qalb al-wujūd*), just as the Sūrat Yā Sīn is known as the heart of the Quran.[97] Finally, the Imam also describes the Muhammadan Reality using the familiar Akbarian image of the Cloud (*ʿamāʾ*), which emanates from the Breath of the All-Merciful (*nafas al-raḥmān*).[98]

---

94 Al-Saqqāf, *Miʿrāj al-arwāḥ* 110. See also al-Saqqāf, *Miʿrāj al-arwāḥ* 457–458.

95 Al-Saqqāf, *Miʿrāj al-arwāḥ* 306.

96 See al-Saqqāf, *Miʿrāj al-arwāḥ* 64, 110–111, 124, 131, 443–445; al-Saqqāf, *Fatḥ bāb al-mawāhib* 26, 59.

97 Al-Saqqāf, *Miʿrāj al-arwāḥ* 306–307. It must be noted in this context that Yā Sīn is also one of the celebrated names of the Prophet Muhammad.

98 Al-Saqqāf, *Miʿrāj al-arwāḥ* 124. The printed edition uses the term *ʿamāʾ* to describe the

Like Ibn ʿArabī, the Imam draws upon several Hadith traditions and the Quran in identifying the Prophet's Spirit with God's All-Inclusive Mercy. As God declares in Q 7:156, "My Mercy encompasses all thing," and in Q 21:107, "We have not sent you but as a Mercy to the worlds." The Reality of Muhammad thus represents the immutable entity that is the locus of God's all-inclusive Mercy, and this Mercy stems from God's original love for Muhammad, out of which the phenomenal world was created. As the Imam explains, God's Mercy is the primordial and ontological foundation of the cosmos, and it is manifested in an all-inclusive (*ʿāmm*) as well as an exclusive (*khāṣṣ*) form, the former of which is identified with the Muhammadan Reality,

> The exclusive Mercy (*al-raḥma al-khāṣṣa*) is what is dispensed by God to His servants during certain specific moments, and the all-inclusive Mercy (*al-raḥma al-ʿāmma*) is the Reality of Muhammad, God's Peace and Blessings be upon him, for he is the locus of manifestation for all the creation … and for this reason, God's Mercy precedes His Wrath, because the entirety of the phenomenal world is a replica (*nuskha*) of the Beloved, and the Beloved is bestowed with [God's] Mercy; thus, the ruling of [God's] Mercy in existence is necessary (*lāzim*), while the ruling of [His] Wrath is accidental (*ʿāriḍ*), as Mercy is among the Attributes of the Divine Essence, while justice is but a [Divine] Act.[99]

Given the cosmic significance and primordial function of the Muhammadan Reality, it follows that all the realized knowledge of the Sufis, and even the knowledge of the Prophets, is but the fruit of being synchronized with the Prophet (*al-muwāfaqa li-l-nabī*), for he is the most complete and singular source of all realized knowledge. Accordingly, the Prophets and the saints (*awl-*

Prophet's Reality before God's creation of the phenomenal world, which spelled in this way indicates blindness or darkness. This is possibly a minor typographical error of the more commonly used Akbarian term *ʿamāʾ* (cloud), which is vocalized with a *hamza* at the end. For Ibn ʿArabī's description of the Muhammadan Reality as a Cloud and its association with the Breath of the All-Merciful, see the discussion in Chapter 371 of the fourth section (*faṣl*) of Ibn ʿArabī, *al-Futūḥāt* vi, 149–150. See also Chittick, *The Sufi path* 125–132. For Shaykh Abū Bakr b. Sālim's discussion on the Breath of the All-Merciful, see al-Saqqāf, *Miʿrāj al-arwāḥ* 54, 111, 116–117, 229–230, 239, 256, 258, 285, 382, 392–393, 398, 443; al-Saqqāf, *Fatḥ bāb al-mawāhib* 39, 105–106, 198–199, 295.

99 Al-Saqqāf, *Fatḥ bāb al-mawāhib* 105–106. The all-inclusive Mercy is ontologically prior and is represented by the Name *al-raḥmān*, while the exclusive Mercy is represented by the Name *al-raḥīm* and is granted to God's worthy servants and the believers. As the Imam and Ibn ʿArabī point out, both Mercies are alluded to in Q 7:156. See Chittick, *The Sufi path* 130–132.

iyā') are able to draw from the Light of Muhammad in accordance with their differing capacities, for their self-disclosures (*tajalliyyāt*) are those of the Divine Attributes (*ṣifāt*), while Muhammad's self-disclosure is that of the Singular Divine Essence (*al-dhāt al-aḥadī*). As the Imam explains,

> the Muhammadan Reality unites all the Prophets, Peace be upon them, for each of them manifested some of the Names and Attributes, and if you were to consider their Reality, and upon realizing that they all return to the Singular Presence (*al-ḥaḍra al-wāḥida*) on account of your being overpowered by the rulings of this Unity, you would uphold their unity and the unity of that with which they came: "We make no distinction between them" [Q 2:285].[100]

It thus follows that Muhammad is not only the seal of the Prophets but is also the seal of absolute sainthood (*al-walāya al-muṭlaqa*), and all knowledge stems from his knowledge.[101] As such, his realized spiritual inheritors (*al-waratha al-muḥaqqiqīn*) inherit from him in varying degrees, according to their different spiritual openings (*fatḥ*), etiquettes (*adab*), and levels of spiritual preparedness (*istiʿdād*), and in their reality, they are no more than translators or interpreters for the Messenger (*tarjumān rasūl Allāh*).[102]

Given that Muhammad is the only Prophet able to be manifest the Reality of the All-Comprehensive Name, he is also distinguished above the Prophets and saints in one other fundamental respect: the traces of his human quality (*bashariyya*) are completely neutralized and effaced (*maʿdūma*) before the Light of God, making him the most complete receptacle and reflection of the Divine Names. As for the Prophets and saints, on the other hand, traces of their human quality always remain, and the disappearance of this quality before God's self-disclosures is likened to the disappearance of the stars before the sun once it has risen. As such, in the case of Muhammad alone, his knowledge of God is equated with God's knowledge of Himself.[103]

100 Al-Saqqāf, *Miʿrāj al-arwāḥ* 130.

101 Al-Saqqāf, *Miʿrāj al-arwāḥ* 28, 30–33, 53, 86, 94, 249, 280; al-Saqqāf, *Fatḥ bāb al-mawāhib* 111–112, 125. For more on Abū Bakr b. Sālim's doctrine of sainthood (*wilāya*) and its Akbarian parallels, see al-Saqqāf, *Miʿrāj al-arwāḥ* 53, 67–68, 78–79, 347–348, 412–413, 458–462, 475–476; al-Saqqāf, *Fatḥ bāb al-mawāhib* 26–28, 92–93, 111–112, 120–121. Cf. Ibn ʿArabī's views in Chodkiewicz, *Seal*, ch. 3, 5, 7 and 9.

102 Al-Saqqāf, *Miʿrāj al-arwāḥ* 58, 208–209, 214, 218.

103 Al-Saqqāf, *Miʿrāj al-arwāḥ* 436; al-Saqqāf, *Fatḥ bāb al-mawāhib* 185–186.

5 The Complete Human

In discussing the Muhammadan Reality, Shaykh Abū Bakr b. Sālim also expounds upon the associated and complementary doctrine of the Complete Human (*al-insān al-kāmil*), which is commonly associated with the function of the spiritual pole (*quṭb*) in any given age.[104] In explicating this classic Sufi doctrine, the Imam employs various titles to describe the Complete Human. Thus, as the microcosmic representation of the macrocosm, he is the Replica of the great world (*nuskhat al-ʿālam al-kabīr*). He is also the Form of God (*ṣūrat al-ilāh*), the Shadow of God (*ẓill al-ilāh*), and the Fount of the world (*ʿayn al-ʿālam*), for being realized in the Divine Names and being able to reflect them throughout the creation, while in his intermediary role between God and creation, he represents the Reality of the Great Isthmus (*al-ḥaqīqa al-barzakhiyya al-kubrā*).[105] Elsewhere, the Imam seems to use the terms *al-insān al-kāmil* and *al-ḥaqīqa al-Muḥammadiyya* interchangeably, which is likely meant to affirm the Complete Human or spiritual Pole (*quṭb*) as the only adequate individual capable of fully assuming the cosmic function and attributes of the Muhammadan Reality.[106]

Among these descriptions, the Imam also expounds upon Ibn ʿArabī's view of the Complete Human's intermediary position within the cosmic hierarchy

---

104 I prefer the "Complete Human," as *kamāl* in Arabic has the primary meaning of arriving at a sense of completion or fulfilment, where one becomes realized in their full human potential. As such, the ideas of perfection and universalism would appear to be secondary and derivative connotations of this understanding. For more on this classic Sufi doctrine, see Chittick, *The Sufi path* 27–30, 276–278; Chittick, William C., *In search of the lost heart: Explorations in Islamic thought*, ed. Mohammed Rustom, Atif Khalil, and Kazuyo Murata, Albany, NY: SUNY Press, 2012, 143–152; Takeshita, Masataka, *Ibn ʿArabī's theory of the perfect man and its place in the history of Islamic thought*, Tokyo (PhD Diss.): Tokyo Institute for the Study of Languages and Cultures of Asia and Africa, 1987; Nicholson, Reynold A., *Studies in Islamic Mysticism*, Cambridge: Cambridge University Press, 1921, ch. 2; Lumbard, Joseph, "*al-Insān al-kāmil*: Doctrine and practice," in *IQ* 38.4 (1994), 261–282.

105 Al-Saqqāf, *Miʿrāj al-arwāḥ* 118–119, 217, 283, 292, 386, 401, 426, 443; al-Saqqāf, *Fatḥ bāb al-mawāhib* 26, 48, 59.

106 As Chodkiewicz helpfully explains, "the terms *ḥaqīqa Muḥammadiyya* and *insān kāmil* are not purely synonymous but express differing views of man, the first seeing him in terms of his primordiality and the second in terms of his finality." Chodkiewicz, *Seal* 69. This understanding is indirectly alluded it to by the Imam when he states, "The pole (*quṭb*), who is at the epicenter of the circle of existence (*markaz dāʾirat al-wujūd*) since pre-eternity and forever, is one when the ruling of unity is considered, and he is also the Muhammadan Reality when the multiplicity in all its numerousness is considered." Al-Saqqāf, *Miʿrāj al-arwāḥ* 280–281; al-Saqqāf, *Fatḥ bāb al-mawāhib* 60–61.

as the confluence of the two seas (*majmaʿ al-baḥrayn*), an expression borrowed from Q 18:60. This title is intended to highlight the Complete Human's uniqueness in his ability to encompass and assume the two realities of Lordship (*rubūbiyya*) and servitude (*ʿubūdiyya*) as the Supreme Intermediary (*barzakh*) between the Real (*al-ḥaqq*) and the creation (*al-khalq*), a capacity that qualifies the human being to become God's vicegerent (*khalīfa*) and steward of the earth. This unique intermediary capacity is particularly attributed to the potential of the believer's heart to experience and contain God's self-disclosure and to reflect the Divine Names, where the Prophet's heart is the most vast and complete human archetype. This doctrine is grounded via frequent recourse to the popular *ḥadīth* wherein God declares, "Neither the heavens nor the earth can contain Me, but the heart of My faithful and humble servant can contain Me."[107] In this sense, even the delimited nature of Muhammad's humanity (*bashariyya*), which is necessarily subject to the same limitations and dictates of the created world, is itself a sign of the Prophet's completeness and ontological perfection since it reflects his ability to experience and relate to both the higher and the lower realms as the most complete and conscious being at the epicenter of the cosmic hierarchy.[108] Given this unique ontological status of the Complete Human as the finality and microcosmic representation of the Muhammadan Reality, every living thing draws its life from his life, and through gazing upon his heart, God bestows His Mercy upon all of existence. As the Imam, thus, asserts on numerous occasions, "The Reality of the Complete Human necessarily courses (*tasrī*) through all the worlds and existent things, just as the Real (*al-ḥaqq*) runs through His creation."[109]

---

107 See ʿAyn al-Quḍāt, *The essence of reality: A defense of philosophical Sufism*, ed. and trans. Mohammed Rustom, New York: New York University Press, 2022, 151.

108 Al-Saqqāf, *Miʿrāj al-arwāḥ* 262, 280, 306–307, 415; al-Saqqāf, *Fatḥ bāb al-mawāhib* 26, 59, 255.

109 See al-Saqqāf, *Miʿrāj al-arwāḥ* 56, 71, 77, 84, 110, 443, 458; al-Saqqāf, *Fatḥ bāb al-mawāhib* 24–25. This understanding is frequently supported with reference to the Complete Human's ability to reflect the encompassing Reality of the Divine Names in Q 57:3, "He is the First (*al-awwal*) and the Last (*al-ākhir*), the Outermost (*al-ẓāhir*) and Innermost (*al-bāṭin*), and He has Knowledge (*ʿalīm*) of all things." While, more precisely, this is a reference to the function of the Muhammadan Reality, which is occasionally referred to as the Reality of the Complete Human (*ḥaqīqat al-insān al-kāmil*), elsewhere, the Imam appears to drop this subtle distinction and to describe this all-encompassing feature as a quality of the Complete Human himself. It is quite likely that in such instances, however, *al-insān al-kāmil* is employed as a synonym for *al-ḥaqīqa al-Muḥammadiyya*.

6 Conclusion

As one of the ʿAlawīs' most celebrated exponents of philosophical Sufism, the famous *manṣab* of ʿĪnāt Shaykh Abū Bakr b. Sālim represents a high point in the *sāda*'s intellectual tradition, and his two major works of Sufi *ḥaqāʾiq*, *Miʿrāj al-arwāḥ* and *Fatḥ bāb al-mawāhib*, have remained practically unknown within the academic study of Yemeni Sufism. While traditional biographies do not mention much about his immediate family and early spiritual training, it is nonetheless known that he was a contemporary of the famous shaykh Ḥusayn Bā Faḍl, the famous author of Sufi *ḥaqāʾiq* and great admirer of Ibn ʿArabī. Since both were disciples of the famous ʿAlawī Sufi master of Tarīm Imam Aḥmad b. ʿAlawī Bā Jaḥdab, it is highly conceivable that these two major Hadhrami Sufis would have met and studied with one another. Thus, aside from his studies and spiritual training with Shaykh Maʿrūf Bā Jammāl, this connection suggests that Shaykh Abū Bakr b. Sālim had received his exposure to Sufi *ḥaqāʾiq* and the works of Ibn ʿArabī through these contacts, pointing once again to the likelihood that Ibn ʿArabī's works were more widely received among Hadhramawt's scholarly elite than we are initially led to believe.

Both of Shaykh Abū Bakr's works on theoretical gnosis are remarkable in their intellectual breadth and sophistication and their technical Sufi vocabulary, displaying an intimate and unmistakable mastery of Ibn ʿArabī's *Futūḥat* and *Fūṣūṣ*. The bulk of this study was devoted to a synopsis of both works' overarching themes, with a special focus on the Imam's Akbarian vocabulary, his gnostic epistemology that privileged the inspired knowledge of the Sufi mystics (*al-ʿilm al-ladunī*), his ontology and theology that expounded upon the doctrine of *waḥdat al-wujūd*, his explication of the Sufi concepts of annihiliation (*fanāʾ*) and subsistence (*baqāʾ*) in God, and his conception of the major Sufi doctrines of *al-ḥaqīqa al-Muḥammadiyya* and *al-insān al-kāmil.*

As one of the most influential ʿAlawī saints of the 10th/16th century, Shaykh Abū Bakr b. Sālim's positive reception and assimilation of Ibn ʿArabī's thought is neither a marginal example nor a surprising discovery for the intellectual historian of Sufism, and further studies into the intellectual history of Hadhramawt and the *sāda*'s spiritual tradition are bound to yield similar Akbarian engagements with Sufi metaphysics and the wider tradition of philosophical Sufism. Indeed, despite his historically controversial status, al-Shaykh al-Akbar's influence on the tradition of philosophical Sufism tradition remains in many ways analogous to Avicenna's towering position within the field of Islamic philosophy: one cannot be considered a serious scholarly inheritor of these two respective intellectual traditions without having mastered the works of their preeminent and most influential intellectual authorities.[110] Such observations thus suggest a need for further research so as to help refine our current understanding of the reception of Ibn ʿArabī and the scope of his historical influence on the intellectual and spiritual landscape of the Yemen and the Hijaz.

Bibliography

Abushouk, Ahmed I. and Hassan A. Ibrahim (eds.), *The Hadhrami diaspora in Southeast Asia: Identity, maintenance or assimilation?*, Leiden: Brill, 2009.

al-ʿAṭṭās, ʿAbdallāh b. ʿAlawī b. Ḥasan, *al-ʿAlam al-nibrās fī l-tanbīh ʿalā manhaj al-akyās*, Tarīm: Zāwiyat al-ʿAydarūs al-ʿIlmiyya, n.d.

al-ʿAydarūs, ʿAbd al-Qādir b. Shaykh b. ʿAbdallāh, *al-Nūr al-sāfir ʿan akhbār al-qarn al-ʿāshir*, ed. Aḥmad Ḥālū, Maḥmūd al-Arnāʾūṭ and Akram al-Būshī, Beirut: Dār Ṣādir, 2001.

ʿAyn al-Quḍāt, *The essence of reality: A defense of philosophical Sufism*, ed. and trans. Mohammed Rustom, New York: New York University Press, 2022.

Bā ʿAlawī, ʿĀbd al-Raḥmān b. Muḥammad and ʿAlī Bā Ṣabrīn, *Bughyat al-mustarshidīn fī talkhīṣ fatāwā baʿḍ al-aʾimma min al-ʿulamāʾ al-mutaʾakhkhirīn*, 4 vols., Tarīm: Dār al-Faqīh, 2009.

Bā Dhīb, Muḥammad, *Juhūd fuqahāʾ Ḥaḍramawt fī khidmat al-madhhab al-Shāfiʿī*, 2 vols., Amman: Dār al-Fatḥ, 2009.

al-Badawī, Mostafa, *A blessed valley: Wadi Hadramawt & the Alawi tradition*, UK: Guidance Media, 2013.

Bang, Anne K., *Sufis and scholars of the sea: Family networks in East Africa, 1860–1925*, London: RoutledgeCurzon, 2003.

Boxberger, Linda, *On the edge of empire: Hadhramawt, emigration, and the Indian Ocean, 1880s–1930s*, Albany, NY: SUNY Press, 2002.

Brehony, Noel (ed.), *Hadhramaut and its diaspora: Yemeni politics, identity and migration*, London: I.B. Tauris, 2017.

Bujra, Abdalla S., *The politics of stratification: A study of political change in a South Arabian town*, Oxford: Clarendon Press, 1971.

Buxton, Amin, *Imams of the valley*, Western Cape: Dār al-Turāth al-Islāmī, 2012.

110 As Chodkiewicz insightfully observes, the Shaykh's work continues to be taken seriously and exhibit a global influence over the spiritual heritage of Sufism, despite all the controversy surrounding his image, due to its one abiding characteristic: "it has a response to everything." Chodkiewicz, *Ocean* 18.

Chittick, William C., *The Sufi path of knowledge: Ibn al-ʿArabī's metaphysics of imagination*, Albany, NY: SUNY Press, 1989.

Chittick, William C., *In search of the lost heart: Explorations in Islamic thought*, ed. Mohammed Rustom, Atif Khalil, and Kazuyo Murata, Albany, NY: SUNY Press, 2012.

Chodkiewicz, Michel, *An ocean without shore: Ibn ʿArabī, the book, and the law*, trans. David Streight, Albany, NY: SUNY Press, 1993.

Chodkiewicz, Michel, *Seal of the saints: Prophethood and sainthood in the doctrine of Ibn ʿArabī*, trans. Liadain Sherrard, Cambridge: Islamic Texts Society, 1993.

Collins, Brinston B., *Ḥaḍramawt: Crisis and intervention, 1866–1881*, Princeton (PhD Diss.): Princeton University, 1969.

De Nicola, Bruno, "The ladies of Rūm: A hagiographic view of women in thirteenth- and fourteenth-century Anatolia," in *Journal of Sufi Studies* 3.2 (2014), 132–156.

Dostal, Walter, "The saints of Hadramawt," in Walter Dostal and Wolfgang Kraus (eds.), *Shattering tradition: Custom, law, and the individual in the Muslim Mediterranean*, London: I.B. Tauris, 2005, 233–253.

Edaibat, Omar, "Muḥyī l-Dīn Ibn ʿArabī's personalist theory of the *sharīʿa*: An examination of his legal doctrine," in *Journal of Sufi Studies* 6.1 (2017), 1–46.

Edaibat, Omar, *The Bā ʿAlawī sāda of the Hadhramaut valley: An intellectual and social history from tenth-century origins till the late-sixteenth century*, Montreal (PhD Diss.): McGill Institute of Islamic Studies, 2021.

al-Fāsī, Yūsuf b. ʿĀbid b. Muḥammad, *Riḥlat Ibn ʿĀbid al-Fāsī min al-Maghrib ilā Ḥaḍramawt*, ed. Ibrāhīm al-Sāmrāʾī and ʿAbdallāh b. Muḥammad al-Ḥabshī, Beirut: Dār al-Gharb al-Islāmī, 1993.

Freitag, Ulrike and William G. Clarence-Smith (eds.), *Hadhrami traders, scholars, and statesmen in the Indian Ocean, 1750s–1960s*, Leiden: Brill, 1997.

Freitag, Ulrike, *Indian Ocean migrants and state formation in Hadhramaut: Reforming the homeland*, Leiden: Brill, 2003.

al-Ḥaddād, ʿAlawī b. Ṭāhir, *ʿUqūd al-almās bi-manāqib shaykh al-ṭarīqa al-Ḥabīb Aḥmad b. Ḥasan b. ʿAbdallāh al-ʿAṭṭās*, Tarīm: Tarīm li-l-Dirāsāt wa-l-Nashr, n.d.

al-Ḥaddād, ʿAlawī b. Ṭāhir, *Janī l-shamārīkh: Jawāb asʾila fī l-tārīkh*, ed. Muḥammad Yaslam ʿAbd al-Nūr, Tarīm: Tarīm li-l-Dirāsāt wa-l-Nashr, 2012.

al-Ḥāmid, Ṣāliḥ, *Tārīkh Ḥaḍramawt*, 2 vols., Sanaa: Maktabat al-Irshād, 2003.

Hartwig, Friedhelm, "Expansion, state foundation and reform: The contest for power in Hadhramaut in the nineteenth century," in Ulrike Freitag and William G. Clarence-Smith (eds.), *Hadhrami traders, scholars, and statesmen in the Indian Ocean, 1750s–1960s*, Leiden: Brill, 1997, 35–50.

Ho, Engseng, *The graves of Tarim: Genealogy and mobility across the Indian Ocean*, Berkeley, CA: University of California Press, 2006.

Ibn ʿArabī, Muḥyī al-Dīn, *al-Futūḥāt al-Makkiyya*, ed. Nawwāf al-Jarrāḥ, 9 vols., Beirut: Dār Ṣādir, 2004.

Ibn ʿArabī, Muḥyī al-Dīn, *Fuṣūṣ al-ḥikam*, Cairo: Dār Afāq, 2016.

Ibn Hishām, Muḥammad, *Tārīkh al-dawla al-Kathīriyya*, ed. Muḥammad ʿAlī al-Jifrī, Tarīm: Tarīm li-l-Dirāsāt wa-l-Nashr, 2002.

Khirid, Muḥammad b. ʿAlī, *Ghurar al-bahāʾ al-ḍawī wa-durar al-jamāl al-badīʿ al-bahī*, ed. ʿAbd al-Qādir al-Jīlānī b. Sālim Khirid, Cairo: al-Maktaba al-Azhariyya li-l-Turāth, 2002.

Knysh, Alexander, *Ibn ʿArabi in the later Islamic tradition: The making of a polemical image in medieval Islam*, Albany, NY: SUNY Press, 1999.

Knysh, Alexander, "The Sāda in history: A critical essay on Ḥaḍramī historiography," in *JRAS* 9.2 (1999), 215–222.

Knysh, Alexander, "The 'tariqa' on a landcruiser: The resurgence of Sufism in Yemen," in *Middle East Journal* 55.3 (2001), 399–414.

Lekon, Christian, *Time, space and globalization: Hadhramaut and the Indian Ocean rim 1863–1967*, Gleichen: Muster-Schmidt, 2014.

Lumbard, Joseph, "*al-Insān al-kāmil*: Doctrine and practice," in *IQ* 38.4 (1994), 261–282.

al-Mashhūr, ʿAbd al-Raḥman b. Muḥammad, *al-Shams al-ẓahīra fī nasab ahl al-bayt min Banī ʿAlawī*, ed. Muḥammad Ḍiyāʾ Shihāb, 2 vols., Jeddah: ʿĀlam al-Maʿrifa, 1984.

al-Mashhūr, Abū Bakr, "al-Shaykh Maʿrūf Bā Jammāl," in *Silsilat aʿlām Ḥaḍramawt al-kāmila*, Aden: Arbiṭat al-Tarbiya al-Islāmiyya (Farʿ al-Dirāsāt wa-Khidmat al-Turāth), 2002, 272–302.

Motoki, Yamaguchi, "Debate on the status of *sayyid/sharīfs* in the modern era: The ʿAlawī Irshādī dispute and Islamic reformists in the Middle East," in Morimoto Kazuo (ed.), *Sayyids and sharifs in Muslim societies: The living links to the Prophet*, London: Routledge, 2012, 49–71.

al-Nawawī, Yaḥyā b. Sharaf and Ibn Rajab, *al-Arbaʿīn al-Nawawiyya wa-tatimmatuhā*, ed. ʿUmar ʿAbd al-Jabbār, Mecca: Maktabat al-Iqtiṣād, n.d.

Nicholson, Reynold A., *Studies in Islamic Mysticism*, Cambridge: Cambridge University Press, 1921.

Peskes, Esther, "Der Heilige und die Dimension seiner Macht: Abū Bakr al-ʿAydarūs (gest. 1509) und die Saiyid-Sūfīs von Ḥaḍramaut," in *QSA* 13 (1995), 41–72.

Peskes, Esther, *al-ʿAidarūs und seine Erben: Eine Untersuchung zu Geschichte und Sufismus einer ḥaḍramitischen Sāda-Gruppe vom fünfzehnten bis zum achtzehnten Jahrhundert*, Stuttgart: Steiner, 2005.

Peskes, Esther, "Sainthood as patrimony: ʿAbd Allāh al-ʿAydarūs (d. 1461) and his descendants," in Alexandre Papas and Catherine Mayeur-Jaouen (eds.), *Family portraits with saints*, Berlin: DeGruyter, 2020, 125–157.

Renard, John, *Friends of God: Islamic images of piety, commitment, and servanthood*, Berkeley, CA: University of California Press, 2008.

Rustom, Mohammed, "Dāwūd al-Qayṣarī: Notes on his life, influence, and reflections on the Muḥammadan Reality," in *Journal of Muhyiddin Ibn ʿArabi Society* 38 (2005), 51–64.

Rustom, Mohammed, "The cosmology of the Muhammadan Reality," in *Ishrāq: Islamic Philosophy Yearbook* 4 (2013), 540–545.

al-Saqqāf, Abū Bakr b. Sālim, *Miftāḥ al-sarā'ir wa-kanz al-dhakhā'ir*, Cairo: al-Bayyina li-l-Nashr wa-l-Abḥāth, 1994.

al-Saqqāf, Abū Bakr b. Sālim, *Miʿrāj al-arwāḥ wa-l-manhaj al-waḍḍāḥ*, ed. Aḥmad Farīd al-Mazīdī, Beirut: Kitāb Nāshirūn, 2013.

al-Saqqāf, Abū Bakr b. Sālim, *Fatḥ bāb al-mawāhib wa-bughyat maṭlab al-maṭālib*, ed. Aḥmad Farīd al-Mazīdī, Beirut: Kitāb Nāshirūn, 2019.

Serjeant, Robert B., "Materials for South Arabian history: Notes on new MSS from Ḥadramawt," in *BSOAS* 13.2 (1950), 281–307.

Serjeant, Robert B., "Materials for South Arabian history: Notes on new MSS from Ḥadramawt (Part II)," in *BSOAS* 13.3 (1950), 581–601.

Serjeant, Robert B., *The saiyids of Ḥaḍramawt*, London: School of Oriental and African Studies, 1957.

Serjeant, Robert B., "Historians and historiography of Ḥaḍramawt," in *BSOAS* 25.1/3 (1962), 239–261.

Serjeant, Robert B., "*Haram* and *hawtah*, the sacred enclave in Arabia," in Francis E. Peters (ed.), *The Arabs and Arabia on the eve of Islam*, Aldershot: Ashgate, 1999, 167–184.

al-Shāṭirī, Muḥammad b. Aḥmad b. ʿUmar, *Adwār al-tārīkh al-Ḥaḍramī*, 2 vols., Tarīm: Dār al-Muhājir, 1994.

al-Shillī, Muḥammad b. Abī Bakr, *al-Mashraʿ al-rawī fī manāqib al-sāda al-kirām Āl Abī ʿAlawī*, 2 vols., Egypt: al-Maṭbaʿa al-ʿĀmira al-Sharafiyya, 1901.

al-Shillī, Muḥammad b. Abī Bakr, *ʿIqd al-jawāhir wa-l-durar fī akhbār al-qarn al-ḥādī ʿashara*, ed. Ibrāhīm Aḥmad al-Maqḥafī, Sanaa: Maktabat al-Irshād, 2003.

al-Shillī, Muḥammad b. Abī Bakr, *al-Sanā' al-bāhir bi-takmīl al-nūr al-sāfir*, ed. Ibrāhīm Aḥmad al-Maqḥafī, Sanaa: Maktabat al-Irshād, 2004.

Sylvaine, Camelin, "Reflections on the system of social stratification in Hadhramaut," in Ulrike Freitag and William G. Clarence-Smith (eds.), *Hadhrami traders, scholars, and statesmen in the Indian Ocean, 1750s–1960s*, Leiden: Brill, 1997, 147–156.

Takeshita, Masataka, *Ibn ʿArabī's theory of the perfect man and its place in the history of Islamic thought*, Tokyo (PhD Diss.): Tokyo Institute for the Study of Languages and Cultures of Asia and Africa, 1987.

CHAPTER 13

A Sufi Vocabulary from the Sokoto Caliphate: Shaykh Dan Tafa's *Poem on Sufi Nomenclature* (*al-Manẓūma li-l-iṣṭilāḥ al-ṣūfiyya*)

Oludamini Ogunnaike

إني وإن لم ألحق بركاتهم   لمكثر في ذكره ومطول
ومرءٌ في ذكرهم متمتع   منه وحثوا الركاب وأجفلوا
حسبي وإن خلفت فرداً بعدهم   أني بهم متوسلٌ متطفلٌ

And if their baraka I've not achieved
I'll mention it at length and frequently
There's joy in 'membering them repeatedly
It spurs the rider on and gives him speed
If after them, I'm left alone, enough for me
Is that I cling to them dependently

SHAYKH DAN TAFA[1]

∵

This short didactic poem and auto-commentary entitled *al-Manẓūma li-l-iṣṭilāḥ al-ṣūfiyya* (*A poem on Sufi nomenclature*)[2] was written by ʿAbd al-Qādir b. Muṣṭafā (d. 1280/1864) (known as "Dan Tafa"), the grandson of the legendary Sufi, scholar, and founder of the Sokoto Caliphate, Usman dan Fodio. Dan Tafa

1 This appears to be a poem of Dan Tafa's, which he used to conclude the work translated in this chapter.

2 Muhammad Shareef of the Sankore Institute edited the manuscript of this text, and this translation is based upon his edition. His translation of this work, along with many other digitized manuscripts and translations of writings of scholars form the Sokoto Caliphate can be found on the website of the Sankore Institute: www.siiasi.org (last accessed: 2 December 2021).

 | DOI:10.1163/9789004529038_014

authored this work when he was only 17 lunar years old, after studying ʿAbd al-Karīm al-Jīlī's magnum opus, *al-Insān al-kāmil* (*The universal man*) with his maternal uncle and Sufi master, Muḥammad Sambo (d. 1242/1826), the son of Usman dan Fodio (d. 1232/1817).

Dan Tafa was born in the middle of the *hijra* (emigration) that marked the beginning of the Sokoto Caliphate, which became the largest polity and one of the most important centers of Islamic scholarship in 13th/19th-century West Africa.[3] Usman dan Fodio, the Sufi scholar and leader of the *jihād* movement, actually halted their *hijra* so that his daughter Khadīja could give birth to Dan Tafa.[4] Khadīja was also an acclaimed scholar and Sufi, having translated the famous Maliki *fiqh* manual, the *Mukhtaṣar* of al-Khalīl into Fulfulde. Dan Tafa's father, Muṣṭafā b. Muḥammad al-Tūrūdī (d. 1261/1845), known as Mallam Tafa, was Usman dan Fodio's personal secretary and student. Mallam Tafa was one of the most respected scholars in Dan Fodio's circle and founded the school of Salame, just outside the city of Sokoto, in what is today Northwestern Nigeria. Dan Tafa received his early education from his parents, and at the age of fifteen, was initiated into Sufism by Muhammad Sambo. In his works, Dan Tafa describes studying Aḥmad al-Zarrūq's (d. 899/1493) *Uṣūl al-ṭarīqa*, Ibn ʿAṭāʾ Allāh al-Iskandarī's (d. 709/1309) *Ḥikam*, and especially al-Jīlī's *al-Insān al-kāmil* with Muḥammad Sambo, who studied these works with Usman dan Fodio. Dan Tafa went on to study an impressive array of Islamic sciences (Arabic linguistics, rhetoric, poetry, Hadith, Islamic law, jurisprudence, Quranic commentary, theology, logic, philosophy, mathematics, history, geography, physics, botany, astronomy, medicine, oneirology, Sufism, the science of letters, and numerous occult sciences) with the cohort of scholars Dan Fodio recruited and trained in the early years of his movement. In short, Dan Tafa was trained in virtually all of the Islamic sciences circulating in West Africa in the 13th/19th century. Indeed, the German explorer Heinrich Barth, whom Dan Tafa met in 1853, described him as "the most learned of the present generations of the inhabitants of Sokoto … on whose stores of knowledge I drew eagerly."[5]

---

3 See Hiskett, Mervyn, *The sword of truth: The life and times of the Shehu Usuman dan Fodio*, New York: Oxford University Press, 1972.

4 The *hijra* dan Fodio and his community began when they left Degel on Thursday the 12th of Dhū l-Qaʿda 1218 AH; they halted at Fankaaji on Tuesday the 17th, and Dan Tafa was born on the 19th of the same month. Boyd, Jean, *The caliph's sister: Nana Asma'u, (1793–1865): Teacher, poet, and Islamic leader*, London: Frank Cass, 1989, 12.

5 See Ogunnaike, Oludamini, "A treatise on practical and theoretical Sufism in the Sokoto Caliphate: Shaykh Dan Tafa's *Exposition of devotions* (*Bayān al-taʿabbudāt*)," in *Journal of*

Shaykh Dan Tafa never held (and seemed to never have vied for) a high political office in the Sokoto state,[6] merely succeeding his father in governing the town of Salame and running its school, which became highly regarded during his lifetime. However, Dan Tafa does seem to have been an important advisor of the Amirs, Wazirs, and Sultans of the Sokoto Caliphate, as well as being widely regarded as its foremost scholar, corresponding widely (and sometimes critically) with other polities and scholars beyond the borders of the Sokoto state.[7] As mentioned, upon his father's death in 1261/1845, Dan Tafa took over his father's school in Salame and taught there until his own passing two decades later. He authored numerous works in various disciplines during his lifetime,[8] many of which seem to have been lost when the brutal French Voulet-Chanoine expedition of 1898 burned the school of Salame to the ground.[9] However, many of his works have been preserved and catalogued by Dan Tafa's descendants in Salame, Sokoto, and in the caliphate-in-exile in Maiurno, Sudan, and also by

---

Sufi Studies 10.1–2 (2021), 152–173; Ogunnaike, Oludamini, "Philosophical Sufism in the Sokoto Caliphate: The case of Shaykh Dan Tafa," in Ousmane Kane (ed.), *New directions in the study of Islamic scholarship in Africa*, Rochester, NY: James Currey, 2021, 136–168; Shareef, Muhammad, *The life of Shaykh Dan Tafa: The life and times of one of Africa's leading scholars and statesmen and a history of the intellectual traditions that produced him*, Maiurno: Sankore Institute of Islamic-African Studies, n.d. for more information on Shaykh Dan Tafa's life and works.

6 According to an oral tradition recorded by Murray Last in *The Sokoto Caliphate*, Dan Tafa became close friends with Aḥmad b. Abī Bakr Atiku, the son of the third Sultan of Sokoto. Aḥmad promised to make Dan Tafa his *wazīr* if he ever became Sultan, but ʿAbd al-Qādir b. Gidado, the then-*wazīr* of the fourth Sultan of Sokoto (ʿAlī Babba Ibn Bello), wanted his own son, Ibrāhīm Khalīlu, to become *wazīr* after him. So when ʿAbd al-Qādir Ibn Gidado got wind of Dan Tafa's arrangement with Aḥmad, he refused to support the latter's bid to become Sultan unless he rescinded his offer to Dan Tafa and promised to make Ibrāhīm Khalīlu b. ʿAbd al-Qādir his *wazīr* instead. Aḥmad agreed and with Ibn Gidado's backing, became the next sultan after death of Sultan ʿAlī Babba Ibn Bello. ʿAbd al-Qādir Ibn Gidado served as *wazīr* under the new Sultan, Aḥmad b. Abī Bakr Atiku, for only forty days, whereupon he died. Upon ʿAbd al-Qādir's death, Sultan Aḥmad honored his promise to the late *wazīr* and appointed Ibrāhīm Khalīlu to his late father's post. Dan Tafa seems to have not contested this change of fortune. See Last, Murray, *The Sokoto Caliphate*, New York: Humanities Press, 1967, 162–165.

7 See Nobili, Mauro, *The sultan, caliph and the renewer of the faith: Ahmad Lobbo, the* Tārīkh al-fattāsh *and the making of an Islamic state in West Africa*, New York: Cambridge University Press, 2020, 218–223.

8 Hunwick records 72 titles (including works of poetry, although some of these are duplicates) in his *Arabic literature of Africa* volume and the Sankore Institute has recorded 44 unique titles. See Hunwick, John and Rex O'Fahey, *The Arabic literature of Africa*. II. *The writings of Central Sudanic Africa*, Leiden: Brill, 1995, 221–230.

9 Last, *The Sokoto Caliphate* 140.

the late Waziri Junaidu, the Sokoto History Bureau,[10] John Hunwick's Arabic Literature of Africa project, and most recently by Shaykh Muhammad Shareeef of the Sankore Institute, who studied and digitized Dan Tafa's works with the latter's descendants in both Sudan and Nigeria. Shareef has done much to preserve and transmit Dan Tafa's legacy into the 21st century, and it is thanks to his efforts that we were able to obtain copies of Shaykh Dan Tafa's manuscripts. While Dan Tafa's historical and legal works[11] have the widest attestation in manuscript collections across the region and have attracted the most attention in Europhone scholarship, his numerous other works on philosophical Sufism, theology, and occult sciences such as his treatise on "The superiority of men to angels" and commentary on al-Ghazālī's famous dictum on the best of possible worlds, await translation and study.[12]

∴

In the Name of God, the Merciful the Compassionate, Praise be to God, Lord of the worlds and the best of prayers and most complete greetings of peace be upon our lord Muhammad and his family and all of his companions. So says the

---

10 See Kani, Ahmed M., "The private library of 'Abd al-Qadir b. al-Mustafā (d. 1864)," in *Sixth interim report, 1979–1981*, Zaria: Northern History Research Scheme, 1987.

11 Dan Tafa's treatise discussing ten legal matters on which Usman dan Fodio and his brother 'Abdullahi dan Fodio disagreed as well as the rulings implemented by Muhammad Bello, Usman dan Fodio's son and political successor, remains a touchstone of Mālikī jurisprudence (*uṣūl al-fiqh*) and legal history for the region. Even more popular are his historical works, *Rawḍāt al-afkār* (*Gardens of toughts*) and the *Mawṣūfat al-Sūdān* (*Description of the Sudan*), which is a translation and augmentation of a Fulfuude poem of Nana Asmā'u describing the *jihād* of dan Fodio and events up to the date of its writing in 1842. The *Rawḍāt al-afkār* describes the various states of the Western and Central Sudan in the period leading up to dan Fodio's 1804 *jihād*, the *jihād* and the establishment of the Sokoto caliphate, and various events therein until the writing of the work in 1824. Interestingly, the work dates years from 1804 onwards in terms of years after 'Uthmān dan Fodio's *hijra*. See Ogunnaike, "Philosophical Sufism in the Sokoto Caliphate" 144; Shareef, *The life of Shaykh Dan Tafa*; Naylor, Paul, *From rebels to rulers: Writing legitimacy in the early Sokoto state*, Rochester, NY: James Currey, 2021; and Zehnle, Stephanie, *A geography of jihad: Sokoto Jihadism and the Islamic frontier in West Africa*, Boston: de Gruyter, 2020.

12 Shaykh Muhammad Shareef's lengthy commentary on Dan Tafa's poem *Shukr al-wāhib* provides an excellent introduction to the many dimensions of Dan Tafa's oeuvre. See Shareef, Muhammad, *'Ilāwat al-muṭālib fī shukr al-wāhib al-mufīḍ al-mawāhib*, Maiurno: Sankore Institute of Islamic-African Studies International, 2013. See Ogunnaike, "Philosophical Sufism in the Sokoto Caliphate" and Ogunnaike, "A treatise" for studies of Dan Tafa's work in this genre.

faqīr before God Most High, ʿAbd al-Qādir the son of Muṣṭafā b. Muḥammad b. Muḥammad, may God pardon them all.

These are words and their meanings which we have composed into an introductory poem on the technical vocabulary of the Sufis since perhaps some of their meanings are hidden from some people who have not attained the root of this technical vocabulary. For they [the Sufis] have not forbidden looking into the science of *taṣawwuf*. Our goal in this is to alert them [to the nature of the science of *taṣawwuf*] and to increase them in benefits, advancement, and attainment. And God is He whose help is sought.

So says ʿAbd al-Qādir b. Muṣṭafā
    In recognition of what I have reaped and harvested
Hoping for the mercy of his Lord, the Eternally Self-Sufficient
    Seeking by it to manifest what had been intended
Praise be to God who has spread
    on the basis of the Folk, the lights of mindfulness
And prayers upon Muhammad
    And his Companions and whosoever, by his religion, is guided
And so: this is a summary poem
    On the technical vocabulary of the Folk—whosoever knows it, succeeds
Explaining and unveiling their meanings
    Uncovering the expressions as it is known
by the Lord of the Throne and He is my sufficiency
    and His pleasure is my desire and my reward.

I say, and with God is success: I began my poem with my name and the name of my father because that is what is required. This father of mine is Muṣṭafā b. Muḥammad b. Muḥammad b. Ibrāhīm b. ʿAlī, written as ʿĀl. He was a notable scholar, a storehouse of brilliant understanding in the high arts of Arabic and in the precise arts of religion, he was a scholar of Hadith (Prophetic traditions), *tafsīr* (Quranic exegesis), *uṣūl al-fiqh* (jurisprudence), and *fiqh* (Islamic law). He was a master of all of the sciences and the rest of the arts. He had a mastery of the science of Hadith, and a high standing in the knowledge of the sciences of theology (*kalām*), law (*fiqh*), and legal judgements. He was a superlative master of these arts. He was gentle, patient, virtuous, and distinguished, possessing a knowledge of the science of the arcana (*ʿilm al-ghawāmiḍ*), as we have mentioned in our book, *The delightful call regarding the scholars of the time* (*Iṭrāb al-adhān fī ʿulamāʾ al-zamān*). So if you like, you can consult it.

The words on the meaning of "praise" (*ḥamd*) and the difference between it and "gratitude" (*shukr*) and the meaning of "prayer" (*ṣalāt*) are among those things [which the previously mentioned scholars] have written upon extensively. My statement "explaining" applies to the entirety of the work, that is, uncovering the veils from it.

> The Essence is what supports the Attributes
> The ground of definition and specification
> The Name is what specifies the Named
> So seek and you will find the sought with it
> The Quality is what points to the state of the Attribute
> Censured is whomever attains it or opposes it.

I mean that the Essence is the thing which supports the Attributes and the Names in their essence, not in their existence. Each name relies upon something, and that thing is the Essence. The Essence of God is an expression designating Himself by which He exists.

I say: know that the Essence of God is the non-manifest Unicity (*al-aḥadiyya*) to which all expressions correspond, although not in a way that exhausts Its meaning from many perspectives. For It [the Divine Essence] is not comprehended by what is understood from any expression nor is It understood by what is known from any allusion. This is because a thing is known by what is related to it, contrasted to what is contrary and so opposite to it. However, the Divine Essence has no relation to anything in existence, nor contrast, nor contrary, nor opposite.

My statement, "The Name is what specifies the Named ..." to the end of the verse means that the name is the thing which designates the named in understanding, conceptualizing it in the imagination, and making it present in the soul. And "the Quality" with the meaning of "the Attribute," here it is what takes you to the state of the described. By it [the Divine Attribute], you will attain understanding of His/its meaning and knowledge of His/its state. So knowledge of it will suffice you as you gather it in your affair and clarify it in your thinking and draw near to it in your intellect, for then you will taste the state of the one described by His Attribute. So then, either the nature [of the one realizing this] is predisposed towards It due to the existence of compatibility (*malā'im*), or it flees from It due to experiencing contradiction. This is the meaning of our statement "Censured (*lā'im*) is he who attains it or opposes it."

> The totality of the opposites and loci
> Is called the Divinity (*al-ulūhiyya*) of the Possessor of Majesty

The Unicity (*al-aḥadiyya*) of the One (*al-wāḥid*) in Sufism
Is what combines everything, but it is different from them
For there is nothing other than the Divine Essence manifest in it
He who has learned this lesson has attained the secrets
The Names and the Attributes are combined
In its Oneness, but by virtue of the Divine Essence.

I mean that Divinity (*al-ulūhiyya*) is the comprehensive level between the Real and created existence and the impossible and possible non-existence. "Allāh" is the name of this level and it has an all-embracing comprehensiveness of the places of manifestation and an overseeing control over each Attribute and Divine Name, and this is the meaning of my statement, "It includes the opposites and loci" etc. Unicity (*al-aḥadiyya*) is a level like the level of Divinity (*al-ulūhiyya*), but it is a descent from the level of Divinity because the level of Divinity gives each thing its right and puts each thing in its place, whereas Unicity combines everything in it without manifesting them. This is because it is the treasurer of the Divine Essence by virtue of [Its] self-disclosure (*tajallī*), and there is neither Name nor Quality in it, nor any trace of them. It [the level of Unicity] is the first of the descents of the Divine Essence from the obscurity of the Cloud (*al-ʿamāʾ*)[13] into the realm of manifestation, so understand and beware of error! This is the meaning of the two verses.

As for Oneness (*al-wāḥidiyya*) in the last verse it is a level including all effects, but not the totality of the Essence, because the Essence manifests the Attribute in it [the level of Oneness], while the Attribute is a manifestation of the Essence.

The difference between Oneness and Unicity in Divinity is that the Names and Attributes are manifest in Divinity by virtue of what is required of each one of the totality. Whereas nothing of the Divine Names and Attributes are manifest in Unicity. That is an allusion to the absolute purity of the Divine Essence, the purity in the affairs of the Essence. The Divine Names and Attributes are manifest in Oneness, but by virtue of the Essence, not by virtue of their separation, so understand. The level of Divinity is a locus of self-disclosure (*majlan*) that gives each thing its right, and Unicity is the locus of self-disclosure where "God was and there was nothing with Him, and He is now even as He was."

---

13 According to the *ḥadīth* of Abū Razīn al-ʿUqaylī, the Prophet was asked, "Where was our Lord before He created creation?" He replied, "He was in a cloud, neither above nor below which was any air (*hawāʾ*)." Related in Ibn Ḥanbal and al-Tirmidhī; see Chittick, William C., *The Sufi path of knowledge: Ibn al-ʿArabī's metaphysics of imagination* Albany, NY: SUNY Press, 1989, 125.

That in which the Divine Attributes are summarized
  And that which has a face [turned towards] the created effects
That is the Mercifulness (*al-raḥmāniyya*) of the Merciful (*al-raḥmān*)
  May we be entered among the group of Its protection
That which is ever turned towards the created
  That is Lordship in its transcendence.

I mean the level which comprises the Attributes, in which the Real Most High summarizes them. Between the Divine Attributes and that which has a face turned towards the world, there is something which is combined with those things which have an effect in creation, and it is called Mercifulness (*al-raḥmāniyya*) according to the technical vocabulary of the Sufis. That is, the Mercifulness is a locus of manifestation of the reality of the all-inclusive Names and Attributes in their totality summarized by the Real in the Names of the Essence. [These Names of the Essence] do not have a face turned towards the creatures like the Divine Names the Knowing, the Hearing, the Powerful, and the Seeing and others like them by which the existential realities are realized.

Mercifulness (*al-raḥmāniyya*) is a name for all of the levels of reality, but not for the level of creation, which has no share in it [the Mercifulness]. Thus it [Mercifulness] is more specific than Divinity due to its isolation by which the Real, Most High, is isolated, whereas, Divinity is a combination of the governing principles (*al-aḥkām*) of the Realness and Createdness. For universality belongs to Divinity and particularity belongs to Mercifulness. So understand!

As for Lordship (*rubūbiyya*) it is a level necessitated by the Names which require existents. The Names the Knowing, the Hearing, the Seeing, the Powerful, the Willer, the King, and those that resemble them among the Divine Names and Qualities fall under this level. For the Knower requires the known and the Powerful requires that over which power is exercised, etc.

So it is apparent that what we have established here is that Lordship includes the Names shared between it and its creation and specified for creation with a specificity of having effects therein. The Names the Knowing, the Hearing, and the Seeing are among the primary category of these names, while the Powerful, the Creator, the Provider are among the secondary category.[14]

The reality of realities is the Cloud (*al-ʿamāʾ*)
  According to the vocabulary of the eminent

---

14 The primary category of Names does not necessarily have an effect on their objects of action (you can know, hear, or see something without affecting it), whereas the secondary category of Names has a clear effect on their objects of action.

The uniqueness of the Guardian (*al-muhaymin*) is His transcendence
And the forms of manifestation, call them His immanence
His Beauty is His Beautifulness (*al-jamāliyya*)
While His Majesty is His Majesticalness (*al-jalāliyya*).

I mean that the Cloud (*al-ʿamāʾ*) is an expression designating the reality of realities which cannot be described by either Realness or createdness. It is the Divine Essence made present because it has no relationship with Realness nor with createdness. The difference between it and Unicity is that Unicity has the purity of the Essence by virtue of [Its] self-disclosure as we have previously stated, while the Cloud has the purity of the Essence by virtue of [Its] self-concealment. So understand and beware of error!

As for His transcendence, it is an expression designating the eternal uniqueness of His Qualities and Names and Essence from what He requires form Himself for Himself in the way of integrity and exaltedness. As for His immanence it is an expression that designates the forms of manifestation through the self-disclosures of the Names and Attributes. Beauty is an expression that designates His Beautifulness, in general. As for its specific meaning, its examples are [the attributes] of knowing, forgiving, compassion, bestowing, opening, providing, gentleness, blessing, and expanding. Majesty is also an expression that designates His Majesticalness, in general. And as for its specific meaning, its examples are [the attributes] of greatness, domination, supremacy, mightiness, debasing, avenging, withholding, harming, restricting, and what resembles them among the among the Names in the two categories (Beauty and Majesty).

His unseen (*ghayb*), by this they mean His "He-ness" (*huwiyyatuhu*)
It has its opposite in "I-ness" (*al-aniyya*)
The priority of perfection is not preceded
By the time of His beginninglessness (*azal*), so understand
His archetype (*mithāl*) and eternity (*qidam*) are in His endlessness (*abad*)
As is His Essential Necessity, and He knows best
His Days are those self-disclosures
Known by the greatest of authorities
The Attribute of the Powerful whenever it reveals itself
Is the clanging of the bell[15] as it is named amongst them

15 Most likely a reference to the Prophet's description of one of the manners in which the

The Mother refers to the quiddity of realities
  An expression among the statements of each of the foremost
The Absoluteness of Being is called a Book
  So let you have no doubts about that.

Know that "He-ness" according to the vocabulary of the Sufis is His unseen (*ghaybihi*) which cannot be manifested. It is the reality of His Essence and the reality of His Attributes with regard to their concealment (*ghuyūba*). "I-ness" is an expression designating the reality of His Essence and the reality of His Attributes with regard to the manifestation of them to Him. That is the meaning of our statement "It has its opposite in His 'I-ness.'"

As for "beginninglessness," it is an expression for the dominion of the unseen of that over which dominion is held by God, the Mighty and Majestic from the perspective of His Perfection, not from the perspective of his priority to the temporally created by temporal duration. And my statement, "His archetype in endlessness"—"endlessness" is an expression for the dominion of the unseen of that over which dominion is held by God, the Mighty and Majestic from the perspective of His Perfection, not from the perspective of temporal duration.[16]

As for "eternity" (*qidam*) it is an expression for the Essential Being. The Essential Being is that which manifests the name "the Eternal" to the Real, not from His being necessary by His Essence, because He was not preceded by non-existence. That which is not preceded by non-existence must necessarily be eternal. "The Days of God" are His self-disclosures and His manifestations which His essence requires by virtue of the various kinds of [Its] perfection. For each of His self-disclosures there is a divine principle designated by the term "affair" (*sha'n*). That principle in existence is an effect suitable to this Affair. So the differences in existence, by which I mean its changes in every time, are only the effects of that Divine Affair.[17]

Revelation would come to him, "Sometimes it comes to me in the likeness of a bell's clanging and that is the most difficult for me. Then it breaks away from me, but I have retained it in my memory." Cf. Ibn 'Arabī's discussion of this *ḥadīth* and the same terminology in Chittick, *The Sufi path* 112.

16 *Azal*, which I translate as "beginninglessness," designates eternity in its aspect of being "before" time (*a parte ante*), while *abad*, translated as "endlessness," designates eternity in its aspect of being "after" time (*a parte post*). They both name the same reality outside of time, but seen from two different perspectives.

17 This whole discussion refers implicitly to the verse of the Quran, "Every day He is upon an affair." (Q 55:29), which in Ibn 'Arabī's school refers to the perpetual, never-repeating self-disclosures of the Divine. Cf. Chittick, *The Sufi path* 18.

As for the "clanging of the bell" it is an expression for the unveiling of the Attribute of Powerfulness from its severity[18] by way of its self-disclosure, which is a kind of Magnificence, and this is the meaning of the verse.

"The Mother" is an expression for the quiddity of the realities and it is the core of the Essence to which no name, attribute, adjective, existence, non-existence, creation, or reality can apply. As for my statement: "The Absoluteness of Being is called a Book," "Book" is an expression for the Absolute Being which has no non-existence in It. The quiddity of the core is the Mother of the Book and the Absolute Being is the Book because existence is contained in it just as letters are contained in the ink.

The self-disclosure of the Essence, call it the Quran
Heaven in the Attribute, call it the *Furqān* (discernment)
Their Torah is the response to the Divine Attributes
Their Psalms (*Zabūr*) concerns the Divine Act, O firmly established
The Gospel (*Injīl*) concerns the Name and the heavenly couch (*sarīr*)[19]
A level of The Merciful, O devotee
Their crown is from the non-existence of limitations
Their Oddness is the call of the presence of God
His manifestations mean descents
But there is no incarnation with regard to His Qualities
Concerning the Divine place (*makāna*), call it
Their cushion (*rafraf*)[20] without considering it to be physical, for that is an error.

Know that "Quran" in the vocabulary of the Sufis is an expression for the self-disclosure of the Essence which includes all of the Names and Attributes in it, while "*Furqān*" is an expression for the reality of the Names and Attributes. "The Torah" is an expression for the self-disclosures of the Attributes, and that is the manifestation of the Real in the loci of manifestation of the Real, and it is from that perspective that the difference between it and the "*Furqān*" is realized. As for "the Psalms," it is an expression for the self-disclosures of the attributes of the acts only. "The Gospel" is an expression for the self-disclosure of the Name of the Essence only.[21] As for "the couch," it is an expression for the

18 Literally "from the leg" (*'an sāq*) a shorter form of the Quranic idiom "On the day when the leg is bared (*yukshafu 'an sāq*) [when things become severe]" (Q 68:42).

19 Q 43:34.

20 Q 55:76.

21 For more on al-Jīlī's symbolic use of pre-Quranic scriptures, see Morrissey, Fitzroy, *Sufism*

level of mercifulness which is the Divine place, while "the crown" is an expression for the non-existence of limitation in place and glory, in accordance with what His Essence requires. As for "the descent" it is an expression for the descent of the Real in every atom of the atoms of existence. As for "the cushion" it is an expression for the Divine place amongst the existents.

Realness and createdness are the two feet
  And mercy and blessing the two sandals
The first of entifications (*ta'ayyunāt*) is the Pen
  According to the vocabulary of the those who understand
And the Tablet, amongst the Folk, is the Real Light
  Inscribed upon it, is the Light of creation
The Attributes of the Acts are the Pedestal
  While His locus of manifestation is called His Holy Throne
[The Divine] place (*makāna*) is where spiritual zeal stops
  Meaning by that, the precinct of the Lote Tree
The origin of torment and bliss
  Is the form of the Noble Chosen One (*al-muṣṭafā l-karīm*)
And what we have desired to put in verse has ended here
  And praise be to God without end
Prayers upon His Noble Messenger
  Our master, characterized by compassion
And upon his companions and whosoever follows [them]
  To the day when forelocks and backs are seized.

I mean that "the Two Feet" are an expression for the two essential opposing rulings such as Realness and createdness, and "the Two Sandals" is an expression for the two opposing qualities of the acts, such as mercy and vengeance. As for "the Pen," I mean by it an expression for the first of the entifications of the created loci of manifestation according to the vocabulary of the Sufis.

As for "the Tablet," it is the Real light evident in a created place of witnessing upon which is inscribed all existing things. As for "the Pedestal," it is an expression for the locus of self-disclosure of all of the Attributes of the Divine Acts, so it is the place of the authority of the command and prohibition, as well as the place of manifestation of the Divine potency. As for "the Throne," according to verification, it is the place of manifestation of magnificence and the rank of

---

and the scriptures: Metaphysics and sacred history in the thought of 'Abd al-Karīm al-Jīlī, New York: Bloomsbury Publishing, 2020.

glory. It is a particularity of the Essence and is equivalent to the Divine Presence and its place. However, it is a place that transcends the six directions [i.e., it is outside of space]. As for "the Lote Tree" it is the utmost place that the servant reaches on his journey to God. There is nothing after it except the place designated for the Real alone. For created things have no place [lit. "have no foot"] here.

As for "the Muhammadan Form," the best of prayers and endless peace be upon its possessor, it is an expression for the light from which God created the Garden and Hell, and the origin of the torment and bliss found therein.

Here I conclude by the grace of God and with His aid I have explained these words. I have made this commentary very condensed as a precaution against unwanted incursion and dissension (*fitna*). In this commentary, I relied on the excellent book of the saint (*wālī*), the knower by God (*ʿārif bi-Llāh*), ʿAbd al-Karīm Jīlānī, *The perfect man*. If not for the universal mercy of God, His boundless favors and solicitude for me, where would I be in this? But the gift of the Real is beneficial, at every moment, and never ceases, time after time. Praise is due to God, the Lord of the worlds.

I ask God that whosoever looks into these words, may he do so with the eye of contentment and overlook any mistake he comes upon in it in terms of language or meaning. For these examples of this Divine knowledge are particular to a folk, the like of whom are rarely found, especially in these times in which good has diminished and evil has spread and naught remains of religion save its name, and of the Quran, its writing. Glory be to God, *verily from God we come and to him we are returning*. I was only driven to undertake this composition in order to seek benefit and to benefit others, and to encourage the spiritual zeal of those who possess the desire and hope for goodness/beauty and increase.

A poem:
And if their *baraka* I've not achieved
I'll mention it at length and frequently
There's joy in 'membering them repeatedly
It spurs the rider on and gives him speed
If after them, I'm left alone, enough for me
Is that I cling to them dependently.

Praise be to God, Lord of the Worlds and prayers and peace be upon the Master of the Messengers. This commentary was completed by my hand on Friday, with nine nights remaining of the month of God, Dhū l-Qaʿda (the 21st of the month) in the year 1236 after the *hijra* of the Prophet [approx. 17th August

1821 CE], upon him be the best prayers and purest peace as long as the kingdom of God remains.

—By the hand of the author, ʿAbd al-Qādir b. Muṣṭafā

Bibliography

Boyd, Jean, *The caliph's sister: Nana Asma'u, (1793–1865): Teacher, poet, and Islamic leader*, London: Frank Cass, 1989.

Chittick, William C., *The Sufi path of knowledge: Ibn al-ʿArabī's metaphysics of imagination*, Albany, NY: SUNY Press, 1989.

ʿAbd al-Qādir b. Muṣṭafā, *al-Manẓūma li-l-iṣṭilāḥ al-ṣūfiyya*, ed. Muhammad Shareef, Maiurno: Sankore Institute of Islamic-African Studies International, 2008.

Hiskett, Mervyn, *The sword of truth: The life and times of the Shehu Usuman dan Fodio*, New York: Oxford University Press, 1972.

Hunwick, John and Rex O'Fahey, *The Arabic literature of Africa*. II. *The writings of Central Sudanic Africa*, Leiden: Brill, 1995.

Kani, Ahmed M., "The private library of ʿAbd al-Qadir b. al-Mustafā (d. 1864)," in *Sixth interim report, 1979–1981*, Zaria: Northern History Research Scheme, 1987.

Last, Murray, *The Sokoto Caliphate*, New York: Humanities Press, 1967.

Morrissey, Fitzroy, *Sufism and the scriptures: Metaphysics and sacred history in the thought of ʿAbd al-Karīm al-Jīlī*, New York: Bloomsbury Publishing, 2020.

Naylor, Paul, *From rebels to rulers: Writing legitimacy in the early Sokoto state*, Rochester, NY: James Currey, 2021.

Nobili, Mauro, *The sultan, caliph and the renewer of the faith: Ahmad Lobbo, the* Tārīkh al-fattāsh *and the making of an Islamic state in West Africa*, New York: Cambridge University Press, 2020, 218–223.

Ogunnaike, Oludamini, "A treatise on practical and theoretical Sufism in the Sokoto Caliphate: Shaykh Dan Tafa's *Exposition of devotions* (*Bayān al-taʿabbudāt*)," in *Journal of Sufi Studies* 10.1–2 (2021), 152–173.

Ogunnaike, Oludamini, "Philosophical Sufism in the Sokoto Caliphate: The case of Shaykh Dan Tafa," in Ousmane Kane (ed.), *New directions in the study of Islamic scholarship in Africa*, Rochester, NY: James Currey, 2021, 136–168.

Shareef, Muhammad, *The life of Shaykh Dan Tafa: The life and times of one of Africa's leading scholars and statesmen and a history of the intellectual traditions that produced him*, Maiurno: Sankore Institute of Islamic-African Studies, n.d.

Shareef, Muhammad, *ʿIlāwat al-muṭālib fī shukr al-wāhib al-mufīḍ al-mawāhib*, Maiurno: Sankore Institute of Islamic-African Studies International, 2013.

Zehnle, Stephanie, *A geography of jihad: Sokoto Jihadism and the Islamic frontier in West Africa*, Boston: DeGruyter, 2020.

PART 3

Islamic Philosophy and Cosmology

CHAPTER 14

Neoplatonic Prayer: The Ismaʿili Hermeneutics of *ṣalāt* according to al-Sijistānī and Nāṣir-i Khusraw

Khalil Andani

While I never had the honor of directly studying under Professor Chittick, I have been fortunate enough to learn from his illustrious students and engage deeply with his writings. Among the many topics on which Professor Chittick has extensively published are Islamic Neoplatonism and the spiritual dimensions of Islamic prayer. On the former topic, Chittick's work on the philosophy and cosmology of Afḍal al-Dīn al-Kāshānī (d. ca. 610/1213–1214) and Ṣadr al-Dīn al-Qūnawī (d. 673/1274) stand out in the field. While many scholars of Islamic studies have expounded on Islamic Neoplatonic thought, Chittick's contribution lies in his argument that to merely label such thinkers as "Neoplatonists" somewhat misses the mark. Bābā Afḍal and al-Qūnawī were not simply "lifting" Neoplatonic terminology from Greek texts as mere window dressing for their onto-cosmological visions. Rather, they spoke of realities like the First Intellect and Universal Soul to denote cosmic spiritual entities that they themselves had directly intuited and experienced through a philosophical and/or mystical way of life. Thus, Chittick's lesson for all of us is to pay closer attention to how so-called Neoplatonic onto-cosmology functions in the worldview and spiritual life of Islamic thinkers when they are studied on their own terms.[1]

With respect to prayer, Professor Chittick translated *al-Ṣaḥīfa al-sajjādiyya* (*The psalms of Islam*) of Imam Zayn al-ʿĀbidīn (61–94/680–713). One of gems of this work, apart from the Imam's supplications, is Chittick's own introduction wherein he explains the larger pietistic and spiritual context of the Imam's prayers. Chittick particularly focuses on why the Prophet Muhammad and Imam Zayn al-ʿĀbidīn, who are protected from sins (*maʿṣūm*) according to Shiʿi theology, would engage in countless supplications of *istighfār*—commonly rendered into English as "seeking forgiveness" from God—and *tawba* (turning toward God)—usually translated as "repentance." In considering this terminology, Chittick patiently explains that *maghfira* in Arabic has a much wider connotation than merely "forgiveness" but refers to God's "covering over" or "conc-

1 Chittick, William C., *In search of the lost heart: Explorations in Islamic thought*, ed. Mohammed Rustom, Atif Khalil, and Kazuyo Murata, Albany, NY: SUNY Press, 2012, ch. 11.

 DOI:10.1163/9789004529038_015

ealing" one's creaturely shortcomings. As Friends of God (*awliyāʾ Allāh*) who have inwardly realized the Islamic *shahāda* and thereby realized their ontological dependence upon God, the Prophet and the Imam—while being sinless—exist in a natural spiritual orientation of seeking and receiving God's protective "covering" over their creaturely limitations, whether they vocalize this through devotional supplication or not. Imam Zayn al-ʿĀbidīn's intense supplications—far from implicating him as a sinner—are expressive of the Imam's constant realization of his own creaturely contingency and spiritual poverty in the face of God's ontological infinitude.[2] In honor of Professor Chittick's contributions on these two topics—Islamic Neoplatonism and prayer—this chapter offers a window into how Shiʿi Ismaʿili Muslim theologians envisioned a uniquely Neoplatonic understanding of the Islamic ritual prayer (*ṣalāt*) by way of the Ismaʿili Quranic hermeneutics known as *taʾwīl* (revelatory exegesis).

⁘

Before turning to Ismaʿili perspectives on prayer, it is helpful to survey views from other Islamic thinkers. Broadly speaking, one can identify two major theological paradigms concerning the nature and modality of God's response to prayer: the "reactive" paradigm and the "receptive" paradigm. The Quran declares unequivocally that God responds to those who supplicate Him: "I answer the supplication (*daʿwa*) of the supplicant (*dāʿī*) when he calls upon Me" (Q 2:186); "Call upon Me and I will answer you" (Q 40:60). Despite the linguistic clarity of these verses, Muslim thinkers differ on the precise nature and conditions of God's response to the prayers of His worshippers. On one hand, there are more literalist understandings that posit a God who responds to prayers by reacting in real-time. According to this "reactive paradigm" espoused by major theologians (*mutakallimūn*), Quranic exegetes (*mufassirūn*), and some Sufi ascetics, God responds to individual prayers and supplications by performing discrete divine actions at a particular moment in time, which is distinct from other moments in which He was not performing these actions. According to a widespread view within this paradigm, God responds to the servant's act of calling upon Him with paradisal reward and forgiveness.[3] Within these theological and exegetical perspectives, God's response to prayers may take one of many forms, as Atif Khalil observes:

2 Zayn al-ʿĀbidīn, ʿAlī b. al-Ḥusayn, *The psalms of Islam*, trans. William C. Chittick, London: Muhammadi Trust, 1988, translator's introduction.

3 Khalil, Atif, "Is God obliged to answer prayers of petition (*duʿa*)? The response of classical Sufis and Qur'anic exegetes," in *Journal of Medieval Religious Cultures* 37.2 (2011), 93–109, 96.

> He may grant the request one has made, in this world; He may deny it here but grant it or its equivalent in the next world; He may grant something else in this world; and finally, He may divert an affliction through the merit of the prayer itself, in either this world or the next.[4]

Sometimes, God withholds responding to a worshipper in this world and rewards him in the afterlife. Overall, in this "reactive" paradigm, God interacts with His creatures temporally and reacts to prayers through performing specific actions.

A second Islamic conception of the metaphysics of prayer is the "receptive paradigm." The receptive paradigm is most pronounced in the teachings of Ibn Sīnā (d. 428/1037) and Ibn ʿArabī (d. 638/1240) and his school. Within the Avicennan and Akbarian theological worldviews, God is immutable and changeless; His Essence and action transcend space, time, and change. Therefore, God bestows His blessings and favors upon His creatures eternally without cessation. As Ibn Sīnā explains:

> No perfections ... are withheld (*mabkhūl*) by the First Principle, but ... that the realization of everything depends on one's preparation to receive them. This is the meaning indicated by the Prophet's saying (upon whom be peace): "In the days of your life, fragrant breezes (*nafaḥāt*) of mercy waft on you from your Lord. Behold! Present yourselves to them (*alā! fataʿarraḍū lahā*)."[5] It is therefore evident that the diffusion of blessings (*nafaḥāt al-alṭāf*) is ceaseless. And this verifies the established teaching that no perfections ... are withheld (*mabkhūl*) by the First Principle, but ... that the realization of everything depends on one's preparation to receive them.[6]

In Ibn Sīnā's view, God—the First Principle and Necessary Being—constantly emanates perfection, existence, and blessings upon contingent existents (creatures). However, every creaturely existent possesses a different level of receptivity to God's continuous blessings. Therefore, how much of God's blessings a particular creature receives at any given moment is constrained by the creature's

4 Khalil, "Is God obliged" 102–103.

5 I have amended Dube's translation of this sentence.

6 Ibn Sīnā, *Kitāb al-Hidāya*, quoted in Dube, Jonathan S., *Pure generosity, divine providence, and the perfection of the soul in the philosophy of Ibn Sīnā (Avicenna)*, Montreal (Masters Diss.): McGill Institute of Islamic Studies, 2014, 32.

receptive capacity and degree of preparation. In this view, the prayer of a supplicant causes no change or alteration in God's perpetual emanation of blessings. Rather, the act of praying and supplicating causes a change within the soul of the supplicant and serves to increase his or her receptivity to God:

> The reception of the guiding effusion … is due to a cause in the receiver [in such a way that] for the soul the request consists in its acquiring the preparation to receive this guidance in a perfect way. … Thus, [what is received] is not something which would occur if there was no request.[7]

In the Avicennan view, God does not respond to one's prayer by doing something different than He was already doing; rather, God is already and always providing His creatures with whatever they require for their self-actualization—before and after they supplicate Him.

One finds similar ideas espoused by the Sufi sage Ibn ʿArabī. In his comments on Q 17:20, "the gift of your Lord is not withheld," Ibn ʿArabī speaks about created beings possessing different levels of a "preparedness" or "predisposition" (*istiʿdād*) towards receiving God's bounties and favors:

> God is saying that He gives constantly, while the loci receive in the measure of the realities of their preparedness. In the same way we say the Sun spreads its rays over the existent things. It is not miserly toward anything. The loci receive the light in the measure of their preparedness … Once you understand this, you will know the gift of God is not withheld. But you want Him to give you something that your preparedness cannot receive. Then you attribute the withholding to Him in that which you seek from Him, and you do not turn your attention toward the preparedness. It is possible that a person has the preparedness to ask, but he does not have the preparedness to receive what he asks for—if it were given to him in place of being withheld.[8]

For Ibn ʿArabī—in a manner similar to Ibn Sīnā—every creature possesses a preparedness to receive the emanation of being (*wujūd*) from God and serve as a locus of manifestation (*maẓhar*) of the Names of God. God bestows being or existence upon all of the loci of manifestation (*maẓāhir*) without restriction

7 Ibn Sīnā, *Kitāb al-Hidāya*, quoted in Dube, *Pure generosity* 32–33.

8 Ibn ʿArabī quoted in Chittick, William C., *The Sufi path of knowledge: Ibn al-ʿArabī's metaphysics of imagination*, Albany, NY: SUNY Press, 1989, 91–92.

or preference. But each locus or *mazhar* receives and manifests God's Being only according to its preparedness. This idea has a direct bearing on Ibn ʿArabī's understanding of prayer. For example, when a person prays and invokes God as *al-raḥmān* (the infinitely compassionate) and pleads for God's compassion (*raḥma*), the true understanding of this prayer differs from that of the common people:

> Those to whom God remains veiled pray to God, who in their belief is their Lord, to have compassion on them. But the People of Unveiling (*ahl al-kashf*) ask that divine Compassion be fulfilled [come into being, exist] through them.[9]

The late Henry Corbin, in explicating Ibn ʿArabī's view of prayer, puts the matter as follows:

> In other words, the Gnostic's prayer does not tend to provoke a change in a being outside him who would subsequently take pity on him. No, his prayer tends to actualize this divine Being as He aspires to be through and for him who is praying and who 'in his very prayer' is the organ of His passion. The Gnostic's prayer means: 'Make of us, let us be, Compassionate ones.'[10]

In other words, the Akbarian perspective entails that to call upon *al-raḥmān* is to make oneself more receptive to God's *raḥma*. Thus, according to Ibn ʿArabī, the act of prayer as understood by the People of Unveiling (*ahl al-kashf*) is directed towards increasing one's level of preparedness to receive the divine self-manifestation.

Finally, it is also worth considering al-Ghazālī's (d. 505/1111) understanding of supplicatory prayer. In his worldview, God's eternal decree (*qaḍāʾ*) and measuring out (*qadar*) of causes and effects that comprise His creatures never change. However, al-Ghazālī explained that the supplications of human beings are among those causes that God's preordained decree and determination have connected to specific effects: "You should know that the revocation of an affliction by supplication is itself a part of Preordination. Supplication is a cause

9 Ibn ʿArabī quoted, in Corbin, Henry, *Alone with the alone*, trans. Ralph Manheim, Princeton: Princeton University Press, 1998, 117. I have modified the wording here to better accord with the technical discussion that follows.

10 Ibn ʿArabī quoted in Corbin, *Alone* 117.

for the revocation of the affliction and the procurement of mercy."[11] In other words, for al-Ghazālī, the supplications of a supplicant do result in that person receiving more of God's mercy only because God primordially decreed that the said supplications are to function as secondary causes (*sabab*) for specific effects. His view rings similar to the ideas of Thomas Aquinas, who wrote about the concept of prayer over a century later: "We do not pray in order to change the decree of divine providence, rather we pray in order to impetrate those things which God has determined would be obtained only through our prayers."[12]

Despite their different theological frameworks, the approach to supplicatory prayer taken by Ibn Sīnā, Ibn ʿArabī, and al-Ghazālī are quite similar; their views all fall under what I have termed the "receptive" paradigm of prayer in Islamic thought. They each emphasize that a person's supplication entails no change for God—whether in God's attributes or God's actions—and that the effects of prayer only pertain to the supplicant's reception of God's blessings and favors. The Ismaʿili Muslim understanding of prayer fits squarely within this receptive paradigm. The distinctiveness of the Ismaʿili conception of prayer comprises two key dimensions. The first is the strongly Neoplatonic orientation of Ismaʿili interpretations of Islamic ritual prayer. The second is the Ismaʿili spiritual hermeneutics or *taʾwīl* of the gestures of the ritual prayer (*ṣalāt*)—such as *takbīr* (recitation of "God is greater"), bowing (*rukūʿ*), and prostration (*sujūd*). In summary, the Ismaʿili approach to prayer involves the worshipper performing the ritual prayer while also recognizing the inner meaning or *taʾwīl* of the recitations, supplications, and gestures of prayer—all of which symbolize one of the spiritual ranks of the Neoplatonic intelligible world or a personal rank in the earthly Ismaʿili *daʿwa*. In attaining to the recognition of the cosmic spiritual and religious hierarchies, the Ismaʿili aspirant simultaneously attains to a fuller understanding of the absolute unitary transcendence of God through which his or her soul comes to resemble the spiritual ranks of the Neoplatonic cosmos—namely the essence and activity of the Universal Soul. As the soul of the Ismaʿili aspirant comes closer to the Universal Soul in terms of semblance and attributes, it becomes more and more receptive to God's eternally flowing blessings that radiate through the Universal Intellect upon the Universal Soul

11 Al-Ghazālī, Abū Ḥāmid, *Invocations and supplications: Book IX of the Revival of the religious sciences*, trans. Kojiro Nakamura, Cambridge, UK: Islamic Texts Society, 1990, 153.

12 Aquinas, Thomas, *Summa theologiae*, ed. Kevin D. O'Rourke, 61 vols., xxxix, Cambridge: Cambridge University Press, 2006, Q. 83, Article 1, 53.

and human souls. Since the Isma'ili Muslim approach is permeated by Neoplatonic references, it is necessary to sketch out the Neoplatonic model of reality that most classical and some contemporary Isma'ili philosophical theologians subscribed to.

∵

According to the classical Isma'ili Neoplatonic theology espoused by various Isma'ili *dāʿīs* like Abū Yaʿqūb al-Sijistānī (d. 361/971), al-Mu'ayyad fī l-Dīn al-Shīrāzī (d. 470/1078), and Nāṣir-i Khusraw (d. ca. 462–481/1070–1088), God is absolutely one, simple, eternal, transcendent, and immutable. This strongly differs from Ashʿari and Maturidi theologies that affirm several ontological divine attributes—life, knowledge, power, will, speech, hearing, and seeing—as distinct qualities (*maʿnā*) or attributes (*ṣifāt*) that subsist (*qā'ima*) in God's Essence. It also differs from Muʿtazili theologies that affirm God's performance of temporal actions. Isma'ili thinkers employed double negation when speaking about God to elevate Him beyond real-distinct attributes and privations: God is neither knowing nor ignorant; God is neither powerful nor powerless; God is neither existent nor non-existent, but rather, He originates existence. God creates and sustains all existents through an eternal and timeless creative action known as God's Word (*kalima*) or God's Command (*amr*).[13] For al-Sijistānī, God's creative action is the actualization of His will in the form of pure goodness (*al-jūd al-maḥḍ*) and perfect wisdom, which necessarily produces harmonious existence. All contingent existents subsist through the creative activity that is the Word of God. Unlike classical Sunni *kalām* theology where all created things are temporally originated (*muḥdath*) and corporeal (*jismānī*), the Isma'ilis upheld the existence of both spiritual (*rūḥānī*) and corporeal (*jismānī*) worlds as products of God's creation. The Word or Command of God, which is His eternal creative act, is the radiation of pure existence (*al-wujūd al-muṭlaq, hast-i muṭlaq*) and pure oneness (*waḥda*) from God. The divine Command or pure being, insofar as it is an action or trace (*athar*) different from God, necessitates and grounds its own perfect quiddity (*māhiyya*) or identity (*huwiyya*), which is always united with it. This union of God's Com-

13 For the doctrine of God's Command or Word, see al-Sijistānī, Abū Yaʿqūb, "Kitāb al-Yanābīʿ," in Paul E. Walker (trans.), *The wellsprings of wisdom: A study of Abū Yaʿqūb al-Sijistānī's* Kitāb al-Yanābīʿ *including a complete English translation with commentary and notes on the Arabic text*, Salt Lake City: University of Utah Press, 1994, 37–112, here 50–52, 55–56, 57–58, 100, 103–104, 107–109.

mand/pure existence and its own quiddity/identity constitute the first originated being (*al-mubdaʿ al-awwal*) or the first contingent reality—known as the First Intellect (*al-ʿaql al-awwal*) or Universal Intellect (*al-ʿaql al-kull*). If God's Command is likened to sunlight, the substance of the First Intellect is like a mirror-like receptacle in which that light subsists and manifests. The Intellect is an eternal, incorporeal, and perfect being that radiates intelligible light and encompasses all that can exist. It contains the universal forms, essences, or archetypes that become manifest in the spiritual and corporeal worlds. The Universal Intellect continuously emanates intelligible forms and spiritual benefits upon all creatures among its direct or indirect effects.[14] The immediate effect that comes into being from the Universal Intellect's eternal emanation is the Universal Soul. The Universal Soul—being the spiritual creation of the Universal Intellect—is less perfect and constantly seeks to realize absolute perfection. The Soul's desire to achieve perfection manifests as goal-directed creation actions through which the Soul accepts intelligible emanations from the Intellect and utilizes these benefits in its creative activity. The Universal Soul emanates human souls, generates Matter and Form, and creates the corporeal world as a means by which human souls achieve perfection. In this cosmological model, the Soul's creation of the corporeal world and human souls facilitate its own spiritual movement from potential perfection to actual perfection. In its production of the spiritual and corporeal worlds, the Universal Soul produces two types of human souls: some human souls are created at the level of actualized perfection—these being the souls of the Prophets and the Imams; other souls are created at the level of potential perfection, which each of them must actualize through the acquisition of knowledge and virtue. Overall, the *telos* of the Universal Soul's creative activity is the perfection of all human souls—through which the Universal Soul itself attains to the perfection of the Universal Intellect.[15]

Before moving forward, given the prevalence of Neoplatonic terminology in Ismaʿili thought and in what follows, it is necessary to take a reminder from Professor Chittick. In the below passage, Chittick advises readers when reading about the so-called "Neoplatonic" elements in an Islamic thinker's worldview:

> When reading historical discussions of Islamic cosmology, we are sometimes left with the impression that the (First) Intellect and the (Universal)

14 Al-Sijistānī, "Kitāb al-Yanābīʿ" 47–61.

15 Khusraw, Nāṣir-i, "Shish faṣl," in Vladimir Ivanov (ed. and trans.), *Six chapters or shish faṣl*, Leiden: Brill for the Ismaili Society, 1949, 25–88, here 19 (Persian), 52 (English).

> Soul—that is, the initial stages of descent from the Origin—were concepts lifted from Neoplatonic sources without much reflection on the part of those who did the lifting. The two can appear as rather odd suppositions that have nothing to do with the real world—though it is understandable, we may be led to believe, that the 'unimaginative Muslims', relying as usual on the Greeks, should borrow this notion as an easy and ostensibly 'rational' explanation for the origin of the universe. But there is no reason to think that these ideas were taken over without critical assimilation on the part of those who took them over ... If we are to make any sense of the Intellect and the Soul as the dual progenitors of the cosmos, we have to stop and reflect on what the philosophers were trying to say. As human beings, we know innately that all things have been born from the Soul, because our own souls embrace nature along with the plant, animal and human faculties. We know innately that the Intellect is the all-embracing origin, because it is precisely our own intelligence that knows all this, arranges all this, becomes all this and embraces all this.[16]

In other words, when Islamic communities like the Ismaʿilis, the Philosophers, or the Sufis employ Neoplatonic terms like the Intellect and Soul, they do so intentionally and critically instead of merely "lifting" Greek terms for cosmetic purposes. As we will see, these metaphysical concepts are integral to Ismaʿili understandings of Islamic ritual practice.

∴

At the individual level, every human soul must self-actualize into an image or likeness of the Universal Soul. In other words, the purpose of human existence is to *imitate* the Universal Soul in virtue and knowledge. This is practically achieved by practicing the exoteric laws and rituals taught by the Prophets and comprehending the esoteric teachings of the Imams, who unveil the inner meaning of the religious laws and revealed scriptures. Nāṣir-i Khusraw relates the ontological affair of the Universal Soul, whose spiritual motion is dynamically present within all human souls:

> the purpose of his realization is to be like (*mānanda shud*) to his own origin and accept the knowledge of the Prophets, who are in the position of the [Universal] Soul in this world in actuality, and when he accepts the

16 Chittick, *In search* 272–273.

> hierarchical ranks (*ḥudūd*) and the recognition of God's oneness (*tawḥīd*), he becomes similar to the Universal Soul and returns to it and receives reward.[17]

The intellectual dimension of the acquisition of perfection climaxes in recognizing God's transcendent oneness through negating all creaturely attributes from Him and properly assigning those attributes to the hierarchy (*ḥudūd*) of God's creation. According to the Ismaʿili understanding of prophetic revelation, the Prophet Muhammad encoded the knowledge of the spiritual and earthly hierarchies (*ḥudūd*) in his religious law (*sharīʿa*) that comprises prescriptions, prohibitions, and rituals. Therefore, an Ismaʿili Muslim must acquire this inner knowledge and internalize it. This is accomplished through performing ritual practices while simultaneously understanding their *taʾwīl* or inner meanings. By combining ritual performance and esoteric comprehension, the human soul gradually develops into a virtual image of the Universal Soul:

> When man strives to put the *sharīʿa* into practice, attains [understanding of] the science of *taʾwīl*, transforms the dense into the subtle, and uses both his organs, the body and the soul, which are given to him [to attain knowledge], he becomes like the Universal Soul. The Universal Soul had the knowledge, then it worked; man works, then acquires the knowledge, thus becoming like the Universal Soul.[18]

Given its Neoplatonic orientations, Ismaʿili theology does not accept the "reactive" paradigm of prayer and supplication. God transcends all creaturely relationships and qualities, including time and change. The creative activities of the Universal Intellect and Universal Soul are likewise unchanging. Therefore, prayer in Ismaʿili philosophical theology does not cause any change or movement in God's essence or God's eternal action. Furthermore, Ismaʿili thought goes further than Ibn Sīnā and al-Ghazālī by maintaining that God transcends all names and attributes. Therefore, the prayer formulas that describe God as *al-raḥmān, al-rahīm, al-ʿalī, al-aʿlā, al-ʿaẓīm, al-qādir, al-ʿālim, al-rabb*, and the like do not literally describe God but instead refer to the highest ranks of created reality; these predications apply to God insofar as He is the originator of these attributes within creaturely reality. Al-Muʾayyad al-Shīrāzī, the highest-ranking

17 Khusraw, "Shish faṣl" 28 (Persian), 63 (English).

18 Khusraw, Nāṣir-i, "Gushāyish wa-rahāyish," in Nāṣir-i Khusraw, *Knowledge and liberation: A treatise on philosophical theology*, ed. and trans. Faquir M. Hunza, London and New York: I.B. Tauris in association with The Institute of Ismaili Studies, 1998, 24–114, 103.

Isma'ili *dāʿī* of his time, glorifies God with respect to His absolute singularity and transcendence as follows:

> He is glorified above entering under a name or an attribute. He is not approached through indications and qualities. It may *not* be said about him that He is living, powerful, knowing, intellecting, perfect, complete, or actual. This is because He is the Originator (*al-mubdiʿ*) of the living, the powerful, the knowing, the intellecting, the perfect, the complete, and the actual.[19]

Instead, the Ismaʿilis consistently applied the literal meaning of various divine names to the Universal Intellect and Soul, who are the highest creations of God. This knowledge is essential to Ismaʿili understandings of prayer where referential meanings of specific prayer formulas are consistently redirected to the hierarchical ranks (*ḥudūd*) of the spiritual and corporeal worlds.

Ismaʿili philosophical theologians produced *taʾwīl* literature in which they disclosed the inner meanings of Islamic prayer invocations and gestures through their Neoplatonic worldview. The Neoplatonic orientation of classical Ismaʿili *taʾwīl* is what distinguishes the Ismaʿili worldview from pre-Islamic Neoplatonism as well as other esoteric approaches to prayer rituals in the wider Sufi tradition. This chapter draws primarily on the writings of al-Sijistāni and Khusraw as case studies in Ismaʿili ritual prayer exegesis. We can begin with al-Sijistānī's explanations of prayer. In his view, the essence of worshipping God is grounded in the Universal Intellect, the highest rank of the spiritual world and the first being originated by God. The Intellect naturally and perpetually worships God, whom it recognizes as the transcendent Originator of its own contingent essence:

> The Intellect glorifies Him beyond the names of the vassals and sanctifies Him from the names of the creatures; had he ever ceased from the glorification and sanctification of the Originator, that would be a stigma flowing upon his substance. However, he is never distracted from his Originator for even an instant.[20]

19 Al-Shīrāzī, quoted in al-Ḥāmidī, Ibrāhīm b. al-Ḥusayn, *Kitāb Kanz al-walad*, Beirut: Dār al-Andalus, 1979, 13–14.

20 Al-Sijistānī, Abū Yaʿqūb, *Ithbāt al-nubuwwāt*, ed. Wilferd Madelung and Paul E. Walker, Tehran: Mīrāth-i Maktūb, 2016, 273.

The Intellect worships God perfectly through negating all creaturely qualities from Him. The Intellect's recognition of God is an affirmation through comprehensive negation. Nāṣir-i Khusraw characterizes the Intellect's perpetual worship as thanksgiving (*shukr*): "Worship to God (*'ibādat*) first comes from the Universal Intellect, which is the worship of thanksgiving (*'ibādat-i shukrī*). No other creature can offer worship such as that. By its greatness, purity, might and wisdom, its worship has no limits."[21] Through the Universal Intellect's worship of God, the Command of God emanates the Universal Soul. The Universal Soul, being less perfect than the Intellect, worships God through its own spiritual motion or activity—which results in the creation and governance of the spiritual and corporeal worlds: "When the Origination descended from the eternality (*azaliyya*) of the Preceder to what His Command settled upon, namely the Follower, her worship of the Originator was not solely by the innate nature of his substance, but rather it was through what the Preceder guided her by."[22] The Soul's creative and demiurgic activity is what brings about its own actualization of perfection. The Universal Soul is continuously guided by the Universal Intellect's intelligible emanations upon it, so its creative activity is constant without any need for discrete changes or interventions. The highest manifestation of the Universal Soul's creative sustenance of the Cosmos is the appearance of Prophets who deliver religious laws and the succession of Imams who interpret them. For this reason, the prayer rituals taught by the Prophet Muhammad symbolically indicate the cosmic motions of the Universal Soul ("Follower") in relation to the Universal Intellect ("Preceder"):

> The journey (*sulūk*) of the Follower within the natures (*al-ṭabī'iyyāt*) was something necessary for the perfection of wisdom and the manifestation of goodness (*al-faḍīla*). This is because it reaches the furthest limit of its objective within natural living beings (*al-mawālīd*)—namely the rational living entity (*al-ḥayy al-nāṭiq*)—which is the essence of the Soul that follows the temperament of the body. This necessitates corporeal Messengers [bringing] laws and statutes in order that they be a reminder for souls and a guidance for them towards the recognition of the worship of God, Exalted be His mention ... The laws also include recitation (*al-qirā'āt*) and speech (*al-kalām*) corresponding to [the fact that] the Follower through [its] supplication and self-abasement towards the Preceder connects (*yaṣilu*) to his allotment from the oneness of his Originator.

21 Khusraw, "Shish faṣl" 24 (Persian), 66 (English).
22 Al-Sijistānī, *Ithbāt* 274.

> [These laws] also include movements like the movement of bodily limbs in ritual prayers (*al-ṣalawāt*) that correspond to [the fact that] the Follower with the motion of being desirous of what is reserved for it from the benefits (*fawāʾid*) of the Preceder comes forth from the rank of potentiality to the rank of actuality.[23]

In the above quotation, al-Sijistānī explains that the Universal Soul sent Prophets or Messengers to reveal laws and commandments to human beings to facilitate their recognition of God. These religious laws include the ritual prayer that comprises Quranic recitations, supplicatory speech, and physical movements of the body. The various prayer actions and invocations symbolize the Universal Soul's cosmic relationship to the Universal Intellect. The supplications of ritual prayer symbolize the metaphysical orientation of the Universal Soul as it humbles itself before the Universal Intellect to receive a share of God's blessings from him. Likewise, the bodily movements like bowing and prostration symbolize the Universal Soul's desire for and receptivity towards the intelligible benefits that emanate from the Intellect. Therefore, the Islamic ritual prayer symbolizes the spiritual states and cosmic functions of the Universal Soul. When an Ismaʿili Muslim believer practices the ritual prayer, he or she imitates the Universal Soul—thereby making her soul more receptive to the intelligible emanations and blessings of the Universal Intellect. The human soul that has attained to this mode of being is a "pure soul" that functions as a spiritual image of the Universal Intellect: "The pure soul receives the benefits of the [Universal] Intellect in their entirety without rejecting anything and the benefits of the Intellect for the soul are nourishment for the appearance of the subtle form (*ṣūrat-i laṭīf*)."[24] The sheer performance of ritual prayer, therefore, embodies the "call" or "invitation" (*daʿwa*) to the absolute unity of God—a knowledge that the Universal Intellect and Soul actualize at the highest degree. In the Ismaʿili interpretation of Islam, this pure knowledge of God's unity is only accessible through obedience and commitment to the Imam of the time, whose pure soul reflects and receives the spiritual emanations of the Universal Intellect and Soul. For this reason, Ismaʿili exegetes explained that ritual prayer as a whole symbolizes the Imam's summons to *tawḥīd* and its performance by the worshipper symbolizes one's submission to the Imam and the journey through the ranks of the Imam's *daʿwa*. According to al-Sijistānī: "Prayer (*al-ṣalāt*) according to us indicates the sovereignty (*walāya*) of the

23 Al-Sijistānī, *Ithbāt* 274.
24 Khusraw, Nāṣir-i, *Wajh-i dīn*, ed. Gholamreza Aavani, Tehran: Anjūman-i Shāhanshāhī-yi Falsafa-yi Īrān, 1977, 98.

Friends (*awliyāʾ*) of God whom people must obey and exemplify."[25] Likewise, Khusraw states that: "The performance of ritual prayer (*namāz*) indicates the performance of the summons (*daʿwa*) to the unification of God and uniting with the Friends of God (*awliyāʾ*)."[26]

∴

The Ismaʿili thinkers provided a Neoplatonic exegesis of the five daily prayer times. According to al-Sijistānī and Khusraw, the five prayers—morning (*fajr*), noon (*ẓuhur*), afternoon (*ʿaṣr*), sunset (*maghrib*), and night (*ʿishāʾ*)—symbolize specific spiritual and earthly ranks (*ḥudūd*). The morning and sunset prayers symbolically indicate the Universal Intellect and Universal Soul respectively. The noon, afternoon, and night prayers respectively represent the Prophet Muhammad, his legatee (*waṣī*) Imam ʿAlī b. Abī Ṭālib, and the Imam of the time. Khusraw's explanations of the inner meaning of the morning and sunset prayers reveals the depths of Ismaʿili exegesis. With respect to the morning prayer that takes place shortly before sunrise, Khusraw writes:

> The morning prayer indicates the First [Intellect] and it was commanded at that time of daybreak [because] the Speaker Prophet indicated that the first light to come into existence from the Command of the Creator was the First, which is called the Pen and the Intellect.[27]

The morning prayer is a likeness of the Universal Intellect because the appearance of sunlight at dawn symbolizes the origination of the Intellect from God's Command or Word; the latter is the pure existence that is united with the Intellect's contingent quiddity. Therefore, the Ismaʿilis perceive the morning prayer as a thanksgiving to God for His eternal bestowal of existence upon the Universal Intellect. This Intellect connects God's Command to all creatures and every human soul possesses an individual intellect that emanates from the Universal Intellect. For this reason, Khusraw situates the Universal Intellect as the true *qibla* (prayer direction) of the morning prayer:

> Since the Creator, may He be glorified and exalted, appointed for us a share of His own light through the mediation of the Intellect, it became

25 Al-Sijistānī, Abū Yaʿqūb, *Kitāb al-Iftikhār*, ed. Ismail K. Poonawala, Beirut: Dār al-Gharb al-Islāmī, 2000, 240.

26 Khusraw, *Wajh-i dīn* 166.

27 Khusraw, *Wajh-i dīn* 166.

> necessary for us at this time—which indicates that great creation who is the *qibla* of the morning prayer—to give thanks to Him, may He be glorified and exalted.[28]

Khusraw offers similar explanations about the sunset prayer in relation to the Universal Soul ("the Second"):

> The evening prayer is the worshipper's gratitude to God for His granting the people a share of the light of the Second. That light is the rational soul of the human being by which he speaks and expresses anything when he indicates to them using names and attributes. Thus, the *qibla* of the evening prayer is the Second.[29]

Ismaʿili hermeneutics of prayer also extend to specific invocations and gestures of worship. Broadly speaking, every stage of one prayer cycle (*rakʿa*) symbolizes a stage in the Ismaʿili *daʿwa*. The *takbīr* when the prayer leader recites "God is greater" symbolizes the Ismaʿili believer pledging the covenant (*mīthāq*) to the Imam of the time, which represents one's formal entry into the Ismaʿili faith. The *qiyām* (standing) represents the believer standing firm by his covenant. The recitation of Sūrat al-Fātiḥa and another Sūra represent the dissemination of esoteric knowledge among the ranks of the *daʿwa*. Khusraw also provides a deeper layer of specific *taʾwīl* for these elements. For example, when one performs the *takbīr* and raises one's hands to the ears, this is an allusion to the absolute transcendence of God above the spiritual and corporeal realms of existence. As Khusraw explains:

> When one says the *takbīr* and raises the hands up to the ears and says *Allāhu akbar*, one indicates that God, the exalted, is greater than the ten corporeal and spiritual ranks—meaning He is neither invisible nor visible like these two categories of creatures. The worshipper's right hand represents the spiritual world and his left hand represents the physical world.[30]

Then the worshipper recites the formula: "*subḥānaka Allāhumma wa-bi-ḥamdika wa-tabāraka ismuka wa-taʿālā jadduka wa-lā ilāha ghayruka*" (Glorified be God and through Your Praise and Your Name is blessed and His majesty is exal-

---

28 Khusraw, *Wajh-i dīn* 168.

29 Khusraw, *Wajh-i dīn* 170.

30 Khusraw, *Wajh-i dīn* 200.

ted and there is no God other than He). Khusraw exegetes the inner meaning of this utterance as follows:

> *Allāhumma* is five letters, meaning God transcends the five spiritual ranks and this is the *tasbīḥ* of the First [Universal Intellect] who says: "my Originator is free from resembling me." And *bi-ḥamdika* (through Your Praise) is the glorification and the magnification of the Second [Universal Soul] where he says [to God]: "Through your Praise, you brought into existence all creatures—meaning through the mediation of the Praise (*al-ḥamd*) that is the Intellect." And "Your Name is self-blessed" means "your Name" is the greatest and by this one intends the Second because He originated it and appointed him [the Soul] as His own Name—meaning that the worship of God is through the First and the Second who are the Names of God in reality (*bi-ḥaqīqat*).[31]

According to Khusraw's elucidation of the *ta'wīl*, the word *Allāhumma* with its five Arabic letters in the glorification symbolically refers to five spiritual ranks created by God: Universal Intellect, Universal Soul, and three spiritual emanations known as Seraphiel (*jadd*), Michael (*fatḥ*), and Gabriel (*khayāl*). Thus, this prayer formula means that God's Essence transcends these give great spiritual ranks. The word *al-ḥamd* (the praise) that belongs to God (*al-ḥamdu li-Llāh*) refers to the Universal Intellect which is God's highest creation that mediates all creaturely relationships with God. The term "Name of God" (*ism Allāh*) refers to the Universal Intellect and Universal Soul, who are the real or ontological names of God through whom God is truly worshipped. In other words, the prayer formulas uttered by the Muslim worshipper are coded references to the absolute transcendence of God and the immanence of the Neoplatonic spiritual hierarchy. The prayer formula's true meaning reflects the knowledge and perspective of the Universal Intellect and Soul, each of whom recognize God's absolute unity through negating the attributes of all creatures, including themselves, from God. Thus, the worshipper who recites this prayer formula and comprehends its inner meaning is imitating the Universal Intellect and Soul in their recognition of God and thereby makes his or her soul into a likeness of them.

The Isma'ili understanding of ritual prayer displays even deeper Neoplatonic resonance in terms of the spiritual exegesis of the acts of bowing (*rukū'*) and prostration (*sujūd*). Prior to bowing, the worshipper recites the seven verses of

---

31 Khusraw, *Wajh-i dīn* 201.

Sūrat al-Fātiḥa and an additional Sūra of the Quran. According to Khusraw, al-Fātiḥa consisting of seven verses symbolizes the seven Imam of a religious cycle and the additional Sūra symbolizes the deputies of the Imam known as *ḥujjas* (proofs) in Ismaʿili vocabulary. Following these recitations, the worshipper engages in bowing, which symbolizes the rank of the Prophet's legatee (*waṣī*) and founder (*asās*), ʿAlī b. Abī Ṭālib, who was the deputy of the Prophet during his lifetime.

When bowing, the worshipper recites *Allāhu akbar* (God is greater). In the Shiʿi perspective as per the teachings of Imam al-Ṣādiq, *Allāhu akbar* means "God is greater than being described."[32] This means that the Founder, ʿAlī b. Abī Ṭālib, taught the absolute transcendence of God. The four letters of *akbar* signify the Universal Intellect, Universal Soul, Speaker Prophet, and Founder—indicating that God transcends the four highest spiritual and earthly ranks of creation. While in the position of bowing, the worshipper then recites: *subḥāna rabbī l-ʿaẓīm wa-bi-ḥamdihi* (glorified is my Sublime Lord and through His praise). Khusraw interprets "my Sublime Lord" (*rabbī l-ʿaẓīm*) in this invocation to be the Universal Soul since the attribute of greatness (*ʿaẓama*) belongs to the Universal Soul, who is the direct creator of the Cosmos: "Through this glorification one declares the greatness (*buzurgwārī*) of the Second (Universal Soul) from whom is the divine support (*taʾyīd*) of the Founder and who is the lord of the composition of this great world."[33] In the same way that bowing is less complete submission than prostration, the rank of the Universal Soul is lower than the rank of the Universal Intellect. For this reason, the divine name *al-ʿaẓīm* that the supplicant recites in bowing indicates the Universal Soul: "[The rank of] the Universal Soul is lower than that of the Universal Intellect. He is the meaning of the glorification of the bowing (*rukūʿ*) … just as bowing is a submission from the servant to God, but it is not as complete as the prostration."[34]

After the completion of the bowing, the worshipper then stands up and recites: *Samiʿa Allāhu li-man ḥamidahu*. According to Khusraw, the inner meaning of this invocation ties back to the exegesis of *al-ḥamd* outlined earlier: "This means that God hears the supplication of the person who praises Him, thanks Him, and recognizes Him through the [Universal] Intellect."[35] Accordingly, the

---

32 Al-Kulaynī, Muḥammad b. Yaʿqūb, *Uṣūl al-kāfī*, ed. ʿAlī A. Ghifārī, Tehran: Dār al-Kutub al-Islāmiyya Murtaḍā Ākhūndī, 1968, 117.

33 Khusraw, *Wajh-i dīn* 202.

34 Khusraw, *Wajh-i dīn* 341. For this passage I have relied on newly edited and translated text provided by Faquir Muhammad Hunzai and Shafique N. Virani whose edition and translation of *Wajh-i dīn* are forthcoming.

35 Khusraw, *Wajh-i dīn* 202.

esoteric meaning of God's Praise (*al-ḥamd*) is the Universal Intellect through which all creatures recognize God and by which creaturely worship is directed towards God. Then the worshipper goes into prostration. The spiritual exegesis of this gesture is that "prostration indicates the Speaker Prophet [Muhammad] through whom is the divine support of the Founder, the Imam, and the *ḥujja*."[36] The earth upon which one submits is a symbol of the Universal Soul: "The earth is a likeness for the Second, who is the sustainer of souls (*parwaranda-yi nafs-hā*), just as the earth is the sustainer of bodies."[37] The believer, when in the act of prostration, imitates the spirituality of the Speaker Prophet, who submits his soul to and unites with the Universal Soul: "This indicates that the Speaker Prophet surrendered all of his convictions at once to the Second when he perceived the vision of the spiritual world."[38] While in prostration, the worshipper recites: *Subḥāna rabbī l-aʿlā wa-bi-ḥamdihi* (glorified is my Most Exalted Lord through His praise). In accordance with Ismaʿili hermeneutics, this invocation alludes to the Universal Intellect and not God because He transcends all likeness and description. As Khusraw explains, the phrase "my Most Exalted Lord" (*rabbī l-aʿlā*) refers to the Universal Intellect and its superiority over all other creatures:

> By this "lord" (*parwardigār*) who is exalted above all things, one intends the Universal Intellect, who is higher than all the spiritual and corporeal ranks while the Creator transcends being similar to the First (Intellect) and since He is dissimilar to the First, it follows that none of the higher or lower ranks are similar to Him.[39]

Like the prior exegesis, the Ismaʿili exegesis of bowing and prostration and the corresponding invocations highlights the absolute transcendence of God and also direct the worshipper to properly recognize that the divine names *al-aʿlā* (the Exalted) and *al-ʿaẓīm* (the Sublime) as properly belonging to the Universal Intellect and Universal Soul. At the same time, the worshipper attests to the absolute unity and transcendence of God, who is the originator of the Universal Intellect and is incomparable to His creation.

36 Khusraw, *Wajh-i dīn* 203.
37 Khusraw, *Wajh-i dīn* 203.
38 Khusraw, *Wajh-i dīn* 203.
39 Khusraw, *Wajh-i dīn* 203.

The foregoing analysis of Ismaʿili prayer exegesis has shown that the Ismaʿili Muslim worshipper is to conceive ritual prayer (*al-ṣalāt*) as an activity in which one imitates the Universal Soul in its cosmic relationship to the Universal Intellect. The Ismaʿili exegesis of the act, timings, and gestures of ritual prayer focuses on the absolute transcendence of God and the specific merits of God's created hierarchy (*ḥudūd*)—the two highest members of which are the Universal Intellect and Universal Soul in the spiritual world and the Prophet Muhammad and Imam ʿAlī in the corporeal world. The ritual prayer in general, in terms of its recitations and bodily gestures, symbolizes how the Universal Soul orients itself before the Universal Intellect in order to receive an allotment of divine blessings from the latter. The human being who performs the ritual prayer with this inner understanding thereby makes his or her soul like the Universal Soul. This makes the human soul more receptive to the blessings emanating from the Universal Intellect:

> By means of an abiding tranquility that she acquires from Intellect, the soul attains the benefits of intellect, and because of the benefits reaching her from Intellect, an everlasting, eternally enduring spiritual form arises.[40]

The Ismaʿili *ta'wīl* or spiritual exegesis of the components of prayer facilitate the worshipper's spiritual recognition of specific ranks in God's created hierarchy. The *ta'wīl* of the five prayer times situates the morning, noon, afternoon, sunset, and night prayers as symbols for the Universal Intellect, the Speaker Prophet, the Founder, the Universal Soul, and the Imam. The *ta'wīl* of specific prayer actions—such as *takbīr, qiyām*, recitation of the Quran, glorification formulas (*tasbīḥāt*), bowing (*rukūʿ*), and prostration (*sujūd*)—situates these practices as symbols of specific hierarchical ranks in creation while also exalting God above their qualities. Thus, the *takbīr* indicates God's absolute transcendence over the spiritual and corporeal hierarchies; the recitation of Sūrat al-Fātiḥa and other Sūras indicate the rank of the Imams and their deputies; the act of bowing indicates the recognition of the Founder (ʿAlī b. Abī Ṭālib); the corresponding glorification of the "Sublime Lord" (*rabb al-ʿaẓīm*) refers to the Universal Soul through whom the Founder is divinely supported Likewise, the act of prostration indicates recognition of the Speaker Prophet and his spiritual unification with the Universal Soul represented by the earth; while the glorification of the "Most Exalted Lord" (*rabb al-aʿlā*) indicates the Universal Intellect,

40 Al-Sijistānī, "Kitāb al-Yanābīʿ" 64.

whose spiritual rank is the most exalted of all creatures. Whenever the worshipper recognizes the attributes of a particular rank (*ḥadd*) of the spiritual or corporeal world, they simultaneously divest that rank of divinity and attest God's absolute transcendence with respect to it.

As noted earlier, Professor Chittick reminds his readers that the "Neoplatonism" espoused by certain Islamic thinkers never amounted to mere mental gymnastics. Rather, the Islamic mystics and philosophers integrated the Neoplatonic worldview into their Islamic commitments and practice. The Ismaʿili spiritual exegesis of prayer with its various Neoplatonic resonances is a textbook example of Professor Chittick's argument. The Ismaʿili philosophical theologians carefully integrated the Neoplatonic vision of the Universal Intellect and Universal Soul as the highest spiritual creations of the absolute transcendent God into their understanding of worship and supplication. The purpose of prayer for Ismaʿili Muslims is not about provoking a "reaction" from God in real-time; rather, prayer enables the worshipper's spiritual reception of God's perpetually occurring blessings through the mediation of the spiritual and corporeal hierarchies. This is confirmed by Khusraw when he says: "When the believer recognizes God's hierarchical ranks (*ḥudūd-i khudā*), he neither describes God nor ascribes to Him any similarity with creatures. He recognizes the excellence (*faḍl*) of each hierarchical rank (*ḥadd*)."[41] In conclusion, Shiʿi Ismaʿili Muslims approach ritual prayer in its esoteric dimension as an intellectual and spiritual ascension through the hierarchy of God's creation that culminates in the inner recognition or gnosis of God's absolute oneness.

Bibliography

Aquinas, Thomas, *Summa theologiae*, ed. Kevin D. O'Rourke, 61 vols., xxxix, Cambridge: Cambridge University Press, 2006.

Chittick, William C., *The Sufi path of knowledge: Ibn al-ʿArabī's metaphysics of imagination*, Albany, NY: SUNY Press, 1989.

Chittick, William C., *In search of the lost heart: Explorations in Islamic thought*, ed. Mohammed Rustom, Atif Khalil, and Kazuyo Murata, Albany, NY: SUNY Press, 2012.

Corbin, Henry, *Alone with the alone*, trans. Ralph Manheim, Princeton: Princeton University Press, 1998.

Dube, Jonathan S., *Pure generosity, divine providence, and the perfection of the soul in the philosophy of Ibn Sīnā (Avicenna)*, Montreal (PhD Diss.): McGill Institute of Islamic Studies, 2014.

41 Khusraw, *Shish faṣl* 24 (Persian), 60 (English).

al-Ghazālī, Abū Ḥāmid, *Invocations and supplications: Book IX of the Revival of the religious sciences*, trans. Kojiro Nakamura, Cambridge, UK: Islamic Texts Society, 1990.
al-Ḥāmidī, Ibrāhīm b. al-Ḥusayn, *Kitāb Kanz al-walad*, Beirut: Dār al-Andalus, 1979.
Khalil, Atif, "Is God obliged to answer prayers of petition (*duʿa*)? The response of classical Sufis and Qurʾanic exegetes," in *Journal of Medieval Religious Cultures* 37.2 (2011), 93–109.
Khusraw, Nāṣir-i, "Shish faṣl," in Vladimir Ivanov (ed. and trans.), *Six chapters or shish faṣl*, Leiden: Brill for the Ismaili Society, 1949, 25–88.
Khusraw, Nāṣir-i, *Wajh-i dīn*, ed. Gholamreza Aavani, Tehran: Anjuman-i Shāhanshāhī-yi Falsafa-yi Īrān, 1977.
Khusraw, Nāṣir-i, "Gushāyish wa-rahāyish," in Nāṣir-i Khusraw, *Knowledge and liberation: A treatise on philosophical theology*, ed. and trans. Faquir M. Hunzai, London and New York: I.B. Tauris in association with The Institute of Ismaili Studies, 1998, 24–114.
al-Kulaynī, Muḥammad b. Yaʿqūb, *Uṣūl al-kāfī*, ed. ʿAlī A. Ghifārī, Tehran: Dār al-Kutub al-Islāmiyya Murtaḍā Ākhūndī, [3]1968.
al-Sijistānī, Abū Yaʿqūb, "Kitāb al-Yanābīʿ," in Paul E. Walker (trans.), *The wellsprings of wisdom: A study of Abū Yaʿqūb al-Sijistānī's* Kitāb al-Yanābīʿ *including a complete English translation with commentary and notes on the Arabic text*, Salt Lake City: University of Utah Press, 1994, 37–112.
al-Sijistānī, Abū Yaʿqūb, *Kitāb al-Iftikhār*, ed. Ismail K. Poonawala, Beirut: Dār al-Gharb al-Islāmī, 2000.
al-Sijistānī, Abū Yaʿqūb, *Ithbāt al-nubuwwāt*, ed. Wilferd Madelung and Paul E. Walker, Tehran: Mīrāth-i Maktūb, 2016.
Zayn al-ʿĀbidīn, ʿAlī b. al-Ḥusayn, *The psalms of Islam*, trans. William C. Chittick, London: Muhammadi Trust, 1988.

CHAPTER 15

The Necessity of the Return (*al-maʿād*): Avicenna on the Posthumous States of the Human Soul in *Aḍḥawiyya* 6–7

Davlat Dadikhuda

إِنَّ الَّذِي فَرَضَ عَلَيْكَ الْقُرْآنَ لَرَادُّكَ إِلَىٰ مَعَادٍ

1 Introduction

The topic of *maʿād* or eschatology/soteriology occupies a special place in Avicenna's (d. 428/1037) philosophical system. Of the many works in which he treats the issue, one in particular is devoted entirely to the topic, namely *al-Aḍḥawiyya fī l-maʿād* (*The return, on the occasion of* ʿīd al-aḍḥā). The crux of Avicenna's theory of "the Return" in this work is contained in chapters 6 and 7 (translations of which are provided below).

The basic meaning of *maʿād*, as the shaykh states in this work, is to be in some place, depart from it, and then return to it. This sense of the term is then transferred to an eschatological context to mean the place a human being is from and to which he returns upon death:

> As for *al-maʿād* in the language of the Arabs, it is derived from "to go back" (*al-ʿawd*). Its reality is the place or state in which a thing was, then was separated from it, and then returned to it. The [term] was thereafter transferred to the original state or locality to which a human being departs after death.[1]

For the shaykh, as we shall see below, this "Return" of the human being to the original state they left will be explained in terms of the metaphysical status

1 Avicenna, *al-Aḍḥawiyya fī l-maʿād li-Ibn Sīnā*, ed. Ḥasan ʿĀṣī, Beirut: al-Muʾassasa al-Jāmiʿiyya, 1987, 89.

 | DOI:10.1163/9789004529038_016

the soul of that human being comes to possess after bodily death. That is, Avicenna's account of *maʿād* is an account of the kind of life a human soul, now separated from the body, will come to enjoy. And this psychological view of post-mortem existence, according to which the human soul goes back to the source it came from, he thinks has scriptural warrant:

> Indeed, in the Book of God the exalted that descended upon His chosen prophet, Muhammad (God's blessings and peace upon him and his family), there is a clear witness for this—namely, His statement, exalted be He, "Oh tranquil soul, return to your Lord, well-pleased and pleasing" [Q 89:27–286]. And "returning" is not said except of a place from which there is a 'coming.'[2]

The two chapters of the *Aḍḥawiyya* that are the focus here deal with two different aspects of this Return. Chapter 6 is about why the Return *must* obtain for the human soul—against those who either deny it outright or simply concede that it may take place. Chapter 7 is about the different groups into which human souls will fall post-mortem and the different psychological states each group will be the subject of or, in short, experience—against those who might think the soul's separated existence is "blank" or unconscious, as though a comatose state.

With respect to chapter 6, note that what the *Aḍḥawiyya* evinces is not only the shaykh's commitment to the mere possibility of the Return but, more strongly, to its necessity. That is, he is of the view that any given human soul will inevitably have a life post-mortem. So there is no escaping the Return; it will occur for the human soul whether one likes it or not. With respect to chapter 7, Avicenna clarifies in some detail that there will be something it-is-like to live this posthumous life; for it will be essentially cognitive in nature, involving a heightened consciousness, and rich in content that is conceptual, phenomenal, hedonic, and horrid (depending on certain factors). The reason why the shaykh structures these two chapters in the way that he does is to understand something about the nature of the good and bad states belonging to various human souls after separation, i.e., from the body; thus one first needs to understand why they necessarily enjoy such states after this separation.

The positions the shaykh maintains in these two chapters of the *Aḍḥawiyya* stand in stark contrast to those whom he called "the Westerners" (*al-maghribiyyīn*)—represented by the Aristotelian commentators (Greek and

2 Avicenna, *al-Aḍḥawiyya* i, 90.

Arabic) who either denied or were unclear about one or both of these two theses which the shaykh's account proposes. For on the principles of "the Easterners" (*al-mashriqiyyīn*)—represented by Avicenna himself—the *maʿād* constitutes a distinct and essential part of the discipline concerned with 'divine matters', namely metaphysics (*al-ilāhiyyāt*). The importance and centrality of this topic in Avicenna's work is indicated, among other reasons, by the fact that he calls it the "fruit" of the discipline concerned with "natural matters" (*al-ṭabīʿiyyat*), that is, natural philosophy: "The fruit of the science concerned with natural matters is the knowledge of the survival of the human soul, and that it has a return."[3]

Avicenna even goes so far as to say that all knowledge acquisition, both the theoretical and practical, is geared toward an eschatological end, i.e., the human soul's perfection insofar as this bears on its posthumous states: "All the sciences have a single benefit in common, which is the attainment of the perfection of the human soul in actuality, preparing it for happiness in the life hereafter."[4]

On the basis of these and similar passages, we see that for the shaykh knowledge has an ultimately soteriological purpose, and human flourishing or felicity, grounded in such knowledge, is fundamentally something otherworldly. If so, it makes good sense why the human soul's post-mortem subsistence and states should be a distinct and vital topic of investigation for Avicenna, and why he made it one of his principal concerns by giving it extensive and consistent treatment throughout his life.

The shaykh's theory of the Return has a number of crucial elements, each of which deserves separate and sustained treatment, not only to better understand them in relation to each other, but also in relation to the rest of his philosophy. Based on one consideration, we can broadly divide the elements of his theory into two sorts; some of those elements constitute fundamental principles, while others amount to corollaries of those principles.

The discussions in *Aḍḥawiyya* 6–7 presuppose a number of such fundamental principles and corollaries. Of the fundamentals, three stand out in particular for our purposes: (i) that the human soul enjoys awareness or cognition of itself independent of the body; (ii) that the human soul is incorruptible; and (iii) that the good of a thing is what perfects a thing, given its nature. As for

3 Avicenna, *al-Mabdaʾ wa-l-maʿād li-l-shaykh al-raʾīs*, ed. ʿAbdallāh Nūrānī, Tehran: The Institute of Islamic Studies, 1984, 1.

4 Avicenna, *The metaphysics of the healing*, ed. and trans. Michael E. Marmura, Provo, UT: Brigham Young University Press, 2005.

the corollaries of these fundamentals, they are as follows: a corollary of (ii) is (ii)* that the human soul survives bodily death; a corollary of (i) is (i)* that, post-mortem, the human soul is conscious of itself. From (iii), we have two corollaries: (iii)* that the good of a capacity is its proper object; and (iii)** that, in the case of a cognitive agent, the cognition of its good is pleasurable (and, correlatively, of what is not its good is unpleasant).

In *Aḍḥawiyya* 6, the shaykh attempts to fulfill two aims. First, to establish (ii) and thereby derive (ii)* from it. And second, show that, post-mortem, the human soul will necessarily be subject to either pleasure or pain. To establish the latter, he will presuppose all of the abovementioned fundamentals and corollaries. Then, in *Aḍḥawiyya* 7, he will further elucidate the soul's Return (i.e., its post-mortem experiences) in light of the abovementioned fundamentals and corollaries, as well as by drawing support from additional ones.

Before presenting the translations of *Aḍḥawiyya* 6–7, let me summarize the case Avicenna puts forward for the second of the two aims just noted. With regard to the first aim, I have dealt with what he says on the topic in some detail elsewhere.[5]

The shaykh begins thus:

> Necessarily, every persisting and cognitive substance is either in repose, pleased, or pained. Hence, in the second life, the soul is either in repose, pleased, or pained.

In light of the above fundamentals and corollaries, we can then parse the reasoning he goes on to give in the following way:

Given that the human soul survives death, in its post-mortem condition wherein the human soul has cognition of itself, we can legitimately ask if that self-consciousness will be accompanied by:

a. A pleasant state
b. A painful state, or
c. Some kind of repose

For any such persistent, self-cognitive agent necessarily enjoys one of these states during the normal course of events. And so if (i)* and (iii)** are true, then a self-aware agent like the human soul is necessarily in one of these states post-mortem as well.

5 Dadikhuda, Davlat, "Not that simple: Avicenna, Rāzī, and Ṭūsī on the incorruptibility of the human soul at *Ishārāt* VII.6," in Abdelkader Al Ghouz (ed.), *Islamic philosophy from the 12th to the 14th century*, Göttingen: V&R Unipress, 2018, 279–307.

The a)–c) division is exhaustive. The first two states are well-known; so what it means, and what it is like, for the soul to be in them requires no explanation. However, with regards to (c), the state of repose, this may be less known. In brief, it is supposed to be, in a sense, a privative condition (i.e., in that it is a state that is non-painful)—for it involves an absence of pain—but in such way that it is not a pleasurable state proper. Qualitatively speaking then, it is a non-painful and non-pleasant state. However, in itself it would still be a positively qualitative state so that there is something it is like to be in that state; and we can best characterize it as some sort of a neutral state of rest or ease (*rāḥa*) between states (a) and (b).

Here, one might object and say: "but why think state (c) would still be something qualitatively positive in nature? In other words, why not say (c) is a state devoid of any qualitative feel, as in something like a comatose condition?"

The shaykh resists this sort of alternative on grounds of (iii), (iii)*, and (iii)**; the proper object of a cognitive capacity is its good. Now the proper object of the soul's capacity for self-awareness, i.e., its own self, is available to itself post-mortem. As such, either the soul will cognize or experience that object as good or not. Whatever the case, all this is just to say the experiential condition will have a qualitative feel to it. Thus, the self's post-mortem experience of itself cannot possibly be empty and blank.

Let us then suppose that indeed the separated human soul is in a state like (c). What would this state be like? One of two options present themselves: in its post-mortem neutral state (c), when the soul engages in self-cognition, either

A. It will find that activity somehow agreeable or joyous, or

B. It will find it somehow disagreeable

The shaykh then rules out disjunct (B) and concludes to (A). Option (B) cannot be the case for the simple reason that disagreeableness and the like are states in conflict with, or opposed to, a state like (c) and what is similar to it; for disagreeableness and the like are basically painful states. State (c), however, is supposed to be one lacking in pain. But if not (B), then (A) is true—there being no third alternative. It thus turns out that to have a cognitive experience that involves a positively qualitative character that is non-painful is, basically, to have an experience that is pleasant in nature. Therefore, as option (A) has it, if the soul in state (c) post-mortem will necessarily find some sort of satisfaction, joy, or the like, then it is enjoying a pleasant state. For insofar as states such as "agreeableness" or "satisfaction" are all clearly good conditions, the soul in state (c) is, therefore, necessarily in some pleasant state. And so, on analysis, it turns out that state (c), the repose neutral state, reduces to state (a) i.e., the pleasant state. In sum, therefore, the soul post-mortem will necessarily be in one of two states, not three: either having (a) a pleasant experience or (b) a painful/unpleasant one.

And these two states, in the language of the *sharʿ*, are nothing but the heavenly and hellish states of felicity and misery respectively. If so, then the upshot is: the heavenly and hellish states of felicity and misery will necessarily obtain for souls in the Afterlife. And this is just what "the Return" amounts to on the principles of the Islamic philosophers (*al-ḥukamāʾ*).

The syllogistic order of the shaykh's argument can be stated as follows:

> If the soul has self-cognition post-mortem, then it will find this either pleasant, painful, or neutral
> The soul has self-cognition post-mortem
> Therefore, post-mortem the soul is either in a pleasant state, a painful state, or a neutral state
> If the soul is in a neutral state, then it is in a pleasant state
> Therefore, post-mortem the soul is either in a pleasant state or a painful state
> Pleasure that lasts is felicity, and pain that lasts is misery
> Therefore, post-mortem, the soul is either felicitous or miserable

2 Translation

Chapter 6
On the Necessity of *maʿād*

I say that if the human soul is a separate immaterial form, then it is eternal and incorruptible. For a thing that exists, when it comes to exist, is either such that it is necessary in existence or contingent in existence. If it is contingent in existence, then its essence has both the potential to be and not to be. And so being is no more apt for it than not being, and hence we find that it at times exists and at times does not exist. It is describable by both descriptions.

It is impossible that in all states it is characterizable by both [descriptions] in a unified way. Rather, it has factor and state in [virtue of] which it is existent no doubt; a factor and a state in [virtue of] which it is non-existent; and a factor and a state which bears [the potential for] both factors. And there is no doubt that the factor bearing the two [other] factors persists in both states; for it is impossible that a thing bear something else and yet be non-existent. Hence, the factor persisting in both cases is matter; the factor by which and upon which [the thing] is existent in actuality is form; and the third factor is nonexistence.

Therefore, everything that does not have matter is not receptive of nonexistence at all and corruptibility. Indeed, all that is receptive of them is either [composed] of matter or is in matter. Therefore, the human soul and the intellect is incorruptible and hence persists after death.

Necessarily, every persisting and cognitive substance is either in repose (*mustarīḥ*), pleased (*mutaladhdhadh*), or pained (*muta'allam*). Hence, in the second life, the soul is either in repose, pleased, or pained. And everything in repose, when it cognizes itself, is either glad (*mughtabiṭ*) with itself or grieved (*maḥzūn*) with respect to itself. And so likewise, the soul in the state of repose is either glad or grieved. But, further, it is impossible that it be grieved; for grief is opposed to repose. Therefore, [the soul] will be glad. And gladness is a certain good and a pleasure; therefore, in the state of repose, [the soul] is pleased. Thus, the [initial] division is not tripartite but bipartite: [the soul in the second life is either] pained or pleased. And eternal pain is misery (*shaqāwa*), and untarnished, substantial eternal pleasure is felicity (*sa'āda*). Hence, the soul after death is either miserable or felicitous. And that is the Return (*al-ma'ād*).

Chapter 7
On Making Known the States of Classes of People after Death and the Verification of the Second Life

One ought to know that not all pleasure is sensible. On the contrary, among pleasures there is what is neither sensible nor does the sensible approach it. And likewise with pains.

In fact, pleasure is the cognition of what is agreeable; and the agreeable is what pertains to the perfection of the substance of a thing and the completion of its act. So the sensible-agreeable then is what perfects the substance of the sense and its act; and the irascible-agreeable, appetitive-agreeable, imaginative-agreeable, thought-agreeable, and the memory-agreeable are all each analogous to that. Were it not for the fact that explaining this in detail would greatly prolong the discourse, I would have taken it up.

However, in a general way, I say [the following]: that every cognitive faculty was made for the purpose of an activity or for [the purpose of something] other than an activity. The thing, then, that reaches [the faculty] and what makes it attain that purpose is the agreeable and the pleasant. So for the [faculty of] taste, it is sweetness; for it is more nutritious than all. And taste is for the sake of nutrition. And for the auditory [faculty], it is a smooth sound, balanced in heaviness and lightness so as not to scatter too much nor gather too much. And for the tactile [faculty], it is the soft and balanced to the touch, for the very same reason. The cause of this is that the activity proper to a thing is the purpose of its substance. And the operations of these things mentioned [above] are in subjects external to them; as long as they do not reach them, they will not act. If they do reach, and are not hurt, then there is pleasure and agreeableness ….

It is evident from all this, then, that pleasures are by cognition of agreeable things, and agreeable things are perfecters of substances and their activities. The relations of some pleasures to others, then, is the relations of cognitive powers, agreeable things, perfecters, and cognitions.

Now, it is self-evidently known that the rational soul is cognitive. Further, its substance is more excellent than the substances of the other powers. For it is simple absolutely and separate from matter in every manner of separation; but they are attached to matter, and receptive of composition and division due to matter.

Further, [the rational soul's] cognition is more excellent than the cognition of the senses; for the soul's cognition is certain, universal, necessary, and eternal, and the cognition of sense is superficial, particular, and ephemeral.

Further, [the rational soul's] agreeable objects of cognition are more excellent; for its objects of cognition are stable meanings, and spiritual forms, and the First Principle of all existence in His majesty and greatness, as well as the lordly angels, the realities of the celestial bodies, and the elements and their essences.

Further, [the rational soul's] perfections are more excellent than the perfections of the sense powers. For its perfection is that it become a world free from change and multiplicity, in which there is the form of every existent as separate from matter. It then is a world opposite the [external] world and parallel to it, except that its make-up is spiritual, lordly, subtle, and holy, while the make-up of the corporeal world is sensible, mixed with viciousness, potentiality, privation, and is dense and polluted. So what sort of comparison can these four meanings belonging to the human soul have to their analogues belonging to the animal soul?

It is clear then that the pleasure which belongs to the human substance—I mean his soul—upon the Return, if it is perfected, is not something to which can be compared any pleasure at all that exists in this our world. *Subḥān Allāh*! Can the good and pleasure that is proper to the substances of the angels be comparable to the good and pleasure which is proper to the substances of the animals and beasts of prey? The human soul is no doubt of an angelic substance, if it be perfected; for it is a separable, intellectual form and this is the same as the form of the angels. However, we do not sense this pleasure while we are embodied; for the bodily powers overpower the rational soul, until the soul is forgetful of itself, and even until power and sovereignty belong to the senses, the estimation, the irascible [faculty], and the concupiscent [faculty].

Evidence for that is the decrease in the sovereignty of the rational soul upon increase in the sovereignty of these [faculties].

Thus, the existence of that [intellectual] pleasure is necessary, though we do not sense it while we are in the body. And the cause of that is the body. An example of this exists in the case of the sense powers; for the bilious finds the sweet thing bitter and dislikes it. Also, it is not objectionable that there is a pleasure whose existence one believes in, but whose what-it-is-like one neither conceptualizes nor experiences at present. For the impotent believes in the existence of the pleasure of copulation, but does not experience it; and the deaf believes in the existence of the pleasure of hearing, and the blind in the existence of the pleasure of beautiful images, but they do not experience them.

Moreover, perception and awareness of that [intellectual] pleasure is based on the extent to which the human and animal faculties subdue one another. So one who strengthens the sovereignty of his rational soul in this world over the sovereignty of the animal faculties begins to experience and feel something of that [intellectual] pleasure in variegated ways. And those granted that in natural-disposition and supported in the mastery of their rational faculty over the animal [faculties], and the internal [faculties] over the external [ones]—such that the animal and external [faculties] do not gain supremacy over them—it may be that a worthy portion of that pleasure will belong to them in this world. But as for [having it] unrestrictedly, there is no way to that except in the Hereafter.

Hence, otherworldly felicity, upon the liberty of the soul from the body, the traces of nature, and its abstraction, is perfect in pleasures [wherein the soul] gazes, in an intellectual manner, at the essence of the One who possesses the mighty kingdom, and at the spiritual entities which worship Him, and at the lofty world, and at the arrival of its perfection to it. Sublime pleasure takes place thereupon; and otherworldly misery takes place with the contrary of that. Just as that felicity is very great, likewise the misery that is its opposite is very painful.

And because the soul is not in the body like form in matter, it is not the body that is the impediment between it and that felicity; rather, it is the traces and dispositions deeply inserted in it from [the side of] the body. So if the bodily dispositions—like appetite, anger, and wishing for what is undesirable from among worldly things—are established in the soul, and take root in it, and it separates from the body while they are stable in it, it is then prevented from true perfection and real felicity, and is as if it were still in the body. And it is this that the sages among the philosophers have referred to as "transmigration."

There is no way to a removal from that except by moderation. For the moderate [person] is someone from whom the two extremes have both been negated and his substance subsists free from both [contrary] natures. So [for example] the moderate in heat and coolness is nothing but that which, becoming neither hot nor cold at all, is one in account. For this reason, [the human soul] is commanded to moderation. And one of the things that purify the soul from the blemishes of nature is worship of the divine and the performance of that towards which the Prophetic *sharīʿa* calls. For it is a fortress and a protection for the soul from this predicament.

The souls separate from bodies are of various classes:

[A] Souls that are perfect and pure. These have absolute felicity.

[B] Souls that are perfect but impure; these are in an intermediate-barrier state, which is between them and their desire, and [their] total abstraction and liberation. Base dispositions prevent [such a soul] from achieving absolute felicity. And because its preoccupying activities come to an end by the separation of the body, the soul braces for awareness of felicity but is barred from it by the base dispositions. And so that then makes it suffer intensely.

However, these dispositions do not belong to [such a soul] substantially; and so they do not pain it for all eternity. Rather, they vanish from it and it finally arrives at true happiness in the end. And because these dispositions are established as a result of motions towards different species of good and bad, whose substance [consisted in] pursuit of animal pleasure, and which have [now] been lost, then that too is among the soul's pains in the Afterlife.

[C1] Souls that are imperfect but pure, and to whom, during their [embodied] life, it occurred that they have a perfection. But they did not seek it; they denied and opposed it, and believed what is untrue. These [souls] are pained by their imperfection eternally.

[C2] Souls that are imperfect but pure, and to whom it did not occur that they have a perfection at all, nor do they have a state other than from the contract placed before them by the Messengers. And so they neither sought [that perfection], nor were they proposed it so that they denied it.

[C3] Souls that are imperfect but pure, and to whom that did not occur, nor did any thought occur to them that they have a perfection which does not exist for them—like the souls of the simple-minded and children.

Each one of these two classes [C2–3] subsists [post-mortem]. And they possess neither unqualified felicity, nor unqualified misery; for they are not aware of the perfection so that they could yearn for it and seek it substantially, and so be pained by the deficiency of that perfection and its loss, like the way the starving [person] is [pained] by hunger. Nor are they pained by the traces and dispositions of nature that are contrary to the substance of the soul; for they are pure. The former class [C2], to the extent that it is aware of the principles, has some trace proceeding from traces of felicity.

[D] Souls that are imperfect and impure. If they are aware that they have some perfection, then theirs is a state of unqualified misery, nor will it abate. If their deficient [state] is devoid of the awareness of the fact that they have that [perfection], they will be pained in accordance with the base dispositions that they've inherited from the world of nature.

That which follows from the doctrine of Alexander is that unqualifiedly imperfect souls corrupt with the corruption of the body. That is something not true, nor is it the doctrine of Aristotle. For the human soul, on the basis of what we established, subsists [post-mortem] necessarily.

Some of the learned say that good souls increase in pleasure and good by mutual encounter, and bad souls increase pain and evil by mutual encounter. For each class [of soul] contacts, in an intellectual manner, its qualitative and dispositional similar. And that the pleasure and pain of mutual encounter is non-finite. By this is meant that when virtuous souls are contacted by [other] virtuous souls, they are pleased by it; and the contrary of that with vicious souls. Each one of the intellectual souls cognizes itself and cognizes what is like itself, exponentially; do you not see it cognizes the intellectual principles which are its causes?

Some of the learned say that although transmigration is impossible, it is not impossible that some souls contact others by way of influencing them either in a bad or good manner. For it is not improbable that there comes about a mixture close to the mixture of the body [that the separated soul] was in, and it then attaches to [that mixture] due the cause that was in the first body from which it separated. However, it is impossible, for the reasons mentioned, that it attaches to [an embodied soul] totally. Among those reasons is the impossibility of two souls in one body. So it attaches to [the embodied soul] by an attachment other than that [kind], which is that it contacts its soul in a spiritual manner. [The embodied] soul is then increased in evil, if [the separated soul] was evil, or in good, if it was good. And from the contact of the two, [various] kinds of intentions and character traits come to be in embodied souls from the two.

A group of them say that the estimative faculty [of the separated soul] connects to matter by the mediation and cause of the rational faculty, and it then is able to view all the meanings existing in the world of sense and nature—not the pure intelligible meanings—since the sensible world then becomes like a body for [that separated soul], and it is imprisoned in it and cannot go beyond it to the higher world. Then, by the looking into all the particular causes in the world, since none of them is more apt for that than others, knowledge of the events which the particular motions lead to is then presented to it. And the embodied soul in contact with [that separated soul] then benefits from the knowledge of events displayed [to it].

They [further] say that the malignant souls from among [the separated souls] are more effective in doing the evil that is possible for them [to do]; for they've departed from the matter by whose motions they were captivated, and have become stuck [acting] in a single way—if it is bad, then they are evil, and if it is good, then they are good. And they are agreed that the evil ones are devils, while the good ones of this deficient class are *jinn*. They postulate for the devils and *jinn* an attachment to people and spiritual actions from which natural actions generate, and make separation from matter an additional [cause] of their power for bringing about an action in conformity with their disposition, whether it is base or noble.

And the best of the learned were of the view that the perfect and pure souls have no regard toward the sensible things.

Some of the learned say that when the soul separates from the body and carries the estimative faculty along with itself in the way mentioned, it is impossible that it be free from the body [and] purified in such a way that nothing of the dispositions of nature accompany it. Hence, at the time of death it is aware of death, and after death it imagines itself in the form of the human being that died, just as it imagines in a dream. And it imagines itself as buried, and imagines the pains that reach it by way of the commonly known sensible punishments, and imagines all it believed in the present life that will belong to it [in the Afterlife] or was commonly-known to be of that form. So if it is happy, it will imagine it in a laudable form in a sensible form and in the form it believed and was familiar with as belonging to those in a state of felicity. They said that this is the punishment of the grave and its reward; and that the second life is [the soul's] removal of the garment of these dispositions and its grave are these dispositions. They [further] said: so do not be astonished that it imagines a beautiful, laudable form and there manifests to it in the Hereafter, before the second life and after it, all the states mentioned in the books of the prophets (upon them be peace) pertaining to the Garden, the wide-eyed houris, and the like of that.

As for [discussion of] the symbols and mysteries mentioned not according to the doctrine of one who proclaims them and believes them, they amount to more than can be enumerated.

Thābit b. Qurra has a strange doctrine, which is his belief that the soul separates from the body into a subtle body. That is something for which there is no reason, unless he was speaking symbolically, like in the other cases.

Having reached this point, let us then conclude this treatise and praise God for [completing] that toward which we have applied ourselves. And we ask the trustworthy shaykh (my benefactor)—may God perpetuate his dynasty—to regard [this work] with a charitable eye and to correct the errors contained therein, *in shāʾ Allāh*.

Praise belongs to God alone, and may His blessings be upon our Prophet Muhammad the chosen one, and all of his family. God alone is sufficient for us.

Bibliography

Avicenna, *al-Mabdaʾ wa-l-maʿād li-l-shaykh al-raʾīs*, ed. ʿAbdallāh Nūrānī, Tehran: The Institute of Islamic Studies, 1984.

Avicenna, *al-Aḍḥawiyya fī l-maʿād li-Ibn Sīnā*, ed. Ḥasan ʿĀṣī, Beirut: al-Muʾassasa al-Jāmiʿiyya, 1987.

Avicenna, *The metaphysics of the healing*, ed. and trans. Michael E. Marmura, Provo, UT: Brigham Young University Press, 2005.

Dadikhuda, Davlat, "Not that simple: Avicenna, Rāzī, and Ṭūsī on the incorruptibility of the human soul at *Ishārāt* VII.6," in Abdelkader Al Ghouz (ed.), *Islamic philosophy from the 12th to the 14th century*, Göttingen: V&R Unipress, 2018, 279–307.

CHAPTER 16

Greek Philosophy and Sufism in Mecdi's Ottoman Turkish *Gardens of Peonies*

Rosabel Ansari

As the works of William Chittick and Sachiko Murata have taught countless students and scholars, the study of religious and philosophical texts from different language traditions opens up worldviews and perspectives on life that differ fundamentally from that of the contemporary world. Translations and studies of such texts not only transfer words and ideas from one language into another, but serve as conductors for different ways of thinking. In this respect, the study of Ottoman Turkish texts, particularly from the classical period of Ottoman intellectual life during the 9th/15th and 10th/16th centuries, is incisive. In its literary and intellectual production, the Ottoman Turkish textual tradition fuses many aspects of Islamic thought into a creative synthesis, and in the interlacing of Arabic and Persian into Turkish, it melds together multiple discourses and perspectives on perennial questions. The Ottoman biographical dictionary *Gardens of peonies* (*Ḥadāʾiq al-shaqāʾiq*) by the scholar and litterateur Mehmed Mecdi (d. 999/1591) is an example of this tradition.*

∴

1 Introduction

Best known in Turkish as the *Tercüme-yi şekayık-ı nuʿmaniye* (*Translation of the crimson peonies*), Mecdi's *Gardens of peonies* is a Turkish translation-cum-adaptation of Tasköprüzade's (d. 968/1561) famous Arabic biographical dictionary of the scholars of the Ottoman Empire, *The crimson peonies among scholars of the Ottoman state* (*al-Shaqāʾiq al-nuʿmāniyya fī ʿulamāʾ al-dawla al-ʿUthmāniyya*). In his introduction to the text, Mecdi provides a philosophical and mystical account of the creation of Adam that serves as a reflection on the

* I give thanks to Betül Başaran for reading Mecdi with me. The American Association of Teachers of Turkic Languages supported this research with a travel grant in Fall 2017.

DOI:10.1163/9789004529038_017

nature and capacity of human knowledge, based on the fusion of the Islamic Peripatetic and Akbarian Sufi traditions.

The fusion of these two traditions in Mecdi's account of the creation of Adam, evident in both the terminology and the theoretical concepts of the text, is illustrative of an integrated perspective on the ways that the human being can know the world. Moreover, it reveals a perspective on the basic philosophical question of what constitutes the sources of knowledge. In specific, the relationship between rational and mystical sources of knowledges appears to be harmonious in Mecdi's anthropology and epistemology. In contrast, the relationship between rational and mystical ways of knowing, especially important for both societal and anthropological concerns, is today not always considered self-evident and is at the crux of many further issues. While on the societal level there is the need for knowledge to be verifiable, on the anthropological level this question pertains to the very substance of the human being. What avenues are available to us, as human beings, to know our place in the world? This question inevitably relates to the nature and substance of the human being, and at the basic level, what it means to be human.

Mecdi's introduction to the text begins with an account of the creation of Adam that fuses Greek philosophical and Akbarian Sufi concepts into a narrative using verses from the Quran and Hadith as well as Persian poetry. The integration of technical concepts and vocabulary from these traditions exemplifies their integration in Mecdi's anthropology and epistemology. Beginning with philosophical concepts to describe the physical and intellectual formation of Adam as a sublime substance, Mecdi's account progresses to the Akbarian theory of Adam as a manifestation of the Divine Names. In particular, Mecdi tells us that it is through the intellectual faculty and the rational soul, themselves obtaining from the Holy Spirit, that Adam is able to become a locus of manifestation for the Divine Names. The structure of the account and the interrelations between the philosophical and Sufi concepts symbolizes the harmony and compatibility between different sources of knowledge in the Ottoman intellectual culture of the time.

2 A Turkish Literary Text

Completed in the year 995/1587, Mecdi's *Gardens of peonies* belongs to the "classical age" of Ottoman literature between the years 857–1008/1453–1600, during which Turkish began to increasingly dominate over Arabic and Persian as a language of high culture, literature and poetry.[1] During this time, authors took

1 Kuru, Selim, "The literature of Rum: The making of a literary tradition (1450–1600)," in Suraiya

pride in producing a higher register of Turkish that used Arabic and Persian morphological and syntactical units within Turkish sentences, likening use of such language to a religiously meritorious act (*mustaḥabb*).[2] It is within this context that Mecdi endeavoured to adapt and expand the deliberately simple Arabic of Tasköprüzade's *Crimson peonies* into an elevated, literary Turkish.[3] Mecdi's text incorporated not only Arabic and Persian units into Turkish sentences, but also used terminology and concepts that presupposed a thorough knowledge of the Islamic philosophical and mystical traditions. It is uncontroversial to say that Mecdi's Turkish adaptation of the *Crimson peonies* is far more challenging than the Arabic original. In fact, Mecdi explains in his introduction that he named his translation of Tasköprüzade's *Crimson peonies* as *Gardens of peonies* in order to symbolize that his text is fuller and more complete than that of Tasköprüzade.[4]

Mecdi's *Gardens of peonies* is closer to literary prose than discursive philosophy or Sufism. Yet, as an example of literary prose it is also illustrative of the intellectual culture and harmony that fused the traditions of philosophy and Sufism in the Ottoman world. This study examines Mecdi's use of philosophical concepts and technical terms that emerged during the Graeco-Arabic translation movement, fused with Akbarian Sufi concepts, as a gateway to revealing that intellectual culture. Moreover, the structure and fusion of these traditions in Mecdi's account of the creation of Adam is symbolic of an anthropology and journey of human realization according to which man moves from the material, to the intelligible, to the divine.[5]

N. Faroqhi and Kate Fleet (eds.), *The Cambridge history of Turkey*, ii, Cambridge: Cambridge University Press, 2013, 548–592, 550–551.

2 Kuru, "The literature" 557, quoting Gelibolulu Mustafa Ali (d. 1600) as found in Fleischer, Cornell H., *Bureaucrat and intellectual in the Ottoman Empire: The historian Mustafa Ali (1541–1600)*, Princeton: Princeton University Press, 1986, 22.

3 Tasköprüzade protested at Âşık Çelebi's translation of his text into Turkish, arguing that he had used a simple Arabic and there is no need to translate it: "O scholar, I have written it like Turkish; you bothered [to translate it] in vain." (Kuru, "The literature" 559). As Kuru explains, "when Taşköprüzade says that the Arabic he employed was 'like Turkish' (Türki gibi), he reveals the fact that Taşköprüzade distinguished among different levels of written Arabic from easy to difficult." (Kuru, "The literature" 559). Despite the fact that Taşköprüzade composed the text in a deliberately simple Arabic there were many translations into Turkish, on which see Gönül, Behçet, "İstanbul kütüphânelerinde al-Şakā'ik al-nuʿmâniya tercüme ve zeyilleri," in *Türkiyat Mecmuası* 7–8 (1945), 136–178. As the trend towards an elevated register of Turkish indicates, the reason for the translation of the text is not likely to have been due to the difficulty of Arabic, but rather due to the tastes of the urban literary class.

4 Mecdi, Mehmed, *Tercüme-yi Şakayık-ı nuʿmaniye*, Istanbul: Daru't-Tıbaati'l-Amire, 1852, 12–13.

5 This journey finds its origin in the Islamic philosophical tradition. A clear articulation of

3 The Assembly of Adam

Mecdi's account of the creation of Adam in the *Gardens of peonies* begins immediately following the opening invocations and salutary blessings on the Prophet. His narrative weaves verses of the Quran and Hadith into a Turkish commentary that itself is replete with technical, and sometimes even archaic, Arabic philosophical concepts and vocabulary, and is further interspersed with Persian poetry. The account of Adam's assembly (*maʿşer-i Adem*) is structured around four stages through which Adam is born from the placenta of non-being (*meşime-yi ʿademden*): 1) the kneading of earth and the harmonizing of the elements; 2) matter finding form; 3) substance becoming a theophany of the Divine Names; 4) God teaching Adam the names and the affairs.

In the first stage of Adam's assembly Mecdi describes two preparatory acts in the physical realm: the kneading of clay and the harmonizing of the four elements. He begins with the *ḥadīth qudsī* according to which God says, "I kneaded the clay of Adam with My hands for forty mornings."[6] Explaining the *ḥadīth* in Turkish, Mecdi tells us that the pure earth (*hak-ı pak*) of Adam was kneaded with the Hand of Power (*yed-i kudretli tahmir olub*), pointing to the divine charge with which the creation of man began. Through use of the Turkish subordinating suffix (*-ub*), Mecdi connects the kneading of earth to the harmonizing of the elements which immediately follows: "The four different elements (*usṭuḳsat*), which are characterized as opposing mixtures, differing

the first two stages is found in Abū Naṣr al-Fārābī. On this see Jabbour, Jawdath, *De la matière à l'intellect: L'âme et la substance de l'homme dans l'oeuvre d'al-Fārābī*, Paris: Vrin, 2021.

6 This appears to be a variation of a report initially found in the Arabic historical works of Ibn Saʿd (d. 230/845) and al-Ṭabarī (d. 310/923) in which the Prophet Muhammad's companion Salmān al-Fārisī (d. 32/652–653) reports (and according to Ibn Saʿd, on the basis of Ibn Masʿūd) that "God, glorified and exalted be He, kneaded the clay of Adam for forty nights (or forty days). Then He struck it with His Hand and all the good came out in the right hand and all the bad came out in the left hand. Then He mixed them together. From there He brings forth the living from the dead and the dead from the living." Ibn Saʿd, Muḥammad, *Kitāb al-Ṭabaqāt al-kabīr*, ed. ʿAlī Muḥammad ʿUmar, 11 vols., i, Cairo: Maktabat al-Khanjī, 2001, 10–11, and with minor variations in al-Ṭabarī, Muḥammad b. Jarīr, *Tārīkh al-Ṭabarī*, ed. Muḥammad Ibrāhīm, 11 vols., i, Cairo: Dār al-Maʿārif, 1990, 93. The report then appears in ʿAbd al-Razzāq al-Kāshānī (d. 730/1330) in the shortened form that Mecdi would use: "I kneaded the clay of Adam with My Hand for forty mornings" which Kāshānī refers to it as a *ḥadīth rabbānī*, i.e., *ḥadīth qudsī* in his exegesis of Q 38:34, often mistakenly attributed to Ibn ʿArabī ([Ps.-]Muḥyī al-Dīn Ibn ʿArabī, *Tafsīr Ibn ʿArabī*, ed. ʿAbd al-Wārith Muḥammad ʿAlī, 2 vols., ii, Beirut: Dār al-Kutub al-ʿIlmiyya, 2001, 180). I thank Irene Kirchner for help tracking the history of this report.

qualities, varying natures, and contrary individual existences (*inniyyāt*), were harmonized according to the best stature."[7]

The harmonizing of the four contrary elements as a preparatory stage for man's coming into being is a basic Avicennan doctrine.[8] For in the human being, Avicenna (d. 428/1037) tells us, the four elements exist closest to a real equilibrium.[9] Thus, having described the kneading of clay, Mecdi combines the Islamic account of the creation of Adam from clay with the philosophical theory that matter is composed of various combinations of the four elements.[10] In the assembly of Adam, the four elements are harmonized according to the "most beautiful stature" (*aḥsen-i taqwīm*), a reference to Q 95:4 in which God says that He created man in the *aḥsan taqwīm*. Here the two accounts of the physical moulding of the matter are woven together seamlessly and integrated into the Quranic narrative of man's creation in the most beautiful stature.

Moreover, in integrating these accounts of the physical moulding of matter, Mecdi uses technical vocabulary pertaining to the philosophical tradition. Most strikingly, Mecdi makes use of the unusual term *usṭuḳsat* (Ar. *usṭuqsāt*), an Arabic transliteration of the Greek *stoicheia* to mean "elements" that originated in the Graeco-Arabic translation movement of the 3rd–5th/9th–11th

7 Mecdi, *Tercüme* 3.6–7.

8 See Avicenna, *Kitāb al-Najāt*, Cairo: Maṭbaʿat al-Saʿāda, 1912–1913, 256–257 [Avicenna, *Avicenna's psychology: An English translation of* Kitāb al-Najāt, *book II, chapter VI*, trans. Fazlur Rahman, London: Oxford University Press, 1952, 24].

9 Avicenna, *al-Qānūn fī l-ṭibb*, ed. Muḥammad A. al-Ḍinnāwī, 3 vols., i, Beirut: Dār al-Kutub al-ʿIlmiyya, 1999, 21.

10 In some sense, these parallel processes are different ways of describing the preparation of matter. In *The physics* 1.2 Avicenna equates matter to both clay and the elements. He tells us that matter (*hayūlā*) is called "clay" (*ṭīna*) from the perspective that it is common to all forms and that it can also be called "element" (*usṭuqus*) because it can be analysed as a part of a whole (Avicenna, *The physics of the healing books I & II: A parallel English-Arabic text*, trans. Jon McGinnis, Provo, UT: Brigham Young University Press, 2009, 14). Furthermore, Ibn Ḥazm (d. 456/1064) reports that some philosophers refer to "matter" as *ṭīna* and *khamīra* ("leaven"), all with the same meaning (Ibn Ḥazm, ʿAlī b. Aḥmad, *Kitāb al-Fiṣal fī l-milal wa-l-ahwāʾ wa-l-niḥal*, v, Cairo: al-Maṭbaʿa al-Adabiyya, 1902–1903, 70). Resultingly, Mecdi's connecting the *ḥadīth* of kneading Adam's clay with the mixing of the elements might be seen as two different descriptions (one Islamic and one Peripatetic) of the same process. Importantly, in his exegesis of Q 2:260 the astronomer Niẓām al-Dīn al-Naysabūrī (d. c. 730/1330) describes how the clay of man was kneaded (*khummirat ṭīnat al-insān*) from the four elements which, when mixed together, produce differing qualities (al-Naysabūrī, Niẓām al-Dīn, *Gharāʾib al-Qurʾān wa-raghāʾib al-furqān*, ed. Zakariyyā ʿUmayrāt, ii, Beirut: Dār al-Kutub al-ʿIlmiyya, 1996, 33). Al-Naysabūrī's exegesis thus already makes the connection found in Mecdi between the act of kneading clay and the mixing of the different elements.

centuries. Having been replaced by the Arabic *ʿanāṣir* (sing. *ʿunṣur*), still found in modern Turkish, use of the term *usṭuḳsat* stands out as archaic and signals the incorporation of the Greek philosophical tradition. Similarly, Mecdi's use of the Arabic term *inniyyāt* (individual existences), also coined during the Graeco-Arabic translation movement, is highly technical and indicative of the philosophical tradition.[11] It points to the philosophical theory that matter is produced by the mixing of the different elements with contrary qualities, and it is through the perfect harmonization of these contrary qualities that the matter of Adam would come to be.

In the second stage of Adam's assembly Mecdi introduces the Aristotelian theory of hylomorphism according to which matter finds form and the material is joined with the immaterial. He tells us that the human composition (*terkib-i beşeri*), the most noble of the three kingdoms, born from the wombs of divine will with the mixing of the heavenly and earthly causes, was formed according to the most beautiful form, integrating Q 40:64: "He formed you and made beautiful your forms." Mecdi then explains this Quranic notion of beautiful formation using hylomorphism whereby matter finds form: "By gentle creation and command, and beautiful fashioning and erection, human matter (*heyula*) found many forms."[12]

In this passage Mecdi describes the formation of human matter in terms of Aristotelian hylomorphism whereby the underlying matter finds the immaterial form. Hylomorphism, as a theory developed by Aristotle, explains that things are composed of both their physical matter and their intelligible, immaterial forms that give unity and structure, or even purpose, to the underlying matter. In this passage, like the previous one, Mecdi also uses technical vocabulary from the philosophical tradition. His choice of *heyula* (Ar. *hayūlā*) to mean

11 In its literal meaning *inniyya* (or alternatively *anniyya*) means "that-ness" in contrast to "what-ness" (*māhiyya* or "quiddity") and is sometimes translated technically as "ipseity." It refers to the individual existence of a thing, or what makes it that thing, as opposed to something else in the same genus [Avicenna, *The healing, logic: Isagoge. A new edition, translation and commentary of the* Kitāb al-Madḫal *of Avicenna's* Kitāb al-Šifāʾ, ed. and trans. Silvia di Vincenzo, Berlin: DeGruyter, 2021, 92–96 using *ayyiyya* instead of *inniyya*]. For an explanation of this term in both philosophy and Sufism, see Mayer, Toby, "Anniyya," in *EI*[3] *Online*, http://dx.doi.org/10.1163/1573-3912_ei3_COM_22817 (last accessed: 3 December 2021). On the history of the term, in the Plotiniana Arabica, al-Fārābī and Avicenna respectively see d'Ancona, Cristina, "Platonic and Neoplatonic terminology for being in Arabic translation," in *Studia Graeco-Arabica* 1 (2011), 23–46; Abed, Shukri, *Aristotelian logic and the Arabic language in Alfārābī*, Albany, NY: SUNY Press, 1991, 67–68; De Haan, Daniel, *Necessary existence and the doctrine of being in Avicenna's metaphysics of the healing*, Leiden: Brill, 2020, 50–51.

12 Mecdi, *Tercüme* 3.10–11.

"matter" is also an archaic term originating in the Graeco-Arabic translation movement as an Arabic transliteration of the Greek *hyle*. As in the previous examples, *heyula* stands out as a specific choice to affirm the basis of Mecdi's account in the philosophical tradition, and especially its classical heritage.

Having already moved from the physical realm to the intelligible, the third stage of Mecdi's account of Adam's assembly moves from the intelligible to the divine. In this stage Mecdi uses noetic and metaphysical theories from the philosophical tradition to account for Adam becoming a vessel for divine manifestation. In this process it is the rational soul, itself obtaining through a divine emanation, that is the nexus connecting Adam, the primordial man, to the divine: "With the power of the rational soul and the intellectual faculty that obtain from the continual help of the Holy Spirit's eternal emanation, that sublime substance became a theophany of the [divine] names."[13]

In symbolizing the progression from the intelligible to the divine, Mecdi describes Adam using the Aristotelian terminology of a "substance" (*cevher*) who becomes a "theophany" (*mazhar*), a reference to the Akbarian theory of divine manifestation. According to Aristotle, "substance" (Gr. *ousia*) is the individual thing composed of matter and form. In contrast to accidents, a substance is that which is not in anything else and thus has an ontological priority and essential unity. *Cevher* (Ar. *jawhar*) was the translation for this term in Arabic. As Mecdi had already described the joining of matter and form, the use of *cevher* is clearly indicative of the Aristotelian theory of substance. Similarly, Mecdi's use of the term *mazhar* (Ar. *maẓhar*) testifies to an Akbarian Sufi framework according to which everything in the world is a manifestation of the divine.[14] Mecdi's account of Adam's passage from a *cevher* to a *mazhar* is thus rich with symbolism of the journey from the intelligible to the divine.

Moreover, the passage from *cevher* to *mazhar* points to the roles of both rational and mystical knowledge and the interrelations between them in Mecdi's thought as well as the broader intellectual culture of his time. On this issue the symbolism within this passage is multi-layered and needs some breaking down. Firstly, Adam's movement from a substance to a theophany takes place through the power of the rational soul and the intellectual faculty. It is thus the power of the intellect, which according to the philosophical tradition is what makes us human, that also makes Adam a locus for the divine.

13 Mecdi, *Tercüme* 3.13.

14 On *maẓhar* in Ibn ʿArabī, see Chittick, William C., *The Sufi path of knowledge: Ibn al-ʿArabī's metaphysics of imagination*, Albany, NY: SUNY Press, 1989, 89–91. For a recent study on Ibn ʿArabī's theory of theophany, see Koca, Ozgur, "The world as a theophany and causality: Ibn ʿArabī, causes and freedom," in *Sophia* 59.4 (2020), 713–731.

Yet, secondly, as this intellect is obtained through the eternal emanation of the Holy Spirit, the intellect itself comes from divine provenance. As such, it is through the intellect within Adam that, due to its divine provenance, substance becomes theophany.

Nonetheless, as a final layer of symbolism, Mecdi's reference to the "eternal emanation of the Holy Spirit" (*ruhu-l-ḳudüsin feyżan-ı sermedisi*) is a reference to the philosophical theory of the Active Intellect's emanation (*fayḍ*) to human beings in their apprehension of intelligibles. Borrowing from Islamic imagery, the philosophical tradition beginning with Abū Naṣr al-Fārābī (d. 339/950) equated the Active Intellect to the Holy Spirit.[15] In this tradition, the Active Intellect is the last of the celestial intellects that governs over the terrestrial realm and serves as the nexus between man and the divine. Through apprehending intelligibles, man comes into contact with the Active Intellect, which emanates intelligibles upon his soul. In this way, knowledge is both an endeavour of human acquisition, and simultaneously an emanation, flow, or effluence from the celestial spheres to the human soul.[16]

In referring to the emanation of the Holy Spirit, Mecdi not only makes use of Avicennan noetics for explaining Adam's passage from substance to theophany, he also signals that this passage takes place through the dual function of the human intellect and divine effluence. In the layers of symbolism in Mecdi's language he tells us that Adam's transformation into a higher being, a theophany, is through a compatibility and harmony between his rational soul and the emanation of the Holy Spirit, i.e., Active Intellect, the source of all intelligibles and the last in a chain of celestial intellects that desire and strive for the First Cause (God). Mecdi reinforces this message with a line of Persian poetry taken from Kamāl Khujandī (d. 803/1400–1401) in which, through divine wisdom, religion is given as a guide to the intellect:

---

15 Al-Fārābī, Abū Naṣr Muḥammad, *al-Siyāsa al-madaniyya*, ed. Fawzī Najjār, Beirut: al-Maṭbaʿa al-Kāthūlīkiyya, 1964, 32.

16 The standard monograph on emanation and intellection in Arabic noetics is Davidson, Herbert A., *Alfarabi, Avicenna, and Averroes on intellect: Their cosmologies, theories of the active intellect, and theories of human intellect*, Oxford: Oxford University Press, 1992. For a recent study on the debate and perspective specifically on Avicenna, see Ogden, Stephen, "Avicenna's emanated abstraction," in *Philosophers' Imprint* 20.10 (2020), 1–26. As Ogden explains, the debate concerns whether knowledge is something humans acquire themselves or receive from a divine source. While scholars have tended to fall into one camp or another, Ogden proposes to reconcile the two. He argues that the Active Intellect does not emanate intelligibles themselves, rather it emanates the power of abstraction which the intellect uses to acquire knowledge. This reading seems similar to Mecdi's presentation of the human intellect as possessing that a power that it obtains from the Holy Spirit's emanation.

> It is His Wisdom that gave the guide of religion to the intellect
> So that it may put the candle of guidance in the chamber of misguidance.[17]

The term *pervane* (translated as "guide") in the first part of the verse also has the meaning of "moth," a motif paired with the candle. Just as the moth seeks the light of the candle, divine wisdom has given religion as a guide to the intellect to seek out the light of guidance in the dark chamber of misguidance. Mecdi's use of this verse thus poetically reinforces the Avicennan noetics just discussed. Just as knowledge is attained through the human intellect's apprehension of intelligibles together with divine emanation, the poetry points to religion gifted by divine wisdom as a guide to the intellect. The human intellect and divine emanation function together in the acquisition of knowledge, as the human intellect and revealed religion function together in the quest for guidance. As such, a separation between the human intellect and the divine appears conceptually impossible.

In the fourth stage of his assembly God teaches Adam the names and affairs of the theophanies. Quoting and then explaining the Quranic verses, "And He taught Adam all the names" (Q 2:31) and "And He taught man what he did not know" (Q 96:5), Mecdi tells us that God informed Adam (*inha ve inba eyledi*) of the supreme essences' sublime names (*zevat-ı aliyatin esma-ı esmasını*) as well as the affairs (*şuun*) of the ways of God's announcements (*müstecmaʿu-l-kemalatın enha-ı enbasını*). Both the essences and the affairs are theophanies (*mezahir* and *mecali* respectively) of God's names and attributes. In other words, having made Adam himself a theophany for the Divine Names, in Mecdi's account God now teaches Adam to recognise the theophanies in both the things of the world and the unfolding of events that take place according to God's announcements. Through the intellect in himself Adam becomes a theo-

17 Khujandī, Kamāl al-Dīn Masʿūd, *Dīwān*, ed. ʿAzīz Dawlatābādī, Tabriz: Intishārāt-i Kitābfurūshī-yi Tihrān, 1958, 2. The Ottoman edition of Mecdi's text gives the final word of the verse as *jalāl* (majesty), however the Persian editions of Khujandī's poetry as well as its indirect recension give *ḍalāl* (misguidance) (e.g., Samarqandī, Dawlatshāh, *Tadhkiratu 'sh-shuʿará ("Memoirs of the poets") of Dawlatsháh bin ʿAláʾu 'd-Dawla Bakhtísháh al-Ghází of Samarqand*, ed. Edward G. Browne, Leiden: Brill, 1901, 1). In view of both recension and meaning, it seems that *ḍalāl* is the correct reading as it refers to the capacity to find guidance even in the quarters of misguidance. The Ottoman edition is most likely a typographical mistake, although manuscript study would have to determine this. It is significant that Mecdi appears to follow Dawlatshāh Samarqandī (d. 900/1494 or 913/1507), who also quotes the same lines of poetry in the opening page of his *Memoirs of the poets*, a biographical dictionary of poets in the Timurid Empire. I thank Mohsen Saber for reading Khujandī's poetry with me and helping to unpack its meaning.

phany of the Divine Names, and it is at this point that he can see that all things and all happenings are reflections of God's names and attributes, mirrors of the Essence.

4 Rationality and Mysticism

Mecdi's account of the creation of Adam fuses the Akbarian Sufi tradition with that of Greek of philosophy through both terminology and a conceptual framework. In its epistemology, this account tells us that it is the intellect, itself of divine provenance, that is the source of Adam's becoming a receptacle for divine knowledge. It is thus through harnessing the divine gift within him, i.e., the intellect that is obtained through the emanation of the Holy Spirit, that Adam can know the unfolding of divine realities. In other words, it is from within that Adam can know what is from without, and it is through the conjoining of his rational faculty with the emanation of the Holy Spirit that Adam can become a site of divine manifestation.

Anthropologically, Mecdi's account of the creation of Adam also tells us about the formation of the human self. Beginning with the material self, there is a perfect harmonization of the elements and an aesthetic shaping of the body. Secondly, the material body finds its immaterial form and telos in order to be actualized as a substance. Thirdly, the intellectual faculty properly trained conjoins with divine emanation. At this point the human self is actualized as a theophany and learns the realities of things. The formation of the human self thus comprises material harmonization and aesthetics, immaterial form and telos, and the intellectual faculty and divine emanation.

Although not a philosophical text itself, Mecdi's account illustrates an intellectual culture that took the compatibility of the rational and mystical sources of knowledge as a basic premise of epistemology and anthropology. In Mecdi's text the fusion of the Greek philosophical tradition, as it was naturalized in the Islamic world, with the Akbarian Sufi tradition points to the view that these traditions contribute to the same body of knowledge concerning the human understanding of the world and our place in it. Furthermore, Mecdi's use of technical terminology and theories particular to these two traditions clearly indicates his command of both these bodies of learning. The use of Arabized Greek words and terminology that grew out of the Graeco-Arabic translation movement also suggests that the texts going back to that period were known and used. Mecdi's command and fusion of the Islamic philosophical and mystical traditions is therefore a further example that helps to break down the assumed distinctions between philosophy and Sufism in Islam.

Bibliography

Abed, Shukri, *Aristotelian logic and the Arabic language in Alfārābī*, Albany, NY: SUNY Press, 1991.

Avicenna, *Kitāb al-Najāt*, Cairo: Maṭbaʿat al-Saʿāda, 1912–1913.

Avicenna, *Avicenna's psychology: An English translation of* Kitāb al-Najāt, *book II, chapter VI*, trans. Fazlur Rahman, London: Oxford University Press, 1952.

Avicenna, *al-Qānūn fī l-ṭibb*, ed. Muḥammad A. al-Ḍinnāwī, 3 vols., Beirut: Dār al-Kutub al-ʿIlmiyya, 1999.

Avicenna, *The physics of the healing books I & II: A parallel English-Arabic text*, trans. Jon McGinnis, Provo, UT: Brigham Young University Press, 2009.

Avicenna, *The healing, logic: Isagoge. A new edition, translation and commentary of the* Kitāb al-Madḫal *of Avicenna's* Kitāb al-Šifāʾ, ed. and trans. Silvia di Vincenzo, Berlin: DeGruyter, 2021.

Chittick, William C., *The Sufi path of knowledge: Ibn al-ʿArabī's metaphysics of imagination*, Albany, NY: SUNY Press, 1989.

d'Ancona, Cristina, "Platonic and Neoplatonic terminology for being in Arabic translation," in *Studia Graeco-Arabica* 1 (2011), 23–46.

Davidson, Herbert A., *Alfarabi, Avicenna, and Averroes on intellect: Their cosmologies, theories of the active intellect, and theories of human intellect*, Oxford: Oxford University Press, 1992.

De Haan, Daniel, *Necessary existence and the doctrine of being in Avicenna's metaphysics of the healing*, Leiden: Brill, 2020.

al-Fārābī, Abū Naṣr Muḥammad, *al-Siyāsa al-madaniyya*, ed. Fawzī Najjār, Beirut: al-Maṭbaʿa al-Kāthūlīkiyya, 1964.

Fleischer, Cornell H., *Bureaucrat and intellectual in the Ottoman Empire: The historian Mustafa Ali (1541–1600)*, Princeton: Princeton University Press, 1986.

Gönül, Behçet, "İstanbul kütüphânelerinde al-Şakāʾik al-nuʿmâniya tercüme ve zeyilleri", in *Türkiyat Mecmuası* 7–8 (1945), 136–178.

[Ps.-] Ibn ʿArabī, Muḥyī al-Dīn, *Tafsīr Ibn ʿArabī*, ed. ʿA.M. ʿAlī, 2 vols., Beirut: Dār al-Kutub al-ʿIlmiyya, 2001.

Ibn Ḥazm, ʿAlī b. Aḥmad, *Kitāb al-Fiṣal fī l-milal wa-l-ahwāʾ wa-l-niḥal*, Cairo: al-Maṭbaʿa al-Adabiyya, 1902–1903.

Ibn Saʿd, Muḥammad, *Kitāb al-Ṭabaqāt al-kabīr*, ed. ʿAlī Muḥammad ʿUmar, 11 vols., Cairo: Maktabat al-Khanjī, 2001.

Jabbour, Jawdath, *De la matière à l'intellect: L'âme et la substance de l'homme dans l'oeuvre d'al-Fārābī*, Paris: Vrin, 2021.

Kāshānī, ʿAbd al-Razzāq, see [Ps.-] Ibn ʿArabī, Muḥyī al-Dīn.

Khujandī, Kamāl al-Dīn Masʿūd, *Dīwān*, ed. ʿAzīz Dawlatābādī, Tabriz: Intishārāt-i Kitābfurūshī-yi Tihrān, 1958.

Koca, Ozgur, "The world as a theophany and causality: Ibn ʿArabī, causes and freedom," in *Sophia* 59.4 (2020), 713–731.

Kuru, Selim, "The literature of Rum: The making of a literary tradition (1450–1600)," in Suraiya N. Faroqhi and Kate Fleet (eds.), *The Cambridge history of Turkey*, ii, Cambridge: Cambridge University Press, 2013, 548–592.

Mayer, Toby, "Anniyya," in *EI³ Online*, http://dx.doi.org/10.1163/1573-3912_ei3_COM_22817 (last accessed: 3 December 2021).

Mecdi, Mehmed, *Tercüme-yi Şakayık-ı nuʿmaniye*, Istanbul: Daru't-Tıbaati'l-Amire, 1852.

al-Naysabūrī, Niẓām al-Dīn, *Gharāʾib al-Qurʾān wa-raghāʾib al-furqān*, ed. Zakariyyā ʿUmayrāt, Beirut: Dār al-Kutub al-ʿIlmiyya, 1996.

Ogden, Stephen, "Avicenna's emanated abstraction," in *Philosophers' Imprint* 20.10 (2020), 1–26.

Samarqandī, Dawlatshāh, *Tadhkiratu ʾsh-shuʿará* (*"Memoirs of the poets"*) *of Dawlatsháh bin ʿAláʾu ʾd-Dawla Bakhtísháh al-Ghází of Samarqand*, ed. Edward G. Browne, Leiden: Brill, 1901.

al-Ṭabarī, Muḥammad b. Jarīr, *Tārīkh al-Ṭabarī*, ed. Muḥammad Ibrāhīm, 11 vols., Cairo: Dār al-Maʿārif, 1990.

CHAPTER 17

Sufism and Philosophy in the Mughal-Safavid Era: Shāh Walī Allāh and the End of Selfhood

Muhammad U. Faruque

1 Introduction: Between Persia and India

In his *The reconstruction of religious thought in Islam*, the late philosopher Muhammad Iqbal (d. 1938) writes of Shāḥ Walī Allāh of Delhi (d. 1176/1762) as "the first Muslim who felt the urge of a new spirit in him" in the great task of rethinking "the whole system of Islam without completely breaking with the past."[1] Whether or not Walī Allāh was indeed the first intellectual to have felt the urge of a new spirit on the cusp of colonial modernity in 12th/18th-century India, there is no denying that he was a wide-ranging thinker who dealt with some of the major intellectual dimensions of Islam.[2] As a prolific writer, he composed over fifty works (including five collections of letters and epistles) ranging from Sufi metaphysics, philosophical theology, *fiqh*, *uṣūl al-fiqh*, and *ʿilm al-ḥadīth*, to philosophy of self and biographical treatises, in which he sought to create a synthetic paradigm for the purposes of rejuvenating the Islamic tradition of his day.[3] The intellectual contribution of this major intellec-

1 Iqbal, Muhammad, *The reconstruction of religious thought in Islam*, ed. and annotated by Saeed Sheikh, Stanford: Stanford University Press, 2013, 78.

2 For Walī Allāh's autobiography, see Allāh, Shāh Walī, *Anfas al-ʿārifīn* [Urdu translation of the Persian original], ed. Sayyid Muḥammad Farūqī al-Qādirī, Lahore: al-Maʿārif, 1974 (*al-juz' al-laṭīf fī tarjamat al-ʿabd al-ḍaʿīf*); Husain, M. Hidayat, "The Persian autobiography of Shāh Walīullāh bin ʿAbd al-Raḥīm al-Dihlavī," in *Journal of the Asiatic Society of Bengal* 14 (1912), 161–176. On his life, see al-Lakhnawī, ʿAbd al-Ḥayy b. Fakhr al-Dīn, *Nuzhat al-khawāṭir bahjat al-masāmiʿ wa-l-nawāẓir*, vi, Multan: Idārat-i Taʾlīfāt-i Ashrafiyya, 1993, 398–415; Rizvi, Sayyid A.A., *Shāh Walī-Allāh and his times: A study of eighteenth century Islām, politics and society in India*, Canberra: Maʿrifat, 1980, 203–228; Jalbani, Ghulam Hussain, *Life of Shah Waliyullah*, Lahore: Ashraf, 1978, 1–14; Allāh, Shāh Walī, *The conclusive argument from God: Shāh Walī Allāh of Delhi's* Ḥujjat Allāh al-bāligha, trans. Marcia K. Hermansen, Leiden: Brill, 1996, xxiii–xxxvi, xxii–xxxiii.

3 On Walī Allāh's revivalist project, see, e.g., Brown, Jonathan A.C., *Misquoting Muhammad: The challenge and choices of interpreting the Prophet's legacy*, London: Oneworld Publications, 2014, *passim*; Nadwī, Abū l-Ḥasan ʿA., *Saviours of Islamic spirit*. IV. *Hakim-ul-islam Shah Waliullah*, Lucknow: Academy of Islamic Research and Publications, 2004, 91–114.

 | DOI:10.1163/9789004529038_018

tual is relatively well-known in the West,[4] although in the Subcontinent itself, there is no lacuna of books written on his thought in Urdu, Hindi, Bengali, and other Indian languages.[5] He is long held as an important precursor to Islamic reformist movements such as Jamaʿāt-i Islāmī and The Muslim Brotherhood.[6]

In the present chapter I aim to probe Shāh Walī Allāh's account of selfhood and subjectivity (i.e., phenomenal experiences involving the first-person pronoun "I") through the "subtle fields of consciousness" known as the *laṭā'if*. I will begin with a brief survey of the state of philosophy and mysticism in the Mughal-Safavid era in order to situate Walī Allāh's thought in relation to the normative Islamic intellectual tradition. A large part of Walī Allāh's writings is devoted to explicating the nature of the self through the *laṭā'if* and one's spiritual journey within them. That is to say, the *laṭā'if* must be discovered, deciphered, and cultivated through the spiritual exercises, as they reveal the true nature of the self. Accordingly, I will examine the nature of ultimate selfhood and the process of its realization through one's understanding of the *laṭā'if*. In the main, I will argue that Walī Allāh develops a highly original model of the self that synthesizes elements from Stoicism, Islamic philosophy, Graeco-Islamic medical tradition, and Sufism.

Research on the nature and development of Islamic philosophy (i.e., various schools of Islamic philosophy including philosophical Sufism) in India is still in its early days, even though bio-bibliographical literature lists hundreds of names with thousands of texts, most of which consist of commentaries and glosses that are still in manuscript form.[7] Therefore, recent scholarship is right to suggest that

---

4 Apart from Rizvi, *Shāh Walī Allāh*, op. cit., and Baljon, Johannes M.S., *Religion and thought of Shāh Walī Allāh Dihlavi*, Leiden: Brill, 1986, there is no other scholarly monograph devoted to Walī Allāh in English. This is rather surprising in that Walī Allāh's oeuvre contains no dearth of ideas, especially in the areas of Sufi metaphysics and philosophical theology.

5 The following book edited by Chaghatai provides an overview of Walī Allāh's reception in some of these languages: Chaghatai, Muḥammad I. (ed.), *Shah Waliullah: His religious and political thought*, Lahore: Sang-e-Meel Publications, 2005, *passim*.

6 For more information, see Mawdūdī, Sayyid Abū l-Aʿlā (Jamaʿāt-i Islāmī), *Tajdīd wa-iḥyā-yi dīn*, Lahore: Islamic Publisher Ltd., 1999, 89.

7 Recent scholarship has seen a boom in post-Avicennan studies after Ernest Renan's (d. 1892) infamous thesis that philosophy in the Islamic lands had disappeared after Averroes. However, it is noteworthy that just as Renan's study asserts a false myth concerning the fate of philosophy in the Islamic world after the classical period (ca. 800–1200), some contemporary scholars tend to give the impression that after Averroes (or gradually after al-Ghazālī's famous attack on *falsafa*) Islamic philosophy had *only* continued in Persia. This seems like the beginning of another myth that is flatly contradicted by the facts on the ground, as the studies of many contemporary scholars, such as Robert Wisnovsky, Khaled al-Rouayheb, Saj-

> at this stage of research ... the tradition be gauged in a preliminary fashion from three related angles: socio-intellectual networks of relevant scholars; a tally of the most significant texts; and brief references to prominent debates and to the contribution of certain outstanding personalities.[8]

Thankfully, a series of pioneering articles (and a book) by Asad Ahmed now fills this desideratum in part by providing maps of the most important scholarly networks and the texts that were studied in *madrasas*.[9]

In any event, when scholars narrate the story of Islamic philosophy in India, they usually trace its source and transmission to two Iranian scholars, namely Fatḥ Allāh al-Shīrāzī (d. 997/1589)[10] and Mīrzā Jān Ḥabīb Allāh al-Bāghnawī

---

jad Rizvi, and Asad Ahmed have shown, demonstrating how philosophical activity continued in various Islamic lands such as Egypt, Ottoman Turkey, and Muslim India up to the 20th century. For a wide-ranging critique of the Orientalist view that Islamic intellectual thought was marked by stagnation in the post-classical period, and that *taqlīd* was the order of the day, see the excellent recent study by El-Rouayheb, Khaled, *Islamic intellectual history in the seventeenth century: Scholarly currents in the Ottoman Empire and the Maghreb*, Cambridge: Cambridge University Press, 2015, 173 and 357–358.

8 Ahmed, Asad and Reza Pourjavady, "Islamic theology in India," in Sabine Schmidtke (ed.), *Oxford handbook of Islamic theology*, Oxford: Oxford University Press, 2016, 607.

9 See Ahmed, Asad, *Palimpsests of themselves: Logic and commentary in postclassical Muslim South Asia*, Oakland, CA: University of California Press, 2022; Ahmed, Asad, "The *Mawāqif of* ʿAḍud al-Dīn Ījī in India," in Ayman Shihadeh and Jan Thiele (eds.), *Philosophical Theology in Islam: Later Ashʿarism East and West*, Leiden: Brill, 2020, 397–412; Ahmed, Asad, "The *Sullam al-ʿulūm* of Muḥibballāh al-Bihārī," in Khaled El-Rouayheb and Sabine Schmidtke (eds.), *Oxford handbook of Islamic philosophy*, Oxford: Oxford University Press, 2017; Ahmed, Asad, "Post-classical philosophical commentaries/glosses: Innovation in the margins," in *Oriens* 41.3–4 (2013), 317–348. See also Malik, Jamal, *Islamische Gelehrtenkultur in Nordindien: Entwicklungsgeschichte und Tendenzen am Beispiel von Lucknow*, Leiden: Brill, 1997, 70 ff.

10 Some have identified the significant role of Fatḥ Allāh al-Shīrāzī, a philosopher trained in the school of Shīrāz and a student of Mīr Ghiyāth al-Dīn Dashtakī (d. 949/1542), and an emigrant to the court of Akbar (r. 963–1013/1556–1605). Numerous works, both academic and popular, stress his role as the foremost philosopher and scientist of his time in the Persianate world, and attribute to him a series of important technological innovations and reforms of the administration, including the adoption of Persian as the official language of the Mughal chancellery. He is also regarded as the main conduit for a serious study of philosophy and theology in India, laying the foundations for the *dars-i niẓāmī* method of education, which emphasized the study of the intellectual disciplines (*maʿqūlāt*). For more information, see Ahmed and Pourjavady, "Islamic theology" 612; ʿAlī, Raḥmān, *Tuḥfat al-fuḍalāʾ fī tarājim al-kumalāʾ*, Lucknow: Nawal Kishore, 1914, 160; Bilgrāmī, Sayyid Ghulām, *Maʾāthir-i kirām*, ed. M. Lyallpūrī, Lahore: Maktaba-yi Iḥyāʾ-i ʿUlūm-i Sharqiyya, 1971, 226, 228–229; al-Lakhnawī, *Nuzhat al-khawāṭir* v, 155–156; v, 539–544; Malik, *Islamische*

(d. 995/1587).[11] Both of these scholars originally hailed from Shīrāz and studied with the two foremost philosophers of the city, namely Jalāl al-Dīn al-Dawānī (d. 908/1502) and Ghiyāth al-Dīn al-Dashtakī (d. 949/1542).[12] Bāghnawī and Fatḥ Allāh al-Shīrāzī represent the two rival intellectual lineages and perspectives of al-Dawānī and al-Dashtakī respectively, which became significant in the trajectory of philosophy in India through the mediating role of the all-too-important but the neglected figure of Mīr Zāhid al-Harawī (d. 1101/1689).[13] Al-Harawī, who was appointed as judge of the Mughal army and granted the administrative leadership (*ṣidārat*) of Kabul later in his life, studied with Mullā

Gelehrtenkultur 86–95; Rizvi, Sajjad, "Mīr Dāmād in India: Islamic philosophical traditions and the problem of creation," in *JAOS* 131.1 (2011), 9–23, 9–10.

11 However, one should also note the intrusion of other currents of Islamic philosophy such as Suhrawardī's Illuminationism that has had a long career in India. For instance, both van Lit and Muḥammad Karīmī mention the possible connection between Suhrawardī and Walī Allāh. And Muḥammad Karīmī notes that Walī Allāh mentions the imaginal places of Jābulqā and Jābursā and the imaginal word (*ʿālam al-mithāl*) in various contexts that indicates that he might have been familiar with Suhrawardī's writings. See Zanjānī Aṣl, Muḥammad Karīmī, *Ḥikmat-i ishrāqī dar Hind*, Tehran: Intishārāt-i Iṭṭalāʿāt, 2007, 69–74; van Lit, Lambertus W.C., *The world of image in Islamic philosophy: Ibn Sīnā, Suhrawardī, Shahrazūrī, and beyond*, Edinburgh: Edinburgh University Press, 2017, 166–167. For some pertinent literature on the penetration of the *ishrāqī* philosophy, see the aforementioned Aṣl, *Ḥikmat-i ishrāqī;* van Lit, *World of image;* and Ernst, Carl, "Fayzī's illuminationist interpretation of Vedanta: The *Shāriq al-maʿrifa*," in *Comparative Studies of South Asia, Africa and the Middle East* 30.3 (2010), 356–364. In his article, Ernst argues that the Mogul court poet Fayẓī (954–1003/1547–1595), who composed the *Shāriq al-maʿrifa*, offers an interpretation of Indian philosophy by drawing on the light symbolism of Suhrawardī's Illuminationism.

12 On these two figures, see Kākāʾī, Qāsim, *Ghiyāth al-Dīn Manṣūr Dashtakī wa-falsafa-yi ʿirfān* (with a critical edition of *Manāzil al-sāʾirīn wa-maqāmat al-ʿārifīn*), Tehran: Intishārāt-i Farhangistān-i Hunar, 2007; Kākāʾī, Qāsim, "Āshnāyī bā maktab-i Shīrāz: Mīr Ghiyāth al-Dīn Dashtakī (1)," in *Khiradnāma-yi Ṣadrā* 5–6 (1996–1997), 83–90; Kākāʾī, Qāsim, "Āshnāyī bā maktab-i Shīrāz: Mīr Ghiyāth al-Dīn Dashtakī (2)," in *Khiradnāma-yi Ṣadrā* 7 (1997), 59–67; Kākāʾī, Qāsim, "Āshnāyī bā maktab-i Shīrāz: Ṣadr al-Dīn Dashtakī (Sayyid-i Sanad)," in *Khiradnāma-yi Ṣadrā* 3 (1996–1997), 82–89; Pourjavady, Reza, *Philosophy in early Safavid Iran: Najm al-Dīn Maḥmūd al-Nayrīzī and his writings*, Leiden: Brill, 2011, 1–44.

13 But the importance of Fatḥ Allāh al-Shīrāzī should not be underestimated, since he was the main channel for a serious philosophical undertaking in India. For this reason, historians of Islamic thought in India trace a lineage from Fatḥ Allāh al-Shīrāzī to the scholars of the Farangī Maḥall in the 12th/18th century. See Ahmed and Pourjavady, "Islamic theology" 612. For a detailed presentation of al-Harawī's life and works, see al-Harawī, Mīr Zāhid, *Sharḥ al-risāla al-maʿmūla fī l-taṣawwur wa-l-taṣdīq wa-taʿlīqātuhu*, ed. Mahdī Sharīʿatī, Qom: Maktabat al-Shahīd Sharīʿatī, 2000, 7–69; Khān, ʿAbd al-Salām, *Barr-i ṣaghīr kī ʿulamāʾ-i maʿqūlāt awr un kī taṣnīfāt*, Patna: Khudā Bakhsh Oriental Public Library, 1996, 27–31; Ahmed, "*Mawāqif of* Ījī" 4.

TABLE 17.1 Intellectual Genealogy Connecting Shāh Walī Allāh to the Persian Tradition[14]

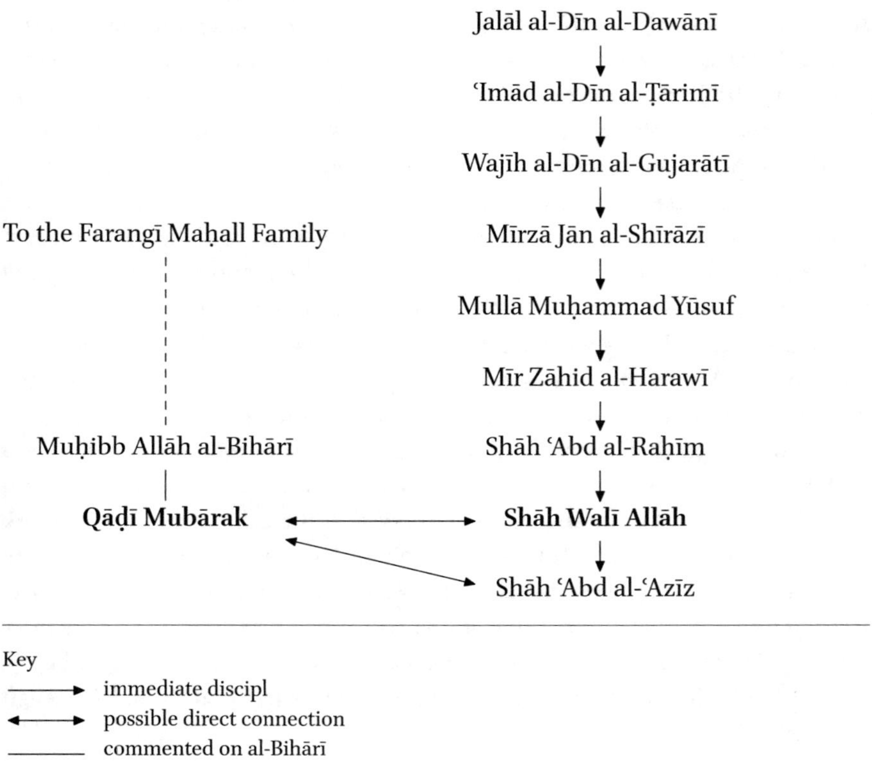

Muḥammad Yūsuf who himself was a student of Bāghnawī.[15] One way to establish the link between Shāh Walī Allāh and the Persian tradition would be to follow the intellectual genealogy of al-Harawī, which includes Walī Allāh's own father, Shāh ʿAbd al-Raḥīm (d. 1131/1719), as he was an immediate disciple of al-Harawī (see Table 17.1 above).

Al-Harawī, the author of a number of important glosses, wrote mainly on theology and philosophy including works such as a gloss on al-Sayyid al-Sharīf al-Jurjānī's commentary on al-Ījī's *Mawāqif*.[16] He also composed a gloss on

14 This table is largely based on the findings of Ahmed, "*Mawāqif of* Ījī" 5–7.

15 Ahmed, "*Mawāqif of* Ījī" 4–8.

16 See al-Harawī, *Sharḥ al-risāla* 28; al-Harawī, Mīr Zāhid, *Ḥawāshī ʿalā fann al-umūr al-ʿāmma min sharḥ al-Mawāqif*, MS Arab SM4154, Houghton Library, Harvard University; al-Khayrābādī, ʿAbd al-Ḥaqq, *Sharḥ ḥāshiyat Mīr Zāhid umūr ʿāmma*, Kanpur: Niẓāmī Press, 1881. For a scholarly treatment of al-Ījī's *Mawāqif*, see Dhanani, Alnoor, "*Al-Mawāqif fī ʿilm al-kalām* by ʿAḍud al-Dīn al-Ījī (d. 1355), and its commentaries," in Khaled El-Rouayheb

Shams al-Dīn al-Iṣfahānī's (d. 749/1348) commentary on *Tajrīd al-iʿtiqād* (*The purification of theology*).[17] In addition, he authored a highly influential commentary on Quṭb al-Dīn al-Taḥtānī's (d. 766/1364) *al-Risāla fī l-taṣawwur wa-l-taṣdīq* (*Treatise on conception and assent*), which generated numerous further glosses in the later tradition.[18] Furthermore, al-Harawī composed a gloss on al-Dawānī's commentary on Suhrawardī's *Hayākil al-nūr* (*The configuration of light*), and penned a commentary on the Quran, among others.[19] In his commentary on *al-Risāla fī l-taṣawwur wa-l-taṣdīq*, al-Harawī engages both with Mīr Dāmād (d. 1040/1631) and Mullā Ṣadrā (d. 1050/1640) and reserves for them honorifics such as *min al-afāḍil* (from the ranks of the virtuous) or *baʿḍ al-afāḍil* (some of the virtuous scholars).[20] This aforementioned commentary, which is a logico-epistemological work, deals with issues such as the difference between conception (*taṣawwur*) and assent (*taṣdīq*), the relation between presential and representational knowledge (*al-ʿilm al-ḥuṣūlī* and *al-ʿilm al-ḥuḍūrī*), God's knowledge of particulars, and relational existence (*al-wujūd al-rābiṭī*)—all of which were also discussed extensively in Ṣadrā's various works.[21] Apart from the Bāghnawī-Harawī intellectual chain (*silsila*), the other scholarly network which might have made Ṣadrā and his school familiar to Walī Allāh was the famous Farangī Maḥall.[22] This is because some of the leading figures of the Farangī Maḥall wrote commentaries on Ṣadrā's *Sharḥ al-hidāya* (*Commentary on the guidance*), and one of the scholars associated with the Farangī Maḥall, namely Qāḍī Mubārak Gūpāmawī (d. 1162/1749) was in Delhi when Walī Allāh was active.[23]

However, before we provide more details on this, it is necessary to say a word about Ṣadrā's influence in India concerning which much ink has been spilled in secondary literature.[24] Probably, the first person who made Mullā Ṣadrā known

---

and Sabine Schmidtke (eds.), *Oxford handbook of Islamic philosophy*, Oxford: Oxford University Press, 2017, 375–396.

17 Al-Harawī, *Sharḥ al-risāla* 30.

18 See al-Harawī, *Sharḥ al-risāla* 41–50. It is to be noted that a gloss on this commentary of al-Harawī by Ghulām Yaḥyā b. Najm al-Dīn al-Bihārī (d. 1180/1766) came to be of great interest for discussions of the nature of God's knowledge.

19 Al-Harawī, *Sharḥ al-risāla* 30.

20 Al-Harawī, *Sharḥ al-risāla* 92, 109, 121, 123, 138, 173, 221, 241, 252, 283, and 287.

21 Al-Harawī, *Sharḥ al-risāla* 91, 200–213.

22 On Farangī Maḥall, see Robinson, Francis, *The ʿulama of Farangi Mahall and Islamic culture in South Asia*, New Delhi: Permanent Black, 2001.

23 For more information on this, see Thubūt, Akbar, *Filsūf-i Shīrāzī dar Hind*, Tehran: Hermis, 2000, 49.

24 On Mullā Ṣadrā in India, see Robinson, *ʿUlama of Farangi Mahall* 14–50, 215–218, 221, 245; Thubūt, *Filsūf-i Shīrāzī*; and Rizvi, "Mīr Dāmād" 449–474.

in India was Maḥmūd Fārūqī Jawnpūrī (d. 1072/1662), who was a student of Mīr Ḍāmād.[25] More importantly, it was Niẓām al-Dīn Sihālawī (d. 1161/1748), the fountainhead of the *dars-i niẓāmī* method of education, who wrote a commentary on Ṣadrā's *Sharḥ al-hidāya*, which was also one of the core texts that was studied and commented upon.[26] In his commentary, Niẓām al-Dīn's opinion about Ṣadrā seems to show a combination of both critical attitude and measured respect. For instance, he takes issue with Ṣadrā's famous doctrine of substantial motion (*al-ḥaraka al-jawhariyya*) and its demonstrations in the *Asfār* and the *Shawāhid* vis-à-vis the latter's *Sharḥ al-hidāya*, arguing that there are discrepancies between these accounts.[27] But in other contexts, he reverentially mentions Ṣadrā's name: "Perhaps about this matter he [i.e., Ṣadrā] possessed unsurpassable knowledge compared to everyone else including this humble man studying his works. His knowledge is like an ocean without shore."[28] He also uses the honorific *baḥr al-ʿulūm* (the ocean of knowledge) for Ṣadrā.[29] Niẓām al-Dīn's son, the celebrated ʿAbd al-ʿAlī Baḥr al-ʿUlūm (d. 1225/1810), also penned a commentary on Ṣadrā. But unlike his father, Baḥr al-ʿUlūm sometimes levels scathing remarks at Ṣadrā that in fact contains innuendoes. For instance, concerning Ṣadrā's theory of substantial motion, Baḥr al-ʿUlūm writes:

> Know that Ṣadrā accepts the occurrence of motion (*ḥaraka*) in substance (*jawhar*), and in his *Asfār* brings evidence to support this, all of which is nothing more than poetry (*shiʿr*) and sophistry (*mughālaṭa*), although he calls them demonstration (*burhān*); it is a waste (*taḍyīʿ*) of time to recount them.[30]

---

25 For bio-bibliographical notes on this figure, see Ahmed, Asad, "al-Jawnpūrī," in *EI*[3] *Online*, http://dx.doi.org.ezp-prod1.hul.harvard.edu/10.1163/1573-3912_ei3_COM_27005 (last accessed: 17 October 2021); Rizvi, "Mīr Dāmād" 17; Bilgrāmī, *Subḥat* ii, 145.

26 See Wisnovsky, Robert, "The nature and scope of Arabic philosophical commentary in post-classical (ca. 1100–1900 AD) Islamic intellectual history: Some preliminary observations," in Peter Adamson, Han Baltussen and Martin W.F. Stone (eds.), *Philosophy, science, and exegesis in Greek, Arabic, and Latin commentaries*, London: Institute of Classical Studies, 2004, 177–178; For a list of its manuscripts, see Thubūt, *Fīlsūf-i Shīrāzī* 44–47.

27 Niẓām al-Dīn, *Sharḥ-i Ṣadrā* (*Sharḥ al-hidāya*), MS, cited in Thubūt, *Fīlsūf-i Shīrāzī* 41.

28 Niẓām al-Dīn, *Sharḥ-i Ṣadrā*, MS, cited in Thubūt, *Fīlsūf-i Shīrāzī* 41.

29 Niẓām al-Dīn, *Sharḥ-i Ṣadrā* (*Sharḥ al-hidāya*), MS, cited in Thubūt, *Fīlsūf-i Shīrāzī* 41.

30 Baḥr al-ʿUlūm, *Sharḥ-i Ṣadrā*, MS, cited in Thubūt, *Fīlsūf-i Shīrāzī* 119 (the translation is mine). Concerning Baḥr al-ʿUlūm's *Sharḥ-i Ṣadrā* and its manuscript locations, see Thubūt, *Fīlsūf-i Shīrāzī* 123–125.

At times Baḥr al-ʿUlūm engages Ṣadrā in a highly technical polemic. For instance, concerning Ṣadrā's ontology and the theory of secondary causation Baḥr al-ʿUlūm says:

> Ṣadrā goes on to state that existent by essence (*mawjūd bi-l-dhāt*) is being (*wujūd*), whereas quiddities, on account of their unity (*ittiḥād*) with being, are existents by accident (*mawjūdāt bi-l-ʿaraḍ*). Moreover, existent by essence accompanied by simple instauration (*jaʿl basīṭ*) is also being, while being itself is the same between what is shared in common (*mā bihi l-ishtirāk*) and what is different (*mā bihi l-imtiyāz*).[31]
>
> We say: This reasoning is devious (*makhdūsh*) because if being itself (*nafs al-wujūd*) is ascribed to something that is instaurated (*majʿūl*), then the instaurer (*jāʿil*) will be its constituent, which, consequently, will raise its rank to the degree of the reality of being (*ḥaqīqat al-wujūd*), while according to Ṣadrā, being is simple (*basīṭ*) and the property of being an instaurer lies outside of it.[32]

Interestingly, although Baḥr al-ʿUlūm disagrees with Ṣadrā on a number of philosophical issues, his views regarding the perfect human (*al-insān al-kāmil*) and God's self-disclosure (*tajallī*) are paradoxically similar to Ṣadrā. Here is a

---

31 Baḥr al-ʿUlūm, *Sharḥ-i Ṣadrā*, MS, cited in Thubūt, *Fīlsūf-i Shīrāzī* 120 (the translation is mine).

32 Baḥr al-ʿUlūm, *Sharḥ-i Ṣadrā*, MS, cited in Thubūt, *Fīlsūf-i Shīrāzī* 120 (the translation is mine). The word *jaʿl*, translated as "instauration," and its derivatives *jāʿil* and *majʿūl* occupy a special place in Ṣadrā's philosophical vocabulary. It signifies putting something into a specific state or condition in conformity with its essential properties. Ṣadrā divides it into two kinds: simple and composite. Simple instauration refers to the construction of something by itself—when we say, for instance, "man is man." In logic, this corresponds to essential primary predication (*al-ḥaml al-dhātī l-awwalī*). As for composite instauration, it refers to cases where the definition of a quiddity involves the convergence of both essential and accidental properties, such as when we say, "Man is a rational animal" and "Man is a writer." For Ṣadrā, what is instaured by itself (*al-majʿūl bi-l-dhāt*) is not essence, but *wujūd*, because *wujūd* does not need an external agent to make it a specific substance, whereas all essences need some cause external to them in order to exist in the external world. In this sense, essences are instaured, or produced "by accident" (*al-majʿūl bi-l-ʿaraḍ*). See al-Shīrāzī, Ṣadr al-Dīn (Mullā Ṣadrā), *al-Ḥikma al-mutaʿāliya fī l-asfār al-ʿaqliyya al-arbaʿa*, ed. Gholamreza Aavani et al., 9 vols., i, Tehran: Bunyād-i Ḥikmat-i Islāmi-yi Ṣadrā, 2001–2005, 65–66; Lāhījī, Mullā Muḥammad Jaʿfar, *Sharḥ al-mashāʿir*, ed. Sayyid Āshtiyānī, ii, Qom: Būstān-i Kitāb, 2007, 805. See also Ṣadrā's extensive analysis in *Asfār* i, 396–423, concerning conception (*taṣawwur*) and assent (*taṣdīq*) as cases of simple and composite instauration.

short example excerpted from Baḥr al-ʿUlūm's commentary on Rūmī's (d. 671/1273) *Mathnawī*:

> *Chūn bi-nālad zāri bī-shikar wa-gila / uftād andar haft gardūn ghulghula*

> As the perfect human laments without complaint
> Commotion stirs in the seven heavens.

> That is, since the perfect human (*insān-i kāmil*) yearns for pure love (*maḥḍ-i ʿishq*), it causes the earth and the sky to be agitated and ebullient. And no one, except the perfected souls, can understand this ebullience (*jūsh*) [of the earth and sky]. The cause of this lament (*nāla*) is that the Pure Self (*dhāt-i baḥt*) is free from any conditioning whatsoever, who, moreover, in His innermost reality (*kunh-i ḥaqīqat*), is beyond any witnessing (*mashhūd namī-shawad*). And one can only witness Him through the disclosure (*tajallī*) of His names that are infinite (*nahāyatī nīst*). Since the lover (*ʿāshiq*), i.e., the perfect human, witnesses the Real (*ḥaqq*) through one of His manifestations, his thirst remains unquenched. So, he fervently wants more of it, and forever remains thirsty of [His Love].[33]

This is strikingly similar to what Ṣadrā says in his *Asfār* regarding the self-disclosure (*tajallī*) and manifestation (*ẓuhūr*) of God's names and qualities and how the perfect human is able to find Him in all of His manifestations.[34] The reason why both of their views converge regarding philosophical Sufism (*ʿirfān*) is that they both draw from Ibn ʿArabī (d. 638/1240) and his school, which can be gleaned from their explicit references to him. Apart from Baḥr al-ʿUlūm, Shāh Walī Allāh's son, Shāh ʿAbd al-ʿAzīz (d. 1239/1824) also wrote a commentary on Ṣadrā's *Sharḥ al-hidāya* (*Commentary on the guidance*), which is occasionally polemical. For example, regarding Ṣadrā's definition of "philosophy," Shāh ʿAbd al-ʿAzīz quips that the former misconstrues the meaning of the word *falsafa*, which is of Greek origin and means "love of wisdom." But according to ʿAbd al-ʿAzīz, since Ṣadrā was not familiar with Greek, he explains its meaning as "becoming similar to God."[35] Nevertheless, in his *Tuḥfa-yi ithnā ʿashariyya* (*Gift*

33 Baḥr al-ʿUlūm, *Mathnawī-yi Mawlawī bā ḥāshiya-yi chandīn muḥashshī az jumla-yi ʿAbd al-ʿAlī* i, 135, cited in Thubūt, *Fīlsūf-i Shīrāzī* 125–126 (the translation is mine).

34 Mullā Ṣadrā, *Asfār* ii, 361. Cf. Sabzawārī, Mullā Hādī, *Sharḥ al-asmāʾ al-ḥusnā*, Tehran: Manshūrāt-i Maktabat Baṣīratī, 1989, 518–519.

35 ʿAbd al-ʿAzīz, *Sharḥ-i Ṣadrā* (Deoband) 9, cited in Thubūt, *Fīlsūf-i Shīrāzī* 149. On Shāh ʿAbd

of Twelver Shi'ism), he leans heavily on Ṣadrā's doctrine of "bodily resurrection" (*ma'ād jismānī*) and accepts the latter's distinction between two kinds of bodies. 'Abd al-'Azīz writes:

> In his *Shawāhid al-rubūbiyya*, Ṣadrā Shīrāzī says ... there are two kinds of bodies: the first kind is that which is directly controlled (*taṣarruf bi-lā wāsiṭa*) by the soul, while the second kind is that which is controlled by the soul through another body. This body is not perceived by the senses (*iḥsās*) since the senses only perceive bodies that are their receptacle (*maḥall*) such as skin. ... So this body is called the body of light (*badan nūriyya*) that belongs to the afterlife, and it possesses essential life (*ḥayāt dhātī*) that never extinguishes. ... This body is more spacious compared to [the outward] body that exists here and the spirit (*rūḥ*) which is known as the animal spirit (*al-rūḥ al-ḥayawānī*). This is because all of these [bodies], including [the animal spirit], which is subtler than the first, belong to this world; hence they are susceptible to change and will eventually perish. So, these bodies will not have resurrection (*ḥashr*). What we are discussing here pertains to the body of the afterlife, which will be resurrected along the soul (*nafs*). This [body] is entwined with the soul, and subsists with the latter's [i.e., the soul] subsistence (*baqā'*).[36]

Apart from *Sharḥ al-hidāya* commentaries, some Indian scholars also engage with or respond to Ṣadra in their other works. Muḥibb Allāh Bihārī (d. 1119/1707), the author of the famous *Sullam al-'ulūm* (*The ladder of the sciences*) on which more than hundred commentaries have been written, mentions Ṣadrā in relation to some topics in Logic (*manṭiq*).[37] Bihārī's commentator, Qāḍī Mubārak Gūpāmawī, who was known to Shāh Walī Allāh, had a great respect for Ṣadrā's mentor Mīr Dāmād. According to 'Abd al-Ḥayy b. 'Abd al-Ḥalīm Lakhnawī (d. 1304/1886), Qāḍī Mubārak was a follower of Mīr Dāmād throughout

---

al-'Azīz b. Shāh Walī Allāh, see Rizvi, Sajjad A.A., *Shāh 'Abd al-'Azīz: Puritanism, sectarian polemics and jihad*, Canberra: Ma'rifat Publishing House, 1982, 103–173; Khān, *Barr-i ṣaghīr* 47; al-Lakhnawī, *Nuzhat al-khawāṭir* vii, 297.

36 'Abd al-'Azīz, *Tuḥfa-yi ithnā 'ashariyya* 239, cited in Thubūt, *Fīlsūf-i Shīrāzī* 163–164 (the translation is mine).

37 Mubārak, Qāḍī, *Kitāb Sullam al-'ulūm wa-ḥāshiyatihi l-mashhūra bi-l-Qāḍī ma'a munhiyātihi*, Kazan: al-Maṭba'a al-Malakiyya, 1887, 281. The *Sullam* was a culmination of engagements with such concerns that had exercised earlier logicians writing in the Islamic tradition. What distinguishes it from earlier textbooks is that paradoxes that emerge from the possibility of a broader range of conceptualized subject terms are a characteristic feature of the work. For further notes on the *Sullam*, see Ahmed, "*Sullam al-'ulūm*" 488–508.

his life.[38] This is partly evidenced in his commentary on the *Sullam*, which incorporates elements from Dāmād's *Ufuq al-mubīn* (*Clear horizons*) concerning God's knowledge of particulars. Qāḍī Mubārak reserves such glorious titles for Mīr Dāmād as *al-sayyid al-bāqir*, and *al-muʿallim al-awwal li-l-ḥikma al-yamāniyya*.[39] He also refers to Ṣadrā's *Asfār* in the commentary, e.g., "This is what Mīr Dāmad verified in some of his writings and his student followed suit in his *Asfār*."[40] The commentary of Qāḍī Mubārak on the *Sullam* along with his self-commentary (entitled *al-Munhiyāt*) contains discussions on logic and epistemology that one also finds in Ṣadrā's various works. Among some of the notable topics one can mention the famous distinction between presential and representational knowledge,[41] self-knowledge, knowledge of God, and, most of all, Ṣadrā's famous doctrine of the identity of the subject of intellect and the intelligible (*ittiḥād al-ʿāqil wa-l-maʿqūl*). The following text shows Qāḍī Mubārak's views concerning the doctrine of the identity of the intellect and what is intellected:

> So inevitably, He manifests Himself in His Essence, so He is the intellect, the subject of intellect, and the intelligible [all at once] ...; a thing which is sanctified from matter, when it exists by itself, is the intellect, the subject of intellect, and the intelligible (*fa-l-shayʾ al-muqaddas ʿan al-mādda idhā kāna mawjūd*^{an} *bi-nafsihi kāna ʿaql*^{an} *wa-ʿāqil*^{an} *wa-maʿqūl*^{an}).[42]

Apart from Qāḍī Mubārak, there were others who either dealt with Ṣadrā (e.g., ʿAbd al-Ḥayy or Barakāt Aḥmad Ṭūkī, d. 1347/1929) or took into account his *Sharḥ al-hidāya* while discussing topics in natural philosophy (*ṭabīʿiyyāt*) such

38 Lakhnawī, *Miṣbāḥ al-Dijī* 224–225, cited in Thubūt, *Fīlsūf-i Shīrāzī* 50.

39 See Mubārak, *Kitāb Sullam al-ʿulūm* 2, 25, 54, 83, 93–94, 100, 104–105, 125–126, 134, 157. Cf. Thubūt, *Fīlsūf-i Shīrāzī* 50.

40 Mubārak, *Kitāb Sullam al-ʿulūm* 214.

41 However, it should be noted that unlike Ṣadrā, Qāḍī Mubārak places the *ḥudūrī-ḥuṣūlī* distinction under the category of "knowledge by means of essence" (*al-ʿilm bi-kunhihi*), which itself is a counterpart of "knowledge of essence" (*al-ʿilm bi-l-kunh*). As Ahmed rightly notes, the distinction between *bi-l-kunh* and *bi-kunhihi* is specific to the Indian philosophical and logical traditions, since in other contexts these two expressions appear to have the same meaning. The distinction between *bi-l-kunh* and *bi-kunhihi* is introduced in the discussion of human ability to know God. Mubārak asserts that both knowledge of God's Essence and knowledge by means of His Essence are unattainable for humans. However, such a distinction, in turn, leads to the aporia of how knowledge of extramental entities is possible at all, which generated a great deal of discussion in the subsequent tradition. For a sophisticated treatment of this issue, see Ahmed, "Post-classical" 328–329.

42 Mubārak, *Kitāb Sullam al-ʿulūm* 8 (the translation is mine).

as motion or space (e.g., Faḍl-i Ḥaqq al-Khayrābādī, d. 1277/1861).[43] One significant but understudied early 20th-century work that draws on Ṣadrā's works is Barakāt Aḥmad's massive *al-Ḥujja al-bāzigha* (*The shining argument*).[44] A contemporary of Iqbal, Barakāt Aḥmad studied *Sharḥ al-hidāya* with ʿAbd al-Ḥaqq al-Khayrābādī, and in turn, taught this work along with Ṣadrā's *Asfār*.[45] In his magnum opus *al-Ḥujja al-bāzigha*, Barakāt Aḥmad explains various Sadrian doctrines from Ṣadrā's *Asfār*, commentary of the *Shifāʾ*, *Sharḥ al-hidāya*, and his glosses on *Sharh ḥikmat al-ishrāq* of Quṭb al-Dīn al-Shīrāzī (d. 710/1311).[46] He often acts as an adjudicator between Ṣadrā and his opponents such as Āqā Ḥusayn Khwānsārī (d. 1099/1688), Baḥr al-ʿUlūm, and ʿAbd al-Ḥaqq Khayrābādī (d. 1318/1900).[47] Although he follows Khwānsārī in referring to Ṣadrā as *al-fāḍil al-Ṣadr al-Shīrāzī*, or *al-fāḍil Ṣadr al-afāḍil*, at times he uses abrasive language to express his disagreement with Ṣadrā.[48] In any event, he also chooses to defend Ṣadrā regarding the latter's theory of substantial motion against other philosophers by affirming motion in substance. For example, he says, "In contrast to what others have said, there is motion in substance (*jawhar*)."[49]

More can be said of Ṣadrā's influence in India, e.g., Akbar Thubūt's informative study lists seventy independent and more than twenty indirect commentaries and glosses on *Sharḥ al-hidāya*.[50] He also provides manuscript sources

43 See, e.g., Ahmed, Asad and Jon McGinnis, "Faḍl-i Ḥaqq Khayrābādī's (d. 1861), *al-Hadiyya al-saʿīdiyya*," in Khaled El-Rouayheb and Sabine Schmidtke (eds.), *Oxford handbook of Islamic philosophy*, Oxford: Oxford University Press, 2017, 546.

44 See Aḥmad, Barakāt, *al-Ḥujja al-bāzigha fī sharḥ al-ḥikmat al-bāligha*, lithographed ed., Decan: ʿUthmān Baryasī, 1916. See also Aḥmad, Barakāt, *Imām al-kalām fī taḥqīq ḥaqīqat al-ajsām*, lithographed ed., Kanpur: al-Maṭbaʿ al-Anẓāmī, 1915; Aḥmad, Barakāt, *Itqān al-ʿirfān fī taḥqīq māhiyyat al-zamān*, lithographed ed., Lucknow: Shāhī Pirīs, 1919.

45 Khān, *Barr-i ṣaghīr* 67–69.

46 Aḥmad, *al-Ḥujja al-bāzigha* 15–31, 34–38, 42–46, 59–63, 87–91, 96–100, 192–195, and 250–253.

47 Aḥmad, *al-Ḥujja al-bāzigha* 18, 20, 97, 250. On Khwānsārī's opposition to Sadrian philosophy that seems to have had an influence in India, see Moazzen, Maryam, *Formation of a religious landscape: Shiʿi higher learning in Safavid Iran*, Leiden: Brill, 2018, 141–144, 222.

48 Aḥmad, *al-Ḥujja al-bāzigha* 18, 20, 97, 322.

49 Aḥmad, *al-Ḥujja al-bāzigha* 287.

50 Thubūt, *Fīlsūf-i Shīrāzī* 4. Some of the notable commentators of Ṣadrā are as follows: Ḥamdallāh b. Shākir Allāh al-Sandīlwī (d. 1160/1747), Muḥammad Amjad al-Qannūjī (ca. 1112/1718), Muḥammad Ḥasan b. Ghulām Muṣṭafā al-Sihālawī, Sayyid Dildār ʿAlī Naqwī Naṣīrābādī (d. 1235/1820), ʿImād al-Dīn al-ʿUthmānī al-Labkanī (ca. 13th/19th century), Turāb al-ʿAlī b. Shajāʿat ʿAlī al-Lakhnawī (d. 1281/1864), Muḥammad Aʿlam b. al-Sandīlwī, Muḥammad ʿAẓmat Kifāyatallāh al-Fārūqī Gūpamawī, and ʿAbd al-Ḥaqq al-Khayrābādī.

for most of these commentaries and glosses.[51] On the whole, given the state of current research, I would like to make a few brief comments about the penetration of Ṣadrā's philosophy among Indian scholars. First of all, I think that one needs to be careful in using the word "influence," since it can be notoriously vague in some contexts. For instance, if one claims that Ṣadrā was influential in India, does it mean he was as influential as, for instance, Ibn ʿArabī? That is to say, the question of "influence" is a relative one. Moreover, if one claims that Ṣadrā was influential in India, does this also mean his writings had a "positive" influence on Indian scholars? This is crucial to note because if the influence of a philosopher is mostly "negative," it might simply be that his ideas did not gain much traction among the groups concerned, which in turn might suggest that others who engaged him did so mostly to refute his ideas or curb his influence in which case it may not properly be called "influence." To be precise, the purpose of this survey is not to determine Ṣadrā's overall influence in India (positive or negative), since this would require a project of its own. But since one of my aims is to gauge how or whether at all Ṣadrā's philosophy played a role in Walī Allāh's thought, especially because there is much in secondary scholarship that tends to inflate Ṣadrā's influence, it is necessary to say a few words concerning how one should understand his influence in India. So, to come back to the issue of "influence" being relative, it may be useful to compare Ṣadrā with Ibn ʿArabī, since we know much more about the latter's reception in India.[52] All the evidence so far suggests that Ibn ʿArabī was far more influential than Ṣadrā in India, so much so that even scholars who are usually cast as philosophers/theologians such as Baḥr al-ʿUlūm, explicitly

51 Thubūt, *Fīlsūf-i Shīrāzī, passim.*

52 See, inter alia, Chittick, William C., "Notes on Ibn al-ʿArabī's influence in the Subcontinent," in *MW* 82.3–4 (1992), 18–41; Chittick, William C., "*Waḥdat al-wujūd* in India," in *Ishraq: Islamic Philosophy Yearbook* 3 (2012), 29–40; Rizvi, Sayyid A.A., *A history of Sufism in India*, New Delhi: Munshiram Manoharlal, 1978–1983 Knysh, Alexander, *Ibn ʿArabi in the later Islamic tradition: The making of a polemical image in medieval Islam*, Albany, NY: SUNY Press, 1999, 271–278; Lipton, Gregory, "Muḥibb Allāh Ilāhābādī: South Asian heir to Ibn ʿArabī," in *Journal of the Muhyiddin Ibn ʿArabi Society* 45 (2009), 89–119, Faruque, Muhammad U., "Sufism *contra* shariah? Shāh Walī Allāh's metaphysics of *waḥdat al-wujūd*," in *Journal of Sufi Studies* 5.1 (2016), 27–57; Faruque, Muhammad U., "Eternity made temporal: Ashraf ʿAlī Thānavī, a twentieth-century Indian thinker and the revival of classical Sufi thought," in *Brill Journal of Sufi Studies* 9.2 (2020), 215–246; Nair, Shankar, "Muḥibb Allāh Ilāhābādī on ontology: Debates over the nature of being," in Jonardon Ganeri (ed.), *The Oxford handbook of Indian philosophy*, Oxford: Oxford University Press, 2017, 657–692; Nair, Shankar, *Translating wisdom: Hindu-Muslim intellectual interactions in early modern South Asia*, Oakland, CA: University of California Press, 2020, chapter 4.

acknowledge their debt to Ibn ʿArabī, whereas in the case of Ṣadrā it is usually in the context of a specific philosophical debate that such scholars would feel obliged to respond.[53] Moreover, in contrast to Ibn ʿArabī whose influence was usually "positive,"[54] Mullā Ṣadrā's thought had generated a mixed result. Nonetheless, the fact that some of the influential Indian philosophers such as Muḥibb Allāh Bihārī, Qāḍī Mubārak, Muḥammad Ḥasan al-Sihālawī (d. 1199 or 1209/1784 or 1794), Baḥr al-ʿUlūm, Shāh ʿAbd al-ʿAzīz, and ʿAbd al-Ḥayy Lakhnawī mentioned or discussed him in various capacities shows that Ṣadrā's name was well-known, along with his mentor Mīr Dāmād. Moreover, Ṣadrā's main works such as the *Asfār* (*Four journeys*), the *Shawāhid* (*The witnesses*), *Mafātīḥ al-ghayb* (*Keys to the unseen*), commentary on the *Shifāʾ* (*The healing*), and many other treatises were available in various Indian libraries including but not limited to Rampur Raza Library, Khudābakhsh Library (Bankipore), Asiatic Society (Kolkata) Calcutta Madrasa Collection, Mawlānā Āzād Library Aligarh, and Dār al-ʿUlūm Deoband Library.[55]

Given our analysis above, it is perhaps not a great surprise that Shāh Walī Allāh does not mention Ṣadrā in his works, although he must have been familiar with his name. However, there may be a number of reasons for this. First, although Walī Allāh was thoroughly familiar with the technical vocabulary of the philosophers and the physicians, whose terminologies he employs throughout his oeuvre, he refrained from identifying himself as a philosopher or a theologian, as he primarily saw himself as a Sufi metaphysician and did not shy away from expressing where his intellectual and spiritual sympathies lie.[56] Moreover, he hardly mentions any philosopher by name; instead he uses the generic *falāsifa* or *ḥukamāʾ* when referring to the philosophers. Furthermore,

---

53 Dahnhardt, Thomas W., "The doctrine of the unicity of existence in the light of an eighteenth century Indian Ṣūfī treatise: The *Waḥdat al-wujūd* by Baḥr al-ʿUlūm ʿAbd al-ʿAlī Ansārī al-Lakhnawī," in *Oriente Moderno* 92.2 (2012), 323–360.

54 On Sirhindī's views on *waḥdat al-wujūd*, see Friedmann, Yohanan, *Shaikh Ahmad Sirhindi: An outline of his thought and a study of his image in the eyes of posterity*, Montreal: McGill University Press, 1971, 59–67; Sirhindī, Aḥmad, "Maktūbāt Imām Rabbānī," in Arthur Buehler (trans.), *Revealed grace: The juristic Sufism of Ahmad Sirhindi*, Louisville, KY: Fons Vitae, 2011, 106 and 125. It is true that more recent scholarship on Shaykh Aḥmad Sirhindī appears to have tackled such views as evidenced in Buehler, Arthur, "Ahmad Sirhindi: A 21st-century update," in *Der Islam* 86.1 (2009), 122–141 and Damrel, David, "The 'Naqshbandi Reaction' reconsidered," in David Gilmartin and Bruce Lawrence (eds.), *Beyond Turk and Hindu*, Florida: University Press of Florida, 2000, 176–198.

55 See, e.g., Ẓafir al-Dīn, Muḥammad, *Taʿāruf-i makhṭūṭāt Kitābkhāna-yi Dār al-ʿUlūm Deoband*, ii, Deoband: Dār al-ʿUlūm, 1973, 138.

56 See, e.g., Allāh, Shāh Walī, *Alṭāf al-quds*, Gujranwala: Madrasa Nuṣrat al-ʿUlūm, 1964, 133.

he is at times highly critical of the philosophers, and this might explain in part why his son, who was influenced by him, also engages in a polemic against Ṣadrā.

2 A Note on the Texts Used

A word needs to be said concerning the texts I will be using in my analysis of Walī Allāh's theory of the self. The main texts that I will be using in my analysis are *Alṭāf al-quds fī maʿrifat laṭāʾif al-nafs* (written in Persian), *al-Tafhīmāt al-ilāhiyya* (*Divine understandings*), and *al-Budūr al-bāzigha* (*Resplendent full moon*). In addition, I will be drawing upon other texts such as *Ḥujjat Allāh al-bāligha* (*The conclusive argument from God*), *al-Khayr al-kathīr* (*Blessings*), etc. My purpose is to provide a comprehensive account of the self in Walī Allāh's various writings. However, it should be noted that among these treatises some e.g., *Alṭāf al-quds* (*The sacred subtleties*) belong to what we might call Walī Allāh's middle period (i.e., 1735–1745), while others e.g. *al-Tafhīmāt al-ilāhiyya* and *al-Budūr al-bāzigha* are late works, or, in the case of the *Tafhīmāt*, a late compilation (with revision) of earlier treatises.[57] So, I take into account the developments in Walī Allāh's conception of the *laṭāʾif* that one observes between his middle and late period. The advantage of reading Walī Allāh's earlier and later works simultaneously allows one to be cognizant of the developments that one observes in his writings. But this does not mean one would encounter two radically different pictures of the self between *Alṭāf al-quds* and the *Tafhīmāt*. So, it remains the case that *Alṭāf al-quds* is Walī Allāh's most sustained and most sophisticated treatment of the *laṭāʾif* among his corpus. Hence a considerable portion of our analysis is based on this treatise. We also frequently refer to other works either to compare or point out revision concerning a particular issue.

2.1 *Previous Scholarship on the Subtle Bodies*

With the above historical backdrop in place, let me now turn to the treatment of the *laṭāʾif* in Walī Allāh's scholarship. First, it should be noted that although aspects of Walī Allāh's psychology (i.e., the *laṭāʾif*) have been analyzed, his theory of selfhood based on the *laṭāʾif* has never received any sustained scholarly treatment. This is despite the fact that the self has been central to his overall

57 For an extensive chronology of Walī Allāh's works, see Baljon, *Religion* 10–14 and Allāh, Shāh Walī, *al-Tafhīmāt al-ilāhiyya*, i, Hyderabad and Sindh: Shāh Walī Allāh Academy, 1967, 15–38.

metaphysics. In particular, existing scholarship has ignored Walī Allāh's conception of self-knowledge and first-person subjectivity, which the latter analyzes through "presential knowledge" (*al-ʿilm al-ḥuḍūrī*), showing his debt to the Islamic philosophers.[58] One reason why scholars have generally neglected selfhood in Walī Allāh's thought is that the self is often taken to be synonymous with the concept of "soul" or as a constellation of various *laṭāʾif*, rather than as a multidimensional entity.[59] Both Baljon's and Hermansen's treatment of Walī Allāh's psychology suffer from such a conceptual stumbling-block.[60]

In his rather dated study on Walī Allāh's religious thought, Baljon mistakenly suggests that the *laṭāʾif* are composed of *pneuma* (*nasama*), rational soul (*nafs nāṭiqa*), and celestial spirit (*rūḥ-i samāwī*).[61] He also leaves it unexplained how the *laṭāʾif* and *nasama* are symbiotically connected. In addition, his study suffers from a number of translation errors.[62] Nevertheless, Baljon correctly identifies that the *laṭāʾif* represent the inner progress of the wayfarer (*sālik*) from the outermost plane of his self to its inmost core.[63] Hermansen improves on Baljon's study of Walī Allāh's theory of the *laṭāʾif* by providing a better historical context and a conceptual frame to understand them as a sort of subtle body.[64] She correctly explains that although some of the *laṭāʾif* have names

58 For an extensive treatment of Walī Allāh's views on self-knowledge and first-person subjectivity, see Faruque, Muhammad U., *Sculpting the self: Islam, selfhood, and human flourishing*, Ann Arbor: The University of Michigan Press, 2021, 80–84.

59 See Faruque, *Sculpting* 49–56.

60 Baljon, *Religion*; Hermansen, Marcia K., "Shāh Walī Allāh's theory of the subtle spiritual centers (*laṭāʾif*): A Sufi theory of personhood and self-transformation," in *JNES* 47.1 (1988), 1–25.

61 Baljon, *Religion* 64–66.

62 Baljon, *Religion* 68, 71, 73–74. For instance, he renders *ḥusn al-ẓann* as "think well of God," which should be "having a positive opinion of somebody/something;" *kashf* as "mystical revelation," which should be "unveiling;" *tajallī* as "radiance," which should be "manifestation/self-disclosure;" *warāʿ as* "abstemiousness," which should be "heightened piety;" and so on.

63 Baljon, *Religion* 67.

64 Hermansen, "Shāh Walī Allāh's theory" 2. Shāh Walī Allāh goes further than his predecessors in presenting sacred history as the realization or even expansion of potentials inherent in the *laṭāʾif*. In this he correlates the development of the *laṭāʾif* with phases of progress in human spiritual history. In his *Tafhīmāt*, Walī Allāh offers a novel suggestion concerning the *laṭāʾif* by explaining that they have a macrocosmic historical manifestation. So, the development of the *laṭāʾif* began with Adam when there were three *laṭāʾif*: the heart (*qalb*), the intellect (*ʿaql*) and the *nafs*. In Prophet Muhammad's time, the higher *laṭāʾif* of the spirit (*rūḥ*) and secret (*sirr*) were awakened in the ideal human form. At the time of Ibn ʿArabī the potential of the arcanum was available to the human species. Finally, Walī Allāh was chosen by God to reveal two additional *laṭāʾif*, namely the philosopher's stone (*ḥajar-i baḥt*) and selfhood (*anāniyya*). See Hermansen, "Shāh Walī Allāh's theory"

corresponding to body parts or faculties or are sometimes described as being located in specific areas of the body (liver, heart, or brain), they are not to be understood as identical with the organs located there. Rather, the *laṭāʾif* should be understood as local manifestations of identically named parts of a higher realm of the cosmological universe that stands vertically above the physical world.[65] I also agree with her translation of the term *nasama* as *pneuma*, since it refers to the spirit formed from the most subtle humors and is related to the term *pneuma* in the Greek medical tradition. Moreover, she agrees with Baljon in describing the *laṭāʾif* as a paradigm for facilitating the wayfarer's spiritual progress from the physical realm to the higher spiritual realms.[66]

Despite these merits, her study is compromised by a number of serious shortcomings. To begin with, her account of Walī Allāh's description of the *laṭāʾif* is largely interpreted through the Mujaddidī paradigm, which has its own elaborate theory of the *laṭāʾif*.[67] As a result, she asserts that the function of *nasama* or *pneuma* is limited to the lowest set of the *laṭāʾif*, namely *nafs*.[68] As will be seen, this is contradicted by the textual evidence I have presented in this study. One reason why the proper relation between *nasama* and the *laṭāʾif* is not well understood in her study is that like Baljon, her analysis fails to account for the development of these concepts from Walī Allāh's middle-period treatise *Alṭāf al-quds* to his late works such as *al-Budūr al-bāzigha*. More importantly, her argument that through an account of *nasama* as a subtle body Walī Allāh was able to reconcile the theological conception of the spirit (*rūḥ*) as something material and created in time with the philosophical notion that

24. The *ḥajar-i baḥt* was also mentioned by Ibn ʿArabī as an essential point in the heart emanating a marvelous and perplexing light. See Nyberg (ed.), *Kleinere Schriften* 216–217, cited in Hermansen, "Shāh Walī Allāh's theory" 15.

65 Hermansen, "Shāh Walī Allāh's theory" 2. So far *laṭīfa* has been variously translated as "subtlety," "tenuous body," "subtle point," "subtle essence," "subtle field," "subtle substance," "subtle entity," "subtle organ," and "subtle spiritual center." For a critical evaluation of some of these translations, see Buehler, Arthur, *Sufi heirs of the prophet: The Indian Naqshbandiyya and the rise of the mediating Sufi Shaykh*, Columbia, SC: University of South Carolina Press, 1998, 103. The term *laṭīfa* is derived from the Arabic word *laṭīf* meaning "gentle," "sensitive," or "subtle." In Sufi literature, the word *laṭīfa* refers to a nonphysical component of the person which can be awakened through spiritual practices. The expression *laṭīfa* may originate in the concept of a subtle body (*jism laṭīf*), which is not Quranic but seems to have arisen in the third Islamic century. The Sufi concept of *laṭīfa* became increasingly refined and complex and was used to explain psychological and spiritual progress of the spiritual aspirant toward annihilation (*fanāʾ*) or subsistence (*baqāʾ*) in the Divine Essence. See Hermansen, "Shāh Walī Allāh's theory" 1–2.

66 Hermansen, "Shāh Walī Allāh's theory" 6.

67 Buehler, *Sufi heirs* 105–130.

68 Hermansen, "Shāh Walī Allāh's theory" 11.

considered it an immaterial, eternal, spiritual soul, is unfortunately incorrect.[69] This is because Walī Allāh proves the immateriality of the self through first-person experiences, as I have explained elsewhere.[70] Moreover, philosophers consider the self (*nafs*) to be immaterial, while their views on the spirit (*rūḥ*) are variegated.[71] Furthermore, unlike Hermansen's account, Walī Allāh in fact claims that *pneuma* acts as a mediator between the immaterial soul and the material body.[72]

In any event, Walī Allāh's own conception of the *laṭāʾif* presumes that they can only be known through *dhawq*, and not through the senses.[73] Moreover, in his view, the knowledge of the *laṭāʾif* or subtle fields of consciousness is a great scale of balance (*mīzānī ast ʿaẓīm*) that God has bestowed on later day Sufis (*mutaʾakhkhirān-i ṣūfiyya*). So, the better one is acquainted with the subtle fields of consciousness, the better one is able to purify them.[74] To illustrate the difference between someone who possesses the knowledge of the *laṭāʾif* and those people who may have devoted their whole life to Sufism without ever gaining this knowledge, Walī Allāh likens the former to the physician (*ṭabīb*) who is skilled in the diagnosis of various types of illnesses, who knows their causes (*asbāb*), symptoms (*ʿalāmāt*), methods of their treatment (*muʿālajāt*), and all the rules which ancient physicians developed through long, protracted experience, and the latter to someone who is like an unqualified physician who can merely prescribe some medicine on the strength of his own defective experience and incomplete understanding. He further adds that whoever is acquainted with the *laṭāʾif* is like a leader (*rahbar*) who has spent a lifetime wandering in the wilderness and has learnt each hill and dale, each path across it, whether it be well-worn or as yet untrodden.[75] After mentioning that the

69 Hermansen says: "By explaining the spirit in this three-tiered way, Shāh Walī Allāh is able to reconcile traditional theological opinions with the concepts of the philosophers influenced by Hellenistic thought concerning the spirit (*rūḥ*). The orthodox position was generally that it was material and created in time, while the philosophers identified it with an immaterial, eternal, spiritual soul. In his description of the three levels, the lowest level of spirit, the *Pneuma*, fulfills the role of the created spirit while aspects of the rational soul and the heavenly spirit accord with the philosophers' concepts." See Hermansen, "Shāh Walī Allāh's theory" 10–11.

70 See Faruque, *Sculpting* 81–83.

71 See Faruque, Muhammad U., *The labyrinth of subjectivity: Constructions of the self from Mullā Ṣadrā to Muhammad Iqbal*, Berkeley, CA (unpublished PhD Diss.): University of California, 2018, 59–76.

72 Faruque, *Labyrinth* 156–163.

73 Faruque, *Labyrinth* 138–143.

74 Walī Allāh, *Alṭāf al-quds* 14–15.

75 Walī Allāh, *Alṭāf al-quds* 15.

exposition of the true nature and properties of the *laṭāʾif* depends in turn on an understanding of the true nature of the self (*ḥaqīqat-i rūḥ*),[76] he expresses hesitation as to whether or not he should really talk about them.[77] But he eventually decides to disclose the secrets of the *laṭāʾif* due to the particular circumstances of his day. Also, according to Walī Allāh, "the science of the *laṭāʾif* is based on the [question of the real nature of the self], so a real necessity arises, and, as is well known, necessity can render lawful that which would otherwise be unlawful (*al-ḍarūra tabīḥ al-maḥdhūrāt*)."[78]

3 The Vocabulary of the *laṭāʾif*

Given that Walī Allāḥ's conception of the self is based on a robust theory of the five microcosmic *laṭāʾif*, viz., *nafs, rūḥ, qalb, ʿaql,* and *sirr,* and other macrocosmic *laṭāʾif* such as *khāfī* and *akhfā,* it would be useful to lay out how he defines these terms before moving on to the core of his theory of the self. Walī Allāh begins by stating that there is a lot of loose talk in Sufi discourse concerning these terms.[79] It is instructive to note that the inconsistent use of these terms, namely *nafs*, *qalb*, *rūḥ*, and *ʿaql* in the Sufi tradition was observed by al-Ghazālī (d. 505/1111) nearly seven hundred years before Walī Allāh when the former was writing his *Iḥyāʾ ʿulūm al-dīn* (*Revival of the religious sciences*), with which Walī Allāh was intimately familiar.[80] Before delving into Walī Allāh's demystification of these terms, I would like to show what al-Ghazālī says about this. Al-Ghazālī writes:

> But few of the leading scholars have a comprehensive knowledge of these terms (i.e., *nafs*, *rūḥ*, *qalb* and *ʿaql*) and their different meanings. … Most of the mistakes regarding them originate in ignorance of the meaning of these names, and of the way in which they are applied to different objects. … One of these is the term heart (*qalb*), and it is used with two meanings. One of them is the cone-shaped organ of flesh that is located at the left side of the chest. It is a particular sort of flesh within which there is a cavity, and in this cavity there is black blood that is the source and seat of the spirit (*rūḥ*). … Whenever we use the term heart in this book, we do

76 Inconsistent use of *rūḥ* but it means "self" here.
77 Walī Allāh, *Alṭāf al-quds* 22.
78 Walī Allāh, *Alṭāf al-quds* 23.
79 Walī Allāh, *Alṭāf al-quds* 74.
80 For a brief history of the *laṭāʾif*, see Faruque, *Sculpting* 174ff.

not mean this sort of heart. … The second meaning of the heart is a "spiritual lordly *laṭīfa*" (*laṭīfa rabbāniyya rūḥāniyya*), which is connected with the physical heart. This *laṭīfa* is the real essence of human. This heart is the part of the human being that perceives, knows and experiences; it is addressed, punished, rebuked, and held responsible, and it has some connection with the physical heart. … Whenever we use the term heart in this book, we mean by it this *laṭīfa*. … The second term is spirit (*rūḥ*), and it is also used with two meanings relevant to our purpose. One of these meanings refers to a subtle body (*jism laṭīf*) whose source is the cavity of the physical heart, and which spreads by means of the pulsative arteries to all the other parts of the body. … Whenever physicians use the term spirit (*rūḥ*) they have in mind this meaning, which is a subtle vapor (*bukhār laṭīf*) produced by the heat of the heart … The second meaning of [*rūḥ*] is that *laṭīfa* in human which knows and perceives, which we have already explained in one of the meanings of the heart. It is the meaning intended by God, the Exalted, in His statement, "Say: the spirit is my Lord's affair" (17:85) … The third term *nafs* (soul/self), partakes of many meanings, two of which pertain to our purpose. By one is denoted that meaning which includes both the faculty of anger (*ghaḍab*) and of appetence (*shahwa*) in human, which we will explain later. This meaning is prevalent among the Sufis (*ahl al-taṣawwuf*), for they mean by *nafs* that principle in human which includes his blameworthy characters (*ṣifāṭ madhmūma*). … The second meaning is that *laṭīfa* which we have mentioned, which is the real human nature (*ḥaqīqat al-insān*). It is the essence of the human and his self (*hiya nafs al-insān wa-dhātuhu*). But it is described by different descriptions according to its different states. … But the *nafs* according to the second definition is praiseworthy, for it is the human's very self or his essence and real nature, which knows God, the Exalted, and all other knowable things. The fourth term, which is intellect (*ʿaql*), also partakes of various meanings that we have mentioned in the *Book of knowledge*. Of these, two are relevant to our purpose. Intellect may be used with the force of knowledge of real nature of things, and is thus an expression for the quality of knowledge whose seat is the heart. Second, intellect may be used to denote that which perceives knowledge, or the heart in the sense of the *laṭīfa*. … So intellect may be used as meaning the quality of the knower, and it may be used to mean the seat of perception, the mind which perceives. So it is now made clear that to you that there exist the following meanings of these terms: the corporeal heart, the corporeal spirit, the appetitive soul, and noetics (*al-ʿulūm*). These are four meanings that are denoted by four terms. There is also a fifth meaning, which pertains to

> the abovementioned *laṭīfa* in the human that knows and perceives, and all four of these names are successively applied to it.[81] There are then five meanings and four terms, and each term is used with two meanings.[82]

Little remains to be said after such a lucid account. As we shall soon see, Walī Allāh draws significantly from al-Ghazālī's *Iḥyā'* regarding the meanings of the four abovementioned terms, but at the same time, unlike al-Ghazālī, he provides a consistent physical basis for the theory of selfhood through an account of *nasama* (*pneuma*) and the *laṭā'if*. In any event, after acknowledging that words such as *nafs* and *rūḥ* are used in a variety of different ways, Walī Allāh goes on to explain that sometimes the *nafs* is used to mean the principle of life (*mabda'-i ḥayāt*), in which case it is synonymous with the *rūḥ*. But Walī Allāh also maintains that sometimes people use the word "*nafs* to refer to (base) human nature (*ṭabī'at-i bashariyya*), with its need for food and drink, while on other occasions it denotes the appetitive self (*nafs-i shahwānī*). …"[83] Moreover, he goes on to suggest that *nafs* is the sum total of all the vices (*radhā'il*) that result from one's carnal desires when they rule the heart and the intellect and enslave both of them.[84] So, we can see that Walī Allāḥ fully agrees with al-Ghazālī regarding the first meaning of *nafs*, which is "the principle in human that includes his blameworthy characters (*ṣifāṭ-i madhmūma*)" such as appetite and anger. Henceforth, we shall translate *nafs* as the "lower self" whenever it is used in relation to base desires. However, for Walī Allāh, *nafs* can also have a plain sense in which it does not have any associated moral or ethical bearings. In such a case, it will simply be translated as "self," which, for both al-Ghazālī and Walī Allāh, refers to the reality of human nature. Similarly, Walī Allāh states that people use the word *rūḥ* (spirit) to mean the principle of life (*mabda'-i ḥayāt*), and also, the fine air (*nasīm-i ṭayyib*) which percolates

---

81 Although this subtle tenuous substance is connected with and used by the rest of the body as well, yet this connection is by means of the heart, which is why its primary connection is with the heart. Therefore, the Sufi Sahl al-Tustarī has likened the heart to the throne and the breast to the seat. For fundamental texts concerning the nature and function of the "heart" in Sufi psychology, see Murata, Sachiko, *The Tao of Islam: A sourcebook of gender relationships in Islamic thought*, Albany, NY: SUNY Press, 1992, ch. 10. For the "heart" in Ibn 'Arabī's thought in general, see Morris, James, *The reflective heart: Discovering spiritual intelligence in Ibn 'Arabī's Meccan illuminations*, Louisville, KY: Fons Vitae, 2005, 31–140.

82 Al-Ghazālī, Abū Ḥāmid Muḥammad, *Iḥyā' 'ulūm al-dīn*, ed. Muḥammad Ḥusayn, viii, Cairo: al-Maktaba al-Thaqāfī, 1937, 1343–1346; translation modified from Skellie, Walter J. (trans.), *Kitāb Sharḥ 'ajā'ib al-qalb = The marvels of the heart: Book 21 of* the Iḥyā' 'ulūm al-dīn, *the Revival of the religious sciences*, Louisville, KY: Fons Vitae, 2010, 5–10.

83 Walī Allāh, *Alṭāf al-quds* 73–74.

84 Walī Allāh, *Alṭāf al-quds* 74.

throughout the body.[85] And at other times they use it to refer to the angelic spirit (*rūḥ-i malakūt*), which was created thousands of years before the creation of human.[86] But he informs the reader that he is using the word *rūḥ* to mean "the heart (*qalb*) after it has abandoned its base instincts (*aḥkām-i suflāniyya*), and when its kinship with the angelic and rational souls (*rūḥ-i malakūt wa-nafs-i nāṭiqa*) becomes predominant" (Fig. 17.1).[87] However, unfortunately, as we will have numerous occasions to observe, he does not always follow his own advice, and often uses *rūḥ* synonymously with *nafs* to mean "self" (i.e., the second meaning of *nafs*).

Moreover, taking leads from al-Ghazālī's *Iḥyā'*, he notes that when people mention the heart (*qalb*), they sometimes refer to the cone-shaped lump of flesh, while at other times they intend to convey the idea of a mental faculty (*laṭīfa-yi darrāka*), synonymous with the intellect (*ʿaql*). Again, much like al-Ghazālī, he defines *qalb* to mean "the spirits of the heart (*arwāḥ-i qalbiyya*) that possess such mental attributes (*ṣifāt-i nafsāniyya*) as anger and shame (*ḥayā'*)."[88] Next, Walī Allāh mentions that the word intellect (*ʿaql*) sometimes refers to knowing (*dānistan*) or the faculty which gives rise to knowing. In this sense, intellect becomes merely an accidental corporeal property (*ʿaraḍī*), and not a self-subsistent substance (*jawhar qā'im bi-nafsihi*). Elsewhere, he observes that people use the term *ʿaql* to mean the substance of the self (*jawhar-i rūḥ*), since some of its functions include understanding (*idrāk*).[89] Then he goes on to assert that intellect for him denotes

> the perceptive faculty which conceptualizes and gives assent to things, so that the heart (*qalb*) and the lower self (*nafs*) may follow its lead, and a coordinating function may arise in the constitution of the perceptive faculty to which the heart and the lower self (*nafs*) lend their support.[90]

He further comments that "these three *laṭā'if* (i.e., *nafs*, *qalb*, and *ʿaql*) permeate the whole body, although the heart is located in the physical heart, the

85 Walī Allāh, *Alṭāf al-quds* 75. Cf. Allāh, Shāh Walī, *Ḥujjat Allāh al-bāligha*, ed. Muḥammad Hāshim, i, Beirut: Dār al-Kutub al-ʿIlmiyya, 1995, 38, which also says the *rūḥ* is the source of life in the animal, which is alive due to the breathing of the *rūḥ* into it and dies when it is separated from it.

86 Walī Allāh, *Alṭāf al-quds* 75.

87 Walī Allāh, *Alṭāf al-quds* 75.

88 Walī Allāh, *Alṭāf al-quds* 74.

89 Walī Allāh, *Alṭāf al-quds* 74.

90 Walī Allāh, *Alṭāf al-quds* 74.

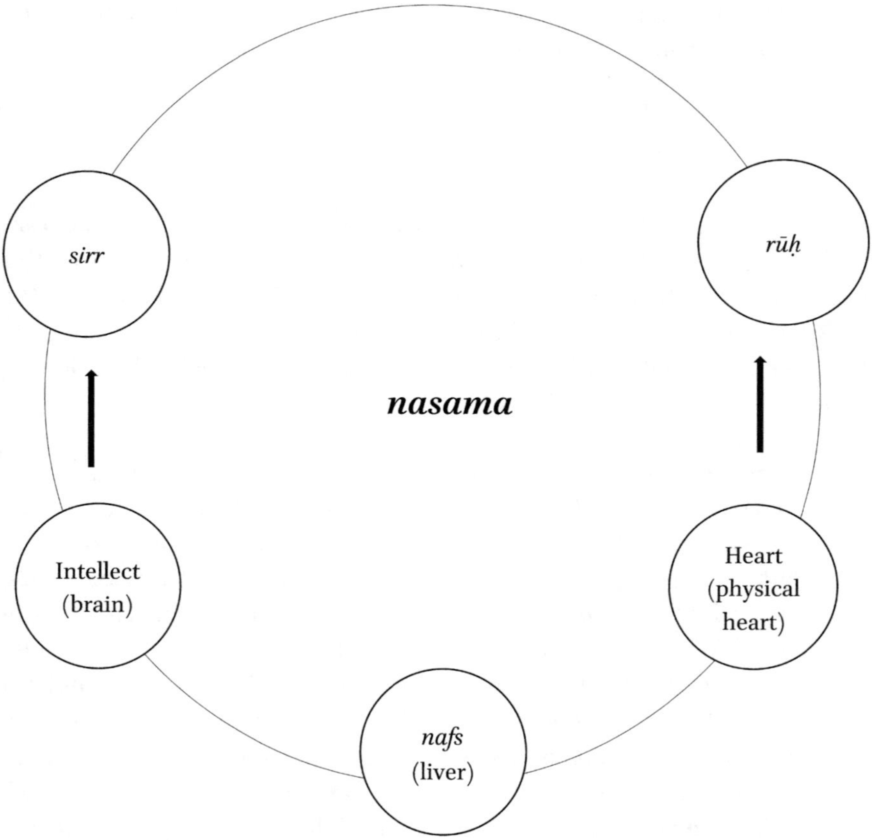

FIGURE 17.1 The branches of *nasama*

self (*nafs*) in the liver, and the intellect in the brain" (Fig. 17.1).[91] Likewise, the word *sirr*, as Walī Allāh explains, indicates concealment. But he quickly follows up by saying that each one of the *laṭāʾif* is concealed, which is why people sometimes refer to the intellect (*ʿaql*) and sometimes to the spirit (*rūḥ*) as *sirr*.[92] According to Walī Allāh, however, "*sirr* is the intellect (*ʿaql*) after it has given up earthly inclinations and is governed by the impulses of the sublime world, thereby attaining vision of the supreme manifestation (*tajallī-yi aʿẓam*) (Fig. 17.1)."[93] Finally, the word *rūḥ*, when used as one of the *laṭāʾif*, means the higher aspect of the heart (*qalb*), when it is purified of its passional

91 Walī Allāh, *Alṭāf al-quds* 74–75.
92 Walī Allāh, *Alṭāf al-quds* 75.
93 Walī Allāh, *Alṭāf al-quds* 75.

elements.[94] It would also be useful to remember that, although both *rūḥ* and *sirr* have a physical locus, they are incorporeal.[95]

4 An Inward Turn through the Subtle Bodies

With all these preliminaries, we should ask now what exactly lies at the basis of the *laṭāʾif*? In a nutshell, the answer would be *nasama* or *pneuma*. But this only begs the further question, what is *pneuma* in Walī Allāh's theory of the self? Again, one can answer it with a word: the rational soul, which is the self. However, to unpack all this step by step, let me first begin with the following quote:

> What I find in my self (*mā wajadtuhu fī dhātī*) regarding human nature, its eyes, hands and feet is that the human being is not an [entity] that comes into existence all at once (*anna l-insān laysa bi-mawjūd marra wāḥida*). Rather in him lie many dimensions (*bal fīhi ṭabaqāt kathīra*) and levels, and each of these levels has an appointed time from its inception until its end. Whoever looks at only his particular level and does not consider other levels thinks human knowledge is confined thus. So the visible level (*al-ṭabaqa al-ẓāhira*) or dimension is the body (*al-badan*), which is the lowest dimension … It is followed by the level of the *laṭīfa* called *pneuma* … The human in reality is this *pneuma* (*fa-l-insān fī l-ḥaqīqa huwa hādhihi l-nasama*), while his body is like an envelope above that protects him. When the body is severed [at death], the *pneuma* endures with its states, and attaches itself to the moral qualities (*al-akhlāq*) and the externa and internal senses (*al-iḥsās al-ẓāhir wa-l-bāṭin*).[96]

In this very important passage, Walī Allāh outlines the framework for his theory of the self in relation to the *laṭāʾif*. He asserts that the self is a *multidimensional* reality, having many levels, each having an appointed time from its beginning

94 Walī Allāh, *Alṭāf al-quds* 75–76.

95 Walī Allāh, *Alṭāf al-quds* 75–76.

96 Walī Allāh, *al-Tafhīmāt al-ilāhiyya* i, 229. The multidimensionality of the self is affirmed in *al-Khayr al-kathīr* as well: "Know that the self (*al-nafs*) has various modes of being (*nashaʾāt*), and each one of these modes has a particular name. If the self clothes itself with the imagination (*al-khayāl*), estimation (*al-wahm*) and perception (*al-idrāk*), then it is named *nasama* and the *nafs* according to the common usage (*iṣṭilāḥ al-qawm*). If it is considered free from matter (*tajarraduhu*), along with spiritual training, it is called *nafs* in the terminology of the philosophers (*iṣṭilāḥ al-falsafa*) and *rūḥ* according to common usage." Allāh, Shāh Walī, *al-Khayr al-kathīr*, Cairo: Maktabat al-Qāhira, 1974, 61.

until its end. In my recent book, I argue that the multidimensionality of the self is best captured through the notion of "spectrum" from which one can derive both its descriptive and normative dimensions. The descriptive self can be further analyzed in terms of its bio-physiological, socio-cultural, and cognito-experiential dimensions, while the normative in terms of its ethical and spiritual dimensions.[97] This can be seen by Walī Allāh's statement that "the human being is not an [entity] that comes into existence all at once," implying that there is a developmental aspect to the reality of the self. Moreover, the lowest dimension of human nature is the body, which is followed by the dimension or level of *pneuma* that underlies the human self. For Walī Allāh, *pneuma*, much like the Stoics, survives death of the body with all the external and internal senses (*al-iḥsās al-ẓāhir wa-l-bāṭin*). But this still leaves the question of the nature of *pneuma* as such. We are told that it is something other than the visible body, but does it mean it is completely immaterial or something between the material and the immaterial? Moreover, what is the precise relationship between this *pneuma* and the self (or the rational soul), which for Walī Allāh is decidedly immaterial? The text below seeks to provide a response to these inquiries:

> Know that the rational soul (*al-nafs al-nāṭiqa*) is the individuating form (*al-ṣūra al-shakhṣiyya*) through which every human acquires his individuality. This [individuality] depends on a subtle body (*jism laṭīf*) produced from the vapor (*bukhār*) of the humors (*al-akhlāṭ*). This is because the nature of the forms is to be dependent on suitable matter (*al-hayūlā al-munāsaba*) possessing a prepared configuration (*al-hay'a al-mustaʿidda*) that will be conferred on it. Since the self (*al-nafs*) is the most subtle, most pure, and most solid of all the forms, it cannot but be dependent on a body which is the most subtle of all bodies (*alṭaf al-ajsām*), maturing at the finest degree of subtlety and equilibrium (*iʿtidāl*) .... We will call this subtle body (*jism laṭīf*) *pneuma* (*nasama*), which pervades (*al-sārī*) the dense body (*al-badan al-kathīf*) in order to manifest the perfections of the self (*kamālāt al-nafs*) in it.[98]

In this seminal text, one can see how the synthesis of the Graeco-Arabic medical tradition, Platonizing Aristotelianism, and Stoicism comes into play in Walī

97 Faruque, *Sculpting*.

98 Allāh, Shāh Walī, *al-Budūr al-bāzigha*, Hyderabad and Sindh: Shāh Walī Allāh Academy, 1970, 38. Cf. Walī Allāḥ, *Ḥujjat Allāh* i, 65, which states that *pneuma* pervade the entire body as a substratum.

Allāh's theory of the self.[99] So the rational soul is the individuating form by which every human acquires his individuality or his specific I-ness.[100] This is more or less standard Aristotelianism. However, Walī Allāh goes on to note that the individuality or the I-ness of every human in turn depends on a on a subtle body (*jism laṭīf*) produced from the vapor (*bukhār*) of the humors (*al-akhlāṭ*).[101] And this is a complex synthesis of Stoicism and the Galenic tradition, with some notable differences. Next, Walī Allāh argues that the self, unlike the version in Stoicism or Galenism, being immaterial and the most subtle of all the forms, cannot but be dependent on a *body* which is also the most subtle of all bodies maturing at the finest degree of subtlety and equilibrium. And Walī Allāh calls this "subtle body" *nasama* or *pneuma*, which is an intermediary between the self (immaterial) and the body (material), and whose function is to manifest the perfections of the self in the body.

Furthermore, from al-Ghazālī's long text quoted earlier, we witnessed that "the second meaning of the heart (*qalb*) is a spiritual lordly *laṭīfa* (*laṭīfa rabbāniyya rūḥāniyya*), which is connected with the physical heart." And al-Ghazālī affirms that this *laṭīfa* is "the real essence of the human and the heart (*qalb*) is that which perceives, knows, and experiences."[102] But al-Ghazālī does not provide any details of the physical constitution of the *laṭīfa*, which is responsible for knowledge and perception, even though he does intimate that the *laṭīfa* of the heart rules all the parts of the body. Al-Ghazālī says:

> Know that the seat of knowledge (*ʿilm*) is the heart, by which I mean the *laṭīfa* that rules all the parts of the body and is obeyed and served by all its members. In its relationship to the real nature of known objects (*maʿlūmāt*), it is like a mirror in its relationship to the forms (*ṣuwar*) of changing appearances. ... The knower is an expression for the heart in which there exists the image of the specific natures of things. Knowledge is an expression for the representation of the image in the mirror. Even as the act of grasping, for example, requires that which grasps, such as the

99 For more information on the Galenic and Stoic background, see Faruque, *Sculpting* 170–178.

100 Cf. Aristotle, *De anima* 412a27.

101 In the *Ḥujjat*, Walī Allāh notes that there is a subtle vapor (*bukhār laṭīf*) in the body, which is produced in the heart from a quintessence of the humors (*khulāṣat al-akhlāṭ*). It carries the faculties of perception, movement, and the distribution of food according to the dictates of medicine. The various states of this vapor, whether fine or thick or pure or turbid has a particular effect on the faculties and the functions that proceed from these faculties. Walī Allāḥ, *Ḥujjat Allāh* i, 38.

102 See Faruque, *Labyrinth* 131–132.

> hand, and that which is grasped, such as the sword in the hand, which is called the act of grasping, so also the coming of the image of the known object into the heart is called knowledge.[103]

Shāh Walī Allāh retains part of al-Ghazālī's model by incorporating the heart (*qalb*) as one of the *laṭāʾif*, as opposed to making it "the" *laṭīfa*. However, what's more important in Walī Allāh's theory is that he fills the "physiological" gaps of the *laṭāʾif* theory through an original synthesis of Stoic-Galenic-Islamic traditions, which, as far as I am aware, is original with him. However, unlike the Stoics, the *pneuma*, for Walī Allāh, is not the self as such; rather it is the *corporal basis* (i.e., matter) of the immaterial self (i.e., form).[104] Nevertheless, to a large extent like the Stoics, Walī Allāh's *nasama* penetrates all the faculties of perception.

To further clarify the nature of *pneuma*, Walī Allāh states that it has three branches.[105] According to his classification, the first branch corresponds to what is called *nafs* in the language of the Sufis (*fī kalām al-ṣūfiyya*), which is like an aperture through which Satan inspires it to incline toward evil (*sharr*), wickedness (*khabth*) and bestiality (*waḥsha*). He further notes that the same term, i.e., *nafs*, is called *al-nafs al-shahwiyya* (the appetitive self) by the philosophers (*al-falāsifa*). The second branch is called *qalb* in the language of the Sufis, while it is called *al-nafs al-sabʿiyya* (the animalistic self) by the philosophers. Similarly, the third branch of *pneuma* is known as *ʿaql* (intellect), which is the same in both Sufis and philosophers' terminology. Walī Allāh then goes on to claim that all of these branches of *nasama*, i.e., the *laṭāʾif*, are accepted by the Sufis, philosophers, and the folk of the transmitted sciences:

> These are the three *laṭāʾif* in all humans which are affirmed by the philosophers, the folk of the transmitted sciences, and the folk of inner intuition [i.e., the Sufis] (*fa-hādhihi thalāth laṭāʾif fī kulli insān ittafaqa ʿalā ithbātihā l-falāsifa wa-ahl al-naql wa-ahl al-wijdān*).[106]

At this point, it would be pertinent to show the contrast between this developed model of the *laṭāʾif* and the early model, which is found in Walī Allāh's middle-period work *Alṭāf al-quds*. In *Alṭāf al-quds*, Walī Allāh uses a slightly different

103 Al-Ghazālī, *Iḥyāʾ ʿulūm al-dīn* viii, 1360, trans. (modified) Skellie, *The marvels of the heart* 35.

104 See Walī Allāḥ, *Ḥujjat Allāh* i, 66.

105 Walī Allāh, *al-Tafhīmāt al-ilāhiyya* i, 229–231.

106 Walī Allāh, *al-Tafhīmāt al-ilāhiyya* i, 232.

scheme to elucidate the basic structure of the self. Also, one observes that he struggles to find the right vocabulary to express the relationship between the self and the *laṭāʾif*. First, he states that the self (*rūḥ*) is composed of three parts (*az sih juzʾ ast*): *nasama* or the airy soul (*rūḥ-i hawāʾī*), the rational soul (*nafs-i nāṭiqa*) and the angelic spirit (*rūḥ-i malakūt*). However, his bio-physiological description of the *nasama* there differs slightly from the account given in his late works such as the *Budūr* and the *Tafhīmāt* in terms of its refinement:

> First, there is the fine air (*nasīm-i ṭayyib*) arising from the subtle vapors (*bukhār-i laṭīf*) of the various elements in digested food. It possesses the capacity for nutrition (*taghdhiyya*), growth (*tanmiyya*), and sense perception (*idrāk*). This is called *pneuma* (*nasama*), the natural soul (*rūḥ-i ṭabīʿī*) or the airy body (*badan-i hawāʾī*). It permeates flesh and bones like the fire in charcoal or the perfume in a rose. It is by virtue of the airy soul (*rūḥ-i hawāʾī*) that the soul is connected with the body. Just as the body tastes death when severed from the soul, the latter suffers a similar death-like pain (*maqāsāt*) when separated from the body. The original source of this subtle vapor lies in the heart, brain, and liver. It arises from the boiling of the blood in the heart which is confirmed by the method and observation of the physicians. That is, when they observe blood turning thick or thin, pure or impure, increasing or decreasing.[107]

As one can see, terms such as *rūḥ-i hawāʾī* or *badan-i hawāʾī* do not occur in the late works. Instead, we have more refined terms such as subtle air (*hawāʾ laṭīf*) that are heuristically more useful, since the word *rūḥ* has so many overlapping meanings with the word *nafs*. More importantly, *pneuma* (*nasama*) is not one of the parts of the self, as the late works make it plain, rather it is its corporal basis. This becomes clearer as we move on to his explanation of the second branch of the self in this early model, namely the rational soul. Concerning the rational soul, Walī Allāh gives the analogy of a date-stone (*nawāt*) and its biological life-cycles (e.g., growth and disintegration) to make the point that if a single date-stone can control its own independent growth, alongside the fact that every tree has its own distinct order (*niẓām*), then reason is compelled to acknowledge the existence of a self (*nafs*) possessing the requisite faculties (*quwā*) in humans, which is called the rational soul (*nafs-i nāṭiqa*).[108] Similarly, the third part is the angelic spirit (*rūḥ-i malakūt*), whose distinctive property is that it remains in the presence of the sacred spirit (*rūḥ al-qudus*), which is

107 Walī Allāh, *Alṭāf al-quds* 24.
108 Walī Allāh, *Alṭāf al-quds* 25–26.

anchored in the heavenly fold (*ḥaẓīrat al-quds*). The angelic spirit maintains this link at all times (*ittiṣāl paydā mī kunad*) and is firmly established in the highest assembly (*mala' al-aʿlā*), where it is able to converse with the angels according to its preparedness (*istiʿdād*).[109]

Now one can see why there are certain inconsistencies in this particular schema. On the one hand, if we conceive of *rūḥ* as spirit, instead of self, which consists of three parts, we run into a mereological fallacy, since the third part of the *rūḥ* is definitely a sort of spirit, namely the angelic spirit. So "spirit" cannot itself be another "spirit," especially since we are not talking about "spirit" and its various kinds such as the natural spirit (*rūḥ-i ṭabīʿī*) and the animal spirit (*rūḥ-i ḥayawānī*). This is because the second part of this *rūḥ* is not called *rūḥ-i nāṭiqa*, instead of *nafs-i nāṭiqa*. Moreover, in numerous other contexts, *nafs-i nāṭiqa* is described as a substance and a non-physical entity that can only be understood as self (not its part), as I have shown in the preceding sections. Therefore, terminological inconsistencies remain in the early model, whether one understands the *rūḥ* to be a spirit or self. Still, one can perhaps hope to reconcile this early model (see Fig. 17.2) with the more matured model (see Fig. 17.3) by a charitable hermeneutical move (see the next section).

After explaining a basic structure of the self (i.e., *rūḥ*), Walī Allāh goes on to discuss the functions and attributes of various parts of the self (*rūḥ*). He acknowledges that every part of the self (*rūḥ*) has its own separate properties. Moreover, each combination of parts has further distinct properties of their own. More significantly, he notes that the airy soul (i.e., *pneuma*) has affinity with the lower soul (*nafs*),[110] while the rational soul with the heart (*qalb*) and the angelic spirit with the intellect (*ʿaql*).[111] Thus we come back three main *laṭā'if*, which comprises the self whose bodily basis is *nasama*. And there is good textual evidence to support this interpretation, since Walī Allāh maintains that the five *laṭā'if* (i.e., including *sirr* and *rūḥ*) are generated from a combination of *pneuma*, the rational soul and the angelic spirit, thereby suggesting here the rational soul and the angelic spirit can be understood in the sense of a *laṭīfa* as well.[112] Moreover, in keeping with late works, he attributes various external and internal senses such as the common sense, the imagination, memory etc., to *pneuma*.[113]

---

109 Walī Allāh, *Alṭāf al-quds* 31.

110 I.e., with the appetitive soul (*nafs-i shahwī*), which is an aspect of the lower soul.

111 Walī Allāh, *Alṭāf al-quds* 34–25.

112 Walī Allāh, *Alṭāf al-quds* 34.

113 Walī Allāh, *Alṭāf al-quds* 34. Airy soul (*nafs-i hawā'ī*) or *nasama* contains three parts: *nafs*, *qalb*, and *ʿaql*. See Walī Allāh, *Alṭāf al-quds* 35.

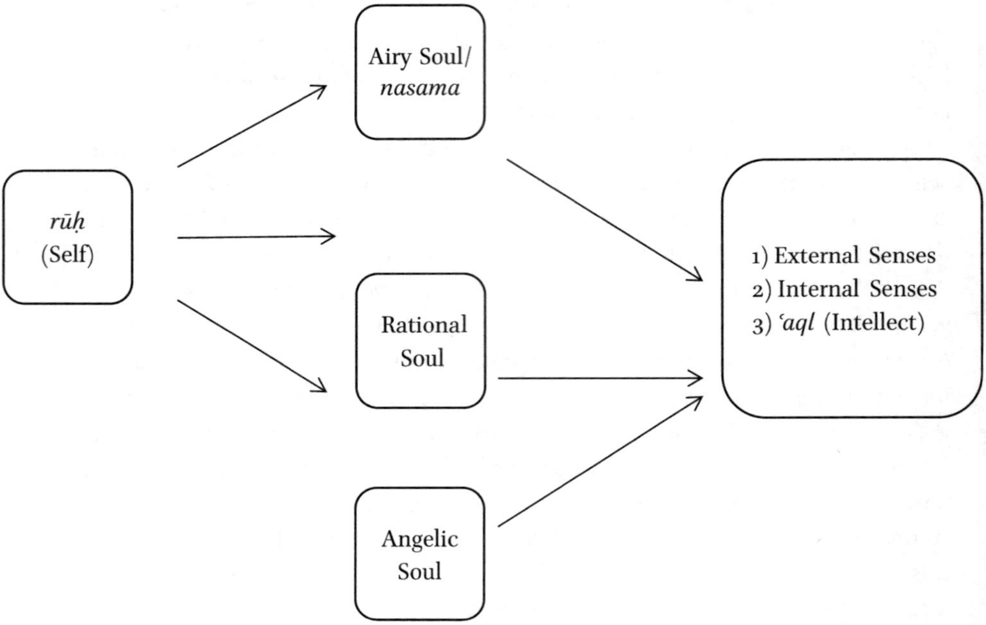

FIGURE 17.2 Early model of the Self

Be that as it may, to give a better *overall* psycho-spiritual sense of the *laṭāʾif* and why it makes more sense to conceive of them as "subtle fields of consciousness," let us consider how Walī Allāh describes their functions. In his account, the *laṭīfa* of the *nafs* is characterized by its ability to form the intention to carry out a particular action, entertain feelings of love and hatred, regulate the carnal desires, and pursue pleasures. In addition, it has to maintain the constitution of the body in accordance with the latter's requirements and has to discharge what the body naturally discharges. Furthermore, basic physical needs such as hunger and thirst, fatigue and pain, and sexual urge that are necessary for the continuation of life are all connected with the lower self (*nafs*).[114] Next, the *laṭīfa* of the *qalb* has to do with emotions such as showing courage or cowardice (*jubn*), anger (*ghaḍab*), shame (*khajālat*), fear (*khawf*), courage (*jurʾat*), generosity (*sakhāwat*), avarice (*shuḥḥ*), love (*ḥubb*), and hatred (*bughḍ*). Walī Allāh illustrates this by arguing that "every person undoubtedly recognizes how he dislikes a thing," why his heart burns with a desire to repel it, why his spirits (*arwāḥ*) seem almost on the point of leaving his body, and why his veins dilate, and his skin turns red. Similarly, in times of fear, he knows why his heart trembles, making his spirits recede into his body, and why his face

114 Walī Allāh, *Alṭāf al-quds* 38–39.

becomes pale and his mouth goes dry.[115] That is to say, the natural sensations and feelings that one goes through due to the stirring of his emotions and passions, are to be attributed to the *laṭīfa* of the heart. Likewise, the functions of the *laṭīfa* of the intellect (*ʿaql*) are comprehension (*fahm*), knowledge (*maʿrifat*), and the capacity to execute decisions. Moreover, the intellect has the feature of recollecting things of the past and making plans for the future.[116]

One notices how the above description systematically attributes both agency-related capacities such as the ability to make decisions and perceptual capacities such as the ability to experience various emotions and make judgements about their moral content to the self, which is difficult to imagine without some form of "consciousness" in the background (see Fig. 17.4). To wit, it is not possible to attribute "agency-related" actions or states to human beings, while not admitting some sort of consciousness. That is the reason I find it most suitable to render the *laṭāʾif* as subtle fields of consciousness. They are "subtle" because they have a subtle bodily basis, while it is more plausible to think of them as "fields" rather than "points," since they "pervade the whole body" and interpenetrate each other. But as Walī Allāh stresses frequently, although there are "seven" such subtle fields of consciousness, it does not entail that there are "seven selves" sitting behind them.[117] This is why the idea of the "multidimensionality" of the self, explicitly asserted by Walī Allāh, can be so crucial in delineating a theory of the self. Walī Allāh writes:

> Every person always experiences these realities. In one sense, these three categories [i.e., the *laṭāʾif*] are separate from each other, while in another sense they are united together.[118]
>
> We have already discussed the cause of their differentiation; the cause of their unity (*wajh-i ittiḥād*) lies in the fact that, although the rational soul directs these various faculties and functions (*shaʿb*), it is itself fundamentally a single entity (*yakī ast*), and fundamentally, its constitution (*mizāj*) is one.[119]

That is to say, *the self is one at the level of its substance-hood or as an immaterial entity, but multiple at the level of its functions, states, and actions*. For this

115 Walī Allāh, *Alṭāf al-quds* 39–40.
116 Walī Allāh, *Alṭāf al-quds* 40.
117 See, e.g., Walī Allāh, *Alṭāf al-quds* 35–36 and 146.
118 Walī Allāh, *Alṭāf al-quds* 40.
119 Walī Allāh, *Alṭāf al-quds* 41.

reason, a spectrum model of selfhood containing multiple dimensions can be heuristically helpful, as it offers a way of reading the *apparently disconnected* reflections on the self in a *coherent* and *unified* way.

Moreover, the self is both a spectrum and an aspirational concept. That is, part of the self is given (i.e., the bio-physiological dimension) but part of it exists only as a potential that one aspires to achieve.[120] Considered thus, the nature of the self constituted by the subtle fields of consciousness (*laṭāʾif*) must be cultivated and purified in order to attain ultimate selfhood (*anāniyya kubrā*). Also, since the *laṭāʾif* form the matrix of one's given subjectivity, it would be helpful to use the metaphor of taking an "inward turn" or journeying within these fields, as they lead to the ultimate destination of the self, which is identity with the divine as we shall see in the next section.

In his *Alṭāf al-quds*, Walī Allāh suggests that in Sufi terminology (*dar iṣṭilāḥ-i ṣūfiyya*), the purification of the lower self, the heart, and the intellect (*tahdhīb-i nafs, qalb wa-ʿaql*) is known as the way (*ṭarīqat*), while that of the spirit and the secret (*tahdhīb-i rūḥ wa-sirr*) is termed gnosis (*maʿrifat*).[121] That is to say, what is known as *ṭarīqat* or the practice of the Sufi way in common Sufi parlance is nothing other than purifying all the *laṭāʾif* of the self. As Walī Allāh explains:

> The whole point of engaging oneself in spiritual activities and exercises is that every *laṭīfa* should be cultivated (*parwarish*) and that due consideration should be given to every stage.[122]

Also, Walī Allāh claims that the real nature and the effects of these *laṭāʾif* are unfamiliar to most minds, and most people do not benefit from being informed of them. Nonetheless, there are two types of people who might benefit from hearing about these things. The first is someone who has already come close to perfecting them completely, and who has acquired the preparedness to purify them. If such a person turns his attention to this present discussion, the conception of the forms of these things will be the correct one, and it will open the door to success. The second type is someone who has been blessed with a

---

120 Faruque, *Sculpting* 44–48.

121 Walī Allāh, *Alṭāf al-quds* 73.

122 Walī Allāh, *Alṭāf al-quds* 87. In Walī Allāh's view, when the wayfarer is released from the influence of the lower self (*nafs*), he should focus his attention on the other *laṭāʾif*, namely *qalb* and *ʿaql*. At this point, his heart becomes his spirit (*rūḥ*) and his intellect becomes his *sirr*. See Walī Allāh, *Alṭāf al-quds* 35. Moreover, when the seeker has completed the purification of the self, the heart, and the intellect, and has gained the benefits accruing from this, the next requirement is the purification yet again of the self, but this time in conjunction with the spirit and the secret faculty. See Walī Allāh, *Alṭāf al-quds* 98.

general knowledge of the *laṭāʾif* but lacks the capacity to understand them in detail. If such a person reads this discussion, Walī Allāh says, his general knowledge will be transformed into a detailed one.[123] Moreover, Walī Allāh notes that since there are so many variations in the types of human selves (*nufūs-i banī ādam*), the means of purification for each of them will also differ, thereby making its scope vast.[124]

However, one may wonder why is there a need to purify one's self or the *laṭāʾif* that comprise it? To answer this Walī Allāh argues that without such a purification, one would not be able to know the real nature of the self and how this differs from what we ordinarily perceive, think, and treat the self to be.[125] Since the *laṭāʾif* also manifest various emotions, Walī Allāh broaches the heart (*qalb*) that plays a crucial role in the purification of the self:

> The heart rules over the bodily organs, and by virtue of its love modify their patterns of behavior. When this quality becomes innate in the heart and is maintained for a long time in close association with continuous worshipping, then a stage is created between these two attributes. ... As a result, [the disciple's] bodily organs become submissive (*khāshiʿ*), and he begins to show courtesy and deference in speech and treat all those who are related to the Beloved (*maḥbūb*) as his own respected friends.[126]

Among many spiritual exercises that Walī Allāh suggests are self-examination (*muḥāsiba-yi nafs*), which is attending to the self moment by moment and remaining constantly aware of its state (*yaʿnī har zamānī waqif-i ḥāl-i khūd bāshad*) to see whether its time is being wasted in negligence (*ghaflat*) and sin, or it is spent in acts of devotion (*ṭāʿat*). If the desired objective is achieved, Walī Allāh continues, we should thank God, and think hard of ways to continue this trend and enhance this practice. But if it is the reverse, we should repent.[127] After mentioning self-examination, Walī Allāh elucidates four cardinal virtues that the self (*nafs*) should cultivate in order to purify itself from the temptations of the lower self. The first of these cardinal virtues is purity (*ṭahārat*) through which the self is related to angels, while the second is humility (*khuḍūʿ*) through which the self acquires an affinity with the highest assembly (*malaʾ al-aʿlā*). The third is generosity (*samāḥat*), by means of which the self obliterates stains left

---

123 Walī Allāh, *Alṭāf al-quds* 112.
124 Walī Allāh, *Alṭāf al-quds* 47.
125 Cf. Walī Allāh, *al-Budūr al-bāzigha* 154.
126 Walī Allāh, *Alṭāf al-quds* 90.
127 Walī Allāh, *Alṭāf al-quds* 81–82; cf. Walī Allāh, *al-Budūr al-bāzigha* 154.

by base human nature such as animal-like behavior (*af'āl-i sab'iyya*) and lust (*shahwiyya*). The fourth is justice (*'adālat*) through which the self may appear pleasing to the highest assembly, may gain favor with it, and receive its mercy and blessings.[128]

Finally, Walī Allāh recommends a host of Sufi spiritual practices, some of which are associated with the Naqshbandī order. Among these practices, he suggests the invocation (*dhikr*), beating one's chest, breath-control (*ḥabs-i nafas*),[129] the secret lesson (*sabq-i bāṭinī*) which is a legacy of the masters of the Naqshbandi school, listening to spiritual music (*samā'*), and contemplating aesthetically pleasing patterns (*naqsh-hā-yi shawq-angīz*).[130] In Walī Allāh's view, all of these spiritual exercises excite longing in the heart and bring it to life. Moreover, the observance of purity at all times (*dawām-i ṭahārat*), the serene light of Quranic recitation, Sufi *wird*, and the cultivation (*parwarish*) of the Uwaysi relationship with the spirits of the saints, all provide nourishment to the self (*nafs*). In the same way, he continues, contemplating attributes of God and meditating on His names (*fikr-i tadabbur-i asmā'*) transport the intellect to the seat of splendor. Lastly, in order to awaken higher *laṭā'if* such as *sirr*, one should practice "pure remembrance," which is the Naqshbandī practice of soundlessly and wordlessly remembering God (*yād dāsht-i ṣirf bī-ṣawt wa-ḥarf kih ma'mūl-i naqshbandiyya ast*).[131]

4.1 *The End of Selfhood*

So far, we have learned that the there are five subtle fields of consciousness (*laṭā'if*) that constitute the individual self, and that one can journey through them—in the sense of discovering them within oneself—in order to reach ultimate selfhood. The next question that arises is what is the nature of ultimate selfhood and how does one attain it? Moreover, how does such a transformed

---

128 Walī Allāh, *Alṭāf al-quds* 52–53.

129 Faruque, *Labyrinth* 195–201.

130 See also, Walī Allāh, *Ḥujjat Allāh* i, 104–105, for a detailed treatment of the Sufi virtues that are essential to purification.

131 Walī Allāh, *Alṭāf al-quds* 108. Continuous worshipping (*dawām-i 'ubūdiyyat*) falls into two categories. The first category is concerned with the limbs and organs of the body and the tongue. This entails spending one's life in prayer and reading the Quran with one's thoughts collected and one's heart concentrated. Walī Allāh asserts that this is one of the fundamental principles of Sufism, which has been explained in such books as Abū Ṭālib al-Makkī's *Qūt al-qulūb*, al-Ghazālī's *Iḥyā' 'ulūm al-dīn*, Jīlānī's *Ghunyat al-ṭālibīn*, and Suhrawardī's *'Awārif al-ma'ārif*. The second category relates to the heart and the intellect. Here the heart is occupied with the love of the Beloved and close attachment to the Beloved. The intellect is occupied with remembrance and awareness while suspending breath (*ḥabs-i nafas*). See Walī Allāh, *Alṭāf al-quds* 86–87.

state of the self look like? Is the individual self dissolved in such a state, or is there still some form of individuality that is retained? Moreover, what does the *sharīʿa* say about such transcendent states? In other words, where does normative Islam stand in all this? Let us, then, proceed to answer all these questions in sequence, and in doing so, bring Walī Allāh's conception of the self to a culmination.

Being an authority on legal matters (i.e., matters pertaining to the *sharīʿa*), in addition to being a Sufi, Walī Allāh seems mindful of the fact that many of his abstruse reflections on the nature of ultimate selfhood might appear unsettling to the uninitiated or the ordinary believer. Thus he begins by asserting that the purpose of the *sharīʿa* is to deliver the self from the punishment of the grave and the Day of Judgment, rather than enabling it to attain the mystical states of annihilation and subsistence:

> If you want to understand the true nature of the *sharīʿa*, then know that human beings are trapped in the grip of the evil-inciting self [i.e., the lower self] …. And the remedy of this situation is provided in view of the entire species [i.e., humanity as a whole], hence it [i.e., the remedy] pertains to the species as a whole, and not to the specific potential that some individual [selves] possess. So, the final purpose of this [i.e., the *sharīʿa*] is to save the [individual] from being devastated in the world, alongside the punishment of the grave and the Day of Judgment. Its purpose is not to enable the self to attain the station of annihilation and permanence for each of the *laṭāʾif*, nor the rank of absolute permanence and perfect settlement (*ḥaqīqat-i sharīʿat agar khwāhī kih bi-fahmī bi-dān kih banī ādam dar qayd-i nafs-i ammāra giriftār shudah būdand …. wa-iltifāt darīn iʿlāj bi-ṣūrat-i nawʿiyya wa-khwāṣṣ-i kulliyya-yi ān nawʿ ast nah bi-istiʿdādāt-i khāṣṣa bar juzwi-yī fardī wa ʿillat-i ghāyat-i ān ikhlāṣ az tazālum dar dunyā mubtalā shudan bi-ʿadhāb-i qabr wa-rūz-i ḥashr ast nah wuṣul-i fanāʾ wa-baqāʾ-yi har laṭīfa wa-ḥuṣūl-i martaba-yi baqāʾ-yi muṭlaq wa-tamkīn-i tāmm*).[132]

After mentioning the above, Walī Allāh adds that whoever thinks otherwise has not understood the Prophet's aims (*maqāṣid*), beneficial strategies (*maṣāliḥ*), commands (*awāmir*), and prohibitions (*nawāhī*). That is to say, the commands and prohibitions of the *sharīʿa* are sufficient to save the self from the punishment of hell or enjoy the blessedness of paradise. But these commands and

132 Walī Allāh, *Alṭāf al-quds* 48–49.

prohibitions of the *sharīʿa* are generic in the sense that they do not take into account "individual potentials" (*istiʿdādāt-i fardī*) that contain the possibilities of realizing the higher states of being through *fanāʾ* and *baqāʾ*. For Walī Allāh, the self has modes of being above and beyond the ordinary teachings of the *sharīʿa*, and, as we shall soon see, he goes to great lengths to elucidate the higher states of the self, some of which might appear rather antinomian from the outward *sharīʿa* perspective. It is also important to note that these passages where Walī Allāh expounds on the higher reality of the self would challenge the existing scholarship, which seeks to present an uncontested, reform-minded image of Shāh Walī Allāh.

In any event, in Walī Allāh's metaphysical anthropology, the nature of the self is bound up with its ontological origin, i.e., the Universal Soul (*nafs-i kulliyya*). Walī Allāh mentions that the goal of "the rational soul (*nafs-i nāṭiqa*) in relation to its origin (*aṣl*) is to be melted in the Universal Soul, which enables it to receive the impulse (*dāʿiya*) of ultimate selfhood."[133] I shall explain the attributes of ultimate selfhood in a moment, but it is crucial to note that for Walī Allāh, the ultimate destination of the self is not the Universal Soul, even though the above citation seems to suggest so. So he sets out to narrate that there is a state in which a divine impulse (*dāʿiya-yi ilāhiyya*) is transmitted, either from the supreme manifestation (*tajallī-yi aʿẓam*) or from the Universal Soul, or from a place where there is no differentiation whatsoever into the supreme manifestation and the Universal Soul—"a place where all is oneness in oneness, simplicity in simplicity (*waḥdat dar waḥdat wa-bisāṭat dar bisāṭat*)" (Fig. 17.4).[134] This divine impulse pours down from one of these sublime regions, attaches itself to the individual selfhood (*anāniyyat-i khāṣṣ*), and mingles with the substance (*jawhar*) of this bubble.[135] In referring to the place which is beyond the degree of the Universal Soul and which is characterized by its utter simplicity, Walī Allāh has in mind the Divine Self, which he sometimes calls the Supreme Self (*dhāt-i baḥt*) or the First of the First (*awwal al-awāʾil*):

> There are others who have passed beyond the Universal Soul and understood the Supreme Self as the First of the First, and the Universal Soul as the first emanation (*ṣādir-i awwal*) and deployed being (*wujūd munbasiṭ*) upon the temples of existents.[136]

133 Walī Allāh, *Alṭāf al-quds* 34.
134 Walī Allāh, *Alṭāf al-quds* 129.
135 Walī Allāh, *Alṭāf al-quds* 129.
136 Walī Allāh, *Alṭāf al-quds* 155.

One question that might arise in this context is how is the perfect human, which is usually conceived as the highest realizable self, related to the Universal Soul? The following text casts light on such concerns:

> The perfect human (*insān-i kāmil*) is a distinct species (*nawʿ-i ʿalāḥida*) among the various kinds of humans, just as human is a distinct species (*nawʿ-i ʿalāḥida*) within its own genus. Just as the human is deemed superior to animals by virtue of his universal outlook (*kullī wa-tafṣīl*), so too is the perfect human vis-à-vis other humans by virtue of the development of his (*laṭāʾif*), which is realized when the Universal Soul manifests itself in his particular selfhood (*anāniyyat-i khāṣṣ*) and made the latter a subservient to its will. The perfect human has many such characteristics, a full account of which would take too long to accomplish. In short, the perfect human is the nearest of all the individual selves to the Universal Soul (*bi-l-jumla insān-i kāmil aqrab-i nufūs-i juzʾiyya ast bi-nafs-i kulliyya*).[137]

It is to be noted that in Walī Allāh's metaphysics of the self, the doctrine of the perfect human does not make much appearance, although he seems to have accepted its general function, as the above passage points out. Nonetheless, Walī Allāh's innovative vocabularies such as *anāniyya kubrā* or *anāniyya muṭlaq* do seem to capture the essential features of the perfect human as the highest attainable self. One innovative move in Walī Allāh's account of the perfect human, however, is that the self attains to the degree of the perfect human through the development of its *laṭāʾif* or the subtle fields of consciousness. This brings us back to Fig. 17.3 (below), in which Walī Allāh illustrates how the self progresses from the microcosmic *laṭāʾif* such as *nafs*, *qalb* and *ʿaql* to the macrocosmic *laṭāʾif*. Now the crucial point to note is that there are two ways one may reach absolute selfhood (*anāniyya muṭlaq*): 1) the path of ultimate sainthood (*al-wilāya al-kubrā*) and 2) the path of prophetic inheritance (*al-wirātha al-nubuwwa*) [indicated by the black pointed arcs in the diagram]. However, as Walī Allāh underlines, "whatever the path may be, Prophetic inheritance or ultimate sainthood, it makes little difference," since what matters is the destination.[138]

As was mentioned earlier, one can reach the pinnacle of selfhood through two distinct routes. First, one should note that the rational soul or the self is the junction (*mawḍiʿ*) between the microcosmic and the macrocosmic *laṭāʾif*.

137 Walī Allāh, *Alṭāf al-quds* 116.
138 Walī Allāh, *Alṭāf al-quds* 123–124. Cf. the black arcs in Fig. 17.3.

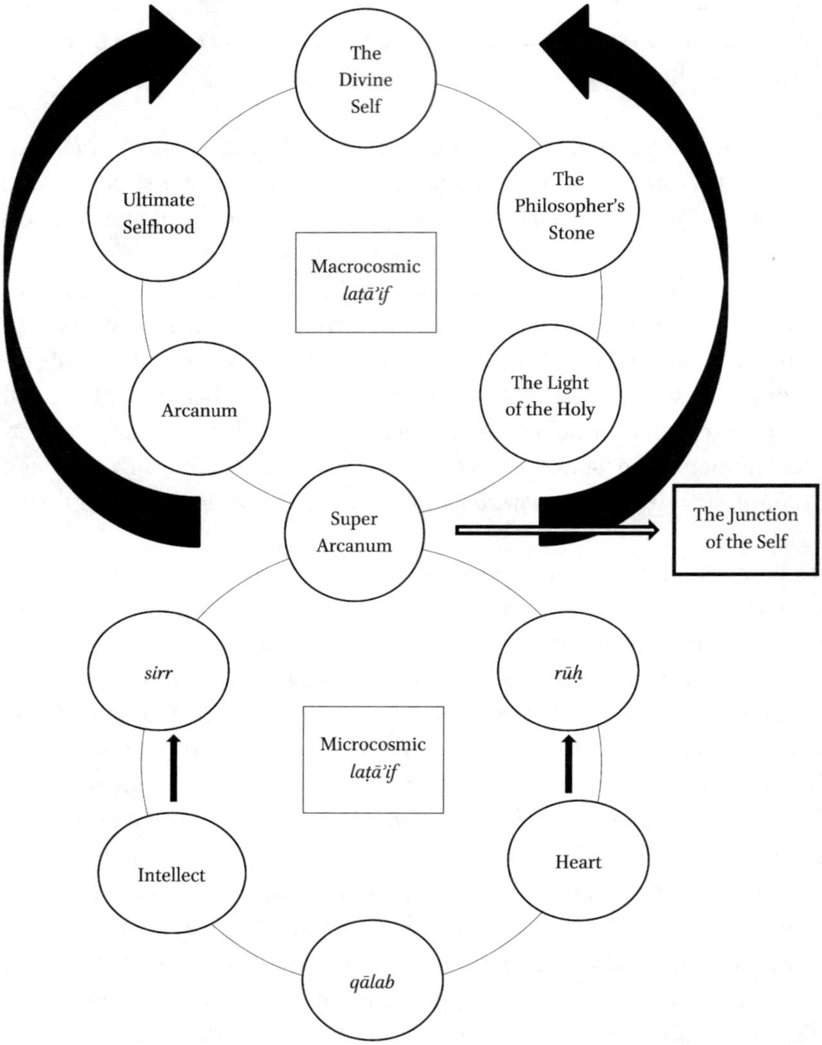

FIGURE 17.3 The *laṭā'if* and selfhood
Note: Based on Walī Allāh's own diagram with some modification; see Walī Allāh, *al-Tafhīmāt al-ilāhiyya* i, 244. In his own commentary on this diagram, Walī Allāh explicitly mentions the rational soul (*al-nafs al-nāṭiqa*) or the self as the junction between the microcosmic and the macrocosmic *laṭā'if*. He states that the rational soul has four frames of reference (*anẓār*), two of which are branched into *rūḥ* and *sirr* below it, while two of them are branched into *khafī* and *nūr al-quds* above it. But the rational soul itself is stationed at the junction of *akhfā* (super arcanum) (*wa-kāna al-nafs al-nāṭiqa innamā hiya fī mawḍiʿ al-akhfā*). See Walī Allāh, *al-Tafhīmāt al-ilāhiyya* i, 244.
BASED ON WALĪ ALLĀH'S OWN DIAGRAM

This junction is also identified with the subtle field *akhfā*, as in Fig. 17.3 From the junction of *akhfā* or the rational soul (which is yet to realize its macrocosmic states), the self can either reach the Supreme Self through the *laṭāʾif* of the arcanum (*khafī*) and ultimate selfhood, or it can traverse the *laṭāʾif* of the light of the holy (*nūr al-quds*) and the philosopher's stone (*ḥajar-i baḥt*)[139] to reach Divinity, and become annihilated in and subsisted through It.

A related issue that emerges from the journey through the *laṭāʾif* and degrees of annihilation that marks every waystation of the *laṭāʾif* is what we stated at the beginning of this section, namely how is reality perceived in such transformed states of the self? Is the individual self dissolved in such a state, or is the state of individuality still retained? The passage below answers this by first asserting that there is a level of selfhood beyond the degree of the Universal Soul:

> Either the individual selfhood (*anāniyyat-i khāṣṣ*) subsists through absolute selfhood (*anāniyyat-i muṭlaq*) or [the gnostic regards] individual selfhood as absolute selfhood, or else, he becomes oblivious to his individual selfhood (*anāniyyat-i khāṣṣ*), neither affirming nor denying it. He neither puts absolute selfhood in place of his individual selfhood nor does he recall it as a separate entity. In the terminology of the folk of wayfaring, this is called the self-disclosure of the Self (*tajallī-yi dhāt*). The ultimate vision of the gnostic in this state is the Universal Soul (*nafs-i kulliyya*). From there he ascends (*ṣuʿūd mī-kunad*) to the Supreme Self (*dhāt-i baḥt*) and gains something from It (*chīzī az ān bi-dastash āyad*) but does not know how to describe it (*nadānad kih barā-yi ān chih ʿibārat gūyad*) … or how to express that which lies beyond the beyond (*warāʾ al-warāʾ*).[140]

Before commenting on this crucial passage, let me also quote the text, in which Walī Allāh explains the nature of the Divine Essence or, to use his own term, the Supreme Self (*dhāt-i baḥt*):

> The distinctive feature of the Supreme Self (*dhāt-i baḥt*) is that on the one hand it remains engrossed in the simplitude of Its Self-Identity (*bi-ṣirāfati huwiyyat-i khūd*), while, on the other, despite its simplitude (*baḥtiyyat*),

139 The "philosopher's stone" is used with reference to this *laṭīfa* because of its marvelous and perplexing nature. Originally, the *ḥajar-i baḥt* indicated a mysterious substance which used to be presented as a gift to the princes and nobles, and was not classifiable as being vegetal, mineral, and so on.

140 Walī Allāh, *Alṭāf al-quds* 123.

> it descends (*tanazzul farmāyad*) or projects outward. However, in the course of its descent it loses none of its simplitude—unlike other things the simplitude of which opposes such a descent. Or, it could be said that when the gnostic turns his gaze upon himself (*naẓar-i khūd bi-khūd uftad*) and plunges deep into the contemplation of the ultimate source of his origin (*aṣl-i uṣūl-i khūdash khawḍ namāyad*), then the utmost limit of his vision is that essential shining point (*muntahī-yi naẓarash nuqṭa-yi shaʿshaʿāniyya-yi dhātiyya būd*). He conceives of this point as the center of his own self (*dar miyān-i rūḥ-i way ast*) whereas it dwells, in its unalloyed simplitude (*bisāṭat-i khūd*), in an eminent place.[141]

Since these two passages represent the culmination of Walī Allāh's theory of selfhood, let me elaborate on them in relation to what has been discussed so far. Walī Allāh calls attention to the fact that the individual selfhood (*anāniyyat-i khāṣṣ*) of every self is subsisted through the absolute selfhood (*anāniyya muṭlaq*) of God. In other words, in Walī Allāh's multidimensional theory of selfhood, God, who is the Supreme Self, stands at the apex. Then, as Walī Allāh maintains elsewhere, the first emanation of the Divine Self is the self-unfolding existence (*al-wujūd al-munbasiṭ*) or the Universal Soul.[142] So when the self reaches the station of the Universal Soul, it either regards its individual selfhood (*anāniyyat-i khāṣṣ*) as absolute selfhood, or it becomes oblivious to its individual selfhood, neither affirming nor denying it. In other words, the self, at that level, is both "I" and not "I." However, the degree of the Universal Soul is still not the quintessence of Divine Reality, which is Supreme Selfhood. Now the Supreme Selfhood of divinity is a state of utter simplitude that is devoid of any duality. In other words, it is a state of absolute oneness. In contrast to many Sufis and theologians who argue that the human self can never attain the Supreme Self of God because of Its utter transcendence, Walī Allāh asserts that when the gnostic turns its gaze upon himself, and plunges deep into the contemplation of his ultimate origin, he comes to recognize the immanent divinity within himself, which is like a shining point that resides at the center of his own self. It is noteworthy that Walī Allāh chooses the metaphor of "point," which is a mathematical abstraction having no one-to-one correspondence in external reality. That is to say, to describe such a reality or the experience of it, which is ineffable or lies beyond the beyond (*warāʾ al-warāʾ*), one reaches the bounds of language.[143] The passage, nonetheless, does not fail to underscore that the

141 Walī Allāh, *Alṭāf al-quds* 119.

142 See Faruque, "Sufism *contra* shariah."

143 As Walī Allāh says: "From the Supreme Self he attains something, which is beyond descrip-

very heart of the Divine Self lies at the deepest core of one's selfhood, which is beyond words, yet attainable through annihilation (*fanāʾ*). But does this experience of the Divine Self as one's deepest core make one God? It seems, for Walī Allāh, the answer is in the negative:

> The inner intuition (*al-wijdān*) explicitly affirms that the servant remains the servant when he progresses [toward God] and the Lord remains the Lord when He descends (*al-ṣarīḥ yaḥkum bi-anna al-ʿabd ʿabd wa-in taraqqā, wa-l-rabb rabb wa-in tanazzala*), and the servant can never take on either the attributes of necessity (*wujūb*) or the attributes emanating from it. He does not know the unseen except which is imprinted on the tablet of his breast (*fī lawḥ ṣadrihi*).[144]

That is, the individual self remains an individual despite the realization of its identity with the Divine Self. The best way to account for this paradoxical situation, where one simultaneously affirms and denies any point of contact with the divine, would be to use the heuristic of "identity and difference." That is, although the identity of every individual "I" is clear and distinct and can be affirmed through presential knowledge, the identity of the same "I" can be ambiguous at the point of its contact with the divine "I," for at that level, the "I" is also "not I." It can be simultaneously affirmed and negated. It is thus a situation of "identity and difference," which, as Walī Allāh admits, only arouses bewilderment (*ḥayra*). For this reason, he says that "there is no point in saying more than this. All in all, we should better be advised to take a step back from this abyss (*waraṭa*)."[145] But since as scholars, we have to carry on our hermeneutical task, I would say that for Walī Allāh, the "end" (in the sense of termination) of selfhood is the end of individual selfhood, but at the same time, the 'end' (in the sense of *telos*) to which it aspires, as it opens unto the realm of meta-individual selfhood.

---

tion and interpretation. If it is called witnessing, it is not really witnessing, or if it is called union, it is actually beyond the category of union. It is like a dream that one soon forgets. However, he knows for certain that "It" is something (i.e., Its existence is affirmed), although Its nature cannot be explained in words." (*Chīzī az dhāt-i baḥt bi-dast āyad kih az ān taʿbīr natawān kard. Agar mushāhida gūyad ān khūd mushāhida nīst wa-agar wuṣūl nāmad ān rā khūd az maqūla-yi wuṣūl natawān guft, khwābī ast farāmūsh. Īnqadr mīdānad kih chīzī hast wa-sharḥ-i ān natawān kard*). See Walī Allāh, *Alṭāf al-quds* 122.

144 Walī Allāh, *al-Tafhīmāt al-ilāhiyya* i, 245.

145 Walī Allāh, *Alṭāf al-quds* 132.

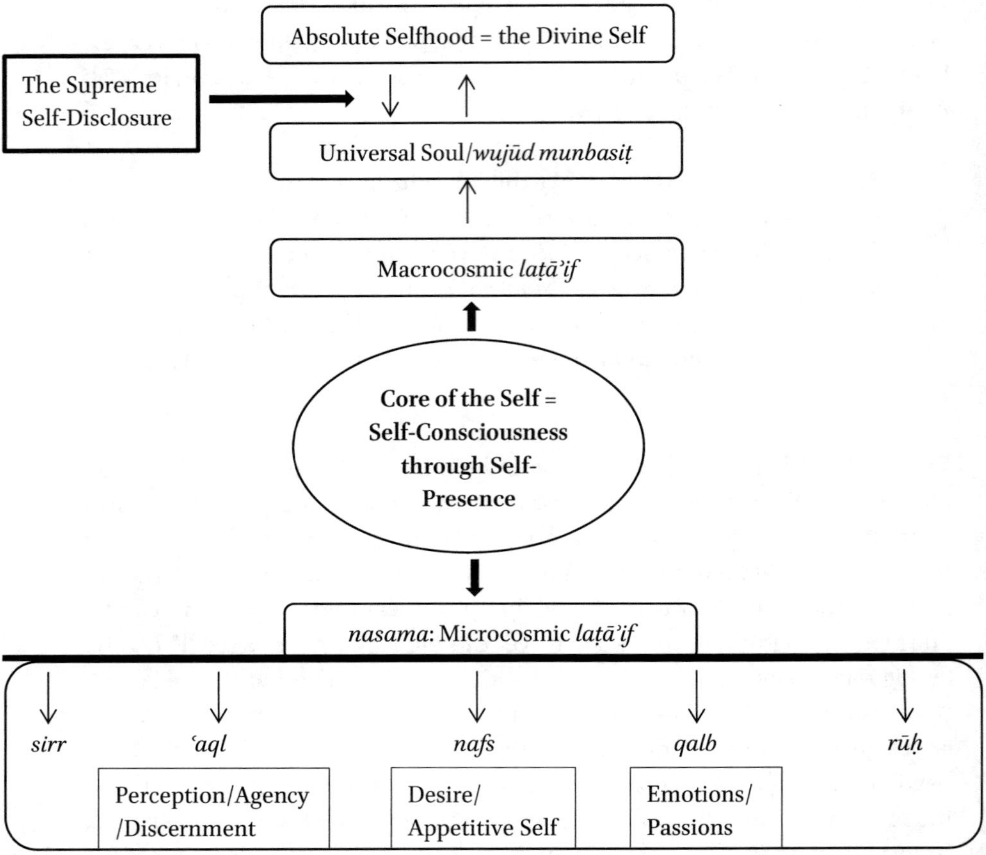

FIGURE 17.4 Shāh Walī Allāh's model of the Self

5 Conclusion

This study explored Shāh Walī Allāh's conception of the self from multiple vantage points. In the end, the feature that stands out in Walī Allāh's philosophy of the self is his penchant for developing original syntheses. It was mentioned earlier that Walī Allāh draws on a panoply of sources ranging over Stoicism, Islamic Neoplatonism, Graeco-Islamic-Indian medical traditions, and Sufism. However, the idea of the self found in some of these intellectual currents stands opposed to one another. For instance, the Stoic self (i.e., *pneuma*) is a material (or quasi-material) entity, which is antithetical to the Avicennan self because of its immateriality. So Walī Allāh argues that the self, being immaterial and the most subtle of all the forms, cannot but be dependent on a *body* which is also the most subtle of all bodies (*alṭaf al-ajsām*) maturing at the finest degree of subtlety and equilibrium. Walī Allāh calls this subtle body *nasama* or *pneuma*, which is an intermediary between the self (immaterial) and the body (material). In this way he was able to resolve the tension between the material *nasama* (*pneuma*) and the immaterial self by reinterpreting Aristotelian hylomorphism so that *pneuma* becomes the "matter" for the "form" of the immaterial self. What is more, by making skillful use of medical knowledge, Walī Allāh was able to synthesize a conception of the self that is based on the physiology of the humoral theory of *pneuma*. Thus, unlike his Sufi predecessors such as al-Ghazālī, he was able to fill the physiological gaps of the *laṭāʾif* theory through a novel synthesis of the Galenic-Islamic medical tradition by mooring the *laṭāʾif* on a corporal base.

At any rate, the many novelties in Walī Allāh's account of selfhood should not cause us to think that he was driven by a "reformist ideology" while constructing such a notion of the self. According to Hermansen, Walī Allāh's theory of the *laṭāʾif* evokes "a mood of reform and heightened individual responsibility."[146] In my reading of Walī Allāh this is far from the case. In fact, Walī Allāh's extensive borrowing from his predecessors and endorsing of their key ideas such as *fanāʾ* and *baqāʾ*, *ʿilm al-ḥuḍūrī*, *laṭāʾif*, *al-nafs al-nāṭiqa*, *al-nafs al-kullī*, *tajallī*, *waḥdat al-wujūd*, *al-wujūd al-munbasiṭ* etc., show that he had little motivation to "reform" conceptions of selfhood in Sufism. If being "original" and "creative" are considered synonymous with being a "reformist," then names such as al-Ghazālī, Ibn ʿArabī, and Mullā Ṣadrā should count first among the foremost reformers of Islam. So a better way to characterize Walī Allāh's thought would be to say that he was a creative thinker, much like Ṣadrā before him, who was able to synthesize elements from different traditions in an original manner.

In the end, it would be fair to claim that Walī Allāh presents a complex, multidimensional understanding of the self that cannot be pinned down to a set of fixed, unchanging features. This means, unlike previous scholarship, one should not just analyze the self in terms of the *laṭāʾif*, even though they may be an important part of it. As Fig. 17.4 summarizes, the center of Walī Allāh's self is defined by self-consciousness, which is known *directly* through self-presence. That is to say, the self, on this account, is present to itself, hence known *directly* (i.e., not as an object). After this one may point to its "spectrum" features (the arrow pointing below) such as the decision making power or agency and various cognitive and emotional capacities. Yet the self can manifest aspirational

146 Hermansen, "Shāh Walī Allāh's theory" 24.

ideals when it undergoes a spiritual journey within the macrocosmic *laṭāʾif*, which are but the self's higher states of consciousness. And, as was explained, at the end of this inward journey lies the Divine Self, which is, paradoxically, nothing other than the individual self that "initiated" the journey from an individual standpoint. It is at that level, through the mystical states of *fanāʾ* and *baqāʾ*, that the identity of the self becomes apophatic in that it simultaneously becomes the "I" and the "not-I," defying any either/or categories (as its reality opens unto the infinite). Thus, one may say that the "end" of selfhood is also its "beginning."

Bibliography

Aḥmad, Barakāt, *Imām al-kalām fī taḥqīq ḥaqīqat al-ajsām*, lithographed ed., Kanpur: al-Maṭbaʿ al-Anẓāmī, 1915.

Aḥmad, Barakāt, *al-Ḥujja al-bāzigha fī sharḥ al-ḥikmat al-bāligha*, lithographed ed., Decan: ʿUthmān Baryasī, 1916.

Aḥmad, Barakāt, *Itqān al-ʿirfān fī taḥqīq māhiyyat al-zamān*, lithographed ed., Lucknow: Shāhī Pirīs, 1919.

Ahmed, Asad, "Post-classical philosophical commentaries/glosses: Innovation in the margins," in *Oriens* 41.3–4 (2013), 317–348.

Ahmed, Asad, "The *Sullam al-ʿulūm* of Muḥibballāh al-Bihārī," in Khaled El-Rouayheb and Sabine Schmidtke (eds.), *Oxford handbook of Islamic philosophy*, Oxford: Oxford University Press, 2017, 488–508.

Ahmed, Asad, "The *Mawāqif of* ʿAḍud al-Dīn Ījī in India," in Ayman Shihadeh and Jan Thiele (eds.), *Philosophical Theology in Islam: Later Ashʿarism East and West*, Leiden: Brill, 2020, 397–412.

Ahmed, Asad, "al-Jawnpūrī," in *EI*³ *Online*, http://dx.doi.org.ezp-prod1.hul.harvard.edu/10.1163/1573-3912_ei3_COM_27005 (last accessed: 17 October 2021).

Ahmed, Asad, *Palimpsests of themselves: Logic and commentary in postclassical Muslim South Asia*, Oakland, CA: University of California Press, 2022.

Ahmed, Asad and Jon McGinnis, "Faḍl-i Ḥaqq Khayrābādī's (d. 1861), *al-Hadiyya al-saʿīdiyya*," in Khaled El-Rouayheb and Sabine Schmidtke (eds.), *Oxford handbook of Islamic philosophy*, Oxford: Oxford University Press, 2017, 535–559.

Ahmed, Asad and Reza Pourjavady, "Islamic theology in India," in Sabine Schmidtke (ed.), *Oxford handbook of Islamic theology*, Oxford: Oxford University Press, 2016, 606–624.

ʿAlī, Raḥmān, *Tuḥfat al-fuḍalāʾ fī tarājim al-kumalāʾ*, Lucknow: Nawal Kishore, 1914.

Alvi, M.A. and A. Rahman, *Fatḥ Allāh Shīrāzī: A sixteenth century Indian scientist*, Delhi: National Institute of the Sciences of India, 1968.

Aristotle, *The complete works of Aristotle: The revised Oxford translation*, ed. Jonathan Barnes, Princeton: Princeton University Press, 1984.

Baljon, Johannes M.S., *Religion and thought of Shāh Walī Allāh Dihlavi*, Leiden: Brill, 1986.

Bilgrāmī, Sayyid Ghulām, *Maʾāthir-i kirām*, ed. Muḥammad Lyallpūrī, Lahore: Maktaba-yi Iḥyāʾ-i ʿUlūm-i Sharqiyya, 1971.

Bilgrāmī, Sayyid Ghulām, *Subḥat al-marjān fī āthār Hindustān*, ed. M. Fazl al-Raḥmān Nadwī, Aligarh: Institute of Islamic Studies, Aligarh Muslim University, 1972.

Brown, Jonathan A.C., *Misquoting Muhammad: The challenge and choices of interpreting the Prophet's legacy*, London: Oneworld Publications, 2014.

Buehler, Arthur, *Sufi heirs of the prophet: The Indian Naqshbandiyya and the rise of the mediating Sufi Shaykh*, Columbia, SC: University of South Carolina Press, 1998.

Buehler, Arthur, "Ahmad Sirhindi: A 21st-century update," in *Der Islam* 86.1 (2009), 122–141.

Chaghatai, Muḥammad I. (ed.), *Shah Waliullah: His religious and political thought*, Lahore: Sang-e-Meel Publications, 2005.

Chittick, William C., "Notes on Ibn al-ʿArabī's influence in the Subcontinent," in MW 82.3–4 (1992), 18–41.

Chittick, William C., "*Waḥdat al-wujūd* in India," in *Ishraq: Islamic Philosophy Yearbook* 3 (2012), 29–40.

Dahnhardt, Thomas W., "The doctrine of the unicity of existence in the light of an eighteenth century Indian Ṣūfī treatise: The *Waḥdat al-wujūd* by Baḥr al-ʿUlūm ʿAbd al-ʿAlī Ansārī al-Lakhnawī," in *Oriente Moderno* 92.2 (2012), 323–360.

Damrel, David, "The 'Naqshbandi Reaction' reconsidered," in David Gilmartin and Bruce Lawrence (eds.), *Beyond Turk and Hindu*, Florida: University Press of Florida, 2000, 176–198.

Dhanani, Alnoor, "*Al-Mawāqif fī ʿilm al-kalām* by ʿAḍud al-Dīn al-Ījī (d. 1355), and its commentaries," in Khaled El-Rouayheb and Sabine Schmidtke (eds.), *Oxford handbook of Islamic philosophy*, Oxford: Oxford University Press, 2017, 375–396.

El-Rouayheb, Khaled, *Islamic intellectual history in the seventeenth century: Scholarly currents in the Ottoman Empire and the Maghreb*, Cambridge: Cambridge University Press, 2015.

Ernst, Carl, "Fayzī's illuminationist interpretation of Vedanta: The *Shāriq al-maʿrifa*," in *Comparative Studies of South Asia, Africa and the Middle East* 30.3 (2010), 356–364.

Faruque, Muhammad U., "Sufism *contra* shariah? Shāh Walī Allāh's metaphysics of *waḥdat al-wujūd*," in *Journal of Sufi Studies* 5.1 (2016), 27–57.

Faruque, Muhammad U., *The labyrinth of subjectivity: Constructions of the self from Mullā Ṣadrā to Muhammad Iqbal*, Berkeley, CA (unpublished PhD Diss.): University of California, 2018.

Faruque, Muhammad U., "Eternity made temporal: Ashraf ʿAlī Thānavī, a twentieth-century Indian thinker and the revival of classical Sufi thought," in *Brill Journal of Sufi Studies* 9.2 (2020), 215–246.

Faruque, Muhammad U., *Sculpting the self: Islam, selfhood, and human flourishing*, Ann Arbor: The University of Michigan Press, 2021.

Friedmann, Yohanan, *Shaikh Ahmad Sirhindi: An outline of his thought and a study of his image in the eyes of posterity*, Montreal: McGill University Press, 1971.

al-Ghazālī, Abū Ḥāmid Muḥammad, *Iḥyāʾ ʿulūm al-dīn*, ed. Muḥammad Ḥusayn, Cairo: al-Maktaba al-Thaqāfī, 1937.

al-Ghazālī, Abū Ḥāmid Muḥammad, *Kitāb Sharḥ ʿajāʾib al-qalb*, see Skellie (trans.), *The marvels*.

al-Harawī, Mīr Zāhid, *Ḥawāshī ʿalā fann al-umūr al-ʿāmma min sharḥ al-Mawāqif*, MS Arab SM4154, Houghton Library, Harvard University.

al-Harawī, Mīr Zāhid, *Sharḥ al-risāla al-maʿmūla fī l-taṣawwur wa-l-taṣdīq wa-taʿlīqātuhu*, ed. Mahdī Sharīʿatī, Qom: Maktabat al-Shahīd Sharīʿatī, 2000.

Hermansen, Marcia K., "Shāh Walī Allāh's theory of the subtle spiritual centers (*laṭāʾif*): A Sufi theory of personhood and self-transformation," in *JNES* 47.1 (1988), 1–25.

Husain, M. Hidayat, "The Persian autobiography of Shāh Walīullāh bin ʿAbd al-Raḥīm al-Dihlavī," in *Journal of the Asiatic Society of Bengal* 14 (1912), 161–176.

Iqbal, Muhammad, *The reconstruction of religious thought in Islam*, ed. and annotated by Saeed Sheikh, Stanford: Stanford University Press, 2013.

Jalbani, Ghulam Hussain, *Life of Shah Waliyullah*, Lahore: Ashraf, 1978.

Kākāʾī, Qāsim, "Āshnāyī bā maktab-i Shīrāz: Ṣadr al-Dīn Dashtakī (Sayyid-i Sanad)," in *Khiradnāma-yi Ṣadrā* 3 (1996–1997), 82–89.

Kākāʾī, Qāsim, "Āshnāyī bā maktab-i Shīrāz: Mīr Ghiyāth al-Dīn Dashtakī (1)," in *Khiradnāma-yi Ṣadrā* 5–6 (1996–1997), 83–90.

Kākāʾī, Qāsim, "Āshnāyī bā maktab-i Shīrāz: Mīr Ghiyāth al-Dīn Dashtakī (2)," in *Khiradnāma-yi Ṣadrā* 7 (1997), 59–67.

Kākāʾī, Qāsim, *Ghiyāth al-Dīn Manṣūr Dashtakī wa-falsafa-yi ʿirfān* (with a critical edition of *Manāzil al-sāʾirīn wa-maqāmat al-ʿārifīn*), Tehran: Intishārāt-i Farhangistān-i Hunar, 2007.

Khān, ʿAbd al-Salām, *Barr-i ṣaghīr kī ʿulamāʾ-i maʿqūlāt awr un kī taṣnīfāt*, Patna: Khudā Bakhsh Oriental Public Library, 1996.

al-Khayrābādī, ʿAbd al-Ḥaqq, *Sharḥ ḥāshiyat Mīr Zāhid umūr ʿāmma*, Kanpur: Niẓāmī Press, 1881.

Knysh, Alexander, *Ibn ʿArabi in the later Islamic tradition: The making of a polemical image in medieval Islam*, Albany, NY: SUNY Press, 1999.

Lāhījī, Mullā Muḥammad Jaʿfar, *Sharḥ al-mashāʿir*, ed. Sayyid Āshtiyānī, Qom: Būstān-i Kitāb, 2007.

al-Lakhnawī, ʿAbd al-Ḥayy b. Fakhr al-Dīn, *Nuzhat al-khawāṭir bahjat al-masāmiʿ wa-l-nawāẓir*, Multan: Idārat-i Taʾlīfāt-i Ashrafiyya, 1993.

Lipton, Gregory, "Muḥibb Allāh Ilāhābādī: South Asian heir to Ibn ʿArabī," in *Journal of the Muhyiddin Ibn ʿArabi Society* 45 (2009), 89–119.

Malik, Jamal, *Islamische Gelehrtenkultur in Nordindien: Entwicklungsgeschichte und Tendenzen am Beispiel von Lucknow*, Leiden: Brill, 1997.

Mawdūdī, Sayyid Abū l-Aʿlā, *Tajdīd wa-iḥyā-yi dīn*, Lahore: Islamic Publisher Ltd., 1999.

Moazzen, Maryam, *Formation of a religious landscape: Shiʿi higher learning in Safavid Iran*, Leiden: Brill, 2018.

Morris, James, *The reflective heart: Discovering spiritual intelligence in Ibn ʿArabī's Meccan illuminations*, Louisville, KY: Fons Vitae, 2005.

Mubārak, Qāḍī, *Kitāb Sullam al-ʿulūm wa-ḥāshiyatihi l-mashhūra bi-l-Qāḍī maʿa munhiyātihi*, Kazan: al-Maṭbaʿa al-Malakiyya, 1887.

Murata, Sachiko, *The Tao of Islam: A sourcebook of gender relationships in Islamic thought*, Albany, NY: SUNY Press, 1992.

Nadwī, Abū l-Ḥasan ʿA., *Saviours of Islamic spirit*. IV. *Hakim-ul-islam Shah Waliullah*, Lucknow: Academy of Islamic Research and Publications, 2004.

Nair, Shankar, "Muḥibb Allāh Ilāhābādī on ontology: Debates over the nature of being," in Jonardon Ganeri (ed.), *The Oxford handbook of Indian philosophy*, Oxford: Oxford University Press, 2017, 657–692.

Nair, Shankar, *Translating wisdom: Hindu-Muslim intellectual interactions in early modern South Asia*, Oakland, CA: University of California Press, 2020.

Pourjavady, Reza, *Philosophy in early Safavid Iran: Najm al-Dīn Maḥmūd al-Nayrīzī and his writings*, Leiden: Brill, 2011.

Rizvi, Sayyid A.A., *A history of Sufism in India*, New Delhi: Munshiram Manoharlal, 1978–1983.

Rizvi, Sayyid A.A., *Shāh Walī-Allāh and his times: A study of eighteenth century Islām, politics and society in India*, Canberra: Maʿrifat Publishing House, 1980.

Rizvi, Sayyid A.A., *Shāh ʿAbd al-ʿAzīz: Puritanism, sectarian polemics and jihad*, Canberra: Maʿrifat Publishing House, 1982.

Rizvi, Sajjad, "Mīr Dāmād in India: Islamic philosophical traditions and the problem of creation," in *JAOS* 131.1 (2011), 9–23.

Robinson, Francis, *The ʿulama of Farangi Mahall and Islamic culture in South Asia*, New Delhi: Permanent Black, 2001.

Sabzawārī, Mullā Hādī, *Sharḥ al-asmāʾ al-ḥusnā*, Tehran: Manshūrāt-i Maktabat Baṣīratī, 1989.

al-Shīrāzī, Ṣadr al-Dīn (Mullā Ṣadrā), *al-Ḥikma al-mutaʿāliya fī l-asfār al-ʿaqliyya al-arbaʿa*, ed. Gholamreza Aavani et al., 9 vols., Tehran: Bunyād-i Ḥikmat-i Islāmi-yi Ṣadrā, 2001–2005.

Sirhindī, Aḥmad, "Maktūbāt Imām Rabbānī," in Arthur Buehler (trans.), *Revealed grace: The juristic Sufism of Ahmad Sirhindi*, Louisville, KY: Fons Vitae, 2011.

Skellie, Walter J. (trans.), *The marvels of the heart: Book 21 of the* Iḥyāʾ ʿulūm al-dīn, *the Revival of the religious sciences*, Louisville, KY: Fons Vitae, 2010.

Thubūt, Akbar, *Filsūf-i Shīrāzī dar Hind*, Tehran: Hermis, 2000.

van Lit, Lambertus W.C., *The world of image in Islamic philosophy: Ibn Sīnā, Suhrawardī, Shahrazūrī, and beyond*, Edinburgh: Edinburgh University Press, 2017.

Walī Allāh, Shāh, *Alṭāf al-quds*, Gujranwala: Madrasa Nuṣrat al-ʿUlūm, 1964.

Walī Allāh, Shāh, *al-Tafhīmāt al-ilāhiyya*, Hyderabad and Sindh: Shāh Walī Allāh Academy, 1967.

Walī Allāh, Shāh, *al-Budūr al-bāzigha*, Hyderabad and Sindh: Shāh Walī Allāh Academy, 1970.

Walī Allāh, Shāh, *Anfas al-ʿārifīn* [Urdu translation of the Persian original], ed. Sayyid Muḥammad Farūqī al-Qādirī, Lahore: al-Maʿārif, 1974.

Walī Allāh, Shāh, *al-Khayr al-kathīr*, Cairo: Maktabat al-Qāhira, 1974.

Walī Allāh, Shāh, *Ḥujjat Allāh al-bāligha*, ed. Muḥammad Hāshim, Beirut: Dār al-Kutub al-ʿIlmiyya, 1995.

Walī Allāh, Shāh, *The conclusive argument from God: Shāh Walī Allāh of Delhi's* Ḥujjat Allāh al-bāligha, trans. Marcia K. Hermansen, Leiden: Brill, 1996.

Wisnovsky, Robert, "The nature and scope of Arabic philosophical commentary in post-classical (ca. 1100–1900 AD) Islamic intellectual history: Some preliminary observations," in Peter Adamson, Han Baltussen and Martin W.F. Stone (eds.), *Philosophy, science, and exegesis in Greek, Arabic, and Latin commentaries*, London: Institute of Classical Studies, 2004.

Ẓafīr al-Dīn, Muḥammad, *Taʿāruf-i makhṭūṭāt Kitābkhāna-yi Dār al-ʿUlūm Deoband*, Deoband: Dār al-ʿUlūm, 1973.

Zanjānī Aṣl, Muḥammad Karīmī, *Ḥikmat-i ishrāqī dar Hind*, Tehran: Intishārāt-i Iṭṭalāʿāt, 2007.

CHAPTER 18

Light/Darkness Dualism and Islamic Metaphysics in Persianate Context

Sayeh Meisami

Many years ago when I was still living in Tehran, I translated an article about Professor Chittick's teachings on cosmology by Mohammed Rustom. This led to our correspondence and fruitful years of friendship and scholarly collaboration, including most recently his invitation to write for this volume. In celebration of Professor Chittick and Professor Murata's precious contributions to the study of philosophy in its Persianate context, I offer in this essay a new narrative concerning the formation of the dual concepts of existence/essence during the classical and post-classical periods of Islamic philosophy.

∵

To begin, a rigid demarcation between mythology and philosophy is neither informative nor useful. It is not informative because it disregards their common source that is human productive imagination;[1] and certainly not useful because it veils the important ways the two may build on each other. As a legacy of the so called "enlightenment" in the modern West, the separation of logos from mythos is premised on the bifurcation of the human epistemic endeavors into that which is valuable due to its "objective" results in correspondence with reality, and that which is the work of imagination both individual and collective with its dubious place in the grand narrative of progress. It is within the Eurocentric metanarrative of progress that the logos/mythos binary opposition has been overemphasized and the history of ideas has been characterized as the evolvement of human knowledge about the world from the immaturity of the mythical imagination to the maturity of philosophical intellection. Despite the post-enlightenment critiques of this approach including the postmodern

1 I emphasize the productive power of imagination as a capacity over and above its reproductive or representational power. This is inspired by Jennifer Gosetti-Ferencei's position on imagination "as the presentational and transformational capacity of consciousness" in her fine interdisciplinary study of imagination. See Gosetti-Ferencei, Jennifer A., *The life of imagination: Revealing and making the world*, New York: Columbia University Press, 2018, 5.

 | DOI:10.1163/9789004529038_019

skepticism of essentialist attempts to define areas of knowledge as separate phenomena, the dominant Western academic discourse on the boundaries of Islamic philosophy still follows the separation paradigm for the most part. In this essay, I challenge this discourse by revisiting the existence/essence conceptualization of reality in Islamic philosophy in view of its affinity with light/darkness dualism in Persian mythology.

Informed by the postmodern method of discourse analysis, first, my account of the connection between mythological and philosophical narratives does not take into consideration the intentionality behind incorporating mythological narratives by the Islamic philosophers at issue. Secondly, my alternative narrative does not imply an understatement of either the Greek or the Quranic influences on the development of Islamic metaphysics, but simply suggests an additional perspective. Thirdly, in my approach to the development of Islamic metaphysics I avoid the essentialist glorification/mystification of "the Persian mind," pace Iqbal,[2] or Corbin's romantic celebration of "the Persian genius"[3] and simply inquire into discourse formation. Lastly, in my account, I avoid any historical or meta-historical claims to the effect that philosophy was born in Persia and suspend judgments on what is the "true" history of philosophy. In general, my arguments are premised on my understanding of both mythology and philosophy as fields of discourse formation which attract, integrate, and modify narratives and conceptual schemes created by human productive imagination over a long period of time, especially those in their cultural vicinity.

The Persian myth of light and darkness as the central narrative of Zoroastrian traditions offers a metaphysical visualization of reality based on tension and resolution. Major scholarships on Zoroastrian texts show that Persian creation myths revolve around antagonism between polar forces of light and darkness, the good spirt and the evil spirit, the limitless and the limited,

---

2 Iqbal essentializes "the Persian mind" and uses a Hegelian tone to build a narrative of its progress from dualism to monism. In his narrative, Iqbal invokes the Zoroastrian dualism of light and darkness in relation to the development of Neoplatonism in Persia and argues that: "The old Iranian idea of the dualism of Light and Darkness, does not act as a determining factor in the progress of Neo-Platonic ideas in Persia, which borrowed independent life for a time, and eventually merged their separate existence in the general current of Persian speculation." See Iqbal, Muhammad, *The development of metaphysics in Persia*, London: Luzac, 1908, 45.

3 For example, Corbin refers to "the Persian genius" that "excels in metaphysics and mysticism." See Corbin, Henry, *History of Islamic philosophy*, New York: Kegan Paul, 1993, 311. He has famously argued for the continuity between Zoroastrian angelology and Avicennan cosmology and believes that "the restoration or re-enlistment of Zoroastrian 'motifs' by the philosophy of Ishrāq is also discernable in the Avicennan line." See Corbin, Henry, *Avicenna and the visionary recital*, trans. Willard Trask, Irving, TX: Spring Publications, 1980, 58.

and truth and falsity, with the final victory belonging to light, the good spirit, the limitless, and truth. Roughly speaking, the Zoroastrian discourse on the origin and composition of the universe revolves around two rivaling narratives. The Older Avesta, namely the *Gathas*, together with the Younger Avesta, which consists mainly of the exegesis of the *Gathas* and other Zoroastrian traditions, picture the cosmic dynamics as a battle between Ohrmazd, the god of light, and Ahriman, the god of darkness. But, already in the *Gathas*, the omniscience, goodness, and power of Ohrmazd qualify him as *the* true God, and on this account some scholars consider the creation narrative of the *Gathas* as monotheistic.[4] The other narrative, which becomes popular during the Sassanian Empire, regards Ohrmazd and Ahriman as the twin sons of infinite time, namely Zurvān.[5] Regardless of differences over the origin of the dark force, these Persian creation narratives construe the dynamics of the natural and the spiritual worlds in terms of the opposition between light and darkness.[6] For example, we read in the *Greater Bundahishn*:

> It is thus revealed in the Good Religion that Ohrmazd was on high in omniscience and goodness. For boundless time He was ever in the light. That light is the space and place of Ohrmazd. Some call it Endless Light. Ahriman was abased in slowness of knowledge and the lust to smite. The lust to smite was his sheath and darkness his place. Some call it Endless Darkness.[7]

The antagonism is extended to all facets of natural, spiritual, and moral life:

---

4 For example, see Boyce, Mary, *Textual sources for the study of Zoroastrianism*, Totowa, NJ: Barnes and Noble, 1984, 12; Aminrazavi, Mehdi, "Introduction," in Seyyed Hossein Nasr and Mehdi Aminrazavi (eds.), *An anthology of philosophy in Persia*, 5 vols., i, London: I.B. Tauris in association with The Institute of Ismaili Studies, 2008–2015, 13–15, 15. In contrast, for Jean Kellens, "There cannot be—and perhaps there never has been—any clear dividing line between polytheism and monotheism." See, Schwartz, Martin et al., "Interpretations of Zarathustra and the *Gāthās*," in Michael Stausberg, Yuhan S-D Vevaina, and Anna Tessmann (eds.), *The Wiley Blackwell companion to Zoroastrianism*, Chichester: Wiley Blackwell, 2015, 39–67, 49.

5 For an account about the development of this idea, see Zaehner, Robert C., *Zurvan, a Zoroastrian dilemma*, Oxford: Clarendon Press, 1955, 54–79.

6 Helmut Humbach refers to this aspect of Zarathustra's world-view as "pan-dualism." While acknowledging Ohrmazd as "the supreme being," Humbach states that "the beings of both the spiritual and the material world, the things they produce and the processes they effect, either belong to the good or to the evil side." See Schwartz et al., "Interpretations" 41.

7 Nasr, Seyyed Hossein and Mehdi Aminrazavi (eds.), *An anthology of philosophy in Persia*, 5 vols., i, London: I.B. Tauris in association with The Institute of Ismaili Studies, 2008–2015, 55–56.

> Bad thought, word and deed are against good thought, word and deed, ... aimless lust against innate wisdom, ... idleness against diligence, sloth against (needful) sleep, vengefulness against peace, pain against pleasure, stench against fragrance, darkness against light, poison against ambrosia, bitterness against sweetness, parsimony against generosity, avarice against discriminate giving, winter against summer, cold against heat ...[8]

To approach the existence/essence dualism of Islamic metaphysics from the point of view of the Persian creation myth I will first argue that Avicenna's (d. 428/1037) famous crafting of this dualism can be interpreted as a continuation or new dimension of the Persian myth of light and darkness. Then I will proceed to revisit the post-Avicennan development of the existence/essence relation in the Illuminationist and Transcendentalist discourses, which are best represented respectively by Shihāb al-Dīn Suhrawardī (d. 587/1191) and Mullā Ṣadrā Shīrāzī (d. 1050/1640), from the perspective of tension between light and darkness.

Avicenna's existence/essence dualism took shape within a cultural and intellectual context which had retained its Persian character during the Islamic rule. One can mention the flourishing of Zoroastrian ideas in Central Asia during the 4th/10th century, most prominently in the city of Samarqand,[9] with its cultural reputation in Persianate history along with Bukhara, the capital of the Samanid dynasty. We know that Avicenna's father worked for the last Samanid Amir, Nūḥ b. Manṣūr (r. 365–387/975–997),[10] and later Avicenna himself served as the Amir's physician and was permitted to use his library.[11] Famously, it was during the Samanid period that discourses on Persian revivalism became prevalent. One example of this revivalism was the reappearance of Persian mythology through the poetry of Daqīqī (d. ca. 366/976) who was possibly a Zoroastrian. Even the next dynasty, the Ghaznavids, who were Turkic by descent, contributed to this movement and the most celebrated Persian poet, Firdawsī of Ṭūs (d. 416/1025), belongs to the latter period.[12] Among

8 Nasr and Aminrazavi (eds.), *An anthology* i, 61–62.

9 Grenet, Frantz, "Zoroastrianism in Central Asia," in Michael Stausberg, Yuhan S-D Vevaina, and Anna Tessmann (eds.), *The Wiley Blackwell companion to Zoroastrianism*, Chichester: Wiley Blackwell, 2015, 129–146, 145.

10 Gohlman, William E., *The life of Ibn Sina: A critical edition and annotated translation*, Albany, NY: SUNY Press, 1974, 17.

11 Gohlman, *The life* 36–37.

12 Afnan, Soheil M., *Avicenna: His life and works*, London: Allen & Unwin, 1956, 46–48; for the intellectual and historical features of Avicenna's age, see McGinnis, Jon, *Avicenna*, Oxford: Oxford University Press, 2010, 3–16.

Avicenna's own followers and interlocutors we come across Bahmanyār b. Marzbān (d. 458/1066) who came from a Zoroastrian background, and Ibn Zayla (d. 440/1047) of a dubious association with Zoroastrianism.[13] To cut an otherwise long historical account short, Avicenna's worldview cannot be fully appreciated without considering the discursive spirit of the age. From this perspective, I revisit Avicenna's modification of Aristotle's metaphysics in view of the Persian myth of light and darkness.

Under the influence of Avicenna the dominant discourse of metaphysics in Islamic Persia was characterized by a narrative that consisted of the dual concepts of existence and essence in their hierarchical relation to each other. These two concepts were initially formulated by Aristotle in several of his works, most importantly his *Metaphysics*. For Aristotle, the "essence" of a thing is the "what it is to be" of it that is stated by its definition. For example, if we define human being as a "rational animal," these two terms signify two concepts that refer to the essential properties of a real human being. Unlike "essence" that captures the reality of what is there in the extra-mental world, whether it be natural or supernatural, "existence" for Aristotle does not refer to a reality in addition to essence, and to say that something exists is the same as saying that something is a substance.[14] That said, Aristotle's use of the two concepts in his study of reality does not comprise a dualism. But Avicenna deviates from him by distinguishing between the referents of the two concepts.

Although he borrows the terms "existence" and "essence" from Aristotle, his view of existence and its relation to essence is unique on three counts.[15] First, for Avicenna, "Existence is neither a thing's quiddity, nor a part of its quiddity."[16] Existence is distinct from essence and it must be affirmed of (*ithbāt*) essence/quiddity (*al-māhiyya*) for something to be regarded as an entity (*shay'*). He states in *al-Ilāhiyyāt min al-shifā'* (*The Metaphysics of the healing*) that "It is known that the reality proper [i.e., quiddity] to each thing is other than the existence that corresponds to what is affirmed."[17] As Robert Wisnovsky

13 For Bahmanyār and Ibn Zayla, see Reisman, David C., *The making of the Avicennan tradition*, Leiden: Brill, 2002, 185–198.

14 Aristotle, *Metaphysics*: *Books Z and H*, trans. David Bostock, New York: Clarendon Press, 1997, Z i, 1028b, 2–4.

15 McGinnis correctly states that "Even if the distinction is already present in al-Fārābī's thought, it was Avicenna who thoroughly explored and developed it." McGinnis, *Avicenna* 247.

16 Avicenna, *al-Ishārāt wa-l-tanbīhāt*, ed. Sulaymān Dunyā, 3 vols., iii, Cairo: Dār al-Maʿārif, 1983–1994, 49.

17 Avicenna, *The metaphysics of the healing*, ed. and trans. Michael E. Marmura, Provo, UT: Brigham Young University Press, 2005, 24.

explains, "To predicate affirmative existence of an entity is to assert that the entity [or thing] is, not what the entity is," and since "Existence that is specific [i.e. the essence] is distinct from affirmative existence, it follows that whatness is distinct from affirmative existence. In other words, essence is distinct from existence."[18] Secondly, in Avicenna's existence/essence dualism existence is metaphysically prioritized since essence or quiddity is not sufficient for "specification" (*takhṣīṣ*) for which quiddity needs a cause which specifies it by conferring existence to it.[19] In other words, while essence and existence are co-extensional in the extra-mental world, it is assumed that without existence bestowed on essence, there would be no specific entity that counts as a reality. Thirdly, for Avicenna, there can be existence without quiddity as in the case of the first cause of the universe that is pure existence. According to him, "the First has no quiddity other than His individual existence."[20]

Now, if we accept that Avicenna's account of the relation between existence and essence is different from Aristotle's, what would be our discursive ground for also suggesting that the former's account reflects the Zoroastrian narrative of light/darkness dualism? Starting with the mythological dualism, "Light" is life-giving in the creative sense of the term. In the language of the Avesta, "Ohrmazd fashioned forth the form of His creatures from His own self, from the substance of light."[21] In its creative aspect, Ohrmazd is comparable to Avicenna's "First Principle" (*al-mabdaʾ al-awwal*) since all existents are originally emanated from the latter. Furthermore, Avicenna describes the First Principle as "Truth" (*ḥaqq*) and "pure good" (*khayr maḥḍ*) that creates through intermediaries which are referred to as "intellects."[22] Similarly, Ohrmazd is associated with truth and goodness, and it creates through the angelic powers of the "Amishā Spentā."[23] Moreover, both Ohrmazd and the First Principle of Avicenna create through thinking. For Avicenna, "that which is known by It [the First Principle] is brought into existence," and "Its ability is identical with Its knowledge of the order of things."[24] On the Zoroastrian end, for example,

18 Wisnovsky, Robert, "Notes on Avicenna's concept of thingness (*šayʾiyya*)," in *ASP* 10.2 (2000), 181–221, 193.

19 Avicenna, *The metaphysics* 31–32.

20 Avicenna, *The metaphysics* 274.

21 Nasr and Aminrazavi (eds.), *An anthology* i, 57.

22 Avicenna, *The metaphysics* 21.

23 See Boyce, *Textual sources* 12–13 & 47; Nasr and Aminrazavi (eds.), *An anthology* i, 19–20.

24 Nasr and Aminrazavi (eds.), *An anthology* i, 254, 256. He says in the same text that "Moreover, Its will proceeds from knowledge in the following manner. It knows that the being of something is in itself good and is pleasant, and the being of such a thing should be in a manner which is good and virtuous, and the existence of such a thing is better than

the *Gathas* addresses Ohrmazd by saying that "... thou didst fashion for us in the beginning, by Thy thought, creatures and inner selves and intentions ..."[25] Most importantly for my comparison, the power of Avicenna's First Principle and that of Ohrmazd's similarly reach as far as what is possible: Ohrmazd cannot turn good what is essentially evil, i.e., Ahriman, and Avicenna's First Principle cannot make existent what is essentially impossible such as a parent who is younger than her child.[26] According to a 3rd/9th century apologist of Zoroastrianism:

> The omnipotence of Ohrmazd [middle Persian for Ahurā Mazdā affects all that which can be and which is determined. As for what cannot be, there is no question of being able or not able to do it. Were I to say that Ohrmazd the Creator had the power to restrain Ahriman [middle Persian for Angra Mainyu] from the wickedness which is his constant nature (this would mean that) it is possible to turn that devilish nature into a divine one, and the divine into a devilish; and that darkness can be made light, and light darkness. Those who say that essence itself can be changed, know nothing of essence, and account wolf and reptile as beneficent.[27]

Likewise, for Avicenna only what is possible in itself can become existent through its cause. I'm here referring to Avicenna's famous development of modalities in connection to metaphysics. According to his *al-Najāt* (*The salvation*):

> In terms of the thing itself on its own, it is something that must exist necessarily, possibly or impossibly. Now, it cannot be something that must exist impossibly, because anything whose existence is impossible through itself is neither through itself nor through another. Nor is it something that must exist necessarily, for we have already said that whatever exists necessarily through itself simply cannot have the necessity of its existence through another. So it remains that with respect to the thing itself, it exists possibly; with respect to introducing an association with that

its nonexistence. Then, It needs no other thing [i.e., no intervening desire, inclination or instrument], because that which is known by It is brought into existence. Thus, in knowing a thing to be, It brings into being all things and brings into being the best possible world which this world has the ability to be, [and this] is the requisite cause for all things such as are to come to exist."

25 Boyce, *Textual sources* 39.

26 On the limit of Ohrmazd's power, see Kronen, John and Sandra Menssen, "The defensibility of Zoroastrian dualism," in *Religious Studies* 46.2 (2010), 185–205, 192–193.

27 Boyce, *Textual sources* 102 cited by Kronen and Menssen, "The defensibility" 193.

> other, it exists necessarily; and with respect to disrupting the association with that other, it exists impossibly. It itself, however—in itself without condition—exists possibly.[28]

The above-mentioned similarities between the Zoroastrian Ohrmazd and Avicenna's First Principle reinforce the comparison of light with existence since Ohrmazd is the creator of light and the First Principle or Necessary Being is the ultimate source of existence. In accordance with this similarity, the light of Ohrmazd and the existence that proceeds from the Necessary Being cannot function in the face of metaphysical impossibility. As light cannot be injected into darkness to make it luminous, existence cannot be added to an essence that is not possible in itself.

Given the above association between the mythological and philosophical narratives about the ultimate reality, it is no accident that the two major metaphysical discourses which appeared in the wake of Avicennan philosophy in Iran, with their strong positions on the existence/essence dualism, i.e., Illuminationism (*ḥikmat al-ishrāq*) and Transcendentalism (*al-ḥikma al-mutaʿāliya*) depend heavily on the concept of light.[29] It is true that Illuminationists such as Suhrawardī try to remove the existence/essence dualism in favor of essence and Mullā Ṣadrā's transcendental philosophy favors existence over essence, but, reality is similarly identified as light in both these traditions. The identification may seem more obvious in Suhrawardī's texts since he proposes an ontology of lights and traces it back to "the teaching of Persian philosophers such as Jamasp, Frashostar, Bozorgmehr, and others before them."[30] However, I argue that although in Mullā Ṣadrā's texts light seems to have a more figurative status, the function of light in his metaphysics is more substantial than a figure of speech or analogical tool. In effect, Mullā Ṣadrā's description of existence for the most part matches Suhrawardī's characterization of reality as light, as I will explain later.

In his *Ḥikmat al-ishrāq*, Suhrawardī sets up an ontology of lights based on his description of light as "that which is evident in its own reality (*al-ẓāhir fī ḥaqīqat nafsihi*) and by essence makes another evident (*al-muẓhir li-ghayrihi*

28 McGinnis, Jon and David C. Reisman (trans.), *Classical Arabic philosophy: An anthology of sources*, Indianapolis: Hackett Publishing, 2007, 212.

29 This claim does not contradict the dominant narrative which explains the use of light imagery under the influence of Neoplatonism since Neoplatonic light motifs can also be interpreted in their coherence and continuation with Persian mythology.

30 Suhrawardī, Shihāb al-Dīn, *The philosophy of illumination*, ed. and trans. John Walbridge and Hossein Ziai, Provo, UT: Brigham Young University Press, 1999, 2. His reference is followed by a disclaimer regarding what he considers as the 'heretical' anthropomorphic teachings of the Magi and Mani.

bi-dhātihi) … thus [it is] more evident in itself than anything to whose reality being evident is superadded."[31] Suhrawardī's focus on light has precedence in Persian philosophical Sufism, for example, in the works of Abū Ḥamid al-Ghazālī (d. 505/1111) and ʿAyn al-Quḍāt Hamadānī (d. 525/1131).[32] In his concise Sufi text, *Mishkāt al-anwār* (*The niche of lights*), Ghazālī, describes light as "that which is manifest and makes manifest" (*al-ẓāhir al-muẓhir*) and he relies on light imagery to promote "a proper perception of the relationship between God and the world" in terms of "His presence."[33] Although he refers to the Quran as his main source for his Sufi interpretation of God-world relationship, it is hard to ignore the Persian undertone of his narrative of light/darkness dialectic despite his Islamic reservations about Zoroastrianism. For example, Ghazālī classifies different forms of worshipping God based on his interpretation of the *ḥadīth* of Veils: "God has seventy veils of lights and darkness: were He to lift them, the august glory of His face would burn up everyone whose eyesight perceived Him."[34] According to his interpretation of this *ḥadīth*, worshippers are of three kinds: those who are veiled by darkness; those who are veiled by a mixture of light and darkness; and those who are veiled by light. It is in this context that Ghazālī refers to Zoroastrian dualists (*al-thanawiyya*) as among those who are veiled from the reality of Light/God by a mixture of light and darkness.[35] Yet, according to him, the Dualists' understanding of light is superior to others in their group such as those who worship fire or the sun because unlike them, the Dualists worship "The unlimited light" and ascribe to Him all the good things in the world.[36]

Among the Sufi followers of Ghazālī, ʿAyn al-Quḍāt Hamadānī's critical engagement with the Zoroastrian narrative of light/darkness is noteworthy. His texts are built on the Sufi metanarrative of monism that entails confrontation with a major interpretation of Zoroastrian dualism, i.e., the rivalry between two gods, one good and one evil. In ʿAyn al-Quḍāt's writings, God is the only real existence and the rest is a manifestation of Him, just like the rays of light are

31 Suhrawardī, *The philosophy* 81.

32 For Ghazālī's influence on ʿAyn al-Quḍāt, see Maghsoudlou, Salimeh, "La pensée de ʿAyn al-Qudāt al-Hamadānī (m. 525/1132), entre avicennisme et héritage ġazâlien," Paris (PhD Diss.): École Pratique des Hautes Études, 2016 and Rustom, Mohammed, *Inrushes of the heart: The Sufi philosophy of ʿAyn al-Quḍāt*, Albany, NY: SUNY Press, 2023.

33 Chittick, William C., "Foreword," in Abū Ḥāmid Muḥammad al-Ghazālī, *The niche of lights*, trans. David Buchman, Provo, UT: Brigham Young University Press, 1998, xiii.

34 Al-Ghazālī, Abū Ḥāmid Muḥammad, *The niche of lights*, trans. David Buchman, Provo, UT: Brigham Young University Press, 1998, 44.

35 Al-Ghazālī, *The niche* 44–53.

36 Al-Ghazālī, *The niche* 49.

manifestations of the light.[37] He characterizes God as the source of lights who is not manifest in His "substance," with the whole of His creation being "accidental" lights which point to God as the hidden source:

> Substance is an expression of the source of existence, whereas an accident has the sense of subsisting in a substance. I am not referring to the substance and accident of the sensible world. I am speaking about the real [*ḥaqīqī*] substance and accident. You cannot understand? Alas! God is existent. Thus, He is a substance. But a substance cannot be without accident. Thus, God's existence is a substance, and light is an accident of that substance.[38]

Notwithstanding, the metanarrative of oneness accommodates the light/darkness dialectic. ʿAyn al-Quḍāt's main usage of the light/darkness relation is in his theory of evil and Satanology where light and darkness which are respectively associated with Muhammad and Iblīs are from the same source and complement each other:

> O dear friend! This is wisdom: Whatever is, was, and will be must not and cannot be otherwise. Whiteness could never be without blackness. Heaven cannot be without earth. Substance is inconceivable without accident. Muhammad could never be without Iblis. Obedience without disobedience and unbelief without faith are inconceivable. So too is it the case with every opposite. This is the meaning of, "Things are distinguished through their opposites."[39]

ʿAyn al-Quḍāt also interprets the light and darkness dialectic in theological terms. In *Tamhīdāt* (*Paving the path*), the white light of Muhammad and the black light of Iblīs respectively point to the attributes of beauty (*ṣifāt-i jamāl*) such as divine mercy, and the attributes of majesty (*ṣifāt-i jalāl*) such as divine compulsion. In this regard, ʿAyn al-Quḍāt says, "Have you ever heard that God has two names? One is the All-Merciful, the Compassionate [Q 59:22] and the other is the Compeller, the Proud [Q 59:23]."[40] An alternative though problematic perspective is to look at this dialectic in ʿAyn al-Quḍāt's works through the

37 Rustom, Mohammed, "Devil's advocate: ʿAyn al-Quḍāt's defense of Iblis in context," in *SI* 115.1 (2020), 65–100, 70–73.
38 Rustom, "Devil's advocate" 84.
39 Rustom, "Devil's advocate" 86.
40 Rustom, "Devil's advocate" 87.

lens of the Avestan opposition between the Bounteous Spirit (Spenta Mainyu) and the Hostile Spirit (Angra Mainyu). The origin of the twin spirits and their opposition has been interpreted differently by Zoroastrian theologians over a long period of time. According to Mary Boyce, in some interpretations "Spənta Mainyu appears as the active principle by which Ahurā Mazdā accomplished the acts of creation."[41] The function of Angra Mainyu is destruction and hostility toward the Bounteous Spirit. Angra Mainyu that is identified as Ahriman in several Zoroastrian texts, is the twin of the Spenta Mainyu in Zurvanism, a monist sect within Zoroastrianism. In this regard, Landolt claims that among the different branches of Zoroastrianism, ʿAyn al-Quḍāt's treatment of light and darkness is more in line with Zurvanism according to which Ohrmazd and Ahriman are created by the same god.[42] We read in the *ʿUlamāʾ-i Islām*, which enshrines the replies by a Zurvanite scholar to questions posed by some Muslim theologians, that "except Time all other things are created. Time is the creator; and Time has no limit, neither top nor bottom. It has always been and shall be for evermore."[43] However, any characterization of the Creator as Time is out of question for ʿAyn al-Quḍāt and it is hardly possible to attribute Zurvanism to his system. All we can support based on the above observations is the significance of the two concepts of light and darkness in his narrative of creation, which seems to have prepared the ground for Suhrawardī.

Suhrawardī's texts not only reflect familiarity with Persian mythology, but also actively incorporate its concepts and narratives. While he distinguishes the aforesaid narratives from "The doctrine of the infidel Magi" and "The heresy of Mani,"[44] at the heart of what he considers the true teachings of the ancient Persians lies the light/darkness dialectic. Suhrawardī categorizes light into "pure light" (*al-nūr al-maḥḍ*) which is self-sufficient, and "accidental light" (*al-nūr al-ʿāriḍ*), which depends on pure light.[45] This may sound similar to ʿAyn al-Quḍāt's employment of the terms "substance" and "accident;" but he identifies substantial light with God, while for Suhrawardī the referent of independent or "pure light" is any light that is incorporeal. In any case, Suhrawardī is adam-

41 Boyce, Mary, "Ahūrā Mazdā," in *EIr*.

42 Landolt, Hermann, "Two types of mystical thought in Muslim Iran," in Ian R. Netton (ed.), *Islamic philosophy and theology: Critical concepts in Islamic thought*, 4 vols., iv, New York: Routledge, 2007, 81–96, 91. Such an attribution of Zoroastrian beliefs to ʿAyn al-Quḍāt is challenged by Rustom's account of ʿAyn al-Quḍāt's rejection of Zoroastrian "ontological dualism." Based on evidence from ʿAyn al-Quḍāt's writings, Rustom argues that "Iblis' darkness is, in fact, not darkness but overshadowed light." See Rustom, *Inrushes*, ch. 9.

43 Zaehner, *Zurvan* 409.

44 Suhrawardī, *The philosophy* 2.

45 Suhrawardī, *The philosophy* 77.

ant that anything other than light, is darkness (*ẓulma*). It is true that in several places he states that darkness is the absence of light, but his cosmology is nevertheless built on the dynamics between light and darkness and the latter seems to be 'present' in the cosmic picture he draws. For one thing, the material world is described as a dusky and shadowy realm due to the permeation of darkness, which he also describes as the domain of "contingency." Moreover, in Suhrawardī's cosmological narrative, except for "the Light of lights" (*nūr al-anwār*) or God, light is essentially accompanied with darkness or shadow. Thus, as far up on the ranks of illumination as the incorporeal lights which proceed from the Light of lights (God), there is also darkness:

> By the manifestation to itself of its dependence (*faqr*) and the darkening of its own essence in its contemplation of the glory of the Light of lights in relation to itself, a *shadow* results from [the incorporeal light] … But with respect to its independence and its necessity by the Light of lights and its contemplation of its glory and might, it brings into being another incorporeal light … its *shadow* is only due to the *darkness* of its dependence.[46]

If we compare Suhrawardī's narrative of the hierarchy of lights with Avicenna's Intellects, then in retrospect we may juxtapose Avicenna's use of "existence" with light and that of "essence" with darkness. Despite Suhrawardī's equation of reality with "essence," his general metaphysical discourse is the same as the Avicennan discourse which has only become more conscious of its Persian background. Moreover, Suhrawardī's use of the concept of "dependence" in the above quotation resonates with the Avicennan coupling of contingency with essence and necessity with existence. Lastly, Suhrawardī's characterization of the ultimate reality as "light" makes it sound more like "existence" in Avicenna's metaphysics despite the former's preference for "essence." But, this is a subject which deserves to be studied further in another article.

Suhrawardī's systematic visualization of the ultimate reality as light vividly informs the two rivalling metaphysical discourses of the Safavid period, which are represented by Muḥammad Bāqir Mīr Dāmād's (d. 1040/1631) essentialism and Mullā Ṣadrā's existentialism. Within the confines of the present essay, it would suffice to note the centrality of light in Mīr Dāmād's metaphysics, which is suggested even by the title of his major treatises such as *al-Qabasāt* (*The firebrands*), and *al-Jadhawāt* (*The burning firewood*). In these two treatises, sim-

46 Suhrawardī, *The philosophy* 95. Italics are mine.

ilar to Suhrawardī, Mīr Dāmād bases his creation narrative on "light" and he develops two cosmic orders, a descending (*nuzūlī*) order and an ascending (*ṣuʿūdī*) one.[47] For Mīr Dāmād, the origin and end of the cosmos is the "Light of lights,"[48] a doctrine which together with his innovative hierarchy of three types of time partially explains why his two students Sayyid Aḥmad ʿAlawī (d. ca. 1060/1650) and Quṭb al-Dīn Ashkiwarī (d. ca. 1088/1678) incorporate Zoroastrian, especially Zurvanite, narratives in their texts.[49] As for Mīr Dāmād's more famous student, Mullā Ṣadrā, he too retains the Illuminationist narrative of creation though for him it is "existence" that best fits into this narrative. He states that, "in truth, the reality of light and existence is the same thing."[50] In Mullā Ṣadrā's texts, not only is "existence" similar to "light" in its self-sufficient luminosity and different degrees of intensity, but also "essence" appears as a shadow of existence, hence the reappearance of light/darkness dialectic in Sadrian metaphysics. Let me start with a passage from *al-Asfār al-arbaʿa* (*The four journeys*) which echoes the Illuminationist tradition but it also exemplifies the association of light with existence and darkness with essence:

> Existence (*wujūd*) is like "light" which is sometimes applied and intended to have an infinitive sense (*al-maʿnā al-maṣdarī*), namely luminosity (*nūrāniyya*) for something, and [in this sense] it is not one of the things in the extra-mental world (*al-aʿyān*) but only exists in the minds; and sometimes it is applied and intended as that which is evident in its own reality (*al-ẓāhir bi-dhātihi*) and makes another evident (*al-muẓhir li-ghayrihi*), namely the luminous realities such as the Transcendent Necessary (*al-wājib taʿālā*), the intellects and the souls, and the accidental lights both the intelligible and the sensible ones, like the light of stars and lamps.

---

47 For a brief survey of these two treatises, see Dabashi, Hamid, "Mīr Dāmād," in Seyyed Hossein Nasr and Oliver Leaman (eds.), *History of Islamic philosophy*, 2 vols., ii, New York: Routledge, 1996, 597–634, 609–614. The above cosmic order is discussed in the ninth *qabas* Mīr Dāmād's treatise. See Mīr Dāmād, Muḥammad Bāqir, *Kitāb al-Qabasāt*: *The book of blazing brands*, trans. Keven Brown, New York: Global Scholarly Publications, 2009, 365–424. For the context and reception of *Kitāb al-Qabasāt* and an analysis of Mīr Dāmād's creation theory, see Rizvi, Sajjad, "Mīr Dāmād's (d. 1631) *al-Qabasāt*: The problem of the eternity of the cosmos," in Khaled El-Rouayheb and Sabine Schmidtke (eds.), *The Oxford handbook of Islamic philosophy*, New York: Oxford University Press, 2017, 438–464, 448–461.

48 Mīr Dāmād, *Kitāb al-Qabasāt* 393–394.

49 For a brief discussion of the Zoroastrian ideas in ʿAlawī and Ashkiwarī, see Corbin, Henry, *En Islam iranien*, 4 vols., iv, Paris: Gallimard, 1971–1972, 49–50.

50 Shīrāzī, Mullā Ṣadrā, *On the hermeneutics of the light verse of the Qurʾān*, trans. Latimah-Parvin Peerwani, London: ICAS Press, 2004, 43.

> [In this second sense] light exists in the extra-mental world rather than in the minds ... and it is identical with the luminous realities (*al-ḥaqāʾiq al-nūriyya*) in their differences which are due to perfection and imperfection, potency and weakness ... And each degree of imperfection or shortness from the perfection of that Light which has no limits in greatness, majesty, glory and beauty, is corresponded with a degree of darkness (*martaba min marātib al-ẓulumāt*) and non-existents (*al-aʿdām*) which are called contingent quiddities (*al-māhiyyāt al-imkāniyya*).[51]

In addition to "darkness," Mullā Ṣadrā's metaphysical narrative associates "quiddity" with "obscurity" (*ibhām*), "latency" (*kumūn*),[52] and "impurity" (*shawb*).[53] Throughout Mullā Ṣadrā's texts, the negative description of quiddity in its contradistinction to existence as perfect and pure seems to bring us close to light/darkness dualism. One apparent impediment to this reading is that Mullā Ṣadrā's metaphysics is known for its existential monism since it considers existence as the only authentic reality with quiddity to be epiphenomenal. One way to address this paradox is to distinguish Mullā Ṣadrā's "monism" from the essentialist monism of Suhrawardī and Mīr Dāmād. It is true that Mullā Ṣadrā's discourse on existence and essence (quiddity) presents existence as the only authentic reality, but quiddities are not merely considerations of the mind (*al-amr al-iʿtibārī*) of the same status as that of "existence" in Suhrawardī's narrative.[54] In other words, Mullā Ṣadrā's "essence" is not an empty term which he could dispose of through logical analysis as does Suhrawardī with respect to "existence." Rather, Mullā Ṣadrā's "essence" applies to different grades of the one Reality or Existence as we read in the quotation above from *al-Asfār*. Quiddities are diversities within the unity of existence and without them there would remain only one undifferentiated simple reality. Moreover, quiddities as such also enjoy mental existence which is the epistemic ground of our knowledge of diversity in unity.[55] To use an analogy by Mullā Ṣadrā, quiddities are as real as numbers which are "an assemblage of units (*al-waḥdāt*) that are similar to one another."[56] With all this in mind, in Mullā Ṣadrā's ontology, essence or quiddity

51 Shīrāzī, *al-Ḥikma al-mutaʿāliya fī l-asfār al-ʿaqliyya al-arbaʿa*, ed. Muḥammad Riḍā Muẓaffar et al., 9 vols., i, Beirut: Dār Iḥyāʾ al-Turāth al-ʿArabī, 1999, 63–64.

52 Shīrāzī, *al-Ḥikma al-mutaʿāliya* i, 68.

53 Shīrāzī, Mullā Ṣadrā, *The book of metaphysical penetrations*, trans. Seyyed Hossein Nasr, ed. Ibrahim Kalin, Provo, UT: Brigham Young University Press, 2014, 12.

54 Suhrawardī, *The philosophy* 45.

55 On this topic, see Meisami, Sayeh, *Mulla Sadra*, Oxford: Oneworld, 2013, 27–35.

56 Shīrāzī, *The book of metaphysical penetrations* 39.

has a subordinate reality as the shadow of existence, rather than being a mental construct which could be disposed of, hence the possibility of comparing it to darkness in Zoroastrian dualism where darkness is there but it is eventually subordinate to light.

With the above in mind, one can argue that Mullā Ṣadrā's discourse on existence/essence, despite the dominance of the Illuminationist terminology of light, is in fact a new dimension of Avicennan dualist metaphysics, and Mullā Ṣadrā's frequent citations of Avicenna reinforces this argument.[57] For example, in his *al-Mashāʿir* (*Metaphysical penetrations*), which is dedicated to proving the authenticity of existence and how it is related to quiddity, Mullā Ṣadrā cites Avicenna to support not only the authenticity of existence but also his own position on quiddities as reflections of the different grades of existence. In this regard, he interprets a passage from Avicenna's *al-Mubāḥathāt* (*The discussions*) on the differences among existing things based on their different species by using number analogy. There he argues that with respect to different numbers which are said to result from the mere "assemblage" of similar units,

> It is equally correct to say that they are differentiated [from one another] as far as their respective essential meanings are concerned, since from each degree (*martaba*) [of numbers] the intellect can abstract qualities and essential properties that are not proven for others. And they have effects and differentiated characteristics which result from this degree … They are therefore like particular existences (*al-wujūdāt al-khāṣṣa*) in the sense that the subject to which these essential structures and universal qualities are attributed is essentially the respective essences of each of these numbers.[58]

What I would like to infer from the above observations about Mullā Ṣadrā's understanding of Avicenna is that similar to the latter, Mullā Ṣadrā's narrative of the existence/essence relation is a continuation of the light/darkness tension in Persianate discursive contexts. The tension starts with Avicenna and takes several directions with a form of resolution in the essentialism of Suhrawardī and Mīr Dāmād, but it reappears in the metaphysics of Mullā Ṣadrā through the narrative of existence as light and quiddity as darkness or shadow of existence. Nevertheless, in spite of the apparent contrast between Mullā Ṣadrā's identific-

57 Mullā Ṣadrā argues that for the majority of later philosophers such as Mīr Dāmād, a misinterpretation of Avicenna led them to deny the authentic reality of existence. See Shīrāzī, *The book of metaphysical penetrations* 37.

58 Shīrāzī, *The book of metaphysical penetrations* 39.

ation of reality with existence and his Illuminationist predecessors' equation of reality with essence, their metaphysical discourses are connected due to their visualization of the ultimate reality as light in its gradations.

In this essay I have attempted to revisit the discursive formation of Islamic metaphysics in its Persianate context through the lens of Persian mythology. Given that ancient mythological narratives do not die out in the passage of time but continue to live in religious, literary, and philosophical discourses, I have suggested that existence/essence dualism in Islamic philosophy or *logos*, is a continuation and expansion of the Persian *mythos* of light/darkness that is central to Zoroastrian scriptures. From this perspective, I have argued that the classical narrative about ultimate reality, most importantly the Avicennan one, can be revisited vis-à-vis its situatedness in Persianate discursive contexts which were informed by the myth of the tension between light and darkness. In this regard, I juxtaposed Avicenna's "existence" with light and his "essence" with darkness based on the creative power of the former and its application to what is "possible." I also tried to show that this *mythos-logos* relation was retained in its Persianate context, culminating in the Illuminationist tradition which offers an ontology of light and darkness with obvious references to Persian myth. I finished my account with Mullā Ṣadrā, whose synthetic discourse on reality takes in the Illuminationist metaphysics of light while restoring Avicenna's "existence" as its philosophical counterpart, thereby creating room, however constricted, for "essence." By bringing the mythological backdrop of Islamic metaphysics in the Persianate world to the fore, my account creates space for the possibility of understanding philosophical accounts from alternative perspectives in order to overcome the hegemony of particularized, and therefore limited, approaches to intellectual history.

Bibliography

Afnan, Soheil M., *Avicenna: His life and works*, London: Allen & Unwin, 1956.

Aminrazavi, Mehdi, "Introduction," in Seyyed Hossein Nasr and Mehdi Aminrazavi (eds.), *An anthology of philosophy in Persia*, 5 vols., i, London: I.B. Tauris in association with The Institute of Ismaili Studies, 2008–2015, 13–15.

Aristotle, *Metaphysics: Books Z and H*, trans. David Bostock, New York: Clarendon Press, 1997.

Avicenna, *al-Ishārāt wa-l-tanbīhāt*, ed. Sulaymān Dunyā, 3 vols., Cairo: Dār al-Maʿārif, 1983–1994.

Avicenna, *The metaphysics of the healing*, ed. and trans. Michael E. Marmura, Provo, UT: Brigham Young University Press, 2005.

Boyce, Mary, "Ahūrā Mazdā," in *EI Online*, http://www.iranicaonline.org/articles/ahura-mazda (last accessed: 4 June 2021).

Boyce, Mary, *Textual sources for the study of Zoroastrianism*, Totowa, NJ: Barnes and Noble, 1984.

Chittick, William C., "Foreword," in Abū Ḥāmid Muḥammad al-Ghazālī, *The niche of lights*, trans. David Buchman, Provo, UT: Brigham Young University Press, 1998.

Corbin, Henry, *En Islam iranien*, 4 vols., Paris: Gallimard, 1971–1972.

Corbin, Henry, *Avicenna and the visionary recital*, trans. Willard Trask, Irving, TX: Spring Publications, 1980.

Corbin, Henry, *History of Islamic philosophy*, New York: Kegan Paul, 1993.

Dabashi, Hamid, "Mīr Dāmād," in Seyyed Hossein Nasr and Oliver Leaman (eds.), *History of Islamic philosophy*, 2 vols., ii, New York: Routledge, 1996, 597–634.

al-Ghazālī, Abū Ḥāmid Muḥammad, *The niche of lights*, trans. David Buchman, Provo, UT: Brigham Young University Press, 1998.

Gohlman, William E., *The life of Ibn Sina: A critical edition and annotated translation*, Albany, NY: SUNY Press, 1974.

Gosetti-Ferencei, Jennifer A., *The life of imagination: Revealing and making the world*, New York: Columbia University Press, 2018.

Grenet, Frantz, "Zoroastrianism in Central Asia," in Michael Stausberg, Yuhan S-D Vevaina, and Anna Tessmann (eds.), *The Wiley Blackwell companion to Zoroastrianism*, Chichester: Wiley Blackwell, 2015, 129–146.

Iqbal, Muhammad, *The development of metaphysics in Persia*, London: Luzac, 1908.

Kronen, John and Sandra Menssen, "The defensibility of Zoroastrian dualism," in *Religious Studies* 46.2 (2010), 185–205.

Landolt, Hermann, "Two types of mystical thought in Muslim Iran," in Ian R. Netton (ed.), *Islamic philosophy and theology: Critical concepts in Islamic thought*, 4 vols., iv, New York: Routledge, 2007, 81–96.

Maghsoudlou, Salimeh, "La pensée de ʿAyn al-Quḍāt al-Hamadānī (m. 525/1132), entre avicennisme et héritage ġazâlien," Paris (PhD Diss.): École Pratique des Hautes Études, 2016.

McGinnis, Jon, *Avicenna*, Oxford: Oxford University Press, 2010.

McGinnis, Jon and David C. Reisman (trans.), *Classical Arabic philosophy: An anthology of sources*, Indianapolis: Hackett Publishing, 2007.

Meisami, Sayeh, *Mulla Sadra*, Oxford: Oneworld, 2013.

Mīr Dāmād, Muḥammad Bāqir, *Kitāb al-Qabasāt: The book of blazing brands*, trans. Keven Brown, New York: Global Scholarly Publications, 2009.

Nasr, Seyyed Hossein and Mehdi Aminrazavi (eds.), *An anthology of philosophy in Persia*, 5 vols., London: I.B. Tauris in association with The Institute of Ismaili Studies, 2008–2015.

Reisman, David C., *The making of the Avicennan tradition*, Leiden: Brill, 2002.

Rizvi, Sajjad, "Mīr Dāmād's (d. 1631) *al-Qabasāt*: The problem of the eternity of the cosmos," in Khaled El-Rouayheb and Sabine Schmidtke (eds.), *The Oxford handbook of Islamic philosophy*, New York: Oxford University Press, 2017, 438–464.

Rustom, Mohammed, "Devil's advocate: ʿAyn al-Quḍāt's defense of Iblis in context," in *SI* 115.1 (2020), 65–100.

Rustom, Mohammed, *Inrushes of the heart: The Sufi philosophy of ʿAyn al-Quḍāt*, Albany, NY: SUNY Press, 2023.

Schwartz, Martin et al., "Interpretations of Zarathustra and the *Gāthās*," in Michael Stausberg, Yuhan S-D Vevaina, and Anna Tessmann (eds.), *The Wiley Blackwell companion to Zoroastrianism*, Chichester: Wiley Blackwell, 2015, 39–67.

Shīrāzī, Mullā Ṣadrā, *al-Ḥikma al-mutaʿāliya fī l-asfār al-ʿaqliyya al-arbaʿa*, ed. Muḥammad Riḍā Muẓaffar et al., 9 vols., Beirut: Dār Iḥyāʾ al-Turāth al-ʿArabī, 1999.

Shīrāzī, Mullā Ṣadrā, *On the hermeneutics of the light verse of the Qurʾān*, trans. Latimah-Parvin Peerwani, London: ICAS Press, 2004.

Shīrāzī, Mullā Ṣadrā, *The book of metaphysical penetrations*, trans. Seyyed Hossein Nasr, ed. Ibrahim Kalin, Provo, UT: Brigham Young University Press, 2014.

Suhrawardī, Shihāb al-Dīn, *The philosophy of illumination*, ed. and trans. John Walbridge and Hossein Ziai, Provo, UT: Brigham Young University Press, 1999.

Wisnovsky, Robert, "Notes on Avicenna's concept of thingness (*šayʾiyya*)," in *ASP* 10.2 (2000), 181–221.

Zaehner, Robert C., *Zurvan, a Zoroastrian dilemma*, Oxford: Clarendon Press, 1955.

CHAPTER 19

Asad Allāh Qazwīnī's Cosmology of the *ahl al-bayt*: A Study and Critical Edition of *Kitāb-i Walāyat-i muṭlaqa*

Cyrus Ali Zargar (*Introduction*) *and Alireza Asghari* (*Edition*)

1 Introduction

The author of the text highlighted here—Asad Allāh Qazwīnī—lived in the mid-13th/19th century. Contemporary author al-Sayyid Aḥmad al-Ḥusaynī, in his biographical dictionary *Tarājim al-rijāl* (*The biographies of men*), describes Qazwīnī as a pious, ascetic, and learned man, albeit one "inclined toward the Sufis" and clearly devoted to Shaykh Aḥmad Aḥsāʾī (d. 1241/1826), "whom he mentions … using every variety of praise and respect."[1] While such a description would not seem pejorative under other circumstances, it would certainly cast a skeptical light on his writings in normative Twelver Shiʿi scholarly circles, in which both the Shaykhī school and Sufism are suspect designations, a point that will be discussed. Qazwīnī was, according to al-Ḥusaynī, "preoccupied with supplications, litanies, and the occult sciences," while transmitting devotional formulas and supplications from his spiritual master, namely Mullā Abū Ṭālib al-Ṭihrānī (d. circa 13th/19th century).[2] From the author's own account, we do know that Qazwīnī completed the treatise presented here, *Kitāb-i Walāyat-i muṭlaqa* (*The book of absolute* walāya), in Rajab of 1262/June or July of 1846. Moreover, we know that Qazwīnī's primary concern as an author was the spiritual wayfarer's contemplation of the cosmological position of the *ahl al-bayt*, that is, the Prophet Muhammad, his daughter Fāṭima, and the twelve imams, especially, of course, Imam ʿAlī.

Asad Allāh Qazwīnī wrote during an important juncture in Shiʿi Islamic thought. The Uṣūlī school of jurisprudence had established itself as "official" in two major ways: First, its advocates—especially Muḥammad Bāqir Bihbihānī (d. 1205/1790)—had successfully defended the necessity of studying the principles of jurisprudence (*uṣūl al-fiqh*) in Shiʿi seminaries. Second, Uṣūlī *ʿulamāʾ*

1 Al-Ḥusaynī, al-Sayyid Aḥmad, *Tarājim al-rijāl*, i, Qom: Ṣadr, 1993–1994, 96.
2 Al-Ḥusaynī does not provide new information about this teacher in the short entry given to him; see al-Ḥusaynī, *Tarājim* i, 38. He is the only source we have on this figure.

 | DOI:10.1163/9789004529038_020

and the ruling Qajar tribe had carved out separate but complementary modes of authority in Persia. In some ways, when seen by its adversaries, the Uṣūlī argument for *ijtihād* (jurisprudential reasoning) curtailed the moral direction of the Shiʿa by limiting interpretive authority to those who had it.[3] Clerical resistance to Uṣūlī authority in the Qajar period did exist in many forms, but perhaps most powerfully in the form of intuitive and mystical interpretations of Shiʿi narrations. In the realm of philosophy, the Sadrian school (that is, the school based on the philosophy Mullā Ṣadrā, d. 1050/1640) was on the verge of acquiring authority as the established Twelver Shiʿi school of philosophy. In this climate, careful and sometimes esoteric readings of Shiʿi narrations offered a philosophical alternative.[4] Qazwīnī's time was one in which Twelver Shiʿi scholarship was finding a more fixed identity. In fact, following the ascendancy of the Uṣūlī school, the next significant disagreement among Shiʿi scholars surrounded the figure whose thought has been elaborated in the writings of Qazwīnī: Shaykh Aḥmad Aḥsāʾī, the eponym of what was to become known as the "Shaykhī" school.

The pillars of Aḥsāʾī's thought, which forms the basis of Qazwīnī's writings, stand on a claim to privileged knowledge of the imams' teachings, whether through dreams or through intuition, a claim that played no small part in both his popularity and his infamy. Indeed, the end of Aḥsāʾī's intellectual and saintly career was marked by tumult, to some degree because of his philosophical shift away from a traditional understanding of corporeal resurrection.[5] Aḥsāʾī presented a cosmology that was syncretic, in that it borrowed from philosophy, Sufism, Hadith literature, and even, according to al-Aḥsāʾī himself, from Iraqi Sabeanism/Mandeanism (as a source for the important term *hūrqalyā*). His is also, however, very clearly an original system inspired by Shiʿi Hadith.[6] In

---

3 Amanat, Abbas, *Resurrection and renewal: The making of the Babi movement in Iran, 1844–1850*, Ithaca and London: Cornell University Press, 1989, 37.

4 Sajjad Rizvi has argued convincingly that the consolidation of Sadrian philosophy in Shiʿi scholarly circles can best be attributed to the classes and commentaries of Mullā Hādī Sabzawārī (d. 1289/1873), who did in fact spend two months studying under Aḥsāʾī but was affected by another teacher's (namely, Mullā Ismāʿīl Darbkūshkī Iṣfahānī, d. 1268/1853) arguments against Aḥsāʾī's commentary on Mullā Ṣadrā's *al-Ḥikma al-ʿarshiyya* (*Wisdom of the throne*). See Rizvi, Sajjad, "*Hikma mutaʿaliya* in Qajar Iran: Locating the life and work of Mulla Hadi Sabzawari (d. 1289/1873)," in *IS* 44.4 (2011), 473–496, 479.

5 Bayat, Mangol, *Mysticism and dissent: Socioreligious thought in Qajar Iran*, Syracuse, NY: Syracuse University Press, 1982, 38–40.

6 This cosmology has been discussed by Henry Corbin in his *Terre céleste et corps de resurrection*, Paris: Buchet/Chastel, 1960, as well as by Juan Cole in "The world as text: Cosmologies of Shaykh Ahmad al-Aḥsāʾī," in *SI* 80 (1994), 145–163. See also MacEoin, Denis M., "Cosmogony and cosmology. VII. In Shaikhism," in *EIr*.

opposition to the Sadrian system, al-Aḥsāʾī rejected a unity of being, envisioning the universe united not by existence but rather by the Muhammadan Reality (*al-ḥaqīqa al-Muḥammadiyya*), which is a vessel for the divine wish that brings all things into being.[7] This cosmology, as conceived by its founder al-Aḥsāʾī and as described by Denis MacEoin, lays "heavy emphasis on the role of the imams as creators and sustainers of the universe," such that al-Aḥsāʾī offers a detailed account of the imams as the four Aristotelian causes of the universe.[8] These themes form the basis of Qazwīnī's thought.

2 Introducing Qazwīnī's Writings and Thought

Published here as a critical edition for the first time, *Walāyat-i muṭlaqa* captures major themes found in Qazwīnī's other writings on cosmology. While research on Qazwīnī is still in its infancy, Alireza Asghari, the editor of this treatise, has provided me with a useful list of his compositions as known to us. All of them exist as manuscripts in the famous Ayatollah Marʿashī-Najafī library, located in Qom, Iran:

1. *Dhikr al-aʿlā*, in 250 sections, each of which is called a *karāmat* ("saintly paranormal deed"). The book contains formulae for remembering God, supplications, and certain prayers that—when repeated a certain number of times or under certain conditions—grant the requests of the supplicant (called *khutūmāt*), MS 14555.
2. *Gharāʾib al-asrār wa-shawāriq al-anwār*, MS 7517-1.
3. *Sirr al-asrār wa-mabdaʾ al-anwār*, MS 3377-2.
4. *al-Ḥujja al-bāligha wa-l-barāhīn al-qāṭiʿa*, MS 3377-1.
5. *Mirʾāt al-aḥkām fī bayān al-ḥalāl wa-l-ḥarām*, concerning ritual purity, the prescribed daily prayers, fasting, *zakāt* (obligatory alms), and the *ḥajj* pilgrimage, MS 280-9.
6. *Walāyat-i muṭlaqa*, MS 3377-3.
7. *Miṣbāḥ al-sālikīn*, concerning the path of spiritual wayfaring, perpetual remembrance, and the sayings of those considered "knowers of God" or those affiliated with Sufi orders, MS 7517-2.

Qazwīnī's writings offer explanations of creation and terms found in Hadith using a cosmological model at variance with the cosmology of Mullā Ṣadrā with which so many students of Islamic philosophy are familiar. The most funda-

---

7 Fuyūḍāt, al-Mīrzā Ḥasan, *Madkhal ilā falsafat al-Shaykh al-Aḥsāʾī*, ed. with an introduction by Tawfīq Nāṣir al-Būʿalī, Beirut: Dār al-Amīra, 2011, 87–89.

8 MacEoin, "Cosmogony."

mental of all cosmological principles, as Qazwīnī presents it, is God's wish, for the divine wish is the first agent and act of creation. This idea has solid footing in a Shiʿi tradition that the author cites and alludes to frequently, one taken from al-Ṣadūq's (d. 381/991) *al-Tawḥīd* (*Declaring God's Oneness*): "God created the things through the wish and created the wish through itself."[9] This "wish" (*mashīʾa*) is an act, and it is the first act by which all other things come into creation. Of course, God's wish cannot be an intention, a desire, a hope, or even a precursor to action. Rather, God's wish is the very act of creation itself, as is supported in a tradition attributed to the eighth Shiʿi imam, al-Imām ʿAlī b. Mūsā al-Riḍā:

> His desire (*irāda*) is His origination of things, nothing else, because He does not deliberate, nor decide, nor contemplate. Rather, he only says to a thing, "Be," and it is, without uttering anything, and without any conceivable properties in that, just as there are no conceivable properties when it comes to Him.[10]

As Qazwīnī explains, the Sufis and others (which would include Mullā Ṣadrā) who describe creation as an emanation of the divine essence or a realization of pure existence have missed the point; the essence remains undivided and untouched by the process of creation, which is simply a fulfillment or unfolding of the divine wish. That which emanates is the divine act, or, in other words, the effects of God, not His essence. Moreover, as the Shiʿi Hadith tradition maintains, those effects find their origins in God's first and finest creation, that from which His own wish radiates, that which can be described as light, words, or meanings, but ultimately is none other than the Prophet Muhammad and his *ahl al-bayt*.

In his *Sirr al-asrār wa-mabdaʾ al-anwār* (*The secret of secrets and the origination of lights*), Qazwīnī expands on these narrations to establish the relationship between God's essence, His wish, and His actions and the equation of the divine wish with the realities represented by the Prophet Muhammad and the *ahl al-bayt*. His readings weave together narrations from various sources, often making enterprising use of supplications, especially *duʿāʾ al-simāt* ("Prayer of the traits"), *al-ziyāra al-jāmiʿa* ("The comprehensive visitation"), and the famous supplication recited during the pre-dawn hours of the month of Ramadan,

9 Al-Ṣadūq, Muḥammad b. ʿAlī b. Bābawayh al-Shaykh, *al-Tawḥīd*, ed. Hāshim Ḥusaynī, Qom: Jāmiʿat al-Mudarrisīn, 1977–1978, 148.

10 Al-Kulaynī, Muḥammad b. Yaʿqūb b. Isḥāq, *al-Kāfī*, ed ʿAlī-Akbar Ghaffārī and Muḥammad Ākhūndī, i, Tehran: Dār al-Kutub al-Islāmiyya, 1987–1988, 109–110.

known as *duʿāʾ al-bahāʾ* ("Prayer of the splendor") or simply *duʿāʾ al-saḥar* ("The dawn prayer"). Qazwīnī strives to be truer to the language of these scriptural sources than that found in the philosophy of Mullā Ṣadrā, though he often makes assumptions not necessarily warranted by the text, assumptions essential to his argument. Thus, for example, Qazwīnī uses a narration from al-Kulaynī's (d. 329/941) *al-Kāfī* (*The sufficient book*) to support his claim that God's temporal knowledge precedes His wish: "It was said to the imam, 'How does God know?' The imam replied, 'He knows and wishes and desires and determines and decrees and executes.'"[11] Qazwīnī reads these verbs as occurring in sequence. For Qazwīnī, since God's essential knowledge cannot be reckoned as "before" or "after" anything else, this *ḥadīth* tells us that God's temporal knowledge precedes his wish. This divine temporal knowledge is "created and possible" as opposed to His essential knowledge, which is eternal and necessary. Of course, the *ḥadīth* in question might not concern a temporal process at all. Rather, causation can exist divorced from time, a point consistently ignored in Qazwīnī's writings. In that case, there becomes little need to suppose a separate category for God's temporal versus His essential knowledge.

Of course, Qazwīnī's goal seems to be to present a cosmology that mirrors the narrations of the *ahl al-bayt* and takes as little recourse to extra-scriptural philosophical arguments as possible. His writings also seem to aim at clarity and simplicity, since his Persian writing style avoids ornate and unnecessary constructions. Indeed, in this regard, Qazwīnī's writings should be considered as valuable contributions to Persian-language philosophy.

Such simplicity also characterizes Qazwīnī's *Kitāb-i Walāyat-i muṭlaqa*. The term *walāya* is famously difficult to translate, but is characterized in Qazwīnī's treatise as a divine unlimited administration (*taṣarruf*) that God has and delegates to those worthy of it through the principle of love, one requiring association, reverence, and obedience. Qazwīnī uses narrations and supplications from Shiʿi sources to construct a cosmological narrative of *walāya*: God's wish, which is the reality of Muhammad, becomes realized in ʿAlī. Muhammad is the principle of silence, while ʿAlī is the principle of speech. In this, Qazwīnī offers an alternative to the Active Intellect and Universal Soul as found in philosophical and Sufi writings, heavily influenced by Neoplatonism. Most significant to Qazwīnī's concept of *walāya* is the sense of servitude and humility that

11 Qazwīnī mentions this in *Sirr al-asrār wa-mabdaʾ al-anwār* (*The secret of secrets and the origin of lights*), as of yet only available in manuscript form. See also al-Kulaynī, *al-Kāfī* i, 148. The discussion of God's wish in *Sirr al-asrār* is even more detailed than that found in the treatise published in the present article.

characterizes those who possess it. The servitude and humility of the Prophet Muhammad, ʿAlī, Fāṭima, and the imams merit *walāya*. Their high status results directly from their knowledge of their place vis-à-vis God. While acknowledging that ʿAlī's reality aided the Biblical prophets when they were in their greatest moments of need, and even equating ʿAlī with the principle of revelation, Qazwīnī rejects the idea that ʿAlī might be superior to the Prophet Muhammad, for God's effects begin with Muhammad. He also makes clear that the Prophet and the *ahl al-bayt*, as created entities, cannot be taken as lords, but they do function as God's faculties, His eyes, hands, ears, and tongue, simply because of the purity of their perception: They are conduits for God's awareness of Himself because they have achieved the status of complete servitude. Similarly, the followers of these possessors of *walāya*, namely, the Shiʿa, should function as faculties for the Prophet and the *ahl al-bayt*. The Shiʿa serve as eyes, hands, ears, and tongues for those whose existence as rays of light allows God to be recognized, as mentioned in the famous *ḥadīth* of the Hidden Treasure, wherein God proclaims, "I was a Hidden Treasure, and I loved to be recognized, so I created the creatures that they might recognize Me."[12]

3 The Historical Significance of Qazwīnī's Shaykhī Writings

One can certainly categorize Qazwīnī's writings as "Shaykhī," as long as the difficulties of that designation are borne in mind as well. While Aḥsāʾī's thought pervades Qazwīnī's work, often making it seem as though Qazwīnī belongs to an established school of thought, Shaykh Aḥsāʾī did not establish a well-defined and separate school of thought during his lifetime. Nevertheless, before his death, Aḥsāʾī had named a successor, namely, his protégé and foremost student Sayyid Kāẓim Rashtī (d. 1259/1844), who, in 1243/1828, was forced to repudiate his master's doctrines, though he did so using the dictates of *taqiyya*.[13] This was a major blow to those who sympathized with the teachings of Aḥsāʾī; persecution followed Rashtī's public pronouncement.[14] Since the Bābī and Bahāʾī religions relied heavily on Shaykhī thought, the association between the Shaykhī

12 Qazwīnī often alludes to the *ḥadīth* of the Hidden Treasure, which, although not found in the authoritative Shiʿi or Sunni Hadith sources, has always been popular among those inclined to knowledge-acquisition through *kashf* or "unveiling." For a discussion of this tradition, see William Chittick's gloss in Samʿānī, Aḥmad, *The repose of the spirits: A Sufi commentary on the divine names*, trans. William C. Chittick, Albany, NY: SUNY Press, 2019, 513, note 521.

13 Amanat, *Resurrection* 41. See also Eschraghi, Armin, "Kāẓem Rašti," in *EIr*.

14 Amanat, *Resurrection* 42.

school and religions distinct from traditional Twelver Shiʿi Islam solidified. Yet Aḥsāʾī passed away before being able to see or comment upon the newer religious movements that made use of his teachings.

Qazwīnī's writings—because of the course of Shiʿi political and historical history that followed—thus represent an alternate mode of Shiʿi thought, which, while ignored for some time, have recently aroused interest in Shiʿi scholarly circles. The current interest in alternates to the philosophy of Mullā Ṣadrā can be seen—to name the most prominent example—in a movement that Sajjad Rizvi has called "fideist," one that seeks to place assertions about existence, the soul, the afterlife, and knowledge firmly within scripture.[15] In many ways, advocates of this movement—the Maktab-i Tafkīk—challenge a philosophical approach that they see as threatening to become canonical, despite its lack of conformity with the teaching of the infallible Imams and its basis in Greek thought and the writings of the Sufi thinker Muḥyī al-Dīn Ibn ʿArabī (d. 638/1240). In this, their view corresponds to that of Asad Allāh Qazwīnī, who presents a cosmology, ontology, and epistemology that derives from the very language of Shiʿi Hadith and the Quran.

The dismissal of Shaykhī thought as heterodox by certain Twelver Shiʿi scholars makes even less sense when one encounters writings such as that of Qazwīnī, or, for that matter, Aḥsāʾī himself. While there were peculiarities, as Denis M. MacEoin discusses, many of the most controversial points attributed to the school's eponym were complete fabrications. Moreover, there is no real reason why Shaykhī thought could not have been integrated into mainstream Shiʿi thought, much like the integration of the thought of Mullā Ṣadrā, which also makes claims that might be seen as contrary to the dictates of traditional Shiʿi theology.[16]

Rather, sensitivity to such ideas must be understood in its historical context. This context is perhaps best exemplified in the life of Mīrzā Muḥammad Nīshāpūrī Akhbārī (d. 1232/1817) who, while not a Shaykhī, represents potential dangers of charismatic and distinctive interpretations of the Shiʿi Hadith canon. It was not Akhbārī's allegiance to scriptural Shiʿism (the Akhbārī school from which he assumed his nickname), nor was it his constant haranguing of Uṣūlī clerics, that brought the Shiʿi masses to listen to him. Rather, it was his seeming legitimacy as a man of unveiling (*kashf*). Indeed, Akhbārī even offered to use his magical abilities to bring to the Qajar ruler of his day, Fatḥ-ʿAlī Shāh (r. 1212–1250/1797–1834), the head of a Russian commander, Pavel Tsitsianov

---

15 Rizvi, Sajjad, "'Only the Imam knows best': The Maktab-e Tafkīk's attack on the legitimacy of philosophy in Iran," in *JRAS* 22.3–4 (2012), 487–503, 493.

16 MacEoin, Denis M., "Aḥsāʾī, Shaikh Aḥmad," in *EIr*.

(d. 1806), in exchange for the removal of royal support for the Uṣūlī *ʿulamāʾ* and state adherence to the Akhbārī school, an offer that Fatḥ-ʿAlī Shāh accepted and Akhbārī fulfilled, for the head, or at least hand, of the commander was sent to Tehran.[17] This was one move among many that prompted the Uṣūlī edict leading to his death. Akhbārī's designs on the monarch's allegiance made his scholarly aspirations more threatening. His claim to mystical insight regarding the words of the imams was also a claim to power, since Akhbārī declared that one with esoteric knowledge of the living twelfth imam would be a gateway to the imam's knowledge (*bāb al-ʿilm*). In all of this, at least to those opposed to him, Aḥsāʾī might have resembled Akhbārī. As Hamid Algar has discussed, the admiration that Fatḥ-ʿAlī Shāh expressed for Aḥsāʾī, as well as the favors that the king lavished upon him, might have contributed to the declaration of heresy (*takfīr*) that the *ʿulamāʾ* made against Aḥsāʾī, and, without that declaration, it is possible that the idea of a separate "Shaykhī" school may never have existed.[18]

Considering the political, historical, and somewhat arbitrary factors that led to the marginalization of Shaykhī thought, the treatise below should matter to all those who study Iranian intellectual history, especially those with an interest in Islamic cosmologies. Moreover, this sample of Qazwīnī's writings comes at an opportune time in Shiʿi Studies, one of increased attention to the most profound implications of canonical narrations among Shiʿi seminarians and devotees alike. Reflection upon these writings will encourage the reader to return to important questions about Shiʿi cosmology and theology, as well as the development of Twelver Shiʿi philosophical schools.

4 Manuscript of *Kitāb-i Walāyat-i muṭlaqa*

What follows is the first edited publication of *Kitāb-i Walāyat-i muṭlaqa*. There is only one manuscript of this text. Fortunately, it has been written preserved in the author's own hand (in *naskh* script). It is to be found at the Ayatollah Marʿashī-Najafī library, number 3377-3, pages 69–75, measuring 21×15.5 centimeters, 17 lines to a page. The entire treatise is extant and was completed, as mentioned above, in Rajab 1262/June–July 1846.

17 Algar, Hamid, *Religion and state in Iran 1785–1906: The role of the ulama in the Qajar period*, Berkeley: University of California Press, 1969/1980, 65.

18 Algar, *Religion and state* 68–69.

FIGURE 19.1 The first page of *Kitāb-i Walāyat-i muṭlaqa* BY THE AUTHOR'S OWN HAND

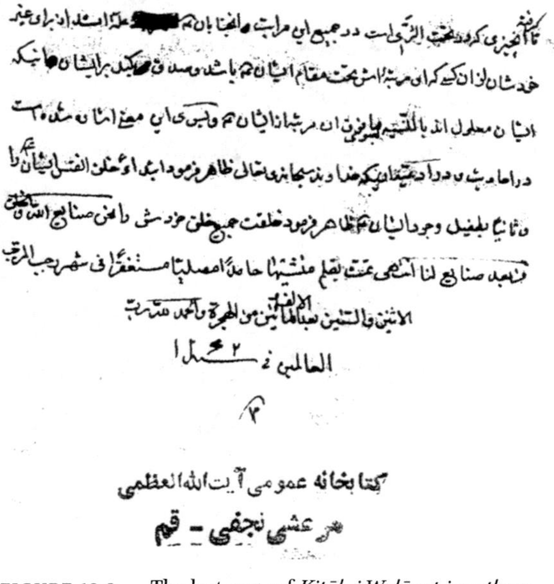

FIGURE 19.2 The last page of *Kitāb-i Walāyat-i muṭlaqa* BY THE AUTHOR'S OWN HAND

5 Edition

کتاب ولایت مطلقه

بسم الله الرحمن الرحیم و به نستعین

عجائب أمر تسرّ المؤمن المتّقي و تضرّ المنافق الشقي

معنای ولایت مطلقه و سلطنت عامّه

در بیان ولایت مطلقه که یکی از اطلاقات اسامی وجود مطلق است.

بدان که مراد به ولایت مطلقه آن سلطنت عامّه‌ای است که عموم دارد آن سلطنت و پادشاهی از برای جمیع ذرّات وجودیّه، و از برای کلّ اشیاء است؛ یعنی آن اشیایی که داخل شده باشند در مُلك خداوندی در آن چیزی که باید متعلّق شود به او اراده الهی، پس در آنها ولی الله ولایت دارد. و معنای این ولایت مطلقه مثل معنای حقیقت محمّدیّه ـ صلی الله علیه وآله ـ است که یك مرتبه اطلاق می کردند و مقامات اسم فاعل را می‌خواستند، ویك مرتبه اطلاق می‌نمودند و از آن اثر مشیّت کونیّه را اراده می‌نمودند. این هم مثل اوست؛ زیرا که حقیقت محمّدیّه ـ صلی الله علیه وآله ـ و ولایت مطلقه دو اسمی هستند بر معنی واحد در نزد قواعد اهل بیت ـ علیهم السلام.

بلی، مختلف می‌شود مفهوم این دو حقیقت به حسب اعتبارات و لحاظات، و به نحو بیانات و تحقیقات.

لوامع علوی

بیان مراتب ثلاثه ولایت و انحصارش در علی علیه السلام

بدان که ولایت، سه ولایت[19] است:

19 بدان که حضرت خاتم الأنبیاء ـ صلی الله علیه وآله ـ را چهار منصب است: نبوت ورسالت و امامت وولایت. ماده اشتقاق نبوت از نبأ است یعنی خبر. و نبی کسی را می گویند که از جانب خدا به او خبر داده شده باشد بدون واسطه بشری، چه دارای شریعت باشد مانند پیغمبر اکرم و سایر پیغمبران مرسل ـ علیه و علیهم السلام ـ یا صاحب شریعت نباشد مانند حضرت یحیی. منصب دوم آن حضرت که رسالت باشد به معنی پیغام رساندن از جانب خدا به بندگان او. و به این اعتبار رسول نامیده شده

يك ولاية اللّهى است، و يك ولاية الرسولى [است]؛ و يك ولاية الوليّ [است].

امّا ولاية الله اشاره به او است قوله تعالى: هُنَالِكَ الْوَلَايَةُ لِلّٰهِ الحَقِّ (18: 44)؛ و امّا ولاية الرسول اشاره به او است قوله تعالى: النَّبِي أَوْلَى بِالمُؤْمِنِينَ مِنْ أَنفُسِهِمْ (33: 6)؛ و امّا ولاية الوليّ كه ولايت علوى ـ عليه السلام ـ است اشاره به او است قوله تعالى: إِنَّمَا وَلِيكُمُ اللّٰهُ وَرَسُولُهُ وَالَّذِينَ آمَنُوا الَّذِينَ يُقِيمُونَ الصَّلَاةَ وَيُؤْتُونَ الزَّكَاةَ وَهُمْ رَاكِعُونَ (5: 55).

و در بسيارى از آيات در قرآن به نام رسول ياد شده و مشرّف به نداى يَا أَيُّهَا الرَّسُولُ (5: 41) گرديده. منصب سوم آن حضرت كه امامت باشد به معناى پيشوايى و استحقاق پيشوا و مقتدا بودن بر خلق است. و بر همه مردمان واجب است به اين منصب به حضرتش اقتدا و تأسى كنند چنانچه در قرآن مجيد است كه: لَكُمْ فِي رَسُولِ اللّٰهِ أُسْوَةٌ حَسَنَةٌ (33: 21)، مَنْ يطِعِ الرَّسُولَ فَقَدْ أَطَاعَ اللّٰهَ (4: 80)، أَطِيعُوا اللّٰهَ وَأَطِيعُوا الرَّسُولَ وَأُولِي الْأَمْرِ مِنكُمْ (4: 59)، مَا آتَاكُمُ الرَّسُولُ فَخُذُوهُ وَمَا نَهَاكُمْ عَنْهُ فَانْتَهُوا (59: 7)، قُلْ إِنْ كُنتُمْ تُحِبُّونَ اللّٰهَ فَاتَّبِعُونِي يحْبِبْكُمُ اللّٰهُ (3: 31). منصب امامت آن جناب از منصب رسالت او بالاتر است؛ زيرا كه مقام نبوت "بشرط لا" خبرى است كه از جانب خدا به او مى‌رسد. ومقام رسالت "بشرط لا" پيغام آوردن او است از جانب خدا. و اين هر دو، مقام ظاهر و مقام قول است. و امّا مقام امامت "بشرط لا" به اعتبار آن است كه آن حضرت از جانب خدا مقتدا به خلق قرار داده شده؛ يعنى بر خلق واجب كرده كه در جميع امور معاش و معاد خود پيرو و تابع او باشند و او را طريق به سوى خدا و محلّ اقتدا و اتباع بدانند و در هيچ امرى از حكم و فرمان او بيرون نباشند.

حاصل آنكه: امامت، رياست الهيّه است بر جميع مخلوق از جانب خالق.

منصب چهارم آن حضرت ولايت باشد؛ يعنى اولى به تصرف و آن براى اين است كه خدا او را اولى از مؤمنين قرار داده از خودشان به دليل آيه مباركه: النَّبِي أَوْلَى بِالمُؤْمِنِينَ مِنْ أَنْفُسِهِمْ (33: 6) به طورى كه حكم پيغمبر اكرم نافذتر بود بر نفوس خلقش از خود خلق به نفوس خود. و اين دو منصب كه امامت و ولايت باشد، مقام باطن و مقام فعل است. و مقام باطن و فعل افضل باشد از مقام ظاهر كه نبوت و رسالت باشد.

و بدان كه مرتبه نبوت و رسالت با مرتبه امامت و ولايت در آن حضرت لازم و ملزوم يكديگرند و انفكاك آنها از يكديگر بر وجه حقيقت متصوّر نيست و اين ظاهر و باطن از يكديگر جدا نمى‌شوند. پس هر وقت كه اطلاق نبى يا رسول به آن حضرت شود "بشرط لا" نيست بلكه به "شرط شىء" است؛ يعنى به شرط مراتب ديگر. رك: ولايت كليّه، سيد محمّد حسن ميرجهانى، ص 11-13.

لکن نيك که ملاحظه می کنی ولایت، همان ولاية الله است و بس که احدی او را متصرّف نیست الّا الله وحده. وآن دو ولایت هم راجع به سوی ولاية الله است که هُنَالِكَ الْوَلَايَةُ لِلّٰهِ الحَقِّ (18: 44).

بلی، ظهور آن ولاية الله در دو مرتبه شده است: یکی در مقام رسول الله ـ صلی الله علیه وآله ـ و یکی در مقام ولیّ الله. مثل آنکه لسان تو وقتی ملاحظه می کنی هیچ ولایت ندارد در مملکت بدن تو، چه لسان در جنب تو لیس بشیء است. لکن ظهور ولایت تو به زبان تو است.

پس این ولایتی که این دو بزرگوار ـ روحی لهما الفداء وعلیهما السلام ـ دارند بالنسبه به ما سوی الله وقتی خوب ملاحظه می کنی همان ولاية الله است و ایشان را عِبَادٌ مُكْرَمُونَ لَا يَسْبِقُونَهُ بِالْقَوْلِ وَهُمْ بِأَمْرِهِ يَعْمَلُونَ (21: 26–27) می‌بینی، لکن از این بابتی که حق تعالی ذات بذاته‌اش أقدس و أجلّ و أشرف و أعزّ و أکرم است از مباشرت و مخالطت و مقارنت با اشیاء، لهذا ولاية الله را مظهری باید، پس مظهر ولاية الله در میان سلسله موجودات نيك که ملاحظه می کنی آن اتمّ و اكمل و اشرف مخلوقات او باید مظهر ولایت او شود. و ما نمی‌بینیم در میان جمیع ما سوی الله أقدم و أسبق و أعزّ و أشرف از ایشان ـ علیهم السلام ـ احدی را به دلایلی که سابقا محقّق شد.

پس آن جناب ـ صلی الله علیه وآله ـ مظهر ولاية الله شده است. و چون که رسول الله ـ صلی الله علیه وآله ـ مقامش مقام عرش است؛ یعنی مقامش، مقام اجمال و مقام صمت است، و آیت عظمی و دلیل کبرای حق است، و او ـ صلی الله علیه وآله ـ هم اجلّ و اکرم از ظهور است، پس ثالثاً کسی باید مظهر ولاية الله شود که مقامش مقام تفصیل و مقام کرسی و مقام نطق و انبساط باشد[20] حتّی یعطي کلّ ذي حقّ حقّه، ویسوق إلی کلّ مخلوق رزقه، اعمّ از آنکه ارزاق ظاهری باشد یا ارزاق معنوی. و این رتبه جلیله و شأن جمیل را به هم نرسانیدند ایشان ـ علیهم السلام ـ مگر به کثرت عبودیّت[21] و ذلّت و به زیادتی خضوع و خشوع و انکساری که بالنسبه به واجب تعالی داشتند. و چون ایشان ـ علیهم السلام ـ چنین کردند، پس خداوند ایشان ـ علیهم السلام ـ را به این مقام و مرتبه رسانید کما قال تعالی: وَوَجَدَكَ عَائِلاً فَأَغْنَى (93: 8)؛ یعنی چون خداوند تو را عایل و

20 و به وجهی فرموده‌اند که رسالت، مقام ظهور و ولایت، مقام بطون است. و شاهد آن قدر ناشناسی امّت از مقام ولایت است.

21 این شأن جمیل، ملازمه با مقام عبودیّت مطلقه دارد که مقام کثرت عبودیّت و خضوع و خشوع، از ظهورات آن در عالم ناسوت است.

فقیر و عبد خاضع خاشع و ذلیل و محتاج دید، پس تو را غنی گردانید. و غنای خداوندی ایشان را غنای اعطاء مال و منال دنیوی نبود، بلکه غنای خداوندی مر ایشان را این بود که ایشان ـ علیهم السلام ـ را واسطه در کلّ فیوضات قرار داد، و ایشان را قائم مقام و خلیفه خود گردانید، کما قال ـ علیه السلام ـ في وصف النبي ـ صلى الله علیه وآله ـ "استخلصه الله في القدم على سائر الأمم أقامه مقامه في سائر عوالمه في الأداء".[22]

بلی، از این است که خداوند می‌فرماید: وَالسَّمَاءَ رَفَعَهَا (55:7)؛ یعنی خداوند سماء را که عبارت از سماء حقیقی این عالم می‌باشد رفیع و بلند گردانید، ولکن میزان که عبارت از امیرالمؤمنین ـ علیه السلام ـ باشد در او صنع فرمود و منبسط گردانید و تفصیل داد و در زمین گذاشت. و فی الزیارة له ـ علیه السلام ـ "عليّ میزان الأعمال، ومقلّب الأحوال"[23] إلى آخره. پس اگر رسول الله ـ صلى الله علیه وآله ـ را خداوند در شب معراج به قطع سیر، رفع حجب و استار از او فرموده، و او را رفیع و بلند گردانید، و جمیع اشیاء را به وی نمود، لکن ولیّ را در زمین که بود کشف حجب و استار از وی فرمود: "رأى ما رأى النبي ـ صلى الله علیه وآله ـ" این بود که آن جناب ـ صلى الله علیه وآله ـ وقتی به زمین تشریف آوردند آنچه دیده بودند ولیّ، مطابق واقع توصیف و تعریف فرمود. و سخن در اینجا بسیار و در این مختصر استقصاء نتوان نمود؛ زیرا که از مطلب باز می‌مانیم.

و همچنین به سبب عبودیّت و خضوع و انکسارشان الی الله ـ سبحانه و تعالی ـ [خداوند] ایشان را یک عزّت و سلطنت و یک علوّ و استعلاء و برتری عطا فرمود که نه اوّل او را حدّی است و نه آخر او را نهایتی که ساقط شده‌اند اشیاء نزد او و حقیر و کوچک گشته‌اند ما سوی الله بالنسبه به آن جنابان ـ علیهما السلام.

بیان علوّ و استعلاء و برتری ایشان ـ علیهم السلام ـ بالنسبة به ما سوی الله

وهذا معنى كلام مولانا و سيّدنا السجاد ـ عليه السلام و روحي له الفداء ـ في الصحيفة في دعاء صلاة الليل:[24] "عزّ سلطانك عزّاً لا حدّ له بأوّليّته، ولا منتهى له بآخريّته، واستعلى ملكك علوّاً

22 بحار الأنوار، ج 94، ص 113، نقلاً عن مصباح الزائر؛ إقبال الأعمال، فصل فيما نذكره من فضل عيد الغدير عند أهل العقول من طريق المنقول، ص 255.

23 المزار للمشهدي، ص 184، الباب 12، التوجّه إلى مشهد أمير المؤمنين ـ عليه السلام.

24 ظاهر عبارت صحیفه توصیف معطاة و مسبّب عبودیّت نیست، بلکه توصیف معبود است.

سقطت الأشياء دون بلوغ أمده، ولا يبلغ أدنى ما استأثرت به من ذلك أقصى نعت الناعتين ...".[25] كه نمی‌رسد به ادنی پایه آن علوّ و بزرگواری، اقصی و بلندی وصف وصف کنندگان. و از جمله واصفین، انبیاء و اولیاء و ملایکه مقرّبین و سایر عباد الله صالحین‌اند. و لذا قال عليّ ـ عليه السلام ـ "ينحدر عنّي السيل ولا يرقى إليّ الطير"[26]، یعنی منحدر و جاری شده است از من سیل‌های علوم و اسرار و انهار حکمت و انوار و ینابیع محبّت و معرفت در جمیع اوطار و اطوار، و هیچ مرغی از مرغ‌های عقول و اوهام خواصّ و عوام به مقام و مرتبه من نمی‌رسد، و هیچ وصف واصفی به کنه حقیقت معرفت من نمی‌رسد، هر قدر که خواهد سیر کند.

و من ذلك قال عليّ ـ عليه السلام ـ في حديث النورانيّة لسلمان و أباذرّ:

أنا عبد الله عزّ وجلّ وخليفته على عباده، لا تجعلونا أرباباً وقولوا في فضلنا ما شئتم، فإنّكم لا تبلغوا كنه ما فينا و لا نهايته، فإنّ الله عزّ وجلّ قد أعطانا أكبر وأعظم ولم يصفه واصفكم أو يخطر على قلب أحدكم. يا سلمان و يا جندب، قالا: لبيك يا أميرالمؤمنين قال ـ عليه السلام ـ: لقد أعطانا الله ربّنا ما هو أجل وأعظم وأعلى وأكبر من هذا كلّه. قالا: يا أميرالمؤمنين ما الذي أعطاكم ما هو أعظم وأجل من هذا كلّه؟ قال ـ عليه السلام ـ: قد أعطانا ربّنا عزّ وجلّ علّمنا الاسم الأعظم الذي لو شئنا خرقنا السماوات والأرض والجنّة والنار ونعرج به إلى السماء ونهبط به الأرض ونغرب ونشرق وننتهي به إلى العرش، نجلس عليه بين يدي الله عزّ وجلّ ويطيعنا كلّ شيء حتّى السماوات والأرض، والشمس والقمر والنجوم، والجبال والشجر والدواب والبحار، والجنّة والنار، أعطانا الله ذلك كلّه بالاسم الأعظم الذي علّمنا وخصّنا به، ومع ذلك كلّه نأكل ونشرب ونمشي في الأسواق و نعمل هذه الأشياء بأمر ربّنا، ونحن عباد الله المكرمون الذين لا يسبقونه بالقول و هم بأمره يعملون. و جعلنا معصومين مطهّرين وفضّلنا على كثير من عباده المؤمنين، فنحن نقول: الْحَمْدُ لِلّٰهِ الَّذِي هَدَانَا لِهَذَا وَمَا كُنَّا لِنَهْتَدِيَ لَوْلَا أَنْ هَدَانَا اللّٰهُ (7:43) و حَقَّتْ كَلِمَةُ الْعَذَابِ عَلَى الْكَافِرِينَ (39:71)، أعني الجاحدين بكلّ ما أعطانا الله من الفضل والإحسان[27] إلى آخر الحديث.

25 الصحيفة السجّاديّة، دعاؤه ـ عليه السلام ـ بعد الفراغ من صلاة الليل لنفسه في الاعتراف بالذنب.

26 نهج البلاغة، ومن خطبة له وهي المعروفة بالشقشقيّة.

27 بحار الأنوار، ج 26، ص 6، ح 1، باب نادر في معرفتهم ـ صلوات الله عليهم ـ بالنورانيّة.

و در حديث ديگر است از آن جناب كه فرمودند: "ظاهري ولاية[28] لا يملك وباطني غيب لا يدرك".[29]

و في خطبة التطنجيّة عنه ـ عليه السلام ـ أيضاً قوله ـ عليه السلام.

ولقد كشف لي فعرفت، وعلّمني ربّي فتعلّمت، ألا فعوا ولا تضجوا ولا ترتجوا، فلولا خوفي عليكم أن تقولوا جن أو ارتدّ لأخبرتكم بما كانوا وما أنتم فيه وما تلقونه إلى يوم القيامة، علم أوعز إليّ فعلمت، ولقد ستر علمه عن جميع النبيّين إلّا صاحب شريعتكم هذه ـ صلوات الله عليه وآله و سلّم ـ، فعلّمني علمه، وعلّمته علمي. ألا وإنّا نحن النذر الأولى، ونحن نذر الآخرة والأولى، ونذر كلّ زمان وأوان، وبنا هلك من هلك، وبنا نجا من نجا، فلا تستطيعوا ذلك فينا، فو الذي فلق الحبّة، وبرأ النسمة، وتفرّد بالجبروت والعظمة، لقد سخرت لي الرياح والهواء والطير، وأعرضت على الدنيا، فأعرضت عنها، أنا كأب الدنيا لوجهها فخنى، متى يلحق بي اللواحق، لقد علمت ما فوق الفردوس الأعلى، وما تحت السابعة السفلى، وما في السماوات العلى، وما بينهما وما تحت الثرى. كلّ ذلك علم إحاطة لا علم إخبار، أقسم بربّ العرش العظيم، لو شئت أخبرتكم بآبائكم وأسلافكم أين كانوا، وممّن كانوا، وأين هم الآن، وما صاروا إليه[30] انتهى.

بيان قصور افهام خلق در معرفت ايشان ـ عليهم السلام ـ به دليل واضح

اى عزيز، چرا بايد نتوانند وصف كنند ايشان را واصفين و ناعتين؟ به جهت آن است كه ايشان به منزله و مرتبه شعاعند. و شعاع كى تواند خود را به مرتبه و مقام منير رسانيده تا آنكه او را بتواند وصف نمايد. پس هر چه وصف كنند واصفين، وصف خودشان است نه وصف ايشان ـ عليهم السلام ـ و وصف ايشان در خور جلال ايشان ـ عليهم السلام ـ نيست. قال ـ عليه السلام ـ "إنّما تحدّ الأدوات أنفسها، وتشير الآلة إلى نظائرها".[31] اين است نكته آيه شريفه كه خداوند فرموده: وَالسَّمَاءَ رَفَعَهَا (55: 7).

28 في البحار: أمر.

29 بحار الأنوار، ج 25، ص 169، ح 38؛ مشارق أنوار اليقين، ص 177.

30 مشارق أنوار اليقين، ص 264.

31 نهج البلاغة، خطبه 186، ومن خطبة له ـ عليه السلام ـ في التوحيد وتجمع هذه الخطبة من أصول العلم ما لا تجمعه خطبة.

و حدّی و انتهایی از برای این علوّ و رفعت قرار نداد تا آنکه بفهمند خلایق که از برای محبّت و معرفت و قرب و علم او، ختمی و نهایتی نیست. قال تعالی في الحديث القدسي في حديث الأسرار: "كلّما رفعت لهم علماً وضعت لهم حلماً ليس لمحبّتي غاية و لا نهاية".[32] پس سلطنت الهی و مُلك او و علوّ او ایشانند. و الیه الاشارة فی دعاء سحر شهر رمضان: "اللّهمّ إنّي أسألك من سلطانك بأدومه وكلّ سلطانك دائم"، و قوله ـ علیه السلام ـ "اللّهمّ إنّي أسألك من ملكك بأفخره وكلّ ملكك فاخر"، و قوله: "اللّهم إنّي أسألك من علوّك بأعلاه وكلّ علوّك عال".[33]

نکته: بیان آنکه انتها از برای رفعت و علوّ ایشان ـ علیهم السلام ـ نیست

بدان که اعلی علوّ خداوندی، آن اوّل صادر[34] از فعل او و اوّل مصنوع او است که رسول الله ـ صلی الله علیه وآله ـ باشد؛ زیرا که آن جناب ـ صلی الله علیه وآله ـ بالنسبه به سایر اهل بیت ـ علیهم السلام ـ اعلی و اشرف و افخر است. و حال آنکه کلّ اهل بیت دائم و عالی و فاخر و شریفند، فافهم المقال و لا تكثر القيل والقال، فإنّ "العلم نقطة كثّرها الجاهلون".[35]

و اینکه گفتیم مقام رسول الله ـ صلی الله علیه وآله ـ مقام صمت است، و مقام امیرالمؤمنین ـ علیه السلام ـ مقام نطق است،[36] إليه الإشارة حديث النورانيّة: "يا سلمان ويا جندب صار محمّد الصامت وصرت أنا الناطق، وصار محمّد المنذر وصرت أنا الهادي". قال تعالی: إِنَّمَا أَنْتَ مُنْذِرٌ وَلِكُلِّ قَوْمٍ هَادٍ (13: 7).

32 الجواهر السنيّة، ص 191، الباب الحادي عشر فيما وردت في شأن محمّد بن عبدالله ـ عليه السلام ـ؛ بحار الأنوار، ج 74، ص 21، ح 6، نقلاً عن كتاب إرشاد القلوب للديلمي.

33 إقبال الأعمال، ج 1، ص 96.

34 مقام صادر اوّل، مقام جمع اهل بیت ـ علیهم السلام ـ است، یعنی مقام "أشهد أنّ أرواحكم ونوركم وطينتكم واحدة" بنا بر اینکه وحدت سنخی مراد نباشد منحصراً.

35 عوالي اللئالي، ج 4، ص 129، ح 223؛ كشف الخفاء، ج 2، ص 67، ح 1760؛ ينابيع المودّة، ج 1، ص 213، ح 16.

36 ظاهر بر عکس است و در بحار ج 26، ص 4 هم بر عکس است: "صار محمّد الناطق وصرت أنا الصامت".

بيان سرّ ظهور ولاية الله و مقامات الله و مقامات النبيّ ـ صلّى الله عليه وآله ـ در عليّ عليه السلام

الحاصل، پس از اين تحقيقات كافيه و تدقيقات وافيه و بيانات شافيه مبرهن و ظاهر شدكه به چه جهت بايد ولاية الله و ولاية الرسول ظهورش در جناب امير ـ عليه السلام ـ باشد.

پس به يك لحاظ گفتيم ولايت، سه ولايت است. و به يك لحاظ كه مى‌آبى و فناء و اضمحلال ايشان را مى‌بينى و ملاحظه مى كنى كه ايشان ـ عليهم السلام ـ عبد مرزوق خداوندى هستند كه لَا يَمْلِكُونَ لِأَنْفُسِهِمْ نَفْعاً وَلَا ضَرّاً (13:16) و هميشه مى گويند: "يا ربّ بيدك لا بيد غيرك، زيادتي ونقصي ونفعي وضرّي"[37] ولايت را منحصر در ولاية الله مى‌بينى و بس. و به يك لحاظ كه ملاحظه مى كنى نمى‌بينى ظهور آن دو ولايت را مگر در علىّ ـ عليه السلام ـ از اين است كه رسول ـ صلى الله عليه وآله ـ مقامش مقام نبىّ شد، و امير ـ عليه السلام ـ مقامش مقام ولىّ. و خلافى است بين علماء كه آيا نبىّ مقدّم بر ولىّ است يا ولىّ مقدّم بر نبىّ است؟ ولكن حقّ مسأله اين است كه مى گوييم اوّل مخلوق حقّ تعالى كه او فى الحقيقة آيه او و مترجم كلام او است نيست مگر نبىّ ـ صلى الله عليه وآله.

بلى، ظهور مقامات نبىّ ـ صلى الله عليه وآله ـ در جناب علىّ ـ عليه السلام ـ شده است. و از اين است كه جميع افعال ربوبيّت ظهورش در علىّ ـ عليه السلام ـ شده است. مثل سقايت كوثر و قسمت جنّت و نار، و قسمت ارزاق عباد، و تميّز بين حقّ و باطل، اگر چه مكرّر گفتيم كه: "لا مؤثّر في الوجود إلّا الله" لكن خداوند نمى‌آيد ذات بذاته‌اش [را] مباشر اشياء نمايد به اين معنى كه بيايد و بر سر حوض كوثر بايستد و ساقى مردم شود، بلكه ظهور اين در اميرالمؤمنين ـ عليه السلام ـ شده است. و يك معناى كوثر هم عبارت از ولايت ولىّ الله است.

و ايضاً اين ولايتى كه آن جناب دارد اين همان ولايتى است كه اشاره به اوست قوله ـ عليه السلام ـ في الزيارة: "السلام على نعمة الله على الأبرار ونقمته على الفجّار".[38] قال تعالى: فَضُرِبَ بَيْنَهُمْ بِسُورٍ لَهُ بَابٌ بَاطِنُهُ فِيهِ الرَّحْمَةُ وَظَاهِرُهُ مِنْ قِبَلِهِ الْعَذَابُ (57:13).

37 إقبال الأعمال، ج 3، ص 296، فيما نذكره من الدعاء في شعبان.

38 المزار، ص 217، زيارة أخرى لأمير المؤمنين.

معنى خليفه بودن علىّ عليه السلام

الحاصل، پس هر كس ولاية الله را حامل است و مظهر است، او خليفة الله است. و او است که معطى كلّ ذى حق حقّه است. و سلطنت الهى و خليفة اللّهى از براى احدى صادق نيست الّا از براى او؛ چه خليفة الله به معنى جانشين و قائم مقام خداوندى بودن است؛ يعنى همان كارى كه خداوند مى‌خواهد جارى فرمايد او نيز جارى فرمايد. اين است معنى "إعطاء كلّ ذي حقّ حقّه، و السوق إلى كلّ مخلوق رزقه".

و ايصال كلّ فيوضات از وجود و رزق و حيات و ممات ايشان ـ چه در دنيا و چه در آخرت ـ در جميع عوالم الهيّه به ايشان [است]. و اين است معناى وجه الله و عين الله و يد الله و لسان الله.

معنى عين الله و يد الله و أُذُن الله و وجه الله و لسان الله بودن علىّ عليه السلام

پس اگر ولىّ الله آن چشمى نداشته باشد كه جميع ما سوى الله را از غيب و شهادت ببيند همچنان كه خداوند مى‌بيند، اين "عين الله" نيست. و اگر نشنوند اصوات جميع ما سوى الله را حالاً و مقالاً او را "أُذن الله الواعية" و "أُذن الله السامعة" كه در زيارت آن جناب في قوله ـ عليه السلام ـ "السلام عليك يا عين الله الناظرة ويده الباسطة وأذنه الواعية"[39] اشاره بدان شده نمى‌نامند. و اگر او در همه جا نباشد كه جميع ما سوى الله را ببيند به رأى العين از كجا او را "وجه اللّهى" كه در كلام الله اشاره بدان شده فى قوله تعالى: فَأَيْنَمَا تُوَلُّوا فَثَمَّ وَجْهُ اللهِ (2:115) مى‌نامند. و اگر اعطا كلّ ذى حقّ حقّه نكند او را چگونه "يد الله الباسطة" گويند. و اگر مقامش مقام "لا يشغله شأن عن شأن" نباشد او را چگونه "سرّ الله" گويند. و اگر ايشان علم حادثى مخلوقى الهى و خزنه علم او نباشند ـ كما فى حديث جابر المتقدّم ـ معلوم مى‌شود كه بايد خداوند چيزى را عالم نباشد.

خلاصه، پس هر كس كه لسانش لسان الله، و عينش عين الله، و يدش يد الله است او خليفة الله است. و ساير انبياء ـ عليهم السلام ـ را كه خليفة الله كردند هم به واسطه آن خليفة الله العظمى بود. چنانكه حديث است كه خداوند عقول انبياء ـ عليهم السلام ـ را از اشعه اجساد ايشان خلق فرمود. و انبياء ـ عليهم السلام ـ هم أيادى و ألسنه ايشانند؛ يعنى هر فيضى و كرامتى و مقام عظيم و معجزه باهرى كه از ايشان ناشى مى‌شد كلاّ از فاضل و شعاع فيوضات و كرامات ايشان ـ عليهم السلام ـ بود. و هر چه را دارا بودند از ايشان دارا بودند.

---

39 المزار للمشهدي، ص 217؛ بحار الأنوار، ج 97، ص 305.

بیان آنکه انبیاء و اولیاء و کمّلین عباد الله هر چه را دارا بودند از فواضل علوم و از اشعّه شعاع و فیوضات ایشان - علیهم السلام - بود

وإليه الإشارة في الحديث النورانيّة خطاباً لسلمان و أباذرّ - رضي الله عنه -:

يا سلمان ويا جندب قالا: لبيك يا أميرالمؤمنين - عليه السلام - قال: أنا الذي حملت نوحاً في السفينة بأمر ربّي، وأنا الذي أخرجت يونس من بطن الحوت بإذن ربّي، وأنا الذي جاوزت بموسى بن عمران البحر بأمر ربّي، وأنا الذي أخرجت إبراهيم من النار بإذن ربّي، وأنا الذي أجريت أنهارها وفجّرت عيونها وغرست أشجارها بإذن ربّي، وأنا عذاب يوم الظلّة، وأنا المنادي من مكان قريب قد سمعه الثقلان الجنّ والإنس وفهمه قوم إنّي لأسمع كلّ قوم الجبّارين والمنافقين بلغاتهم، وأنا الخضر عالم موسى، وأنا معلّم سليمان بن داود، وأنا ذو القرنين، وأنا قدرة الله عزّ وجلّ.[40]

وقال العسكرى - عليه السلام - "الكليم ألبس حلّة الاصطفاء لمّا عهدنا منه الوفاء، وروح القدس في جنان الصاقورة ذاق من حدائقنا الباكورة"[41].[42]

وفي خطبة الافتخار عن عليّ - عليه السلام - كما في رواية أصبغ بن نباتة:

أنا صاحب القرون الأوّلين، أنا المتكلّم بالوحي، أنا المعطي، أنا المبذل، أنا القابض يدي على القبض، أنا وليّ الرحمان، أنا صاحب الخضر وهارون، أنا صاحب موسى ويوشع بن نون، أنا صاحب شيث بن آدم، أنا صاحب موسى وآدم - إلى أن قال - عليه السلام - ألا وكم عجائب تركتها ودلائل كتمتها لا أجد لها حملة أنا صاحب إبليس بالسجود، أنا معذّبه وجنوده على الكبر والعنود، أنا رافع إدريس مكانا عليّاً، أنا مُنطق عيسى في المهد صبيّاً، أنا ميدان الميادين وواضع الأرض، أنا صاحب الطور، أنا ذلك النور الظاهر، أنا ذلك البرهان الباهر، وكلّ ذلك بعلم من الله ذي الجلال، أنا دليل السماوات، أنا أنيس المسبّحات.[43]

40 بحار الأنوار، ج 26، ص 5، ح 1، باب نادر في معرفتهم - صلوات الله عليهم.

41 الباكورة: أوّل ما يدرك من الفاكهة.

42 بحار الأنوار، ج 26، ص 265، ح 50، باب جوامع مناقبهم و فضائلهم 3.

43 مشارق أنوار اليقين، ص 261.

بیان آنکه ولیّ الله تصرّف دارد در ملك خداوندی در آن چیزی که اراده الهی به آن تعلّق گیرد

ای عزیز! از این قبیل از کلمات آن جناب ـ علیه السلام ـ در خطب و در طی کلمات و اخبار ایشان ـ علیه السلام ـ اکثر من أن تستصقی است. و در حدیث نبوی ـ صلی الله علیه وآله ـ است که فرمودند: "یا عليّ إنّ الله أيّد بك النبيّين سرّاً، وأيّدني بك جهراً".[44]

از بزرگواری پرسیدم که سرّ این چیست که عقول انبیاء ـ علیهم السلام ـ که از فاضل و شعاع ایشان ـ علیهم السلام ـ خلق شده‌اند وحی بر ایشان نازل می‌شود و جبرئیل ـ علیهم السلام ـ از آسمان بر ایشان نازل گردد و جناب امیر ـ علیه السلام ـ که جمیع انبیاء و اولیاء پرتوی از شعاع نور جمال وی‌اند بر او وحی نازل نشود؟

جواب داد که: چرا رشته امر را از دست می‌دهی. آیا فراموش نموده‌ای معنی "ولیّ الله" بودن را که به معنای این است که زمام جمیع امورات در دست او است؟ و فراموش نموده‌ای معنی "لسان الله" بودن و "ید الله" بودن آن جناب ـ علیه السلام ـ را، و واسطه در کلّ فیوضات بودن آن جناب ـ علیه السلام ـ را، و معنی آن حدیثی که فرمودند: "أنا كلمة الله الناطق، أنا آخذ العهد على الأروح في الأزل، أنا الحيّ الذي لا يموت، أنا المفوّض إليّ أمر الخلائق" و امثال این کلمات را؟ پس کسی که "کلمة الله الناطق"، و لسان خداوند، و سبب اعظم، و واسطه در کلّ فیوضات باشد، و تفویض شده باشد به او امر خلایق، تصوّر نما که وحی الهی به انبیاء کی[45] واسطه‌اش بود. اگر گویی بلاواسطه به جبرئیل می‌رسید کلامی است فاسد، و نقض می کند مر مقامات ایشان ـ علیهم السلام ـ را، و معنی واسطه بودن و سبب اعظم بودن ایشان را. و اگر گویی واسطه وحی امیرالمؤمنین ـ علیه السلام ـ بود، فقد ثبت المطلوب، چون که خداوند ذات بذاته‌اش اجل و اکرم و اشرف از مخالطت و مباشرت و مقارنت با اشیاء است، و سببی او را لازم است. پس اوّل واسطه و سبب اوّل و سبب اعظم امیر المؤمنین ـ علیه السلام ـ است لا غیر. و او است مبلّغ وحی و مترجم کلام او، فافهم.

الحاصل، پس انبیاء هر چه را دارا بودند همگی از فاضل مراتب و مقامات آن جنابان ـ علیهم السلام ـ بود. و همچنین هر شیعه کامل و محبّ صادقی که منقطع به سوی ایشان ـ علیهم السلام ـ بوده، و متبع باشد مر افعال و اقوال و احوال و اخلاق و سلوك ایشان ـ علیهم السلام ـ را، یعنی آن

44 حلیة الأبرار، ج 2، ص 17؛ مدینة المعاجز، ج 1، ص 144، ح 86.

45 یعنی: چه کسی.

اشخاصی که به نور علم و عمل رابطه و آشنایی و انسی با اهل بیت ـ علیهم السلام ـ در این عالم پیدا کردند ومی کنند، آنها هم هر چه را دارا هستند از فاضل فاضل و شعاع شعاع ایشان ـ علیهم السلام ـ است. و ایشان هم لسان‌اند و هم یداند ایشان ـ علیهم السلام ـ را، و لکن لسان الله و ید الله و آیة الله و عین الله حقیقی منحصر به ایشان است، و سایر ما سوی خدّام و عین و لسان و ید ایشان ـ علیهم السلام ـ اند. ولکن از آنجایی که آیه آیه هم آیه است، پس اشیاء هر کدام حرکتشان بر وفق رضا و محبّت الهی شد، و در جمیع افعال و اعمال و اقوال و احوال مطابق با ایشان ـ علیهم السلام ـ شد، از ید ایشان و لسان ایشان و عین ایشان ـ علیهم السلام ـ است. و هر گاه مخالف با ایشان ـ علیهم السلام ـ شد، شکّی نیست که آن در آن حال، لسان اعداء ایشان است. مثلاً شخص در وقتی که سبّ می کند و فحش می گوید، یا طفل یتیم را می‌زند، آن وقت لسان او و ید او، ید ایشان ـ علیهم السلام ـ نیست، بلکه در آن حال لسان او و ید او لسان و ید اعداء ایشان است.

بناءً علی هذا، واضح شد که در حین اطاعت، انسان، لسان و ید ایشان می‌شود، و سبب است در اسباب جزئیّه در این عالم. و در چنین حالت، ولا یت او رأسی است از رؤس ولا یت، و شأنی است از شئونات آن ولا یت کلیّه. و هرگاه مخالف شد، لسان او و ید او شأنی است از شؤونات لسان و ید اعداء ایشان ـ علیهم السلام.

و این معنی بر احدی مخفی و پوشیده نیست که بعد از آنکه ایشان ـ علیهم السلام ـ "شهداء دار الفناء"، و "خزنة علم الله"، و "عباد مکرمون" خداوند شدند، ایشان ـ علیهم السلام ـ هم شاهدند بر کلّ ما سوی الله، به علّت آنکه خلیفة الله کسی است که مصداق "لا یشغله شأن عن شأن" در عالم خلق باشد، چه تو هر قدر عظمت از برای خداوند ثابت می کنی باید از برای ایشان ـ علیهم السلام ـ نیز ثابت باشد، به علّت آنکه خلیفه بودن هر کسی مناسب مقام آقای او است، پس خلیفه الهی باید اجلّ خلفا باشد، و باید کسی ولیّ الله و خلیفة الله باشد که او را سلطنت عامّه باشد در مُلك خداوندی در آنچه باید متعلّق شود به او اراده الهی که تمام عالم کبیر را و تمام این هزار هزار عالم و هزار هزار آدم را، چه در دنیا و چه در آخرت و چه در برزخ و چه در بعث و چه در نشور و چه در جنّت و عوالم آن در جمیع ما سوی الله خلیفة الله باشد. این است بعد از آنکه راوی از امام ـ علیه السلام ـ سؤال نمود که بعد از آنکه اهل جنّت در جنّت و اهل نار در نار مستقر شدند دیگر خداوند خلقی خلق می‌فرماید؟ فرمودند: بلی. عرض کرد: "فمن الحجّة علیهم؟ قال ـ علیه السلام ـ نحن الحجّة علی الأوّلین والآخرین"، فافهم. ولقد فتحت لك بابا ینفتح منه ألف باب، فخذه وکن من الشا کرین والحمد لله ربّ العالمین.

و بالجمله، از برای این حقیقت مقدّسه و مشیّت مبارکه به این اسماء مبارکه که ذکر شد و غیر آن از امثال این اسماء، آن اوّل وجود است بر جهت اطلاق در عالم خلق و در عالم ایجاد و حدوث؛ به علّت آنکه وقتی که ملاحظه می کنی می‌بینی که عالم قائم است به دو شیء: به فعلی و به مفعولی. و مقصود از فاعل خداوند ـ سبحانه و تعالی ـ است. و مراد از فعل آن حقیقت مقدّسه‌ای است که اشاره بدان شد. و مراد از مفعول حقایق موجودات و ذوات کاینات است از عقل اوّل کلّی گرفته تا آخر مراتب سفلیه از مراتب وجود که مرتبه جماد باشد. و چون که این فعل الله ظاهر و متحقّق نمی‌شد، بلکه ممکن نبود ظهور و تحقّق آن مگر به متعلّقات و به محلّش که تعبیر از او به انفعال و انوجاد نموده‌اند؛ یعنی انوجاد و انفعالی که کسر و انکسار باشد، و چون که ایضا محلّ فعل و متعلّق آن خود حقیقت محمدیّه ـ صلی الله علیه وآله ـ بود که موجود می‌شد به این حقیقت محمدیّه تمام فعل و مشیّت الهیّه و حقیقت محمدیّه ـ صلی الله علیه وآله ـ هم اوّل وجودات و اوّل ما صدر از او و اوّل موجودات و مخلوقات و محل بود، واجب شد اینکه بوده باشد این حقیقت محمدیّه از سنخ حالّ که اگر محلّ شیء از سنخ حالّ در آن فعل نباشد هر آینه زایل می گردد مناسبت، و ممتنع می گردد محلّ بودن آن.

بیان مقامات و مراتب ایشان ـ علیهم السلام ـ در مقام نقطه و الف و حروف و کلمه

الحاصل، از برای این حقیقت مقدّسه ـ کما بیّنّا سابقاً ـ دو اطلاق است در دو مقام:

یکی مقام اجمال، و یکی مقام تفصیل. و در مقام اجمال اراده می‌شود در محلّ بودن ایشان فعل الله را مجموع قصبه یاقوت که عبارت از چهارده نفر معصومین ـ علیهم السلام ـ باشند.

و امّا در مقام ثانی که مقام تفصیل باشد، جناب رسول ـ صلی الله علیه وآله ـ خصوصیت دارد بر سیزده تن ـ علیهم السلام ـ پس در مقام اوّل چون که بودند ایشان ـ علیهم السلام ـ آن کلمه علیا و کلمه تقوا و کلمه توحید، پس از برای ایشان ـ علیهم السلام ـ چهار مرتبه حاصل شد:

مقام اوّل: مقام نقطه است در مقام کلمه. مقام دویم: مقام الف است. سیّم: مقام حروف عالیات است در کلمه. چهارم: مقام تمام کلمه است. پس نقطه عبارت از جناب محمّد ـ صلی الله علیه وآله ـ است، و الف عبارت از علیّ ـ علیه السلام ـ است. و حروف عالیات عبارت از سایر ائمّه ـ علیهم السلام ـ است. و تمام کلمه عبارت از صدیقه کبری فاطمه زهرا ـ سلام الله علیها ـ است.

و بعبارة أخری، مقام نقطه اشاره به مقام مشیّت، و دویم مقام اراده، و سیوم مقام قَدَر، و چهارم مقام قضا است که تمامیّت شیء به این چهار متحقق می‌شود، کما برهنا سابقاً.

بعبارة أخرى، مقام اوّل که مقام نقطه باشد عبارت از نقطه بسم الله الرحمن الرحیم است. و دوم مقام باء "بسم الله" است. و سیوم مقام حروف "بسم الله" است. و چهارم مقام کلمه مبارکه است.

تکریر و تقرین للتوضیح

بدان که در این مقام مناسب آمد آن سؤالی که شخص از جناب شیخ[46] ـ أعلی الله مقامه ـ نموده بود در مشیّت و بیان مقامات ایشان ـ علیهم السلام ـ ذکر شود. و ما به ذکر ترجمه آن پرداخته، متعرّض ظاهر عبارت عربیّت او نشدیم لیفید الخواصّ و العوامّ جمیعاً.

مسئول منه ـ أعلی الله مقامه ـ: اگر گویی که چگونه اطلاق می‌شود حقیقت محمّدیّه ـ صلی الله علیه وآله ـ بر مشیّت که بگوییم: آن حقیقت مقدّسه خود مشیّت است چنانکه سابقاً تحقیق نمودی. و چگونه می‌شود که ایشان ـ علیهم السلام ـ مقامات خداوندی باشند؛ یعنی آن مقاماتی که واقع می‌شود بر او اسامی وجود حق مثل ذات بحت و مجهول النعت و عین الکافور، وذات ساذج بلا اعتبار، ومجهول مطلق، وذات بحت، وشمس الأزل ومنقطع الاشارات والواجب الحقّ واللّا تعیّن والکنز المخفي والمنقطع الوحداني.[47] و همچنین سایر اسمایی که او را هست. پس اگر گویی که ایشان ـ علیهم السلام ـ وجودشان وجود مطلق است، پس نمی‌فهمیم ما معنای او را. پس چگونه می‌توان جمع نمود میانه حقیقت محمّدیّه و میانه آنکه فرمود: "خلق الله الأشیاء کلّها بالمشیّة" و حال آنکه ایشان ـ علیهم السلام ـ هم از جمله اشیاء هستند. و اگر ایشان غیر از این مرتبه باشند، پس محتاج به بیان است.

جواب عنه ـ رحمه الله ـ این مسأله آن است که می گوییم: اطلاق حقیقت محمّدیّه ـ صلی الله علیه وآله ـ بر مشیّت می‌شود و می‌توانی بگویی که حقیقت محمّدیّه ـ صلی الله علیه وآله ـ خود مشیّت است چنانچه سابقاً بیان نمودیم. لکن به دو احتمال:

اوّل آنکه: قائل شوی بر اینکه حقیقت محمّدیّه ـ صلی الله علیه وآله ـ عبارت از مشیّت است؛ یعنی حقیقت ایشان را خود مشیّت دانی لا غیر. آن مشیّتی که او را اسامی متعدّده می‌باشد. چنانچه ذکر کثیری از اسماء او را حقیر نمودم. این یك اطلاق.

و ثانی آنکه: قائل شوی بر اینکه نسبت حقیقت محمّدیّه ـ صلی الله علیه وآله ـ بالنسبة به مشیّت مثل نسبت انکسار است به کسر، چه انکسار مقام انفعال فعل است در حینی که فاعل، او را منفعل

---

46 شیخ احمد احسایی ـ أعلی الله مقامه.

47 در نسخه: الوجداني.

و منکسر می‌سازد. بلی، اطلاق می‌شود به سبیل حقیقت اینکه بگویی آن مشیّتی که مخلوق است به نفس خود و معلول است به علّت خود، آن خود حقیقت محمّدیّه ـ صلی الله علیه وآله ـ است و این نفس مشیّت عبارت از خود مشیّت است. پس قول حضرت ـ علیه السلام ـ که فرمودند خداوند خلق فرمود اشیاء را به مشیّت معنای او چنین می‌شود: یعنی خداوند خلق فرمود خلق را به شعاع حقیقت محمّدیّه ـ صلی الله علیه وآله ـ یا خلق فرمود خلق را به نفس آن حقیقت به اعتبار آنکه گفتیم آن نفس محلّ مشیّت است آن مشیّتی که آن، نفس حقیقت است کما قال تعالی: لَا يَسْبِقُونَهُ بِالْقَوْلِ وَهُمْ بِأَمْرِهِ يَعْمَلُونَ يَعْلَمُ مَا بَيْنَ أَيْدِيهِمْ وَمَا خَلْفَهُمْ (21: 27–28)، یا آنکه به عکس بوده باشد که بگویی حقیقت محمّدیّه ـ صلی الله علیه وآله ـ نفس مشیّت است. پس در این هنگام مشیّت مخلوق می‌باشد به آن حقیقت به این معنی که بگویی مشیّت عبارت از قابل است، و قابل عبارت از فاعل است؛ یعنی آن فاعلی که این فعل به جهت او است کما قال تعالی: كُنْ فَيَكُونُ (2: 117). پس "کن" عبارت از فعل است، و "یکون" عبارت از مفعول.

بیان عنوان "الله" بودن ایشان

و امّا معنی آنکه ایشان ـ علیهم السلام ـ "مقامات الله" و "علامات الله" هستند که اسامی وجود حق بر ایشان ـ علیهم السلام ـ اطلاق می‌شود آن هم مثل همان است که گفتیم. و معنای او این است که می گوییم: خداوند تعالی که بود کنز مخفی، معروف نبود ابداً، پس چون که دوست داشت که شناخته شود و معروف گردد، ظاهر شد از برای ایشان به خود ایشان، و ظاهر شد از برای هر شیء به نفس خود آن شیء. پس ایشان ـ علیهم السلام ـ به اعتبار آنکه مظاهر علیای خداوندی هستند اطلاق وجود مطلق بر ایشان ـ علیهم السلام ـ می‌شود چنانچه سابقاً عرض نمودیم.

و امّا وقوع اسامی مذکوره بر ایشان ـ علیهم السلام ـ پس از آنجایی که آن اسامی اطلاق می‌شود بر معنایی که آن معنا عنوان حق ـ سبحانه و تعالی ـ است، پس حقایق ایشان ـ علیهم السلام ـ عبارت از همین عنوان است. و اسماء لفظیّه هم اسماء این عنوان هستند. و این عنوان اسم است از برای ذات غیب بحت. و این اسم آن اسمی است که در دعا اشاره به آن شد: "وأسألك باسمك الذي استقرّ في ظلّك، فلا يخرج منك إلى غيرك".[48] و معنی آنکه مستقر است در ظلّ خودش؛ یعنی قرار گرفته و استقرار یافته است در ظلّ خداوند سبحانه، پس خارج نمی‌شود از ظلّ خداوند به سوی غیر او.

48 "وهذا رجب المرجّب الذي أكرمتنا به أوّل أشهر الحرم أكرمتنا به من بين الأمم يا ذا الجود والكرم،

و این ظلّ عبارت از همان اسم است، یعنی اینکه خداوند اقامه فرموده و برپا داشته است او را به نفس خودش، یعنی بلا مادّة او را خلق فرموده است.

و معنی دیگر اینکه می گوییم: اسم عبارت از خود مشیّت است. و ظلّ عبارت از حقیقت محمدیّه ـ صلی الله علیه وآله ـ است، أو بالعکس علی ما أشرنا سابقاً.

و امّا ظهور ایشان و بودن ایشان ـ علیهم السلام ـ از اشیاء، پس لازم نمی آید اینکه ایشان ـ علیهم السلام ـ علّت اشیاء نبوده باشند، تجمعهم صفة وتفرقهم صفة. پس آن صفت جامعی که از برای اشیاء است عبارت از شیئیّت است، لکن صدق می کند بر آن شیء به حقیقت، و بر شیء دیگر به حقیقت بعد از حقیقت، یعنی به حقیقت اضافی.

و امّا صفت مفرقه آن است که می گوییم: اینکه شیئیّت بر دو قسم است: یك شیئیّتی است به نفس خود، و یك شیئیّتی است به غیر نفس خود. آن شیئیّتی که به نفس خود است آن علّت است، و آن شیئیّتی که به غیر نفس خود است آن معلول است. و از برای ایشان ـ علیهم السلام ـ مراتب چندی است از وجود مطلق گرفته تا آن چیزی که در تحت الثری است. در جمیع این مراتب آن جنابان ـ علیهما السلام ـ علّت‌اند از برای غیر خودشان از آن کسی که او مرتبه‌اش تحت مقام ایشان ـ علیهم السلام ـ باشد و صدق کند بر ایشان اینکه ایشان معلول‌اند بالنسبه به سوی ما فوق آن مرتبه از ایشان ـ علیهم السلام ـ و به سوی این معنی اشاره شده است در احادیث و در ادعیه آنکه خداوند ـ سبحانه و تعالی ـ ظاهر فرمود ابتداءً خلق انفس ایشان ـ علیهم السلام ـ را، و ثانیاً به طفیل وجود ایشان ـ علیهم السلام ـ ظاهر فرمود خلقت جمیع خلق خودش را: "نحن صنائع الله والخلق من بعدُ صنائع لنا".[49]

تمّت بقلم منشیها حامداً مصلیّاً مستغفراً في شهر رجب المرجّب الاثنین والستّین بعد الألف والمئتین من الهجرة والحمد لله ربّ العالمین في سنة ١٢٦٢.

فنسألك به وباسمك الأعظم الأجل الأكرم الذي خلقته فاستقرّ في ظلّك فلا يخرج منك إلى غيرك" إلى آخر الدعاء. [مصباح المتهجّد، ص 816، العمل في أوّل ليلة من رجب، ح 20/877].

49 در نهج البلاغه چنین آمده است: "فإنّا صنائع ربّنا والناس بعد صنائع لنا". [نهج البلاغة، ومن كتاب له إلى معاوية جواباً واحتجاجاً].

Bibliography

al-Aḥsāʾī, Muḥammad b. ʿAlī b. Ibrāhīm, *ʿAwālī l-laʾālī l-ʿazīziyya fī l-aḥādīth al-dīniyya*, ed. Mujtabā ʿIrāqī, Qom: Maṭbaʿat Sayyid al-Shuhadāʾ, 1983.

Algar, Hamid, *Religion and state in Iran 1785–1906: The role of the ulama in the Qajar period*, Berkeley: University of California Press, 1969/1980.

Amanat, Abbas, *Resurrection and renewal: The making of the Babi movement in Iran, 1844–1850*, Ithaca and London: Cornell University Press, 1989.

al-Baḥrānī, Hāshim, *Ḥilyat al-abrār*, ed. Riḍā al-Burūjirdī, Qom: al-Maʿārif al-Islāmiyya, 1990–1991.

al-Baḥrānī, Hāshim, *Madīnat al-maʿājiz*, ed. ʿIzzat-Allāh Hamadānī, Qom: al-Maʿārif al-Islāmiyya, 1992–1993.

Bayat, Mangol, *Mysticism and dissent: Socioreligious thought in Qajar Iran*, Syracuse, NY: Syracuse University Press, 1982.

al-Bursī, al-Ḥāfiẓ Rajab, *Mashāriq anwār al-yaqīn*, ed. ʿAlī ʿĀshūr, Beirut: al-Aʿlamī, 1999.

Cole, Juan, "The world as text: Cosmologies of Shaykh Ahmad al-Aḥsāʾī," in *SI* 80 (1994), 145–163.

Corbin, Henry, *Terre céleste et corps de resurrection*, Paris: Buchet/Chastel, 1960.

Eschraghi, Armin, "Kāẓem Rašti," in *EIr*.

Fuyūḍāt, al-Mīrzā Ḥasan, *Madkhal ilā falsafat al-Shaykh al-Aḥsāʾī*, ed. with an introduction by Tawfīq Nāṣir al-BūʿAlī, Beirut: Dār al-Amīra, 2011.

al-Ḥurr al-ʿĀmilī, Muḥammad b. al-Ḥusayn, *al-Jawāhir al-sinniyya*, Najaf: Maktabat al-Mufīd, 1964.

al-Ḥusaynī, al-Sayyid Aḥmad, *Tarājim al-rijāl*, Qom: Ṣadr, 1993–1994.

Ibn Ṭāwūs, Raḍī al-Dīn ʿAlī b. Mūsā b. Jaʿfar, *Iqbāl al-aʿmāl*, ed. Jawād Qayyūmī Iṣfahānī, Najaf: al-Nuʿmān, 1993–1994.

al-Kafʿamī, Ibrāhīm, *Miṣbāḥ al-mutahajjid*, Beirut: Fiqh al-Shīʿa, 1983.

al-Kulaynī, Muḥammad b. Yaʿqūb b. Isḥāq, *al-Kāfī*, ed ʿAlī-Akbar Ghaffārī and Muḥammad Ākhūndī, Tehran: Dār al-Kutub al-Islāmiyya, 1987–1988.

MacEoin, Denis M., "Aḥsāʾī, Shaikh Aḥmad," in *EIr*.

MacEoin, Denis M., "Cosmogony and cosmology. VII. In Shaikhism," in *EIr*.

Majlisī, Muḥammad Bāqir, *Biḥār al-anwār*, ed. Yaḥyā al-ʿĀbidī, Beirut: al-Wafāʾ, 1983.

al-Mashhadī, Muḥammad b. Jaʿfar, *al-Mazār*, ed. Jawād Qayyūmī Iṣfahānī, Qom: al-Nashr al-Islāmī, 1998–1999.

Mīr-Jahānī, Sayyid Muḥammad Ḥasan, *Wilāyat-i kulliyya*, ms., in the author's hand, private collection.

Rizvi, Sajjad, "*Hikma mutaʿaliya* in Qajar Iran: Locating the life and work of Mulla Hadi Sabzawari (d. 1289/1873)," in *IS* 44.4 (2011), 473–496.

Rizvi, Sajjad, "'Only the Imam knows best': The Maktab-e Tafkīk's attack on the legitimacy of philosophy in Iran," in *JRAS* 22.3–4 (2012), 487–503.

Samʿānī, Aḥmad, *The repose of the spirits: A Sufi commentary on the divine names*, trans. William C. Chittick, Albany, NY: SUNY Press, 2019.

al-Ṣadūq, Muḥammad b. ʿAlī b. Bābawayh al-Shaykh, *al-Tawḥīd*, ed. Hāshim Ḥusaynī, Qom: Jāmiʿa-yi Mudarrisīn, 1977–1978.

al-Sharīf al-Raḍī, Abū l-Ḥasan al-Mūsawī, *Nahj al-balāgha*, ed. Muḥammad ʿAbduh, Qom: Dār al-Dhakhāʾir, 1991–1992.

PART 4

Hermeneutics and Cross-Cultural Translation

CHAPTER 20

Observations on Embodiment and Cross-Cultural Translation

Amer Latif

> The more you think about it, the more it should become clear that most important questions cannot be answered "yes" or "no."
>
> SACHIKO MURATA AND WILLIAM CHITTICK[1]

∴

As I contemplated what to write for this *Festschrift* in honor of Professors Murata and Chittick, the choice was clear. It had to be something on how they have helped so many of us understand the nuances, complexity, and mutual complementarity of the poles that are set up whenever we consider questions of existential significance. I came to study with them from an undergraduate background in physics and saw their treatment of Islam informed by the kind of "both-and" logic familiar to me from discussions of reality in quantum physics. In my experience as their teaching assistant in multiple courses and in my own teaching, I have continued to see deep appreciation expressed by students for their style of writing that keeps illuminating the relative truths within complementarity perspectives on any given issue.

In what follows, I give an overview of the way in which Murata and Chittick have presented the importance of nuance and complexity in understanding Islamic conceptions of God. I also provide a summary of how they have used this approach as a model to frame and practice the translation of Islamic texts, in particular the Quran and Sufi literature. Modernity has inherited dualistic models of human nature and perception that rose out of enlightenment rationality (the blank slate theory of human nature, for example). But recent research in the cognitive sciences shows the limitations of modern dualistic models.

1 Murata, Sachiko and William C. Chittick, *The vision of Islam*, New York: Paragon House, 1994, 68.

 | DOI:10.1163/9789004529038_021

This research, though it operates purely at the level of material causation, paints a picture of human nature that is closer to the models of human nature and perception one finds in the classic Islamic texts of a Rūmī (d. 672/1273) or an Ibn ʿArabī (d. 638/1240). I conclude by examining some of the ways in which cognitive science can be helpful in understanding the logic of "both-and" as presented in the writings of Professors Murata and Chittick.

∵

In summing up the focus on the body in Islamic education, Murata and Chittick note that the body is "the indispensable support for everything human, not least the mind and heart."[2] Their observation that "most important questions cannot be answered 'yes' or 'no'" seems to arise from the fact of human embodiment. Most definitions of a human include reference to embodiment as the feature that we share with all other creatures. Along with the old definition, "Man is a rational animal," attributed to Aristotle, we find modern versions such as: "Humans are animals with opposable thumbs" or "Human beings are storytelling animals."

Sages like Rūmī provide us with a number of imagistic reflections on the consequences of our embodiment, especially the experience of humans as sites of tensions and contradictions. In describing our self-quarreling natures, Rūmī says: "Poor humans ... are compounded of intellect and appetite. They are half angel and half beast; half snake and half fish. Their fish pulls them toward water, and their snake pulls them toward dry land. They are engaged in strife and war."[3]

To this duality at the level of motivation and desire, we can add another equally powerful duality at the level of knowledge. Do we trust our everyday perception or do we rely on our rationality to go against the apparent evidence of our own senses?

In order to learn that the earth is round, we have to suspend the evidence of our eyes—the same eyes that we have to trust in order to step out of the way of an oncoming bus so as not to get crushed. It takes a while but a verified/scientific view of the world does take hold if the culture repeats it enough and if it is represented visually in texts and in movies. But for all that, we live in a world that appears flat to us. It also appears that the earth is at the center of the world—to our naked eye, the sun and the stars revolve around the earth.

---

2 Murata and Chittick, *The vision of Islam* xxxviii.

3 Rūmī, Jalāl al-Dīn, *Fīhi mā fīhi*, ed. Badīʿ al-Zamān Furūzānfar, Tehran: Amīr Kabīr, 1969, 78.

The same tension between a verified/scientific truth and our sensed/perceptual truth exists at the level of our consciousness and self. The Buddha verified for himself and taught the truth of "no self." But the idea that the self is not real does not initially sit well with people's everyday experience. "What do you mean there's no self? I can't show it to you, but I know it's here" is a common response at encountering this Buddhist idea. On this count, modern neuroscience concurs with the Buddha: Consciousness is a hallucination created moment by moment by our brain-bodies.[4]

As a final example of this phenomenon where we are told that our senses deceive us and that our everyday experience obfuscates reality, let us consider the stability of the physical world. Our everyday experience as mediated by our bodies and our senses gives us confidence that all bodies are stable to a degree; yes, there are changes in all bodies but these happen over a period of time. But here too we have modern physics telling us that at the quantum level everything in the cosmos is coming into existence and being annihilated multiple times within one second. This is similar to the Quranically inspired doctrine of the continuous renewal of creation in Sufi metaphysics.

Clearly at times we must trust our senses and at others we must not trust them. Appearances are both true and false at the same time. True from the perspective of everyday apparent experience, but false from the perspective of a deeper and verified perspective based on research. The appropriate logic for our embodied human condition is "both-and," the logic of paradox and contradiction, of being pulled in opposite directions.

While their focus on the logic of "both-and" is connected with embodiment, it also follows from the methodology that Murata and Chittick adopt in studying and teaching Islam. Put simply, their method is to approach Islam and premodern Muslim writers on their own terms. As they articulate in the preface to their introductory text *The vision of Islam*:

> If we did not take seriously the Muslim intellectuals' own understanding of their religion, we would have to replace it with the perspectives of modern Western intellectuals. Then we would be reading the tradition with the help of critical methodologies that have developed within the elitist circles of Western universities. But why should an elitist and alien perspective, one usually hostile to religion in general, be preferable to an indigenous perspective …?[5]

4 For example, https://www.ted.com/talks/anil_seth_your_brain_hallucinates_your_conscious_reality/ (last accessed: 22 December 2021).

5 Murata and Chittick, *The vision of Islam* xiii.

By adopting this simple yet radical approach, *The vision of Islam* brings across the universe of discourse that allows the nuanced logic of "both-and" to make sense in an Islamic and broadly human context.

Successful representation of others hinges around the degree to which researchers or translators allow the voices of their sources to come through, which is based on an awareness of the degree to which their own biases and agendas are refracting the source material. By not using prevalent sociological or psychological models, most of which are reductionist in some way or another, Murata and Chittick work with the exact terms and categories used by the Muslim authors whom they study. By listening carefully to Muslim voices in Islamic texts written in Arabic, Persian, and Chinese, they have introduced a new level of precision and consistency in translating Islamic concepts into English. The result is an enrichment of theoretical resources available to students of Islam, world religions, and philosophy.

The vision of Islam is matched by few, if any, introductory texts on Islam for using a theoretical approach ("the *ḥadīth* of Gabriel") that arises entirely out of the Islamic tradition. The three dimensions of action/*sharīʿa*, understanding/*īmān*, and intentionality/*iḥsān* constitute a simple yet sophisticated model that is easy to grasp yet adept in achieving analytic depth and coherence. The categories of action, understanding, and intentionality abstracted from "the *ḥadīth* of Gabriel" can profitably be used for studying other religious traditions as well.

In explicating the fundamental Islamic doctrine of the oneness of God, *tawḥīd*, Professor Murata and Chittick's methodology really shines. In interpreting the meaning of *tawḥīd* they highlight the interplay of the two complementary modes of difference and sameness in understanding God's oneness. The witnessing and assertion of God's oneness: There is no god but God (*lā ilāha illā Allāh*) is composed of an affirmation followed by a negation.

The negation of "no god" declares God incomparable to and different from all of creation. This perspective, called *tanzīh*, "affirms God's oneness by declaring that God is one and God alone is Real. Hence everything other than God is unreal and not worthy of consideration. God's single reality excludes all unreality."[6] In contrast, the affirmation of "but God," called *tashbīh*, "declares that God's oneness is such that his one reality embraces all creatures. The world, which appears as unreality and illusion, is in fact nothing but the One Real showing his signs. Rather than excluding all things, God's unity includes them."[7]

6 Murata and Chittick, *The vision of Islam* 71.

7 Murata and Chittick, *The vision of Islam* 71.

Through this presentation they bring their readers to appreciate the need for a perspective that affirms the truth of both God's sameness and God's difference:

> … neither *tanzih* nor *tashbih* provide a complete picture of reality. The universe needs to be understood in terms of both perspectives simultaneously … Then we see that each thing is at once near to God and far from him, at once similar to God and incomparable with him. Each thing is confronted simultaneously with mercy and wrath, gentleness and severity, life-giving and slaying, bestowal and withholding, reality and unreality. This is *tawhid*.[8]

Tanzīh and *tashbīh* are presented as two poles of *tawḥīd*: human understanding of God's oneness and the consequent actions based on this understanding move between these two complementary perspectives. A particular strength of Murata and Chittick's exposition of Islam is the quick and clear way in which they relate concepts to practical consequences and actions. In the case of *tawḥīd*, they immediately point out how both of these perspectives can be seen as operative in the daily lives of Muslims:

> The two perspectives of *tanzih* and *tashbih*, or God's distance and nearness, are met constantly in Islamic texts and in the everyday life of Muslims. Let us cite one simple example. We have already referred to the Koranic formula "Praise belongs to God," which is recited by Muslims on all sorts of occasions and in all sorts of contexts, since it expresses gratitude to God. People recite it when anything good happens, when they eat or drink something, when they see something that pleases them … The formula of praise ties blessings back to God. It takes the signs in the cosmos and in the soul and ascribes them to their divine origin. Hence it affirms the perspective of *tashbih*, the nearness of God and his activity in all situations, his care and concern for human beings.[9]

They then offer an example for how Muslims practice *tanzīh* in their everyday life:

> Another commonly recited Koranic formula is "Glory be to God" (*subhanallah*). In contrast to "Praise belongs to God," this formula stresses *tanzih*.

8 Murata and Chittick, *The vision of Islam* 73.

9 Murata and Chittick, *The vision of Islam* 73–74.

> It is uttered when any thought of ill occurs toward God or his activity, or when any suggestion is made that God might have motivations like human beings. The Koran often employs the phrase with this meaning, as when it rejects various opinions of pre-Islamic peoples. For example, "They have set up a kinship between Him and the jinn. … Glory be to God above what they describe!" (37:173).[10]

Students find the examples and analysis given above quite helpful. In my experience, though, the example that makes students stop and that illuminates the Islamic concept and practice of oneness is their discussion of Prophet Muhammad's prayer:

> The Prophet used to pray, "I seek refuge in Thy good-pleasure from Thy anger, I seek refuge in Thy pardon from Thy punishment, I seek refuge in Thee from Thee." When you fear God, you do not run away from him, you run toward him. And when you love God, you also run toward him. This is precisely the implication of *tawhid*. However you approach things, you are led back to God.[11]

In the words of Bābā Zahīn Shāh Tājī,

> Though there is no one else
> Manifesting in all that there is;
> In everything, those looking
> fancy seeing something else.
> You are not other, I am not other
> "No" is not other, "Yes" is not other;
> The Lords of certainty are one thing,
> The companions of surmise something else.
> Whom else will they seek,
> Whom else will they find?
> They will leave your door,
> But can they go anywhere else?[12]

10 Murata and Chittick, *The vision of Islam* 74.

11 Murata and Chittick, *The vision of Islam* 70.

12 Tājī, Zahīn Shāh, *Āyāt-i jamāl*, Karachi: Maktaba-yi Tāj, 1967, 73; cited in Latif, Amer, "Ẕahīn Shāh Tājī's (d. 1978) *Signs of beauty* (*Āyāt-i jamāl*)," in *Journal of Sufi Studies* 10.1–2 (2021), 215–233, 230.

To appreciate the implications of the theoretical insights afforded by an analysis of *tawḥīd* in terms of *tanzīh* and *tashbīh*, let us consider how Murata and Chittick have applied these insights to the process of translation. In the preface to *The self-disclosure of God*, his third major study of Ibn ʿArabī's thought, Chittick shares his reflections on translation in a section titled "The translator's dilemmas."[13] He credits the process of translating Ibn ʿArabī as having made him aware of one of the major issues that confronts anyone who seeks to translate Ibn ʿArabī and the Quran: "This obstacle is the prevalence of abstraction in the English language and in our concepts of what amounts to elegant prose, and the fact that abstraction pushes the understanding in the direction of *tanzīh*."[14] We can say that while distancing via abstraction is baked into the functioning of reason, in contrast, imagination, makes an abstraction palpable and present.

In fact, Ibn ʿArabī's rhetorical purpose in his writings, Chittick suggests, was to connect the two poles of human understanding via reason and imagination. If on the one hand the *kalām* and philosophy folks were too reliant on the abstractions of reason, on the other hand there were forms of Sufism that denigrated reason beyond what Ibn ʿArabī considered proper. In his view both reason and imagination are needed to continuously apprehend the Real. The tension between the competing functions of reason and imagination leads Chittick to ask the question of how to balance the concrete and the abstract in translating Ibn ʿArabī and the Quran. He shares instances of how his views and translational choices have shifted over the years. These changes were made in an "attempt to bring the English closer to the concrete imagery of the original Arabic, or to indicate the etymological connections"[15] between words, that is, to preserve the concrete presence of the root letters within derived words:

> For example, in SPK [*The Sufi path of knowledge*], I translated the term *athar* as "effect." The English word is relatively abstract and suggests that it is contrasted with the Arabic word for "cause," which it is not. Here I render the term as "trace." In SPK I translated *tawajjuh* as "to turn the attentiveness" or simply "attentiveness." The term attentive is already abstract, and the suffix *ness* makes it doubly so. In this book I have rendered *tawajjuh* in its literal sense as "to turn the face" or "face-

13 Chittick, William C., *The self-disclosure of God: Principles of Ibn al-ʿArabī's cosmology*, Albany, NY: SUNY Press, 1998, xxxv–xl.

14 Chittick, *The self-disclosure* xxxv.

15 Chittick, *The self-disclosure* xxxvii.

> turning." It may seem strange to hear that God turns desire's face toward something, but not after one has thought about the implications of God's Koranic ascription of the term face (*wajh*) to Himself.[16]

An important effect of paying attention to concreteness in translational choices is the preservation of the imagistic and hence presence-inducing effects of the original.

Recent research in the broad field of cognitive science provides insight into understanding the importance of embodiment for human knowledge and perception. Broadly speaking, there seems to be general consensus in the scientific community that "even quite abstract concepts are based in sensory-motor images" and are in fact structured by the sensory motor systems that give rise to them.[17] "Conscious awareness is fundamentally structured by a set of dynamic 'somato-motor' maps anchored in the body, which serves as the basic 'yardstick' for the various neural processes that we experience as the mind."[18] Edward Slingerland cites the pioneering work of Mark Johnson to give an example of how "somato-motor" maps or image schemas structure our experience of the world. Considering the activity of balancing, Johnson says the following:

> "It is crucially important to see that balancing is an activity we learn with our bodies and not by grasping a set of rules or concepts ... The meaning of balance begins to emerge through our acts of balancing and through our experience of systemic processes and states within our bodies". Having developed this image schema, Balance, as a result of our embodied experience in the world, we inevitably begin to project it onto more abstract domains of experience—perceiving, understanding, and feeling these domains through the filter of the Balance schema. Our understanding of what constitutes a "balanced" life, a "balanced" argument, moral or legal "balance," and the "balance" we perceive in a pleasing work of art is thus fundamentally structured by our sensory-motor sense of physical Balance, and this embodied feeling cannot be fully captured in an amodal, formal definition.[19]

---

16 Chittick, *The self-disclosure* xxxviii.

17 Slingerland, Edward, *What science offers the humanities: Integrating body and culture*, Cambridge: Cambridge University Press, 2008, 162.

18 Slingerland, *What science offers* 163.

19 Slingerland, *What science offers* 164–165.

Embodiment gives rise to and structures abstract thought. Metaphorical or analogical thinking in which we use one concrete situation to conceptualize something different lies at the heart of human cognition and problem solving. According to Lovett and Forbus, "analogy is the cornerstone of human intelligence."[20]

In a paper with far reaching consequences for the philosophy of religion, Daniel Gilbert suggests that

> findings from a multitude of research literatures converge on a single point: People are credulous creatures who find it very easy to believe and very difficult to doubt. In fact, believing is so easy, and perhaps so inevitable, that it may be more like involuntary comprehension than it is like rational assessment.[21]

Gilbert notes that humans "immediately believe what they see and only question their percepts subsequently and occasionally."[22] What ties this discussion perfectly with the way in which Chittick has applied the notion of *tashbīh*/presence to concreteness in translational choices is the cause identified by Gilbert for belief being the default state of the human body-mind: "the correlation between a perceptual representation (i.e., one's mental image of an object) and the presence of that object is nearly perfect. Organisms need not question percepts, because percepts are for the most part faithful representations of reality."[23]

In light of these insights from cognitive science, we can draw the following conclusions: *Tashbīh* is grounded in the body; it is pre-verbal and a constitutive part of being human. It also appears that *tashbīh* is more primary than *tanzīh* because abstract thought builds on the foundations of our basic experience of living as embodied creatures. In the domain of translation, then, it is important to preserve the images within the original texts and the concreteness of their language. By preserving these features, translators ensure that possible meanings present in the original text are not foreclosed by an abstracted choice. As Chittick puts it:

---

20 Lovett, Andrew and Kenneth Forbus, "Modeling visual problem solving as analogical reasoning," in *Psychological Review* 124.1 (2017), 60–90.

21 Gilbert, Daniel T., "How mental systems believe," in *American Psychologist* 46.2 (1991), 107–119, 117.

22 Gilbert, "How mental systems believe" 116.

23 Gilbert, "How mental systems believe" 116.

> The mysteries of the universe do not lie primarily in the universal laws and principles, even though these are mysterious enough. What is *most* mysterious and miraculous about the universe is its concrete particularity, its every object and inhabitant, each of which is uniquely and ultimately unfathomable. The more we derive our abstract principles and lift them beyond everyday minuteness, the more we depart from the universe *as it actually is*. God is disclosed in the details, in the molecules and atoms, just as He appears in the grand, overarching syntheses and unities. Yes, reality is found in the grand abstractions achieved by reason, but it is also found in the concrete things that we experience, and *these have an even greater claim to be called the reality of the Real.*[24]

Bibliography

Chittick, William C., *The self-disclosure of God: Principles of Ibn al-ʿArabī's cosmology*, Albany, NY: SUNY Press, 1998.

Gilbert, Daniel T., "How mental systems believe," in *American Psychologist* 46.2 (1991), 107–119.

Latif, Amer, "Ẕahīn Shāh Tājī's (d. 1978) *Signs of beauty* (*Āyāt-i jamāl*)," in *Journal of Sufi Studies* 10.1–2 (2021), 215–233.

Lovett, Andrew and Kenneth Forbus, "Modeling visual problem solving as analogical reasoning," in *Psychological Review* 124.1 (2017), 60–90.

Murata, Sachiko and William C. Chittick, *The vision of Islam*, New York: Paragon House, 1994.

Rūmī, Jalāl al-Dīn, *Fīhi mā fīhi*, ed. Badīʿ al-Zamān Furūzānfar, Tehran: Amīr Kabīr, 1969.

Slingerland, Edward, *What science offers the humanities: Integrating body and culture*, Cambridge: Cambridge University Press, 2008.

Tājī, Zahīn Shāh, *Āyāt-i jamāl*, Karachi: Maktaba-yi Tāj, 1967.

24 Chittick, *The self-disclosure* xxxvii. Emphases are mine.

CHAPTER 21

Translating Islamic Metaphysical Texts: Some Reflections on Knowledge Transmission

Mukhtar H. Ali

1 Introduction

This reflective essay on knowledge transmission investigates translation in the Islamic metaphysical tradition. If we are to observe a basic typology of Islamic texts, certain works are the "texts" (*matn*) and others are the "commentaries" (*sharḥ*). The former type is dense, technical and recondite, while the latter is discursive and explanatory. Muḥyī al-Dīn Ibn ʿArabī's (d. 638/1240) *Fuṣūṣ al-ḥikam* (*The ringstones of wisdom*) and ʿAbdallāh Anṣārī's (d. 481/1089) *Manāzil al-sāʾirīn* (*The stations of the wayfarers*) are prime examples of the elliptical and pithy style of the *matn* which, without commentaries or a teacher to explain their meanings, are extremely difficult to comprehend. Some works such as the *Manāzil* are composed in concise rhymed prose, a very particular style of Arabic rhetoric called *sajʿ* used extensively in sacred literature. The Arabic is mellifluous and easy to remember but translating this type of text—except for the gifted translator—is all but futile because there is no counterpart in English for their use of Arabic rhetorical devices. Replete with the technical terms of Sufi metaphysics, it becomes critical then to translate their attending commentaries and supply the reader with extensive annotations. Commentaries, on the other hand, are discursive and explanatory yet often prohibitively long. Inspired by the *matn*-style discourse of premodern Islamic scholarship, this essay focuses on the art of translating metaphysical texts and its connection to the transmission of spiritual knowledge. It addresses spiritual languages, the types of translators and ends with a few remarks on the practical concerns and challenges of translating this genre.

2 The Prophet as God's Translator

As most people are not conversant in divine discourse, there is a need in every age for a translator of spiritual language, whether it be a written word, an outward sign, or an inward self-disclosure. To this end, God sent prophets so

 | DOI:10.1163/9789004529038_022

that His signs were communicated to the people in their own language and according to their capacities. Since the prophets received from God directly, "We revealed it to you on the Night of Destiny" (Q 97:1), and through His existential signs, "We will show them Our signs on the horizons and in themselves so it becomes clear to them that it is the truth" (Q 41:53), they became fluent in God's language. This enabled them to speak to God directly and come to know the true nature of existence, as the Prophet prayed, "O God! Show us things as they truly are."[1] Furthermore, they came to know the languages that pertain to the outward and inward dimensions of the human being. The body, soul, imagination, intellect, heart and spirit each speak a language specific to their worlds.

Muslims uniformly agree that the Quran and Hadith form the twin sources of Islamic knowledge, both of which rely on the veracity of the Prophet, even if the former are the words of God and the latter are the words of the Prophet. This integral relationship between divinity and prophethood is principally established in the Islamic profession of faith, the *kalima*, which attests to divine unity coupled with the messengership of the Prophet. Belief in divine Unity is secured by acknowledging the one who disclosed this gnosis and personified it. If this is not self-evident, then the Quran clarifies the issue of obedience to the Prophet, "O believers, obey God and His Messenger and do not turn away from him while you hear his call" (Q 8:20), and "You who believe, obey God and the Messenger, and those in authority among you" (Q 4:59), and "Accept whatever the Messenger gives you, and abstain from whatever he forbids you" (Q 59:7). Similarly, the Prophet said, "I leave behind two weighty things, which if you hold fast to, you will never go astray, the Book of God and the members of my household"[2] or in some sources, "my *sunna*." In either version, the import is the same: the Book of God is conjoined with its messenger and its interpreters, which in this case refers to the members of his household.

The need for the messenger is highlighted again in the verse, "It is not for any man that God should speak to him except through revelation or from behind a veil, or by sending a messenger to reveal by His command what He wills: He is Sublime and Wise" (Q 42:51). The Quran partly alludes to the reason in the next verse by asserting that revelation occurs from the world of command, which is

1 Āmulī, Ḥaydar, *Jāmiʿ al-asrār wa-manbaʿ al-anwār*, ed. Henry Corbin and Osman Yahya, Beirut: Muʾassasat Taʾrīkh al-ʿArabī, 1969, 287.

2 Al-Bukhārī, Muḥammad, *Ṣaḥīḥ al-Bukhārī*, ed. M.D. al-Bughā, 6 vols., Damascus: Dār Ibn Kathīr, 1987, Book 44, *ḥadīth* 55. This famous tradition is reported in the standard Sunni collections, *Saḥīḥ al-Tirmidhī* and *Musnad* of Aḥmad b. Ḥanbal (d. 241/855).

the world of luminous spirits,[3] "Therefore, we revealed to you a spirit from Our command. You did not even know what the Scripture or faith was, but We made it a light, guiding with it whoever We will of Our servants" (Q 42:52). However, it is not explicit in the verse why God would speak to a prophet directly but not to all people. What is the need to speak behind a veil or via messenger, as the Quran describes? The answer perhaps lies in the two divine attributes, Sublime and Wise (mentioned in the verse), governing this phenomenon. God, the Sublime, the Wise, speaks to those of sublime character and wisdom dictates that speech be directed towards the worthy, namely, those who possess understanding. Since God's words are sublime and wise, the recipient must first understand God's language and discourse, which, at the highest level are the divine names. Only those who possess sublimity and wisdom are capable of being addressed by God directly.

In the following enigmatic description, Imam Jaʿfar al-Ṣādiq (d. 148/765) comments on the divine names insofar as they represent the underlying structure of inviolable divine language and hence reality:

> God Almighty created the names through letters that do not possess an utterance, through a word that is not spoken, through a figure that is not corporeal, through an allegory that is indescribable, through a color that has no tint, negating all notions of dimension, far removed from limits, veiled from the senses of the imagination, concealed but not hidden.[4]

These divine realities which are described as letters, words, allegories, figures, and colors do not have a counterpart in creation except via manifestation or theophany. On the divine plane, it is God's language in His own terms which then descends on the plane of human language. The foremost among humanity who speak God's language are the prophets, then the inheriting saints who must then translate it for the common folk.[5]

---

3 Commentators of the Quran explain that the word "command" (*amr*) here means the World of Command (*al-ʿālam al-amr*), which is a luminous world that originates from the engendering command "Be!" It is also mentioned in the Quran and the Hadith to mean Gabriel, the Trusted Spirit (*al-rūḥ al-amīn*) and the Holy Spirit (*al-rūḥ al-qudus*), the angels, the power by which the body is sustained and is living, and the human faculty of rationality through which man recognizes his selfhood.

4 Al-Kulaynī, Muḥammad b. Yaʿqūb, *Uṣūl al-kāfī*, ed. ʿAlī Akbar al-Ghaffārī, 8 vols., i, Tehran: Dār al-Kutub al-Islāmiyya, 1983–1984, 166, cited in Tabrīzī, Javād Malikī, *Risāla-yi liqāʾ Allāh*, ed. Ṣādiq Ḥusaynzāda, Qom: Intishārāt Āl-i ʿAlī, 2002, 19.

5 This refers to the famous *ḥadīth* related by al-Tirmidhī (d. 279/892), Abū Dāwūd (d. 275/889),

3 The Types of Language

Spiritual languages include revelation, inspiration, and unveiling, some of which are specific to the prophets and others encompass all of creation, as the verses allude, "Your Lord inspired the bee" (Q 16:68), and "We inspired the mother of Moses" (Q 28:7). Indeed, God speaks to all creation, each according to its capacity, as in, "When your Lord took out the offspring from the loins of the Children of Adam and made them bear witness about themselves, He said, 'Am I not your Lord?' and they replied, 'Yes, we bear witness.' Lest you say on the Day of Resurrection, 'We were not aware of this.'" (Q 7:176). The Quran also uses the term *bayān* to denote expression, as in "The Merciful, taught the Quran, created man, taught him expression (*bayān*)" (Q 55:1–4). *Bayān* includes all types of expression, literal, figurative and real, and the Quran possesses each type, as Imam Jaʿfar al-Ṣādiq states,

> The book of God, Almighty has four aspects: the expression (*ʿibāra*), the allusion (*ishāra*), subtleties (*laṭāʾif*), and realities (*ḥaqāʾiq*). The expression is for laypersons (*ʿawāmm*), the allusion for the elite (*khawāṣṣ*), the subtlety for the saints (*awliyāʾ*), and the reality for the prophets (*anbiyāʾ*).[6]

There are other forms of *bayān* such as clairvoyance (*firāsa*), dreams (*manām*) and imagination (*mithāl*). In fact, all things in existence possess speech and expression, "God, who gave speech to everything, has given us speech" (Q 41:21).

Building on this hierarchy, the types of expression can also be categorized as the language of expression and the language of meaning, which respectively denote the outward and inward aspects of language. Some words have intrinsic meaning, so their meanings are their inward aspects and spirits. Just as the words denoting the divine names relate to their realities, some words are the manifestation of their realities. Such words open existential doors, which is why the Quran exhorts one to invoke God's names (*adhkār*), as they are sacred utterances and numinous sounds that have real effects in existence. "O believers, remember/mention God abundantly" (Q 33:41). It is significant

---

Nasāʾī (d. 303/915), Ibn Māja (d. 273/887) and Aḥmad b. Ḥanbal, "The scholars are the inheritors of the prophets." See Ḥaydar Āmulī's discussion on sainthood in his *Jāmiʿ al-asrār*.

6 See Mayer, Farhana (trans.), *Spiritual gems: The mystical Qurʾān commentary ascribed to Jaʿfar al-Ṣādiq as contained in Sulamī's Ḥaqāʾiq al-tafsīr from the text of Paul Nwyia*, Louisville, KY: Fons Vitae, 2011, xxi, and Keeler, Annabel, *Sufi hermeneutics: The Qur'an commentary of Rashīd al-Dīn Maybudī*, Oxford: Oxford University Press, 2017, 55.

that the word *dhikr* in Arabic means both remembrance in the heart and utterance on the tongue.

The Quran combines both types of language. Its appeal is both its eloquence and the beauty of its meaning, since not everything beautiful in form is beautiful in meaning. Just as God speaks to mankind through the Quran,[7] responding to God requires knowledge of the language of meaning, since one converses with God in the world of meanings. The language of meaning is the language of the heart; expression cannot encompass it because the heart is vast. That is, there are realities of the heart that cannot be expressed in words, so another form of language must be used. For this reason, the Sufis often chose poetry as the medium to describe the subtleties of the heart, invoking the imagination through symbols and sublimating the rational discourse of the intellect. In other words, when expressions reach their endpoints, one attends only to meanings.

The language of meaning is cultivated through *adab*, which refers not only to the refinement of language, but also good manners, etiquette and propriety. It is the aesthetic, subtle and emotive aspect that applies to both types of language: expression and meaning. Meaning also demands *dhawq* which refers to sensibility, discernment, cultivation and refinement. Both *adab* and *dhawq* are key qualities in grasping allusions, subtleties and realities. In the art of decorating, for example, one discerns the internal language of aesthetics, style, color, placement and energetics as these produce a certain effect on the viewer or enhance the experience in subtle ways.

Beyond the language of meaning, there is the language of reality (*ḥaqīqa*) and engendered existence (*takwīn*). God and the angels speak to the people of reality (*ahl al-ḥaqīqa*) in the language of reality. *Takwīn* is also the language of primordial nature (*fiṭra*), mentioned in the verse, "Set your face (*wajh*) to the religion, uprightly (*ḥanīf*), in the divine nature (*fiṭrat Allāh*) upon which He originated mankind—there is no altering God's creation. That is the upright religion, but most people do not know" (Q 30:30). "Face" refers to essence and identity, and true religion which is the totality of man's activity in this world is equated with a God-given human nature.[8] Thus, the language of reality is the existential movement of one's whole being and identity.

7 Imam ʿAlī says, "God has disclosed Himself to His servants in His Word, but they do not see." *Nahj al-balāgha*, ed. Ṣubḥī al-Ṣāliḥ, Beirut: Dār al-Kutub al-Lubnānī, 2004, sermon 147; see Rayshahrī, Muḥammad, *Mīzān al-ḥikma*, 12 vols., viii, Beirut: Dār Iḥyāʾ al-Turāth al-ʿArabī, 2001, 3326, no. 16417.

8 See the commentary on this verse in Nasr, Seyyed Hossein et al. (eds.), *The study Quran: A new translation and commentary*, New York: HarperOne, 2015.

In this hierarchy of language, the lowest level is expression which corresponds with the imaginal plane (*khayāl*), then the language of meaning which reflects realities and corresponds with the intellect and heart, then the language of reality itself. If words are the forms of the language of expression, then meanings are the forms of the language of reality. So, it returns to three things: words, meanings and realities.

4 Types of Translators

Traditionally, Muslims describe God as the speaker and the Prophet as the messenger, but we can equally regard each as a translator. Translation in this context means the transmission of knowledge from a higher order to a lower one, the transference of meaning from one plane of reality to another, or in the terminology of the Sufis, the gradual descent (*tanazzulāt*) of realities, theophanies (*tajalliyyāt*), individuations (*taʿayyunāt*), effusion (*fayḍ*), and manifestation (*ẓuhūr*). God speaks through His signs, so by extension, He "translates" the attributes of perfection in the forms of creation. These are existential words, as the verses mentions, "If all the trees on earth were pens and all the seas, with seven more seas besides, [were ink,] still God's words would not be exhausted" (Q 31:27). Linguistically, He speaks through revelation, "We have sent it down as an Arabic Quran so people may understand" (Q 12:2), which is God's own translation of the perfections of His Being through allegories, stories and commandments, all of which reflect how the Prophet addressed his people, "We have not sent any messenger except with the language of his people so He can make things clear to them" (Q 14:4). Thereafter, the sage or guiding master (*shaykh*), having inherited spiritual authority from a prophet becomes the link between God and man. This is because he has fluency in the languages of meaning and reality, and can translate divine signs, correlate the outward with the inward and help the disciple move deftly through the spiritual worlds. The *shaykh's* gaze is oriented both outwardly in the "horizons" and inwardly in the souls, so he translates theophany and forges it into his teaching. By reading the divine signs, he instructs the disciples to harnesses their spiritual energies, traverse the path, and attain *adab* with their Lord. Thus, a spiritual guide is necessary in every age, as Imam al-Ṣādiq warned, "He who does not have a sage to guide him, perishes,"[9] because theophany is perpetual, "Every day He is in a

9 Majlisī, Muḥammad Bāqir, *Biḥār al-anwār li-durar akhbār al-aʾimma al-aṭhār*, Beirut: Muʾassasat al-Wafāʾ, 1983, lxxviii, 159, no. 10.

new manifestation" (Q 55:29). Each renewed manifestation requires a reading, a translation and an instruction and an application.

Finally, man is a translator of himself since he is the comprehensive book of existence, as Imam ʿAlī says,

Do you suppose that you are a small particle	While the Great World is enfolded within you?
You are the Manifest Book whose	Letters bring forth the hidden.[10]

The Quran affirms that the soul is a book and a witness, "Read your Book! Your soul suffices as reckoner against you this day" (Q 17:14) and "man is a witness against himself" (Q 75:14). With respect to these verses, reading is distinct from translating, since the former refers to direct experience and witnessing, and the latter refers to transference of one form to another, in the way that a dream is interpreted.

With respect to man's outer form, the body's needs are translated through the soul's desires. Each of the body parts have a meaning and correspondence in existence and with God. That is why Imam ʿAlī said, "I am the face of God, the right hand of God."[11] The back (*ẓahr*), for example, signifies the outward and the belly (*baṭn*) signifies the inward. The inner meaning (*sirr*) of the back is safety (*amān*) and affection (*ḥanān*), or close relatives, since the seed originates from the back according to the Quran, "So let man consider from what he is created. He is created from a gushing fluid. Then he emerges from between the backbone and breastbone" (Q 86:5–7). The inner meaning of the belly is one's parents, but primarily the mother since the belly relates to the womb, whereas the back relates to the father and the loins. Some human faculties do not compete with others, such as sight and hearing as each has its own domain of activity. But there are also contrary powers such as desire and intellect, each try to gain dominance over the other, and sometimes there is a conflict in the soul itself when, for example, the blaming soul (*lawwāma*) censures the commanding soul (*ammāra*). The limbs have inner meanings as all things have an inner meaning, so a sound understanding of their existential significances leads one to establish the correct relationships and correspondences.

Finally, the tongue is the translator of the intellect, the intellect is the translator of the heart, and the heart is the translator of God, for the heart is the seat

10 Imam ʿAlī's famous poem describes the human comprehensiveness which became the mainstay of Ibn ʿArabī's doctrine of the perfect human (*al-insān al-kāmil*).

11 This is known as the Sermon of Disclosure cited in Āmulī, *Jāmiʿ al-asrār* 411–563.

of vision and communion with God. Thus, the famous *ḥadīth* states, "Neither My earth nor heavens embrace Me, but the heart of My pure, pious servant with faith does embrace Me."[12] To embrace God in the heart is to meet Him and converse with Him through the language of meaning. When the illuminated heart receives theophany (*majlā*), it speaks with its spirit and light. Receiving directly from God, it becomes the reflection of His self-disclosure. So, if the gnostic speaks about a theophany that he witnesses in his heart, he becomes the translator of God's self-disclosure insofar as he speaks through its spirit and light.

5 Knowledge Transmission

The abovementioned classification of the function of a translator also holds true from a phenomenological perspective. This is because knowledge transmission ultimately entails the distillation of knowledge from one form to another according to the various degrees and modalities of existence. The transmission of knowledge is its translation and transformation into a new form, since not all concepts apply in every realm. Just as drowning does not apply to fish, conflict, hatred, and bloodshed do not apply to the intellectual world, rather they apply to the material world which is bound by space and time. So concepts must be translated from one world to another in keeping with the limitations of each world.

Knowledge transmission also depends on the giver, the recipient and the correspondence between the two. Even if the giver is magnanimous and the giving is abundant, the transmission is limited only by the receptivity of the vessel. Each degree of transmission colors its meanings in the same way that existence is colored by each descending degree of manifestation. Realities in the intellect are translated into imaginal form but also find their way into the external world. Conversely,

> Whatever exists in the sensory realm has a form in the Imaginal World, and all that exists in the Imaginal World has a form and reality on the plane of Lordship, and all that exists on the plane of Lordship has a form and name on the plane of the divine names.[13]

12 Kāshānī, Fayḍ, *Maḥajjat al-bayḍā'*, v, Beirut: Dār al-Maḥajjat al-Bayḍā', 2005, 26.

13 Jāmī, ʿAbd al-Raḥmān, *Naqd al-nuṣūṣ fī sharḥ Naqsh al-fuṣūṣ*, ed. William C. Chittick, Tehran: Intishārāt-i Anjuman-i Shāhanshāhī-yi Falsafa-yi Īrān, 2001, 181.

Undoubtedly, language and meaning evolve over time. The language of the revelation (*shar*ʿ) or the Quranic style that emerged from the cultural context of the Prophet, its imagery drawn from the desert environment of pre-Islamic Arabia, is clearly different from the language of mysticism and philosophy which developed much later. The Quran speaks of God and His attributes, but the Sufi philosopher uses the terms such as Being and its perfections. The Pen and Tablet of the Quran are the Universal Intellect and Soul in the language of philosophy. As every age and discipline has its language and style of discourse, knowledge is correctly transmitted when the translator is attuned to the nuances of meaning as they evolve over time.

6 Translating Metaphysical Texts

Having described the real translator of divine signs and theophanies and examined a spiritual typology of language, let us turn our attention to a few practical aspects of translating metaphysical and spiritual texts in contemporary Sufi Studies. We often find that these texts are revelatory in nature, transcribed from flashes of inspiration that describe visionary states and spiritual realities, as Ibn ʿArabī admits,

> In what I have written, I have never had a set purpose, as other writers. Flashes of divine inspiration used to come upon me and almost overwhelm me, so that I could only put them from my mind by committing to paper what they revealed to me. If my works evince any form of composition, that form was unintentional.[14]

As Sufi metaphysical texts primarily describe realities attained through spiritual experience, they use symbolic language to express something only their authors and their likes perceive. This then is the great challenge for the contemporary translator: to come to terms with a vision, perspective, and experience of reality that is commensurate with the worldview of the author whose work is being translated, despite the many confines of our contemporary languages. Members of the school of Ibn ʿArabī, for example, have coined many new technical terms often in conversation with rational theology and philosophy but used in ways consistent with their metaphysical worldview. For example, the

14 Ibn ʿArabī, Muḥyī al-Dīn, *al-Futūḥāt al-Makkiyya*, 4 vols., Beirut: Dār Iḥyāʾ al-Turāth al-ʿArabī, 1998, cited in Austin, Ralph W.J., *Sufis of Andalusia: The 'Rūḥ al-quds' and 'al-Durrat al-fākhirah' of Ibn 'Arabī*, London: George Allen and Unwin, 1971, 48.

Arabic word *ʿayn*, can mean thing, entity, identity, essence, quiddity, eye, spring, spy and self. From this root structure, the school of Ibn ʿArabī employs two key terms, one of which is *taʿayyun*. This word can be translated as individuation, or as Professor Chittick renders it, "entification." Technically, *taʿayyun* is the particularization of the Essence in its descending degrees, that is, existence is the successive particularizations and individuations of the Essence, even if the Essence *qua* Essence is absolute and undetermined. Thus, *taʿayyun* is any type of specification or individuation, not only that of entities. The second term is *aʿyān al-thābita*, which are the forms of realities or essences in the divine knowledge, that is, "the forms of the divine names and the realities of external entities."[15] Professor Izutsu translates it as the "permanent archetypes" and Professor Chittick as the "fixed entities." Neither the Arabic term nor the translation can adequately capture what Ibn ʿArabī meant when he said,

> The *aʿyān* are essentially characterized by non-existence (*ʿadam*). Surely, they are permanently subsistent (*thābita*), but they are permanently subsistent only in a state of non-existence; they have not even smelled the fragrance of existence. Thus, they remain eternally in that state despite the multiplicity of the forms which they manifest in the existing things.[16]

Another key word that is less ambiguous but has interesting semantic implications is the term *wujūd*, which comes from the Arabic root letters *w-j-d* and denotes both "existing" and "finding." This double meaning is significant insofar as existence is something that is to be found, or that which if found, exists. The Arabic word conveniently links the complementary disciplines of ontology and epistemology, like the word *ʿālam* (world). The root letters *ʿ-l-m* of the word *ʿālam* (world) signify "to know" and relates to the word *ʿalāma*, which means sign or token. So, the world is "that through which something is known," or the signs through which God is known; the world is also "everything other than God."[17] Thus, if the translator does indeed grasp the meaning, he must negotiate between form and meaning, the form being the expression, terminology and structure of the language, and meaning being the metaphysical reality indicated.

15 Al-Qayṣarī, Dāwūd b. Maḥmūd, *The horizons of being: The metaphysics of Ibn al-ʿArabī in the Muqaddimat al-Qayṣarī*, trans. Mukhtar H. Ali, Leiden: Brill, 2020, 103.

16 Ibn ʿArabī, Muḥyī al-Dīn, *Fuṣūṣ al-ḥikam*, ed. Abū l-ʿAlāʾ ʿAfīfī, Beirut: Dār al-Kutub al-ʿArabī, 1980, 63, cited in Izutsu, Toshihiko, *Sufism and Taoism: A comparative study of key philosophical concepts*, Berkeley, CA: University of California Press, 1983, 161.

17 Al-Qayṣarī, *The horizons* 133.

In short, translation at the highest level is the art of spiritual literacy whereby one perceives the theophany of the divine names, grasps its import, then relates it to the people according to their capacity. At the lowest level, it is a literary exercise conveying the outer forms of expression in various languages. Yet, all types of translation are invaluable for knowledge transmission, and each benefits according to his receptivity. Surely, those who engage in the pursuit and transmission of knowledge receive a share of its blessing, as the Prophet has stated,

> One who follows a path in the pursuit of knowledge, follows a path to paradise. The angels spread their wings for the seekers of knowledge out of delight. All in the heaven and the earth asks forgiveness for the seeker of knowledge, even the fish in the sea. The excellence of the learned over the devout is like the excellence of the moon over the stars on a full-moon night. The learned are the heirs of the prophets, for the prophets did not leave behind a *dīnār* or *dirham* but left the legacy of knowledge. So, whoever partakes of it obtains an abundant share.[18]

7 Concluding Remarks

I hope that this set of reflections sheds light on some of the challenges and promises that the contemporary translator of Islamic metaphysical texts will invariably encounter. Truly, the translations of Professors Chittick and Murata faithfully convey the spiritual and metaphysical concerns of the past masters and their exalted visions of reality. As contemporary scholars and students of Islamic metaphysics, we are therefore eternally grateful to Chittick and Murata for sharing their knowledge with us through their countless contributions, and for inspiring us to carry on the tradition.

Bibliography

ʿAlī b. Abī Ṭālib, *Nahj al-balāgha*, ed. Subḥī al-Ṣāliḥ, Beirut: Dār al-Kutub al-Lubnānī, 2004.

Āmulī, Ḥaydar, *Jāmiʿ al-asrār wa-manbaʿ al-anwār*, ed. Henry Corbin and Osman Yahya, Beirut: Muʾassasat Taʾrīkh al-ʿArabī, 1969.

18 Al-Kulaynī, *Uṣūl al-kāfī* i, *ḥadīth* 1.

Austin, Ralph W.J., *Sufis of Andalusia: The 'Rūḥ al-quds' and 'al-Durrat al-fākhirah' of Ibn ʿArabī*, London: George Allen and Unwin, 1971.

al-Bukhārī, Muḥammad, *Ṣaḥīḥ al-Bukhārī*, ed. M.D. al-Bughā, 6 vols., Damascus: Dār Ibn Kathīr, 1987.

Chittick, William C., *The Sufi path of knowledge: Ibn al-ʿArabī's metaphysics of imagination*, Albany, NY: SUNY Press, 1989.

al-Ghazālī, Abū Ḥāmid, *Iḥyāʾ ʿulūm al-dīn*, ed. ʿAbd al-ʿAziz al-Sayrawān, 5 vols., Beirut: Dār al-Qalam, n.d.

Ibn ʿArabī, Muḥyī al-Dīn, *Fuṣūṣ al-ḥikam*, ed. Abū l-ʿAlāʾ ʿAfīfī, Beirut: Dār al-Kutub al-ʿArabī, 1980.

Ibn ʿArabī, Muḥyī al-Dīn, *al-Futūḥāt al-Makkiyya*, 4 vols., Beirut: Dār Iḥyāʾ al-Turāth al-ʿArabī, 1998.

Izutsu, Toshihiko, *Sufism and Taoism: A comparative study of key philosophical concepts*, Berkeley, CA: University of California Press, 1983.

Jāmī, ʿAbd al-Raḥmān, *Naqd al-nuṣūṣ fī sharḥ Naqsh al-fuṣūṣ*, ed. William C. Chittick, Tehran: Intishārāt-i Anjuman-i Shāhanshāhī-yi Falsafa-yi Īrān, 2001.

Kāshānī, Fayḍ, *Maḥajjat al-bayḍāʾ*, Beirut: Dār al-Maḥajjat al-Bayḍāʾ, 2005.

Keeler, Annabel, *Sufi hermeneutics: The Qurʾan commentary of Rashīd al-Dīn Maybudī*, Oxford: Oxford University Press, 2017.

al-Kulaynī, Muḥammad b. Yaʿqūb, *Uṣūl al-kāfī*, ed. ʿAlī Akbar al-Ghaffārī, 8 vols., Tehran: Dār al-Kutub al-Islāmiyya, 1983–1984.

Majlisī, Muḥammad Bāqir, *Biḥār al-anwār li-durar akhbār al-aʾimma al-aṭhār*, Beirut: Muʾassasat al-Wafāʾ, 1983.

Mayer, Farhana (trans.), *Spiritual gems: The mystical Qurʾān commentary ascribed to Jaʿfar al-Ṣādiq as contained in Sulamī's Ḥaqāʾiq al-tafsīr from the text of Paul Nwyia*, Louisville, KY: Fons Vitae, 2011.

Nasr, Seyyed Hossein et al. (eds.), *The study Quran: A new translation and commentary*, New York: HarperOne, 2015.

al-Qayṣarī, Dāwūd b. Maḥmūd, *The horizons of being: The metaphysics of Ibn al-ʿArabī in the Muqaddimat al-Qayṣarī*, trans. Mukhtar H. Ali, Leiden: Brill, 2020.

Rayshahrī, Muḥammad, *Mīzān al-ḥikma*, 12 vols., Beirut: Dār Iḥyāʾ al-Turāth al-ʿArabī, 2001.

Tabrīzī, Javād Malikī, *Risāla-yi liqāʾ Allāh*, ed. Ṣādiq. Ḥasanzāda, Qom: Intishārāt Āl-i ʿAlī, 2002.

CHAPTER 22

Historical Imagination: Voicing Silences in Early Sufi Texts through Narrative

Laury Silvers

"How can narrative embody life in words
and at the same time respect what we cannot know?"
SAIDIYA HARTMAN, "Venus in two acts"

∵

1 Introduction

When I started my life as an academic in the study of Sufism, I believed in "objective scholarship" as if it were a pure being that lived in an ivory tower away from the world.[1] I gave my best historical takes on the material before me whether or not the analysis supported my Muslim faith, my Sufi path, and my experiences as a woman, and without a care for its effects beyond the scope of the field and my promotion file. When I diverged from that narrow path, I said so.[2] It was only as I was working on gender in Sufism that I understood my academic writing arose out of my position in the world and objectivity was a fairy tale.[3] I admitted I was telling stories about the past—however crit-

1 Thanks to Saliha DeVoe, Sara Abdel-Latif, Kecia Ali, and Megan Goodwin for their insights and guidance.

2 Silvers, Laury, "'In the book we have left out nothing': The ethical problem of the existence of verse 4:34 in the Qur'an," in *Comparative Islamic Studies* 2.2 (2006), 171–180, 178n2.

3 While a grounding assumption in fields such as Gender, Post-Colonial, and African American Studies, the impossibility of detached objectivity remains controversial in the field of Islamic studies. See Aaron Hughes, who decries the introduction of "identity politics" into the field of Islam following the impact of Edward Said's *Orientalism*. Hughes, Aaron W., *Islam and the tyranny of authenticity: An inquiry into disciplinary apologetics*, Sheffield: Equinox, 2016; Hughes, Aaron W., *Theorizing Islam: Disciplinary deconstruction and reconstruction*, London: Acumen, 2014 and the varied responses to Hughes in Sheedy, Matt (ed.), *Identity, politics and the study of Islam: Current dilemmas in the study of religions*, Sheffield: Equinox, 2018.

 | DOI:10.1163/9789004529038_023

ically analyzed—and my writing had an impact beyond my professional life. Muslims, especially Muslim women, were reading my work on early pious, mystic, and Sufi women. It mattered to them and sometimes it disturbed them. I realized I was little different from the transmitters, editors, and authors of the works I studied. All of us were weaving narratives that might serve as credible resources of thought for our audiences. I just never grasped the breadth of my audience and, to the degree I was able, I needed to take responsibility for the impact of my work on the communities around me. I began to engage with non-academic readers and translate my findings in conversation with them.[4] When I left the academy and turned to writing fiction, the responsibility to critically examine what I wanted to do with history in my stories was even more plain. I write detective novels set in the early 4th/10th-century Sufi communities in Baghdad that not only ask "whodunit," but also how Muslim tradition arises from the social worlds and intentions of its authors, depicts the impact of the authors' work then, and, by analogy, now, and considers the nature of historical writing in and out of the academy.[5]

Historical authenticity was not the primary value of medieval Muslim accounts of the pious, the saintly, and even the scholarly. Rather, the accounts were intended to tell a good story to a desired end. Najam Haider describes how even historians, like Abū Jaʿfar al-Ṭabarī (d. 310/923), rhetoricized their framing of events, endowing narratives with significance, and presenting them in an edifying form. Haider writes, "The result was a meaningful rendering of the past that was deemed more truthful than a documentary recitation of figures or events."[6] Biographers likewise relied on their audience having a broad familiarity with events, figures, and tropes, allowing them leeway to construct the material at hand to their personal and institutional intentions.[7] So much more

4 I have taken part in public facing scholarship on the "Feminism and Religion" blog, in community talks in the United States, Canada, and South Africa, then later, on Twitter, Facebook, in my novels, and in the blog section of my website (http://www.llsilvers.com/blog).

5 It is not unusual for historians who write fiction to address historical questions in their work. For example, Umberto Eco's *The name of the rose* is a historical mystery about semiotics depicted through debates on interpretation of doctrine and clues to a murder. The mystery is set within a literal archive, a library, and explores the idea of a conceptual archive by asking what books belong there and why. Kecia Ali called my attention to Black authors, such as Beverly Jenkins, who take up historical questions in African American historical romance. See Dandridge, Rita B., "The African American historical romance: An interview with Beverly Jenkins," in *Journal of Popular Romance Studies* 1.1 (2010), 1–11.

6 Haider, Najam, *The rebel and the Imām in early Islam: Explorations in Muslim historiography*, Cambridge: Cambridge University Press, 2019, 4.

7 See Richardson, Kristina, "The evolving biographical legacy of two late Mamluk Ḥanbalī judges," in Stephan Conermann (ed.), *History and society during the Mamluk period (1250 to*

the case when we leave behind genres with an assumed concern for historicity, however defined, for Sufi and piety literature in which moral pedagogy is the stated concern and experiences of the unseen are the currency of authenticity and authority.[8]

The compilers, authors, and editors of these early texts contribute these narratives of meaning to an "archive" acting as a credible resource for understanding and action.[9] The archive is not a library, although libraries play a role in its life. Rather, the archive is the sum total of a community's approved texts, oral traditions, material, social, cultural, and ritual practices.[10] Repetition of approved traditions guarantees those meaningful renderings of the past retain their reliability for the future. If a particular rendering is no longer shared textually, orally, in practice, or becomes marginalized or even excluded, it stops being a credible source.[11] But accidents of history also play a role in the life of the archive. Political and institutional change, the effects of floods, worms, and fire on libraries, destruction of mausoleums, changes in oral traditions and regional practices, or the challenge of making meaning out of widespread disease, for instance, does its own work in transforming the resources people have to hand and are encouraged to rely upon.[12]

1517), Bonn: Bonn University Press, 2014, 29–50, and Reid, Megan, *Law and piety in medieval Islam*, Cambridge: Cambridge University Press, 2013 for a discussion of how changing biographies shape the legacies of their subjects through narrative means.

8 Cooperson, Michael, *Classical Arabic biography: The heirs of the prophets in the age of al-Maʾmūn*, Cambridge: Cambridge University Press, 2004, esp. 154–187; Knight, Michael M., *Muhammad's body: Baraka networks and the Prophetic assemblage*, Chapel Hill, NC: The University of North Carolina Press, 2020.

9 Osborne, Thomas, "The ordinariness of the archive," in *History of the Human Sciences* 12.2 (1999), 51–64.

10 Bora, Fozia, *Writing history in the medieval Islamic world: The value of chronicles as archives*, London: I.B. Tauris, 2019; Knight, *Muhammad's body*; Vansina, Jan, *Oral tradition as history*, Madison: University of Wisconsin Press, 1985; Vaknin, Judy, Karyn Stukey and Victoria Lane (eds.), *All this stuff: Archiving the artist*, Oxfordshire: Libri Publishing, 2013.

11 Geissinger, [Ash], *Gender and Muslim constructions of exegetical authority: A rereading of the classical genre of Qurʾān commentary*, Leiden: Brill, 2015; Geissinger, [Ash], "Umm al-Dardāʾ sat in *tashahhud* like man: Towards the historical contextualization of a portrayal of female religious authority," in *MW* 103 (2013), 305–319.

12 Biran, Michal, "Libraries, books, and transmission of knowledge in Ilkhanid Baghdad," in *JESHO* 62 (2019), 464–502; Mulder, Stephennie, "The mausoleum of Imam al-Shafiʿi," in *Muqarnas* 23 (2006), 15–46; Safi, Omid, *The politics of knowledge in premodern Islam: Negotiating ideology and religious inquiry*, Chapel Hill, NC: University of North Carolina Press, 2009; Stearns, Justin K., *Infectious ideas: Contagion in premodern Islamic and Christian thought in the western Mediterranean*, Baltimore: Johns Hopkins University Press, 2011.

As historians, we study these living archives and we contribute to them whether we are aware or even interested in their existence. We assess these complexities, intentions, and accidents to produce narratives arising from our considered understanding of what may have happened and what may be at work in a particular text or texts. But no matter how considered and careful we may be, no matter our political, theoretical, religious, or secular loyalties, our scholarly productions are also rhetoricizing acts.[13] By arguing one reading of history is more credible than another, we hope to shape the archive of our field to our desired ends so that it will serve as a resource for future scholars. This is the nature of academic debate, but the stakes in our work extend beyond the state of the field. The stories we tell about history affect real-world consequences in similar ways to the narratives produced by those we study.[14] It may be used by political entities to create or support credible archives for action or attitudes.[15] Even the work of secular or religious scholars in areas such as Sufism, Hadith, Quran, and theology may contribute to a transformation in the structure of the archive of Islamic tradition itself.[16] Thus, I need to take responsibility for how I tell my stories.

---

13 See Knysh, Alexander, "Historiography of Sufi Studies in the West," in Youssef M. Choueiri (ed.), *A companion to the history of the Middle East*, Malden, MA: Blackwell, 2005, 106–132.

14 For instance, see Chaudhry, Ayesha S., "Islamic legal studies: A critical historiography," in Anver M. Emon and Rumee Ahmed (eds.), *The Oxford handbook of Islamic law*, Oxford: Oxford University Press, 2017, 1–40 and Morgenstein Fuerst, Ilyse, "Job ads don't add up: Arabic + Middle East + texts ≠ Islam," in *Journal of the American Academy of Religion* 88.4 (2020), 915–946.

15 On the role scholarship on Sufism plays in contemporary North American Sufi communities, see Sharify-Funk, Meena, William R. Dickson, and Merin S. Xavier, *Contemporary Sufism: Piety, politics, and popular culture*, New York: Routledge, 2018; Hamid Dabashi gives a summary of the impact of Edward Said's *Orientalism* (Dabashi, Hamid, "Edward Said's *Orientalism*: Forty years later," in *al-Jazeera* (3 May 2018), https://www.aljazeera.com/opinions/2018/5/3/edward-saids-orientalism-forty-years-later (last accessed: 24 September 2021)). Finally, see the debate between Graeme Woods and Kecia Ali concerning ethical responsibility and scholarship on ISIS and Slavery in Woods, Graeme, "What ISIS really wants," in *The Atlantic* (2015), https://www.theatlantic.com/magazine/archive/2015/03/what-isis-really-wants/384980/ (last accessed: 24 September 2021) and Ali, Kecia, "Redeeming slavery: The 'Islamic State' and the quest for Islamic morality," in *Mizan* 1.1 (2016), https://mizanproject.org/journal-post/redeeming-slavery/ (last accessed: 24 September 2021).

16 Knysh, "Historiography" 211. Also on Sufism see, Hermansen, Marcia, "The academic study of Sufism at American universities," in *AJISS* 24.3 (2007), 24–45; Hammer, Juliane, "Sufism in North America," in Lloyd Ridgeon (ed.), *Routledge handbook on Sufism*, London: Routledge, 2020, 514–530; Funk, Dickson, and Xavier, *Contemporary Sufism*. Also see Facebook groups "Studies in Islamic mysticism," "Sufi literature," and "The Muhyiddin Ibn

After reading *The lover*, the first novel in my series, Saliha DeVoe called my attention to the work of historian, Saidiya Hartman, pointing out echoes of Hartman's work in my own. Hartman's "Venus in two acts" articulates the historical method of critical fabulation at play in her searing memoir of the history and legacy of enslavement in the Americas, *Lose your mother: A journey along the Atlantic slave route*. She uses fictional and first-person narrative to call attention to the rhetoricizing acts of slave ship records, slavers' biographies, medical records, and other sources. Her work teases out the history of African women enslaved in the Americas and, at the same time, marks the impossibility of telling their stories at all. Hartman retrieves the lives of enslaved women from an archive meant to erase their humanity, but she does not tell a consoling story of resilience, heroism, or vulnerability. To do that would only erase the history of violence that made the narrative work necessary in the first place. Rather, she tells their stories in such a way as to call attention to their silencing and remark on how that silencing carries forward in time, entrenching racialized violence into the present, and to make space for liberation.

I am limited to broad strokes in my application of Hartman's use of critical fabulation to articulate the work I am doing in my novels. While the accounts of early pious and Sufi women are also mediated by transmitters and silenced in the later historical records, resulting in the structural marginalization of women in Sufism to the present—and even though some of the pious and mystic women depicted were enslaved or, whether free or enslaved, sometimes treated as non-consenting, lesser, objects of inspiration by men—they were, nevertheless, presented as spiritual elites in the texts. By marking the differences, I am not arguing for ethical relativism regarding enslavement in Muslim lands or racism as compared to the Americas. The bulk of this essay will raise a few of the particular vulnerabilities of the lowest status elite women in their social worlds and in the texts. Here, I solely mark that the sources I work with differ from Hartman's because the depicted status of the women in those sources differs. I offer this harrowing selection from "Venus in two acts" to make the point of difference in depiction perfectly clear.

> One cannot ask, "Who is Venus?" because it would be impossible to answer such a question. There are hundreds of thousands of other girls who share her circumstances and these circumstances have generated few stories. And the stories that exist are not about them, but rather about

---

al-Arabi society," for example, in which practitioners of Sufism actively engage academic scholarship on Sufism in understanding and forming their paths.

> the violence, excess, mendacity, and reason that seized hold of their lives, transformed them into commodities and corpses, and identified them with names tossed-off as insults and crass jokes. The archive is, in this case, a death sentence, a tomb, a display of the violated body, an inventory of property, a medical treatise on gonorrhea, a few lines about a whore's life, an asterisk in the grand narrative of history. Given this, it is doubtless impossible to ever grasp [these lives] again in themselves, as they might have been 'in a free state.'[17]

As DeVoe rightly put it, there are only echoes of Hartman's method in the stories I tell but the echoes resound in their own way. The novels in *The Sufi mysteries quartet* act as a non-consoling critical fabulation, a rhetoricizing fictive analysis that brings early mystic women to life in a way that comments on their near erasure from the primary sources and our own scholarship, which diminishes their authority as reliable sources in the archive, and the impact of that silencing over time.

2 Rhetoricizing Sources

Saidiya Hartman writes of the afterlife of slavery, meaning the harm of slavery that continues to this day as thwarted opportunity, structural inequality, and social and institutional brutality.

> If slavery persists as an issue in the political life of black America, it is not because of an antiquarian obsession with bygone days or the burden of a too-long memory, but because black lives are still imperiled and devalued by a racial calculus and a political arithmetic that were entrenched centuries ago. This is the afterlife of slavery—skewed life chances, limited access to health and education, premature death, incarceration, and impoverishment. I, too, am the afterlife of slavery.[18]

In Sufism, the near erasure of Sufi women from the biographical literature and manuals has resulted in its own afterlife: women's relative marginalization on the path itself. Biographical and piety literature is mediated by the trans-

17 Hartman, Saidiya, "Venus in two acts," in *Small Axe: A Caribbean Journal of Criticism* 26 (2008), 2–14, 2.

18 Hartman, Saidiya, *Lose your mother: A journey along the Atlantic slave route*, New York: Farrar, Straus and Giroux, 2008, 6.

mitters of the reports, then the editors and compilers, and even the copyists of the texts themselves and may be more useful in understanding the world of the men who produced them than the women's lives which they depict. Compilers gathered oral and written reports of an individual's pious behaviour and sayings, assessed their value according to their own methods of historical plausibility and the usefulness of the account to their particular projects, then reframed them for transmission.[19] Women's accounts were treated in significantly different ways than men's.[20] Transmitters, compilers, and editors might change the nature of the account to vouch for a woman's respectability, compile multiple accounts under one broadly acceptable woman's name, place a woman's saying in a man's mouth, or most often let her story go entirely.[21] The written history of women's practices, teachings, and testimonies to their authority are the collateral damage of such efforts, which has after-effects to this day.

Early pious and mystic communities were largely gender inclusive, but the growing scholarly expectation that women should lead lives of private worship affected how Sufis presented the path to the outside world. In one salient example, Sara Abdel-Latif shows that Abū ʿAbd al-Raḥmān al-Sulamī (d. 412/1021) and Abū l-Qāsim al-Qushayrī (d. 465/1072) treated accounts of women in their works in keeping with their distinct approaches to the growing institutionalization of Sufism. While al-Sulamī complied and edited biographies and accounts of both men and women to "create a canon of mystical predecessors

---

19 See Cornell, Rkia E., *Rabiʿa from narrative to myth: The many faces of Islam's most famous woman saint, Rabiʿa al-ʿAdawiyya*, London: Oneworld Academic, 2019; Reid, *Law and piety*; Geissinger, [Ash], "Female figures, marginality, and Qur'anic exegesis in Ibn al-Jawzi's *Ṣifat al-ṣafwa*," in Yasmin Amin and Nevin Reda (eds.), *Islamic interpretive tradition and gender justice: Processes of canonization, subversion, and change*, Montreal: McGill-Queen's University Press, 2020, 151–178; Cooperson, *Classical Arabic biography*; Bashir, Shahzad, *Sufi bodies: Religion and society in medieval Islam*, New York: Columbia University Press, 2011.

20 By women, I mean those who are categorized as such under headings and sections naming them "women," enslaved or free, in the piety and biographical literature. Nevertheless, gender in the premodern sources was not strictly binary in practice and understanding. It was a hierarchy in which elite males, however defined, were "men," and women, young men, the enslaved, and non-elite males of African descent were "not men." These "not men" were also treated differently in the sources no matter the headings under which they are mentioned. While a more inclusive understanding of gender is outside the scope of the discussion in this chapter, the social hierarchy of identities is not. For a full treatment, see Abdel-Latif, Sara, "Narrativizing early mystic and Sufi women: Mechanisms of gendering in Sufi hagiographies in Ridgeon," in Lloyd Ridgeon (ed.), *Routledge handbook on Sufism*, London: Routledge, 2020, 132–145.

21 Silvers, Laury, "Early pious, mystic, and Sufi women," in Lloyd Ridgeon (ed.), *Cambridge companion to Sufism*, Cambridge: Cambridge University Press, 2014, 24–52, 24–29.

from whom to draw chains of transmissions," al-Qushayrī seems to have limited "that pool of predecessors to those he could definitively argue were in alignment with the ethics and moral values of Shafiʿī Islamic jurisprudence."[22] In fact, Abdel-Latif shows that al-Qushayrī treats al-Ḥusayn b. Manṣūr al-Ḥallāj (d. 309/922) similarly to the women, dropping him from the biographical section as well, thus excluding him as predecessor, but including his aphorisms in the manual section. Al-Qushayrī seems to have found women and al-Ḥallāj too controversial for comprehensive inclusion due to the tense scholarly factionalism of Khurasan.[23] Compound editorial acts like these with broader institutional disinterest over the years in copying al-Sulamī's biographical work on women, *Dhikr al-niswa al-mutaʿabbidāt al-ṣūfiyyāt* (*Memorial of Sufi Women Devotees*) compared to the wide reception of *al-Risāla al-Qushayriyya* (*al-Qushayri's Epistle*), and much of women's practices, teaching, and authority were no longer in view.[24]

While early pious and mystic women taught men and women in public and private, formally and informally, and accounts of their lives and teachings were eagerly sought out, they are almost entirely absent from the later tradition, excluding them from the foundational texts that came to define Sufism.[25] This may seem equivocal as men's sayings underwent the same kinds of intervention, including their names being dropped from the primary sources, but as I point out in my piece on the social worlds of early pious, mystic, Sufi women, there is a difference.

> Certainly, men's names have been dropped from the sources. But the sheer number of extant reports of men compared to women in the formative literature means that women are read as marginal to the development, transmission, and preservation of Sufi practices, knowledge, and teaching.[26]

If women are marginal, then only men are necessary for the successful transmission of Sufism. The result is that women are effectively removed from the

---

22 Abdel-Latif, "Narrativizing" 134–135.

23 Abdel-Latif, "Narrativizing" 134–135. On Sulamī's willingness to include even the most controversial Sufis in his works and an analysis of his biographical collection *Dhikr al-niswa*, see Salamah-Qudsi, Arin, *Sufism and early Islamic piety: Personal and communal dynamics*, Cambridge: Cambridge University Press, 2019, 60–77.

24 Al-Sulamī, Abū ʿAbd ar-Raḥmān, *Early Sufi women*: Dhikr an-niswa al-mutaʿabbidāt aṣ-ṣūfiyyāt, trans. Rkia E. Cornell, Louisville, KY: Fons Vitae, 2000, 43–47.

25 For exact numbers, see Silvers, "Early pious" 24n2.

26 Silvers, "Early pious" 25.

archival history of predecessors and exist only as exceptions. Such exclusions work alongside with and reinforce gendered social segregation in worship and learning that developed in the first century after the Prophet's death.[27] The afterlife of the mediated silencing of women in the sources has resulted in systematic measures over time that have almost entirely barred women from institutional authority within Sufism, have in some cases sidelined them from rituals and access to in-person guidance, and have restricted their entrance onto the path at all.[28]

3 Rhetoricizing Silences

Saidiya Hartman uses the term "silences" to indicate gaps in the sources that need to be voiced using the historical tools available to us and to point to the process of erasure. She writes,

> The intention here isn't anything as miraculous as recovering the lives of the enslaved or redeeming the dead, but rather laboring to paint as full a picture of the lives of the captives as possible. This double gesture can be described as straining against the limits of the archive to write a cultural history of the captive, and, at the same time, enacting the impossibility of representing the lives of the captives precisely through the process of narration.[29]

In my scholarly work, I recovered aspects of early pious and mystic women's lives from the silences in the texts by reading against the transmitters' rhetoricizing grain. To read and write academically against the grain, one must be familiar with the primary sources, obviously, but also the social, political, and religious worlds in which they were produced, and the editorial efforts at work in the text. To write fiction against the grain, I must reframe those probabilities

27 See Halevi, Leor, *Muhammad's grave: Death rites and the making of Islamic society*, New York: Columbia University Press, 2007; Sadeghi, Behnam, "The traveling tradition test: A method for dating traditions," in *Der Islam* 85.1 (2009), 203–242; Geissinger, "Umm al-Dardāʾ;" Sayeed, Asma, *Women and the transmission of religious knowledge*, Cambridge: Cambridge University Press, 2013; Katz, Marion, *Women in the mosque: A history of legal thought and social practice*, New York: Columbia University Press, 2014.

28 Bashir, *Sufi bodies*, 148–163; Malamud, Margaret, "Gender and spiritual self-fashioning: The master-disciple relationship in classical Sufism," in *Journal of the American Academy of Religion* 64.1 (1996), 89–117.

29 Hartman, "Venus" 11.

in my own rhetoricized fictional narrative to bring these hidden lives to light in a way that keeps the historical erasure in view and even comments on their silencing. A critical fabulation is not a story that helps us forget by reclaiming lost lives, but on the contrary, asks us to remember critically the processes of erasure and its systemic afterlife.

All four novels in the series tell the story of women's marginalization from the centre of the Sufi authority to its edge. This narrative arc begins in *The lover* with the introduction of my main characters' mother, a famed ecstatic who wandered the empire, preaching in the streets and graveyards before settling in the Sufi community of Baghdad with her twin children, Zaytuna and Tein (pronounced "teen"). Her character, her dialogue, and the events of her life are adapted from the accounts of named and unnamed early pious and mystic women, reference narrative tropes that have disembodied women from their social worlds and experiences and speak to the systemic loss of women's authority in Sufism over time. Their mother is known only by the sobriquet, "al-Ashiqa as-Sawda." But I do not just withhold their mother's personal name, she does not share her history, even with her own children. She has told Tein and Zaytuna that she is Nubian and she left her home to wander alone with God. Her only possessions are the beads she brought with her on the road that she bartered for food, clothing, or lodging when necessary, and a cherished drum she received as a gift.

In the following passage, I give Zaytuna and Tein the worry that their mother will be forgotten by the Sufis. I hoped passages like this would evoke worry in the reader about her memory and cause them to come to grieve her loss along with Zaytuna and Tein.

> [Tein is sleeping in his sister Zaytuna's rented room, and it is dark.]
> "I don't know if I can sleep anymore. Do you have any oil for the lamp?"
> Tein laughed. "I have to tell you, Zay, your sainthood game is off. Shouldn't you be lighting up the room at night with your luminous soul already?"
> "Mother never lit up at night. If any woman's soul was going to be a lamp, it would have been hers. I complained to Uncle Nuri about these stories once. He laughed at me, thinking they were talking about earthly light. He said, 'When dawn breaks, one no longer needs a lamp.'"
> "Well," Tein replied, "she couldn't see in the dark, either."
> "That's not what he meant."
> "Zay, do you think people will tell stories about her someday?"

She found the lamp. "Sorry Tein. I've got the lamp but no oil. We're stuck in the dark. What did you say?"

"Stories. Will people tell stories of Mother? Will anyone know her name?"

"Why did she never tell us stories of her life before she wandered?" Zaytuna asked, "We know nothing about who we come from. Our family. We've got nothing other than her drum and the beads."

"If we should've known," he said, "she'd have told us. She left all that behind."

"For God."

"Maybe for a different reason."

"I wish I could've asked her."

"Listen, Zaytuna. I meant will the Sufis tell stories about her?"

"I've always heard the aunts and uncles tell stories of the women. Mustafa said he heard an auntie reciting Mother's poetry recently. I can't imagine them forgetting about her, forgetting about the women. If they go the way of the scholars, though ... Women are no better than donkeys and dogs to the likes of them."

"Mustafa is not like that," Tein insisted.

"True, but it seems like the ones who are like that get control of everything."[30]

I could have given al-Ashiqa as-Sawda a name. I could have filled out her details and, as will be discussed below, softened the difficult moments that women like her probably experienced. But for Hartman, narrative restraint and a refusal to provide closure is at the heart of this kind of writing.[31] One should not console the reader with assurances that women like their mother were remembered, thus permitting the reader to forget the silencing of these women's lives. Had I done so, the novel would reiterate the rhetoricizing methods of the early sources: Tell a story heralding mystic women that makes no one uncomfortable. Such a story allows us to forget their loss and uphold women's continued marginalization as natural and necessary to the transmission of Sufi teaching now.

30 Silvers, Laury, *The lover*, Toronto: Self-published, 2019, 101–102.

31 Hartman, "Venus" 12.

4 Rhetoricizing Consolation

For Hartman, voicing silences should never come at the cost of producing consoling narratives. Literary acts of reclamation can erase the experiences and the systems of violence that created them. She considered writing the story of two enslaved girls as if they existed in a free state, but realized she could not. It would have been a betrayal of the fact of their lives only to console herself over their loss.

> But the consolation of this vision—a life recognized and mourned in the embrace of two girls—was at odds with the annihilating violence of the slave ship and with virtually everything I had ever written. Initially I thought I wanted to represent the affiliations severed and remade in the hollow of the slave ship by imagining the two girls as friends, by giving them one another. But in the end I was forced to admit that I wanted to console myself and to escape the slave hold with a vision of something other than the bodies of two girls settling on the floor of the Atlantic. In the end, I could say no more about Venus than I had said about her friend: "I am unsure if it is possible to salvage an existence from a handful of words: the supposed murder of a negro girl." I could not change anything: "The girl 'never will have any existence outside the precarious domicile of words' that allowed her to be murdered." I could not have arrived at another conclusion. So it was better to leave them as I had found them. Two girls, alone.[32]

Interestingly, the transmitters of accounts of early pious and Sufi women did a kind of consoling themselves when faced with the fact of women's experience. As discussed above, the social and political pressures required handling women's narratives with care as their inclusion became controversial. When transmitters retold accounts of women, their narratives tended to vouch for the women's sanctity by assuring the audience that, despite their public behaviour and keeping company with men, they were above sexual reproof. Stories of women upbraiding great men, refusing marriage, ruining their beauty, being honorary men, or having luminous souls that transform sexed bodies into disembodied lamps acted as consoling frames for transmissions of women's wisdom.[33] The transmitters sought to convince their audience that the women and their wisdom should be taken seriously. While these accounts demonstrate the

32 Hartman, "Venus" 8–9.

33 On vouching, see Silvers, "Early pious" 45–47, 50 and Silvers, Laury, "Disappearing women:

highest respect for these women and a desire to preserve their legacies, a long-term effect is stories that distance women from their experiences and the social realities that shaped them.

All of al-Ashiqa as-Sawda's dialogue, history, and behaviour is adapted from these surviving accounts, but also wide-ranging scholarship on the social realities of the day.[34] Zaytuna and Tein's mother is based on accounts of early women who roamed the empire to be alone with the divine lover, who fell into ecstasy and preached in mixed-gender circles in graveyards, on the street, and in private homes, inspiring followers to weep and love God through their own love. Some of these named or unnamed women lived, while others may be inventions or even composites of several women. No matter the case, the accounts are evidence that such women existed and acted as models upon which to construct a tale.[35] While al-Ashiqa as-Sawda is a composite of several early pious and mystic women, African, Arab, and Persian, I want to discuss the consoling account of one woman in particular, Maymūna al-Sawdāʾ, and the possible afterlife of her story today.

Maymūna al-Sawdāʾ was a Black woman consumed with love of God, who sought solitude with her divine lover as a shepherd.[36] She is described as "mad," meaning one who has lost her rational faculties by reason of her behaviour, her unwillingness to conform to social roles, and her language, speaking about God in ways that confuse others. As she wandered alone with her sheep, her mother would come to check on her and bring her food. There would be no record of her except that ʿAbd al-Wāḥid b. Zayd (d. 176/793) dreamt she would be his wife

---

Hafsa bint Sirin and the textual seclusion of early pious and Sufi women," presented at Boston University, February 16, 2012. On the trope of women as honorary men, see Sharify-Funk, Dickson, and Xavier, *Contemporary Sufism* 192–194 and Dakake, Maria, "Walking upon the path of God like men? Women and the feminine in the Islamic mystical tradition," in Jean-Louis Michon and Roger Gaetani (eds.), *Sufism: Love and wisdom*, Bloomington: World Wisdom, 2006, 137–140. Gender is employed at multiple levels of meaning in these accounts, on the qualitative meaning of calling a woman a "man" on the path, rather than the social meaning, which is my point here, see Murata, Sachiko, *The Tao of Islam: A sourcebook of gender relations in Islamic thought*, Albany, NY: SUNY Press, 1992, 316–319.

34 For examples of the primary and secondary sources, see the acknowledgement sections of my novels *The lover*, *The jealous*, *The unseen*, and *The peace* (forthcoming).

35 See El-Cheikh, Nadia M., "Women's history: A study of al-Tanūkhī," in Manuela Marín and Randi Deguilhem (eds.), *Writing the feminine: Women in Arab sources*, London: I.B. Tauris, 2002, 130–148; Geissinger, *Gender*; Bashir, *Sufi bodies*.

36 Black skin is typically marked in the sources with an observation or, like here, with a *laqab*, "The Black Woman." But the *laqab* does not just describe her skin color, it also denotes a distinctive social characteristic of Blackness. As discussed in this section, Blackness in these sources is less a natural descriptor than a social category. Thus, I capitalize "Black" and "Blackness" in these contexts.

in paradise and sought her out.[37] Given what we know about the lives of women like Maymūna, they typically slept rough outdoors, in mosques open to travellers or caravansaries, and under the roofs of strangers. Whether on the road, in cities, or in Maymūna's case, in the countryside, these women would have been subject to fascination, praise, and condemnation, as well as physical and sexual violence.[38]

Maymūna's account hints at the physical violence a woman like her might have experienced as she wandered with her sheep. She reportedly wore a woollen garment embroidered with the words "Not for buying or selling."[39] Maymūna was not alone; a formerly enslaved woman was said to have worn a woollen *jubba* with the same message.[40] The words could be read as a shared statement on the anti-mercantilism of their paths in keeping with the verse, "Those are they that have bought error at the price of guidance, and their commerce has not profited them, and they are not right-guided" (Q 2:16). But if we limit it to that meaning, we miss a more socially grounded message, one possibly intended for those whom the women expected to encounter while wandering. The historical record demonstrates that even in Muslim lands, gangs would abduct vulnerable people off the road, especially targeting Black travellers, and would sell them into slavery.[41]

---

37 On ʿAbd al-Wāḥid, see Javad Shams, Mohammad, "ʿAbd al-Wāḥid b. Zayd al-Baṣrī," trans. S. Umar, in *Encyclopaedia Islamica*.

38 For general remarks on the danger women faced while traveling, see Tolmacheva, Marina, "Medieval Muslim women's travel: Defying distance and danger," in *World History Connected* (2013), n.p., https://worldhistoryconnected.press.uillinois.edu/10.2/forum_tolmacheva.html (last accessed: 22 September 2021). Likewise, see the trope of good rule being marked by the ability of a woman to travel alone safely in Fierro, Maribel, "Violence against women in Andalusi historical sources (third/ninth-seventh/thirteenth centuries)," in Robert Gleave and Istvan Kristo-Nagy (eds.), *Violence in Islamic thought from the Qurʾan to the Mongols*, Edinburgh: Edinburgh University Press, 2015, 155–174, 161. On the violent treatment of women who had lost their rational faculties, see Dols, Michael W., Majnūn: *The madman in medieval Islamic society*, Oxford: Oxford University Press, 1992, 396. Rape was ubiquitous enough in all walks of life that medieval Muslim jurists conceived of multiple categories of offence to narrow down the particularities of each assault. See Badr, Yasmine, *Defining and categorizing "rape": A study of some pre-modern and early modern Islamic legal sources*, Montreal (PhD Diss.): Institute of Islamic Studies McGill University, 2018 and Azam, Hina, *Sexual violation in Islamic law: Substance, evidence, and procedure*, Cambridge: Cambridge University Press, 2015. On sexual violence in warfare, attitudes towards sexual assault in historical literature, and for a plethora of footnotes detailing sexual violence in multiple contexts, see Fierro, "Violence against women," 161.

39 Silvers, "Early pious" 45.

40 Silvers, "Early pious" 45.

41 Bruning, Jelle, "Slave trade dynamics in Abbasid Egypt: The papyrological evidence," in

Maymūna would have been at risk, and the account offers a metaphor for actual sexual violence. When ʿAbd al-Wāḥid finds Maymūna, he declares with surprise that wolves mingle with her sheep and do not attack them. I would argue this part of her story is not about sheep and wolves. Instead, he is vouching for her. He assures his audience that she is his future wife, albeit in paradise, and more importantly, that she was miraculously protected by God from sexual assault. She upbraids him for visiting her unbidden and his surprise at her intimate relationship with God through which she, the sheep, was protected from men, the wolves.

> He said, "I see the wolves are with the sheep! The sheep do not fear the wolves, nor do the wolves eat the sheep. How could that be?"
>
> "Leave me alone! I fixed what is between me and my Master, and so He has taken care of the wolves and the sheep."[42]

I would argue that anyone hearing Maymūna's story in the early and medieval period would know exactly what was meant by "sheep" and "wolves" and might be reassured by a story that permits her sanctity to go unsullied. But over time, this consoling narrative commits a kind of violence by silencing the fact of what she must surely have experienced. It is made worse by the compounded nature of her historical vulnerability to erasure, not just as a woman, but as a Black woman, a poor woman, and a woman who was not in full control of her rational mind.

I try to rectify this textual silencing by bringing Maymūna's experience to al-Ashiqa as-Sawda's story responsibly. Hartman writes about such textual interventions as "jeopardizing the status of the event": "I have attempted to jeopardize the status of the event, to displace the received or authorized account, and to imagine what might have happened or might have been said or might have been done."[43] In *The lover*, I write against the grain of the account of Maymūna's experience by offering a different reading of her words. Words that were once meant to silence her experience as an act of consolation are here said in personal defiance and in narrative recognition of the violence likely perpetrated against her. A defiance that is a mirror of her rejection of the man who interrupts her without invitation and seems to understand so little about God. Further, a defiance that places these Black women, their wisdom, and their

---

JESHO 63 (2020), 682–742, 689–690n46; Tolmacheva, "Medieval Muslim women's travel" [n.p.]; Fierro, "Violence against women" 162–164.

42 Silvers, "Early pious" 45–47.

43 Hartman, "Venus" 11.

experiences at the centre of Sufism.[44] The account no longer suggests that sanctity confers protection from hardship, but rather that one is at peace with God and protected by God, no matter the brutalities of life.

> [al-Ashiqa as-Sawda, with young Zaytuna and Tein in tow, has taken refuge in a mosque overnight. A man has followed them and attempts to rape her.]
>
> Zaytuna sat up and leaned over onto her mother as she pulled her clothes straight. Her mother wound an arm around her and brought her in close. "I have fixed what is between me and God, the sheep no longer fear the wolves."[45]

There are those who have said that I should have followed the transmitters with consoling half-truths and that I have diminished Sufi women by exposing the likelihood of these incidents. But were those early women ashamed that we should cover it up now? Did ʿAbd al-Wāḥid depict her as a woman ashamed? In my reading, his concern was with the assumptions of his audience, not with Maymūna. One account after another of these early mystics depict saintly women who cared about God alone, never sinking to the idolatry of what others think of them. Thus, continuing to uphold these consoling narratives only suggests that the social and bodily vulnerabilities these women experienced are shameful, and further deflects from pointing to an ever-absent perpetrator. To have been raped should not diminish her accomplishments or sanctity. To have fixed what is between her and God in the face of rape is instead an aspirational story for those who have suffered similarly.

5 Rhetoricizing Voicing

For Hartman, the histories of those written out of the archive cannot be told by giving voice to the women, but by giving voice to the impossibility of telling the story itself. But one can write a critical fabulation from the sources, a story that sharpens the point of the losses in articulating what could have been.

---

44 On the role of defiance in telling the histories of Black lives in pre-modern critical race studies, see Hendricks, Margo, "Coloring the past, rewriting our future: RaceB4Race," https://www.folger.edu/institute/scholarly-programs/race-periodization/margo-hendricks (last accessed: 22 September 2021).

45 Silvers, *The lover* 51.

> The intent of this practice is not to *give voice* to the slave, but rather to imagine what cannot be verified, a realm of experience which is situated between two zones of death—social and corporeal death—and to reckon with the precarious lives which are visible only in the moment of their disappearance. It is an impossible writing which attempts to say that which resists being said (since dead girls are unable to speak). It is a history of an unrecoverable past; it is a narrative of what might have been or could have been; it is a history written with and against the archive.[46]

In that vein, why did I choose to depict al-Ashiqa as-Sawda as a woman of Nubian heritage rather than Arab, Persian, or Turkmen? In short, because it is Black Muslims whose histories and presence are silenced most in the Muslim community now.[47] If we were to ask non-Black Muslims living in North America to imagine an early Muslim saint, my guess is that few would imagine a Black woman.[48] Most likely, they would imagine the nearly legendary Rābiʿa al-ʿAdawiyya, who is described as a Persian or Arab woman in the sources and even with fairer skin in some popular depictions.[49] I hoped that al-Ashiqa as-Sawda would pose the question of "what could have been" in a history of Sufi tradition that in large part has not favoured women, Black women, or Blackness.[50]

The low social status of Black people became a metaphor for sanctity in Sufism itself, but this is not favouring Blackness. There is no shortage of proof that Blackness was a social and moral stain in early and medieval Islam. A report that the Prophet Muhammad advised his community in his farewell pilgrimage that they should follow a leader, "*even if* he were an enslaved Abyssin-

46 Hartman, "Venus" 12.

47 On contemporary anti-Blackness in North America and the diaspora, see Curtis Edward E., *The call of Bilal: Islam in the African diaspora*, Chapel Hill, NC: University of North Carolina Press, 2014; Hill, Margari et al. (eds.), *Study of intra-Muslim ethnic relations: Muslim American views on race relations, for the Muslim anti-racism collaborative*, Alta Loma: Muslim ARC, 2015 (https://www.muslimarc.org/interethnic; last accessed: 21 September 2021); Abdul-Khabeer, Suʿad, *Muslim cool: Race, religion, and Hip Hop in the United States*, New York: New York University Press, 2016; Abdullah-Poulos, Layla (ed.), *Black Muslim reads*, New York: NbA Muslims, 2020.

48 I mention these locales because my intention was directed toward my likely readers who, as I expected, overwhelmingly live in the United States and Canada.

49 On Rabiʿa's likely racial background, See Cornell, *Rabiʿa* 45–48.

50 Obviously, this observation only holds in those locales where people of African descent were/are in the minority and/or are marginalized. For the recognition of Black female Sufi guides in Senegal, see, for example, Hill, Joseph, *Wrapping authority women Islamic leaders in a Sufi movement in Dakar, Senegal*, Toronto: University of Toronto Press, 2018.

ian with a head like a raisin," was relayed widely to enforce political quietism.[51] The mention of sin with darkened skin or darkness in the heart in the Quran and Hadith inspired punishments for crimes. Along with other humiliations, non-Black criminals would have their skin blackened with coal and would be paraded through the streets.[52] A Black person might transcend their Blackness through noble Arab lineage, as long as they were among those who knew them well enough to overlook their Blackness for their Arabness.[53] Otherwise, all bets were off. In Sufism, this low worldly status, enslavement too, represented complete subjection to God, the highest aspiration of every ascetic or mystic.[54] Consider the retort of the early mystic Shaʿwāna in the face of unwelcome praise, "I am a sinful black slave."[55] But the subversion of Blackness in Sufism and piety literature is not praise of Black people. On the contrary, it amounts to praise of the subjection of Black people as it only makes sense in a social order in which Blackness is associated with the lowest of the low.[56]

---

51 Al-Bukhārī, Muḥammad *Ṣaḥīḥ al-Bukhārī (Arabic-English)*, trans. Muhammad M. Khan, 9 vols., Medina: Dar Ahya [sic] Us-Sunnah Al-Nabawiýa [sic], 1979, Book 93, *ḥadīth* 6 [emphasis is mine]. Crone, Patricia, "Even an Ethiopian slave: The transformation of a Sunnī tradition," in *BSOAS* 57.1 (1994), 59–67, 60–61.

52 Lange, Christian, "Legal and cultural aspects of ignominious parading (*tashhīr*) in Islam," in *Islamic Law and Society* 14.1 (2007), 84–85; Q 3:106 and Q 10:27; Ibn Māja, Abū ʿAbdallāh Muḥammad b. Yazīd al-Qazwīnī, *Sunan Ibn Māja*, ed. Muḥammad F. ʿAbd al-Bāqī, 2 vols., Beirut: Dār Iḥyāʾ al-Turāth al-ʿArabī, 1975, Book 37, Chapter 29, *ḥadīth* 145.

53 Schine, Rachel, "The racialized other in early Arabic literature: Literature as an institution of community," in Zain Abdullah (ed.), *Routledge handbook on Islam and race*, New York: Routledge (forthcoming). On notions of race relevant to this discussion, also see Richardson, Kristina, *Difference and disability in the medieval Islamic world: Blighted bodies*, Edinburgh: Edinburgh University Press, 2012; McLeod, Nicholas C., *Race rebellion, and Arab Muslim slavery: The Zanj rebellion in Iraq 869–883 C.E.*, Louisville (PhD Diss.): University of Louisville, 2016; El Hamel, Chouki, *Black Morocco: A history of slavery, race, and Islam*, Cambridge: Cambridge University Press, 2014.

54 On the significance of the color black in Sufism with examples see Orfali, Bilal and Nada Saab (eds.), *Sufism, black and white: A critical edition of* Kitāb al-Bayāḍ wa-l-sawād *by Abū l-Ḥasan al-Sīrjānī (d. ca. 470/1077)*, Leiden: Brill, 2012, 12–17; Schimmel, Annemarie, *Mystical dimensions of Islam*, Chapel Hill, NC: University of North Carolina Press, 1975, 123–124. For two more illustrative examples, see Salamah-Qudsi, *Sufism* 245, 257. In some cases, blackening the skin in Sufism refers to mourning rituals in which one blackens the face with coal. For an example see al-Qushayrī, ʿAbd al-Karīm, *al-Qushayri's epistle on Sufism*, trans. Alexander Knysh, Reading: Garnet Publishing, 2007, 137.

55 Silvers, "Early pious" 43. It is an open question whether or not Shaʿwāna was a Black woman, formerly enslaved, enslaved still, or a free Persian woman. The depth of intention in the words would differ given the identity of the speaker and consideration must be given to the role of the transmitter in the wording, but the equivalence between Blackness and perfected humility is the same.

56 Abdel-Latif makes this point and expands the conversation about the gendered depiction

If I were to portray Blackness in keeping with the common subversion trope in Sufism in my novels, I would only embed those widely-held negative associations even further. Instead, I sought out positive associations of Blackness in Sufism spurred by a diagram used by a contemporary Rifaʿi Sufi order. The diagram associates a color with each stage on the path. Black is assigned to the perfected human being (*al-insān al-kāmil*) with the explanation that only black can be fully receptive to the undifferentiated light of God.[57] In his commentary of the Quran, Sahl al-Tustarī (d. ca. 293/896) explains that "night" in the verse, "And by the night when it passes away," refers to "the great blackness," meaning those members of the Prophet's community who are not tainted by this world, unharmed by sin, know only God, and will enter paradise without judgment.[58] Further, some Sufis associate black or an experience of a "black light" with higher levels of the path, and sometimes with human perfection.[59] The conception of the color black as low-thus-high is similar in these schemes, yet different in a crucial way. While black as perfection in these examples results from the abasement of the self in God's self, it has the potential to do so without reference to demeaning social hierarchies, whether or not those who made the association held those views. These interpretations thus displace the oft-used subversion trope as the "credible resource" in the imagined world of my novels with what "could have been" at the centre of the Sufi tradition instead.

In the novels, I adopted the Rifaʿi diagram's colors associated with the distinct levels of the soul and their characteristics. These associations come into play in a number of ways, most notably in a crucial dream sequence. In *The lover*, after Zaytuna wades past colored river stones representing the other stages and psychological challenges she will encounter on the path, she finds

---

of non-elites in early and medieval Sufism, "When women, youths, slaves and black individuals are cast as deviations from the free, elite male norm in these sources, they serve as props for male spiritual advancement." Abdel-Latif, "Narrativizing" 133.

57 The diagram and its interpretation were given to the author at the Canadian Institute of Sufi Studies, Toronto, Ontario, Canada, 2018. This particular diagram is also used by the Helveti-Jerrahi Order of Toronto.

58 Q 89:4; al-Tustarī, Sahl b. ʿAbdallāh, *Tafsīr al-Tustarī*, trans. Annabel Keeler and Ali Keeler, Louisville, KY: Fons Vitae, 2011, 282–283.

59 On "black light," see Corbin, Henry, *Man of light in Iranian Sufism*, New Hampshire: Omega Publications, 1994, 99–110. On the black ink of the Quran, see Rustom, Mohammed, *Inrushes of the heart: The Sufi philosophy of ʿAyn al-Quḍāt*, Albany, NY: SUNY Press, 2023, ch. 8. On the significance of color, including black, in early Kubrawi Sufism from the 7th/13th century, see Abuali, Eyad, "Words clothed in light: *Dhikr* (recollection), color and synaesthesia in early Kubrawi Sufism," in *Iran* 58.2 (2020), 279–292. I am indebted to Alan Godlas for resources and conversation on the color black, "the black light," and the subversion trope in Sufism.

her perfected, Black mother waiting for her. In Zaytuna's dream state, it was as if her mother were the angel Gabriel, inviting her to cross to a higher station.

> The stream's light dimmed as she walked. The city fell away behind her. The world fell away around her. The stones in the bed darkened. A pool was ahead. She could just see it. She walked to it. The water deepened. She was up to her waist in it. The water had no light. The sky had no features. Blackness embraced her. A blackness that accepted all light, rejecting nothing. The edge of the pool went to the horizon. First light arrived in the distance, only a thread of golden blackness illuminating the far, far edge of all things. It grew, the deepest brown, red and golden, slowly filling the sky with its warmth and clarity. Her eyes adjusted, taking in more, taking in every moment until she saw that the golden encompassing blackness was her mother. Her arms filled the horizon from East to West. Her mother's body held every direction.[60]

The scene is an emotional breaking point for Zaytuna, where she finds her connection to her lost mother through the dreamworld and is invited to come to terms with her past in her present moment. Her mother speaks, as if relaying a message from God, telling her to take care of the children at the centre of the case Zaytuna is investigating. "Her words were like a bell sounding, pealing through Zaytuna's every cell. 'My babies. Take care of them.'"[61] Every emotion of the novel has been leading to this moment in which Zaytuna begins to accept the losses of her past, most especially the childhood loss of her mother, to join her mother on a path towards sanctity, and to receive her mother's blessing for her own path seeking justice for the most vulnerable. Rather than a consoling narrative of the sort that Hartman warns against, in the context of the novel to this point, the scene honours the complex lives of mother and daughter with intimacy between themselves and with God.

6 Conclusion

While I intended my mysteries to first and foremost entertain, I also hoped that the historically grounded plots, settings, and character arcs would prompt the reader to question their assumptions about the history of Islam. As discussed in

60 Silvers, *The lover* 139.
61 Silvers, *The lover* 139.

this chapter, my novels are filled with the complexities of gendered and racial hierarchies, popular and elite interpretive communities, ritual practices, social mores, political agendas, doctrines, legal theory and practice, and ethics, but do not try to force a neat story out of them. Whether it be disputes within and between the early Sufi and Hanbali communities in Baghdad arising from internal and external pressures (*The lover*), the nature of justice in ʿAbbasid-era military, jurisprudential, and even popular court systems (*The jealous*), the questions facing a Baghdadi Shiʿa community whose Imam is in hiding (*The unseen*), or the diversity of and tensions within popular and elite Quran culture (*The peace*), my main interest is in depicting the diverse efforts of human beings to make sense of it all. I wanted to explore the Muslim past for the present, perhaps offering a way of thinking that does not look away from the difficulties while celebrating its possibilities.[62] As Hartman writes, "The necessity of trying to represent what we cannot, rather than leading to pessimism or despair must be embraced as the impossibility that conditions our knowledge of the past and animates our desire for a liberated future."[63]

Bibliography

Abdel-Latif, Sara, "Narrativizing early mystic and Sufi women: Mechanisms of gendering in Sufi hagiographies in Ridgeon," in Lloyd Ridgeon (ed.), *Routledge handbook on Sufism*, London: Routledge, 2020, 132–145.

Abdul-Khabeer, Suʿad, *Muslim cool: Race, religion, and Hip Hop in the United States*, New York: New York University Press, 2016.

Abdullah-Poulos, Layla (ed.), *Black Muslim reads*, New York: NbA Muslims, 2020.

Abuali, Eyad, "Words clothed in light: *Dhikr* (recollection), color and synaesthesia in early Kubrawi Sufism," in *Iran* 58.2 (2020), 279–292.

Ali, Kecia, "Redeeming slavery: The 'Islamic State' and the quest for Islamic morality," in *Mizan* 1.1 (2016), https://mizanproject.org/journal-post/redeeming-slavery/ (last accessed: 24 September 2021).

Azam, Hina, *Sexual violation in Islamic law: Substance, evidence, and procedure*, Cambridge: Cambridge University Press, 2015.

Badr, Yasmine, *Defining and categorizing "rape": A study of some pre-modern and early*

62 For an academically critical reconstruction of gender and sexuality in Sufism, see Shaikh, Saʿdiyya, *Sufi narratives of intimacy: Ibn ʿArabi, gender, and sexuality*, Chapel Hill, NC: University of North Carolina Press, 2012.

63 Hartman, "Venus" 12–13.

modern Islamic legal sources, Montreal (PhD Diss.): Institute of Islamic Studies McGill University, 2018.

Bashir, Shahzad, *Sufi bodies: Religion and society in medieval Islam*, New York: Columbia University Press, 2011.

Biran, Michal, "Libraries, books, and transmission of knowledge in Ilkhanid Baghdad," in *JESHO* 62 (2019), 464–502.

Bora, Fozia, *Writing history in the medieval Islamic world: The value of chronicles as archives*, London: I.B. Tauris, 2019.

Bruning, Jelle, "Slave trade dynamics in Abbasid Egypt: The papyrological evidence," in *JESHO* 63 (2020), 682–742.

al-Bukhārī, Muḥammad, *Ṣaḥīḥ al-Bukhārī* (*Arabic-English*), trans. Muhammad M. Khan, 9 vols., Medina: Dar Ahya [sic] Us-Sunnah Al-Nabawiýa [sic], 1979.

Chaudhry, Ayesha S., "Islamic legal studies: A critical historiography," in Anver M. Emon and Rumee Ahmed (eds.), *The Oxford handbook of Islamic law*, Oxford: Oxford University Press, 2017, 1–40.

Cooperson, Michael, *Classical Arabic biography: The heirs of the prophets in the age of al-Maʾmūn*, Cambridge: Cambridge University Press, 2004.

Corbin, Henry, *Man of light in Iranian Sufism*, New Hampshire: Omega Publications, 1994.

Cornell, Rkia E., *Rabiʿa from narrative to myth: The many faces of Islam's most famous woman saint, Rabiʿa al-ʿAdawiyya*, London: Oneworld Academic, 2019.

Crone, Patricia, "Even an Ethiopian slave: The transformation of a Sunnī tradition," in *BSOAS* 57.1 (1994), 59–67.

Curtis, Edward E., *The call of Bilal: Islam in the African diaspora*, Chapel Hill, NC: University of North Carolina Press, 2014.

Dabashi, Hamid, "Edward Said's *Orientalism*: Forty years later," in *al-Jazeera* (3 May 2018), https://www.aljazeera.com/opinions/2018/5/3/edward-saids-orientalism-forty-years-later (last accessed: 24 September 2021).

Dakake, Maria, "Walking upon the path of God like men? Women and the feminine in the Islamic mystical tradition," in Jean-Louis Michon and Roger Gaetani (eds.), *Sufism: Love and wisdom*, Bloomington: World Wisdom, 2006, 131–151.

Dandridge, Rita B., "The African American historical romance: An interview with Beverly Jenkins," in *Journal of Popular Romance Studies* 1.1 (2010), 1–11.

Dols, Michael W., Majnūn: *The madman in medieval Islamic society*, Oxford: Oxford University Press, 1992.

El-Cheikh, Nadia M., "Women's history: A study of al-Tanūkhī," in Manuela Marín and Randi Deguilhem (eds.), *Writing the feminine: Women in Arab sources*, London: I.B. Tauris, 2002, 130–148.

El Hamel, Chouki, *Black Morocco: A history of slavery, race, and Islam*, Cambridge: Cambridge University Press, 2014.

Fierro, Maribel, "Violence against women in Andalusi historical sources (third/ninth-seventh/thirteenth centuries)," in Robert Gleave and Istvan Kristo-Nagy (eds.), *Violence in Islamic thought from the Qur'an to the Mongols*, Edinburgh: Edinburgh University Press, 2015, 155–174.

Geissinger, [Ash], "Umm al-Dardā' sat in *tashahhud* like man: Towards the historical contextualization of a portrayal of female religious authority," in *MW* 103 (2013), 305–319.

Geissinger, [Ash], *Gender and Muslim constructions of exegetical authority: A rereading of the classical genre of Qur'ān commentary*, Leiden: Brill, 2015.

Geissinger, [Ash], "Female figures, marginality, and Qur'anic exegesis in Ibn al-Jawzi's *Ṣifat al-ṣafwa*," in Yasmin Amin and Nevin Reda (eds.), *Islamic interpretive tradition and gender justice: Processes of canonization, subversion, and change*, Montreal: McGill-Queen's University Press, 2020, 151–178.

Haider, Najam, *The rebel and the Imam in early Islam: Explorations in Muslim historiography*, Cambridge: Cambridge University Press, 2019.

Halevi, Leor, *Muhammad's grave: Death rites and the making of Islamic society*, New York: Columbia University Press, 2007.

Hammer, Juliane, "Sufism in North America," in Lloyd Ridgeon (ed.), *Routledge handbook on Sufism*, London: Routledge, 2020, 514–530.

Hartman, Saidiya, *Lose your mother: A journey along the Atlantic slave route*, New York: Farrar, Straus and Giroux, 2008.

Hartman, Saidiya, "Venus in two acts," in *Small Axe: A Caribbean Journal of Criticism* 26 (2008), 2–14.

Hendricks, Margo, "Coloring the past, rewriting our future: RaceB4Race," https://www.folger.edu/institute/scholarly-programs/race-periodization/margo-hendricks (last accessed: 22 September 2021).

Hermansen, Marcia, "The academic study of Sufism at American universities," in *AJISS* 24.3 (2007), 24–45.

Hill, Joseph, *Wrapping authority women Islamic leaders in a Sufi movement in Dakar, Senegal*, Toronto: University of Toronto Press, 2018.

Hill, Margari et al. (eds.), *Study of intra-Muslim ethnic relations: Muslim American views on race relations, for the Muslim anti-racism collaborative*, Alta Loma: Muslim ARC, 2015 (https://www.muslimarc.org/interethnic; last accessed: 21 September 2021).

Hughes, Aaron W., *Theorizing Islam: Disciplinary deconstruction and reconstruction*, London: Acumen, 2014.

Hughes, Aaron W., *Islam and the tyranny of authenticity: An inquiry into disciplinary apologetics*, Sheffield: Equinox, 2016.

Ibn Māja, Abū 'Abdallāh Muḥammad b. Yazīd al-Qazwīnī, *Sunan Ibn Māja*, ed. Muḥammad F. 'Abd al-Bāqī, 2 vols., Beirut: Dār Iḥyā' al-Turāth al-'Arabī 1975.

Javad Shams, Mohammad, "ʿAbd al-Wāḥid b. Zayd al-Baṣrī," trans. S. Umar, in *Encyclopaedia Islamica.*

Katz, Marion, *Women in the mosque: A history of legal thought and social practice*, New York: Columbia University Press, 2014.

Knight, Michael M., *Why I am a Salafi*, Berkeley: Soft Skull Press, 2015.

Knight, Michael M., *Muhammad's body: Baraka networks and the Prophetic assemblage*, Chapel Hill, NC: The University of North Carolina Press, 2020.

Knysh, Alexander, "Historiography of Sufi Studies in the West," in Youssef M. Choueiri (ed.), *A companion to the history of the Middle East*, Malden, MA: Blackwell, 2005, 106–132.

Lange, Christian, "Legal and cultural aspects of ignominious parading (*tashhīr*) in Islam," in *Islamic Law and Society* 14.1 (2007), 81–108.

Malamud, Margaret, "Gender and spiritual self-fashioning: The master-disciple relationship in classical Sufism," in *Journal of the American Academy of Religion* 64.1 (1996), 89–117.

McLeod, Nicholas C., *Race rebellion, and Arab Muslim slavery: The Zanj rebellion in Iraq 869–883 C.E.*, Louisville (PhD Diss.): University of Louisville, 2016.

Morgenstein Fuerst, Ilyse, "Job ads don't add up: Arabic + Middle East + texts ≠ Islam," in *Journal of the American Academy of Religion* 88.4 (2020), 915–946.

Orfali, Bilal and Nada Saab (eds.), *Sufism, black and white: A critical edition of* Kitāb al-Bayāḍ wa-l-sawād *by Abū l-Ḥasan al-Sīrjānī (d. ca. 470/1077)*, Leiden: Brill, 2012.

Mulder, Stephennie, "The mausoleum of Imam al-Shafiʿi," in *Muqarnas* 23 (2006), 15–46.

Murata, Sachiko, *The Tao of Islam: A sourcebook of gender relations in Islamic thought*, Albany, NY: SUNY Press, 1992.

Osborne, Thomas, "The ordinariness of the archive," in *History of the Human Sciences* 12.2 (1999), 51–64.

al-Qushayrī, ʿAbd al-Karīm, *al-Qushayri's epistle on Sufism*, trans. Alexander Knysh, Reading: Garnet Publishing, 2007.

Reid, Megan, *Law and piety in medieval Islam*, Cambridge: Cambridge University Press, 2013.

Richardson, Kristina, "Singing slave girls (*qiyan*) of the ʿAbbasid court in the ninth and tenth centuries," in Gwyn Campbell, Suzanne Miers and Joseph C. Miller (eds.), *Children and slavery through the ages*, Athens: Ohio University Press, 2009, 105–118.

Richardson, Kristina, *Difference and disability in the medieval Islamic world: Blighted bodies*, Edinburgh: Edinburgh University Press, 2012.

Richardson, Kristina, "The evolving biographical legacy of two late Mamluk Ḥanbalī judges," in Stephan Conermann (ed.), *History and society during the Mamluk period (1250 to 1517)*, Bonn: Bonn University Press, 2014, 29–50.

Rustom, Mohammed, *Inrushes of the heart: The Sufi philosophy of ʿAyn al-Quḍāt*, Albany, NY: SUNY Press, 2023.
Sadeghi, Behnam, "The traveling tradition test: A method for dating traditions," in *Der Islam* 85.1 (2009), 203–242.
Safi, Omid, *The politics of knowledge in premodern Islam: Negotiating ideology and religious inquiry*, Chapel Hill, NC: University of North Carolina Press, 2009.
Salamah-Qudsi, Arin, *Sufism and early Islamic piety: Personal and communal dynamics*, Cambridge: Cambridge University Press, 2019.
Sayeed, Asma, *Women and the transmission of religious knowledge*, Cambridge: Cambridge University Press, 2013.
Schine, Rachel, "The racialized other in early Arabic literature: Literature as an institution of community," in Zain Abdullah (ed.), *Routledge handbook on Islam and race*, New York: Routledge (forthcoming).
Shaikh, Saʿdiyya, *Sufi narratives of intimacy: Ibn ʿArabi, gender, and sexuality*, Chapel Hill, NC: University of North Carolina Press, 2012.
Sheedy, Matt (ed.), *Identity, politics and the study of Islam: Current dilemmas in the study of religions*, Sheffield: Equinox, 2018.
Silvers, Laury, "'In the book we have left out nothing': The ethical problem of the existence of verse 4:34 in the Qurʾan," in *Comparative Islamic Studies* 2.2 (2006), 171–180.
Silvers, Laury, "Disappearing women: Hafsa bint Sirin and the textual seclusion of early pious and Sufi women," presented at Boston University, February 16, 2012.
Silvers, Laury, "Early pious, mystic, and Sufi women," in Lloyd Ridgeon (ed.), *Cambridge companion to Sufism*, Cambridge: Cambridge University Press, 2014, 24–52.
Silvers, Laury, *The lover*, Toronto: Self-published, 2019.
Silvers, Laury, *The jealous*, Toronto: Self-published, 2020.
Silvers, Laury, *The unseen*, Toronto: Self-published, 2021.
Silvers, Laury, *The peace*, Toronto: Self-published (forthcoming).
Schimmel, Annemarie, *Mystical dimensions of Islam*, Chapel Hill, NC: University of North Carolina Press, 1975.
Sharify-Funk, Meena, William R. Dickson, and Merin S. Xavier, *Contemporary Sufism: Piety, politics, and popular culture*, New York: Routledge, 2018.
Stearns, Justin K., *Infectious ideas: Contagion in premodern Islamic and Christian thought in the western Mediterranean*, Baltimore: Johns Hopkins University Press, 2011.
al-Sulamī, Abū ʿAbd ar-Raḥmān, *Early Sufi women:* Dhikr an-niswa al-mutaʿabbidāt aṣ-ṣūfiyyāt, trans. Rkia E. Cornell, Louisville, KY: Fons Vitae, 2000.
Tolmacheva, Marina, "Medieval Muslim women's travel: Defying distance and danger," in *World History Connected* (2013), n.p., https://worldhistoryconnected.press.uillinois.edu/10.2/forum_tolmacheva.html (last accessed: 22 September 2021).

al-Tustarī, Sahl b. ʿAbdallāh, *Tafsīr al-Tustarī*, trans. Annabel Keeler and Ali Keeler, Louisville, KY: Fons Vitae, 2011.

Woods, Graeme, "What ISIS really wants," in *The Atlantic* (2015), https://www.theatlantic.com/magazine/archive/2015/03/what-isis-really-wants/384980/ (last accessed: 24 September 2021).

Vaknin, Judy, Karyn Stukey and Victoria Lane (eds.), *All this stuff: Archiving the artist*, Oxfordshire: Libri Publishing, 2013.

Vansina, Jan, *Oral tradition as history*, Madison: University of Wisconsin Press, 1985.

CHAPTER 23

The Tao of *maʿrifa*: Adam's Encounter with Hell in Paradise

Mohammed Mehdi Ali

1 Introduction

Before Professor Sachiko Murata's studies of the historical presence of Islam in China came out, she published her monumental book *The Tao of Islam*. In this comprehensive study, she applied a generalized version of the yin-yang hermeneutic to understand the metaphysical nature of gender relationships in the Islamic sapiential tradition. In this paper, I aim to use Professor Murata's method of reading the Islamic tradition to illustrate the ways in which the nature of *maʿrifa*, or the recognition of human reality, is rooted in the recognition of the duality of God's merciful and wrathful attributes, both of which Murata identifies as the Islamic counterparts to yin and yang. I begin by elucidating the relation that Murata sees between the Tao and its successive process of manifestation, and the nature of God as described by the scheme of Essence, names, and attributes. I emphasize the duality inherent in the conception of the Tao and its repercussions on the nature of the cosmos to suggest its parallels with the complementarity of God's acts, which define the various manifestations of divine reality in creation.

The value of this yin-yang reading for both the present inquiry lies in the fact that it throws the complementary and polar nature of reality in the Islamic worldview into sharp relief. The contribution that I offer is to show how this polarity, inherent in God's attributes, is therefore also essential for a full realization of Adam's nature, since he was made in the divine form. While like Murata herself I use multiple authors to illustrate my own reading, I focus on a single event: the fall of Adam and Eve from Paradise as a result of Iblīs' "deception."

As Murata has shown in her substantial scholarly contribution, the yin-yang reading is relevant to the Islamic intellectual universe because duality is a necessary consequence of God's oneness and is thus manifest at all levels of existence. This paper is also concerned with the polar nature of these dualities, or how twoness resolves into a unity at the highest level of analysis. I argue that this resolution is present in the story of Adam's fall by examining various areas of tension, contradiction, and polarity in the story.

 | DOI:10.1163/9789004529038_024

I begin by showing how the Garden contains a "seed" of the Fire in the form of the tree Adam eats from, as well as the opposite case of a "seed" of the Garden in the Fire, thus demonstrating the logic inherent in the Taoist symbol of yin-yang. The next area of polarity I consider key to understanding the importance of the fall in the Islamic tradition is the mystery of Adam's creation, bringing together the highest and lowest aspects of creation. This all-comprehensiveness helps us understand another aspect of Satan's deception, namely his promise to make Adam and Eve angels (who are simultaneously higher and more limited than humans), which takes advantage of their forgetfulness, another quintessentially human trait.

The main point I demonstrate in the section on the intersection between the command and the decree, or free will and determinism, is how the decree "depends" on Adam's free response to the command (since his disobedience leads to the fulfillment of the decree) as well as how the command determines his place as decreed by God (if Adam did not disobey the command, he would not have been sent to the "lowest of the low," "a wrongdoer, ignorant"). The situation here is paradoxical: Adam was meant to be sent to the earth, but his actions lead him there, meaning that the decree seems to only have been accomplished by the command. On the other hand, the command "justifies" the decree: he is sent to the earth, because he is in the wrong. I point out, however, that the same authors who so eloquently set up this paradox beautifully emphasize the role of mercy in all of this: God's acts are not reactions to His creatures. At the same time, the sources sing the praises of a Lord who grants kindness and severity in keeping with the nature and reality of His creation, giving each one of them wonders beyond their due in the final analysis. There is an enmeshment of activity and receptivity between the command and decree as described by Aḥmad Samʿānī (d. 534/1140) and Rashīd al-Dīn Maybudī (d. ca. 520/1126) such that each is inseparable from the other in the case of Adam, whose distinctive trait is his free will.

I further elucidate the issue of activity and receptivity in thinking about one of Murata's most significant pairings—heaven and earth. Discussing the various ways in which a single reality can be considered either active or receptive, I compare earth, Adam, and women to demonstrate that there is a certain kind of superiority and activity in the state of being receptive to something higher and more exalted. I focus on the relation between God and Adam to make the point that, in a certain respect, the former "needed" the latter in order to make Himself manifest. I bring this back to the discussion of free will and determinism to show that one of the ways in which Adam lives up to what is asked of him by God is precisely by asking for forgiveness for his disobedience, thereby showing a respect for the rights of the various levels of divine reality, which is precisely what God "needed" him to recognize (*ʿarafa*).

The final section focuses on the love that both Adam and God had for recognition (*maʿrifa*). I suggest that the entire story so far can only be understood as a cohesive whole, as a unity transcending the various polarities, the Tao that is undifferentiated over and above its manifestations as yin and yang, when the element of love in this story is highlighted. Many of the passages I quote focus on the love and care with which God creates Adam. That fact should be enough to tell us that there is more to this story than meets the eye at first. Indeed, Satan does deceive Adam and Eve with the tree that he claims will give them immortality and make them into angels, but I argue, based on many of the Islamic sapiential sources that emphasize love, that this is not why Adam and Eve decide to eat from the tree. Rather, from the moment of his creation, Adam was God's familiar: the first thing he saw when God brought him to life was God's infinite beauty. He fell in love, not simply with the gentle acts of God manifested in the Garden but with the entirety of the divine reality, which includes severity, wrath, and mercy among others. He saw that he was in an abode dominated by only some of God's qualities, and as a whole made in the mirror of the divine whole, he yearned for all of God. He only knew that the tree represented severity, the half that the Garden was missing, and he jumped at the chance to become whole again. But he was deceived, since Satan pointed to something outside of his own human reality that could help him find God. The famous alleged prophetic dictum tells us man can only recognize God by recognizing his own self, and I argue that what the Quran tells us when it says "He forgot" was that Adam forgot *this* truth. Other aspects of this story fall into place as well: God told Adam not to approach the tree, but He knew that Adam would be compelled to disobey by the virtue of "his great love." As Samʿānī and Maybudī tell us, love, like the decree, is pre-eternal, while the command is newly arrived in relation to creatures. Adam lived up to what was asked of him by disobeying.

Finally, God did not punish him by sending him to the earth. Rather, the earth is the abode of *taklīf* which is the central point in creation. In terms of this paper, its centrality can be understood as being open to both wrath and mercy, since human actions can result in either destination (as opposed to the predominance of one attribute in the Garden or the Fire), as well as being the place where human beings can fully actualize their nature as central (since they contain all the attributes of God without being dominated by a single type) and earthly creatures. For a finite act of disobedience, Adam was given the chance to see infinite beauty once again.

2 The Tao as Method

The title of this paper invites some explanation. It takes its cue from the title of Sachiko Murata's groundbreaking study *The Tao of Islam* on the metaphysical dimensions of Islam, studied through the lens of duality. She subtitles her work *A sourcebook on gender relationships in Islamic thought* because the study examines lengthy quotations by some of the greatest thinkers in the Islamic tradition to show that discussions of the masculine and feminine involved investigating the very nature of reality itself. It is important to recognize that the problem of gender relationships for Murata *necessitates* investigation into metaphysical issues; she is not simply dealing with the issue of gender in a metaphysical way but arguing that gender is at root a metaphysical issue. Therefore, her project comes down to an investigation of Islamic metaphysics, which is precisely the lens that I want to use for this paper.

Since both my paper and Murata's work are heavily influenced by the concept of the "Tao," it will be helpful to explain what I mean by this word. As Murata mentions, the introductory text for the class from which this book was developed was the Chinese classic the *I Ching*.[1] The definition of the Tao given by this text which provided the foundations for both Confucianism and Taoism in China and has been massively influential for the last 3000 years seems like the most appropriate way to understand this key term. It tells us, "That which lets now the dark, now the light appear is [sic] tao."[2] The dark and the light mentioned here are, of course, the famous yin and yang, symbolized by the well-known circle divided into two halves of dark and light, with a spot of dark in the light and a spot of light in the dark.

Yin and yang are central to the *I Ching* or the *Book of changes*, and as its title suggests, it depicts these two as forces that are constantly in motion, a process of change which creates the universe. "Yin and yang embrace each other in harmony, and their union produces the Ten Thousand Things, which is everything that exists."[3] The constant movement of yin and yang also means that the universe is in a state of perpetual change, something that is perceptible in the changing of the seasons or the alternation of day and night. As these examples suggests, the motion of yin and yang, while seemingly contradictory on their

1 Murata, Sachiko, *The Tao of Islam: A sourcebook on gender relationships in Islamic thought*, Albany, NY: SUNY Press, 1992, 1.

2 Baynes, Cary F. and Richard Wilhelm, (trans.), *The* I Ching *or* Book of changes, Princeton: Princeton University Press, 1983, 297.

3 Murata, *The Tao of Islam* 6–7.

own respective levels, is also harmonious: the night gradually brightens into day, and autumn gradually warms into spring.

The equilibrium of this motion is not found in the opposition of yin and yang itself, but it is determined by what unites the two: the Tao or Tai Chi (the "Great Ultimate"), which was "totally undifferentiated" prior to the manifestation of yin and yang. Heaven is pure yang and earth pure yin. Then, the "two primary forces," "four images," and "eight trigrams" are generated. The eight trigrams represent a "cosmic family" of a father, mother, three sons, and three daughters.[4] The last six of these are combined to form the 64 hexagrams (six-line images) which constitute, along with their commentaries, the text of the *Book of changes*. We see that the process of creative change is ordered and progressive, and therefore, the movement of phenomena in the cosmos, which the hexagrams represent, is similarly balanced. In this way, the *I Ching* constantly tells us to view the world through images that illustrate higher principles.

All of these images put together give us an idea of the nature of the *Book of changes* as it describes the movement of the Tao in the cosmos. The Tao is originally unknown and reveals itself through the movement of yin and yang. This self-disclosure is recognizable to us through heaven and earth, which are the fundamental yin and yang, as well as in their combinations in the form of the sixty-four hexagrams. The role of the *I Ching* then is to remind its readers of the principles that lie behind the world that they see and interact with on a daily basis that are organized around a polarity that resolves into a unity in the final analysis.[5]

The fundamental Islamic duality that Murata is exploring in this book is one derived from the nature of God as described by a wide variety of Islamic thinkers. God is described primarily by the names that scholars have derived from scriptural sources. Roughly, these names fall into three categories: names that describe God in Himself (His Essence), names that describe God's attributes, and names that describe God's acts. Those names that describe God's Essence cannot be ascribed to other than God, such as the name *Allāh*. His attributes include names that do not have opposites such as "Alive, Knowing, Desiring, Powerful, Speaking, Hearing, and Seeing."[6] Those that describe God's activity towards created things fall into complementary pairs such as "Merciful and Wrathful, Gentle and Severe, Beautiful and Majestic, Guider and Misguider, Exalter and Abaser, Forgiver and Avenger, Benefiter and Harmer, Life-giver and

4 Murata, *The Tao of Islam* 7–8.
5 For Murata's discussion of polarity, see Murata, *The Tao of Islam* 22.
6 Murata, *The Tao of Islam* 55.

Slayer, Expander and Contractor."[7] Despite the apparent multiplicity of these descriptions, they all return to God.

In order to understand the relationship of the Tao to Islamic thought in Murata's scheme, it is important to consider the implications of these three categories for describing God. The first *shahāda*, or the statement of *tawḥīd*, tells us that God is the only reality there is, and God's name *al-ḥaqq* or the Real denotes this sense most directly. There is no reality but God. Therefore, the three categories of describing the nature of God are, in fact, names that describe the nature of reality itself. Furthermore, these three categories pertain to different levels at which God is envisioned: the names of the Essence are qualities possessed by God alone, the attributes belong to God, but creatures also partake of them, and the acts describe how God relates to creation. Much of Murata's argument takes advantage of the parallel between the Tao in itself (undifferentiated and therefore, unknown) and its manifestation as yin and yang, which then assumes a relationship with the cosmos it generates and the discussion of the nature of God in Himself who then possesses certain characteristics and activity in relation to the cosmos which He creates.

The complementarity that exists between the names of God's acts listed above further extends this parallel. These names come in pairs which mirrors the importance of the duality in the activity of the Tao. The two-ness of yin and yang becomes four and eight and 64, increasing in multiplicity until one reaches the Ten Thousand Things.[8] Similarly, the polarity of the names of God's acts can be considered in many ways, each relative to a multiplicity of levels. Murata outlines how these names are manifest in the reality of human beings on a horizontal level in terms of their relationships with each other. Life and death, vengeance and forgiveness, exaltation and abasement, wrath and mercy, to name just a few pairs, are found all around us in varieties of different ways:[9] calling them "acts of God" allows us to organize our understanding about the activity in the world and trace their roots in the Real. Murata also mentions the "vertical" level which describes the hierarchy of cosmological levels, such as the distinction between body and spirit, man and God, among others. Within these levels, names like knowledge and ignorance, life and death, exaltation and abasement all have their place, since God is knowledgeable and man ignorant, and the spirit is alive and exalted in relation to the body's death and abasement.[10] Furthermore, "to use an attribute in describing something is to

7 Murata, *The Tao of Islam* 55.
8 Murata, *The Tao of Islam* 59.
9 Murata, *The Tao of Islam* 55.
10 Murata, *The Tao of Islam* 55.

conjure up a relationship … theoretical discussion of these relationships can be drawn out indefinitely."[11] In this line, she creates a parallel between Islamic theology and the Tao's engendering of the Ten Thousand Things, since the multiplicity of the ways in which yin and yang relate to each other generates the cosmos.

I have carefully been using the word "parallel" to describe how Murata thinks about the Tao in relation to Islamic thought to drive home the fact that she is not engaged in a syncretic project. The use of Chinese metaphysics in this context was a careful choice on Murata's part to make her audience, predisposed to viewing Islam as a religion that oppressed women, more receptive to her presentation of gender relationships as rooted in the very nature of things.[12] My own focus is on the inherently polar (and therefore unitary)[13] structure of reality she highlights in making her argument. Jamal Elias nicely sums up the issue in his review of *The Tao of Islam*:

> In articulating her construct of the "Tao of Islam" the author points to certain parallels between Islamic and Chinese cosmology. Murata is not trying to argue for cross-cultural influence or syncretism reminiscent of R.C. Zaehner's *Hindu and Muslim Mysticism* or of numerous works relating Islam to Judaism and Christianity. Her approach is phenomenological, and from this perspective the observation that certain kinds of Islamic thought appear Taoist seems natural and beyond dispute.[14]

My own goal in this paper, then, is to take this same "conceptual grid" and "hermeneutic" and apply it to the story of Adam's fall from the Garden and bring out its implications for the goal of human life. In doing so, I will flesh out the aforementioned scheme of Murata's argument as it relates to my own.

11 Murata, *The Tao of Islam* 57.
12 Murata, *The Tao of Islam* 1–2.
13 Polarity suggests the "poles" of a circle or sphere, and therefore polarity only exists in relation to a unity.
14 Elias, Jamal J., "Review of *The Tao of Islam: A sourcebook on gender relationships in Islamic thought*," in *IrS* 28.1–2 (1995), 94–96, 94. See also the pertinent remarks in Ernst, Carl W., "Review of *The Tao of Islam: A sourcebook on gender relationships in Islamic thought*," in *JAOS* 114.4 (1994), 677–678, 678.

3 Adam's Fall

The story of Adam's fall is of primary importance for the sapiential tradition Murata is representing in her work. As the first human being and the first prophet sent to the earth, Adam's conduct in eating from the tree and repenting for his action both demonstrates human frailty in following God's commandments and the proper response to their weakness: seeking God's Mercy. I will use Quranic verses and terminology to elucidate the various significances of the event of eating from the tree. I then draw upon authors such as Maybudī, Samʿānī, Ibn ʿArabī (d. 638/1240), and Najm al-Dīn Rāzī (d. 654/1256) to point to a deeper reality hidden in this myth about human origins, centering around the alleged prophetic saying "He who recognizes (*ʿarafa*) himself (or "his soul") recognizes (*ʿarafa*) His Lord"[15] as well as the seeming paradox in God's placement of Adam in the Garden after having told the angels He would "place in *the earth* a vicegerent" (Q 2:30).[16] It is from the use of the word *ʿarafa* in the above quoted saying that this paper gets its title: *maʿrifa* being a derivation from the same root that designates the ultimate goal of human striving.

We will begin by looking at a verse which records Satan's (or Iblīs) words to Adam, when tempting him to eat from the tree. He says, "O Adam, shall I point you (*adulluka*) to a tree of everlastingness (*khuld*) …?" (Q 20:120). It is important to recognize the deception in Satan's words to Adam here by focusing on the word "everlastingness (*khuld*)." In the Quran, words derived from the same root (*kh-l-d*) as *khuld* are used 87 times, the vast majority of verses, 80 of them, referring to either the Garden or the Fire.[17] Given that Adam is already in the Garden, Satan's promising him everlastingness if he eats from a tree that God has prohibited him[18] on the pain of being removed from his current home[19] is particularly ironic, since it implies that the Satan is pointing Adam to the only other place that is everlasting: the Fire, a place moreover explicitly associated with Satan himself. This suggestion is strengthened by the fact that in two other verses God tells Adam and Eve that eating from this tree will make them from

15 Murata, *The Tao of Islam* 26.

16 Unless otherwise noted, all translations from the Quran are mine.

17 In the seven times that the Quran uses this word in other contexts, it is referring to the story of Satan tempting Adam (Q 7:20 and Q 20:120), scorning those who think that their stay on earth is everlasting (Q 21:34, Q 26:129, and Q 104:3), one verse that points out the foolishness of one who inclines (*akhlada*) to the earth (Q 7:176), and one verse that denies that prophets are created with everlasting bodies and asserts that they need food and drink (Q 21:8).

18 Q 7:19.

19 Q 20:117.

the *ẓālimūn* or evildoers.[20] The Quran also tells us the Fire is "the recompense of the evildoers" (Q 5:29).

Moreover, Satan is motivated by revenge: after he refuses to prostrate before Adam, God tells Adam and his wife that he is an "enemy" to them.[21] Iblīs promises to misguide God's servants.[22] God then tells him that He will place all those that are misguided in Hell along with Satan.[23] Thus, it accords with the logic of the story that Satan should try to ensure that Adam should be the first to end up in Hell with him, since in his eyes, it is Adam who is at least partially implicated in his fall from grace.[24] Satan's role as an enemy of mankind and specifcally Adam, his association with the Fire, and his use of the word of "everlasting" to trick Adam out of the Garden all connote that Satan was, in fact, trying to draw the first human to the Fire, another abode of everlastingness. The ironic aspect of this whole account should not be forgotten: Satan is attempting to draw Adam away from the abode of bliss (*niʿma*) he is already in to its polar opposite, an abode of chastisement (*ʿadhāb*).

Since we are using the Chinese hermeneutic of the Tao to analyze the "seed" of chastisement present among the overwhelming bliss that characterizes the Garden in which Adam was placed, we should expect the converse situation to be present in Fire: a "seed" of bliss in an abode characterized by chastisement. Indeed, we find this to be the case in an explanation Ibn ʿArabī gives about God's name *al-jāmiʿ* or "the One who brings together." He points out that one can only bring together things if there is a multiplicity of things, which means that the declaration of oneness (*tawḥīd*) necessitates *shirk* or associationism, its opposite. He then applies this lens to various aspects of reality, including bliss and chastisement, telling us that realities can only be appreciated through their opposites. Over the course of this explanation, Ibn ʿArabī makes a good case for the name *al-jāmiʿ* as an Arabic rendition for the Chinese concept of Tao: a reality that creates opposites so its essential unity can be appreciated. He concludes his argument by telling us that some of the people sent to the Fire will be able to appreciate both bliss and chastisement, by finding former in the midst of the latter.

> He who is a companion of security does not know its flavor through tasting. No one knows its measure save the one at whom it arrives while he

---

20 Q 2:35 and Q 7:19.
21 Q 20:117.
22 Q 7:17.
23 Q 7:18.
24 Satan also blames God in Q 7:16.

> is in the state of fear. He finds its flavor through its arrival ... The pleasure of the Companions of the Blaze is magnificent, for they witness the abode, while security is one of its properties. There is no surprise if roses are found in rose gardens. Surprise comes from roses in the pit of the Fire ...
>
> Within the Fire
> a group will be blissful through the chastisement—
> if not for witnessing the opposite,
> they would not be safe.[25]

Since he is talking about a specific group that will experience bliss in the Fire, his argument is not necessarily that everyone will experience bliss in Hell or that it is the predominant characteristic of that abode. Rather, it is the opposite: precisely because the Fire is dominated by chastisement, the people in it can appreciate bliss all the more by knowing the pain of punishment so severely. Therefore, when a certain group within it finds bliss or "roses in the pit of the Fire," their "pleasure ... is magnificent."[26] The force of his argument for this possibility lies in its being necessitated by the name of God as the "One who brings together." Since the names of God are descriptions of the nature of existence, gathering together must occur on every level of existence. This argument is then both an explicit and implicit proof for my own argument: within the framework of the Chinese hermeneutic I am borrowing from Murata, the existence of a seed of Hell in Paradise, or a dot of yang within yin, must find its reflection in the opposite situation: the existence of a seed of Paradise in Hell, or a dot of yin within yang. Implicitly, since God as the "One who brings together" means that the people in the chastisement of the Fire will experience bliss, it can also mean that the people in the bliss of the Garden can experience some of the chastisement of the Fire, a possibility confirmed by my understanding of the story of Adam and the tree of everlastingness.

4 Adamic All-Comprehensiveness

An important difference between Adam and Eve, on one hand, and Iblīs, on the other, is highlighted in Q 7:23, where the progenitors of the human race

25 Chittick, William C., *The self-disclosure of God: Principles of Ibn al-ʿArabī's cosmology*, Albany, NY: SUNY Press, 1998, 178–181.

26 Chittick, *The self-disclosure of God* 181.

admit that: "Our Lord, we have wronged ourselves. And if Thou dost not forgive us and have mercy upon us, we shall surely be amongst the lost."[27] When contrasted with Iblīs' arrogance upon being confronted with his disobedience, Adam and Eve's acceptance of their fault shows a profound humility, which the Quranic account holds up as exemplary for all of their children. Iblīs himself refers to the root cause of this difference in his justification for not bowing down to Adam: "I am better than him. You created me of fire, and You created him of clay" (Q 7:12). As Murata points out, the attributes of earth are lowly, heavy, dark, and ignorant—far removed from the light of the intellect and spirit.[28] As a creature of fire, considered in-between the light of the heavens and the darkness of the earth, Iblīs rightly judged himself as being closer to spiritual realities than clay was. However, fiery nature is such that it is "the form of elemental disequilibrium ... [it] rises up against that which is entified within it. It oversteps its bounds and conceals [*kufr*] it."[29] Since Iblīs is made of fire, he is rebellious by nature. Made of a lower substance, however, Adam and Eve were more receptive to servitude of everything other than God (*mā siwā Allāh*) to God.

Iblīs had "one squint eye" since, like the angels, he did not grasp that the clay of human beings was mixed with the spirit of God.[30] Despite the lowliness of earth, God paid it several honors when He desired to use it mold Adam's body. Rāzī describes some of these in memorable detail:

> The first honor that was bestowed upon the earth was that it was called to God's Presence by several messengers, but it pretended not to care. It said: "We know nothing of the mystery of these words" ... In this state, all the angels were biting the fingers of wonder with the teeth of astonishment: "What kind of mystery is this? Lowly earth has been summoned to the Presence of Inaccessibility with all this honor. In spite of its perfect lowliness and despicableness, the earth keeps on pretending not to care and makes itself unapproachable. Nevertheless, the Presence of Independence, Utter Freedom, and Perfect Jealousy does not leave it."[31]

---

27 This translation of Q 7:23 was undertaken in consultation with Murata, *The Tao of Islam* 275.

28 Murata, *The Tao of Islam* 17.

29 Murata, *The Tao of Islam* 96.

30 Murata, *The Tao of Islam* 42.

31 Murata, *The Tao of Islam* 41.

The reason for the respect that is bestowed towards the earth is made clear when God decides to blow His own spirit into Adam's body.[32] Rāzī again vividly describes the result of this act:

> … this world, the next world, and everything within them are but a microcosm in relation to the infinitude of the World of the Spirit. So look what honors he was given! When the two—spirit and frame—are brought together in a special order, they move on to their own perfection. Who knows what felicity and good fortune will be showered down upon their head? Wretched is the person who is deprived of his own perfection and looks down upon himself with the eye of disdain.[33]

In the quote above, he references the microcosm and its relation to "this world" and the next. The two chief characteristics Murata seeks to highlight in her selection of quotes is the opposition between the earth with which Adam's body was created and the spirit, transcending the cosmos entirely and belonging to God himself, that was blown into him. The on-lookers of these strange events are the angels and Iblīs, who was made of fire and elevated to the ranks of the angels, who were made of light.[34] All of these high beings are thrown into bewilderment by the care and attention God gives to the creation of this mysterious creature, recognizing that they are in some respects higher than Adam and in others, lower. This composition of dualities exemplified by Adam, spanning the whole range of reality, is an ideal object of study for Murata's approach throughout this book, since she is constantly seeking to highlight the different relations in which a single thing can be seen.

But after all this pomp and ceremony, Adam falls from the Garden in which God places him at the hands of his declared enemy. Turning to Q 7:20, we see Satan tempting Adam and Eve with immortality but this time, the Quranic account adds an important detail: "Your Lord has prohibited you from this tree lest you become two angels, or lest you become immortals."[35] We have already seen one kind of deceit when Satan tempted Adam and Eve with an everlasting abode outside of the Garden, but the reference to becoming angels adds another kind of deception which will be instructive to investigate in light of the above quotes from the Islamic sapiential tradition. Despite having been in-blown with God's own spirit, Adam and Eve also partake of an

32 Q 15:29.
33 Murata, *The Tao of Islam* 43.
34 Murata, *The Tao of Islam* 42.
35 This translation of Q 7:20 is taken from Murata, *The Tao of Islam* 275.

earthly, clayish nature. The spirit shares certain similarities with the light from which angels were created but nevertheless, the first two human beings are not purely spiritual beings like angels.[36] In this way, we see how Satan's words are again deceptive: the human being is a compound reality and occupies a special position in the cosmos because of this, but Iblīs attempts to make Adam forgetful of his own nature.

Adam falls to the earth, driven down to the "lowest of the low" seemingly by his own actions, which makes him end up exactly where God promised the angels He would place him.[37] "Surely I am placing in the earth a vicegerent" (Q 2:30). The manner of this fall provides the Islamic sapiential tradition with much to reflect upon. Aḥmad Samʿānī captures the tension between the plan of God and the free will of Adam that placed him on the earth:

> O tree, put up your head next to Adam's throne! O appetite for the fruit, enter into Adam's heart! O accursed one, let loose the reins of your whispering! O Eve, you show the way! O Adam, don't eat the fruit, have self-restraint! O self-restraint, don't come near Adam! O God, God, what is all this? "We want to bring Adam down from the throne of indifference to the earth of need."[38]

This passage highlights a couple of different instances of duality that will serve as useful points of investigation for this paper. Firstly, there is the tension between what Samʿānī terms as "God's command" or religious injunction and "God's decree" which determines what will actually occur. In this case, God's command and His decree were different, which brings up a conflict between determinism and free will.[39] In this passage in particular, Samʿānī depicts the decree as overtaking even the inner faculties of Adam, such as appetite and self-restraint. These statements, such as the ones ordering the tree, Eve, self-restraint, appetite can be taken to refer to the decree, while the one ordering Adam to not eat from the tree belong to the command. Secondly, the last statement of this passage highlights the duality between the bliss of Paradise where Adam and Eve can eat and drink as they please with no commands other than "Don't approach the tree!" and the abode of the command and prescription

---

36 Murata, *The Tao of Islam* 235.

37 Q 95:4–5; Murata, *The Tao of Islam* 42.

38 Murata, *The Tao of Islam* 35.

39 Chittick, William C., *Divine love: Islamic literature and the path to God*, New Haven: Yale University Press, 2013, 88–89.

(*taklīf*) that is the earth.[40] Samʿānī here is implicitly suggesting that God's plan from the beginning was to place Adam in the abode of *taklīf*, a theme that he expands on later, while explaining the importance of and need for the Fall to happen in the way that it did.

"Dear friend, Adam had still not eaten the wheat when they sewed the hat of his election. Iblis had still not rebelled when they moistened the arrow of the curse with the poison of severity."[41] In this passage, we see Samʿānī again emphasizing the perspective of the decree in the actions of Iblīs and Adam, but with the added element of another important polar duality: the "election" of Adam representing God's mercy towards him and the severity of God towards Iblīs, who is outwardly a manifestation of His wrath. When considered in light of the schema of God's Essence, attributes, and acts, this passage is saying something quite remarkable. We saw the mercy-wrath polar opposition in the list of the names of God's acts, which are how God relates to creatures such as Adam and Iblīs. However, the perspective Samʿānī is adopting in this particular passage can be read as preceding even the creation of Adam and Iblīs, and certainly preceding the actions of these two characters of this important myth. Indeed, the decree is "pre-eternal" or *azalī*.[42] God's acts are manifested temporally and with relation to creatures, but here Samʿānī is pointing out that the roots of all the acts are always present in God, which is to say, these acts are outside of time. Therefore, from the perspective of the decree, Adam's eating from the tree, being thrown out of Paradise, Iblīs' whispering, disobedience, arrogance had already happened with respect to God. From this standpoint, Adam's being sent to earth and Iblīs becoming a satan are not responses to their respective actions. They, like everything else in the cosmos from the greatest archangel in the celestial regions to the lowliest ant crawling in a dark subterranean cave, are playing their appointed parts. With relations to the acts, the mercy and wrath being manifested with respect to Adam and Iblīs originate in the Mercy (*raḥma* or *al-raḥmān*) that alone characterizes God's very Self. The acts that come forth from God (whether conceived temporally or not) do so in accordance with God's essentially merciful nature. Therefore, even

40 For the command, see Q 2:35 and for "the command and prescription," see Chittick, *Divine love* 94.

41 Chittick, *Divine love* 84.

42 Chittick, *Divine love* 32. The following quote is from the same page: "In other words, all beings have been decreed. God is saying: Whatever is be-able has come to be, whatever is doable I have done, whatever is runable I have run, whatever is choosable I have chosen, whatever is acceptable I have accepted, whatever is liftable I have lifted, whatever is throwable I have thrown."

the seeming wrath that is displayed in the case of Iblīs and Adam *is* merciful at its root, since mercy "permeates all things."[43] When combining these two perspectives—that of the pre-eternality of everything that pertains to God and His Essential Mercy—we see that the events of the Fall inescapably occurred as a manifestation of God's Mercy towards all His creatures.[44]

It is only because Adam sought God's mercy and forgiveness when confronted with His wrath that he was able to see the mercy in God's actions. This attitude stands in stark contrast to Iblīs' response who arrogantly asserted that God made him disobey and was consequently only able to see the wrath, a characteristic that only appears in relation to the illusory cosmos. God took a special interest in Adam, precisely because of his knowledge of and response to the distinction between these levels. Even though we can say that mercy is present in the things that happened to both Adam and Iblīs, Adam clearly has a special mercy and status accorded to him from the very beginning—the sewing-on of the "hat of election." The first human being received this honor because he displayed courtesy (*adab*) from the very beginning, as we have already seen in the verse where Adam and Eve ask for forgiveness from God. Unlike Iblīs who blames God for his mistake since he realizes that what occurred with him was always meant to be, Adam honors the fact that even though it was because of God's pre-eternal decree that he slipped, he himself still listened to the enemy he was warned against and ate from the tree that led to his downfall.

5 The Priority of Earth Over Heaven: God's Seeking of Adam

Much of Murata's argument in this book—whether in discussing gender relationships or proper human behavior—is about the need to observe the distinction between levels.[45] Moreover, she argues that the existence of these levels is an essential feature of reality since higher levels are in need of lower levels to manifest themselves. Since this book is about the ontological roots of gender

43 Murata, *The Tao of Islam* 55.

44 "As for the prophetic sayings that both of God's hands are right and blessed, this is true out of courtesy [*adab*]. It is also true when we verify the matter in respect of the attribution of two hands to Him, though not in respect of their effect in that which comes into existence through them." In this quote from Murata, *The Tao of Islam* 84, al-Qūnawī is explaining philosophically the issues that lie behind Samʿānī's statement above. God is essentially merciful, but His acts (represented by His hands) are differentiated in the cosmos with respect to mercy and wrath. Samʿānī is combining these two perspectives in the quote, whereas al-Qūnawī is drawing a distinction between various levels.

45 Murata, *The Tao of Islam* 57–58.

relationships, it is interesting to look at the issue of higher and lower levels in terms of the degree men have over women.[46] In the following quote, Ibn ʿArabī is discussing a verse which God sends down regarding a disagreement between the Prophet and two of his wives, which he sees as

> indicat[ing] the strength singled out for the woman in His words concerning ʿĀʾisha and Hafṣa: "If you two support one another against him, God is his protector, and Gabriel, and the righteous amongst the faithful; and, after that, the angels are his supporters" [66:4]. All of this in order to vie in strength with two women! And here God mentions only the strong, those who possess power and strength![47]

And why is it necessary that God's final messenger need all this help? Ibn ʿArabī tells us that

> There is nothing in the created world greater in strength than woman, because of a mystery known only by those who know that within which the cosmos came into existence, by what movement the Real brought it into existence, and the fact that it comes from two premises. For the cosmos is a result. The one who takes into marriage [*nākiḥ*] is a seeker, and a seeker is poor and needy. The one who is taken in marriage is [*mankūḥ*] is the sought, and the sought has the mightiness of being the object of need. And appetite predominates. Thus has been made clear to you the place of woman among the existent things, what it is in the Divine Presence that looks upon her, and why it is that she manifests strength.[48]

The above quotes epitomize Murata's argument in several ways. Firstly, there is a qualitative, cosmological, and even meta-cosmological analogy between creation and women. The author, one of the greatest (according to some, *the* greatest) spokesman of the tradition, is telling us that God seeks the cosmos just as men seek women for marriage. He comes to the latter conclusion about the relationship between men and women *because* "men have a degree over women." And the presence of such a dynamic in Islamic thought is exactly why Murata adopts a Chinese hermeneutic in this book, since this way of thinking tells us that anything that is high is considered "heaven" and anything that is

46 Murata, *The Tao of Islam* 173. See also Q 2:228.
47 Murata, *The Tao of Islam* 177.
48 Murata, *The Tao of Islam* 177.

low is considered "earth." A single reality may be "heaven" from one perspective and "earth" from another. The most important thing to keep in mind when analyzing anything is one's standpoint, since one thing will always be above and active and the other below and receptive. Moreover, what is above only exists in its relation to the receptivity of what is below: "If earth is prior to heaven in a certain respect—even one can say, 'above' heaven—this simply means that the sufficient reason for the existence of heaven is bestow upon the earth."[49] Murata's point here is that heaven, or anything defined in terms of its activity, is in need to something to receive its activity, and so the existence of something active is only possible if there is something to receive its activity, hence the priority of earth over heaven. Similarly, the cosmos is receptive to God's creative self-disclosure and is an "earth," and this is why it is sought. Ibn ʿArabī uses the analogy of God's relation to the cosmos to describe men's relationship to women and concludes that the receptivity women have in relation to men gives them "the mightiness of being the object of need."[50]

Discussing Adam's disobedience in terms of God's "need" to manifest His attributes may seem counter-intuitive but it was a natural—and very important—move for the Islamic tradition and helps illuminate a key aspect of Murata's use of Chinese hermeneutics. The Quran tells us that Adam was taught all the names.[51] One interpretation of this verse is that he was taught all the names of God, which define the very nature of reality.[52] When the angels were asked if they knew what Adam knew, they admitted their ignorance.[53] In light of these verses and highlighting the priority of what is below to what is above, we can analyze a strange-seeming *ḥadīth*: "If you did not sin, God would bring a people who did sin, and then He would forgive them."[54] In the discussion where he quotes this saying, Maybudī tells us, speaking for God, that: "The

49 Murata, *The Tao of Islam* 13.

50 As implied earlier, relationships are only possible with regards to entities (*aʿyān*) or things (*ashyāʾ*). In respect of His names, God is delimited (because He is "God" and not a "vassal") and in this way, He is able to assume relationships with creatures. The Essence, however, is non-entified (*lā taʿayyun*) and therefore, does not assume relationships with the cosmos, or rather, any relationship can be ascribed to it without It being limited by any single one. This dual way of considering the nature of God allows for God to remain utterly independent of the cosmos, while respecting the divine freedom to choose relationality and limitation. The reason for the latter lies in the former: God is "so free of limitations that we cannot limit it by saying that it is free of limitations." See Murata, *The Tao of Islam* 93.

51 Q 2:31.

52 Murata, *The Tao of Islam* 36.

53 Q 2:32.

54 Chittick, *Divine love* 79–80.

treasury of My mercy is full. If no one is disobedient, it will go to waste."[55] In this same vein, Samʿānī suggests that God wasn't happy with only angels to worship Him: "Before Adam was brought into existence, there was a world of full of existent things, creatures, formed things, determined things—all of it a tasteless stew. The salt of pain was missing."[56] God's mercy, which includes forgiveness, is one of His most important attributes and can even be used to describe His reality in Himself.[57] As Maybudī and Samʿānī explain to us, with the creation of Adam, God was able to display His essential attribute. Furthermore, this self-disclosure had precisely to do with Adam and Eve's repentance (*tawba*): because they admitted their fault, God describes Himself as merciful and one who accepts *tawba*.[58] The use of this description illustrates the larger point suggested by the *ḥadīth*: mercy is only ever displayed in response to evil. Angels cannot sin and therefore, are barred from experiencing the mercy and forgiveness essential to God. In disobeying God's command, Adam and Eve demonstrate their unique status among creation as bringing into actuality the precondition necessary for displaying the reality of the essential divine mercy.

6 Loving to Recognize

The Islamic sapiential tradition suggests that Adam's sin was motivated out of passionate love for God.

> Be careful not to think that Adam was taken out of paradise because of his lowliness. It was not that. Rather, it was because of the grandeur of his aspiration. The petitioner of passion came to the door of Adam's breast and said, "O Adam, the beauty of meaning has been unveiled, but you have stayed in the abode of peace." Adam saw an infinite beauty, next to which the beauty of the eight paradises was nothing.[59]

To understand this perspective, let us review some of what our sources have told us. Rāzī, on the basis of the Quranic account, reminds us that God blew of

55 Chittick, *Divine love* 79–80.
56 Chittick, *Divine love* 65.
57 Murata, *The Tao of Islam* 55. See also Murata, *The Tao of Islam* 206–208, 324 for the discussion of the divine feminine and the mercy of existence. For the relation between the womb and mercy, see Murata, *The Tao of Islam* 188.
58 Q 2:37.
59 Chittick, *Divine love* 86.

His own spirit into the frame of Adam, which was molded with special attention. This image is a very intimate one and suggests that the first thing Adam saw or was conscious of was the reality of God. Even if some of His names "stress greatness, power, control, and masculinity," the Quran tells us that all of God's names and therefore, His reality is beautiful.[60] And being that this beauty belongs to God, it is infinite and superlative. After witnessing this, Adam is placed in the Garden, which while beautiful, did not hold a candle to the beauty of God, and he is understandably distressed and decides to remedy the situation.

> His great aspiration tightened its belt and said: "If you ever want to fall in love, you must fall in love with that …" The command came: "Adam, now that you have stepped into the lane of passion, leave paradise, for it is the house of ease. What do the passionate have to do with the safety of the Abode of Peace?"[61]

The last quote points out some characteristics of the nature of the Abode of Peace in which Adam was placed that prevented him from fully recognizing (*maʿrifa*) the reality of God.

God is often discussed as a "Hidden Treasure" on the basis of a *ḥadīth qudsī* where He tells the prophet David that He created creation because He "loved to be known/recognized."[62] In creating the cosmos, God becomes manifest, and many authors, including Samʿānī, from the tradition describe this process of manifestation in terms of complementary names:

> O dervish! He has a gentleness and a severity to perfection, a majesty and a beauty to perfection. He wanted to distribute these treasures. On one person's head He placed the crown of gentleness in the garden of bounty. On another person's liver He placed the brand of severity in the prison of justice. He melts one in the fire of majesty. He caresses another in the light of beauty.[63]

---

60 For wrathful names, see Murata, *The Tao of Islam* 9. For "most beautiful names," see Q 17:110.

61 Chittick, *Divine love* 86.

62 A *ḥadīth qudsī* is a statement made by the Prophet speaking on behalf of God. For this particular *ḥadīth qudsī* see Murata, *The Tao of Islam* 61.

63 Murata, *The Tao of Islam* 61–62.

This quote, especially in its allusion to a garden of bounty, makes it clear why Adam was unsatisfied with the Garden or Paradise in which he was placed: he only experienced what Murata refers to as the yin names.[64] Adam could not see the display of the yang names, such as being imprisoned by justice or being burnt by the fire of majesty, outside of himself. It also explains why he needed to brace himself by tightening the belt of aspiration: he was leaving an abode dominated by gentleness and ease in order to experience the burning pain of passion. This love was for the sake of knowing or recognizing God in His fullness, and it is precisely the reason God created Adam: He knew that this creature would be unsatisfied with the Garden.

Moreover, God created Adam in such a way that he could only be fully himself—fully human—by recognizing the fullness of the Hidden Treasure. The cosmos in its differentiated expanse displays the entirety of the names of God, and the human being, or the microcosm, mirrors the macrocosm by containing within itself all of these names in an undifferentiated mode.[65] The macrocosm contains parts which individually display various attributes of God, but the human being alone is able to bring all of these attributes together in a single reality, potentially becoming a mirror in which God is able to contemplate himself. This potentiality becomes actual when man has recognition (*maʿrifa*) of what he really is: He who recognizes (*ʿarafa*) himself recognizes (*ʿarafa*) His Lord. This adds another dimension to Maybudī's explanation of why Adam was unsatisfied in Paradise: he could not fully be himself there. "The command came: 'The veiled virgin of recognition [*maʿrifa*] wants a mate to be her fiancé.' They sifted the eighteen thousand worlds in looking for a mate without finding one, for the majestic Quran gives news that '*Nothing is as His likeness*' [42:11]."[66] The scriptural proof given here is fascinating and is a reference to the alleged *ḥadīth* about *maʿrifa* above. God has no likeness in all the worlds, but Adam brought all the divine attributes together. As Samʿānī continues, he makes it clear that the human being's "worthiness for union"[67] with God comes from God Himself. He tells us that the rationale that threw the angels, the Throne, the heavens, and Paradise itself out of consideration was the fact that they are already exalted entities[68] and God wanted it to be known that the desire for union comes from Himself, not from the worth of anything else. For this reason, "thrown-down

64 Murata, *The Tao of Islam* 56.
65 Murata, *The Tao of Islam* 34.
66 Chittick, *Divine love* 86.
67 Chittick, *Divine love* 86.
68 Chittick, *Divine love* 86.

dust" which is the lowliest thing in the cosmos—in one respect—was the perfect candidate. God "fired one arrow of eminence from the bow of election" at "Adam's makeup."[69] What was this "arrow" in scriptural terms? It is the "Attributed Spirit" (*al-rūḥ al-iḍāfī*)[70] that God blew into Adam from His own spirit.[71] Notice that before this in-blowing of the spirit into Adam, he was dead and only came to life through God's own breath. His essential reality comes from God's own, and his outward, earthly reality can add no illusion of eminence precisely because it is so low, heavy, and dark. The only thing that it can do is obscure the greatness of what is hidden, even from Adam himself.

And that is exactly what happened in the Garden: Adam "forgot."[72] Even if the authors we have been considering so far have told us that he ate the fruit out of love for God and that this was destined, he still disobeyed God's command. Both he and Eve realized that they had transgressed as soon as they had done the deed and asked for forgiveness. But in light of the more fundamental reality of the human being we have been considering, this sin takes on a different dimension. From our current standpoint, we can say that Adam forgot not merely the shariʿite command but his inner reality which was created in God's image. *Maʿrifa*, as we saw, refers to the recognition of one's own self as having been created in the image of God, which is to say that it is inward looking. Satan pointed to the tree *outside* of Adam and Eve as something that could satisfy their yearning for God and the two of them believed him. That was the real nature of the sin of forgetfulness and is the essential reality of all human disobedience. Adam and Eve were in the abode of peace, of not recognizing God, of distance (*tanzīh*) in the midst of mercy, and they wanted *maʿrifa* of God in Himself, merciful *and* wrathful attributes. In this sense, Iblīs' deception was not that he was luring Adam and Eve out of the Garden unawares in that they did not recognize that he was pointing them towards wrath and disobedience through a tree that symbolized the Fire. Rather, they saw this tree as a seed of wrath in the Garden and approached it but didn't realize that they should not be looking outwards. Once their mistake became clear to them, they asked for forgiveness, and *they were not punished*. In fact, they got what their "great aspiration" had desired in the first place: "a land of exile"[73] where they and their children could take up the path of finding God. You can only find something when you acknowledge that it is lost, and Samʿānī makes it clear that

69 Chittick, *Divine love* 87.
70 Murata, *The Tao of Islam* 212.
71 See note 35.
72 Q 20:115.
73 Chittick, *Divine love* 87.

the gentleness of Paradise was not helping: “A roasted heart will never be content with roast chicken.”[74]

7 Finding the Center: The Earth of *taklīf*

This brings us to the issue of *taklīf* or “prescription.” Earth, as opposed to Heaven, is dominated by prescription because it is the domain of human beings, who are characterized by free will and therefore, need to distinguish between right and wrong. So fundamental is this aspect of human beings that the first humans—Adam and Eve—were given shariʿite commands even in the Garden. While from the perspective of the command they may have disobeyed, from the perspective of the decree, they inescapably acted in the way that God knew was appropriate to their realities: they disobeyed. “We did not find in him [Adam] any constancy” (Q 20:115). On one level, this verse refers to the fact that Adam disobeyed. On another level, it can be taken as expressing a fundamental human reality: they are defined by their potentiality, hence their lack of constancy. The earlier part of this *āya* from the Quran refers to the “covenant of Alast” that God took from the human race when He asked: “Am I not (*alastu*) your Lord?” The children of Adam all replied that they bore witness that He was their Lord.[75] Even though they all agreed that God was their Lord, this world is a place of trial and forgetfulness and God wanted to separate out those who do good, those who don't, and those who remember the covenant by recognizing themselves and their Lord.[76] Therefore, their lack of constancy also gives human beings their ability to distinguish themselves and remember their true natures, which they can only do in the abode of prescription or earth. The Quran describes these three ends by referring to the “people of the right hand” or those going to Paradise, “people of the left” or those going to Hell, and “the outstrippers,” who in this context can be taken as those who have recognized their Lord.[77] But it is important to note that only on earth do human beings have the chance to show their differentiation in this way. In Paradise, they would not have had that option. Their final end would have already been chosen for them, and more importantly, God's desire to be recognized could not have been achieved. This is why He chose Adam: He “found in him no constancy” because

74 Chittick, *Divine love* 72.

75 Q 7:172.

76 For discussion of the various kinds of aspiration that inspired these categories, see Chittick, *Divine love* 178–179, 221–225.

77 Q 56:8–10.

he was tossed about by his burning love of his passion to recognize God.[78] And the first human being lived up to what was asked of him. Adam left Paradise so he could take on the work of recognizing God and achieve the goal of his great love and passion—and give his children that same potential. I will end this paper by stressing the importance of the earth which can lead to the yin of the felicity of Paradise and the yang of the wretchedness of Hell—or the Tao of what is beyond the two of them: love for recognizing the Real.

> Were there no earth, the breast would have no burning! Were there no earth, religion would have no sorrow or joy! Were there no earth, love's fire would not flame up! Were there no earth, who would smell the scent of beginningless love? Were there no earth, who would become the familiar of the Eternal Beloved? Dervish, Iblis's curse marks the perfection of the majesty of earth. Seraphiel's trumpet was prepared for the sake of the yearning of earth ... Riḍwān[79] with all the slaves and serving boys is but earth under the feet of earth ... The pure, incomparable Essence is witnessed by the hearts of earth.[80]

8 Conclusion

The *ḥadīth* of the Hidden Treasure tells us that God created creation because He loved to be recognized. As we saw earlier, the human being is the creature singled out for this purpose. It is the contention of this paper, therefore, that the myth of human origins reflects this desire. The methodology inspired by Murata's pioneering work *The Tao of Islam*, allows us to locate areas of polar opposition, contradiction and tension in order to fully flesh out the richness of this myth. The human being is precisely an indefinite creature, tossed between extremes: he has free will to obey the divine command a certain extent but is constantly running up against the immutability of the divine decree. He has a spirit which transcends the cosmos but is confined by a body made of the lowest and darkest thing in creation. Adam disobeyed by eating from the tree,

78 See Chittick, *Divine love* 92: "He made everyone drunk with the wine of *Am I not your Lord?* [7:172] ... He sent these drunkards into this world of ups and downs ... There is a lame mosquito missing a wing, a leg, and eye, the other eye shut. They throw it into an ocean of fire or an ocean of water. The address comes, 'Hey you, don't burn your wings, don't get wet!'
The king said to me, 'Drink wine, but don't get drunk!'
O king, everyone who drinks wine gets drunk."

79 Riḍwān is the angel who presides over the doors of Paradise.

80 Murata, *The Tao of Islam* 141.

but this was not counted against him. After all, his substance is such that it is "wrongdoing, ignorant;" he was expected to fall short. And indeed, the divine decree was such that he *did* fall short. The clash between determinism and free will, between divine spirit and human body, between severity and gentleness was never about a single act of obedience or disobedience.

The dichotomies discussed in this paper tell us that Adam's action was never what God was looking at because He knew how things would turn out. Rather, He was looking at Adam's nature: he forgot his own nature, sinned, and then asked for forgiveness. Focusing on polar opposites which resolve into a unity shows us that these various acts were motivated by Adam's love to recognize God in himself, which mirrors God's own love for creating Adam. The first human being showed his true colors in all of these deeds and was rewarded with an abode worthy of his "great love:" an earth of *taklīf* where he and his children are placed in the center, between mercy and wrath, Paradise and Hell, and free will and determinism. The children of Adam can choose to go in any direction, but they only truly learn from the story of their father when they cease being distracted by peripheral phenomena and cultivate their recognition of their Beloved.

Bibliography

Baynes, Cary F. and Richard Wilhelm (trans.), *The* I Ching *or* Book of changes, Princeton: Princeton University Press, 1983.

Chittick, William C., *The self-disclosure of God: Principles of Ibn al-ʿArabī's cosmology*, Albany, NY: SUNY Press, 1998.

Chittick, William C., *Divine love: Islamic literature and the path to God*, New Haven: Yale University Press, 2013.

Elias, Jamal J., "Review of *The Tao of Islam: A sourcebook on gender relationships in Islamic thought*," in *IrS* 28.1–2 (1995), 94–96.

Ernst, Carl W., "Review of *The Tao of Islam: A sourcebook on gender relationships in Islamic thought*," in *JAOS* 114.4 (1994), 677–678.

Murata, Sachiko, *The Tao of Islam: A sourcebook on gender relationships in Islamic thought*, Albany, NY: SUNY Press, 1992.

CHAPTER 24

A Supplication for God's Mercy on the Day of ʿArafa by the Fatimid Chief *Dāʿī* al-Muʾayyad al-Shīrāzī

Tahera Qutbuddin

> Pilgrims stand up to supplicate you in this hour at ʿArafāt. They have congregated to your door from every deep valley, speaking different languages and with different forms and ways, covered in dust and earth as though resurrected on judgment day, wrapped in white sheets as though wearing the shrouds of the people of the grave. They pray to you, O lord of the worlds, in fear and in hope, for earthly desires and religious aspirations. They beseech your mercy, O most merciful lord. God, we too are your servants! Even though we are absent from that holy place in body, yet we are present there in soul and faith. God, shower blessings on Muhammad and his descendants, and regard us with the same merciful gaze with which you regard your chosen ones who are present in that holy place.
>
> Excerpt from AL-MUʾAYYAD AL-SHĪRĀZĪ's ʿArafa supplication

∴

After a few lines of reverent address to the Almighty, so begins the impassioned supplication of the Fatimid Chief *Dāʿī* al-Muʾayyad al-Shīrāzī (d. 470/1078) on the day of ʿArafa (also: ʿArafāt). ʿArafa, 9 Dhū l-Ḥijja, is the most important day of the *ḥajj* pilgrimage just before the Great Eid, a day of repentance and renewal when pilgrims stand from morning to night in supplication on Mount ʿArafāt near Mecca, entreating God's forgiveness and mercy.[1] Muʾayyad's ʿArafa supplication comes within a tradition of devotional and literary supplication. Two lines of ʿArafa prayer are attributed to the Prophet Muhammad

1 For more on the *ḥajj* and the standing at ʿArafāt, see Tagliacozzo, Eric and Shawkat M. Toorawa (eds.), *The* hajj*: Pilgrimage in Islam*, New York: Cambridge University Press, 2016; Wensinck, Arent J., Jacques Jomier and Bernard Lewis, "Ḥadjdj," in *EI*[2]; Rubin, Uri, "ʿArafāt," in *EI*[3].

 | DOI:10.1163/9789004529038_025

(d. 11/632) himself,[2] but perhaps the earliest long supplication is attributed to the Prophet's grandson Imam al-Ḥusayn b. ʿAlī (d. 61/680), followed by the equally famous supplication by al-Ḥusayn's son and successor, Imam ʿAlī Zayn al-ʿĀbidīn, also known as al-Imām al-Sajjād (d. 95/714). Professor William Chittick has translated both these supplications with his characteristic flair, the first in ʿAllāma Ṭabāṭabāʾī's *A Shiʿite anthology*, and the second within *The psalms of Islam*, Chittick's translation of Zayn al-ʿĀbidīn's compiled supplications titled *al-Ṣaḥīfa al-Sajjādiyya*.[3] In the present article for Chittick and Murata's *Fests-*

2 "The best supplication is made on the Day of ʿArafa, and the best invocation that I and the Prophets before me have made is, 'There is no god but God. He is one, and has no partner'" (Mālik b. Anas, *al-Muwaṭṭaʾ*, ed. Muḥammad Fuʾād ʿAbd al-Bāqī, 2 vols., i, Cairo: Dār Iḥyāʾ al-Turāth al-ʿArabī, 1985, 215, part 15: *Qurʾān*, ch. 8: *Duʿāʾ*, *ḥadīth* #32). The prophet is also said to have declared that "The most sinful pilgrim on ʿArafāt is the man who leaves thinking he has not been forgiven" (al-Qāḍī al-Nuʿmān, *The pillars of Islam*, trans. Asaf A.A. Fyzee, rev. Ismail K. Poonawala, i, New Delhi: Oxford University Press, 2002, 320), and in this compendium, which is the major Fatimid legal compendium, it is narrated on the authority of the Family of the Prophet that no particular prayer is mandated for ʿArafa, but the pilgrim should "supplicate abundantly and ask God for his favors in this world and the next" (al-Qāḍī al-Nuʿmān, *The pillars* i, 320).

3 Al-Ḥusayn b. ʿAlī, "Duʿāʾ al-Ḥusayn yawm ʿArafa," in al-Qummī, ʿAbbās, *Mafātīḥ al-jinān*, Kuwait: Maktabat al-Faqīh, 2004, 363–379; trans. Chittick as "Prayer for the Day of ʿArafa," in Ṭabāṭabāʾī, Muḥammad Ḥusayn, *A Shiʿite anthology*, trans. William C. Chittick, Albany, NY: SUNY Press, 1981, 93–112. Chittick also mentioned this supplication in his very first English article, "A Shādhilī presence in Shiʿite Islam," in *Sophia Perennis* 1.1 (1975), 97–100; repr. in Chittick, William C., *In search of the lost heart: Explorations in Islamic thought*, ed. Mohammed Rustom, Atif Khalil, and Kazuyo Murata, Albany, NY: SUNY Press, 2012, 39–42. Zayn al-ʿĀbidīn, ʿAlī b. al-Ḥusayn al-Sajjād, *al-Ṣaḥīfa al-Sajjādiyya al-kāmila*, Beirut: Muʾassasat al-Aʿlamī, 1992, 207–229; trans. Chittick as "His supplication on the Day of ʿArafa," in Zayn al-ʿĀbidīn, ʿAlī b. al-Ḥusayn al-Sajjād, *The psalms of Islam*, trans. William C. Chittick, London: Muhammadi Trust, 1988, 339–362. These two supplications are recited by the Shiʿa annually on ʿArafa day. Zayn al-ʿĀbidīn's supplications also include lengthy prayers in times of human need, such as his prayer for rain during drought, or more generally to praise God and ask for forgiveness of sins. See also further supplications by the Prophet Muhammad in al-Quḍāʿī, al-Qāḍī Muḥammad b. Salāma, *Light in the heavens: Sayings of the Prophet Muḥammad*, ed. and trans. Tahera Qutbuddin, New York: New York University Press, 2016, 170–173 (ch. 17: Final chapter containing the Prophet's supplications). See also supplications by Imam ʿAlī (d. 40/661) in al-Quḍāʿī, al-Qāḍī Muḥammad b. Salāma, *A treasury of virtues: Sayings, sermons and teachings of ʿAlī*, ed. and trans. Tahera Qutbuddin, New York: New York University Press, 2013, 176–197 (ch. 8: Prayers and supplications); and Chittick's translation of ʿAlī's supplications in ʿAlī b. Abī Ṭālib, *Supplications (duʿāʾ)*, trans. William C. Chittick, London: Muhammadi Trust, 1982, *passim*. The Quran itself contains several short supplications to God made by prophets and believers. In the Fatimid tradition, the Imam-Caliph al-Muʿizz (r. 341–365/953–975) also composed lengthy supplications. See one such supplication by al-Muʿizz in Guyard, M. Stanislas, *Fragments relatifs à la doctrine des Ismāʿīlīs*, Paris: Imprimerie nationale, 1874, 48–53, 168–182; Massignon, Louis, *Recueil de textes inédits concernant l'histoire de la mystique en pays*

chrift, I am pleased to offer the text, translation, contextualization, and commentary of another exquisite gem from the treasury of *ḥajj* supplications—the ʿArafa supplication by al-Muʾayyad al-Shīrāzī.

∴

1 The Fatimids, al-Muʾayyad al-Shīrāzī, and His Supplications

The Fatimids were an Ismaʿili Shiʿa dynasty who ruled a large part of the Muslim world from the 4th/10th through 6th/12th centuries, with their caliphal seat first in North Africa and then Egypt.[4] They claimed descent from the Prophet Muhammad through his daughter Fāṭima Zahrāʾ and her husband ʿAlī b. Abī Ṭālib, hence their dynastic title. Challenging the ʿAbbasids of Baghdad, they also claimed to be the sole rightful Caliphs and Imams of the Muslim community, who had inherited Muhammad's temporal and spiritual authority. They referred to their religio-political mission as the *daʿwa* (lit. call or invitation), referring to the Quranic verse, "The true *daʿwa* belongs to God" (*lahū daʿwat al-ḥaqq*; Q 13:14). Their *daʿwa* was conducted by the Imam as the highest authority, and under his spiritual aegis, by agents of his *daʿwa*, each called a *dāʿī*.

Al-Muʾayyad al-Shīrāzī was chief *dāʿī* and "chief gate" under the Fatimid Imam-Caliph al-Mustanṣir (r. 427–487/1036–1094).[5] He was born in Shiraz,

---

d'Islam, Paris: Geuthner, 1929, 217. For more on the genre of supplication in Islam, see Padwick, Constance E., *Muslim devotions: A Study of prayer-manuals in common use*, London: SPCK, 1961; Gardet, L., "Duʿāʾ," in *EI*²; Katz, Marion H., *Prayer in Islamic thought and practice*, Cambridge: Cambridge University Press, 2013, 29–43; Ali, Mukhtar H., "The power of the spoken word: Prayer, invocation, and supplication in Islam," in David McPherson (ed.), *Spirituality and the good life: Philosophical approaches*, Cambridge: Cambridge University Press, 2017, 136–154.

4 On Fatimid history, see Walker, Paul E., *Exploring an Islamic empire: Fatimid history and its sources*, London: I.B. Tauris, 2002; Halm, Heinz, *The empire of the Mahdi: The rise of the Fatimids*, trans. Michael Bonner, Leiden: Brill, 1996; Daftary, Farhad, *The Ismaʿilis: Their history and doctrines*, Cambridge: Cambridge University Press, 2007; Brett, Michael, *The Fatimid Empire*, Edinburgh: Edinburgh University Press, 2017; and Jiwa, Shainool, *The Fatimids*. I. *The rise of a Muslim empire*, London: I.B. Tauris, 2018. For a summary of their philosophy, see Walker, Paul E., "The Ismāʿīlīs," in Peter Adamson and Richard Taylor (eds.), *The Cambridge companion to Arabic philosophy*, Cambridge: Cambridge University Press, 2005, 72–91. On their civilizational contributions, see Qutbuddin, Tahera, "Fatimids," in Edward Ramsamy (ed.), *Cultural sociology of the Middle East, Asia, and Africa*, ii, Thousand Oaks, CA: Sage, 2011, 37–40.

5 "Chief gate" (*bāb al-abwāb*) was the highest rank following the Imam in the Fatimid spiritual hierarchy. For al-Muʾayyad's biography, see Qutbuddin, Tahera, "al-Muʾayyad al-Shīrāzī,"

where he lived till the age of fifty and served as *Dāʿī* of Fars, then he migrated to Cairo, where he spent the rest of his life in the direct service of his Imam. Muʾayyad's 800 weekly lectures for the Fatimid congregation—called "assemblies of wisdom" (*majālis al-ḥikma*)—were collected into his magnum opus, the 8-volume *al-Majālis al-Muʾayyadiyya*. A profound scholar and prolific author with a strong individual style, al-Muʾayyad wrote eleven works in several fields: symbolic exegesis of the Quran, Hadith, and *sharīʿa*, metaphysics or "supreme truths," autobiography, poetry (which also includes six poetry supplications, *munājāt*),[6] translation, and the subject of the present study—supplications (*adʿiya*, sing. *duʿāʾ*).[7]

Al-Muʾayyad's prose supplications have been compiled—likely by his Yemeni student, al-Qāḍī Lamak b. Mālik al-Ḥammādī (d. ca. 491/1098), who also probably compiled his *Majālis* and his poetry *Dīwān*—in a volume titled *al-Adʿiya al-Muʾayyadiyya* (*al-Muʾayyad's supplications*).[8] The compilation con-

in *EI*³; Qutbuddin, Tahera, *al-Muʾayyad al-Shīrāzī and Fatimid* daʿwa *poetry: A case of commitment in classical Arabic literature*, Leiden: Brill, 2005, 15–100; and Ḥusayn, "Ḥayāt al-Muʾayyad," in the introduction to his edition of al-Muʾayyad al-Shīrāzī, *Dīwān*, ed. Muḥammad Kāmil Ḥusayn, Cairo: Dār al-Kātib al-Miṣrī, 1949, 17–50. For a personal narrative, see al-Muʾayyad's autobiography, *al-Sīra al-Muʾayyadiyya*, ed. Muḥammad Kāmil Ḥusayn, Cairo: Dār al-Kātib al-Miṣrī, 1949. On al-Muʾayyad's Persian period, see Klemm, Verena, *Memoirs of a mission: The Ismaili scholar, statesman and poet al-Muʾayyad fi'l-Din al-Shirazi*, London: I.B. Tauris, 2003; Howes, Rachel T., "The Qadi, the wazir and the *daʿi*: Religious and ethnic relations in Buyid Shiraz in the eleventh century," in *IrS* 44.6 (2011), 875–894; and Alexandrin, Elizabeth R., "Studying Ismaʿili texts in eleventh-century Shiraz: Al-Muʾayyad and the 'conversion' of the Buyid Amir Abu Kalijar," in *IrS* 44.1 (2011), 99–115.

6 On al-Muʾayyad's *munājāt* poetry, see Qutbuddin, *al-Muʾayyad al-Shīrāzī* 220–235.

7 On al-Muʾayyad's works, see Qutbuddin, "al-Muʾayyad al-Shīrāzī" 124–127; Qutbuddin, *al-Muʾayyad al-Shīrāzī* 358–368; Ḥusayn in the introduction to his edition of al-Muʾayyad, *Dīwān* 58–65; Poonawala, Ismail K., *Biobibliography of Ismāʿīlī literature*, Malibu, CA: Undena Publications, 1977, 103–109; al-Majdūʿ, *Fahrasat al-kutub wa-l-rasāʾil wa-li-man hiya min al-ʿulamāʾ wa-l-aʾimma wa-l-ḥudūd al-afāḍil*, ed. ʿAlī Naqī Munzavī, Tehran: Chāpkhānah-i Dānishgāh, 1966, 41–44, 88, 173–175, 202–204 (with summaries); Ivanow, Wladimir, *Ismaili literature: A bibliographical survey*, Tehran: Asadi, 1963, 45–47.

8 On Lamak's 5-year sojourn and study with al-Muʾayyad in Cairo, and his probable compilation of his master's works, see Qutbuddin, *al-Muʾayyad al-Shīrāzī* 12–13. Some supplications in *al-Adʿiya al-Muʾayyadiyya*, including the ʿArafa supplication, are of al-Muʾayyad's authorship, while others are from the pen of earlier savants; they are included in *al-Adʿiya al-Muʾayyadiyya* because al-Muʾayyad cites them at various places in his *Majālis*, where he attributes them to anonymous *daʿwa* authors: cf., al-Muʾayyad al-Shīrāzī, *al-Adʿiya al-Muʾayyadiyya*, facs. ed. Khuzayma Quṭb al-Dīn, [Mumbai] [1961]; ed. Ḥusām Khaddūr and Muḥammad Ibrāhīm Ḥasan, comp. al-Dāʿī Ṭāhir Sayf al-Dīn, *al-Ṣaḥīfa al-Muʾayyadiyya: al-Adʿiya al-mubāraka*, Salamiyya: Dār al-Ghadīr, 2011, supplication #1 cited in al-Muʾayyad al-Shīrāzī, *al-Majālis al-*

tains twenty-nine supplications to God, varying between one and twenty-three (smaller sized) pages in the facsimile edition, grounded either explicitly or implicitly in Fatimid metaphysics. They praise God and implore intercession from Muhammad and his descendants for forgiveness of sins. They entreat God's succor and describe the supplicant's desperate straits. Several beseech God's aid for his religion, which is described as having become "a ball tossed around by the hands of God's enemies."[9] Some supplications are highly esoteric with heavy use of cosmic symbolism. In contrast, the ʿArafa supplication is deeply personal. While it is framed in the metaphysics of God's transcendence and underpinned by Fatimid doctrines, it turns philosophical musings regarding human frailty and powerlessness into a moving plea to the Almighty for mercy and succor.

2 Al-Muʾayyad al-Shīrāzī's ʿArafa Supplication: Text and Translation

The following is the text and translation of al-Muʾayyad's ʿArafa supplication. The text is transcribed from the facsimile volume edited and inscribed in 1380/1960 by my late revered father, the 53rd Ṭayyibī *Dāʿī* Sayyidna Khuzaima Qutbuddin (d. 2016), for liturgical use in the Ṭayyibī Dāʾūdī Bohra community.[10] The compilation serves as a prayerbook from which they recite a supplication every day in the last ten days of Ramadan following the noon prayer. Within it, they recite al-Muʾayyad's ʿArafa supplication—along with Imam Zayn al-ʿĀbidīn's ʿArafa supplication—annually during ʿArafa.

We can tentatively position the composition of al-Muʾayyad's ʿArafa supplication in Cairo soon after 451/1059, based on internal evidence: Al-Muʾayyad went to Mecca for the *ḥajj* pilgrimage in 446/1054, an obvious setting for such a prayer, but the supplication specifically says, "Our bodies are absent from that

Muʾayyadiyya, 8 vols., i–iv, ed. Ḥātim Ḥamīd al-Dīn (sole critical edition), Bombay and Oxford: Oxford Printers, 1975–2011. Vols. 1–8 ed. Ḥusām Khaddūr, Salamiyya and Damascus: Dār al-Ghadīr, 2008–2017. Vols. 1–3, ed. Muṣṭafā Ghālib, Beirut: Dār al-Andalus, 1974–1984, iv, *majlis* 25; supplication #6 cited in al-Muʾayyad, *al-Majālis* vi, *majlis* 12; supplication #10 cited in al-Muʾayyad, *al-Majālis* iv, *majlis* 43; supplication #18 cited in al-Muʾayyad, *al-Majālis* iv, *majlis* 14; supplication #19 cited in al-Muʾayyad, *al-Majālis* iv, *majlis* 24; supplication #20 cited in al-Muʾayyad, *al-Majālis* iv, *majlis* 22.

9 Al-Muʾayyad, *al-Adʿiya* 179, supplication #18.

10 Al-Muʾayyad, *al-Adʿiya* 207–214, supplication #24. The *basmala* (initial invocation of God's name) and the opening lines of the first supplication are inscribed in the hand of the 51st Ṭayyibī *Dāʿī* Sayyidna Taher Saifuddin (d. 1965).

holy place," so that was not the place or date of composition. Toward the end, al-Mu'ayyad says, "God, you know that we have left our homeland to perform *jihād* in your path," and we know from the historical record that al-Mu'ayyad fled Shiraz in 433/1042, arriving in Cairo in 436–437/1045–1046, so the supplication must be composed after those events. He then mentions having fought oppressors who have "rent the sanctity of Islam," such that "the lands of the Muslims burn with their killings and incarcerations," and these lines also appear to refer to specific historical events. Al-Mu'ayyad had put together a coalition that fought and defeated the ʿAbbasids in 450/1058, and a year later, the Seljuqs retook Baghdad and reinstated the ʿAbbasid caliph. It seems likely that he composed the present supplication in Cairo sometime after the reversal, probably soon afterward, in the wake of bloody reprisals against Fatimid supporters in those lands.

The historical context is important, but the message is timeless, and the supplication is one in which all Muslim devotees, Shiʿa and Sunni, can find personal meaning. It is also one that all scholars of Islam and Arabic literature can read as an exemplary text of Muslim devotion, Arabic erudition, and Fatimid piety.

The text has never before been published in Western academia, and my translation attempts to capture in lucid English some of the literary brilliance, powerful emotion, and nuanced theological themes of Mu'ayyad's devotional Arabic.

In the name of God,
most compassionate, most merciful

بسم الله الرحمن الرحيم

God, you have placed a seal on even the most intelligent heart such that it cannot truly comprehend you. You have hobbled even the most outpacing tongue such that it cannot fully express your greatness. If a man attempts to rise to the heights of your reality, he is betrayed by the wings of his heart and tongue, no matter how hard they beat and flutter.

أَللّٰهُمَّ يا من خَتَمَ دون تحقيقِ معرفتِه على ذَكِيِّ الجَنان. وعَقَلَ دون الإبانة عن كُنْهِ عظمته جَرِيِّ اللسان. فالمرْءُ إذا رامَ الارتقاءَ إليه بأحَدِهما خانَه جَناحا لسانِه وقلبِه الخافِقان.

(*cont.*)

Pilgrims stand up to supplicate you in this hour at ʿArafāt. They have congregated to your door from every deep valley,[11] speaking different languages and with different forms and ways, covered in dust and earth as though resurrected on judgment day, wrapped in white sheets as though wearing the shrouds of the people of the grave. They pray to you, O lord of all the worlds, in fear and in hope,[12] for earthly desires and religious aspirations. They beseech your mercy, O most merciful lord.	أنت الذي وقف لك في هذه الساعة الواقفون بعَرَفَات. محشورين إلى بابك من كلّ فجٍّ عميق على ٱخْتلاف اللُّغات والصفات. شُعْثاً غُبْراً كأنّما أُنْشِروا ليوم النَّشور. مُلْتَفّين في أطْمارٍ كأنّها أَكْفانُ أصحاب القبور. يدعونك يا ربّ العالمين. خوفاً وطَمَعاً للدنيا والدين. ويسترحمونك يا أرحم الراحمين.
God, we too are your servants! Even though we are absent from that holy place in body, yet we are present there in soul and faith.	أللّٰهُمّ ونحن عبيدك وإن كنّا غُيّباً عن ذلك المقام بأبداننا. فنحن حُضورٌ بأنفسنا وأدياننا.
God, shower blessings on Muhammad and his descendants, and regard us with the same merciful gaze with which you regard your chosen ones who are present in that holy place. Grant us an abundant share of the pious supplications they offer to you.	أللّٰهُمّ فصَلِّ على محمّد وآله وَٱلْحَظْنا بِعَين رحمتك التي تَلْحَظ بها أصفياءَك من حاضري ذلك المقام. وٱجعل لنا من صالح ما يدعون به أجْزلَ الأقسام.
God, clothe us in garments of wellbeing in life, and in robes of piety in death.[13] Grant us the sustenance of good deeds whose benefit will remain.[14]	أللّٰهُمّ أَلْبِسْنا لباسَ العافِية للحياة. ولباس التقوى للممات. وٱرْزُقْنا من الباقيات الصالحات.

11 Reference to Q 22:27.
12 Reference to Q 7:56.
13 Reference to Q 7:26.
14 Reference to Q 18:46.

(*cont.*)

God, place us among those whom you have freed from the stranglehold of worldly aspirations and earthly calamities. Record our names in the register of those whom you have prompted to love faith, and in whose hearts you have made it beautiful.[15] Have us draw near to people of discernment "who remember God standing and sitting and when they lay on their sides" [Q 3:191].	أللّٰهُمَّ ٱجْعَلْنا مِمَّن نَفَّسْتَهم عن خِناق همومهم للدنيا وكروبهم. وأَثْبِتْنا في صحيفة مَن حَبَّبْتَ إليهم الإيمانَ وزَيَّنْتَه في قلوبهم. وأَلْحِقْنا بأُولي الألباب ﴿الَّذِينَ يَذْكُرُونَ اللّٰهَ قِيَامًا وَقُعُودًا وَعَلَىٰ جُنُوبِهِمْ﴾.
God, make the occupations of this world the least of our occupations, and knowledge of the hereafter the entirety of our yearnings. "Endow us in our affairs with right guidance" [Q 18:10] by helping us perform good deeds.	أللّٰهُمَّ ٱجْعَلْ شُغل الدنيا أقلّ أشغالنا. وعلم الآخرة مجموعِ آمالنا. ﴿وَهَيِّئْ لَنَا مِنْ أَمْرِنَا رَشَدًا﴾ بصلاح أعمالنا.
God, have mercy on the destitution of one who is dependent on a stalk of vegetation produced by the earth. Have mercy on the captivity of one who is imprisoned by the calamitous hand of the days and the nights. Have mercy on the feebleness of one who is truly weak and powerless facing the sovereignty of death.	أللّٰهُمَّ ٱرْحَمْ فَقْرَ مَن هو إلى نَبْتَةٍ تُغَذِّيه من نَباتِ الأرض فقير. وأَسْرَ مَن هو بِيَدِ تصاريف الأيّام والليالِي أسير. وضُعْفَ مَن هو عند سلطان الموت ضعيفٌ حقير.
God, when this is my lowly condition—a mosquito can pain and hurt me and a gulp can choke and kill me—it is all the more fitting that you look at me with compassion and mercy. Let not the paths of your mercy narrow to exclude me. Let not the bounties of your benevolence pass me by. Let not the pools of your wisdom become muddied as I drink.	أللّٰهُمَّ وإِنَّ مَن كانت هذه حالُه تُؤْلِمُه البَقّة. وتقتله الشَّرْقة. فَحَقيقٌ أَنْ تَنالَه منك الرحمةُ والرِّقّة. فلا يضيق به من مراحمك مَذهب. ولا يفوته من عواطفك مَطلب. ولا يتكدّر عليه من مشارب حِكَمك مَشرب.

15 Reference to Q 49:7.

(*cont.*)

God, house us in your shade in a home that is free from troubles and exempt from suffering. Gift us life secured with the rope of eternity, against which the sharp blades of catastrophe are forever sheathed.

أَللّٰهُمَّ فَأَسْكِنَّا من جِوارك دارًا سليمةً من الآفات. بريئةً من العاهات. وأَوْلِنا منك حياةً تجعلها بِعُقْدَةِ الخلُود معقودة. وقواطِعَ سيوف الحِدثان دونها مغمودة.

God, cover us in robes of your protection for as long as you have us live. Guard us in the fortress of your safety and security for as long as you have us remain on earth.

أَللّٰهُمَّ جَلِّلْنا جِلالَ صَوْنِك ما أَحْيَيْتَنا. وَٱحْمِنا بِحِمٰى أمانك وأَمْنك ما أَبْقَيْتَنا.

God, you know that we have left our homeland to perform *jihād* in your path and please you.[16] You know that we have borne great hardships and tribulations in heart and body. We fight oppressors who have unsheathed the sword of treachery and unfurled banners of error. They have committed great crimes. They have rent the sanctity of Islam. The lands of the Muslims burn with their killings and incarcerations. Muslim women are in the vicious grasp of their immoralities and indecencies.

أَللّٰهُمَّ إنّك تعلم أنّا خرجنا مُجاهدين في سبيلك ٱبْتغاءَ مرضاتك عن أوطاننا. وحملنا عظيم الكُلَف والمشاقّ في نفوسنا وأبداننا. نجاهد الظالمين الذين شَهَروا سيوف البَغْي. ونشروا أعْلام الغَيّ. وتجرّءوا على عظيم الأجرام. وهتكوا حرمة الإسلام. فديار المسلمين في حريق قتلهم وأسرهم. وحريمهم في هَتْكة فُحْشهم ونُكْرهم.

God, shower blessings on Muhammad and his descendants, and let your mighty aid give our hands strength over these oppressors. Let your potency and power help us to strike at their potency and power. Fortify the pillars of the righteous rule of the Prophet's descendants by obliterating the oppressors' unrighteousness. Crush the sinews of

أَللّٰهُمَّ صلّ على محمّد وآل محمّد وطَوِّلْ لنا بنصرك العزيز عليهم يدًا. وٱجْعَلْ لنا من حَوْلك وقوّتك على إيهان حولهم وقوّتهم مَدَدًا. وأَقِمْ لِحقّ آل محمّد صلّى الله عليه وعلى آله بِزَهْق باطلهم عَمَدًا. وفُتَّ يا ربِّ في عَضُد المتّخذين للمُضِلّين منهم عَضُدًا.

16 Reference to Q 2:207.

(*cont.*)

those who take error-mongers as their sinews.[17]	
God, belief has sallied forth to face unbelief, and unbelief has sallied forth to challenge belief. Lord, strike down Satan's banner. Let him run on his heels when the two armies meet. Protect your sacred sanctuary, God, from the might of the cursed elephant.[18] Destroy it and destroy its army, the brethren of devils and demons. Let their bodies receive the blows of death. Let their blood be drunk by thirsty swords. Have mercy on hearts[19] that burn from their oppression, on eyes that stream from their harm, on the blood of Muslims painting their swords, on spirits snatched out of bodies, on women, veils torn, their honor in the grip of the enemy's hand.	أللّٰهُمّ إنّ الإيمان بَرَزَ إلى الكفر والكفر بَرَزَ إلى الإيمان. فنكِّسْ يا ربِّ راية الشيطان. لِيَنْكُصَ على عَقِبَيْهِ إذا تَرَاءَتِ الفِئَتان. وَٱحْفَظِ ٱللّٰهُمَّ حرمك الأمين. من بأس الفيل اللعين. ودَمِّرْ عليه وعلى حَشَدَتِه إخوان الشياطين. وَٱجْعَلْ يا ربِّ أجسامهم مواقع الحُتوف. ودِماءهم مناهل السيوف. وَٱرْحَمْ أكبادًا من ظلمهم حَرّٰى. وعيونًا من اذاهم عبرى. [١٥٠] ودِماءً للمسلمين بسيوفهم مطلولة. وأرواحًا من أجسادهم مسلولة. وحريمًا كُشِفَتْ عنها بأيديهم أستارُها. وأحاط بها في قَبْضَتهم عَوارُها.
God, faces are covered in dust prostrating before your greatness. We place our trust in you, and our faces are covered in dust prostrating before you. Have mercy on our wretched state and answer our prayer that you grant strength to Islam. Grant us your powerful aid, such that we obtain our desires, desires held by people of discernment and conviction who have faith that	أللّٰهُمّ يا من تَعَفَّرَتْ بالسجود لعظمته الخُدود. تَوَكَّلْنا عليك. وهذه خُدودنا مُتَعَفِّرَةٌ بالسجود بين يَدَيْك. فَٱرْحَمْ منّا ذِلّة المقام. وأجِبْ سؤالنا في عزّ الإسلام. وأيِّدْنا من نصرك العزيز بما نَنالُ به مَنالة ذَوي البصائر الموقنين. الذين أيْقَنوا أنّ ﴿وَعْدَكَ الْحَقُّ﴾ حيث قلتَ سبحانك ﴿وَكَانَ حَقًّا عَلَيْنَا نَصْرُ الْمُؤْمِنِينَ﴾.

17 Reference to Q 18:51.

18 Reference to Q 105.

19 Lit. "livers." The liver was deemed the seat of emotions in pre-modern medicine and psychological theory.

(*cont.*)

"your promise is true" [Q 11:45]. For you have said, "In truth, we shall aid believers" [Q 30:47].	
All praise and favors belong to God. May he bestow blessings on our master Muhammad and his descendants who are the best community. May he bless them all.	وللهِ الحمدُ وَالمنّة. وصلّى الله على سيّدنا محمّد وآله خير الأُمّة. وسلّم عليهم أجمعين.

3 Commentary: Prayer, Aesthetics, and Theology

Al-Mu'ayyad's ʿArafa supplication is a *tour de force* of heartfelt prayer and aesthetic brilliance, underpinned by an Islamic theological base with some specifically Fatimid nuances. The entire text is an entreaty for God's mercy (*raḥma*), and as part of God's mercy, for his aid. The word *raḥma* and its derivatives are explicitly used and implicitly evoked throughout the text. In the following sequential commentary on the supplication, I point out aspects of this framing theme, alongside facets of form, style and theology that structurally, aesthetically, and doctrinally underscore the leitmotif of mercy.[20]

The full supplication is a plea addressed directly to God. Each new section begins with a vocative address to the Creator for a total of 15 usages, and the repeated call to God, set up as a frame for the content, emphasizes the supplicant's singular focus on the Deity; the term used is "*Allāhumma*," (O God!), a special Arabic phrase traditionally reserved to address God in prayer, with the unique suffix "*-umma*" appended to the word *Allāh*. Within the sections, the presence of the second-person pronoun of address, "*anta*" (you) is persistent, and alongside the use of the first-person singular and plural for the supplicant, it further emphasizes the personal nature of the supplication, pairing the supplicant with the supplicated lord. Two other common phrases in Islamic

20 In this supplication, al-Mu'ayyad does not explicitly mention forgiveness of sins, a key aspect of the ʿArafa rite in Fatimid religiosity, but presumably it is implicit in his pleas for mercy. He does speak of it in the *Majālis* where he writes that "the heedless who fail to obtain God's forgiveness in Ramadan will not be eligible to receive it until the following Ramadan, unless they stand upon ʿArafa." Al-Mu'ayyad, *al-Majālis* i, *majlis* 36.

supplication are used once within the lines of entreaty: "*Yā arḥama l-rāḥimīn*" (O most merciful lord), and "*Yā rabba l-ʿālamīn*" (O lord of all the worlds), where the word "*rabb*" (lord) also has the semantic sense of "nurturer," and again signals God's mercy.

The address to God is grounded in Fatimid theology which understands God as beyond the grasp of intellect and imagination.[21] The metaphors al-Muʾayyad uses to express the inability of the created to articulate the Creator's transcendent oneness are paradoxically erudite:

> God, you have placed a seal on even the most intelligent heart such that it cannot truly comprehend you. You have hobbled even the most outpacing tongue such that it cannot fully express your greatness. If a man attempts to rise to the heights of your reality, he is betrayed by the wings of his heart and tongue, no matter how hard they beat and flutter.

The Arabic verb *ʿarafa* means literally "to recognize," and it is interesting that a supplication for recitation on the day of ʿArafa, where pilgrims strive to achieve greater awareness of the Creator, begins by stating that we can never really comprehend God, we can never truly recognize him; al-Muʾayyad uses the word *maʿrifa* (recognition) which has the same three-letter root as *ʿarafa*: ʿ-R-F. Based on direct statements elsewhere, al-Muʾayyad's subtext appears to be that the declaration of inability to recognize is itself true recognition of God; that, in fact, understanding that one can never understand is the only true way to understand God.

Following the address which establishes the supplicant as a believer—and thus, presumably, deserving of God's mercy—the supplication opens with *ḥajj* and ʿArafa themes that implicitly yet unambiguously invoke God's mercy: "Pilgrims stand up to supplicate you in this hour at ʿArafāt." The "standing" at ʿArafa which is an essential component of *ḥajj* rites—*waqafa laka l-wāqifūna bi-ʿArafāt* (lit. standers stand before you at ʿArafāt)—is emphasized; and the place is named right at the onset: ʿArafāt. For Muslims, the very name ʿArafāt evokes associations of prayer for God's mercy, of the Prophet Muhammad's standing on the Mount of Mercy (*jabal al-raḥma*) on ʿArafa and lifting his hands in prayer, of the clamor of pilgrims year after year, through the ages, all standing and calling out to God. The land and the day of ʿArafa, believed by Muslims to be the ultimate place and time in which prayers are certain to be heard, provide

21 See more on this concept in, e.g., al-Muʾayyad, *al-Majālis* i, *majlis* 37; ii, *majlis* 99; iii, *majlis* 2; iv, *majlis* 84.

the *raison d'être* of the supplication, and are therefore foregrounded. The picture painted of the pilgrims with vivid descriptions of their white unstitched garments and their dusty mien, their cacophony of languages and features and customs, is graphic and moving:

> They have congregated to your door from every deep valley, speaking different languages and with different forms and ways, covered in dust and earth as though resurrected on judgment day, wrapped in white sheets as though wearing the shrouds of the people of the grave.

Evocative and palpable, the simile of pilgrims standing on the plain likened to the dead resurrected for the accounting on Judgment Day is one that al-Muʾayyad uses often. He paints the same somber image in his *Majālis*, where he explicitly connects the rising from the graves to the standing before the Great Judge, saying, "on the day that they emerge from their graves, beseeching the mercies of … the one who is worshipped, and to whom all affairs return."[22] Why do they stand in this pitiful state? They implore God's mercy. I have already mentioned the earlier explicit address as "O most merciful lord," and the implicit recall of the Prophet's standing on the Mount of Mercy. Here, the sights and sounds evoked by the pilgrims' description are immediately followed by a declaration of the purpose of their standing, of their objective in coming to ʿArafa: "They pray to you, O lord of all the worlds, in fear and in hope, for earthly desires and religious aspirations. They beseech your mercy, O most merciful lord." What the pilgrims beseech, first and foremost, is God's mercy. The word will be used again at the onset of the personal prayer coming next and emphasized yet again at the very end.

The mention of the pilgrims and their prayers segues into the supplicant's personal invocation, with a masterful line of transition that transposes the pilgrims present on ʿArafa with his own self, for though he is not standing on the physical mount of ʿArafa, he is standing there in spirit: "God, we too are your servants! Even though we are absent from that holy place in body, yet we are present there in soul and faith." Physical attendance at ʿArafa garners God's benevolent eye, but for those who want to attend but are unable to do so, they are still present in spirit if they hold true belief. What counts is sincere intention.

On a deeper level, the line embodies the heart of the Fatimid belief system in which the holy places of Islam and the worship acts of the *sharīʿa*, though

22 Al-Muʾayyad, *al-Majālis* i, *majlis* 94; the last phrase is a reference to Q 11:123.

most holy in their physical aspects, serve as symbols for the living guides, the Imams and their appointed rankholders in each age. In this Fatimid belief system of symbolic interpretation (*taʾwīl*),[23] the spiritual counterpart for the Kaʿba, the House of God, is the Imam of the Age. He is the "living, speaking" (*ḥayy, nāṭiq*) House of God. As mentioned earlier, *ʿarafa* means "to recognize." Performing the *ḥajj* and standing on ʿArafa, the major rite of the pilgrimage, symbolizes recognition of and allegiance for the true Imam of the Age. Those who recognize the Imam stand truly on Mount ʿArafāt. In tandem with the physical rites, it is even more important to believe with your heart and to recognize the deeper meanings of the *ḥajj* rites.[24] Furthermore, and connecting ʿArafa with God's mercy, it is notable that in Fatimid symbolic interpretation, Prophet Muhammad is the embodiment of God's mercy, as certified by the Quranic verse, "We have not sent you but as mercy for all the worlds" (Q 21:107). Al-Muʾayyad affirms this doctrine in his *Majālis* and declares further that like Muhammad, a living embodiment of God's mercy is present for people of every age, namely, Muhammad's legatee ʿAlī and the Imams in their line.[25]

---

23 On the Fatimid system of symbolic interpretation (*taʾwīl*), see Qutbuddin, Tahera, "Principles of Fatimid symbolic interpretation (*taʾwīl*): An analysis based on the *Majālis Muʾayyadiyya* of al-Muʾayyad al-Shīrāzī (d. 470/1078)," in Rodrigo Adem and Edmund Hayes (eds.), *Reason, esotericism and authority in Shīʿī Islam*, Leiden: Brill, 2021, 151–189, *passim*.

24 The same concept—of being present in spirit, though absent in body—is articulated by al-Muʾayyad in *al-Majālis*, following on from the *Majālis* segment quoted above in which he speaks of the pilgrims being dressed in shrouds; and here he adds an enigmatic line, "O how many who are present there are in truth absent, and how many who are far away from it are actually very close." Al-Muʾayyad, *al-Majālis* i, *majlis* 94; the part about being present in spirit though absent in body is also reiterated in al-Muʾayyad, *al-Majālis* iv, *majlis* 37. Al-Muʾayyad clarifies this doctrine in the *Majālis* (i, *majlis* 95; ii, *majlis* 54 and 90), where—connecting ʿArafa to the Quranic "people of the peaks" (*aṣḥāb al-aʿrāf*) (Q 7:48) [N.B.: *aʿrāf* and ʿArafa are also derived from the same root: ʿ-R-F]—he declares that ʿArafa symbolizes the Imams. This point is made directly in the ʿArafa poem composed by "the younger Muʾayyad," the Indian Ṭayyibī *Dāʿī* Sayyidna Taher Saifuddin (d. 1385/1965), who declares in his opening line, "Imam of the Age, the man who truly recognizes you (*ʿarafa*) is the man who stands regarding you as the meaning of ʿArafa" (يا امام العصر يا من عرفه—واقفٌ منه بمعنى عرفة), Sayf al-Dīn, Sayyidnā Ṭāhir, *Dīwān: Jawāhir al-balāgha al-laduniyya*, 2 vols., ii, Dubai: Ṭayyibī Daʿwa Publications, 1993, 78. In the same poem, he says further, "Whosoever stands upon the ʿArafāt of [the Imam's] knowledge has learned its sublime truth" (من يقف في عرفات من معارفه لطفًا عليها وقفه), Sayf al-Dīn, *Dīwān* ii, 79. Full poem, translation, and recitation at https://www.fatemidawat.com/prayers/qasidas-marsiyas-and-salaams/%E2%80%98ya-imam-al-asri-ya-man-arafa%E2%80%99-composed-by-syedna-taher-saifuddin-%E2%80%98ya-imam-al-asri-ya-man-arafa (last accessed: 17 May 2022).

25 Al-Muʾayyad, *al-Majālis* ii, *majlis* 70; see also al-Muʾayyad, *al-Majālis* ii, *majlis* 17 & 37, and *passim*. In the lines that I have cited in my previous paragraph (al-Muʾayyad, *al-Majālis* i,

Next, the personal prayer begins, moving from the *ḥajj*-specific to the general. Taking a page from the supplications of Imam ʿAlī Zayn al-ʿĀbidīn, who frequently prefaced entreaties within his supplications with blessings (*ṣalawāt*), it begins with the invocation, "God, shower blessings on Muhammad and his descendants." In Fatimid belief, entreaties to God to shower blessings on Muhammad and his descendants are always heard and answered. Not only do they provide the theological bedrock for all other pleas, being the essential mode of salvation—for whoever invokes these benedictions on the Prophet and his descendants becomes himself linked with them, and, through their intercession, attains an angelic station in the afterlife—but they also ensure that all other pleas are heard and answered.[26] The Fatimids are not mentioned by name, but the invocation of blessings on Muhammad and his descendants clearly refers to them. The transition from the pilgrims to the supplicant continues: "and regard us with the same merciful gaze"—note the plea again for mercy—"with which you regard your chosen ones who are present in that holy place. Grant us an abundant share of the pious supplications they offer to you." Those who know and profess allegiance to the true Imam are the ones who truly stand on ʿArafa, and they are thus partners with the supplicants who physically stand on the holy site.

Now, al-Muʾayyad begins his litany of profound petitions: "God, clothe us in garments of wellbeing in life, and in robes of piety in death." God is the one who grants us health and happiness in our earthly lives, and he is the one who guides us to piety. The antithesis of life and death in these lines underscores the power of God over both, and the human need for his aid in both. Asking for wellbeing (*ʿāfiya*), more specifically, good health, for life, and of piety (*taqwā*) for death is a common binary in Muslim prayer. The two appeals together are an application for God's benevolence always, now and in the hereafter, with the two

---

majlis 94), the "mercies (*marāḥim*)" beseeched by ʿArafa supplicants are entreated from "the one whose sanctified and unsanctified places all speak with the tongue of wisdom"–these ritual places, *ḥaram* and *ḥill*, also symbolize God's messengers and Imams. By following their guidance, believers attain God's ultimate mercy, which is the return to the heavenly abode.

26 On the deep meaning of the *ṣalawāt* benediction in Fatimid theology, see explanation in Qutbuddin, Tahera, "Karbala mourning among the Fāṭimid-Ṭayyibī-Shīʿa of India: Doctrinal and performative aspects of Sayyidnā Ṭāhir Sayf al-Dīn's Arabic lament, 'O King of martyrs' (*Yā Sayyida l-shuhadāʾī*)," in *Shiʿi Studies Review* 5 (2021), 3–46, 28–29; Qutbuddin, Aziz, Taḥmīd: *A literary genre? A study of the Arabic laudatory preamble with a focus on the Fatimid-Ṭayyibī tradition*, London (PhD Diss.): School of Oriental and African Studies, University of London, 2009, 174–181; and in the primary sources al-Muʾayyad, *al-Majālis* ii, *majlis* 63; iv, *majlis* 73; al-Qāḍī al-Nuʿmān, *Taʾwīl al-daʿāʾim*, ed. Muḥammad Ḥasan al-Aʿẓamī, 2 vols., i, Cairo: Dār al-Maʿārif, 1982, 303–304.

things that matter most, and that generate all other good things. It is a prayer for aid to piety in this world, such that following the path of godliness, the supplicant arrives at a good end in the hereafter. Al-Muʾayyad follows this prayer with a line that directly connects this world and the hereafter: "Grant us the sustenance of good deeds whose benefit will remain." Good deeds are the best sustenance, they are the true wealth, for they are the only treasures that we will carry with us into the hereafter. He continues, underscoring the line just voiced with another that says the same thing from the opposite side: "God, place us among those whom you have freed from the stranglehold of worldly aspirations and earthly calamities." We should aspire to good deeds, for their benefit will remain, while shunning the headlong pursuit of worldly aspirations, for worldly benefits, when pursued with no mind to religion and the hereafter, and which have many in their grip, will, by inference, perish with a person's earthly life. Al-Muʾayyad also asks for deliverance from earthly calamities, and with the juxtaposition of earthly calamities with worldly aspirations, it is almost implied that the one causes the other, or, at the very least, that the absence of the one ensures that a person will not be overly affected by the other; he will be able to endure worldly troubles because he knows they are temporary. The focus in all this is squarely on the eternal hereafter. Al-Muʾayyad continues, "Record our names in the register of those whom you have prompted to love faith, and in whose hearts you have made it beautiful."[27] Belief too is a gift from God, and God will grant direction to those who ask him for it. In the next line, he says, "Have us draw near to people of discernment (*ūlū l-albāb*) who"—and this is a verse from the Quran—"remember God standing and sitting and when they lay on their sides" (Q 3:191). In other words, the focus and goal of worldly acts should center on attaining the hereafter. Discernment, reason, intelligence—

27 This line alludes to Q 49:7: "Allah has prompted you to love faith, and made it beautiful in your hearts." The Fatimids' conception of free will and predestination states that, on the one hand, humans are born in this world with a predestined fate, and their destiny is a direct result of their actions in the world of first creation. But, once born, they have complete freedom to make choices, whether for good or for evil, and these choices will determine their path in the afterlife. For an allusive statement to this effect, citing the words of Imam Jaʿfar al-Ṣādiq (d. 148/765), see al-Rāzī, Abū Ḥātim, *The proofs of prophecy*, trans. Tarif Khalidi, Provo, UT: Brigham Young University Press, 2011, 30–32. See also several declarations of free choice in the sense I have outlined in al-Muʾayyad, *al-Majālis* ii, *majlis* 28 & 29; iv, *majlis* 18, 21 & 49. For a succinct presentation of the Fatimid-Ṭayyibī position, see the *majlis* of the 54th Ṭayyibī *Dāʿī* Sayyidna Taher Fakhruddin, "Do we have free will? *Majalis al-ḥikma* Series": https://www.youtube.com/watch?v=qOMKZp-rgOI&list=PLoYKJ1IUTM6peAezs6wWpfyHnAUQv1cbs&index=41 (last accessed: 7 November 2021).

all these are essential themes in al-Muʾayyad's theology that underpin all his prayers, poems and teachings;[28] the most intelligent thing a person of reason can do is to remember God, for believing in God, and supplicating him ensure a person's eternal bliss in God's shade. Following in this same vein of magnifying the hereafter and insisting on the low worth of this world, al-Muʾayyad supplicates, "God, make the occupations of this world the least of our occupations, and knowledge of the hereafter the entirety of our yearnings." He ends this general segment of his supplication by citing a verse from the Quran to make the umbrella plea, "Endow us in our affairs with right guidance by helping us perform good deeds." (Q 18:10). The repetition of the plea for help to perform good deeds accentuates this crucial proposition.

The next segment highlights the petitioner's utter and total powerlessness in supporting his own life and wellbeing, and al-Muʾayyad relies on this pitiful image to solicit—again, and over and over in these next lines—God's mercy:

> God, have mercy on the destitution of one who is dependent on a stalk of vegetation produced by the earth. Have mercy on the captivity of one who is imprisoned by the calamitous hand of the days and the nights. Have mercy on the feebleness of one who is truly weak and powerless facing the sovereignty of death.

The philosophical aspect of human frailty and dependance is masterfully turned into a very personal plea. These lines, and the next, position the supplicant in a manner of utmost and entire dependence on God's mercy: "God, when this is my lowly condition—a mosquito can pain and hurt me and a gulp can choke and kill me—it is all the more fitting that you look at me with compassion and mercy." The very tangible mention of a mosquito and a gulp of water brings the abstract into the realm of the mundane, the metaphysical into the purview of everyday human travails, in an image that is immediately relatable for most people. The word mercy, and its near synonym, benevolence (*ʿaṭf*), is again invoked: "Let not the paths of your mercy narrow to exclude me. Let not the bounties of your benevolence pass me by." And, for al-Muʾayyad, knowledge, learning, rationality, wisdom—all these are never far from the lexical setting of God's mercy, visible here when he juxtaposes the plea for mercy with a plea for a drink from the pools of God's wisdom, particularly notable because of the Fatimid symbolic interpretation of water as divine knowledge, "Let not

28 See, e.g., al-Muʾayyad, *al-Majālis* i, *majlis* 1–2; al-Muʾayyad, *Dīwān* 202, poem 2, v. 63; al-Muʾayyad, *Dīwān* 321, poem 62, vv. 121–122.

the pools of your wisdom become muddied as I drink." The real manifestation of God's mercy, then, is his bestowal of heavenly wisdom that flows from the celestial realm.

The next two pleas deepen the earlier petition for liberation from earthly calamities. Building on the declaration of the supplicant's own inability to deflect any kind of harm from himself, al-Mu'ayyad first asks God for eternal life, which he characterizes as a state in which he will be forever safe from catastrophe and suffering: "God, house us in your shade in a home that is free from troubles and exempt from suffering. Gift us life secured with the rope of eternity, against which the sharp blades of catastrophe are forever sheathed." The metaphor of rope and blade gives a physical presentation to an abstract concept, that of eternity and catastrophe, where the ultimate catastrophe is death. The second plea comes back to the petitioner's earthly life and pleads for God's protection at all times in the here and now: "God, cover us in robes of your protection for as long as you have us live. Guard us in the fortress of your safety and security for as long as you have us remain on earth." As in the earlier pleas for garments of wellbeing and piety in life and death, the supplication asks for "robes of protection," and it adds a further image of a "fortress of safety"—presumably petitioning for both physical protection and spiritual safety.

Now, the supplication moves to a very particular theme, one that is pervasive not only in al-Mu'ayyad's supplications, but also in his poetry and his autobiography, that of his performance of *jihād* in God's path. Likely, he refers to the establishment of the Fatimid *daʿwa* in often hostile territory, and of the sufferings he has endured in this endeavor. Al-Mu'ayyad presses home these points here—as he does in those other genres of his writing—to highlight the urgent need for God's aid against God's enemies. The theme is presented in three segments, each prefaced with the direct address, "God!" The first of the three segments begins with a statement to the effect that the supplicant has faced exile in the path of God, "God, you know that we have left our homeland to perform *jihād* in your path and please you," and this refers specifically, as mentioned earlier, to al-Mu'ayyad's own poignant situation where he was forced out of his homeland, Shiraz, because of his efforts in the land of Fars to establish the Fatimid cause—both religious and political—through pressure exerted on the Buyid king Abū Kālījār (r. 415–440/1024–1048) by the rival ʿAbbasid forces, and compelled to leave behind home and friends and family and flock.[29] It goes on to detail the suffering rained down on believers by God's enemies. The first few lines most likely echo al-Mu'ayyad's own tribulations, in

29 See details and further references in Qutbuddin, *al-Mu'ayyad al-Shīrāzī* 48–56.

addition to their general import: "You know that we have borne great hardships and tribulations in heart and body. We fight oppressors who have unsheathed the sword of treachery and unfurled banners of error." The next lines are condemnatory in an overarching denunciation that signals the ʿAbbasids' atrocities in more universal terms: "They have committed great crimes. They have rent the sanctity of Islam. The lands of the Muslims burn with their killings and incarcerations. Muslim women are in the vicious grasp of their immoralities and indecencies." The language is potent and highlights both the suffering and anguish of the believers and the cruelty and dominance of the enemy. Potentially, as also mentioned earlier, this could be a reference to the Seljuq retake of the ʿAbbasid realm, following the year of Fatimid dominance in 450/1058 achieved at al-Muʾayyad's hand.[30] In these lines, although the Fatimid Imam-Caliphs are not mentioned by name, al-Muʾayyad evokes their fight for Islam implicitly and his own with them.

The second of the three segments regarding *jihād* and God's enemies builds on the desperate straits just outlined to transition to a heartfelt plea for God's aid. For a second time in the supplication, again prefacing this new and specific plea, al-Muʾayyad frames his entreaty with a prayer for blessings to be bestowed on the Prophet and the Imams in his line, "God, shower blessings on Muhammad and his descendants," before going on to plead, "and let your mighty aid give our hands strength over these oppressors. Let your potency and power help us to strike at their potency and power." He again mentions the Prophet's descendants, and although he does not name them, he most certainly refers to the Fatimid Caliph-Imams whom he serves: "Fortify the pillars of the righteous rule of the Prophet's descendants by obliterating the oppressors' unrighteousness. Crush the sinews of those who take error-mongers as their sinews." As is his custom, al-Muʾayyad's language is stylized, and he makes use of tacitly persuasive instruments from the Arabic rhetorical toolbox to achieve his goal. Particularly here he employs the metaphors "fortify the pillars ..." and "crush the sinews ...,"[31] combined with poetic repetition of the word "sinews," one a literal usage for the body part that carries weapons, itself figurative in its denotation of strength, and the other a directly metaphorical use signaling supporters. These aesthetic techniques aid in crafting a powerful plea to God to grant victory to the righteous Fatimid Imams and destroy their evil enemies.

30 See details and further references in Qutbuddin, *al-Muʾayyad al-Shīrāzī* 68–77.
31 Reference to Q 18:51.

The final and third segment regarding *jihād* begins with a declaration, "God, belief has sallied forth to face unbelief, and unbelief has sallied forth to challenge belief," that echoes the Prophet Muhammad's prayer in the Battle of the Trench (*khandaq*) when—as narrated by al-Mu'ayyad himself—the young ʿAlī b. Abī Ṭālib had sallied forth to fight against the famed pagan warrior ʿAmr b. ʿAbd Wadd (d. 5/626), thereby saving the Muslims and Islam from an existential threat.[32] Al-Mu'ayyad's single-lined but immensely forceful pronouncement in his supplication aligns the Fatimid Imam-Caliphs with true belief, and with Muhammad and ʿAlī, and it links their opponents (primarily the ʿAbbasids and the Spanish Umayyads, both dynasties with a Quraysh pedigree) with the pagan Meccan Quraysh who embody unbelief who had fought against the Prophet. The statement also subtly alludes to al-Mu'ayyad's earlier phrase of prayer for God to record his name among those God has prompted to love belief, in other words, to love ʿAlī and the Fatimid Imams in his line. Al-Mu'ayyad builds on this declaration to put forth a litany of entreaties that evoke yet another early Quranic theme:

> Lord, strike down Satan's banner. Let him run on his heels when the two armies meet. Protect your sacred sanctuary, God, from the might of the cursed elephant. Destroy it and destroy its army, the brethren of devils and demons. Let their bodies receive the blows of death. Let their blood be drunk by thirsty swords.

The reference to the Quranic Sūra of the Elephant is unmistakable,[33] an allusion to the historical episode of the Ethiopian-Yemeni general Abraha who brought an army of elephants to demolish the sacred Kaʿba in Mecca in 570 CE, the same year that the Prophet Muhammad would be born. The Quran, as is well known, vaunts God's destruction of those who would destroy the sacred sanctuary of God's House, by sending an army of Abābīl birds who rained down stones of brimstone and fire. The elephant—here possibly the ʿAbbasid-Seljuq ruler—may be mighty in size and strength, but God—whose side the Fatimid Imams represent—is powerful over all. Al-Mu'ayyad's prayer shifts yet again from a tone of reckoning to a timbre of pleading, that echoes the earlier lines of fraught suffering:

> Have mercy on hearts that burn from their oppression, on eyes that stream from their harm, on the blood of Muslims painting their swords,

32 Al-Mu'ayyad, *al-Majālis* iv, *majlis* 13 & 15.

33 Q 105.

on spirits snatched out of bodies, on women, veils torn, their honor in the grip of the enemy's hand.

As already demonstrated briefly earlier, al-Mu'ayyad's ʿArafa supplication is a masterpiece of Arabic belle-lettres, with powerful rhyme and parallelism constituting a pulsing cadence, and vivid imagery. Rhythm is a major driver of the prose, and the lines just cited, like most sets of lines before them in the supplication, are rhythmic and parallel, and each structurally parallel line deepens the sense of despairing need. The main clause addresses God with the imperative verb "have mercy [on]" (*irḥam*)—note again the recurrence of this key lexeme of mercy, as the supplicant's pleas crescendo in the approach to the finale—and the four words, hearts, eyes, blood, and spirit, occupy the identical grammatical slot of direct object in each of the subordinate clauses. The conjunction "and" and the preposition "from" are repeated in each, and the repetition, perhaps ironically, makes them fade away and the substantives pop out. Moreover—and here I refer the reader to the Arabic text provided earlier—the first two words rhyme in R (*ḥarrā, ʿabrā*), and the second set, the third and fourth words, rhyme in L (*maṭlūla, maslūla*), and each of the two pairs is also morphologically equivalent. All this, parallel structure (*izdiwāj*), morphological equivalence (*tawāzun*), and rhyme (*sajʿ*), produces a strong rhythmic cadence. Throughout the text, consecutive groups of two or three or four lines possess near-identical grammatical structure. The text is fully rhymed, and like the parallel structure, the rhyme too changes after every few phrases, as is customary in medieval Arabic chancery prose. Parallelism combined with rhyme is highly prized in stylized prose, and the theorists laud it with the technical literary term, "studding with gems" (*tarṣīʿ*).[34]

The supplication is also rich in literal and metaphorical imagery. The picture painted of the pilgrims at the outset of the text, with stark descriptions of their white wrappers likened to shrouds of the dead, is graphic. The picture painted of the wretchedness of the human condition, with mention of the supplicant's dependance for his very life on a piece of vegetation, and his helplessness against an insect as tiny as a mosquito, is moving. The metaphor in the supplication's opening segment of a high-flying bird unable to reach the heights evoked in the phrase "the fluttering wings of his heart and tongue" gives physical shape to the abstract concept of human inability to comprehend the divine reality.

34 Al-Qalqashandī, Aḥmad b. ʿAlī, *Ṣubḥ al-aʿshā fī ṣināʿat al-inshāʾ*, ed. ʿAbd al-Qādir Zakkār, 14 vols., ii, Damascus: Wizārat al-Thaqāfa wa-l-Irshād al-Qawmī, 1981, 282.

Repetition of key words, especially the word mercy, and repetition of key phrases, especially the benediction on the Prophet Muhammad and his progeny who are the embodiment of God's mercy, drive home the key messages of the supplication.

Profuse citation of the Quran, directly, or by invoking its themes and vocabulary—flagged in my commentary and notes—infuses an Islamic flavor into the entirety of the supplication, as well as injecting an air of doctrinal and perhaps also temporal authority.

Toward the end of the supplication, al-Muʾayyad verbalizes his submission to God, and his trust in God, in abject humbleness, "God, faces are covered in dust prostrating before your greatness. We place our trust in you, and [note the emphatic near repetition] our faces are covered in dust prostrating before you." He also reiterates his plea of mercy, conjoined with a repeated plea for God's aid and victory, "Have mercy on our wretched state and answer our prayer that you grant strength to Islam. Grant us your powerful aid, such that we obtain our desires, desires held by people of discernment and conviction who have faith that 'your promise is true' (Q 11:45). For you have said"—and al-Muʾayyad ends his entreaties with citation of God's words of promise in the Quran—" 'In truth, we shall aid believers'(Q 30:47)."

The supplication ends with praise of God and, once more, blessings on Muhammad and his descendants: "All praise and favors belong to God. May he bestow blessings on our master Muhammad and his descendants who are the best community. May he bless them all."

Bibliography

Alexandrin, Elizabeth R., "Studying Ismaʿili texts in eleventh-century Shiraz: Al-Muʾayyad and the 'conversion' of the Buyid Amir Abu Kalijar," in *IrS* 44.1 (2011), 99–115.

ʿAlī b. Abī Ṭālib, *Supplications* (*duʿāʾ*), trans. William C. Chittick, London: Muhammadi Trust, 1982.

Ali, Mukhtar H., "The power of the spoken word: Prayer, invocation, and supplication in Islam," in David McPherson (ed.), *Spirituality and the good life: Philosophical approaches*, Cambridge: Cambridge University Press, 2017, 136–154.

Brett, Michael, *The Fatimid Empire*, Edinburgh: Edinburgh University Press, 2017.

Chittick, William C., "A Shādhilī presence in Shiʿite Islam," in *Sophia Perennis* 1.1 (1975), 97–100; repr. in Chittick, William C., *In search of the lost heart: Explorations in Islamic thought*, ed. Mohammed Rustom, Atif Khalil, and Kazuyo Murata, Albany, NY: SUNY Press, 2012, 39–42.

Daftary, Farhad, *The Ismaʿilis: Their history and doctrines*, Cambridge: Cambridge University Press, 2007.

Fakhruddin, Sayyidna Taher, "Do we have free will? *Majalis al-ḥikma* Series," https://www.youtube.com/watch?v=qOMKZprgOI&list=PLoYKJ1IUTM6peAezs6wWpfyHnAUQv1cbs&index=41 (last accessed: 7 November 2021).

https://www.fatemidawat.com/prayers/qasidas-marsiyas-and-salaams/%E2%80%98ya-imam-al-asri-ya-man-arafa%E2%80%99-composed-by-syedna-taher-saifuddin-%E2%80%98ya-imam-al-asri-ya-man-arafa (last accessed: 17 May 2022).

Gardet, L., "Duʿāʾ," in *EI*².

Guyard, M. Stanislas, *Fragments relatifs à la doctrine des Ismāʿīlīs*, Paris: Imprimerie nationale, 1874.

Halm, Heinz, *The empire of the Mahdi: The rise of the Fatimids*, trans. Michael Bonner, Leiden: Brill, 1996.

Howes, Rachel T., "The Qadi, the wazir and the *daʿi*: Religious and ethnic relations in Buyid Shiraz in the eleventh century," in *IrS* 44.6 (2011), 875–894.

Ivanow, Wladimir, *Ismaili literature: A bibliographical survey*, Tehran: Asadi, 1963.

Jiwa, Shainool, *The Fatimids*. 1. *The rise of a Muslim empire*, London: I.B. Tauris, 2018.

Katz, Marion H., *Prayer in Islamic thought and practice*, Cambridge: Cambridge University Press, 2013.

Klemm, Verena, *Memoirs of a mission: The Ismaili scholar, statesman and poet al-Muʾayyad fiʾl-Din al-Shirazi*, London: I.B. Tauris, 2003.

al-Majdūʿ, *Fahrasat al-kutub wa-l-rasāʾil wa-li-man hiya min al-ʿulamāʾ wa-l-aʾimma wa-l-ḥudūd al-afāḍil*, ed. ʿAlī Naqī Munzawī, Tehran: Chāpkhānah-i Dānishgāh, 1966.

Mālik b. Anas, *al-Muwaṭṭaʾ*, ed. Muḥammad Fuʾād ʿAbd al-Bāqī, 2 vols., Cairo: Dār Iḥyāʾ al-Turāth al-ʿArabī, 1985.

Massignon, Louis, *Recueil de textes inédits concernant l'histoire de la mystique en pays d'Islam*, Paris: Geuthner, 1929.

al-Muʾayyad al-Shīrāzī, *Dīwān*, ed. Muḥammad Kāmil Ḥusayn, Cairo: Dār al-Kātib al-Miṣrī, 1949.

al-Muʾayyad al-Shīrāzī, *al-Sīra al-Muʾayyadiyya*, ed. Muḥammad Kāmil Ḥusayn, Cairo: Dār al-Kātib al-Miṣrī, 1949.

al-Muʾayyad al-Shīrāzī, *al-Majālis al-Muʾayyadiyya*, 8 vols., i–iv, ed. Ḥātim Ḥamīd al-Dīn (sole critical edition), Bombay and Oxford: Oxford Printers, 1975–2011. Vols. 1–8 ed. noncritical ed. Ḥusām Khaddūr, Salamiyya and Damascus: Dār al-Ghadīr, 2008–2017. Vols. 1–3, noncritical ed. Muṣṭafā Ghālib, Beirut: Dār al-Andalus, 1974–1984. Vol. 1, excerpts from *majlis* 1–20 trans. Jawad Muscati and Bahadur Moulvi, *Life and lectures of the grand missionary al-Muʾayyad-fid-din al-Shirazi*, Karachi: Ismailia Association, 1950. Vol. 1, *majlis* §1, trans. Ali Qutbuddin, "The discourses of al-Muʾayyad: Reason and revelation," in Hermann Landolt, Samira Sheikh and Kutub Kassam (eds.), *An anthology of Ismaili literature: A Shiʿi vision of Islam*, London: Institute of Ismaili Studies, 2008, 131–134.

al-Mu'ayyad al-Shīrāzī, *al-Adʿiya al-Mu'ayyadiyya*, facs. ed. Khuzayma Quṭb al-Dīn, [Mumbai] [1961]; noncritical ed. Ḥusām Khaddūr and Muḥammad Ibrāhīm Ḥasan, comp. al-Dāʿī Ṭāhir Sayf al-Dīn, *al-Ṣaḥīfa al-Mu'ayyadiyya: al-Adʿiya al-mubāraka*, Salamiyya: Dār al-Ghadīr, 2011.

Padwick, Constance E., *Muslim devotions: A study of prayer-manuals in common use*, London: SPCK, 1961.

Poonawala, Ismail K., *Biobibliography of Ismāʿīlī literature*, Malibu, CA: Undena Publications, 1977.

al-Qāḍī al-Nuʿmān, *Ta'wīl al-daʿā'im*, ed. Muḥammad Ḥasan al-Aʿẓamī, 2 vols., Cairo: Dār al-Maʿārif, 1982.

al-Qāḍī al-Nuʿmān, *Daʿā'īm al-Islām*, ed. Asaf A.A. Fyzee, 2 vols., Cairo: Dār al-Maʿārif, 1985.

al-Qāḍī al-Nuʿmān, *The pillars of Islam*, trans. Asaf A.A. Fyzee, rev. Ismail K. Poonawala, New Delhi: Oxford University Press, 2002.

al-Qalqashandī, Aḥmad b. ʿAlī, *Ṣubḥ al-aʿshā fī ṣināʿat al-inshā'*, ed. ʿAbd al-Qādir Zakkār, 14 vols., Damascus: Wizārat al-Thaqāfa wa-l-Irshād al-Qawmī, 1981.

al-Quḍāʿī, al-Qāḍī Muḥammad b. Salāma, *A treasury of virtues: Sayings, sermons and teachings of ʿAlī*, ed. and trans. Tahera Qutbuddin, New York: New York University Press, 2013.

al-Quḍāʿī, al-Qāḍī Muḥammad b. Salāma, *Light in the heavens: Sayings of the Prophet Muḥammad*, ed. and trans. Tahera Qutbuddin, New York: New York University Press, 2016.

al-Qummī, ʿAbbās, *Mafātīḥ al-jinān*, Kuwait: Maktabat al-Faqīh, 2004.

Qutbuddin, Tahera, *al-Mu'ayyad al-Shīrāzī and Fatimid* daʿwa *poetry: A case of commitment in classical Arabic literature*, Leiden: Brill, 2005.

Qutbuddin, Aziz, Taḥmīd*: A literary genre? A study of the Arabic laudatory preamble with a focus on the Fatimid-Ṭayyibī tradition*, London (PhD Diss.): School of Oriental and African Studies, University of London, 2009.

Qutbuddin, Tahera, "Fatimids," in Edward Ramsamy (ed.), *Cultural sociology of the Middle East, Asia, and Africa*, ii, Thousand Oaks, CA: Sage, 2011, 37–40.

Qutbuddin, Tahera, "Karbala mourning among the Fāṭimid-Ṭayyibī-Shīʿa of India: Doctrinal and performative aspects of Sayyidnā Ṭāhir Sayf al-Dīn's Arabic lament, 'O King of martyrs' (*Yā Sayyida l-shuhadā'ī*)," in *Shīʿī Studies Review* 5 (2021), 3–46.

Qutbuddin, Tahera, "Principles of Fatimid symbolic interpretation (*ta'wīl*): An analysis based on the *Majālis Mu'ayyadiyya* of al-Mu'ayyad al-Shīrāzī (d. 470/1078)," in Rodrigo Adem and Edmund Hayes (eds.), *Reason, esotericism and authority in Shīʿī Islam*, Leiden: Brill, 2021, 151–189.

Qutbuddin, Tahera, "al-Mu'ayyad al-Shīrāzī," in *EI*³

al-Rāzī, Abū Ḥātim, *The proofs of prophecy*, trans. Tarif Khalidi, Provo, UT: Brigham Young University Press, 2011.

Rubin, Uri, "ʿArafāt," in *EI*³.

Sayf al-Dīn, Sayyidnā Ṭāhir = Sayyidna Taher Saifuddin, *Dīwān: Jawāhir al-balāgha al-laduniyya*, 2 vols., Dubai: Ṭayyibī Daʿwa Publications, 1993.

Ṭabāṭabāʾī, Muḥammad Ḥusayn, *A Shiʿite anthology*, trans. William C. Chittick, Albany, NY: SUNY Press, 1981.

Tagliacozzo, Eric and Shawkat M. Toorawa (eds.), *The* hajj*: Pilgrimage in Islam*, New York: Cambridge University Press, 2016.

Walker, Paul E., *Exploring an Islamic empire: Fatimid history and its sources*, London: I.B. Tauris, 2002.

Walker, Paul E., "The Ismāʿīlīs," in Peter Adamson and Richard Taylor (eds.), *The Cambridge companion to Arabic philosophy*, Cambridge: Cambridge University Press, 2005, 72–91.

Wensinck, Arent J., Jacques Jomier and Bernard Lewis, "Ḥadjdj," in *EI*².

Zayn al-ʿĀbidīn, ʿAlī b. al-Ḥusayn al-Sajjād, *The psalms of Islam*, trans. William C. Chittick, London: Muhammadi Trust, 1988.

Zayn al-ʿĀbidīn, ʿAlī b. al-Ḥusayn al-Sajjād, *al-Ṣaḥīfa al-Sajjādiyya al-kāmila*, Beirut: Muʾassasat al-Aʿlamī, 1992.

CHAPTER 25

Made in God's Image: A Contemporary Sufi Commentary on Sūrat al-Insān (Q 76) by the Moroccan Shaykh Mohamed Faouzi al-Karkari

Yousef Casewit

1 Introduction

The Karkariyya is a contemporary branch of the Shādhilī Sufi order (*ṭarīqa*) founded by Shaykh Mohamed Faouzi al-Karkari (b. 1974) in 2007 in the small northeastern Moroccan town of el-Aruit, near the coastal city of Nador. Despite its humble beginnings, the Karkariyya has established itself as one of Morocco's most dynamic centers for the dissemination of Sufi teachings. It is based in a large Sufi lodge (*zāwiya*) that accommodates thousands of visitors throughout the year and houses dozens of male and female resident disciples (*mutajarridīn*) who live with the Shaykh for extensive periods of rigorous spiritual training. The order's largest branches are presently located in France, Algeria, Tunisia, and Oman, with a growing presence in various cities of Morocco, West Africa, and North America. The Karkariyya's active outreach on social media platforms has contributed to its growth from a local Moroccan order to an internationally diverse, multicultural, and multilingual network of Sufi seekers.

The major events that shaped the Shaykh's life, including his ascetic practices and decade of wandering throughout Morocco, are described in a hagiographical work penned by his Belgian disciple Jamil Zaghdoudi entitled, *At the service of destiny: A biography of the living Moroccan Sufi master Shaykh Mohamed Faouzi al-Karkari*. Shaykh al-Karkari is heir to the Moroccan Shādhilī-Darqāwī-ʿAlawī lineage, and places himself on par with the prominent 19th and 20th century revivers of North African Sufism, including al-ʿArabī al-Darqāwī (d. 1823) and Aḥmad al-ʿAlawī (d. 1934). As such, the spiritual teachings and practices of Shaykh al-Karkari closely resemble those of the Moroccan Darqāwīs, especially Aḥmad Ibn ʿAjība (d. 1809), with a special emphasis on the direct witnessing (*mushāhada*) of divine light. The Shaykh's works occasionally invoke the writings and teachings of Ibn ʿArabī, although the latter's teachings tend to be channeled through the Shādhilī writings of Ibn ʿAjība.

To date, Shaykh al-Karkari has authored seven Arabic works which attest to both the continuation and revival of the North African Shādhilī tradition. Many

 | DOI:10.1163/9789004529038_026

of his books have been translated into French, English, and Spanish, although three of his works are most important to his teachings. The first, entitled *The foundations of the Karkariyya order* (*al-Kawākib al-durriyya fī bayān al-uṣūl al-nūrāniyya*), articulates the key practices of the order and provides legal justifications and metaphysical expositions of the pact (*al-ʿahd*), the sacred dance (*al-ḥaḍra*), the patched cloak (*al-muraqqaʿa*), the invocation of the divine name (*al-ism*), Sufi wandering (*al-siyāḥa*), the spiritual retreat (*al-khalwa*), and realization of the innermost secret (*al-sirr*). The second, *Introduction to Islamic metaphysics: A contemporary Sufi treatise on the secrets of the divine name* (*Kāf al-astār li-mā fīhā l-jalāla min asrār*), is an exposition of Sufi doctrine and the Shaykh's notion of the seven "readings" (*qirāʾāt*) or degrees of realization of the divine name, *Allāh*. The third, entitled *The Sufi path of light* (*Kitāb al-Maḥajja al-bayḍāʾ*), argues for the centrality of divine light as both a key to and criterion for spiritual wayfaring in the Quran, the *sunna*, and the Sufi tradition. Aside from these three principal works, al-Karkari has also published a series of books based on transcriptions of his spiritual discourses (*mudhākara*) that offer commentaries on the lives of various Quranic prophets including Moses, Jesus, and Solomon.

Below is a translation of *The holy presence: On the human configuration* (*Kitāb al-Ḥaḍra al-quddūsiyya fī l-nashʾa al-insāniyya*). This short treatise was first published in 2015 in a collection of al-Karkari's Sufi poetry and aphorisms entitled *The chalice of spirits* (*Dīwān dinān al-arwāḥ*).[1] The treatise presents the meanings of Sūrat al-Insān (Q 76) from the perspective of God's "holy presence," or in the manner of a holy saying (*ḥadīth qudsī*) pronounced in the divine voice. The treatise is divided under subheadings and describes paradisal delights and infernal torments as disclosures of divine names and attributes. Throughout the treatise, the Shaykh invokes key Sufi themes such as the Perfect Man (*al-insān al-kāmil*), the hidden treasure, disclosures of divine names, the symbolic significance of the letters of the Quran, and the Aeon (*dahr*) which stands between sheer eternity and temporality.

---

1 Al-Karkari, Mohamed Faouzi, *Dīwān dinān al-arwāḥ*, Casablanca: Maṭbaʿat Ṣināʿat al-Kitāb, 2015, 165–182.

2 Translation

The Holy Presence: On the Human Configuration[2]

The Aeon and the Human Being

> Has there come upon man a span of the Aeon in which he was a thing unremembered? [Q 76:1][3]

Dear human being, there *came upon* you *a span of the Aeon* in which you were a *thing unremembered.* You were not subject to the vicissitudes of time, nor restrained within the confinements of space, because you were not a *thing* at all, nor was there even any*thing* like you. Before before-ness you were concealed in the holy invisible heart of the unseen realm. There, you swam within the *Aeon* itself, hallowed beyond time and space. Night did not enfold you, nor did day envelop you, in that Aeonic pre-eternity where the eternal attributes permeate the stages of perfection.

Then, when We desired to descend from the Treasure to bring Our Love into fruition, you manifested in Our image, and We concealed you within the clay of immanence and the water of transcendence, and We molded you with the attributes. Then when you became baked clay, Our omnipotence etched within you the secret of will—"what, then, has deluded you with regard to your noble Lord?" [Q 82:6].

I created your clay with My Hand and etched the realities of your vicegerency upon your form, so that you may become manifest through the wet clay of power, and nonmanifest through the lights of the Presence. Between the pores of your clay, the awesome lights of divine singularity shone forth from behind the veil of might, so that the angelic periphery fell prostrate unto you, for you are the Kaʿba of existence and the manifestation-site of direct witnessing.

For when We were a non-delimited existence that did not accept forms, Our realities had to be reflected in entities and possibilities that were receptive of them, and so each name manifested as a mirror for Our realities. And it was in you that all these realities were brought together, and in you that every name became manifest.

I brought you into manifestation within *a span of the Aeon*, delimited by nondelimited meanings, and I *stretched forth* your *shadow* upon the earth of

2 I am grateful to Khalid Williams for his feedback on this translation.

3 Quran translations are based on Nasr, Seyyed Hossein et al. (eds.), *The study Quran: A new translation and commentary*, New York: HarperOne, 2015.

existence, then I "withdrew you unto Myself, a gentle withdrawal" [Q 25:46]. I made you nondelimited through the secret of supreme vicegerency, so that you became nondelimited in your delimitation, transcendent in your immanence.

So return to the center of your identity for *a span* of your time, and you shall find Me to be *the Aeon* itself. Annihilate the periphery in the center of Will, and you shall discover Me within your nonmanifest Cloud, your hidden core, your nonexistent being.

The Mixture of Divine Power

> Truly We created man from a drop of mixed fluid that We may test him, and We endowed him with hearing, seeing. [Q 76:2]

I *created* you from the *mixture* of opposites, and I proportioned your form with My hand, fusing together the sensory with the suprasensory, *that* I *may test* you with the burden that the heavens and the earth were unable to bear.

The *drop* of will began within the womb of power, and you witnessed the presence without form, while the realities of passion danced around you to the melodies of love, urging you to break out of your treasure-nature and become manifest, chanting the hymns of 'I loved to become known.'

Then you appeared from between the opposites, churning in the isthmus of the two oceans in "the most beautiful stature" [Q 95:4], in Our All-Merciful form and Our holy attributes, "hearing and seeing, so O mankind! What has deluded you with regard to your noble Lord, Who created you, then fashioned you, then proportioned you, assembling you in whatever form He willed?" [Q 82:6–8]. You are seduced by your own self from Me, and the herebelow has wrapped your heart with chains of appetites and pleasures, and the hereafter has shackled you with its palaces and amorous peers. You are a slave of worldly vestiges, a prisoner of separative entities, bound by the rope of your selfish interests, having fallen from the *most beautiful stature to the lowest of the low*.

And when you wished to depart, you only left one realm of being for another, spinning within an infinite orbit without ever standing still for a single moment. You must raise your saintly aspiration toward Our presence and return to Our mighty precinct, for there is none other than Us.

You must strive for the *kāf* of Spiritual Excellence, O human, the *kāf* by which you may see Me with My sight, and hear Me with My hearing, and come to Me with My foot, thereby becoming hearing, seeing, and a luminous lamp. Turn in repentance from yourself, and return to yourself within you. Mount the steed of My Lights so that you may plumb the oceans of My secrets. Pass away from the all, until you see that I am the all.

Guidance upon the Way

> Truly We guided him upon the way, be he grateful or ungrateful. [Q 76:3]

We *guided* you *upon the way* to attainment, clarified for you the foundational principles, and disclosed Ourself to you through the majestic Name. We made you a *book in which there is no doubt*, engraved with Our beautiful names, and wrote you down with the Pen of singularity and the ink of pre-eternity.

The guidance is from yourself to yourself, from your earth to your heaven, from your sensory faculties to your suprasensory reality. "Whoever is guided is only guided to his own soul" [Q 10:108]. Look at yourself and you shall see Me; search within yourself and you shall discover Me; plunge into yourself and you shall find Me. Read your hidden book and know its concealed secret that no angel or jinn can behold. Do not skip a single line, nor underestimate a single vowel or letter.

The *omen* of your secret is *fastened upon* your *neck*, and is closer to you than you are to yourself. So step outside of yourself, remain with yourself and for yourself, and drink the ginger of existence from your "boiling spring" [Q 88:5].

If you are *grateful*, you are *grateful* to yourself; if you are *ungrateful*, it is because of your own delusion. "And whosoever gives thanks, he gives thanks only for his own soul; and whosoever is ungrateful, truly my Lord is Self-Sufficient, Generous" [Q 27:40].

"We have surely prepared for the disbelievers chains, shackles, and a blazing flame" [Q 76:4].

As for the one who denies My commanding reality, and is heedless of My radiant presence, his recompense shall be *chains* of deprivation from My light, *shackles* of veils from My secrets, and the *blazing flame* of distance from the holy presence.

The Cup of the Pious

> Truly the pious drink of a cup mixed with camphor. [Q 76:5]

The *pious* are the servants of the attribute, those who are upon the innate disposition, in whose hearts gush forth the spring of singularity, so that the rivers of love flow within their souls, and the streams of yearning pervade their spirits, and the oceans of servanthood stir in their innermost secret hearts, delivering them from the contaminations of place and confinements of space, so that they see with My eye and hear with My hearing.

I gave them to drink from the *cup* of My gentleness that discloses itself through My holy Lights, mixed with the *camphor* of intense love, a pre-eternal drink from a pre-eternal *cup*, without shape or color. If it were to be unveiled, the people of heaven and earth would prostrate to its beauty; and if they were given to drink one drop of it, they would all be enraptured by the sweetness of its esoteric realities, their intellects dazzled by the pleasure of witnessing. A glance at it erases sin, and a sip from it quenches hearts. Whoever sees it knows Me, and whoever tastes it loves Me.

Its *camphor* (*kāfūr*) is one of My secrets, tasted only by the one who passes away in Me and subsists through Me. Its *kāf* is immanence for the people of faith; its *alif* measures out the constituents of spiritual excellence; its *fāʾ* is knowledge for the people of gnosis; its *wāw* is life for the people of certainty; and its *rāʾ* is an expansion for the servants of the All-Merciful.

The Fountain of God's Servants

> A fountain whereof drink the servants of God, while they make it gush forth abundantly. They fulfill their vows and fear a day whose evil is widespread, and give food, despite loving it, to the indigent, the orphan, and the captive. [Q 76:7–8]

The *fountain of the servants of God* is not mixed with the *camphor*-veils of the dualist attributes. It is transcendent beyond transcendence. Its *drink* is sheer in essence and single-sourced, because for them there is no difference between subjugation and gentleness. To their unitary essences, the attributes resemble one another; they bring together the opposites, and have become liminal entities within the coolness of the spring. They are at once the drinkers and the cup-bearers, *making it gush forth* and then *drinking*.

They *drink* from the spring of the hidden Name, then draw from within their spirits "drinks of diverse hues" [Q 16:69] and stations for the folk of the attributes and acts, *wherein there is healing* for the sickness of beholding other-than-God, a balm for the wounds of separation, and an antidote to the poison of the ego.

They fulfill their vows, willingly sacrificing themselves by passing away in My oneness. They have no existence except through Me, for I am the One and they are the manifestation-sites of My levels.

The Indigent, the Orphan, and the Captive

> And they give food, despite loving it, to the indigent, the orphan, and the captive. [Q 76:8]

The *food* of the presence is beloved to the people of the beatific vision, because it is their inner provision. Whoever gives of what his soul loves pierces through the most intense veils of separation. "You will never attain piety till you spend from that which you love" [Q 3:92]. So *spend from* the lights and gnostic sciences that I have bestowed upon you.

The "indigent is the one whose spiritual provision is limited" [Q 65:7] and is incapable of seeking it for himself because he finds repose in sensory objects. Therefore you must feed him from the holy feasts that were provided to you.

The orphan is the one without an intermediary to support him with the gnostic sciences of the unseen. You must admit him into the protection of your stronghold, and embrace him among the children of the presence, "as progeny, one from another" [Q 3:34].

The captive is the one who is bound by the chains of natural appetites and the attributes of the evil-enjoying soul. You must set free the saintly aspiration within him, so that he may rid himself of the shackles of his earth-nature and break from the fetters of his illusion.

Before feeding them, teach them *in the name of God* so that they may realize its realities. Let them eat from the stations of proximity before them, as was decreed for them in pre-eternity; and let them not encroach upon the stations of others, nor eat from the middle, for that is the locus of the descent and of blessing.

The Face of God

> We feed you only for the Face of God. We do not desire any recompense or thanks from you. [Q 76:9]

My true servants are those who have passed away from the sensory human substance and from the wages of deeds. They aspire through their deeds for My approval, not for amorous peers and palaces, nor out of fear of chains and fires. They seek the neighbor before the house. Their hearts wish to gaze upon the Cup-Bearer on the day of approval and good-pleasure. "Faces that Day shall be radiant, gazing upon their Lord" [Q 75:22–23].

There is no distance between Me and My true servants. They are the intermediary, and they are the veil. They are the manifestation-site of My beauty and mercy. I have permitted to them My beauty, and so they enjoy My Light. I have allowed them to behold My secrets, and so they attain realization of My names. Wherever they turn, they witness pure meaning before sensory object, and so they grasp the allusion and transcend the expression. You see them turning their faces unto the heaven of dominion, so I turn them toward the qibla of the Name: the sacred mosque of pre-eternity.

Radiance and Joy

> "Truly we fear from our Lord a grim, calamitous day." So God has shielded them from the evil of that Day, bestowed upon them radiance and joy. [Q 76:10–11]

Things have no existence alongside the One whom "nothing is like unto Him" [Q 42:11]. Transcend time and you shall enter the stronghold of the Aeon; and I am the Aeon.

There is no past and no future, but only your now. Do not confine My gaze in time, for time is passing away, and I am the Subsistent. Rather, look at yourself and you shall see Me. My signs within you are a concealed and sewn up mass; and on the horizons they are inscribed in unstitched differentiation.

Whoever beholds himself discovers Me, and whoever beholds My traces loves Me; for My traces are proof of My names, and My names are proof of My attributes, and My attributes are a proof of My Essence. Pass away from the engendered realms of being, and behold the Being-Giver; pass away from the cup, and behold the Cup-Bearer.

How could you presume to know Me while you are imprisoned by your spatial directions, confined to your human nature, enthralled by your bodily structure, enraptured with love for that which passes away?

The Light of My Face pervades the heavens and the earth. "No disproportion dost thou see in the All-Merciful's creation" [Q 67:3]. See with the eye of oneness, and you shall behold Me in the all; efface spatial location, and spatial extension will come to naught. Cling to the possessive particle 'My' [in My spirit, *rūḥī*; Q 38:29], that it may bring you back to the original inblowing.

My servants have passed away from time, and burst through the walls of their bodily frames, and penetrated the courtyard of non-spatiality with their inner vision, freeing themselves from the bonds of number and reckoning. I greet them with joy, radiance, nearness, and manifestation. They wander in My beauty, dazzled. Your gaze falls upon them, but you do not see them, for you are veiled by yourself from them. You must travel the path of the people of love, and be among the righteous.

The Garden of the Gnostic Sciences

> And [God has] rewarded them, for having been patient, with a Garden and with silk. Therein they recline upon couches, seeing neither sun nor bitter cold. Its shade shall be close above them, and its clusters shall be made to hang low. [Q 76:12–14]

The *garden* of gnostic sciences is surrounded by the trench of the "I"-letters. Build the bridge of "He" with lowliness, needfulness, repentance, and seeking forgiveness, that you may enter among the ranks of the servants.

Whoever enters the garden of gnostic sciences, I shall clothe in the *silk* of My attributes, and conceal his qualities with My qualities, and cover his characteristics with My characteristic, until he says to a thing, "'Be!,' and it is" [Q 2:117].

He *reclines upon couches* of names and stations, covered by *the shade* of nearness from the *sun* of yearning and the *bitter cold* of spiritual states, with the fruits of pure meaning *hanging low* as he enjoys the delights of abandonment in God.

A Spring Named Salsabīl

> And vessels of silver and goblets of crystal are passed around them—silvern crystal that they have measured out with due measure. Therein they are given to drink of a cup mixed with ginger, a spring therein named Salsabīl. [Q 76:15–18]

They are encircled by attendants in the abode of permanence, because in the herebelow they were the center of the command and the *qibla* of disclosures. They were the Kaʿba of My Lights and the manifestation-site of My secrets.

Vessels of marvelous forms fashioned from the *silver* of My attributes *are passed around them*, and *goblets* of unseen subtleties fashioned from the *silvern* Lights of My Essence; *goblets of* the *crystal* glass of their inner hearts, resplendent planets and lordly suns, *that they have measured out* during their vanishing lives *with due measure*, and filled them up with Lights and secrets.

They are My true servants, and I give them to drink from a *cup mixed with* the hot *ginger* of yearning, and the pleasure of complete absorption in the presence of My attributes. This *mixture* is a *spring* of divine attributes and Essence, tasted by the one who has passed away in the hot *ginger* of yearning as well as the cool *camphor* of plunging, so that he brings together countless opposites, and the Salsabīl of the Eternal One manifests for him.

The Blissful Presence

> Immortal youths wait upon them; when you see them you would suppose them to be scattered pearls. And when thou seest, there thou wilt see bliss and a great kingdom. Upon them are garments of fine green silk and rich brocade. They are adorned with silvern bracelets and their Lord shall give them to drink of a drink most pure. Truly this is a reward for you, and your endeavoring is held in gratitude. [Q 76:19–22]

As they dwell in the gardens of My presence, the *immortal youths* of name-disclosure *wait upon them, pearls* cultivated from the drop of mercy descending from the heaven of My most holy effusion, guarded in the oysters of their breasts.

An incomparable *bliss* in the garden of the presence. Behold, again and again, and you shall *see* what you have never seen: a garden of My presence, not delimited by the cycles of time, closer to you than the straps of your sandals, My *reward* is not a delayed payment.

I clothe them in *garments* of reward, *fine silk* of the names and *rich brocade* of the attributes, and I beautify them *silvern bracelets* of My lordly character traits.

I give them to drink of a drink purified from temporality, squeezed from the pre-eternal wine, that they may purify themselves of their claims, and awaken from their illusions, and be able to *touch* that which is *concealed*, and swim in the "locations of the stars" [Q 56:75–79].

The Name of the Lord

> Truly We have sent down the Quran upon thee as a revelation. So be patient with thy Lord's judgment and obey neither sinner nor disbeliever among them. And invoke the Name of thy Lord morning and evening, prostrate unto Him during the night, and glorify Him by night at length. Truly they love the ephemeral and put a weighty day behind them. [Q 76:23–28]

The engendered realms of being are traces of the differentiated *furqān*, and durations of time are traces of the gathered Quran. The dot of the *bāʾ* is the secret of union, while the letter is the door of duality. Read the stitched non-differentiation within the unstitched differentiation and you shall become a gathered Quran; understand the unstitched differentiation through the stitched non-differentiation, and you shall become a human being.

"Whoever remembers Me, I shall remember him. So remember Me, and I shall remember you" [Q 2:152]. Whomever I remember, I shall remind him of himself, and whomever I remind of himself shall be guided toward Me. I shall make for him a mirror by which he may behold his true nature and know that he is the center of the orbit of transcendence, as well as the periphery of the realm of immanence. For when My Identity desired to disclose Itself from the Treasure, for and by Itself, It manifested through the human reality that encompasses all the names, is adorned by all the attributes, and bears all the properties and levels. When the angels of the heavens saw it, they fell prostrate before the Adamic human form. You are therefore the index of the book of existence, and you are the reality of My supreme name.

Whoever desires to attain Me, let him remember Me *by night at length*, and glorify Me *morning and evening*, till I cover His description with My description, and conceal His attribute with My attribute, and manifest for him knowledge of opposites, and split the *lām* for him into two *alifs*, so that he recognizes the difference between the master and the servant. The one flows through all numbers, and prostration is the dot of conjunction and intimate union: "prostrate and draw nigh" [Q 96:19]. He will fall down in perpetual prostration, and his prayer will be constant and everlasting.

The Reminder

> We created them and made firm their frames; and whensoever We will, We shall exchange them for others like them. Truly this is a reminder; so let him who will, take a way unto his Lord. And you do not will but that God wills. Truly God is Knowing, Wise. He causes whomsoever He will to enter into His Mercy. And as for the wrongdoers, He has prepared for them a painful punishment. [Q 76:28–31]

I have *reminded* you, O forgetful one. I have alerted you, O distracted one. Mount the steed of invocation, and fly away from yourself toward yourself. Remove the secondary connections and causes between Us, so that you may enter into the election of pre-eternity, and the light of your innate disposition may pour into the cup of your heart. This is My *way*.

Expose yourselves to the breezes of union, and halt before the doorstep of My will and the source of My desire. *Take* the *way* of the servants of the presence; the manifestation-sites of My success-giving and My guidance, the guardians of the courtyard of mighty approval, so that you may be "exchanged for others, and be brought into being as another creation," [Q 23:14] in "the most beautiful stature," [Q 95:3] in My merciful form and luminous attributes.

Bibliography

al-Karkari, Mohamed Faouzi, *al-Kawākib al-durriyya fī bayān al-uṣūl al-nūrāniyya*, Casablanca: Maṭbaʿat Ṣināʿat al-Kitāb, 2013.

al-Karkari, Mohamed Faouzi, *Kitāb al-Maḥajja al-bayḍāʾ*, Casablanca: Maṭbaʿat Ṣināʿat al-Kitāb, 2014.

al-Karkari, Mohamed Faouzi, *Dīwān dinān al-arwāḥ*, Casablanca: Maṭbaʿat Ṣināʿat al-Kitāb, 2015.

al-Karkari, Mohamed Faouzi, *al-Tarātīl al-hāʾiyya fī l-āya al-hārūniyya al-mūsāwiyya*, Casablanca: Maṭbaʿat Ṣināʿat al-Kitāb, 2016.

al-Karkari, Mohamed Faouzi, *Afānīn al-sujūd li-alif al-khulūd*, Casablanca: Maṭbaʿat Ṣināʿat al-Kitāb, 2017.

al-Karkari, Mohamed Faouzi, *Kāf al-astār li-mā fīhā l-jalāla min asrār*, Casablanca: Maṭbaʿat Ṣināʿat al-Kitāb, 2018.

al-Karkari, Mohamed Faouzi, *In the footsteps of Moses: A contemporary Sufi commentary on the story of God's confidant* (kalīm Allāh) *in the Qurʾān*, trans. Yousef Casewit, ed. Khalid Williams, Brussels: Les 7 Lectures, 2021.

al-Karkari, Mohamed Faouzi, *Introduction to Islamic metaphysics: A contemporary Sufi treatise on the secrets of the divine name*, trans. Yousef Casewit and Khalid Williams, Brussels: Les 7 Lectures, 2021.

al-Karkari, Mohamed Faouzi, *Sabaʾ al-ins wa-l-jānn fī ḥaḍrat Dāwūd wa-Sulaymān*, Casablanca: Maṭbaʿat Ṣināʿat al-Kitāb, 2021.

al-Karkari, Mohamed Faouzi, *Sufism revived: A contemporary treatise on divine light, prophecy, and sainthood*, trans. Yousef Casewit, ed. Khalid Williams and Tarek Ghanem, Brussels: Les 7 Lectures, 2021.

al-Karkari, Mohamed Faouzi, *The foundations of the Karkariyya order*, trans. Yousef Casewit, Khalid Williams and Jamil Zaghdoudi, Brussels: Les 7 Lectures, 2021.

al-Karkari, Mohamed Faouzi, *The Sufi path of light*, trans. Khalid Williams, ed. Yousef Casewit, (forthcoming).

Nasr, Seyyed Hossein et al. (eds.), *The study Quran: A new translation and commentary*, New York: HarperOne, 2015.

Thibdeau, John, "Visions and virtues: The *minhāj al-tarbiya* of the *ṭarīqa* Karkariyya," in *Journal of Sufi Studies* 11.2 (2022), 251–286.

Zaghdoudi, Jamil, *At the service of destiny: A biography of the living Moroccan Sufi master Shaykh Mohamed Faouzi al-Karkari*, trans. Edin Lohja, ed. Yousef Casewit, Brussels: Les 7 Lectures, 2019.

CHAPTER 26

Remembering Toshihiko Izutsu: Linguist, Islamicist, Philosopher

Atif Khalil

1 Introduction

The publication of this *Festschrift* in honor of Professors William Chittick and Sachiko Murata coincides with the 30-year death anniversary of Toshihiko Izutsu, who was one of their teachers and one of the most remarkable scholars of Islam of the last century. Like Henry Corbin (d. 1978), with whom he forged a close friendship, Izutsu saw himself first and foremost as a philosopher, and in his own particular case, as a "metaphysician of the word."[1] The designation symbolized both his fascination with language and a lifelong preoccupation with the nature of Being to the extent that it emerges as a Word (through the *kun fa-yakūn*, the creative fiat) out of the silence of the formless Absolute, Beyond Being, Non-Being, or Void. In conventional academic parlance, Izutsu might also be described as a philosopher of language, a designation not wholly inaccurate as long as we keep in mind the intricate, intimate relation he believed to exist between human speech, on the one hand, and Being as a repository of meaning, on the other.

Born in Tokyo in 1914 to a businessman who was also deeply committed to Zen and the art of calligraphy, in his early adulthood he gravitated towards the study of language and Greek philosophy. At least some of this impulse stemmed from a reaction to the austere and demanding forms of meditation his father imposed on him in childhood, not to mention his devaluation of thinking, although the precise nature of Izutsu's early relation with Buddhism remains unclear.[2] It was this appreciation for the magic of language that stirred in his

1 Wakamatsu, Eisuke, *Toshihiko Izutsu and the philosophy of word: In search of the spiritual Orient*, trans. Jean C. Hoff, Tokyo: International House of Japan, 2014, xii.

2 On Izutsu's early relationship with both Zen and his father, see Makino, Shinya, "On the originality of 'Izutsu' Oriental philosophy," in Sayyid J. Āshtiyānī et al. (eds.), *Consciousness and reality: Studies in memory of Toshihiko Izutsu*, Leiden: Brill, 2000, 253–254; Nakamura, Kojiro, "The significance of Toshihiko Izutsu's legacy for comparative religion," in *Intellectual Discourse* 17.2 (2009), 147–158, 147–148; Wakamatsu, *Toshihiko Izutsu* 3–6.

 | DOI:10.1163/9789004529038_027

heart a desire to learn Arabic, a wish later fulfilled when he met Abdurreshid Ibrahim (b. 1857) in his early 20s. A Russian Tatar who traced his descent to Bukharans who had migrated to Western Siberia, he moved to Japan in the early 1930s after an initial visit in 1909. Having been imprisoned in the Russian Empire on more than one occasion for his anti-colonial, pan-Islamic activities, Japan seemed like an ideal refuge. The nation had proven itself remarkably resilient in the 1904–1905 war with Russia,[3] and its cultural and moral ethos, in his eyes, was deeply compatible with Islam. Having studied in Medina, Mecca, and Istanbul, the man who had served as *qāḍī* in his own country, was no insignificant figure. Among Japanese journalists, he was sometimes introduced as "the former president of Muslims in Russia." Even though no such office existed, he held a prominent place in the eyes of his co-religionists.[4] Conversant in Japanese, it was perhaps only natural that he would become the first imam of the Tokyo Mosque.[5]

Although Ibrahim had initially declined the young Izutsu's requests for a meeting, he eventually agreed but stubbornly refused to teach him Arabic. When they met, the elderly gentleman said to him, holding an English biography of the Prophet Muhammad in his hand, *hādha kitāb jā'a min Amrīka, afahimta?* (This book has just arrived from America. Do you understand?).[6]

3 In a speech delivered in Japan on his visit in 1909, Shaikh Ibrahim described the plight of his community under Russian rule, along with his newfound fascination with the country, in the following words: "Frankly, before the Russo-Japanese War I knew almost nothing about Japan. Japan's great success in this war affected me so much that I decided to come to Japan. I am sure we can learn many things in Japan which are developing day by day like the rising sun. As to our Tatar people, words cannot describe the various kinds of oppression that we suffered during 450 years under Russian rule. The Russian government has not permitted us to learn our own history. They do not want to have enlightened Muslim subjects; for example, last year alone 15 Tatar schools, built by the people's own efforts and expense, were closed down by the order of the government. You can understand everything by this simple example." Cited in Komatsu, Hisao, "Muslim intellectuals and Japan: A pan-Islamist mediator, Abdurreshid Ibrahim," in Stéphane A. Dudoignon, Hisao Komatsu and Yasushi Kosugi (eds.), *Intellectuals in the modern Islamic world: Transmission, transformation, communication*, London: Routledge, 2006, 273–288, 277.

4 Komatsu, "Muslim intellectuals" 274.

5 On the intersecting political and religious nature of Ibrahim's relationship with Japan, see Esenbel, Selcuk, "Abdürreşid Ibrahim: 'The world of Islam and the spread of Islam in Japan,' 1910," in Sven Saaler and Chistopher W.A. Szpilman (eds.), *Pan-Asianism: A documentary history*. I. *1850–1920*, Lanham, MD: Rowman & Littlefield, 2011, 195–203; Esenbel, Selcuk, "Japan's global claim to Asia and the world of Islam: Transnational nationalism and world power, 1900–1945," in *AHR* 109.4 (2004), 1140–1170, 1148–1154. See also Komatsu, "Muslim intellectuals" 273–288. On the Tokyo Mosque, see below.

6 Wakamatsu, *Toshihiko Izutsu* 50–51.

Izutsu would later recall the "tremendous thrill" he felt on hearing the sound of classical Arabic. The excitement must have impressed itself on him, since he agreed to teach Izutsu, but on one condition: that he also learn the faith of the majority of those who speak it. Originally, the arrangement between them was for Izutsu to come once a week for lessons. Instead, he ended up attending almost every day. Two years later, he had become so immersed in the universe of Islam that Ibrahim could say to him, "You are a natural-born Muslim. Since you were a Muslim from the time of your birth, you are my son."[7] Izutsu's wife, Toyoko, later described her husband's teacher as "an engaging and affable man who ... had a penchant for proverbs."[8] Abdurreshid Ibrahim died in exile in Japan in 1944, in his early 90s—in the same year as Izutsu's father.

It was through the Tokyo Imam that Izutsu would meet one of his protégés, Musa Jarullah (b. 1875), also a Tatar Russian involved in the political and religious resistance movement against the Russians for their incursion into and annexation of Muslim territories.[9] A scholar trained in Maturidi theology and Hanafi law in the *madrasas* of Bukhara in modern Uzbekistan, and having served for some time as the imam of the Great Mosque of St. Petersburg,[10] he was also an advocate of women's rights, promoted a doctrine of universal salvation, and argued that the *ʿulamāʾ* had fallen short of their responsibilities as custodians of the faith.[11] While he (like Ibrahim) has often been described as a *jadīdī* or Muslim reformer,[12] he objected to the term because it was often used as a term of reproach by his critics.[13] In fact, his own thought appeared to combine strands of both traditionalism and reform, conservatism and reconstruction. It was under his tutelage that Izutsu studied the grammar of Sībawayh (d. 180/796), pre-Islamic *jāhilī* poetry, and a range of other

7 Wakamatsu, *Toshihiko Izutsu* 51.

8 Wakamatsu, *Toshihiko Izutsu* 51.

9 The most comprehensive study of his life and influence in English is to be found in Altuntas, Selcuk, *How to be a proper Muslim in the Russian Empire: An intellectual biography of Musa Jaraullah Bigiyev (1875–1949)*, Madison (PhD Diss.): University of Wisconsin-Madison, 2018.

10 Wakamatsu, *Toshihiko Izutsu* 53.

11 Albayrak, Ismail, "The reception of Toshihiko's Izutsu's Qur'anic studies in the Muslim world: With special reference to Turkish Qur'anic scholarship," in *JQS* 14.1 (2012), 73–106, 97n3; Altuntas, *How to be a proper Muslim* 4–5 and 11–13.

12 On the Russian Jadidists, see Fuller, Graham E., *A world without Islam*, New York: Little, Brown and Company, 2010, 173–177. On the fluctuating plight of Muslims in Russia, see ch. 8. As the former vice-chairman of the National Intelligence Council at the CIA, the author brings a unique perspective to his analysis of political Islamic movements.

13 Altuntas, *How to be a proper Muslim* 3.

classical Arabic texts.[14] It was also through Musa Jarullah that Izutsu came to learn of the prodigious powers of memory that were produced in the educational centers where the *ʿulamāʾ* were trained. Once he came to visit Izutsu when he had fallen sick. Noticing his large collection of books, he asked him what he did when he moved, to which the student replied, somewhat sheepishly, that he packed them in a basket and carried them "like a snail." Musa laughed and said a genuine scholar could teach and write anywhere, empty-handed. On one occasion, Izutsu brought some Arabic texts for his teacher. A few days later, when he returned, to his surprise Musa had memorized them all.[15]

Musa would eventually depart Japan, making his way to Cairo where he passed away some years after WWII, in 1949. A decade before his own death, Izutsu penned a short essay in Japanese in his memory, entitled *The wandering pilgrim teacher*. Activist, intellectual, conservative, reformer, Izutsu always respectfully referred to him as "Professor Musa." The man who had traveled throughout the Islamic world after his exile from Russia appeared unable to stay in one land. In a novella by Toyoko featuring her husband, he would say to Izutsu, "To become like a tree rotting in the place it was planted—what a boring life."[16]

While Japan did not have a developed Islamic studies tradition, Izutsu's scholarship of Islam did not emerge, within a Japanese academic context, out of a total vacuum. One formidable influence was Shūmei Ōkawa,[17] director of the East Asian Economic Research Bureau, a think tank for whose journal (*New Asia*) Izutsu regularly contributed. Ōkawa, as Izutsu would state, had a "deeply personal interest" in Islam.[18] As the author of an early introductory book on the subject in Japanese, *Outline of Islam*, he saw the faith as a culmination of the Abrahamic religions, a bridge between East and West, and yet also a manifestation of the "Oriental spirit."[19] While he was familiar with Western scholarship on Islam, he objected to what he felt was the underlying prejudice that animated much of it, rooted in centuries of military conflict with the Muslim world.

14 Albayrak, "The reception" 74.

15 Wakamutsa, *Toshihiko Izutsu* 53.

16 Wakamutsa, *Toshihiko Izutsu* 52.

17 The Japanese convention of placing the last name before the first has not been followed in this paper, for purposes of creating consistency with the citation of non-Japanese names.

18 Cited in Wakamatsu, *Toshihiko Izutsu* 56. For a Saidian analysis of the apparent tensions in his views of Islam, see Aydin, Cemil, *The politics of civilizational identities: Asia, West and Islam in the pan-Asianist thought of Ôkawa Shûmei*, Cambridge, MA (PhD Diss.): Harvard University, 2002, ch. 6.

19 See more on this complex question below.

Some of these attitudes had even percolated into Japanese culture, such as the belief that the religion's founder came with the Quran in one hand and the sword in the other, offering death or conversion. For Ōkawa, the Prophet's earnest desire was not war but peace, and he only resorted to violence as a last resort. "Unfortunately," he wrote, "as a result of Christianity's hostility to all things non-Christian, Islam is always painted black."[20] Ōkawa also pointed out that Muslims developed a pattern of religious toleration wherever they went, unprecedented for the scale and size of their civilization. What particularly attracted him to the faith was the manner in which it sought to synthesize the political, social, economic, private, and spiritual spheres of life into a single rubric.

Although Ōkawa has been described as one of the founders of Islamic studies in Japan,[21] he was not, to be clear, a professionally trained Islamicist. Born in 1886, in high school he had been captivated by Western philosophy. By the time he entered university, however, his interest had shifted to pre-modern Japanese thought, Buddhism, and ancient India. He eventually graduated with a thesis on Nāgārjuna.[22] Largely self-taught when it came to Islam,[23] he published an essay on Sufism in 1910,[24] and a series of articles on "Mohammed and his religion," shortly afterward.[25] His most important works on the faith would only come out closer to the end of his life, including (apart from his introductory book) a translation of the Quran[26] that was completed before his death, not

20 Cited in Wakamatsu, *Toshihiko Izutsu* 56.

21 Aydin, *The politics* 173.

22 Takeuchi, Yoshimi, "Profile of Asian minded man X: Ōkawa Shūmei," in *Developing Economies* 7.3 (1969), 367–379, 370. For a critical appraisal of Takeuchi's article, and some important corrections, see Usuki, Akira, "A Japanese Asianist's view of Islam," in *Annales of Japan Association for Middle East Studies* 28.2 (2013), 59–84. Ōkawa's studies of Indian philosophy took place under the direction of Masaharu Anesaki (1873–1949), the founder of the disciple of Religious Studies in the country. Krämer, Hans M., "Pan-Asianism's religious undercurrents: The reception of Islam and translation of the Qurʾān in twentieth century Japan," in *The Journal of Asian Studies* 73.3 (2014), 619–640, 627.

23 It should be noted that he too had studied with Shaikh Ibrahim, although it is hard to determine the extent of it in the available secondary literature.

24 Usuki, "A Japanese Asianist's view" 66.

25 Usuki, "A Japanese Asianist's view" 82.

26 While he had studied Arabic in his younger days, he was not fluent enough to produce a direct translation and had to rely instead on the available ones in the languages he was fluent in. Describing the process of producing his own rendition of the sacred text, Ōkawa wrote, "I asked that the Arabic edition of the Koran and copies of more than ten foreign translations of the Koran such as Japanese, classic Chinese, English, French and Dutch translations be brought into my study room and my hospital. I began to read them … My illness didn't affect my understanding. On the contrary, I could understand more clearly

long after he had recovered from a mental illness that forced him to become hospitalized at the Matsuzawa Hospital. In his memoir, he said this was the most peaceful time of his life. Curiously, he also reported having visions during this period of the Prophet, "dressed in a green mantle and a turban" declaring "there is only one God: and Muhammad, Christ and the Buddha are all prophets of the same God."[27] He left behind a biography on him that was published posthumously.

Ōkawa's scholarly career cannot be disentangled from his political activities as a Pan-Asianist who saw in Pan-Islamism an ally against Western imperial encroachment—a view shared by many in the government. His fascination with the faith, bordering at times on Islamophilia, was at least partially grounded in the role he felt it could play in the formation of a united Eastern front against the West, with imperial Japan at the center. The seeds for Izutsu's deep sympathy for Islam and his later association, though indirect, with the Traditionalist school, known for its critique of the "desacralization" of the world brought about through secular modernity, may well have been planted, in this respect, by the political and cultural climate of pre-WWI Japan, as well as his close relation to thinkers associated with anti-colonial, anti-Western movements. These were figures with profoundly existential interests in religion and who were grappling with how to preserve tradition in the modern world without at the same time succumbing to the domination of the West.[28] On this question, however, there is a need for more research—research that does not at the same time ignore the truly ecumenical, global vision of Izutsu's own scholarship,[29] and the seeming distance he kept from politics.

Izutsu began to write on Islam and related themes early in his life. His first major article, in Japanese, came out in 1939. It was on Arabic linguistics. A year later, he published another essay on the ethics of the Muʿtazilite Quran commentator al-Zamakhsharī (d. 538/1144). Then in 1941, when he was only 27,

most of the passages that I couldn't understand when I first read them." Cited in Usuki, "A Japanese Asianist's view" 76–77.

27 Cited in Esenbel, "Japan's global claim" 1162.

28 See Esenbel's observations in "Japan's global claim" 1145–1146.

29 Takeuchi notes the vision of a global community, of a united East and West, that may have emerged in Ōkawa's own thought and intellectual career near the end of his life, where Islam played the role not just of an ally of the East, but of a bridge that could bring the two worlds together. "It is conceivable," writes Takeuchui, "that the Islamic religion was a subject of greater interest to Ōkawa than either Christianity, Buddhism or Japan's indigenous religions. Ōkawa had an image of a sphere in which were united religion and politics, of a place which was the point of encounter between East and West; for him, Islam was the manifestation of this ideal. As his research progressed, he became more and more captivated by the Islamic religion. For that very reason, his Islamic studies are outstanding, and even today are a valuable legacy." Takeuchi, "Profile" 373.

he wrote his first book, again in Japanese, *A history of Arabic thought: Islamic theology and philosophy*, a survey that ended with Averroes (d. 595/1198).[30] His scholarly output at this stage took place within an intellectual milieu that saw a rise of Japanese publications on Islam, an outgrowth of deepening relations between Japan's pan-Asianists and anti-colonial Muslim pan-Islamists. The highpoint of this period lay between 1939 and 1941, when according to one count a total of 673 books, articles, and pamphlets were printed on the subject.[31] Interestingly, this three-year span followed the erection of the Tokyo Mosque in 1938 on the occasion of the Prophet's birthday. Built in the style of classical Central Asian architecture, and funded in part by the Japanese government including major corporations such as Mitsubishi, at the opening of the mosque delegates from a range of Muslim countries were present. They included the crown prince of Yemen, envoys from Mecca, Chinese Muslims, and emigres from the USSR.[32] Ibrahim who was invited to assume the role of the mosque's imam, was also present. It was here that Izutsu would often come to continue his studies.

2 The Years Following the Second World War

Five years after the catastrophic tragedies of Hiroshima and Nagasaki, Izutsu became an Assistant Professor at Keio University, although he began working as a researcher and later lecturer at the institution from 1937 onwards. Then in 1952, when he was 38, he wrote a biography of the Prophet (*Mahometto*) in Japanese. However, in the words of Wakamatsu, this work, by Izutsu's own confession, was not strictly speaking a historical study but "a hymn of praise to his spiritual hero and a confession of his inner thoughts."[33] Yet Izutsu also later said of this work on a figure whom he referred to as "the hero of the spiritual world"—the "spiritual world" being, for Izutsu, reality—that it was his "pure starting point."[34] In the same year he married Toyoko, the woman that would become his life-long companion. From 1957–1958, he produced a Japanese translation of the Quran. It was no doubt his painstaking analysis of the

30 Wakamatsu described the study as "the first serious history of Islamic philosophy in Japanese." See Wakamatsu, *Toshihiko Izutsu* 307–308.

31 Aydin, *The politics* 174n2.

32 Esenbel, "Japan's global claim" 1164–1165; Komatsu, "Muslim intellectuals" 282–283.

33 Wakamatsu, *Toshihiko Izutsu* 156. See also Nakamura, Kojiro, "Islamic Studies in Japan," in Gerrie ter Haar and Yoshio Tsuruoka (eds.), *Religion and society: An agenda for the 21st century*, Leiden: Brill, 2007, 261–265, 263.

34 Wakamatusu, *Toshihiko Izutsu* 2, 123, and 156.

scripture that accompanied this task that set the stage, in 1959, for his first English book on Islam, *The structure of ethical terms in the Quran: A study in semantics*. This would lay the foundation for the development of a linguistic method of analyzing the text, and lead to the publication in 1964 of *God and man in the Quran*, and then in 1965, of *The concept of belief in Islamic theology: A semantic analysis of īmān and islām*. Along with *Ethico-religious concepts of the Quran* (a revised version of the earliest of the triad), Izutsu's studies of the language and worldview of Muslim revelation would establish him as an Islamicist of international stature, not to be ignored. It was a testament to his linguistic versatility that, as a scholar entirely trained in Japan, he was able to compose such innovative, ground-breaking studies entirely in English. This is not to say there was no pushback from certain quarters in the West in response to an outsider writing about the faith of Muslims (a subject over which many Orientalists in the guild traditions felt they exercised monopoly). Even when his work was praised, a certain civilizational hubris might lurk in the background, as when one American professor observed in the pages of a leading journal, in what amounted to a backhanded compliment, that one "may perhaps be more surprised to find a Japanese scholar writing on Islamic subjects than to find that he does it well."[35]

Izutsu's Japanese translation of the Quran was the first to be based on the original Arabic. There were at least two others (besides Ōkawa's[36]) that appeared earlier, relying on European languages.[37] The first of these came out in 1920 at the hands of Ken'ichi Sakamoto (d. 1930), a prolific public intellectual responsible for a number of works on European history and a 2,500-page *World history*, not to mention a biography of the Prophet Muhammad published in 1899. For his knowledge of Muslim beliefs, practices, and tradition, he seems to have depended exclusively on Western scholarship, making use of Rodwell's 1861 English Quran for his own. His aim was to render knowledge of the history and religions of the world available to the Japanese middle-class.[38] The other version was completed by Gorō Takahashi (1856–1935) and Amado Ariga (1868–1946). The former was an experienced translator of European religious and philosophical literature, commissioned by the latter, a Japanese convert to

35 Partin, Harry B., "Semantics of the Qurʾān: A consideration of Izutsu's studies," in *History of Religions* 9.4 (1970), 358–362, 358. One problem his work encountered was that it was not operating on the premises of the deeply historicist nature of Western scholarship on the Quran.

36 See fn 26.

37 As noted earlier, Ōkawa made use of a Quran in classical Chinese.

38 Krämer, "Pan-Asianism's religious undercurrents" 621–622.

Islam, to help in producing a Quran that was more accessible than Sakamoto's, which, for Amado, had the unfortunate feature of being too expensive and difficult to understand. He wanted one that could be of "general use" so it could better serve his needs of making the sacred text of Islam accessible to his countrymen and women.[39]

An intriguing figure in the history of Islam in Japan, Amado was born Bunhachirō Ariga, but adopted the name "Ahmad" ("Amado" being a Japanized version) following his conversion, which took place closer to the end of his life. He had been introduced to the religion in India as a young man at the end of the 19th century while serving as a foreign trade representative. An Indian Muslim merchant by the name of Haydar Ali, whom he encountered in his travels, left a deep impression on him, planting the seeds for a formal entry into Islam decades later.[40] Active in Japan's small but growing Muslim community, and part of Ibrahim's broader network, he played a role in the construction not only of the mosque of Tokyo, but also of Nagoya and Kōbe. Like other Japanese converts, he felt that Shinto and Islam were deeply compatible. "In our country's Shinto," he wrote, "we believe in the Great God Amenominakanushi; this deity is identical to the only God in which we [Muslims] believe. For this reason, I think that those people who believe in Amenominakanushi are by nature identical to us believers."[41] This impulse to see in the theology of Islam deep structural simil-

39 Krämer, "Pan-Asianism's religious undercurrents" 624–625.

40 Misawa, Nobuo, "Shintoism and Islam in interwar Japan: How did the Japanese come to believe in Islam?," in *Orient* 46 (2011), 119–140, 130.

41 Citied in Krämer, "Pan-Asianism's religious undercurrents" 627. Generally speaking, Amado was lukewarm about pressing the similarities between Shinto and Islam, unlike another prominent Japanese convert, Nur Muhammad Ippei Tanaka (1882–1934). Some have accused the latter of stressing the converges between the two faiths to the point of syncretism. This was certainly not how he saw it. And even if there were some syncretism present, it probably could not have gone very far, considering his close relation with and tutelage under Shaikh Ibrahim. It should perhaps be noted here that Tanaka had engaged in a deep study of Islam while in China, having been inspired by Liu Zhi's (d. 1730) Chinese biography of the Prophet Muhammad which he translated into Japanese. In many respects, he sought to look at Islam through the lens of Shinto in much the same way that Chinese Muslims had often looked at Islam through the lens of Confucianism. Generally speaking, there is a tendency in much of the secondary literature to overstate the political reasons for Japanese conversions to Islam in the pre-WWII period, while calling into question the knowledge these converts had of the faith they adopted. Misawa's treatment of this problem helps rectify the tendency, at least in some respects, but falls into its own traps. Misawa, "Shintoism and Islam" 119–140. For more on Tanaka, see Dufourmont, Eddy, "Tanaka Ippei: 'Islam and pan-Asianism,' 1924," in Sven Saaler and Christopher W.A. Szpilman (eds.), *Pan-Asianism: A documentary history. II. 1920-Present*, Lanham, MD: Rowman & Littlefield, 2011, 87–91.

arities with the religions of the Far East, a sentiment found among Muslims in this part of the world, would emerge also in Izutsu, although in a much more refined, developed, and nuanced form. Naturally, Izutsu's own translation of the Quran would outstrip all those that preceded it both in its precision and quality for self-evident reasons. Only a scholar of his erudition and mastery of classical Arabic could produce a version of such a caliber, made all the more popular since it was written not in formal literary but colloquial Japanese.[42]

Many have argued that the waning of Japanese interest in Islam after the second world war is proof that it was simply rooted in the geopolitics of the day. While some of this was inevitable as Japan reconfigured its global alliances, and reconstructed its own post-war identity (politically, socially, intellectually, and culturally), the decline of interest was not as steep as often made out. For one thing, the number of works on Islam published from 1950 to 1959 suggests otherwise. There were just a little more than 900 articles, books, and pamphlets produced in those years, almost the same number that emerged between 1905 and 1930.[43] The period is significant since it was after all in the aftermath of Japan's victory over Russia in 1905 that relations began to develop between representatives of Japanese Pan-Asianism and Muslim anti-colonial pan-Islamism.[44] "That interest in Islam endured," observes Krämer, "clearly indicates that Islam was more than a political expedient for at least some Japanese."[45] This was certainly the case with Izutsu, who was on his way to becoming the nation's leading expert on the faith, and who would come out with some of his most lasting scholarly contributions in the decades following WWII.

Izutsu's academic trajectory may appear somewhat unconventional when we consider that he only received his doctorate in 1959, five years after being appointed professor at the Faculty of Letters. It was a mere formality, however, aided by a close friend in the university, to ensure no obstacles would stand in the way of his scholarly work abroad, since his own institution did not require the degree.[46] Two of his previously published works (one being his Quran translation) were submitted in lieu of the dissertation. As for research outside Japan, this was facilitated through a Rockefeller Foundation award that allowed him to travel for the first time beyond the borders of the country of his birth. He visited Lebanon, Syria, and Egypt, experiences that marked his first direct contact with the Islamic world and which afforded him an opportunity to engage

42 Krämer, "Pan-Asianism's religious undercurrents" 632.
43 Aydin, *The politics* 174n2.
44 Esenbel, "Japan's global claim" 1140–1141; Koyagi, "The hajj" 851–852.
45 Krämer, "Pan-Asianism's religious undercurrents" 632.
46 Wakamatsu, *Toshihiko Izutsu* 200.

in dialogue with scholars of Islam from the Middle East. He then traveled to Germany where he met the linguist Leo Weisgerber (1899–1985) whose theories of language he had employed, and would continue to develop, in his own studies of the Quran.[47]

3 The Years at McGill and the Imperial Academy of Philosophy

In 1960 Izutsu visited McGill's Institute of Islamic Studies, established less than a decade earlier by Wilfred C. Smith (1916–2000), a pioneering Canadian scholar of comparative religion and of Islam. In 1962, he took up the position of visiting professor at the Institute, traveling back and forth between Canada and Japan, until he was appointed professor there seven years later. It was in 1962 upon attending a lecture by Seyyed Hossein Nasr, who had come to visit McGill, that an entirely new trajectory of thinking opened up to him. The talk was on the Safavid philosopher Mullā Ṣadrā (d. 1050/1640). It was a watershed moment for Izutsu, catalyzing a new phase of scholarship that would turn his attention to the later Islamic sapiential tradition.[48] If Ṣadrā was, historically speaking, the "synthesizing point" in whom a particular conception of existence was articulated that arrested the mind of Izutsu, then Ibn ʿArabī (d. 638/1240) was its point of origin.[49] It was only natural that in order to adequately grasp this vision of reality, he would have to begin with a careful, meticulous study of the Andalusian mystic. If we are to believe a widely circulated story at McGill, in order to better understand Ibn ʿArabī, Izutsu plunged into a three-month *khalwa* or solitary retreat where he only read him and did nothing else, with Toyoko bringing meals into his study so as not to interrupt the ascent of her husband's mind into the spiritual world of the *walī*. The impact that his immersion into the *weltan-*

---

47 Along with Weisgerber, we cannot also ignore the influence of the American linguists Sapir (1884–1939) and Whorf (1897–1941) on his thinking.

48 Nasr, Seyyed Hossein, "Preface," in Sayyid J. Āshtiyānī et al. (eds.), *Consciousness and reality: Studies in memory of Toshihiko Izutsu*, Leiden: Brill, 2000, xi–xv, xi.

49 "This concept, unity of existence, goes back to a great Arab mystic-philosopher of Spain of the eleventh and twelfth centuries, Ibn ʿArabī (1165–1240). It exercised a tremendous influence upon the majority of Muslim thinkers, particularly in Iran, in the periods extending from the thirteenth century down to the 16th–17th centuries, when the tradition of Islamic metaphysical thinking found its culminating and all-synthesizing point in the thought of Ṣadr al-Dīn Shīrāzī, commonly known as Mullā Ṣadrā (1571–1640)." Izutsu, Toshihiko, "The basic structure of metaphysical thinking in Islam," in Toshihiko Izutsu, *Creation and the timeless order of things: Essays in Islamic mystical philosophy*, Ashland, OR: White Cloud Press, 1994, 1–37, 2.

schauung of arguably Islam's most important Sufi thinker had on Izutsu cannot be underestimated. "Had he not encountered this mystic philosopher," wrote Wakamatsu, "Izutsu's thought would likely have been completely different."[50] In fact, his Japanese biographer went so far as to state that Izutsu's own personal philosophy can be traced to "a line of descent that stretches back to Ibn ʿArabī."[51]

While Izutsu was already familiar with the mystic before he came to Montreal, having published an essay in Japanese on his ontology in 1944,[52] it was through his encounter with Nasr and then two years later, Corbin's student Hermann Landolt, who became his colleague in 1964, that he was able to tread into the universe of Ibn ʿArabī through a doorway quite different from that of conventional Western scholarship. There is no doubt that the captivating and synthetic nature of Nasr's lecture, where he would have outlined the significance of Ibn ʿArabī for Ṣadrā, drawing on a living Persian *ʿirfānī* tradition with which he was in direct contact in Iran, would play an instrumental role in directing Izutsu into the Akbarian school. He had intuited beforehand the momentousness of this new phase of his intellectual life: describing his move to McGill he admitted that he was "urged on by what seemed like an unstoppable existential impulse."[53]

The first significant fruit of this development appeared in 1966–1967, with the two-volume publication of *A comparative study of key philosophical concepts in Sufism and Taoism: Ibn ʿArabī and Lao-Tzū*.[54] While, as the title indicates, it was a comparative study, the section on Ibn ʿArabī alone (a good two-thirds of the study) was a full monograph in its own right. Along with Corbin's *Creative imagination in the Sufism of Ibn ʿArabī*, and the lengthy treatment of the mystic in Nasr's *Three Muslim sages*, these three works were the best introductions to Ibn ʿArabī thus far in the West.[55] In many ways, they complemented each other well. Nasr presented a panoramic view of Ibn ʿArabī's life and thought, Corbin focused on the significance he gave to the *mundus imaginalis*, and Izutsu outlined the mystic's worldview with special attention to the *Fuṣūṣ*

50 Wakamatsu, *Toshihiko Izutsu* 206.

51 Wakamatsu, *Toshihiko Izutsu* 206.

52 Izutsu, Toshihiko, "The ontology of the Islamic mystic philosopher Ibn ʿArabī," in *Tetsugaku* 25–26 (1944), 332–357.

53 Cited in Wakamatsu, *Toshihiko Izutsu* 337.

54 Republished in 1983 as *Sufism and Taoism: A comparative study of key philosophical concepts*.

55 On the limitations of early Western scholarship on Ibn ʿArabī, see Khalil, Atif and Shiraz Sheikh, "Sufism in Western historiography: A brief overview," in *Philosophy East and West* 66.1 (2016), 194–217, 202–203.

and its later commentary tradition. If Corbin offered an inroad into Ibn ʿArabī through the Western tradition (or to be more precise, through what it had lost of the science of the *imaginal*), Izutsu did so through the Far East, by means of the inspired, shamanic (= "prophetic") wisdom of Taoism. It would remain for William Chittick, a student of these three giants, to take Akbarian studies to new heights with his magisterial *The Sufi path of knowledge: Ibn al-ʿArabī's metaphysics of imagination* (1989), arguably the most utilized work in the field of Ibn ʿArabī Studies. SPK would be followed by *The self-disclosure of God: Principles of Ibn al-ʿArabī's cosmology*, and a number of other books and articles.[56]

Nasr observed that Izutsu had the rare gift of mastering the major languages of three major civilizations: Western, Islamic, and Far Eastern.[57] If anything, *Sufism and Taoism*—a study of Chinese and Arabic texts authored in English by a Japanese thinker—was a fitting illustration of this. By all accounts, Izutsu was a linguistic prodigy. There were rumors among students at Keio University that he knew 200 languages. When my own professor Todd Lawson, a student of Landolt at McGill, asked him how many he actually knew, to put the speculations to rest, he replied, "thirty-two," wryly adding, "but I make fewer mistakes in my Japanese."[58] Surprisingly, in middle-school Izutsu was a poor student who hated English. But matters took a turn the day he learned that unlike Japanese, English distinguished between the singular and the plural. In a moment of awakening, it dawned on him that people who speak different languages might well experience the world differently. The simple insight stoked a thirst that was never quite quenched. "The absurd notion kept running through my mind," he wrote, "that I would master all the languages in the world, every single one of them." "As a result of that momentary experience, I stepped into the scholarly world. The fascination of that mysterious thing called scholarship took hold of me as if in premonition of what lay ahead."[59]

The trajectory of Izutsu's acquisition of languages unfolded something like the toppling of dominoes, and was closely tied to his yearning to read the religious, philosophical, and literary classics of the world, in their original forms.

56 We also cannot overlook here the pioneering works of Michel Chodkiewicz (d. 2020).

57 Nasr, "Preface" xii.

58 The question was posed some time in the 80s, in the context of a seminar Izutsu gave at the Institute of Ismaili Studies in London on al-Bīrūnī's (d. 430/1048) commentary on Patanjali's *Yoga-Sutra*. He read the Arabic text alongside the original Sanskrit. See also Landolt, Hermann, "Remembering Toshihiko Izutsu," in *Zindagī nāma wa-khadamat-i ʿilmī wa-farhangī-yi Purūfisūr Tūshihikū Izūtsū*, Tehran: Anjuman-i Āthār wa-Mafākhir-i ʿIlmī, 2006, 1–11, 8–9.

59 Cited in Wakamatsu, *Toshihiko Izutsu* 41.

Plato and Aristotle led him to Greek, Dostoyevsky to Russian, the Old Testament to Hebrew. We may assume that it was the Quran that drew him to Arabic. This, after all, would explain his eagerness to study both together with Shaikh Ibrahim. The title of Izutsu's first English book, *Language and magic: Studies in the magical function of speech* (1956), fittingly captured how deeply the subject arrested his imagination.

Despite his fascination with and mastery of languages, at McGill Izutsu was remembered for the aura he carried of an unassuming silent sage, distinguished, according to his colleague Landolt's account, for his *khāmūshī*.[60] And yet it could be colorfully interspersed with the sound of roaring laughter coming out of a classroom where he might be teaching. His predilection for silence also did not prevent him from an occasional debate, as occurred with the fiercely opinionated Turkish sociologist Niyazi Berkes (1908–1988), who taught at McGill from 1952 to 1975.[61] As a Kemalist who supported the abolition of the caliphate and the eradication of the *sharīʿa*, he was often at odds with Izutsu, who while certainly not an Islamist, had a soft spot for the idea of the "world of Islam"—traces perhaps of the relationship he forged with Shaikh Ibrahim and Musa Jarullah (erstwhile pro-Ottomans), as well as Ōkawa, who felt Ataturk had gone too far in the direction of secularization. While Izutsu was not a simple anti-modernist, he recognized the dehumanizing effects of contemporary industrialized, highly technologized societies, where the human being had lost a sense of meaning and purpose;[62] the threat of nihilism that lurked behind much of modern Western thought;[63] and the "spiritual crisis"

60 Landolt, "Remembering" 2.

61 Shared through personal correspondence with S. Esenbel.

62 Consider Izutsu's following statement: "The technological agglomeration of the life-order in highly industrialized modern society in the West has thrown man into an incurable isolation. The life-order created by technology is in reality a disorder in the sense that it is a vast and elaborate system of meaninglessness or absurdity. Man is forced to live in a huge dehumanized mechanism and meaning he himself does not understand and, which, moreover, constitutes a standing menace to his individuality and personality. In such a situation, modern man necessarily becomes alienated from Nature and his own self." Izutsu, Toshihiko, "Existentialism East and West," in Toshihiko Izutsu, *The concept and reality of existence*, Tokyo: Keio Institute of Cultural and Linguistic Studies, 1971, 25–33, 26. In the same essay, Izutsu also highlights the dangers of not articulating the Islamic philosophical tradition in a way that is relevant to the needs of the modern world. To fail to revive the "creative energy contained in this philosophy" is to ensure that "it will find itself utterly powerless in the presence of contemporary problems." Izutsu, "Existentialism" 32.

63 See Nakamura, "The significance" 149.

of the modern world.[64] It is a curious feature that in many of Izutsu's pictures, whether lecturing or immersed in study, he dons a traditional Japanese kimono. It would be naïve to suggest that this was mere nativism on his part. More than anything, it seems to have reflected his desire not to relinquish the sacred mores of his own tradition, thoughtlessly discarded by his contemporaries in response to the encroachment of secular modernity. In a picture taken of Izutsu in 1949, where he was honored with the Fukuzawa award for his book on the mystical element in Greek philosophy, he stood out as the only one among the dozen photographed to be adorned in classical Japanese garb.[65]

In the same year that Izutsu was appointed full-time professor at McGill, the university opened up a branch of its Institute of Islamic Studies in Tehran, in a beautiful Qajar house. Izutsu took up residence here, a move that allowed him to devote his attention to later Islamic philosophy and mysticism in an environment more conducive to such research because of the presence of important authorities of that tradition. With Mehdi Mohaghegh, an Iranian colleague from the Institute, he authored an English translation of a section of Sabzawārī's (d. 1295/1878) *Sharḥ-i manẓūma* (*Commentary on the Poem on metaphysics*), eventually published in 1977 as *The Metaphysics of Sabzavārī*. This was preceded by their collaborative production of a critical edition of the text eight years before. In 1977, he also published, with Mohaghegh and others, Mīr Dāmād's (d. 1040/1631) *Kitāb al-Qabasāt* (*Book of embers*). Two years before both of these works saw the light of day, however, Nasr invited him to join the teaching staff as a full-time member of the Iranian Academy of Philosophy which had recently been founded under the patronage of Queen Farah Pahlavi. Izutsu accepted, joining Corbin as part of its international faculty, where he would teach courses on Islamic and Far Eastern philosophy. At the recommendation of Nasr, with whom he traveled to many conferences abroad, he wrote *Toward a philosophy of Zen Buddhism* in English, published

64 In 1981, he delivered a paper in Rabat entitled, "Oriental philosophy in face of the spiritual crisis in the contemporary world." Āshtiyānī, Sayyid J. et al. (eds.), *Consciousness and reality: Studies in memory of Toshihiko Izutsu*, Leiden: Brill, 2000, 449. The sentiment was shared by many of his colleagues at Eranos, including his friend Mircea Eliade who was deeply influenced by Guénon, but kept this influence private. Hakl, Hans T., *Eranos: An alternative intellectual history of the twentieth century*, trans. Christopher McIntosh, Montreal: Routledge, 2013, 231. On Izutsu's regular participation in these conferences, beginning with his first lecture in 1967, and continuing involvement for fifteen years thereafter, see 229–230; cf. Wakamatsu, *Toshihiko Izutsu* xviii and other relevant pages.

65 https://www.keio.ac.jp/en/keio-times/features/2021/4/ (last accessed: 25 June 2021).

by the Academy in 1977.[66] While Izutsu recognized that Zen stood opposed to speculative philosophy in the conventional sense, it was nevertheless possible, as he argued in the introduction of the book, to produce a philosophical expression—a "philosophization"—of the Zen experience, and that is what he set out to accomplish in the short work.[67]

The intellectual and spiritual friendship that grew between Nasr and Izutsu, from the time of their first meeting, was perhaps best exemplified by their joint translation of the *Tao Te Ching*, undertaken at the suggestion of Izutsu after an old manuscript of the text was discovered in a Chinese imperial archaeological site. Their schedule was to meet periodically in a beautiful garden in the courtyard of the Academy. Izutsu would first translate from Chinese into English, and then Nasr from English into Persian, taking into consideration Izutsu's exegesis as they proceeded along. By the end, not only did they have a Persian translation, but also an English one as a byproduct of their exercise in cross-cultural philosophy. When Nasr left Iran for a few weeks in 1979, unbeknown to him at the time that he would never return due to the outbreak of the revolution, this was the only work in progress he took with him on the flight. His intention was to continue plugging away at it in his spare moments. The upheavals that followed in the wake of the political events that took the world by surprise prevented him from bringing the project to completion. Now, after more than four decades, this work has been published along with Nasr's Persian commentary.[68]

One of the most significant consequences of Izutsu's stay in Iran was that he was able to train some very important scholars (among them Gholamreza Aavani, William Chittick, James Morris, Sachiko Murata, and Nasrollah Pourjavady), many of whom would play a significant role in charting the trajectory of Islamic studies both abroad and in Iran. Part of their experience as students included reading classical texts with Izutsu line-by-line, such as the *Fuṣūṣ*, which they began in the early 70s and completed some eight years later. His exacting attention to detail, both grammatical and philosophical, must have left an indelible mark, as can be seen from the impressive quality of their scholarship in the years that followed. Murata in particular, as a Japanese student proficient in both the languages of the Islamic world and the Far East, perhaps best exemplifies the legacy of Izutsu. It has been noted that unlike Western scholars, Izutsu's encounter with Islam came through a mind molded

---

66 Nasr, Seyyed Hossein, "Intellectual autobiography," in Edwin Hahn et al. (eds.), *The philosophy of Seyyed Hossein Nasr*, Chicago: Open Court, 2001, 1–85, 52.

67 Izutsu, Toshihiko, *Towards a philosophy of Zen Buddhism*, Tehran: Imperial Iranian Academy of Philosophy, 1977, repr. Boulder: Prajna Press, 1982, x.

68 Laozi, *Tāʾū tih chīng: Ṭarīq wa-faḍāʾil-i ān*, English trans. Toshihiko Izutsu and Seyyed Hossein Nasr; Persian trans. and comm. Seyyed Hossein Nasr, Tehran: Intishārāt-i Iṭṭilāʿāt, 2021.

and shaped by the traditions of the Far East. Nowhere is such an encounter more visible, among those who studied under him, than in Murata's *The Tao of Islam* (1992), an encyclopedic *tour de force* that examines gender in Islam not through the axioms and categories of Western feminism (which is usually the lens through which this thorny subject is broached) but through the "backdoor" of Chinese cosmology, with special attention to the complementary principles of yin-yang. Murata would later explore the development of the Islamic *ḥikma* tradition in China, or more specifically, its encounter with and assimilation of Confucian social teachings, Neo-Confucian metaphysics, Buddhism, and Taoism in *Chinese gleams of Sufi light* (2000). More recently, she published *The first Islamic classic in Chinese* (2017), a translation with introduction and commentary of Wang Diu's *Real commentary on the true teaching*, the first major pre-modern articulation of Islamic thought in Chinese. Like Izutsu, Murata has also written about Islam in Japanese. With his help, she translated the *Maʿālim al-ūṣūl* (*Principles of Islamic law*), a 10th/16th-century text on the principles of jurisprudence, published in 1985 as *Isurāmuhō riron josetsu*. The subject reflected her early interest in law, which she studied as an undergraduate student at Chiba University just outside of Tokyo before moving to Iran to study *fiqh*.[69]

The Iranian years were for Izutsu a time of great productivity. Even as law-and-order began to break down with the unfolding of the early stages of the revolution, Izutsu unremittingly continued his scholarly activities. "Aided by superb colleagues," he wrote, he proceeded with "editing and annotating unpublished Islamic philosophical texts ... In an unusually tense atmosphere, we held regular meetings and enthusiastically pressed ahead with our research."[70] When it became clear that it was too dangerous to remain, Izutsu boarded one of the last Japanese rescue missions and left Iran, never to return. Even though the decision was forced on him by circumstances outside of his control, he would later recount being free of the "slightest feeling of regret," not because he had a personal wish to depart a nation for which he had grown fond, or because he had been treated badly by its people, but due to his belief in an ever-present Agency that guides our lives, especially at key junctures separating different phases.[71] Echoing the Islamic idea of *tawakkul*, of complete and total

69 For some important biographical details about the intellectual interests that brought her to Iran, and her studies with Izutsu, Nasr, and important religious authorities in the country, see Murata, Sachiko, *The Tao of Islam: A sourcebook on gender relationships*, Albany, NY: SUNY Press, 1992, introduction.

70 Cited in Wakamatsu, *Toshihiko Izutsu* 257.

71 Wakamatsu, *Toshihiko Izutsu* 257.

reliance on and trust in God, he had once even described himself as a "fatalist." Had it not been for the tumultuous events that brought Imam Khomeini (d. 1989) into power, it seems improbable that he would have bade farewell to the country in the foreseeable future.

4 Return to the Homeland

On his return to Japan, Izutsu decided that he would now dedicate his intellectual energies to the elaboration of "Oriental philosophy," as he conceived it, primarily in Japanese. This philosophy was not, as sometimes misunderstood, that of the Far East, but of an Orient that included the realms of Islam, particularly Persia. After all, the *ḥikma* of the Ishrāqī "Illuminationist" school of al-Suhrawardī (d. 587/1191) formed part of the "wisdom of the East."

To be clear, Izutsu recognized, before Edward Said, that the so-called East was anything but a repository of a single, unified vision of reality—a single Oriental essence. "There is in the East," he wrote very explicitly, "no ... uniformity. We can only speak of Eastern philosophies in the plural."[72] However, he also felt there were deep conceptual overlaps that could allow for the development of a metaphilosophy of Eastern modes of thinking, one that could serve ultimately as a bridge between East and West, and beyond that, as a pathway to the articulation of a universal vision of reality (curiously also an aim of Ōkawa[73]). Within the confines of the Orient itself, *waḥdat al-wujūd* (the unity of being) was crucial to the formation of such a model. While he recognized the doctrine was simply one among a number of non-Western philosophies, he also felt it had within it the resources for the development of an overarching metasystem or conceptual umbrella that could accommodate various other subsystems of Eastern thinking. If the "fundamental structure" of *waḥdat al-wujūd* could be adequately explicated, it could, he felt, "provide a basic conceptual model by which the majority of Oriental philosophies will be brought up to a certain level of structural uniformity concerning ... their most fundamental aspects." The doctrine and the philosophical possibilities it contained were, to quote his own words,

> representative of a basic structure which is commonly shared by many of the Oriental philosophies going back to divergent historical origins,

---

72 Izutsu, Toshihiko, *The concept and reality of existence*, Tokyo: Keio Institute of Cultural and Linguistic Studies, 1971, 1.

73 But without the political implications (see note 29 above).

> like Vedantism, Buddhism, Taoism and Confucianism. The structure of the philosophy of *waḥdat al-wujūd* would in this perspective be seen to represent one typical pattern—an archetypal form, we might say—of philosophical thinking which one finds developed variously in more or less different forms by outstanding thinkers belonging to different cultural traditions in the East.[74]

As we can glean from the passage, *waḥdat al-wujūd* was, for Izutsu, not exclusive to Islam. But his deep study of the Quran, Arabic, Ibn ʿArabī, and the Islamic philosophical heritage allowed him to discern the presence of such a mode of thinking elsewhere. When Masataka observed about Izutsu, that it was "his long-term research in speculative, philosophical Sufism which enabled him to rediscover a similar tradition in Buddhism,"[75] he was only partially correct. It allowed him to discover similar traditions across the entire spiritual and philosophical landscape of the East.

Izutsu retained an active regimen of writing and scholarship when he returned from Iran. He composed ten books in Japanese from 1979 onwards—at least half of them on (or directly related to) Islam.[76] Only two were in English, *The theory of beauty in the classical aesthetics of Japan* (co-authored with his wife Toyoko), and *Sufism and Taoism* (a revised version of his earlier work). The articles he published in Japanese (twelve in total), and in English or European languages (fourteen), covered a wide range of subjects, with his interest in a metaphilosophy of the East now squarely at the center. Islam was still present, but it was as if what he had synthesized intellectually from his years at McGill and the Imperial Academy was now being used to help him understand the Orient as a whole in a much deeper light.

It was also in this third phase of his life in Japan that Izutsu began to develop an interest in postmodernism. He met Derrida, the French philosopher of deconstruction, who penned a short essay for Izutsu (*Letter to a Japanese friend*) where he provided some schematic reflections on his own terminology. Some, however, have made more of this interest than it warrants, because

---

74 Izutsu, *Concept and reality* 36–37.

75 Masataka, Takeshita, "Toshihiko Izutsu's contribution to Islamic Studies," in *Journal of International Philosophy* 7 (2016), 78–81, 81.

76 *Birth of Islam* (1979), *A fountainhead of Islamic philosophy* (1980), *Islamic culture* (1981), *Reading the Quran* (1983), and *Scope of words: God and man in Judeo-Islamic philosophy* (1991). See Iwami, Takashi, "Bibliography of Toshihiko Izutsu's writings," in Sayyid J. Āshtiyānī et al. (eds.), *Consciousness and reality: Studies in memory of Toshihiko Izutsu*, Leiden: Brill, 2000, 441–442. It is unlikely the first of these was published before he left Iran, though he may well have written most if not all of it before his return to Japan.

Izutsu was if anything a conventional postmodernist. In fact, the aspects of this outlook he was most attracted to were those that grew out of the years he spent meditating on the teachings of Ibn ʿArabī: an awareness of the relative nature of truth, the ineffability of the Real, the limits of reason, and the mind's incapacity, on its own, to fully grasp Reality. But Izutsu's understanding of these matters (like the doctrine of *waḥdat al-wujūd*) went far beyond anything postmodernism could offer, since it recognized not just relativity, but a relativity that was itself a mysterious expression of what Meister Eckhart referred to as "the ground of being." And this is why he could more accurately be described, as one writer has done, as a "post-postmodernist," since beyond Maya's play of words and ideas, there lay an Absolute which, for him, was the object of all human yearning and desire, the alpha and omega of all that is, was, and could ever be. Izutsu was, in this respect, as far from being an agnostic on metaphysics as one can imagine.

The Japanese scholar-sage passed away unexpectedly on the morning of January 7th, 1993, the consequence of a brain hemorrhage after a minor fall at home. But death, as he knew all-too-well, was far from the end. If one had prepared for it in the true mystical sense, through catharsis, knowledge, and inner-illumination, it was a liberation. As he had written years earlier in a meditation on human mortality in words that call to mind the famous couplet of the mystic martyr al-Ḥallāj (d. 309/922):

> While the body lives, the spirit sinks down into the darkness of death; therefore, so long as the body does not die, the spirit cannot live. Until one dies in the flesh, one cannot live in the spirit. For a person to be able to live a life truly worthy of that name, the spirit must first be freed from the tomb of the flesh. As the tragedian Euripides says, 'Who knows but that life be death and death be life?'; to be alive in this world is, in fact, to be dead, and to be dead in this world, conversely, is to be truly alive.[77]

77 Cited in Wakamatsu, *Toshihiko Izutsu* 321.

Bibliography

Albayrak, Ismail, "The reception of Toshihiko's Izutsu's Qur'anic studies in the Muslim world: With special reference to Turkish Qur'anic scholarship," in *JQS* 14.1 (2012), 73–106.

Altuntas, Selcuk, *How to be a proper Muslim in the Russian Empire: An intellectual biography of Musa Jaraullah Bigiyev (1875–1949)*, Madison (PhD Diss.): University of Wisconsin-Madison, 2018.

Āshtiyānī, Sayyid J. et al. (eds.), *Consciousness and reality: Studies in memory of Toshihiko Izutsu*, Leiden: Brill, 2000.

Aydin, Cemil, *The politics of civilizational identities: Asia, West and Islam in the pan-Asianist thought of Ôkawa Shûmei*, Cambridge, MA (PhD Diss.): Harvard University, 2002.

Dufourmont, Eddy, "Tanaka Ippei: 'Islam and pan-Asianism,' 1924," in Sven Saaler and Christopher W.A. Szpilman (eds.), *Pan-Asianism: A documentary history*. II. *1920-Present*, Lanham, MD: Rowman & Littlefield, 2011, 87–91.

Esenbel, Selcuk, "Abdürreşid Ibrahim: 'The world of Islam and the spread of Islam in Japan,' 1910," in Sven Saaler and Chistopher W.A. Szpilman (eds.), *Pan-Asianism: A documentary history*. I. *1850–1920*, Lanham, MD: Rowman & Littlefield, 2011, 195–203.

Esenbel, Selcuk, "Japan's global claim to Asia and the world of Islam: Transnational nationalism and world power, 1900–1945," in *AHR* 109.4 (2004), 1140–1170.

Fuller, Graham E., *A world without Islam*, New York: Little, Brown and Company, 2010.

Hakl, Hans T., *Eranos: An alternative intellectual history of the twentieth century*, trans. Christopher McIntosh, Montreal: Routledge, 2013.

Iwami, Takashi, "Bibliography of Toshihiko Izutsu's writings," in Sayyid J. Āshtiyānī et al. (eds.), *Consciousness and reality: Studies in memory of Toshihiko Izutsu*, Leiden: Brill, 2000, 441–442.

Izutsu, Toshihiko, "The ontology of the Islamic mystic philosopher Ibn ʿArabī," in *Tetsugaku* 25–26 (1944), 332–357.

Izutsu, Toshihiko, *The concept and reality of existence*, Tokyo: Keio Institute of Cultural and Linguistic Studies, 1971.

Izutsu, Toshihiko, "Existentialism East and West," in Toshihiko Izutsu, *The concept and reality of existence*, Tokyo: Keio Institute of Cultural and Linguistic Studies, 1971, 25–33.

Izutsu, Toshihiko, *Towards a philosophy of Zen Buddhism*, Tehran: Imperial Iranian Academy of Philosophy, 1977, repr. Boulder: Prajna Press, 1982.

Izutsu, Toshihiko, "The basic structure of metaphysical thinking in Islam," in Toshihiko Izutsu, *Creation and the timeless order of things: Essays in Islamic mystical philosophy*, Ashland, OR: White Cloud Press, 1994, 1–37.

Khalil, Atif and Shiraz Sheikh, "Sufism in Western historiography: A brief overview," in *Philosophy East and West* 66.1 (2016), 194–217.

Komatsu, Hisao, "Muslim intellectuals and Japan: A pan-Islamist mediator, Abdurreshid Ibrahim," in Stéphane A. Dudoignon, Hisao Komatsu and Yasushi Kosugi (eds.), *Intellectuals in the modern Islamic world: Transmission, transformation, communication*, London: Routledge, 2006, 273–288.

Koyagi, Mikiya, "The hajj by Japanese Muslims in the interwar period: Japan's pan-Asianism and economic interests in the Islamic world," in *Journal of World History* 24.4 (2014), 849–876.

Krämer, Hans M., "Pan-Asianism's religious undercurrents: The reception of Islam and translation of the Qurʾān in twentieth century Japan," in *The Journal of Asian Studies* 73.3 (2014), 619–640.

Landolt, Hermann, "Remembering Toshihiko Izutsu," in *Zindagī nāma wa-khadamāt-i ʿilmī wa-farhangī-yi Purūfisūr Tūshihikū Izūtsū*, Tehran: Anjuman-i Āthār wa-Mafākhir-i ʿIlmī, 2006, 1–11.

Laozi, *Tāʾū tih chīng: Ṭarīq wa-faḍāʾil-i ān*, English trans. Toshihiko Izutsu and Seyyed Hossein Nasr; Persian trans. and comm. Seyyed Hossein Nasr, Tehran: Intishārāt-i Iṭṭilāʿāt, 2021.

Makino, Shinya, "On the originality of 'Izutsu' Oriental philosophy," in Sayyid J. Āshtiyānī et al. (eds.), *Consciousness and reality: Studies in memory of Toshihiko Izutsu*, Leiden: Brill, 2000, 253–254.

Masataka, Takeshita, "Toshihiko Izutsu's contribution to Islamic Studies," in *Journal of International Philosophy* 7 (2016), 78–81.

Misawa, Nobuo, "Shintoism and Islam in interwar Japan: How did the Japanese come to believe in Islam?," in *Orient* 46 (2011), 119–140.

Murata, Sachiko, *The Tao of Islam: A sourcebook on gender relationships*, Albany, NY: SUNY Press, 1992.

Nakamura, Kojiro, "Islamic Studies in Japan," in Gerrie ter Haar and Yoshio Tsuruoka (eds.), *Religion and society: An agenda for the 21st century*, Leiden: Brill, 2007, 261–265.

Nakamura, Kojiro, "The significance of Toshihiko Izutsu's legacy for comparative religion," in *Intellectual Discourse* 17.2 (2009), 147–158.

Nasr, Seyyed Hossein, "Preface," in Sayyid J. Āshtiyānī et al. (eds.), *Consciousness and reality: Studies in memory of Toshihiko Izutsu*, Leiden: Brill, 2000, xi–xv.

Nasr, Seyyed Hossein, "Intellectual autobiography," in Edwin Hahn et al. (eds.), *The philosophy of Seyyed Hossein Nasr*, Chicago: Open Court, 2001, 1–85.

Partin, Harry B., "Semantics of the Qurʾān: A consideration of Izutsu's studies," in *History of Religions* 9.4 (1970), 358–362.

Takeuchi, Yoshimi, "Profile of Asian minded man X: Ōkawa Shūmei," in *Developing Economies* 7.3 (1969), 367–379.

Usuki, Akira, "A Japanese Asianist's view of Islam," in *Annales of Japan Association for Middle East Studies* 28.2 (2013), 59–84.

Wakamatsu, Eisuke, *Toshihiko Izutsu and the philosophy of word: In search of the spiritual Orient*, trans. Jean C. Hoff, Tokyo: International House of Japan, 2014.

Index of Names and Technical Terms

Printed in the United States
by Baker & Taylor Publisher Services